enVisionMATH® 2.0

Authors

Randall I. Charles
Professor Emeritus
Department of Mathematics
San Jose State University
San Jose, California

Janet H. Caldwell
Professor of Mathematics
Rowan University
Glassboro, New Jersey

Juanita Copley
Professor Emerita, College of Education
University of Houston
Houston, Texas

Warren Crown
Professor Emeritus of Mathematics Education
Graduate School of Education
Rutgers University
New Brunswick, New Jersey

Francis (Skip) Fennell
L. Stanley Bowlsbey Professor of Education and Graduate and Professional Studies
McDaniel College
Westminster, Maryland

Stuart J. Murphy
Visual Learning Specialist
Boston, Massachusetts

Kay B. Sammons
Coordinator of Elementary Mathematics
Howard County Public Schools
Ellicott City, Maryland

Jane F. Schielack
Professor of Mathematics
Associate Dean for Assessment and Pre K-12 Education, College of Science
Texas A&M University
College Station, Texas

Mathematicians

Roger Howe
Professor of Mathematics
Yale University
New Haven, Connecticut

Gary Lippman
Professor of Mathematics and Computer Science
California State University East Bay
Hayward, California

Contributing Authors

Zachary Champagne
District Facilitator, Duval County Public Schools
Florida Center for Research in Science, Technology, Engineering, and Mathematics (FCR-STEM)
Jacksonville, Florida

Jonathan A. Wray
Mathematics Instructional Facilitator
Howard County Public Schools
Ellicott City, Maryland

ELL Consultants

Janice Corona
Retired Administrator
Dallas ISD, Multi-Lingual Department
Dallas, Texas

Jim Cummins
Professor
The University of Toronto
Toronto, Canada

Texas Reviewers

Theresa Bathe
Teacher
Fort Bend ISD

Chrissy Beltran
School Wide Project Coordinator
Ysleta ISD

Renee Cutright
Teacher
Amarillo ISD

Sharon Grimm
Teacher
Houston ISD

Esmeralda Herrera
Teacher
San Antonio ISD

Sherry Johnson
Teacher
Round Rock ISD

Elvia Lopez
Teacher
Denton ISD

Antoinese Pride
Instructional Coach
Dallas ISD

Joanna Ratliff
Teacher
Keller ISD

Courtney Jo Ridehuber
Teacher
Mansfield ISD

Nannie D. Scurlock-McKnight
Mathematics Specialist
A.W. Brown Fellowship-Leadership Academy
Dallas, TX

Brian Sinclair
Math Instructional Specialist
Fort Worth ISD

Savvas Learning Company LLC, 15 East Midland Avenue, Paramus, NJ 07652

ISBN-13: 978-0-328-76723-6
ISBN-10: 0-328-76723-9
17 2022

Digital Resources

Look for these digital resources in every lesson!

Go to SavvasTexas.com

Solve

Solve & Share problems plus math tools

Learn

Visual Learning Animation Plus with animation, interaction, and math tools

Glossary

Animated Glossary in English and Spanish

Tools

Math Tools to help you understand

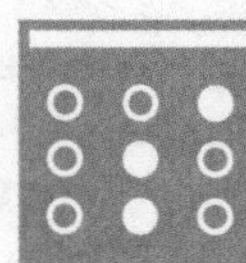

Check

Quick Check for each lesson

Games

Math Games to help you learn

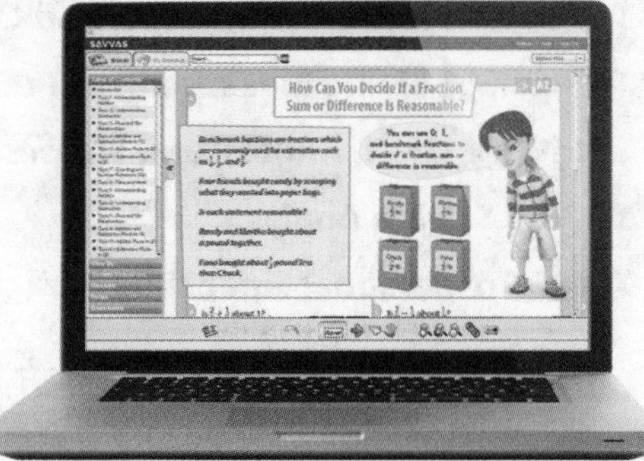

eText
The pages in your book online

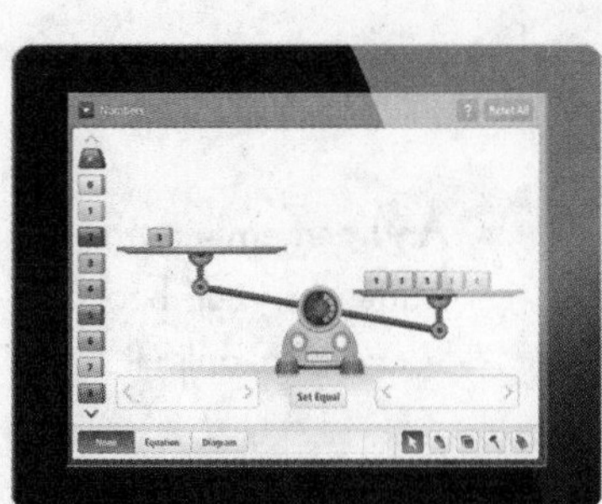

SavvasTexas.com
Everything you need for math anytime, anywhere

Key

Number and Operations
Algebraic Reasoning
Geometry and Measurement
Data Analysis
Personal Financial Literacy

Mathematical Process Standards are found in all lessons.

Digital Resources at SavvasTexas.com

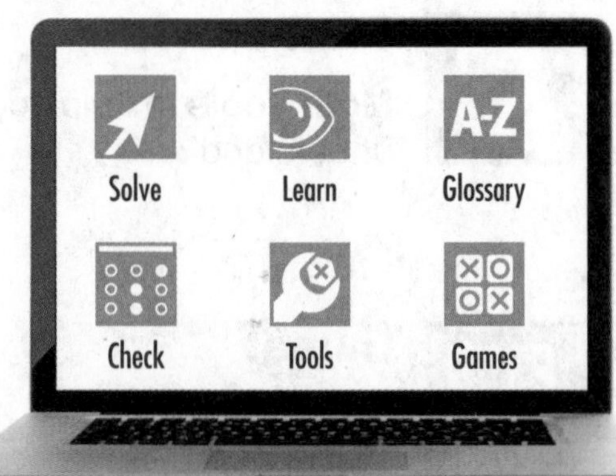

And remember, the pages in your book are also online!

Contents

Topics

VOLUME 1

VOLUME 2

Volume 1

TOPIC 1 Place Value

Hi, I'm Carlos. This shows different ways to represent a decimal.

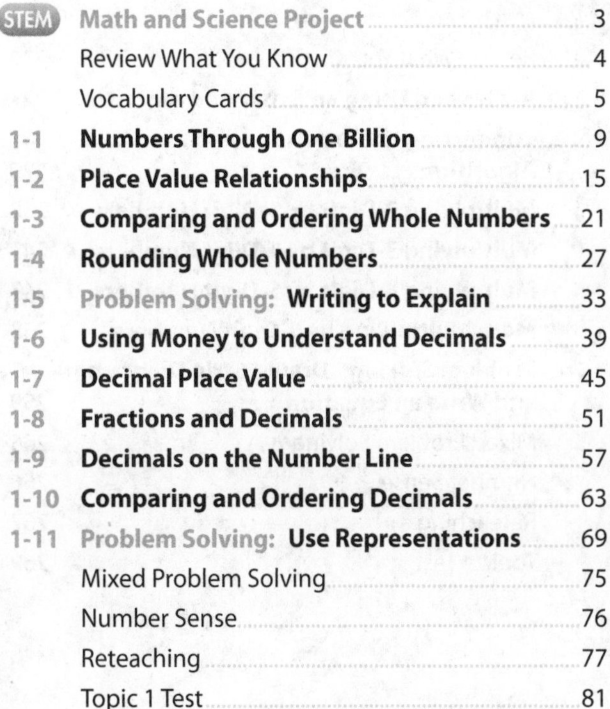

Expanded form: 1 + 0.6 + 0.04
Standard form: 1.64
Word form: one and sixty-four hundredths

TEKS 4.1A, 4.1B, 4.1C, 4.1D, 4.1E, 4.1F, 4.1G, 4.2, 4.2A, 4.2B, 4.2C, 4.2D, 4.2E, 4.2F, 4.2G, 4.2H, 4.3G

TOPIC 2 Adding and Subtracting Whole Numbers and Decimals

Hi, I'm Jada. This shows how you can use place-value grids to add decimals.

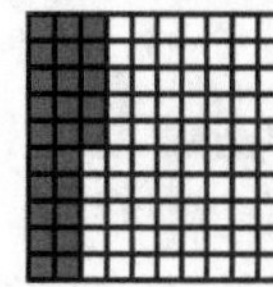

$0.85 + $0.40 = $1.25

TEKS 4.1A, 4.1B, 4.1C, 4.1D, 4.1E, 4.1F, 4.1G, 4.4, 4.4A, 4.4G, 4.5, 4.8C

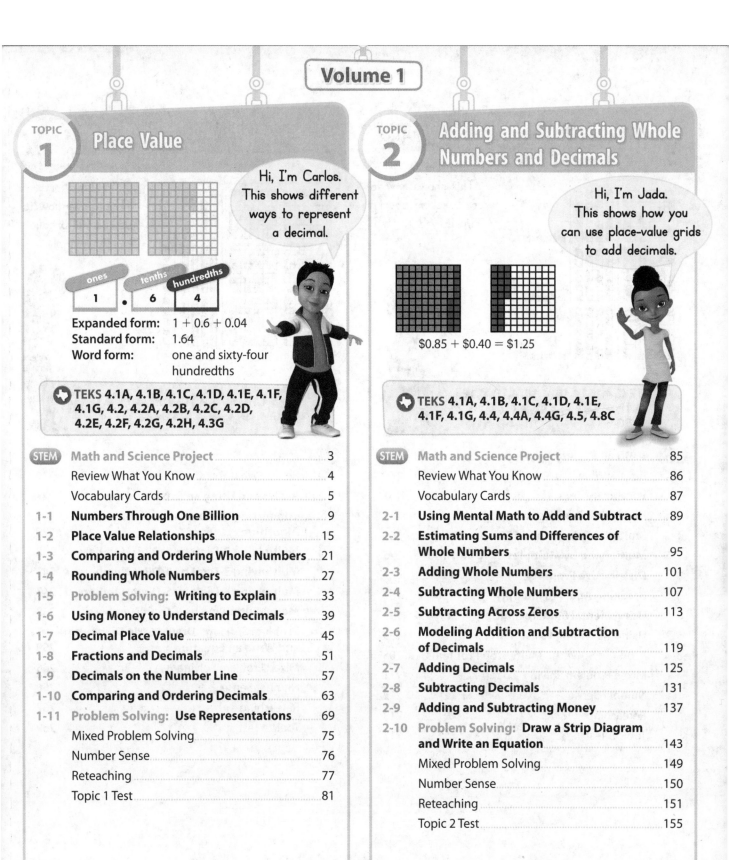

Volume 1

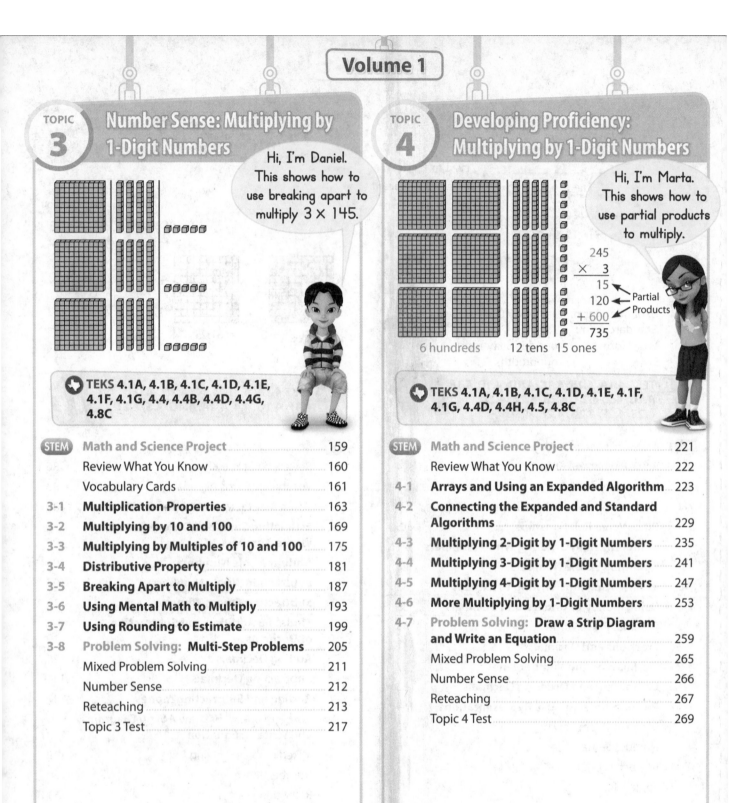

TOPIC 3 Number Sense: Multiplying by 1-Digit Numbers

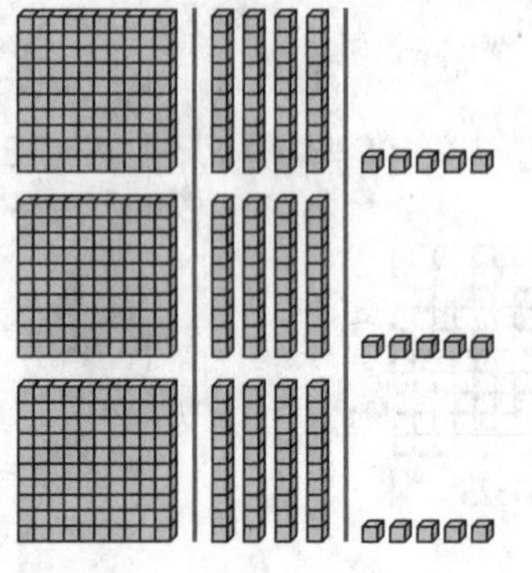

Hi, I'm Daniel. This shows how to use breaking apart to multiply 3 × 145.

TEKS 4.1A, 4.1B, 4.1C, 4.1D, 4.1E, 4.1F, 4.1G, 4.4, 4.4B, 4.4D, 4.4G, 4.8C

TOPIC 4 Developing Proficiency: Multiplying by 1-Digit Numbers

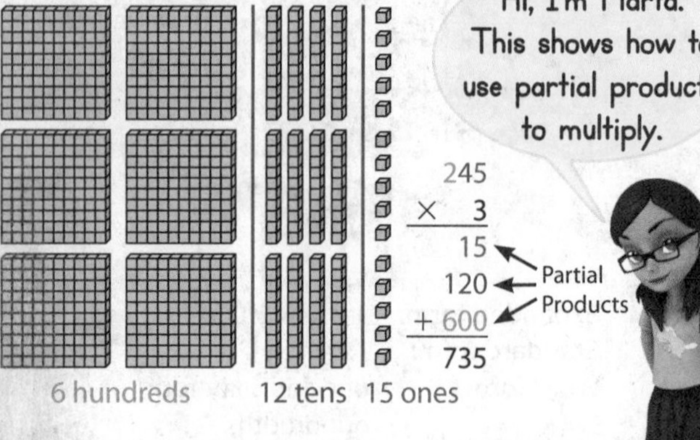

TEKS 4.1A, 4.1B, 4.1C, 4.1D, 4.1E, 4.1F, 4.1G, 4.4D, 4.4H, 4.5, 4.8C

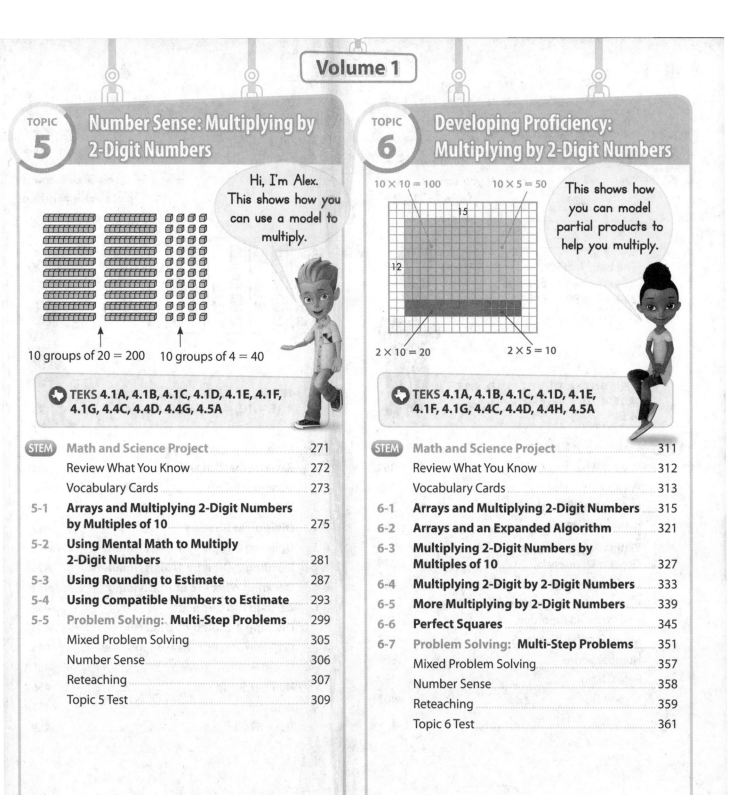

TOPIC 5 Number Sense: Multiplying by 2-Digit Numbers

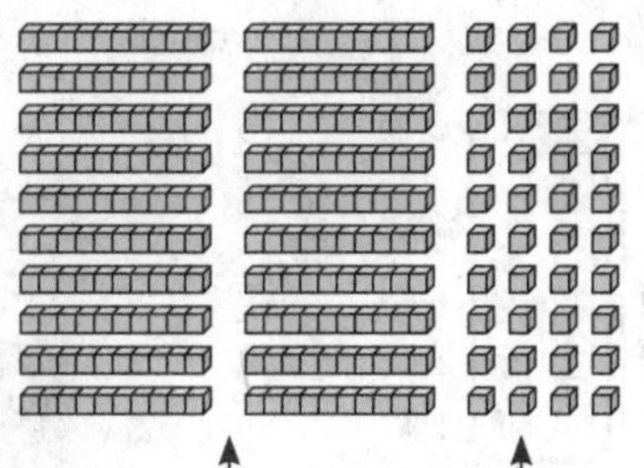
10 groups of 20 = 200
10 groups of 4 = 40

Hi, I'm Alex. This shows how you can use a model to multiply.

TEKS 4.1A, 4.1B, 4.1C, 4.1D, 4.1E, 4.1F, 4.1G, 4.4C, 4.4D, 4.4G, 4.5A

TOPIC 6 Developing Proficiency: Multiplying by 2-Digit Numbers

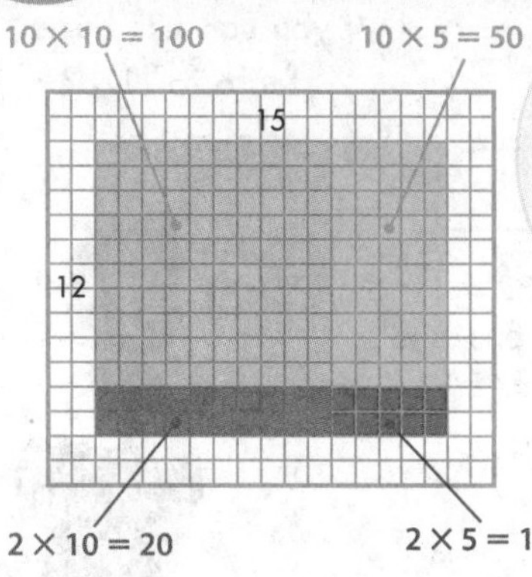
10 × 10 = 100
10 × 5 = 50
15
12
2 × 10 = 20
2 × 5 = 10

This shows how you can model partial products to help you multiply.

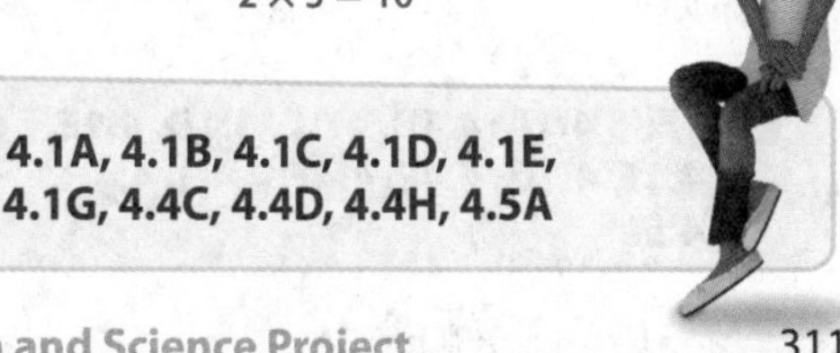
TEKS 4.1A, 4.1B, 4.1C, 4.1D, 4.1E, 4.1F, 4.1G, 4.4C, 4.4D, 4.4H, 4.5A

Volume 1

Number Sense: Dividing by 1-Digit Divisors

This shows how you can use basic facts to divide mentally.

320

?	?	?	?

The basic fact is $32 \div 4 = 8$.
32 tens $\div\ 4 = 8$ tens or 80.
$320 \div 4 = 80$

TEKS **4.1A, 4.1B, 4.1C, 4.1D, 4.1E, 4.1F, 4.1G, 4.4E, 4.4F, 4.4G, 4.4H, 4.5**

TOPIC 8

Developing Proficiency: Dividing by 1-Digit Divisors

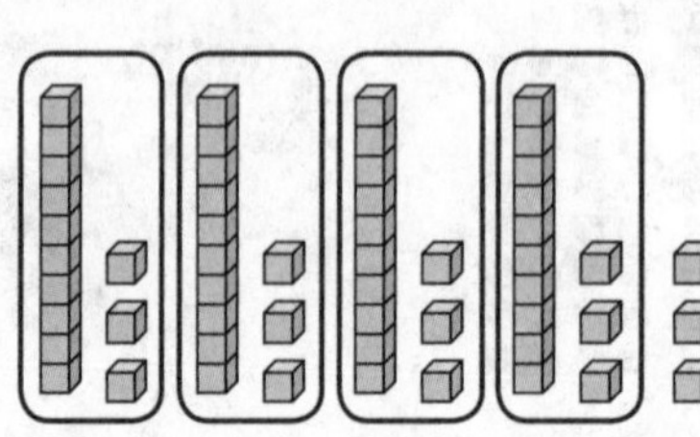

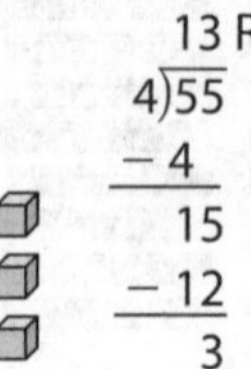

TEKS **4.1A, 4.1B, 4.1C, 4.1D, 4.1E, 4.1F, 4.1G, 4.4E, 4.4F, 4.4G, 4.4H**

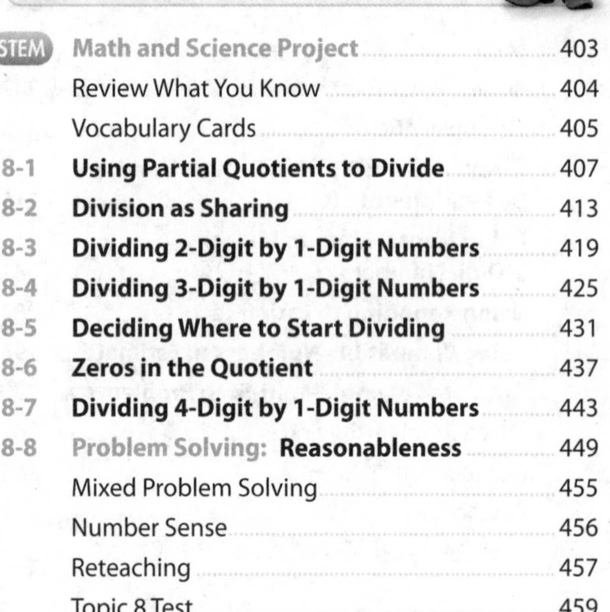

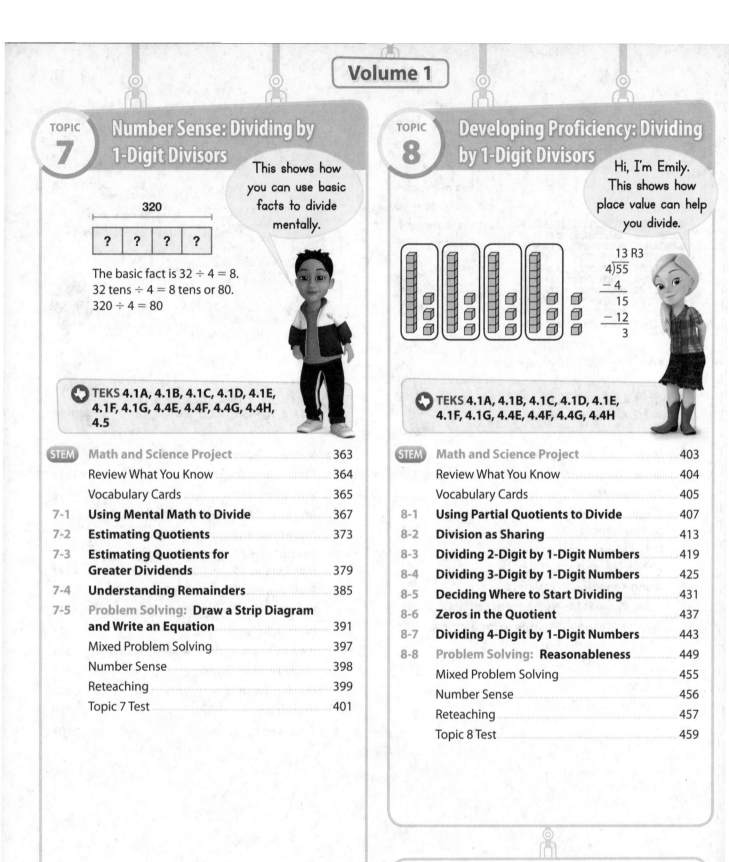

Volume 2

TOPIC 9 Patterns and Equations

Hi, I'm Jackson. This shows how an equation must be balanced and equal on both sides of the equal sign.

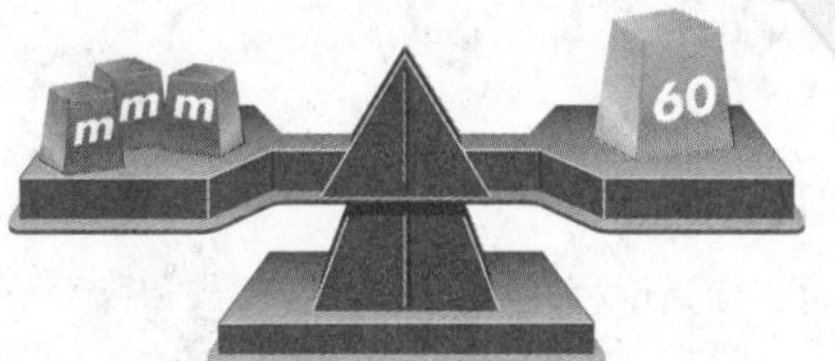

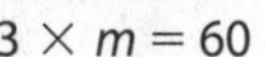

$3 \times m = 60$

TEKS 4.1A, 4.1B, 4.1C, 4.1D, 4.1E, 4.1F, 4.1G, 4.5, 4.5B

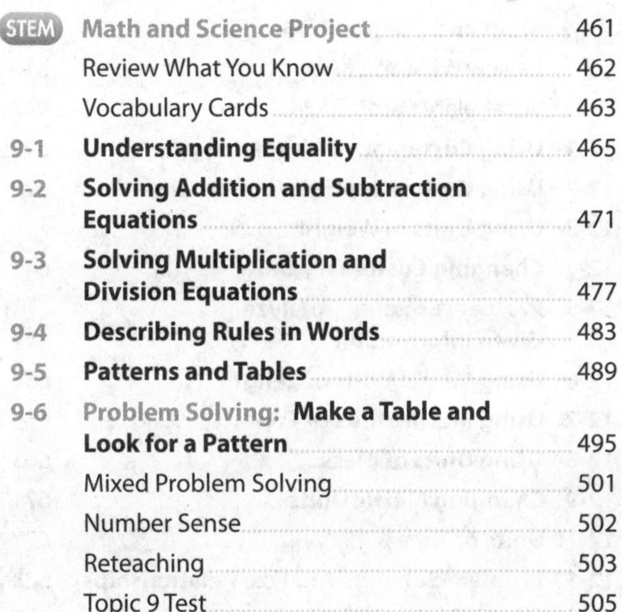

TOPIC 10 Fraction Meanings and Equivalence

This shows how fraction strips can be used to determine equivalent fractions.

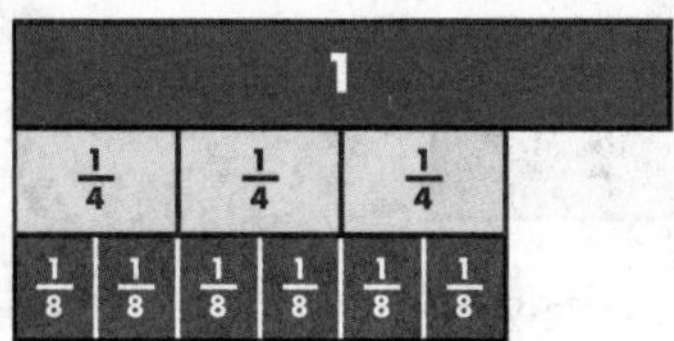

TEKS 4.1A, 4.1B, 4.1C, 4.1D, 4.1E, 4.1F, 4.1G, 4.3A, 4.3C, 4.3D, 4.3G

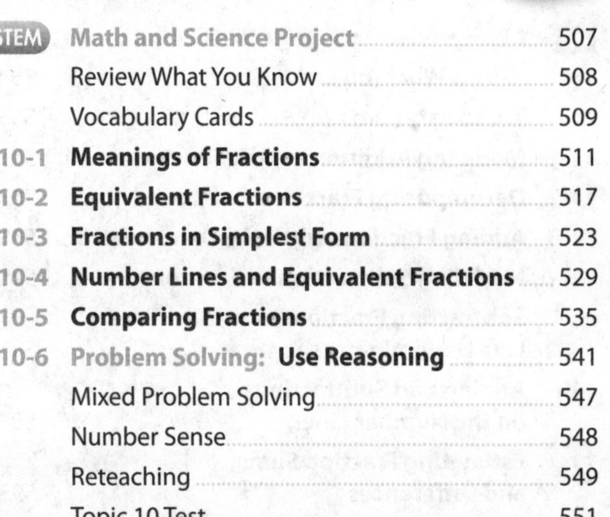

Volume 2

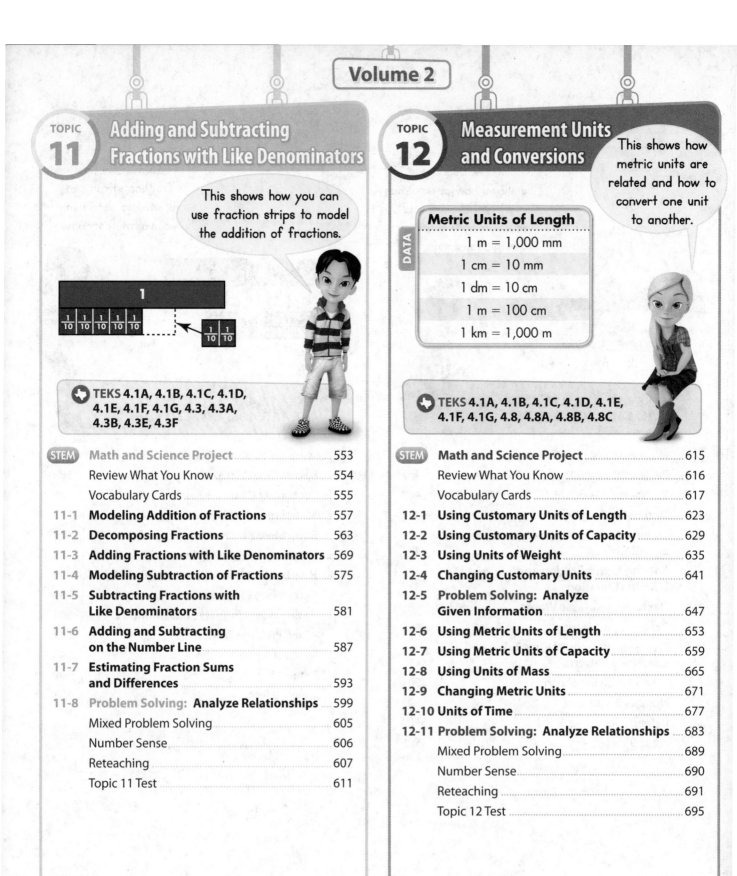

TOPIC 11 Adding and Subtracting Fractions with Like Denominators

This shows how you can use fraction strips to model the addition of fractions.

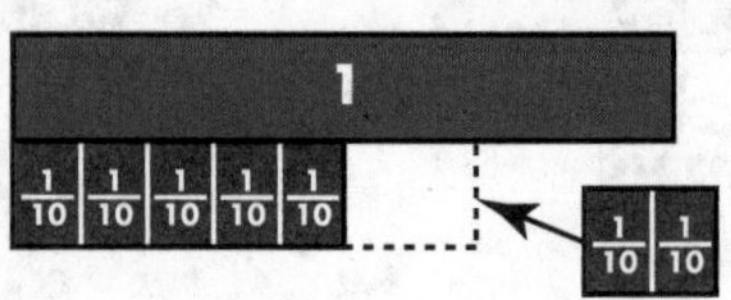

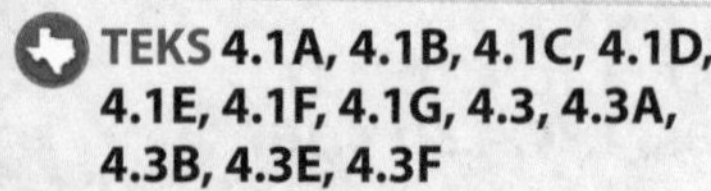

TEKS 4.1A, 4.1B, 4.1C, 4.1D, 4.1E, 4.1F, 4.1G, 4.3, 4.3A, 4.3B, 4.3E, 4.3F

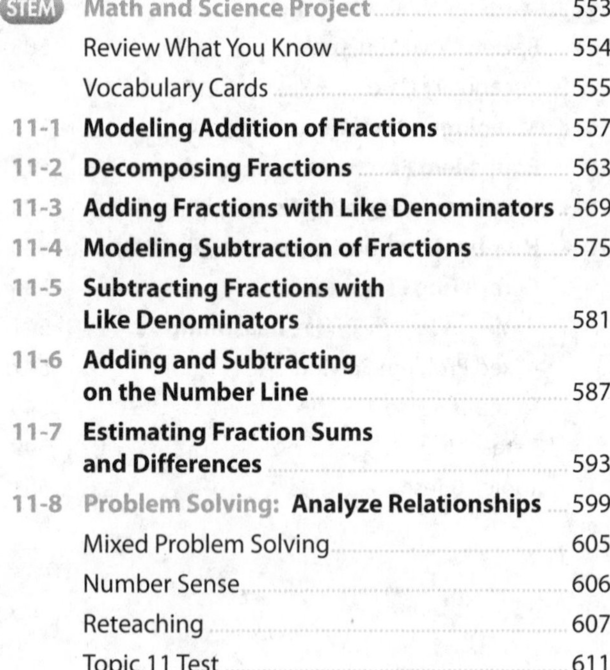

TOPIC 12 Measurement Units and Conversions

This shows how metric units are related and how to convert one unit to another.

DATA

Metric Units of Length
1 m = 1,000 mm
1 cm = 10 mm
1 dm = 10 cm
1 m = 100 cm
1 km = 1,000 m

TEKS 4.1A, 4.1B, 4.1C, 4.1D, 4.1E, 4.1F, 4.1G, 4.8, 4.8A, 4.8B, 4.8C

Volume 2

TOPIC 13 Solving Measurement Problems

8 ft
6 ft
width (w)
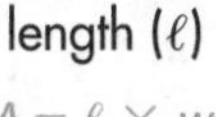
length (ℓ)

$A = \ell \times w$

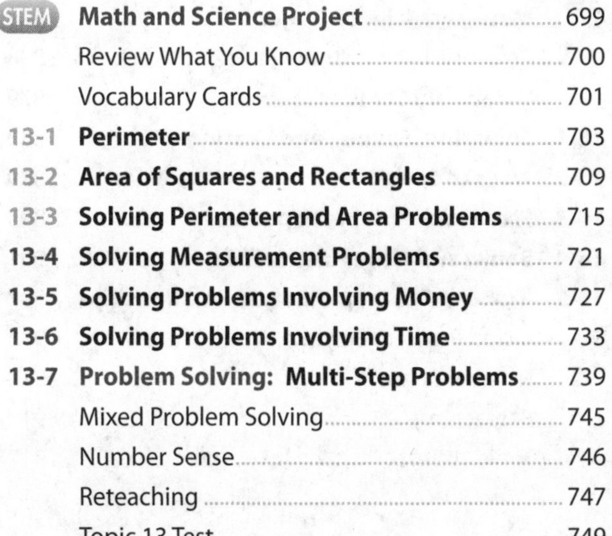
This shows how to calculate the area of a rectangle.

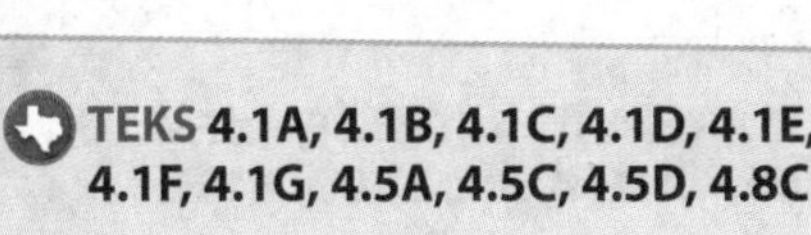

TEKS 4.1A, 4.1B, 4.1C, 4.1D, 4.1E, 4.1F, 4.1G, 4.5A, 4.5C, 4.5D, 4.8C

TOPIC 14 Lines, Angles, and Shapes

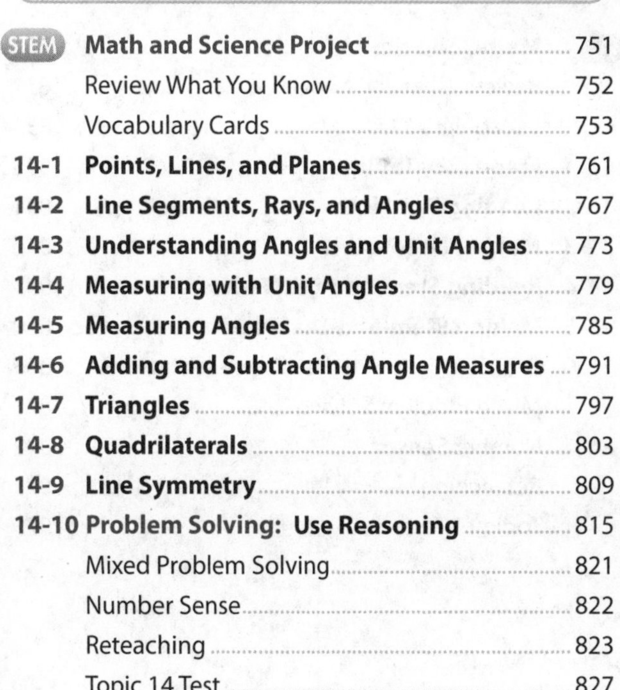
Hi, I'm Zeke. This shows how to measure and draw angles.
W
T
U

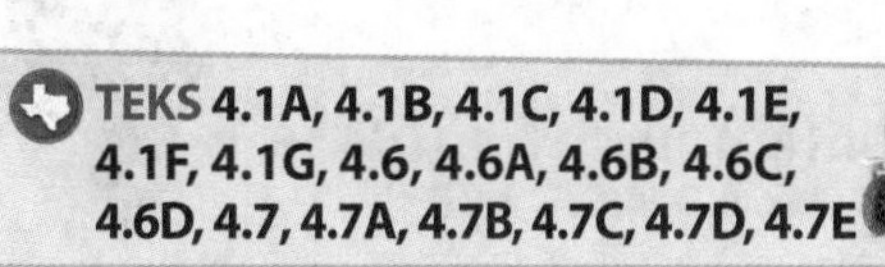

TEKS 4.1A, 4.1B, 4.1C, 4.1D, 4.1E, 4.1F, 4.1G, 4.6, 4.6A, 4.6B, 4.6C, 4.6D, 4.7, 4.7A, 4.7B, 4.7C, 4.7D, 4.7E

Volume 2

TOPIC 15 Data Analysis

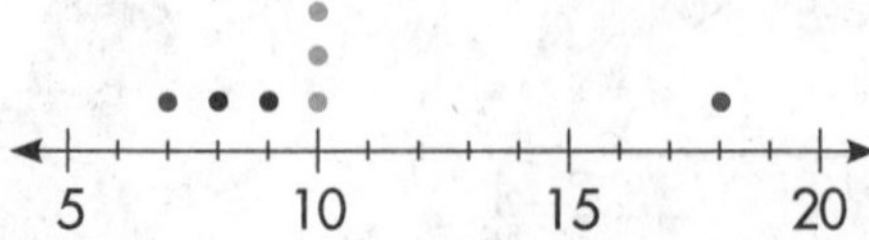

This shows how to create and use a dot plot to solve problems.

TEKS 4.1A, 4.1B, 4.1C, 4.1D, 4.1E, 4.1F, 4.1G, 4.9, 4.9A, 4.9B

TOPIC 16 Personal Financial Literacy

This shows different ways to save money.

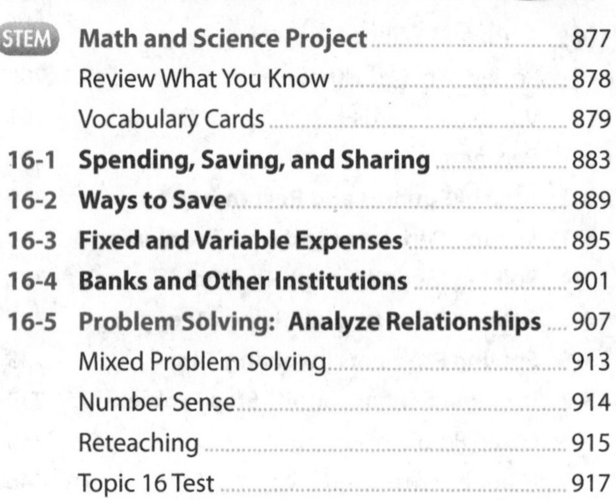

TEKS 4.1A, 4.1B, 4.1C, 4.1D, 4.1E, 4.1F, 4.1G, 4.10, 4.10A, 4.10B, 4.10C, 4.10D, 4.10E

Volume 2

Step Up to Grade 5

These lessons help prepare you for Grade 5.

TEKS 5.1A, 5.1B, 5.1C, 5.1D, 5.1E, 5.1F, 5.1G, 5.3A, 5.3H, 5.3I, 5.3J, 5.4, 5.4H, 5.6A, 5.6B

Have a great year!

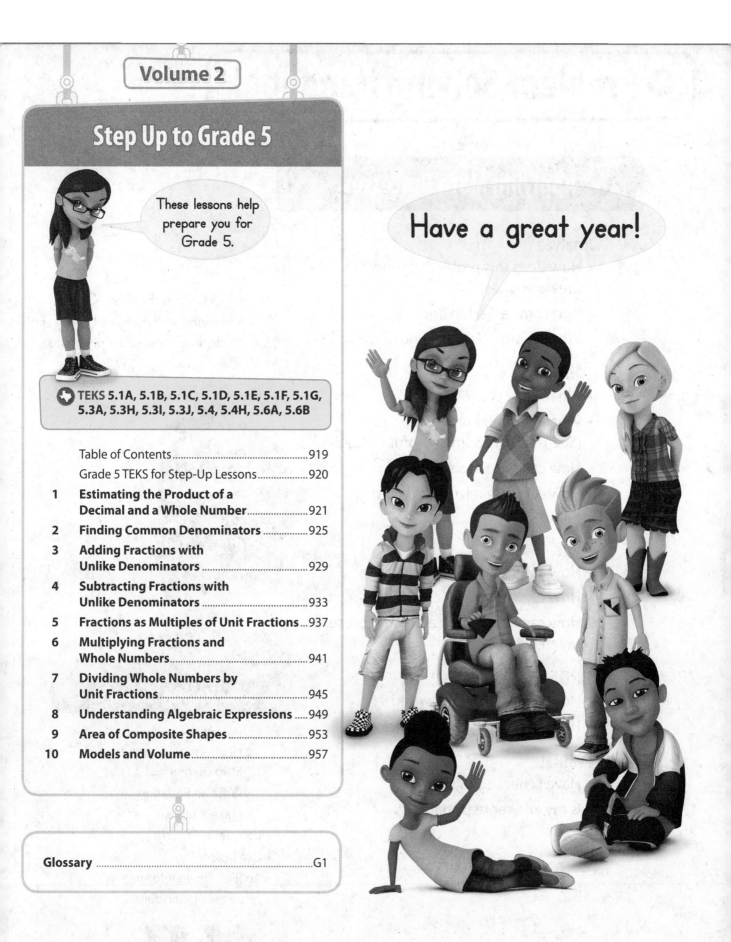

Problem-Solving Handbook

Applying Math Processes

Analyze
- How does this problem connect to previous ones?
- What am I asked to find?
- What information do I know?

Plan
- What is my plan?
- What strategies can I use? (See the list of some helpful strategies.)
- How can I use tools?
- How can I organize and record information?

Solve
- How can I use number sense?
- How can I estimate?
- How can I communicate and represent my thinking?

Justify
- How can I explain my work?
- How can I justify my answer?

Evaluate
- Have I checked my work?
- Is my answer reasonable?

Use this Problem-Solving Handbook throughout the year to help you solve problems.

Some Helpful Strategies

- Represent the Problem
  - Draw a Picture or Strip Diagram
  - Write an Equation
  - Make a Table or List
- Look for a Pattern
- Use Reasoning
- Analyze Given Information
- Analyze Relationships

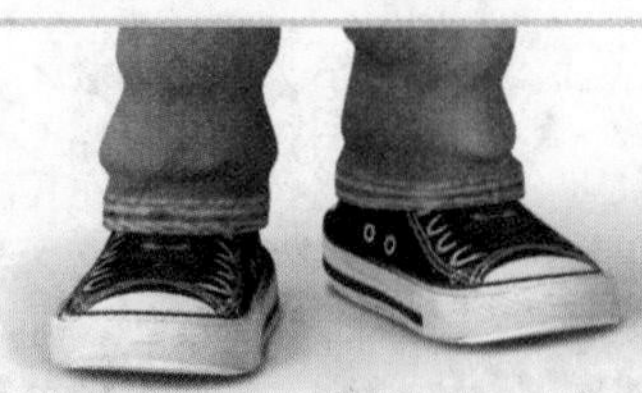

Problem-Solving Tools

Real Objects

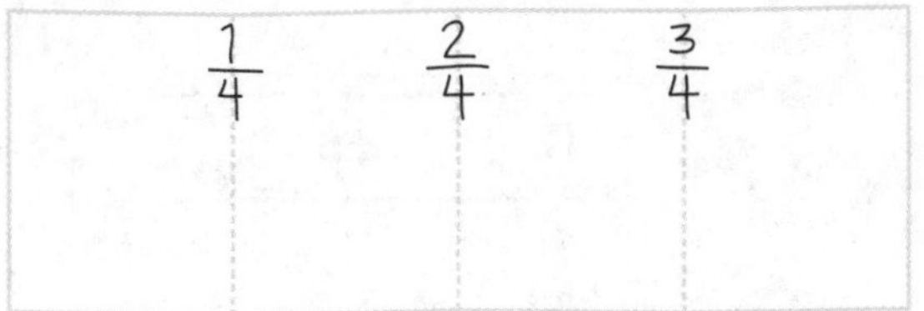

Manipulatives

Distance Run

Ann $\frac{3}{4}$ mile

Tom $\frac{1}{3}$ mile

Maria $\frac{5}{8}$ mile

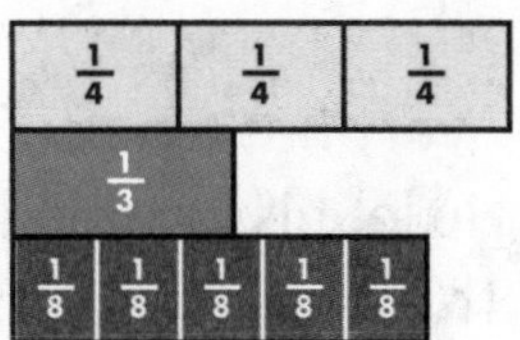

Paper and Pencil

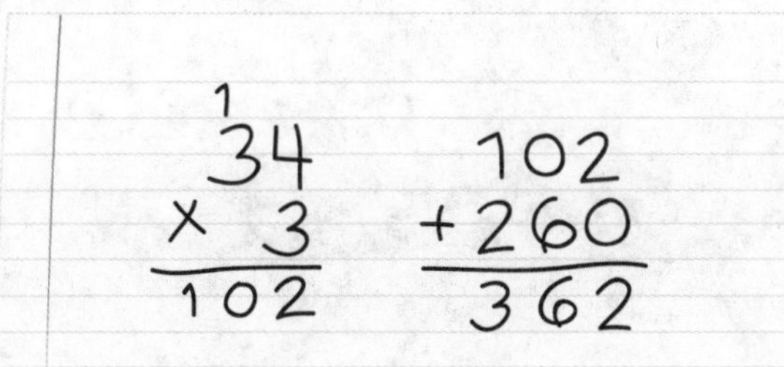

Technology

Problem-Solving Techniques

Mental Math

Sale!

Table...... $129
Chair......... $69
Desk....... $229

129 + 69 + 229 = ?
130 + 70 + 230 = 430
430 − 3 = 427

Estimation

There are 192 seats in a local concert hall. A jazz band plays there 3 nights each week.

192 × 3 = ?
About 200 × 3 =
600 people can see the band each week.

Number Sense

DATA

Students per Grade	
Kindergarten	50
Grade 1	56
Grade 2	58
Grade 3	57
Grade 4	54
Grade 5	55

Each grade has
between 50 and 60 students.
There are 6 grades.
The total number of students
will be between 300 and 360.

You can draw a **strip diagram** to show how the quantities in a problem are related. Then you can write an equation to solve the problem.

Part-Part-Whole: Addition and Subtraction

Draw this **strip diagram** for situations that involve joining parts of a whole or separating a whole into parts.

Whole → 72

17	55
↑ Part	↑ Part

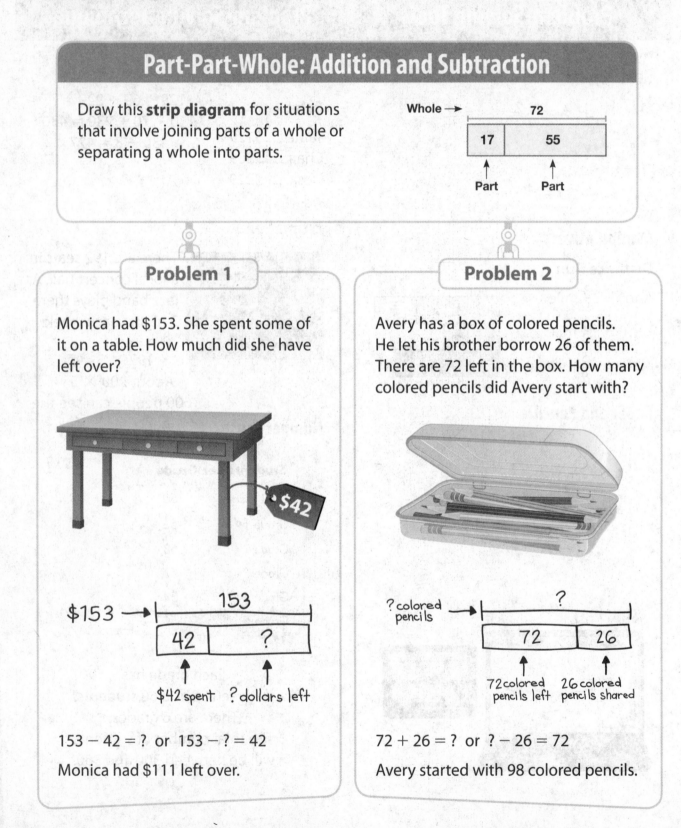

Problem 1

Monica had $153. She spent some of it on a table. How much did she have left over?

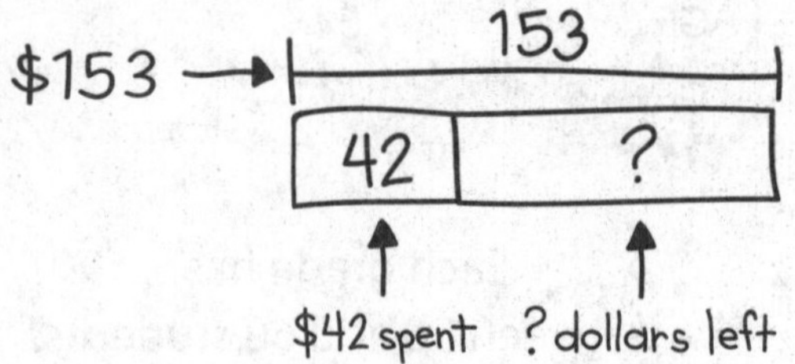

$153 - 42 = ?$ or $153 - ? = 42$

Monica had $111 left over.

Problem 2

Avery has a box of colored pencils. He let his brother borrow 26 of them. There are 72 left in the box. How many colored pencils did Avery start with?

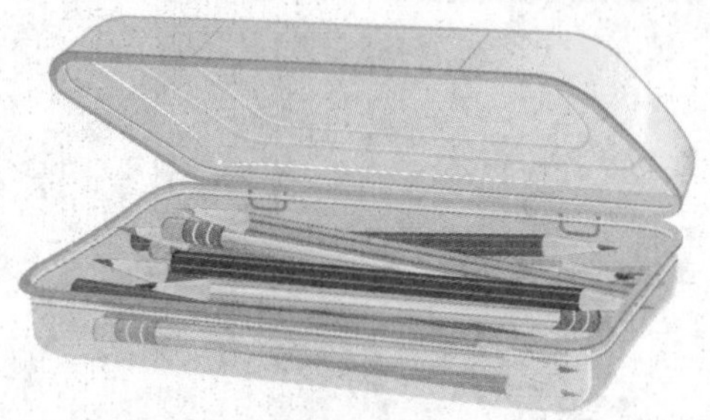

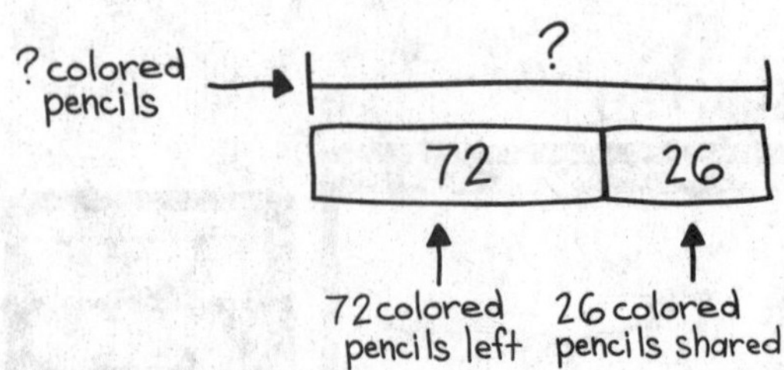

$72 + 26 = ?$ or $? - 26 = 72$

Avery started with 98 colored pencils.

Pictures help you understand.
Don't trust key words in a problem.

Comparison: Addition and Subtraction

Draw this **strip diagram** for comparison situations involving how much more one quantity is than another quantity.

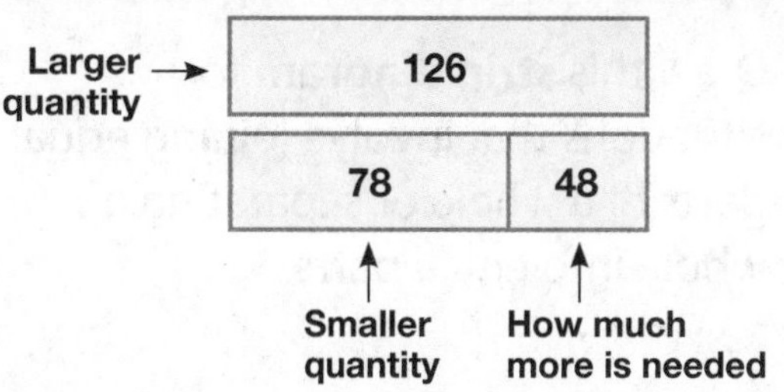

Problem 1

Perri has read the entire book shown below. Jae has read 221 facts in the book. How many more facts has Perri read than Jae?

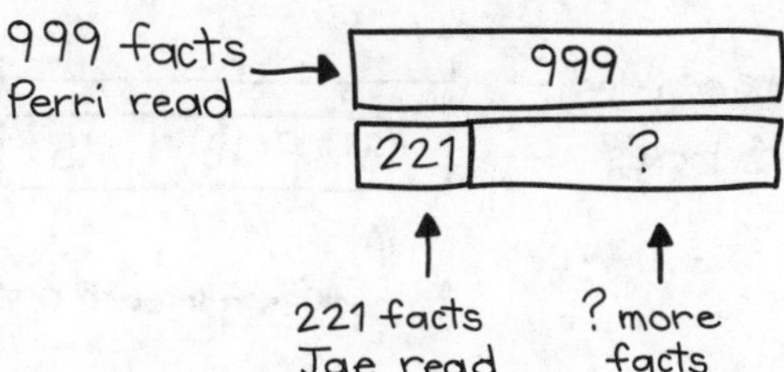

$999 - 221 = ?$

Perri has read 778 more facts than Jae.

Problem 2

Stanley has 128 classical songs on his computer. He has 234 more pop songs than classical songs. How many pop songs does Stanley have?

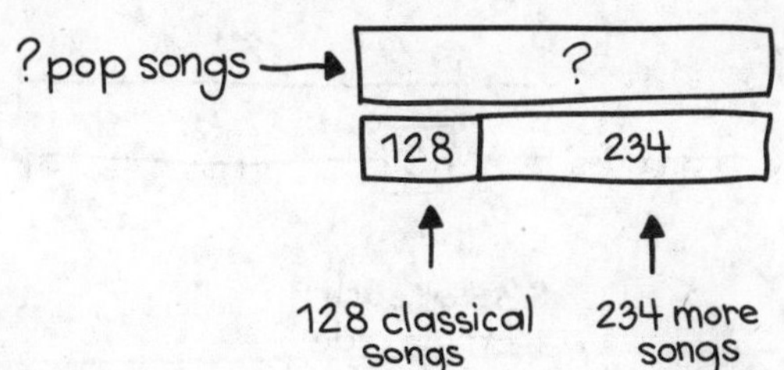

$128 + 234 = ?$

Stanley has 362 pop songs.

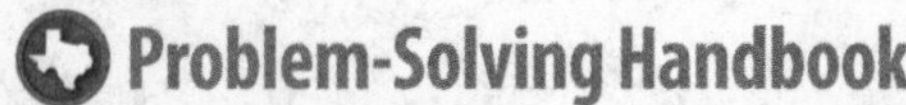

Problem-Solving Handbook

More Strip Diagrams

The **strip diagrams** on these pages can help you solve problems involving multiplication and division.

Equal Parts: Multiplication and Division

Draw this **strip diagram** for situations that involve joining equal parts of a whole or separating a whole into equal parts.

Whole → 84

Number of equal parts → | 28 | 28 | 28 |

↑ Amount for each part

Problem 1

Malik spent $27 riding the train this week. Each train ticket cost $3. How many times did Malik ride the train this week?

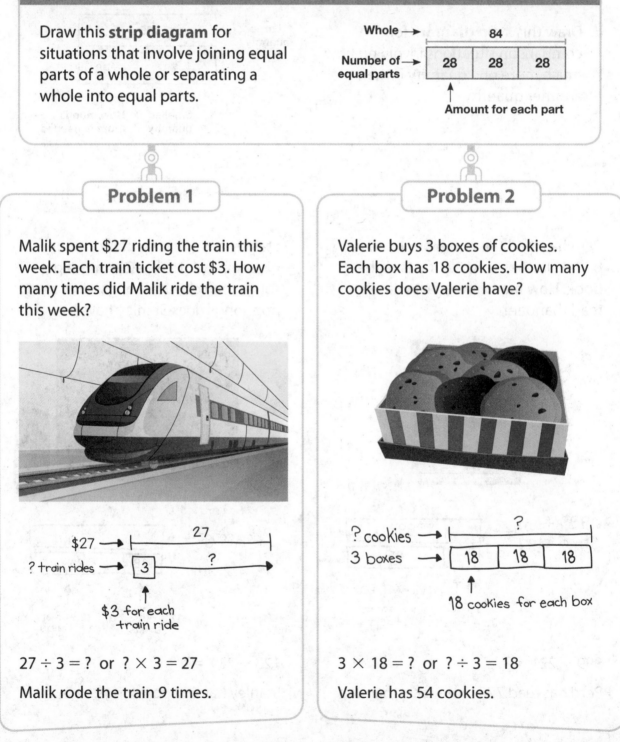

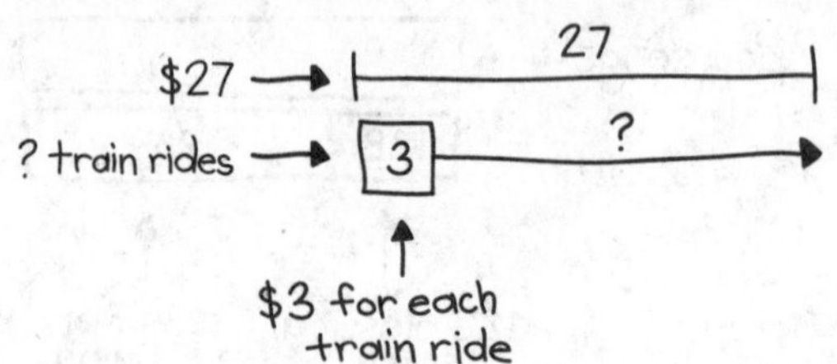

$27 \div 3 = ?$ or $? \times 3 = 27$

Malik rode the train 9 times.

Problem 2

Valerie buys 3 boxes of cookies. Each box has 18 cookies. How many cookies does Valerie have?

? cookies → ?

3 boxes → | 18 | 18 | 18 |

↑ 18 cookies for each box

$3 \times 18 = ?$ or $? \div 3 = 18$

Valerie has 54 cookies.

Multiplication and division are similar to addition and subtraction.

Comparison: Multiplication and Division

Draw this **strip diagram** for comparison situations involving how many times one quantity is of another quantity.

78

Larger quantity → | 26 | 26 | 26 | 3 times as many

Smaller quantity → | 26 |

Problem 1

Cal's jacket costs 4 times as much as his hat cost. Cal spent $40 on his coat. How much did Cal spend on his hat?

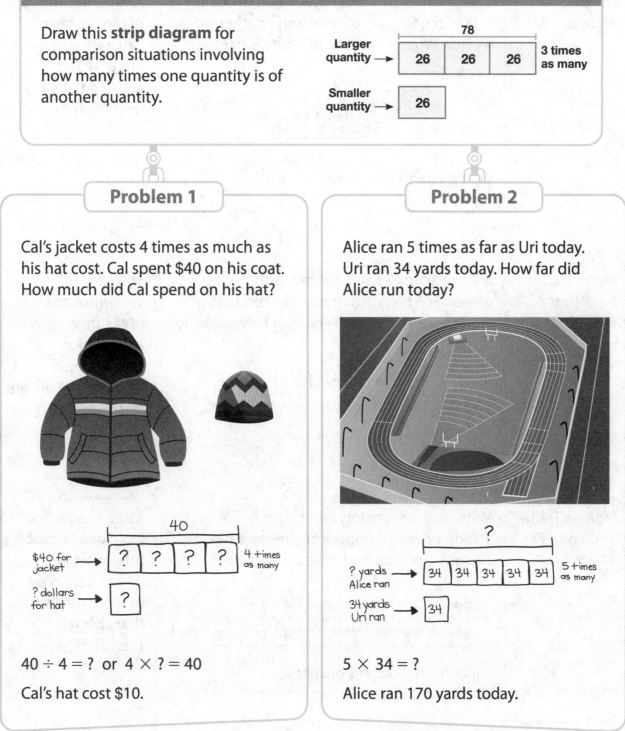

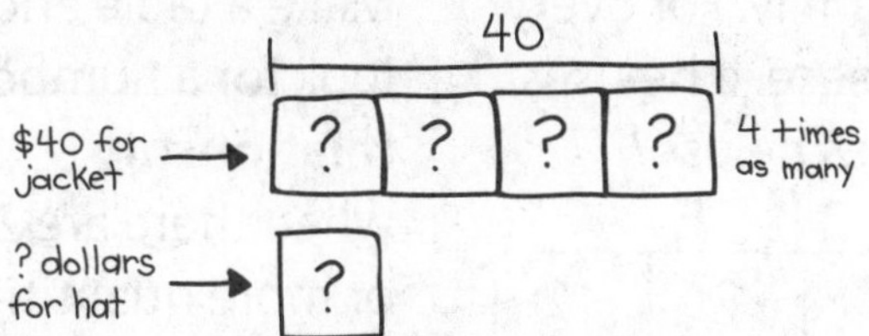

$40 \div 4 = ?$ or $4 \times ? = 40$

Cal's hat cost $10.

Problem 2

Alice ran 5 times as far as Uri today. Uri ran 34 yards today. How far did Alice run today?

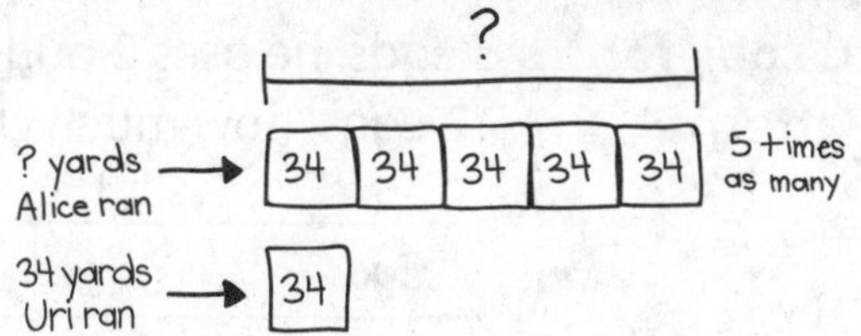

$5 \times 34 = ?$

Alice ran 170 yards today.

Problem-Solving Handbook

Creating a solution plan involves choosing and trying a strategy and then sometimes trying a different strategy.

Strategy	Example	When I Use It
Draw a Picture	Cheryl fences in a rectangular garden. One side of the fence is 8 yards, and another side is 4 yards. What is the area of Cheryl's garden? 8 yards 4 yards Cheryl's garden is 32 square yards.	A **representation** of the problem can help you visualize the facts and identify relationships.
Write an Equation	Brittany earns $9 an hour babysitting. She earned $63 babysitting this weekend. How many hours did Brittany babysit this weekend? Find $63 \div 9 = h$. $h = 7$, so Brittany babysat for 7 hours.	You can **communicate ideas** by writing an equation to describe a situation involving an operation or operations.
Make a Table and Look for a Pattern	Milton makes omelets for his family. For every 3 eggs, he uses 2 ounces of cheese. If he uses 12 eggs, how much cheese does he use? (table below) Milton uses 8 ounces of cheese.	Make a table and look for a number **relationship** when there are 2 or more quantities that change in a predictable way.

Eggs	3	6	9	12
Cheese (ounces)	2	4	6	8

There's almost always more than one way to solve a problem.

Strategy	Example	When I Use It
Use Reasoning	Max has a flight at 7:30 P.M. It takes him 50 minutes to get from his home to the airport. He wants to arrive at the airport $1\frac{1}{2}$ hours before his flight. When is the latest he should leave his home? Time Max leaves home ← 50 minutes ← Time Max gets to airport ← $1\frac{1}{2}$ hours ← Time of Max's flight 7:30 Max should leave his home at 5:10 P.M.	**Reason** with the facts you know to find what actions cause the end result.
Analyze Given Information	Leon bought twelve of the same kind of flower. He spent $48. What type of flower did he buy? 12 × $2 = $24 12 × $3 = $36 12 × $4 = $48 12 × $5 = $60 Leon bought irises.	**Analyze given information** to help find a solution.
Analyze Relationships	A newspaper has 58 articles. Twelve are sports, five are editorials, ten are business, and the rest are news. How many of the articles are news? 12 + 5 + 10 = 27 There are 27 articles that are sports, editorial, or business. 58 − 27 = 31 So, 31 articles are news.	You can **analyze relationships** in information you are given to find unknown information.

DATA

Flower Prices

Flower	Price
Tulip	$2
Rose	$3
Iris	$4
Lily	$5

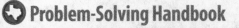

Problem-Solving Handbook

Problem-Solving Recording Sheet

This sheet helps you organize your work and make sense of problems.

Name Carlos

Teaching Tool 1

Problem-Solving Recording Sheet

Problem:

Lynda wants to buy a bike that costs $80. Her father will help by paying for $20. She will earn the rest by walking dogs. She earns $6 for each dog she walks. How many dogs does Lynda need to walk in order to have enough money for the bike?

ANALYZE

Need to Find

Number of dogs

Know

Earns $6 per dog.

Bike costs $80.

Dad's part is $20.

PLAN

Strategies

- ☐ Represent the Problem
  - ☑ Draw a Picture or Strip Diagram
  - ☑ Write an Equation
  - ☐ Make a Table or List
- ☐ Look for a Pattern
- ☐ Use Reasoning
- ☑ Analyze Given Information
- ☐ Analyze Relationships

SOLVE and JUSTIFY

Show Your Work and Answer.

$80

$20	? dollars

Dad's money ↑ Lynda's money ↑

20 + ? = 80, so Lynda must save $60.

Money earned → $60

Dogs walked → $6 ?

60 ÷ 6 = 10, so Lynda must walk 10 dogs.

EVALUATE

Check Your Work. Is Your Answer Reasonable?

I used inverse operations to check my work.

10 × 6 = 60

60 + 20 = 80

My answer is reasonable.

TT1

TOPIC 1 Place Value

Essential Questions:
How are greater numbers written?
How can whole numbers and decimals be compared and ordered?
How are fractions and decimals related?

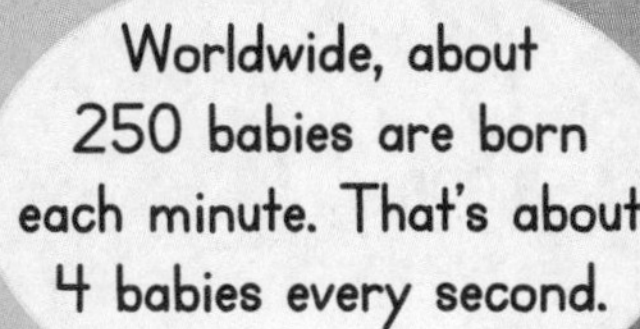

Worldwide, about 250 babies are born each minute. That's about 4 babies every second.

In the official 2010 Census, the population of the United States was 308,745,538.

Some scientists study world populations! Here's a project about population and ordering numbers.

Math and Science Project: Construct Tables and Charts

Do Research Use the Internet or other sources to find the populations in 2010 of five other countries.

Journal: Write a Report Include what you found. Also in your report:

- Make a place-value chart that includes the five populations.
- Write each population in expanded form.
- Make a table that orders the populations from greatest to least.

Name ______________________________

Review What You Know

Vocabulary

Choose the best term from the box. Write it on the blank.

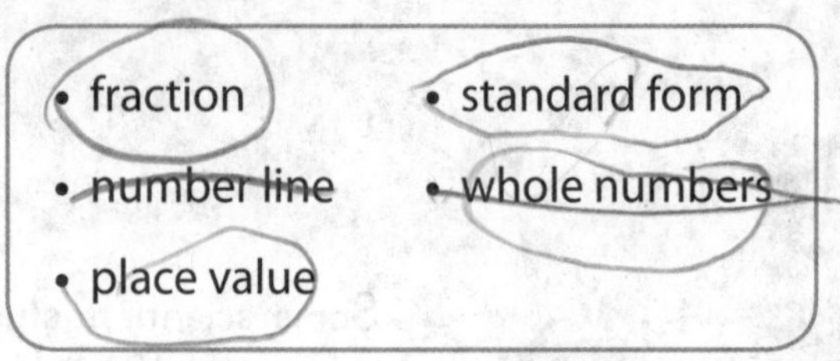

• fraction
• standard form
• number line
• whole numbers
• place value

1. The numbers 0, 1, 2, 3, 4, and so on are called __________.
2. A number written using only digits is in __________.
3. A __________ is a number used to name a part of a whole.
4. The value given to the place of a digit in a number is its __________.

Comparing Numbers

Compare each set of numbers using >, <, or =.

5. 84,201 ◯ 84,021
6. 66,313 ◯ 66,313
7. 4,289 ◯ 4,290
8. 1,007 ◯ 1,070
9. 73,082 ◯ 73,082
10. 90,725 ◯ 89,726

Place Value

Tell if the underlined digit is in the ones, tens, hundreds, thousands, or ten thousands place.

11. 79,482
12. 68,000
13. 41,506
14. 90,005
15. 35,100
16. 24,731
17. 82,997
18. 53,274

Fractions

19. **Represent** In which picture does the blue shaded portion NOT represent the fraction $\frac{5}{8}$?

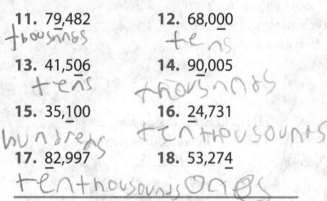

A

B

C

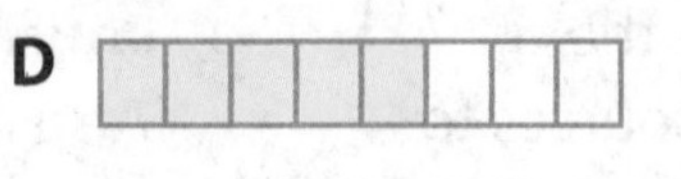

D

Now you are ready to learn more about place value.

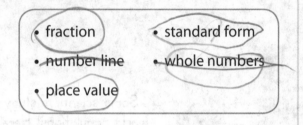

Name ______________________________

Solve & Share

In a recent year, a professional baseball team had an average home attendance of 36,382 fans. Total home attendance for the season was 2,946,949. Write these numbers in word form. ***Solve this problem any way you choose.***

Lesson 1-1

Numbers Through One Billion

TEKS 4.2B Represent the value of the digit in whole numbers through 1,000,000,000 and decimals to the hundredths using expanded notation and numerals. **Mathematical Process Standards** 4.1A, 4.1C, 4.1D, 4.1E, 4.1F, 4.1G

Digital Resources at SavvasTexas.com

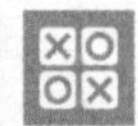

Solve Learn Glossary Check Tools Games

You can **communicate** mathematical ideas. Saying a number out loud can help you write its word form. ***Show your work in the space below!***

36,382
tnirtysix thousanthree Hunred Eithyto

2,946,949
Two millon nine hundred forty six tousand nine hundred forth nine

Look Back!

Connect Where have you seen greater numbers written? Give an example.

bank videogames
checks money casinos
Lotery

What Are Some Ways to Write Numbers to One Billion?

A

The graph shows major league baseball attendance over five years. Write the expanded form and word form of the total attendance during that time.

You can use a place-value chart to help.

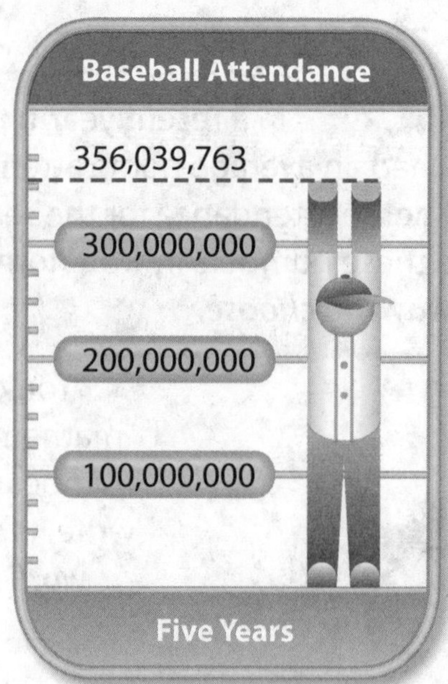

Use expanded form and word form.

B

The chart shows periods of three places, starting from the right and including the millions and billions periods.

Each digit of 356,039,763 is written in its place on the chart. Expanded form shows the sum of the values of each digit.

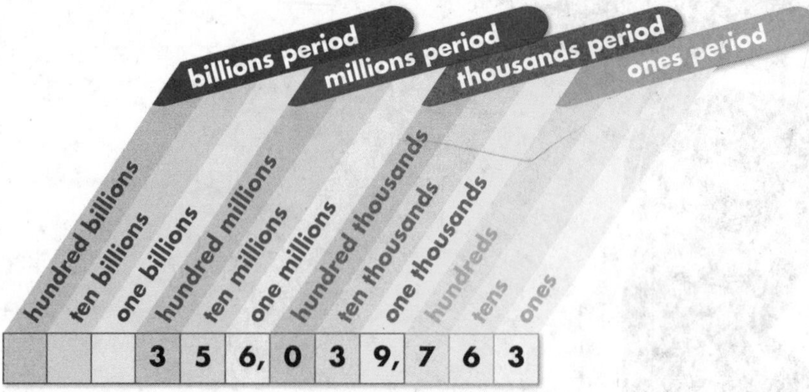

Expanded form: 300,000,000 + 50,000,000 + 6,000,000 + 30,000 + 9,000 + 700 + 60 + 3

Word form: three hundred fifty-six million, thirty-nine thousand, seven hundred sixty-three

Do You Understand?

Convince Me! What pattern exists in the three place values in each period?

Name

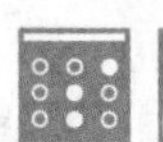

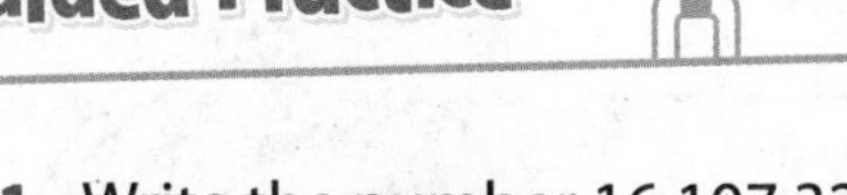

Guided Practice*

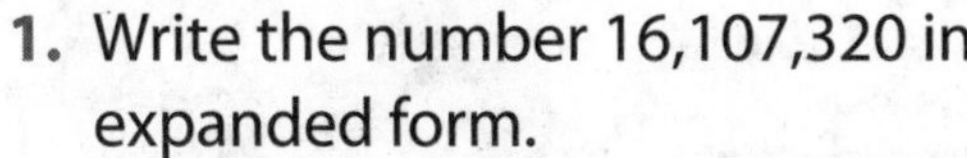

1. Write the number 16,107,320 in expanded form.

2. What is the value of the 5 in 356,039,763?

3. During a recent 10 years, 808,715,710 fans attended major league baseball games. What digit is in the ten millions place in 808,715,710?

4. Write the number 70,000,000 + 400,000 + 10,000 + 8,000 + 500 + 30 + 9 in word form and standard form.

5. What is the least 10-digit whole number? Write the number in word form and in standard form.

Independent Practice

6. Write the number in word form and in standard form.

   300,000,000 + 40,000,000 + 7,000,000 + 300,000 + 10,000 + 6,000 + 20 + 9

In **7** and **8**, write the number in expanded form.

7. 249,104,330

8. 430,290,100

In **9** and **10**, write the value of the red digit in each number.

9. 214,278,216

10. 334,290,652

*For another example, see Set A on page 77.

Problem Solving

11. **Number Sense** Fort Knox holds 147,300,000 ounces of gold. Write the number that is one million more.

12. In 2011, seventy-three million, four hundred eleven thousand, five hundred nineteen fans attended major league baseball games. Which choice shows ten million more?

    A 73,511,519
    B 74,411,519
    C 83,411,519
    D 84,411,519

13. **Connect** Which digit has the same value in both numbers? What is the value of that digit?

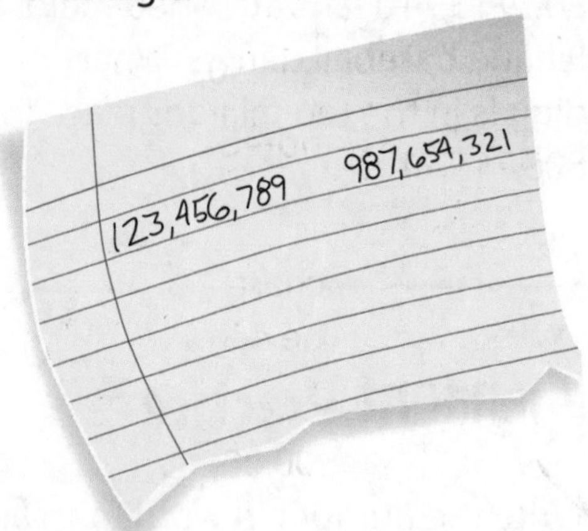

14. Jeff's photo album can hold 12 photos on a page. He has two pages filled. How many photos does he have?

15. **Explain** Which number will take less time to write in expanded form, 800,000,000 or 267,423?

16. **Extend Your Thinking** Two numbers have the same digits in the millions period, the same digits in the thousands period, and the same digits in the ones period. Do these two numbers have the same value? Explain.

17. **Extend Your Thinking** One number has a 7 in the millions period. Another number has an 8 in the millions period. The thousands periods and the ones periods of both numbers are identical. Is the second number one million greater than the first? Explain.

Name ____________________

Solve & Share

In the number 655,000, what is the relationship between the value of the 5 in the ten thousands place compared to the value of the 5 in the thousands place? ***Solve this problem any way you choose.***

Lesson 1-2
Place Value Relationships

TEKS 4.2A Interpret the value of each place-value position as 10 times the position to the right and as one-tenth of the value of the place to its left. Also, 4.2. **Mathematical Process Standards** 4.1C, 4.1D, 4.1E, 4.1F

Digital Resources at SavvasTexas.com

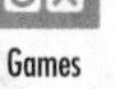

You can **analyze relationships.** Think about how place values relate to each other. ***Show your work in the space below!***

Look Back!

Number Sense What is the relationship between the value of the 5 in the thousands place compared to the value of the 5 in the ten thousands place?

How Are Place-Value Positions Related?

A

The official 2010 Census reported the population of Houston to be 2,099,451.

How are the two 9s in that number related to each other?

Writing the number in a place-value chart can help.

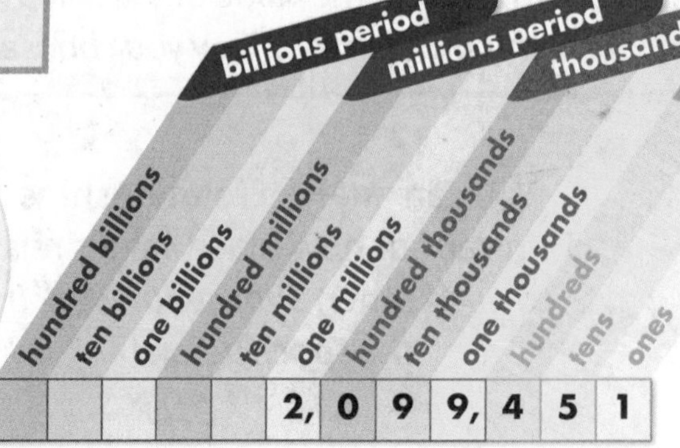

Compare place values to values on the right and on the left.

B

One Way

The value of each place-value position is 10 times the value of the place to its right.

Think about the expanded form of 2,099,451:

2,000,000 + 90,000 + 9,000 + 400 + 50 + 1

The value of the 9 in the ten thousands place is 10 times the value of the 9 in the thousands place.

C

Another Way

The value of each place-value position is one-tenth the value of the place to its left.

Again, think about the expanded form of 2,099,451:

2,000,000 + 90,000 + 9,000 + 400 + 50 + 1

The value of the 9 in the thousands place is one-tenth the value of the 9 in the ten thousands place.

Do You Understand?

Convince Me! True or False? Explain.

The value of the red 4 is 100 times the value of the blue 4 in the number at the right.

4,440

Name ______________________________

Guided Practice*

In **1** and **2**, write whether the value of the red digit is ten times or one-tenth the value of the blue digit.

1. 436,033,281 **2.** 770,652,487

In **3** and **4**, name the values of the given digits in the numbers.

3. The 2s in 302,997,621 **4.** The 1s in 896,541,174

5. Is the value of the second 5 in 450,852,137 one-tenth the value of the first 5? Explain.

6. Is the value of the 7 in 763,419,251 ten times the value of the 6? Explain.

Independent Practice

In **7** through **10**, write whether the value of the red digit is ten times the value of the blue digit, one-tenth the value of the blue digit, or neither.

7. 832,251,760 **8.** 990,326,817

9. 571,726,398 **10.** 216,447,032

You can use a place-value chart to help.

In **11** and **12**, name the values of the given digits in the numbers.

11. The 7s in 775,823,159

12. The 4s in 504,405,623

**For another example, see Set B on page 77.*

Problem Solving

13. Reason Write the number 43,335 in the place-value chart. What can you say about the 3s in the number 43,335?

thousands period			ones period		
hundred thousands	ten thousands	one thousands	hundreds	tens	ones

Can you relate the middle 3 to the 3 to its right and the 3 to its left?

14. In one year, a large airport was used by 5,662,000 passengers. In the number 5,662,000, the value of the 6 in the hundred thousands place is _____ the value of the 6 in the ten thousands place.

A six times
B ten times
C one tenth
D one sixth

15. Mark needs to solve $56 \div 8 = \square$. What multiplication fact can he use to find the missing number in this division fact?

16. Represent Write the expanded form of the number shown in the place-value chart.

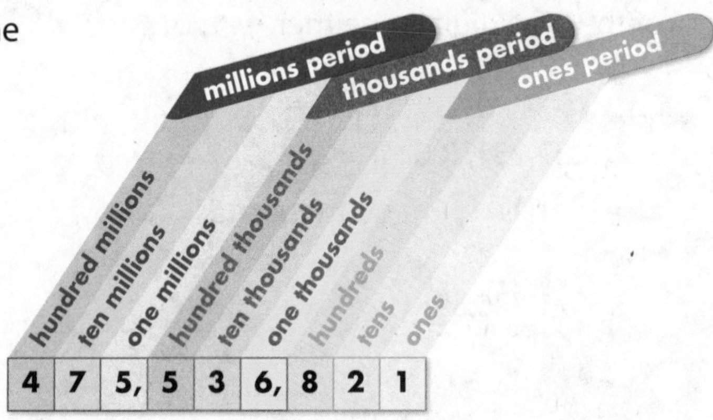

17. Extend Your Thinking Mia says that in the number 55,555,555, all the digits have the same value. Is she correct? Explain.

18. Extend Your Thinking Vin says that in the number 4,346, one 4 is 10 times as great as the other 4. Is he correct? Explain.

Name ______________________

Homework 1-2
Place Value Relationships

Another Look!

According to the 2010 Census, the total population of Florida is 18,801,310. How are the two 8s in that number related to each other?

A place-value chart can help you see the relationship between digits in a number.

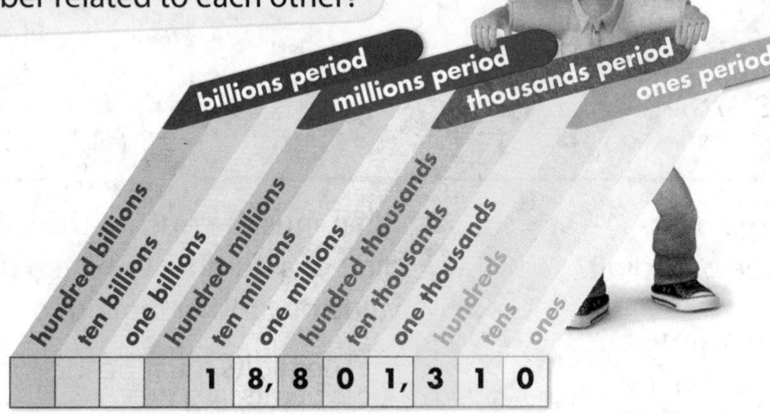

				1	8,	8	0	1,	3	1	0

Write the number in expanded form.
10,000,000 + 8,000,000 + 800,000 + 1,000 + 300 + 10

Look at the number of zeros after each 8.

The value of the 8 in the one millions place is 10 times the value of the 8 in the hundred thousands place.

The value of the 8 in the hundred thousands place is one-tenth the value of the 8 in the one millions place.

1. What is the relationship between the 1s in 911,147,835?
The 1 in the ten millions place is __1,000__ the value of the middle 1.
The 1 in the hundred thousands place is __100__ the value of the middle 1.

In **2** and **3**, relate the value of the red digit to the value of the blue digit.

2. 709,946,107
yes the vele is the same

3. 115,093,628
ai's the same

In **4** and **5**, name the values of the given digits in the numbers.

4. The 5s in 155,523,962
the same vwile

5. The 8s in 126,888,493

6. **Reason** The table shows the number of cards in different numbers of packages.

   a. How many cards will there be in 9 packages?

   b. How many cards will there be in 1 package?

DATA

Number of Packages	Number of Cards
2	10
3	15
6	30

7. In which number is the red digit one-tenth the value of the blue digit?

   A 144,127,288
   B 144,127,288
   C 144,127,288
   D 144,127,288

8. What must be true for the value of one digit of a number to be ten times the value of another digit in that number?

   A The digits must be identical and in the same period.
   B The digits must be identical and in the same number.
   C The digits must be identical and next to each other.
   D The digits must be identical and in different periods.

9. **Extend Your Thinking** In the number 514,482,441, how is the relationship between the first pair of 4s the same as the relationship between the second pair of 4s? How is it different?

10. **Extend Your Thinking** Is the blue digit in 321,568,794 ten times the value of the red digit in 469,751,803? Explain.

Name ______________________________

Solve & Share

A robotic submarine can dive to a depth of 26,000 feet. Which oceans can the sub explore all way to the bottom? ***Solve this problem any way you choose.***

Lesson 1-3

Comparing and Ordering Whole Numbers

TEKS 4.2C Compare and order whole numbers to 1,000,000,000 and represent comparisons using the symbols >, <, or =. Also, 4.2.
Mathematical Process Standards 4.1A, 4.1B, 4.1C, 4.1D, 4.1E

Digital Resources at SavvasTexas.com

Solve

Learn

Glossary

Check

Tools
Games

You can **create and use representations.** A number line or place-value chart can help you show your work. ***Show your work in the space below!***

DATA

Ocean	Depth
Atlantic	28,232 ft
Pacific	35,840 ft
Indian	23,376 ft

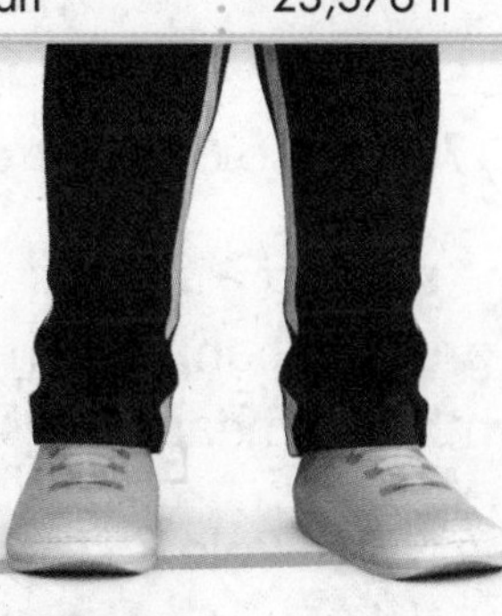

Look Back!

Connect Which of the oceans listed is the shallowest? Which is the deepest?

How Do You Compare Numbers?

A

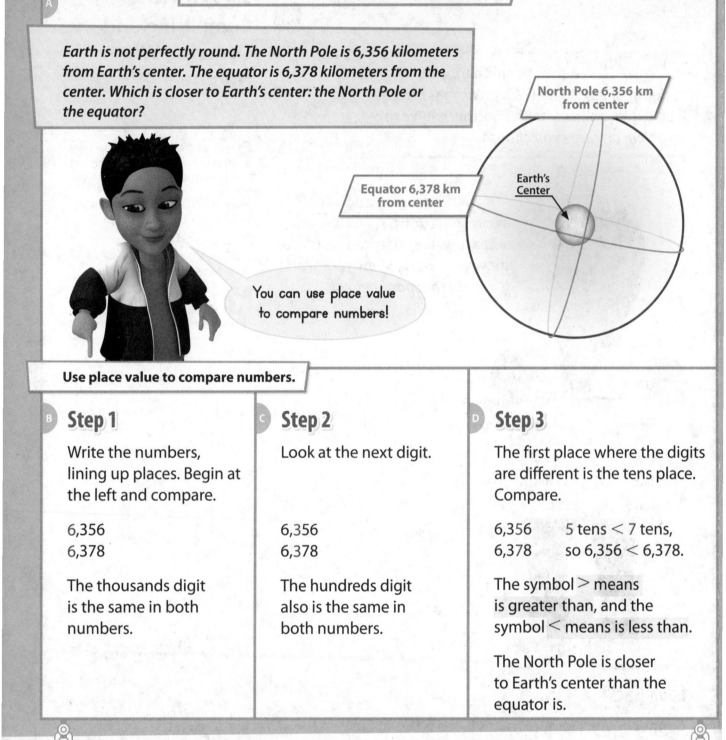

Earth is not perfectly round. The North Pole is 6,356 kilometers from Earth's center. The equator is 6,378 kilometers from the center. Which is closer to Earth's center: the North Pole or the equator?

You can use place value to compare numbers!

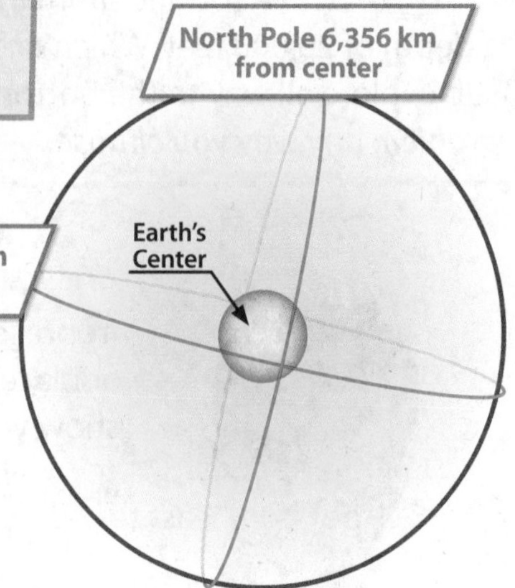

Use place value to compare numbers.

B

Step 1

Write the numbers, lining up places. Begin at the left and compare.

6,356
6,378

The thousands digit is the same in both numbers.

C

Step 2

Look at the next digit.

6,356
6,378

The hundreds digit also is the same in both numbers.

D

Step 3

The first place where the digits are different is the tens place. Compare.

6,356   5 tens $<$ 7 tens,
6,378   so 6,356 $<$ 6,378.

The symbol $>$ means is greater than, and the symbol $<$ means is less than.

The North Pole is closer to Earth's center than the equator is.

Do You Understand?

Convince Me! Is a whole number with 4 digits always greater than or less than a whole number with 3 digits? Explain.

Name

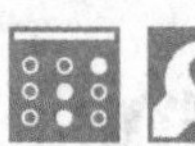

Guided Practice*

In **1** and **2**, complete by writing > or < in each ◯.

1. 2,643 ◯ 2,801

2. 6,519 ◯ 6,582

In **3** and **4**, order the numbers from least to greatest.

3. 7,502,941 6,793,868 6,723,194

4. 80,371 15,048 80,137

5. Number Sense List these continents in order from least to greatest area.

DATA

Continent	Area (in square miles)
Europe	4,010,000
North America	9,450,000
South America	6,890,000

6. Formulate a Plan Which places would you use to order these numbers from greatest to least?
32,463 32,482 32,947

Independent Practice

In **7** through **10**, complete by writing > or < in each ◯.

7. 22,873 ◯ 22,774

8. 1,912,706 ◯ 1,913,898

9. 412,632 ◯ 412,362

10. 999,999,999 ◯ 1,000,000,000

In **11** through **14**, write the numbers in order from least to greatest.

11. 43,783 434,282 64,382

12. 723,433 72,324 72,432

13. 58,028 85,843 77,893

14. 274,849,551 283,940,039 23,485,903

*For another example, see Set C on page 77.

Problem Solving

15. **Number Sense** Which shows the planets in order from the one closest to the sun to the one farthest from the sun?

A Earth, Venus, Jupiter, Mercury, Mars
B Mercury, Venus, Earth, Mars, Jupiter
C Mars, Jupiter, Mercury, Venus, Earth
D Jupiter, Mars, Earth, Venus, Mercury

DATA

The Five Closest Planets to the Sun

Planet	Distance (miles)
Earth	93,000,000
Jupiter	483,000,000
Mars	142,000,000
Mercury	36,000,000
Venus	67,000,000

16. Which place value would you use to compare the numbers 14,321 and 11,941?

A tens
B hundreds
C thousands
D ten thousands

17. **Number Sense** Write three numbers that are greater than 780,000 but less than 781,000.

18. **Reason** Could you use only the millions period to order 462,409,524, 463,409,524, and 463,562,391?

19. **Math and Science** Write the population of Alaska in word form and in expanded form.

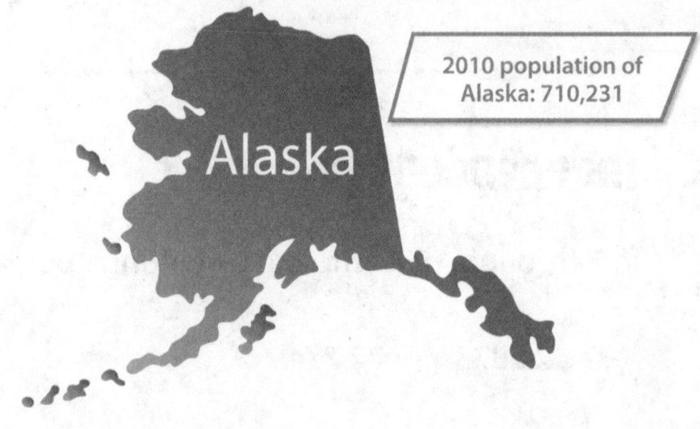

20. **Extend Your Thinking** Describe how to order 7,463, 74,633, and 74,366 from least to greatest.

Name ______________________________

Homework 1-3

Comparing and Ordering Whole Numbers

Another Look!

The distance around Earth depends on whether you measure around the equator or around the North and South Poles.

Distance around the poles: 131,463,255 ft

Earth's Center

Distance around the equator: 131,479,659 ft

Which distance is greater: the distance around the equator or the distance around the North and South Poles?

Step 1	Step 2	Step 3
Write the numbers, lining up the places. Begin at the left and compare. 131,479,659 131,463,255 The hundred millions digit is the same in both numbers.	Continue comparing the digits from left to right. 131,479,659 131,463,255 The ten millions, one millions, and hundred thousands digits are the same.	The first place where the digits are different is the ten thousands. 131,479,659 131,463,255 Compare. 7 ten thousands > 6 ten thousands, so 131,479,659 > 131,463,255. The distance around Earth is greater around the equator.

1. Use place value to order the numbers from greatest to least.

3,922,284   37,544,237   3,921,107   37,544,037

In **2** through **7**, complete by writing > or < in each ◯.

2. 2,854,376 ◯ 2,845,763

3. 6,452,789 ◯ 6,452,876

4. 59,635 ◯ 59,536

5. 29,374,125 ◯ 30,743,225

6. 159,480,000 ◯ 92,418,218

7. 449,321 ◯ 450,123

8. Number Sense Write the names of the oceans in order from least to greatest area. Write a number that is between the two numbers in the middle of the list.

DATA

Ocean	Area (square kilometers)
Atlantic	82,400,000
Pacific	165,760,000
Arctic	14,090,000
Indian	65,526,700

9. Analyze Information If the continents were ordered from greatest to least area, which continent would be in the middle of the list?

DATA

Continent	Area (square kilometers)
Africa	30,065,000
Antarctica	13,209,000
Asia (plus the Middle East)	44,579,000
Australia (plus Oceania)	7,687,000
Europe	9,938,000
North America	24,256,000
South America	17,819,000

10. Number Sense Write the number 39,005 in expanded form.

11. The Atlantic Ocean has an area of 33,420,000 square miles. This area is between which numbers?

A 33,400,000 and 33,440,000
B 33,000,000 and 33,040,000
C 33,100,000 and 33,419,000
D 33,430,000 and 33,500,000

12. Extend Your Thinking If the area of the continent in the middle of the list above in Problem 9 had an area of ten million more square kilometers, would it still be in the middle of an ordered list? Explain.

13. Extend Your Thinking The first digit of two different numbers is in the hundred millions place. Both numbers contain the same digits. Can you determine the greater of the two numbers? Explain.

Name

Guided Practice*

In **1** through **6**, round each number to the place of the underlined digit.

1. 128,955 **2.** 85,639

3. 9,924 **4.** 194,524

5. 160,656 **6.** 149,590

7. Explain Explain how to round a number when 7 is the digit to the right of the rounding place.

8. A city's population is 421,906. Round 421,906 to the nearest hundred thousand and to the nearest thousand.

Independent Practice

In **9** through **28**, round each number to the place of the underlined digit.

9. 493,295 **10.** 39,230 **11.** 277,292 **12.** 54,846

13. 4,028 **14.** 638,365 **15.** 453,280 **16.** 17,909

17. 1,456,000 **18.** 55,460 **19.** 321,679 **20.** 417,547

21. 117,821 **22.** 75,254 **23.** 9,049,999 **24.** 666,821

25. 2,420 **26.** 900,985 **27.** 9,511 **28.** 73,065

**For another example, see Set D on page 78.*

Problem Solving

29. For each zoo in the chart, round the attendance to the nearest hundred thousand.

Zoo Attendance	
Zoo D	234,679
Zoo E	872,544
Zoo F	350,952

30. Number Sense Write four numbers that round to 700,000 when rounded to the nearest hundred thousand.

31. A forest ranger correctly rounded the number of visitors to a park one summer to be 120,000 visitors. Which of the following could have been the actual number of visitors to the park?

A 123,900
B 126,480
C 128,770
D 130,000

32. Analyze Information Amy counted the number of boys and girls at a party. She recorded the results in the tally chart below.

Party	
Girls	///
Boys	𝍸 //

How many more boys than girls were at the party?

33. Connect A fruit market sold 3,849 apples, 3,498 oranges, and 3,894 pears in one day. Round each number to the nearest hundred. Then order the rounded numbers from greatest to least.

34. Extend Your Thinking Liz had attended class every day since she started school as a kindergartner. She said she had been in school for about 1,000 days. What numbers could be the actual number of school days if Liz rounded to the nearest ten?

35. Extend Your Thinking Write a 5-digit number that when rounded to the nearest thousand and hundred will have a result that is the same. Explain.

Name ______________________

Solve & Share

Write to explain why 23,542 rounds to 24,000 when rounded to the nearest thousand.

You can **create and use representations,** such as a number line. ***Show your work in the space below!***

Problem Solving

Lesson 1-5
Writing to Explain

TEKS 4.1G Display, explain, and justify mathematical ideas and arguments using precise mathematical language in written or oral communication.
Mathematical Process Standards 4.1B, 4.1C, 4.1D, 4.1F

Digital Resources at SavvasTexas.com

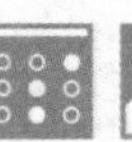

Solve | Learn | Glossary | Check | Tools | Games

Look Back!

Communicate Do you think your written explanation above is a good explanation? Tell why.

How Can You Write a Good Math Explanation?

A-Z

A Analyze

What happens to the area of the rectangle if the lengths of its sides are doubled?

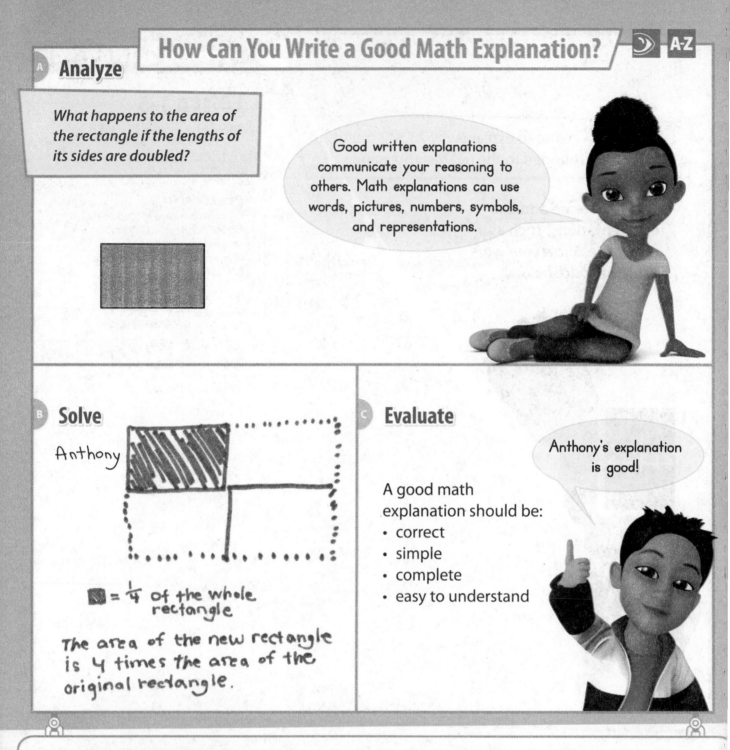

Good written explanations communicate your reasoning to others. Math explanations can use words, pictures, numbers, symbols, and representations.

B Solve

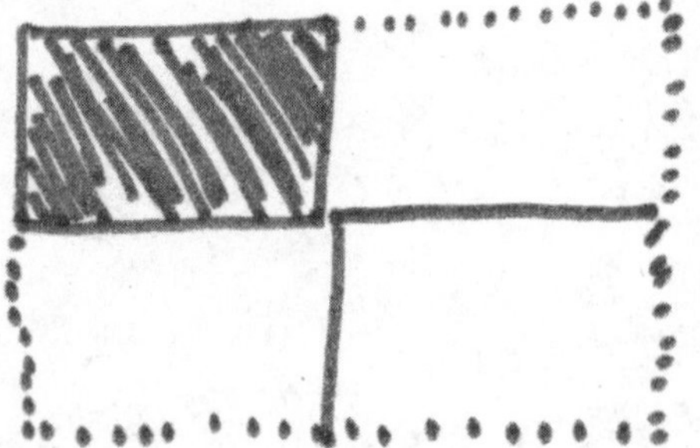
Anthony

■ = 1/4 of the whole rectangle

The area of the new rectangle is 4 times the area of the original rectangle.

C Evaluate

A good math explanation should be:

- correct
- simple
- complete
- easy to understand

Anthony's explanation is good!

Do You Understand?

Convince Me! How could Anthony's explanation be even better?

Name ___

Guided Practice*

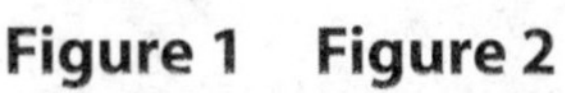

1. **Explain** Complete the table. Look for a pattern. Write and explain how to find the number of small triangles in Figure 4.

Figure 1 **Figure 2** **Figure 3** **Figure 4**

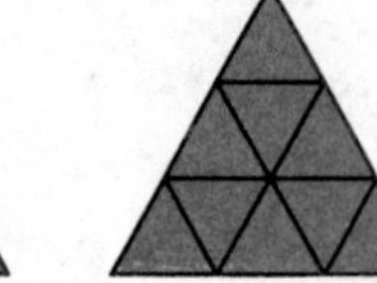
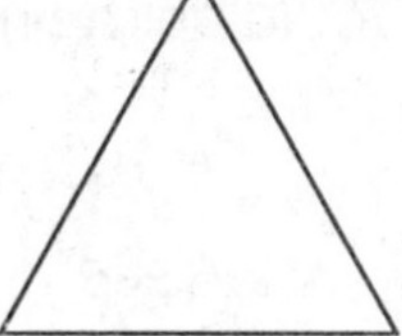

Figure Number	1	2	3	4
Number of Rows	1	2		
Number of Small Triangles				

2. The product of two numbers is 48. When the greater number is divided by the lesser number, the quotient is 3. Write and explain how to find the two numbers.

Independent Practice

3. **Explain** Write and explain the pattern and how to find the number of small cubes in Figure 4.

Figure 1 **Figure 2** **Figure 3** **Figure 4**

4. The Chinese calendar names each year after one of 12 animals. The animals are always repeated in this order: Rat, Ox, Tiger, Rabbit, Dragon, Snake, Horse, Sheep, Monkey, Rooster, Dog, and Pig. 2015 is the Year of the Sheep. How can you find the animal name for the year you were born?

*For another example, see Set E on page 78.

Problem Solving

5. **Reason** Write and explain why it might be easier to place the numbers in Set A in order from least to greatest than it would be the numbers in Set B.

DATA

Set A	Set B
325,865	456,089
45,760	492,111
1,025,680	409,867

6. The numbers below follow a pattern. Four students give explanations for the pattern and how to find the next number. Which explanation is best?

50 500 5,000 50,000 ____

A Each number is 10 times as great as the number before it. The next number is 500,000.

B The pattern uses higher place values to write numbers in the thousands periods.

C I can multiply each number by 10 to find the next number. The pattern repeats 5 times.

D The next number is $10 \times 50,000$, or 500,000.

7. **Number Sense** Jared said, "348 rounds to 350 and 350 rounds to 400. So, 348 rounds to 400." Write and explain if Jared's reasoning is correct.

8. Mr. Juarez has three children. The sum of their ages is 19. The oldest child is twice the age of the youngest child. The middle child is 7 years old. Explain how to find the ages of the oldest and youngest child.

9. **Extend Your Thinking** There is $\frac{5}{8}$ of a pizza left from last night's dinner. Gina wants to share it with her brother. Write and explain how to share the five slices of pizza equally.

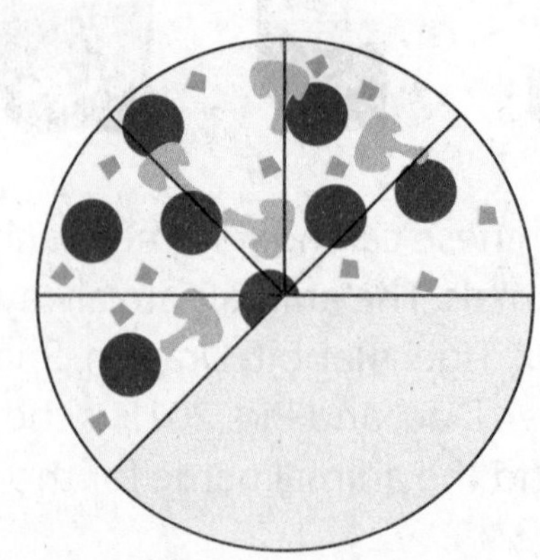

Name

Homework 1-5
Writing to Explain

Another Look!

What happens to the perimeter of a rectangle if the lengths of its sides are doubled?

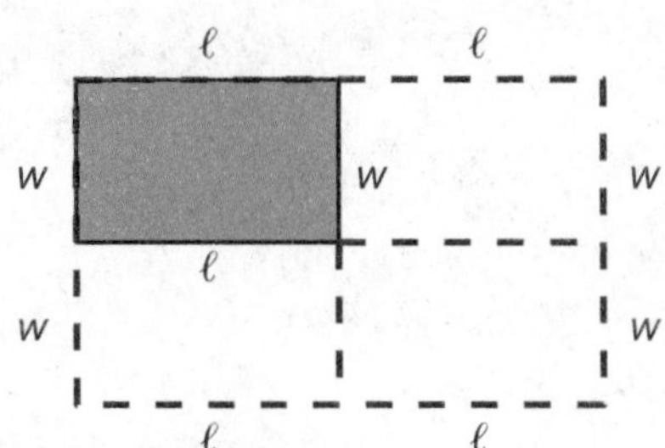

You can draw a diagram to help solve the problem.

Remember
A good math explanation should be:
- correct
- simple
- complete
- easy to understand

The perimeter of the blue rectangle is $P = \ell + \ell + w + w$.

Doubled means each of the side lengths is 2 times greater. So the perimeter will also be 2 times greater.

1. **Explain** Sophie has designed a quilt square using red, blue, and white triangles. Write and explain what fraction of the quilt square each color will be.

2. Heather is writing a 3-digit number. She uses each of the digits 1, 5, and 9 once. What are the possible numbers she can write?

3. **Draw a Picture** If the area of a rectangle is doubled, will the perimeter of the rectangle always be doubled too? Write and explain your reasoning.

4. **Personal Financial Literacy** Yuan earns $5 each week doing yard work. He spends $10 each month on entertainment. He also spends $50 each fall on school clothes and supplies. Yuan deposits the rest of the money in a savings account. How much money does Yuan save in 1 year? (HINT: There are 12 months or 52 weeks in a year.)

5. A magazine has a total of 24 articles and ads. There are 9 ads. How many articles are there?

24 articles and ads

9	?

A 9 articles
B 15 articles
C 24 articles
D 33 articles

6. **Analyze Information** Gerard writes the number seven hundred fifty-two million, three hundred twenty-seven as 752,327,000. Write and explain whether Gerard is correct.

7. **Mental Math** Write and explain how to find the next number in the sequence.

1,000,000,000
10,000,000
100,000
1,000
______

8. Mary says that she ordered the numbers from greatest to least. Write and explain what mistake she may have made.

825,386,927
825,460,926
825,459,925
825,374,924

You can use place value to help find a pattern in this sequence.

9. Simon asked Margaret to guess a number. He gave these hints.

- The number has 3 digits.
- The digit in the hundreds place is less than 2.
- The digit in the tens place is greater than 8.
- The number is even.

What are the possible numbers?

10. **Extend Your Thinking** What do you think would be the place values of the digits 1, 2, and 3 in this number? Write and explain your reasoning.

123,000,000,000

Name ______________________________

Solve & Share

Suppose you have $3.45. List ways you can show this amount using pennies, dimes, and dollar bills. Circle the way that uses the fewest of each kind of bill or coin. ***Solve this problem any way you choose.***

Lesson 1-6
Using Money to Understand Decimals

TEKS 4.2E Represent decimals, including tenths and hundredths, using concrete and visual models and money. Also, 4.2B.
Mathematical Process Standards 4.1A, 4.1B, 4.1C, 4.1E, 4.1G

Digital Resources at SavvasTexas.com

Solve

Learn

Glossary

Check

Tools

Games

You can **select and use tools.** Bills and coins can help you model your work. ***Show your work in the space above!***

Look Back!

Number Sense Is it possible to show $3.45 using only one type of coin or bill? Explain.

How Are Decimals Related to Money?

A

Seth paid six dollars and fifty-two cents for two frozen yogurts.

How can you show the decimal value of money?

A penny is one hundredth of a dollar.

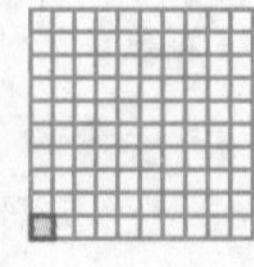

0.01

A dime is one tenth of a dollar.

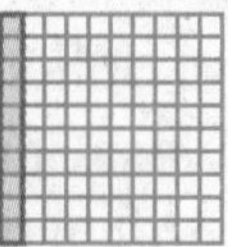

0.1

Use a place-value chart.

B

One Way

You can use a place-value chart to show the decimal value of money.

Dollars (ones)		Dimes (tenths)	Pennies (hundredths)
6	•	5	2

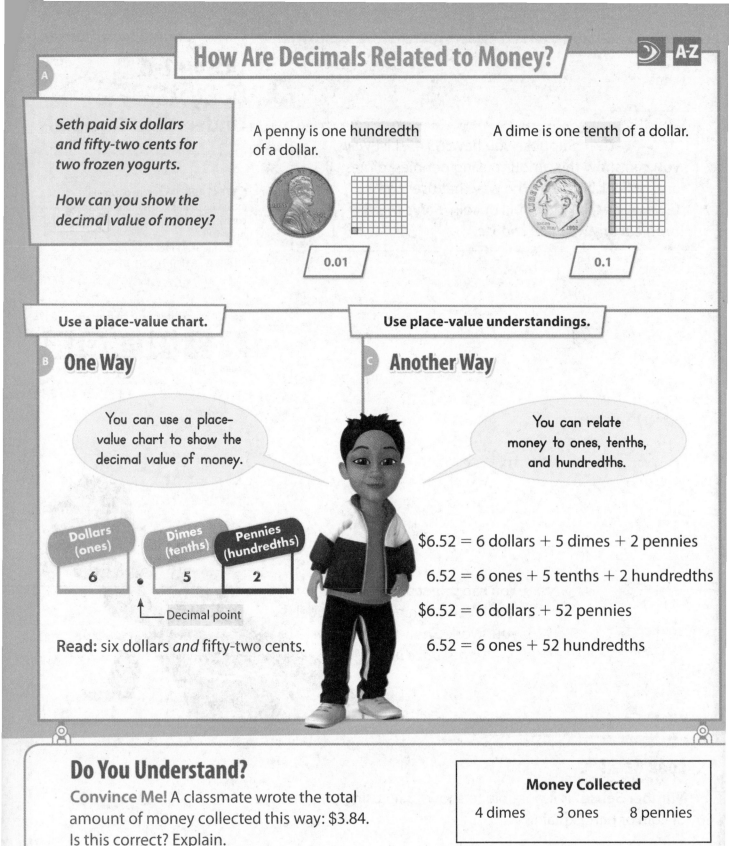

Decimal point

Read: six dollars *and* fifty-two cents.

Use place-value understandings.

C

Another Way

You can relate money to ones, tenths, and hundredths.

\$6.52 = 6 dollars + 5 dimes + 2 pennies

6.52 = 6 ones + 5 tenths + 2 hundredths

\$6.52 = 6 dollars + 52 pennies

6.52 = 6 ones + 52 hundredths

Do You Understand?

Convince Me! A classmate wrote the total amount of money collected this way: \$3.84. Is this correct? Explain.

Money Collected		
4 dimes	3 ones	8 pennies

Name ____________________

Guided Practice*

In **1** and **2**, fill in the blanks to tell how many of each.

1. \$9.75 = ____ dollars + ____ dimes + ____ pennies

9.75 = ____ ones + ____ tenths + ____ hundredths

2. \$3.62 = ____ dollars + ____ pennies

3.62 = ____ ones + ____ hundredths

3. Explain How many hundredths are in one tenth? Explain using pennies and a dime.

4. Tools Gina's allowance is \$2.50. How much is this in dollars and dimes?

Independent Practice

In **5** through **8**, fill in the blanks to tell how many of each.

5. \$5.83 = ____ dollars + ____ pennies

5.83 = ____ ones + ____ hundredths

6. \$7.14 = ____ dollars + ____ pennies

7.14 = ____ ones + ____ hundredths

7. \$2.19 = ____ dollars + ____ dime + ____ pennies

2.19 = ____ ones + ____ tenth + ____ hundredths

8. \$3.24 = ____ dollars + ____ dimes + ____ pennies

3.24 = ____ ones + ____ tenths + ____ hundredths

In **9** through **12**, write the amount with a dollar sign and decimal point.

9. 6 dollars + 9 dimes + 3 pennies

10. 5 dollars + 8 pennies

11. 7 dollars + 3 dimes + 4 pennies

12. 4 dollars + 7 dimes

*For another example, see Set F on page 79.

Problem Solving

13. Connect How could you use the fewest number of dollar bills, dimes, and pennies to buy the bubble blower?

14. Analyze Information The table shows the numbers of magazines sold by four schools in a fundraiser contest. Order the numbers to find which schools came in second place, third place, and fourth place.

School	Magazines Sold	Prize
Jefferson School	1,569	First
Adams School	1,532	
Harding School	1,505	
Hammond School	1,560	

15. Which of the following is equal to 4 hundredths, 3 tenths, and 6 ones?

A $3.36
B $3.64
C $6.34
D $6.43

16. Represent Pablo saves $1.20 each week. Make a table to show how much he saves in dollars and dimes after one week, two weeks, and three weeks.

17. Make a place-value chart to show the value of 5 dollars, 1 dime, and 3 pennies.

18. Extend Your Thinking Barbara has 11 dimes. Evan has 8 dimes and 21 pennies. Who has more money? How much more?

Name ______________________________

Solve & Share

Olivia is making a drawing of a bike path. She made a mark for 0.2 mile because that is the location of a shelter. There is a water fountain at 0.6 mile. Show where Olivia should mark 0.6 mile. Explain your work. ***Solve this problem any way you choose.***

Problem Solving

Lesson 1-11
Use Representations

TEKS 4.1E Create and use representations to organize, record, and communicate mathematical ideas. Also, 4.2H.
Mathematical Process Standards 4.1A, 4.1B, 4.1D, 4.1F, 4.1G

Digital Resources at SavvasTexas.com

Solve Learn Glossary Check Tools Games

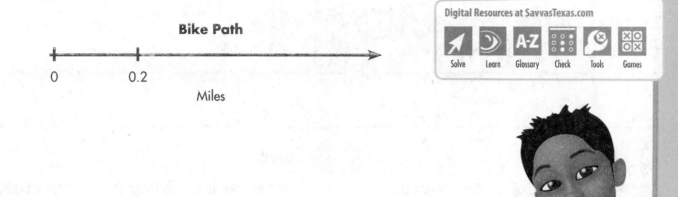

Bike Path

0 0.2

Miles

You can **create and use representations.** You can represent distances on a number line. ***Show your work in the space above!***

Look Back!

Connect Where have you seen drawings showing places, routes to take, and how far apart they are?

How Can a Representation Help You Solve a Problem?

A-Z

A

Analyze

A hiking path is being planned for the local park. The planner started marking the drawing of the path with distances, but stopped. Where should the 1-mile mark be placed?

A picture can help you represent the facts you know.

B

Plan

What do I know?	The hiking path must be 1 mile long. The marker for 0.4 mile is located on the drawing.
What am I asked to find?	Where the 1-mile mark should be located on the drawing

C

Solve

Double the distance from 0 to 0.4 to get 0.8.

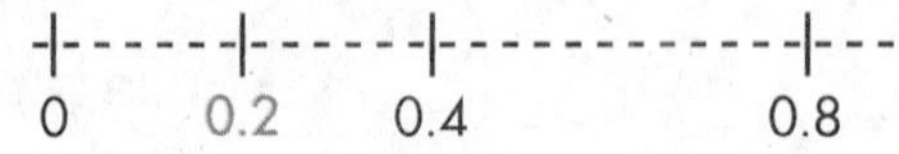

0.2 is halfway from 0 to 0.4

Move 0.2 to the right of 0.8 and get to 1.

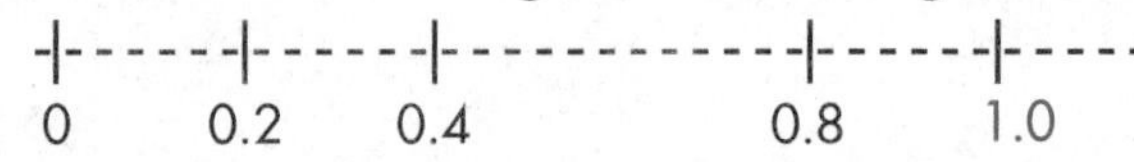

Do You Understand?

Convince Me! How can you use the number line below to show about where 0.5 is located? Explain.

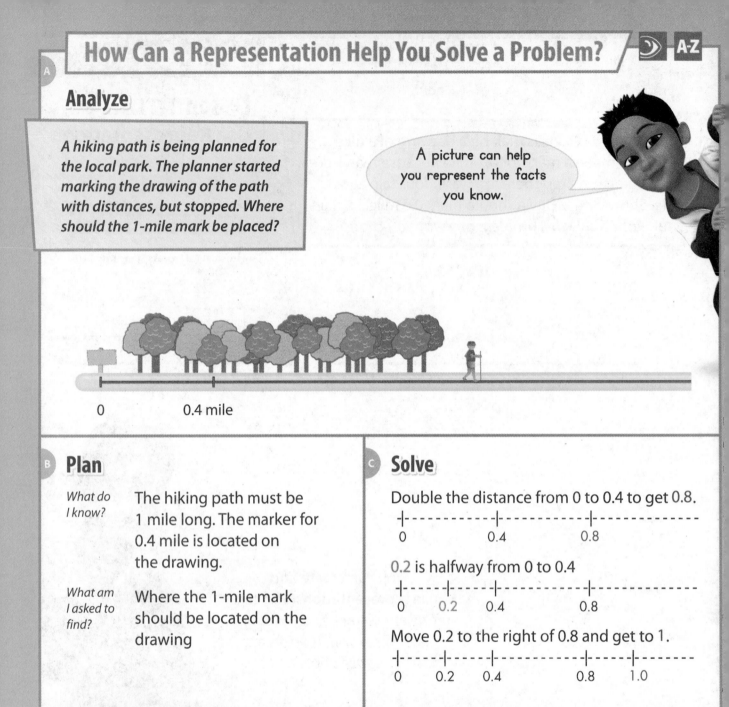

Name ______________________________

Guided Practice*

1. **Connect** Look at the hiking path below. Carla begins at the starting point and walks 0.8 mile. Where on the drawing would Carla end her walk?

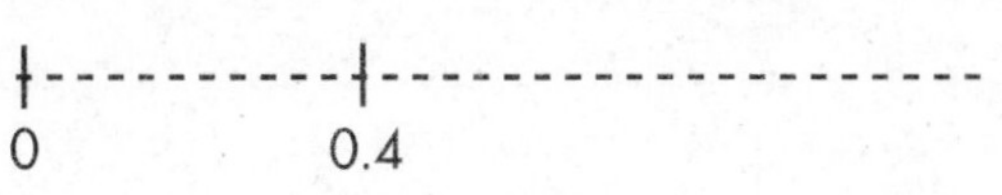

2. **Reason** How are the numbers 0.4 and 0.8 related? How can this help you to find where 0.8 is located on the drawing?

3. **Explain** Explain how you can use the mark on the line to find where 1.0 should be located. Find 1.0.

4. **Communicate** Write a problem that uses the drawing below to solve.

0 0.3

Independent Practice

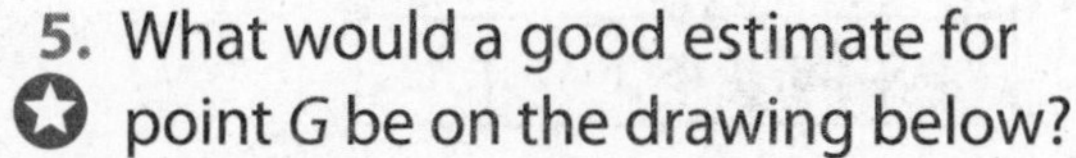

5. What would a good estimate for point *G* be on the drawing below?

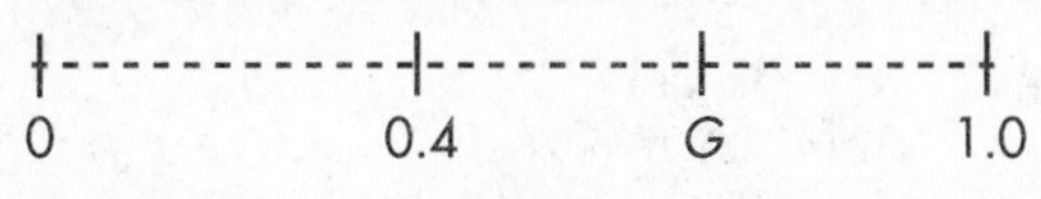

A 0.3
B 0.5
C 0.7
D 0.9

6. **Explain** Blake jogged 0.7 mile one morning. His sister jogged $\frac{75}{100}$ mile that same day. Who jogged farther? Explain.

7. **Reason** Allie needed to design a banner for field day. She wanted her banner to be 2 feet long. Allie marked 0.5 foot on her drawing. How can she use this distance to find 2 feet?

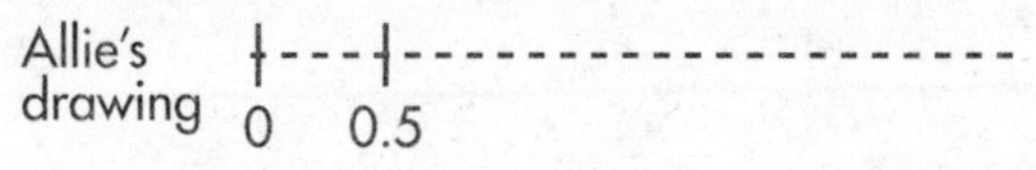

8. **Formulate a Plan** Shawn marked 8 feet on the chalkboard. How can Shawn use this distance to find 20 feet?

Shawn's drawing 0 8

*For another example, see Set K on page 80.

Problem Solving

9. **Represent** Use estimation to show these decimals on the number line. Explain your strategy.

0 0.2 1

10. Which numbers are **NOT** in order from least to greatest?

A 0.3, 0.7, 0.9
B 0.04, 0.09, 0.12
C 0.15, 0.19, 0.23
D 0.24, 0.09, 0.18

11. Dawn has 45 customers on her paper route. She delivers newspapers every day. How many newspapers does she deliver in five days?

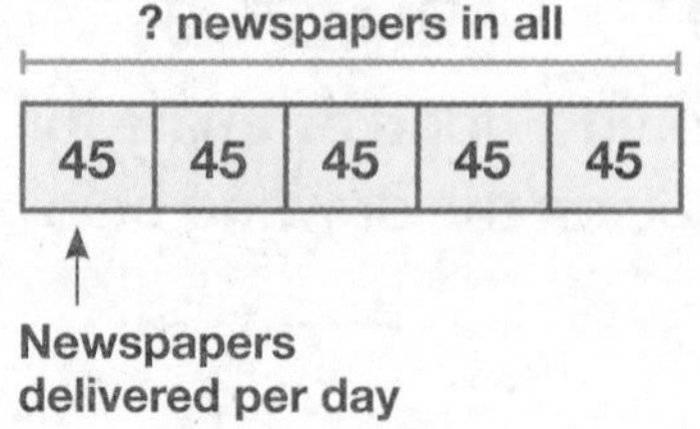

12. **Represent** The length of a rectangular pen is two feet longer than the width. The perimeter of the pen is 28 feet. Complete the table to find the length and width of the pen.

Length	4	5	6		
Width	2	3	4		
Perimeter	12	16	20		

13. **Extend Your Thinking** Jane pulled weeds in the garden 7 times. She was paid \$5 each time she pulled weeds for less than 1 hour and \$6 each time she pulled weeds for more than 1 hour. If Jane received \$36, how many times did she pull weeds for more than 1 hour?

Name ____________________

Homework 1-11
Use Representations

Another Look!

A fence is 20 ft long. It has posts at each end and at every 4 ft along its length. How many fence posts are there?

Analyze

Step 1: What do you know?

The fence is 20 ft long.

There are fence posts at each end.

There are fence posts every 4 ft along the length of the fence.

Step 2: What are you trying to find?

How many posts the fence has.

Plan and Solve

Step 3: What strategy will you use?

Strategy: Draw a picture

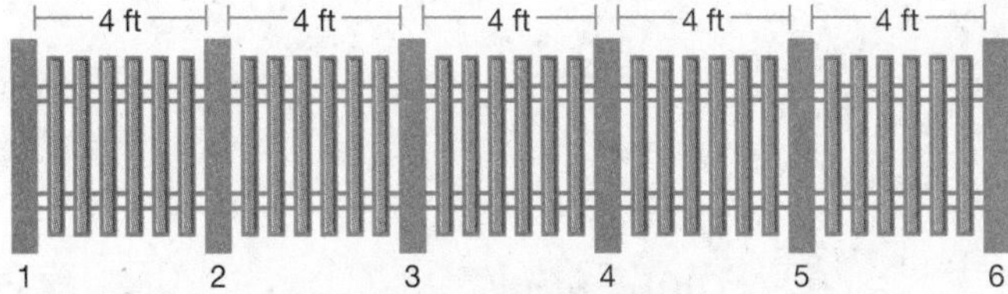

There are 6 fence posts altogether.

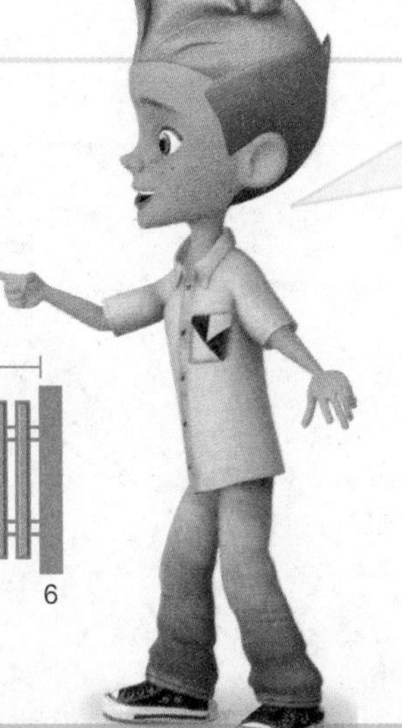

Draw a picture to help organize the information in the problem. Then you can solve it more easily.

1. **Extend Your Thinking** Four fence lengths like the one at the top of the page are used to make a square enclosure. If each side of the fence shares a corner post, how many posts will be needed in all? Explain.

2. **Draw a Picture** Mark is making a quilt with his grandmother. Each row of the quilt has 6 squares. There are 8 rows. Half of the squares are blue. How many blue squares are in the quilt?

3. **Represent** Neil needs to cut 3 long boards into 9 smaller boards. The first long board is 10 ft, the second is 16 ft, and the third is 18 ft. The table lists the smaller boards Neil needs. Use a drawing to show how he can divide the 3 boards so there is no waste.

DATA

Length of Board	Number Needed
4 ft	3
5 ft	4
6 ft	2

10 ft | 16 ft | 18 ft

4. Which has the greatest value?

A 2 quarters, 2 dimes, 16 pennies
B 2 quarters, 5 nickels, 12 pennies
C 1 quarter, 3 dimes, 3 nickels, 15 pennies
D 2 quarters, 1 nickel, 29 pennies

5. Which point on the number line is the best estimate of 0.58?

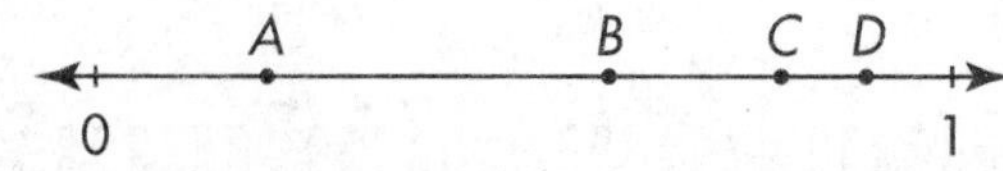

A Point *A*
B Point *B*
C Point *C*
D Point *D*

6. **Extend Your Thinking** During breakfast, the school cafeteria sells half of the milk they have. They sell twice as much milk as orange juice. By the end of breakfast, they have sold 3 gallons of orange juice. Write and explain how to find how much milk the cafeteria had at the beginning of the day.

You may need to solve a smaller problem first.

Name ______________________________

TOPIC 1 Mixed Problem Solving

Applying Math Processes

- How does this problem connect to previous ones?
- What is my plan?
- How can I use tools?
- How can I use number sense?
- How can I communicate and represent my thinking?
- How can I organize and record information?
- How can I explain my work?
- How can I justify my answer?

1. **Number Sense** Write the standard form of an 8-digit number with a 6 in the hundred thousands place and a 3 in the hundreds place.

2. **Personal Financial Literacy** Ross works part-time at a grocery store and cuts grass for Mr. Lopez. Last month, Ross worked 46 hours at the grocery store and cut Mr. Lopez's grass twice. What was his total income last month?

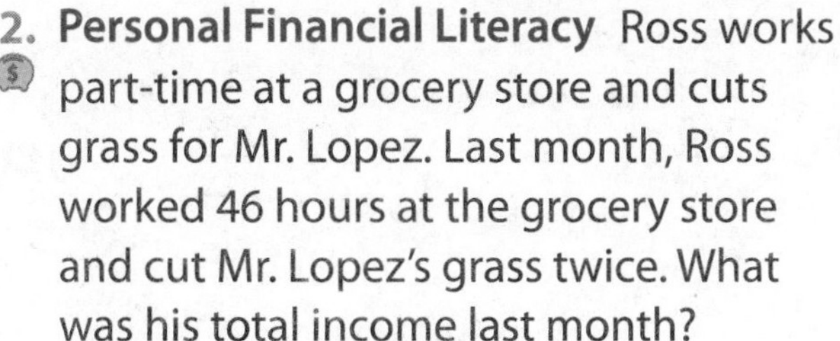

DATA

Ross's Job	Income
Grocery Store	$8 per hour
Cutting grass	$20 each time

3. Use the hundredths grids to model 0.48, 0.6, and 0.07. Then order these decimals from least to greatest.

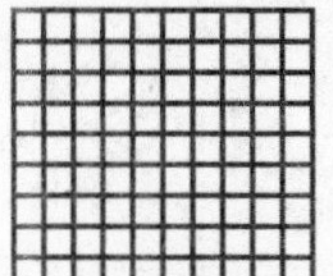 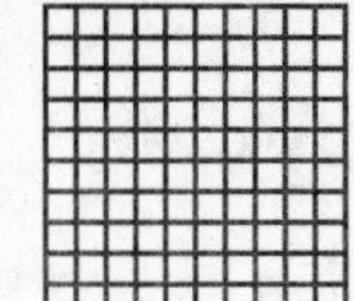 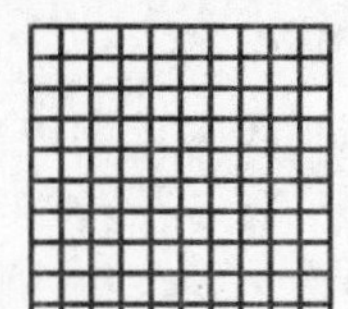

4. **Extend Your Thinking** Describe the relationship between the values of the two 8s in the number 8,380,000.

5. **Reason** Could you use only the ten thousands place to order 345,092, 348,429, and 352,093? Explain.

6. **Number Sense** Earl is thinking of a 4-digit number in which all of the digits are the same. He says that the value of the digit in the hundreds place is 400. How can you find the value of the digit on the left and the right of the hundreds place?

Error Search

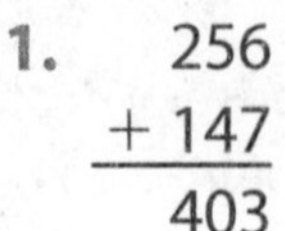

Find each problem that is not correct. Circle what is wrong and rewrite the problem so it is correct.

1. $\begin{array}{r} 256 \\ +\,147 \\ \hline 403 \end{array}$

2. $\begin{array}{r} 507 \\ -\,169 \\ \hline 368 \end{array}$

3. $\begin{array}{r} 685 \\ +\,239 \\ \hline 824 \end{array}$

4. $\begin{array}{r} 450 \\ -\,376 \\ \hline 174 \end{array}$

Reasoning

Write whether each statement is true or false. If you write false, change the numbers or words so that the statement is true.

5. The number 453,951,862 has the digit 3 in the ten millions place.

6. To order the numbers from least to greatest, compare the hundred thousands place.
   849,261,486　　849,560,217　　849,147,413

7. On a number line, 0.7 is closer to 1 than to 0.5.

8. When the same digits are next to each other in a number, the digit on the left has one-tenth the value of the digit on the right.

9. When comparing two decimal numbers, the decimal with the greater number of digits always has the greater value.

Name ___

Set A pages 9–14

Use a place-value chart to write 200,301,400.

Expanded form:
200,000,000 + 300,000 + 1,000 + 400

Word form: two hundred million, three hundred one thousand, four hundred

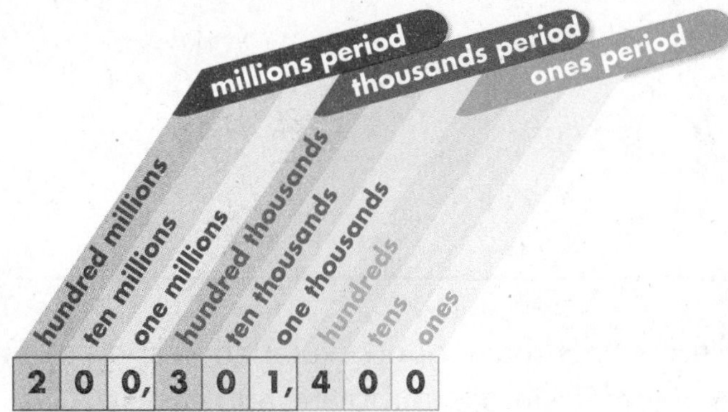

Remember that periods can help you read large numbers.

Write each number in expanded form and word form.

1. 27,549

2. 6,792,065

Set B pages 15–20

Relate the values of the 4s in the number 441.

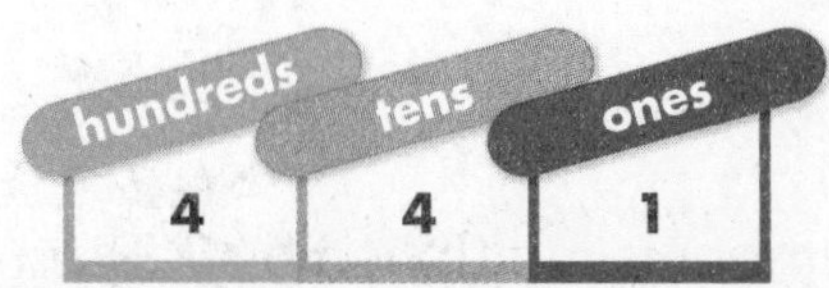

The first 4 is in the hundreds place. Its value is 400.

The second 4 is in the tens place. Its value is 40. The value of the 4 in the hundreds place is 10 times the value of the 4 in the tens place.

Remember that when two digits next to each other in a number are the same, the one on the left is 10 times greater than the one on the right, and the one on the right is one-tenth the value of the one on the left.

In **1** and **2**, name the values of the given digits.

1. the 8s in 5,188 **2.** the 7s in 7,740,000

3. In 687,332,195, how is the value of the three in the ten thousands place related to the value of the 3 in the hundred thousands place?

Set C pages 21–26

Use place value to compare 45,423 and 44,897. Start comparing from the left. Look for the first digit that is different.

45,423 44,897

5 > 4

So, 45,423 > 44,897.

Remember that you can use place value to compare numbers using symbols.

Write < or > in the ◯.

1. 735,291,000 ◯ 735,291,001

Order the numbers from greatest to least.

2. 622,981 614,762 621,046

Set D pages 27–32

Round 764,802 to the nearest hundred thousand.

hundred thousands place

764,802 — The digit to the right of the rounding place is 6.

800,000 — Since 6 > 5, round by adding 1 to the digit in the hundred thousands place.

So, 764,802 rounds to 800,000.

Remember to look at the number to the right of the rounding place. Then change the digits to the right of the rounding place to zeros.

Round each number to the place of the underlined digit.

1. 166,742
2. 76,532
3. 5,861
4. 432,041
5. 132,505
6. 257,931

Set E pages 33–38

Ann says that 785 is greater than 758, and 758 is greater than 685. So, 785 is greater than 685. Write and explain whether her reasoning is correct.

Drawing a picture is often helpful in writing explanations. For this problem, a number line can be included in the explanation.

650 675 700 725 750 775 800

Because 785 > 758, and 758 > 685, then 685 will be to the left of 758 and 785 on the number line. So, 785 > 685. Therefore, Ann's reasoning is correct.

Use digital tools to solve these and other Reteaching problems.

Remember that a good explanation should be correct, simple, complete, and easy to understand. It is sometimes helpful to use words that indicate order like first, then, next, and finally.

Write to explain.

1. A number is multiplied by 2. Then that product is multiplied by 5. Write to explain how you know what digit is in the ones place of the final product.

2. Explain how to round 750,890,002 to the nearest million.

Name ______________________________

Set F pages 39–44

Write 4 dollars, 8 dimes, and 2 pennies with a dollar sign and a decimal point.

Read: four dollars and eighty-two cents

Write: $4.82

Remember that a dime is one tenth of a dollar, and a penny is one hundredth of a dollar.

Write each amount with a dollar sign and a decimal point.

1. 3 dollars + 4 pennies
2. 1 dollar + 5 dimes + 6 pennies
3. 9 dollars + 6 dimes
4. 4 dimes + 9 pennies

Set G pages 45–50

Write the decimal shown in expanded form, standard form, and word form.

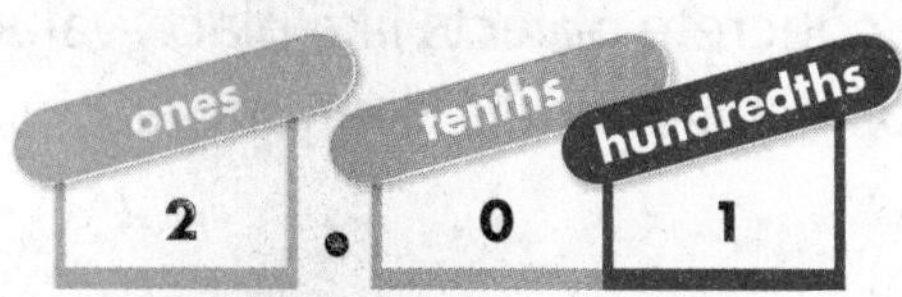

Expanded form: 2 + 0.01

Standard form: 2.01

Word form: Two and one hundredth

Remember to use the word *and* for the decimal point.

Write the following in word form and expanded form.

1. 12.13
2. 11.1
3. What is the value of the 9 in 1.09?

Set H pages 51–56

Write $\frac{1}{100}$ as a decimal.

$\frac{1}{100}$ is one hundredth, or 0.01.

$\frac{1}{100} = 0.01$

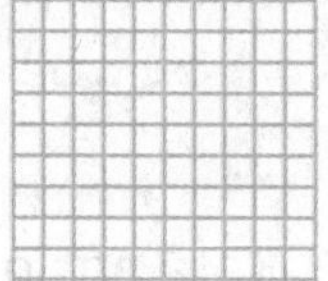

Remember that you can read the decimal and write what you say when writing a decimal as a fraction. You can also read fractions that have 10 or 100 as a denominator to help you write the equivalent decimal form.

Write each fraction as a decimal.

1. $\frac{8}{10}$
2. $\frac{94}{100}$

Write each decimal as a fraction.

3. 0.4
4. 0.53

Set I pages 57–62

Show 7.7 on a number line. Divide the distance from 7 to 8 into 10 equal lengths.

Label the tick marks, and draw a point at 7.7.

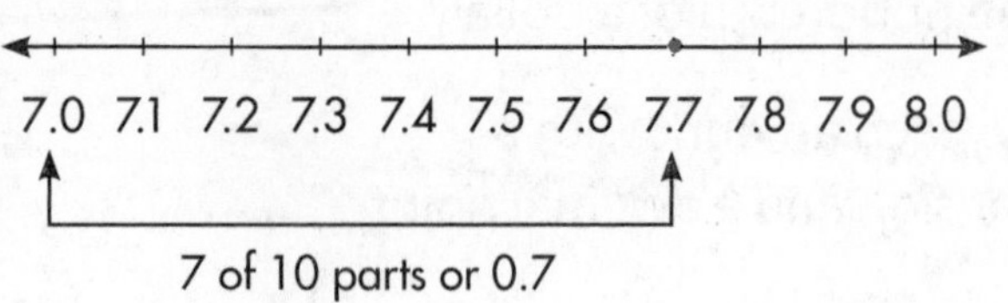

Remember that distances between tick marks are equal.

J K L M N O

5.40 5.45 5.50 5.55 5.60 5.65 5.70

Name the decimal at each point.

1. *K* **2.** *M* **3.** *O*

Name the point for each decimal.

4. 5.6 **5.** 5.5 **6.** 5.42

Set J pages 63–68

Order 0.2, 0.7, and 0.1 from least to greatest.

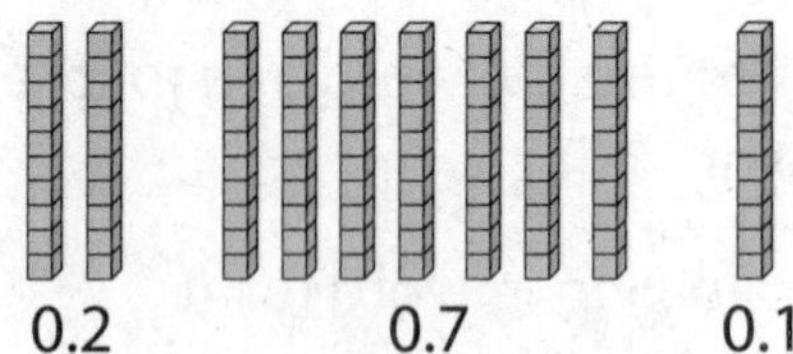

Use the tenths place to order. The least number is 0.1. The greatest number is 0.7. The order from least to greatest is 0.1, 0.2, 0.7.

Remember to check if you are ordering from least to greatest or greatest to least.

Order the numbers from least to greatest. You can use concrete objects like place-value blocks or visual models like hundredths grids to help.

1. 0.6, 0.3, 0.7 **2.** 0.99, 0.09, 0.9

Set K pages 69–74

A biking trail is being planned for a town. Where should the 2-mile marker be placed?

0 0.5 1.0 2.0

What do I know? The biking trail must be at least 2 miles long. The 0.5-mile mark is located on the drawing.

What am I asked to find? Where would the 2-mile mark be located on the drawing?

Think: 1.0 is double 0.5, and 1.0 is half of 2.0.

Measure the distance from 0 to 0.5. Double this distance. Mark 1.0. Now double this distance and mark 2.0.

Remember that you can use a ruler to measure the distance between each mark.

1. Look at the walking path below. Will begins at the starting point and walks 0.6 mile. Where on the path would Will end his walk?

0 0.3

2. Kate has marked a distance of 0.5 ft on a wall. Where would she mark a distance of 3 ft on the wall? How did you determine the location?

0 0.5

Name ______________________________

TOPIC 1 Test

1. Which is the missing number?
$8.36 = 8 dollars + 3 dimes + ☐ pennies
8.36 = 8 ones + 3 tenths + ☐ hundredths

A 2

B 3

C 6

D 8

2. Which decimal is shown in the grid below?

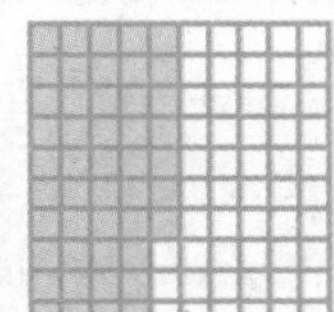

A 7.41

B 1.74

C 1.53

D 1.47

3. Which statement is **NOT** true?

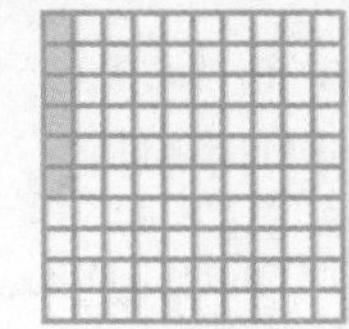
0.06

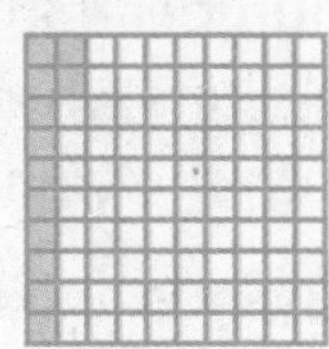
0.12

A 0.12 < 0.06

B 0.06 > 0.12

C 0.06 = 0.12

D All of the above

4. The price of a new refrigerator has the same result, when rounded to the nearest hundred or thousand. Which could be the price of the new refrigerator?

A $1,049

B $1,118

C $1,179

D Not here

5. Which decimal is best represented by point *C* on the number line?

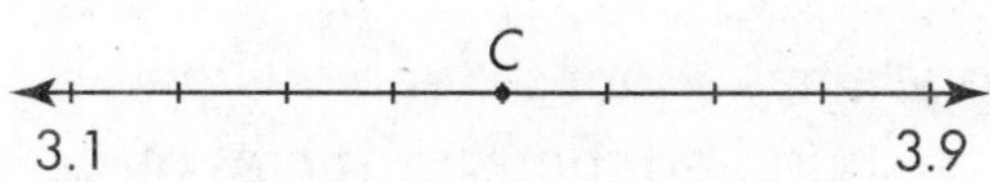

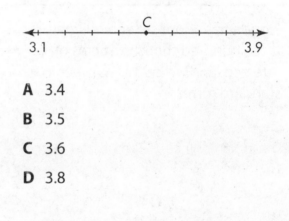

A 3.4

B 3.5

C 3.6

D 3.8

6. Richard marked the point *N* on a number line. Which is the best estimate for the point Richard marked?

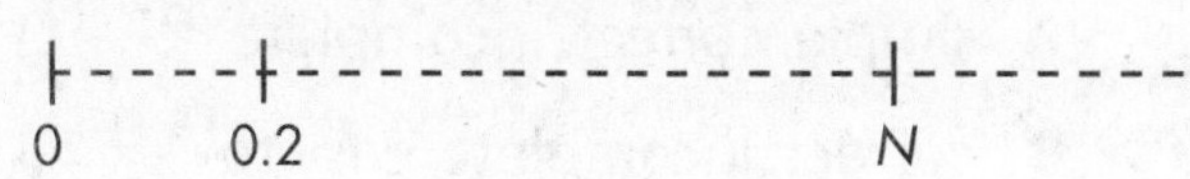

A 0.4

B 0.5

C 0.6

D 0.8

7. How could you use the least amount of $1 bills, dimes, and pennies to pay for the soccer ball?

A 6 dollars, 4 dimes, 9 pennies

B 6 dollars, 40 dimes, 90 pennies

C 6 dollars, 4 dimes, 900 pennies

D 6 dollars, 40 dimes, 900 pennies

8. Florida has about sixteen million, three hundred thousand acres of forested land. Write this number in standard form.

9. Which of the following best describes a good math explanation?

A simple, correct, incomplete

B correct, incomplete, easy to understand

C complete, simple, correct

D easy to understand, complete, incorrect

10. The table shows the areas of four states. Which of the four states has the least area?

DATA

State	Area (sq. mi)
Montana	147,042
Oklahoma	68,898
Oregon	98,381
Wyoming	97,814

A Montana

B Oklahoma

C Oregon

D Wyoming

11. The total area of Earth's land surface is about 148,940,000 square kilometers. In 148,940,000, which digit is in the hundred millions place?

12. In the number 436,621, which places contain digits where one digit is one-tenth the value of the other?

A thousands and ten thousands

B hundreds and thousands

C ones and tens

D ten thousands and hundred thousands

Name ____________________

13. In the kennel, 7 out of the 10 dogs weigh less than 20 pounds. What is $\frac{7}{10}$ written as a decimal?

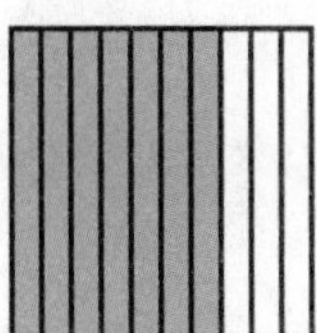

14. Which number is best represented by point *R* on the number line?

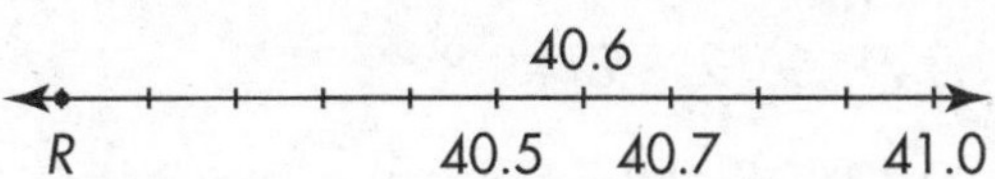

A 40.1

B 40.0

C 39.9

D 39.0

15. Tory saves $2.30 each week. How much money has she saved in dollars and dimes after 3 weeks?

A 2 dollars, 9 dimes

B 6 dollars, 3 dimes

C 6 dollars, 9 dimes

D 9 dollars, 6 dimes

16. Which is another way to write the numeral 14,363?

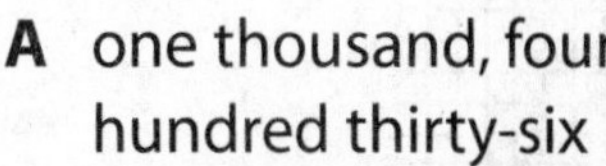

A one thousand, four hundred thirty-six

B fourteen thousand, three hundred thirty-six

C fourteen thousand, three hundred sixty

D fourteen thousand, three hundred sixty-three

17. A jar of coins contains 6,245 pennies. What is 6,245 rounded to the nearest hundred?

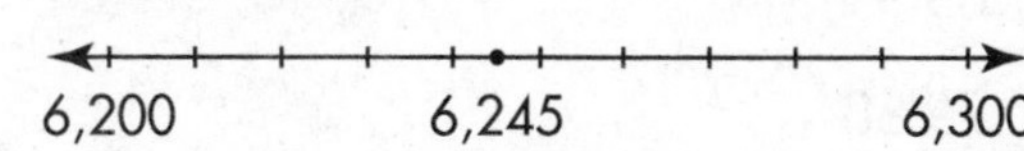

A 7,000

B 6,300

C 6,200

D 6,000

18. Cory used the fewest number of $1 bills, dimes, and pennies to buy a ticket to a movie. Cory used 8 dollars, 7 dimes, and 5 pennies. Write the cost of the movie ticket using a dollar sign and decimal point.

19. What fraction and decimal represent the part that is green?

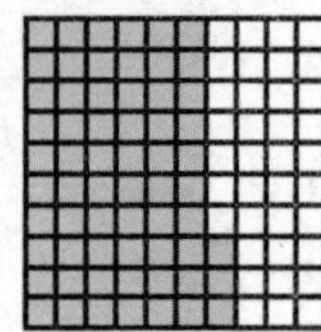

A $\frac{63}{100}$ and 0.63

B $\frac{63}{100}$ and 6.3

C $\frac{63}{10}$ and 0.63

D $\frac{63}{10}$ and 6.3

---

20. Which of the following has a 9 in the hundredths place?

A 28.79

B 65.91

C 79.88

D 926.7

---

21. Farmers produced 654,289,070 bushels of wheat in one year. What is the value of the 7 in the number 654,289,070?

			.		
0	0	0		0	0
1	1	1		1	1
2	2	2		2	2
3	3	3		3	3
4	4	4		4	4
5	5	5		5	5
6	6	6		6	6
7	7	7		7	7
8	8	8		8	8
9	9	9		9	9

22. Which number is between 4,259,921 and 4,329,349?

A 4,359,219

B 4,329,391

C 4,329,319

D 4,259,291

---

23. Which shows the gymnastic scores in order from least to greatest?

A 9.72, 9.8, 9.78, 9.87

B 9.78, 9.72, 9.87, 9.8

C 9.78, 9.8, 9.72, 9.87

D 9.72, 9.78, 9.8, 9.87

---

24. What is the missing number?
$5.47 = 5 dollars + ▢ dimes + 7 pennies
5.47 = 5 ones + ▢ tenths + 7 hundredths

			.		
0	0	0		0	0
1	1	1		1	1
2	2	2		2	2
3	3	3		3	3
4	4	4		4	4
5	5	5		5	5
6	6	6		6	6
7	7	7		7	7
8	8	8		8	8
9	9	9		9	9

Adding and Subtracting Whole Numbers and Decimals

Essential Questions:
How can sums and differences of whole numbers be estimated?
What are standard procedures for adding and subtracting whole numbers and decimals?
How can sums and differences be found mentally?

The world's fastest car can reach a speed of 267 miles per hour!

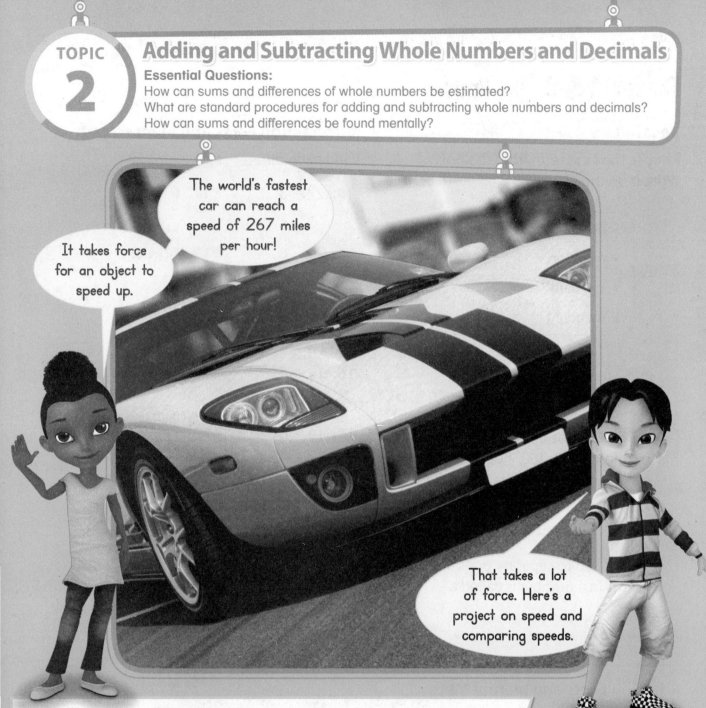

It takes force for an object to speed up.

That takes a lot of force. Here's a project on speed and comparing speeds.

Math and Science Project: The World's Fastest Animals

Do Research Forces can speed things up, and forces can slow things down. Use the Internet or other sources to find the five fastest animals in the world.

Journal: Write a Report Include what you found. Also in your report:

- Make a chart that includes the type of animal, whether the animal moves on land, in water, or through the air, and the speed of the animal.
- Order the speeds from fastest to slowest.
- Calculate the difference between the fastest animal and the slowest animal.

Name ______________________________

Review What You Know

Vocabulary

Choose the best term from the box. Write it on the blank.

- decimal point
- equation
- estimate
- rounding

1. An ______________ is an approximate number or answer.

2. A process that determines which multiple of 10, 100, 1,000, and so on, a number is closest to is called ______________.

3. A dot used to separate ones and tenths in a number is called a ______________.

Addition Facts and Mental Math

Find each sum.

4. 4 + 6
5. 7 + 5
6. 29 + 8
7. 14 + 5
8. 13 + 7
9. 37 + 7

Subtraction Facts and Mental Math

Find each difference.

10. 27 − 3
11. 6 − 4
12. 15 − 8
13. 11 − 8
14. 66 − 2
15. 17 − 8
16. 16 − 4
17. 20 − 5
18. 14 − 6
19. 11 − 6
20. 95 − 10
21. 33 − 7

Decimals

22. **Explain** How does a concrete model, such as place-value blocks, help you compare 0.4 and 0.36?

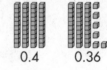

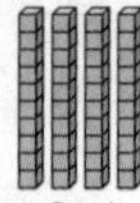

My Word Cards

A-Z

Use the examples for each word on the front of the card to help complete the definitions on the back.

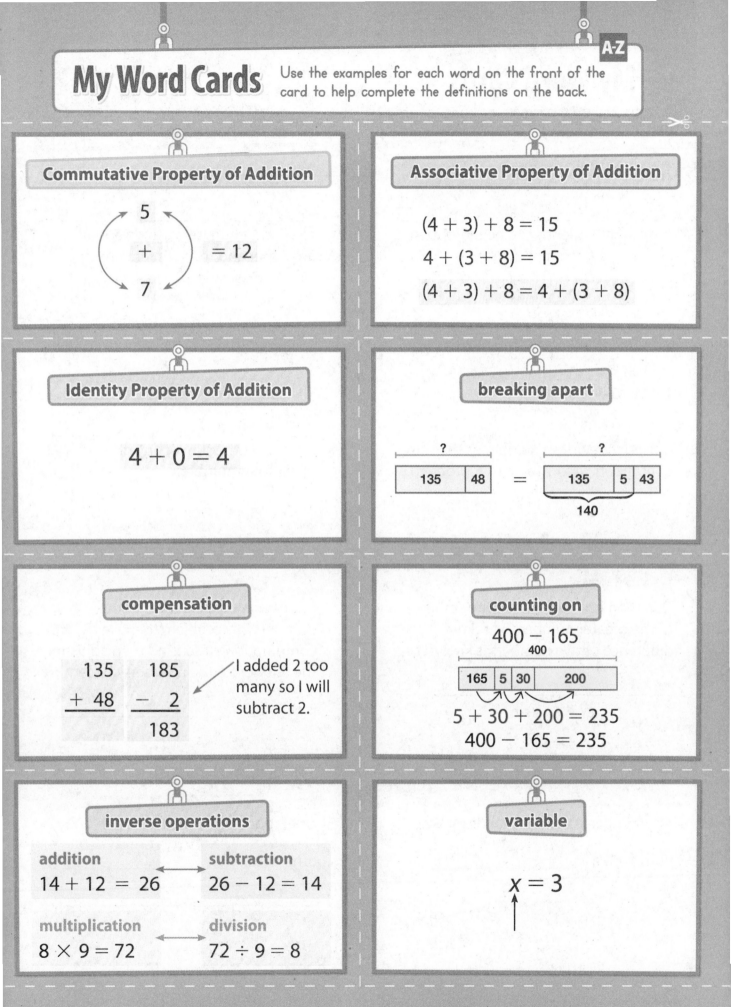

Commutative Property of Addition

5 + 7 = 12

Associative Property of Addition

$(4 + 3) + 8 = 15$

$4 + (3 + 8) = 15$

$(4 + 3) + 8 = 4 + (3 + 8)$

Identity Property of Addition

$4 + 0 = 4$

breaking apart

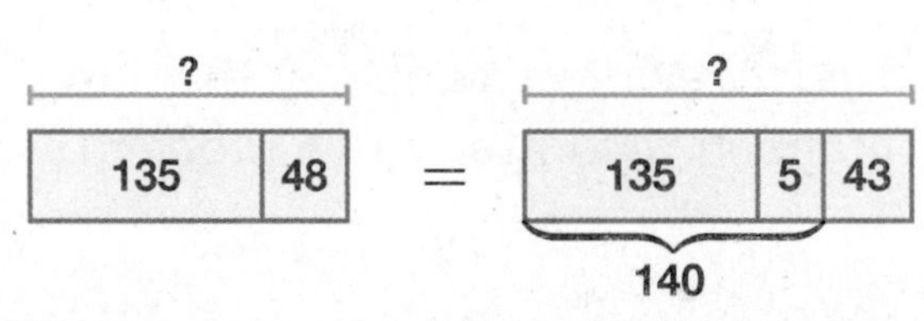

compensation

$$\begin{array}{r} 135 \\ +\ 48 \\ \hline \end{array} \qquad \begin{array}{r} 185 \\ -\ 2 \\ \hline 183 \end{array}$$

I added 2 too many so I will subtract 2.

counting on

$400 - 165$

400

165	5	30	200

$5 + 30 + 200 = 235$

$400 - 165 = 235$

inverse operations

addition ⟷ **subtraction**

$14 + 12 = 26$ ⟷ $26 - 12 = 14$

multiplication ⟷ **division**

$8 \times 9 = 72$ ⟷ $72 \div 9 = 8$

variable

$x = 3$

My Word Cards

Complete each definition. Extend learning by writing your own definitions.

The ______________________

______________________ states that addends can be regrouped and the sum remains the same.

The ______________________

______________________ states that numbers can be added in any order and the sum remains the same.

The mental math method of

______________________ is used to rewrite a number as the sum of numbers to form an easier problem.

The ______________________

______________________ states that the sum of any number and zero is that number.

Counting up from the lesser number to the greater number to find the difference of two numbers is known as

______________________.

Choosing numbers close to the numbers in a problem to make the computation easier, and then adjusting the answer for the numbers chosen

is called ______________________.

A symbol or letter that stands for a

number is a ______________________.

Operations that can undo each

other are ______________________

______________________.

Name ______________________________

Solve & Share

Luke collected 36 baseball cards and 34 football cards. Find the number of cards in his collection. ***Solve this problem any way you choose.***

Lesson 2-1
Using Mental Math to Add and Subtract

TEKS 4.4 Develop and use strategies and methods for whole number computations and decimal sums and differences in order to solve problems with efficiency and accuracy.
Mathematical Process Standards 4.1A, 4.1C, 4.1D, 4.1G

Digital Resources at SavvasTexas.com

Solve

Learn

Glossary
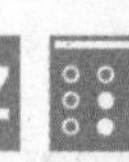
Check
Tools

Games

You can use mental math. Think about breaking the numbers into tens and ones. ***Show your work in the space below!***

Look Back!

Justify Why is $36 + 4 + 30$ an easier problem to solve mentally than $36 + 34$?

How Can You Use Mental Math to Add and Subtract?

A

How many years have Ms. Walston and Mr. Randall been teaching?

What is the total number of years all of the teachers in the chart have been teaching?

DATA

Teacher	Years Teaching
Ms. Walston	12
Mr. Roy	5
Mr. Randall	30

There is more than one way to do mental math.

Use properties and mental math to add.

B

Commutative Property of Addition: You can add two numbers in any order.

42

12	30

$12 + 30 = 30 + 12$

Ms. Walston and Mr. Randall have been teaching a combined total of 42 years.

C

Associative Property of Addition: You can change the grouping of addends.

47

12	30	5

$(12 + 30) + 5 = 12 + (30 + 5)$

The total number of years the three teachers have been teaching is 47 years.

D

Identity Property of Addition: Adding zero does not change the number.

$12 + 0 = 12$

Do You Understand?

Convince Me! Show how to use the Commutative Property to rewrite $(18 + 12) + 25$. Tell why your expression shows the Commutative Property.

Name ______________________________

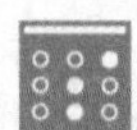

Another Example

Mental math strategies can help you add or subtract.

Find 135 + 48.
Break apart to find a ten:

Adding 5 to 135 is easy.
Break apart 48.

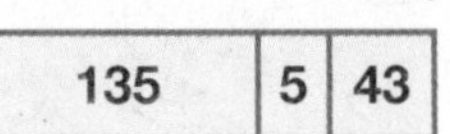

135 + 5 = 140
140 + 43 = 183
So, 135 + 48 = 183.

Find 400 − 165.
Use counting on to subtract:

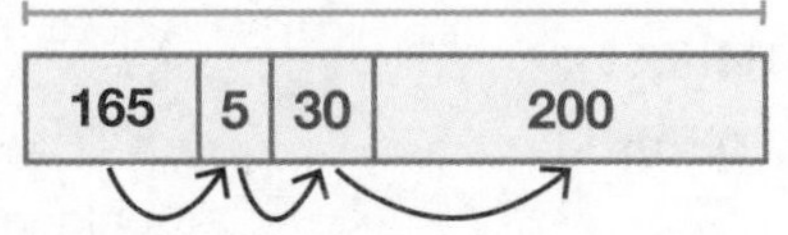

5 + 30 + 200 = 235
So, 400 − 165 = 235.

Find 260 − 17.
Use compensation:

It is easy to subtract 20.

260 − 20 = 240

I subtracted 3 too many, so I will add 3.

240 + 3 = 243
So, 260 − 17 = 243.

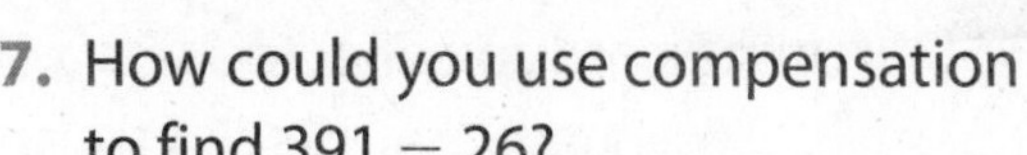

Guided Practice*

In **1** through **6**, use mental math to add or subtract.

1. 86 + 25 **2.** 497 + 0

3. 566 − 359 **4.** 169 − 48

5. 239 + 509 **6.** (40 + 5) + 8

7. How could you use compensation to find 391 − 26?

8. Explain Explain how you used mental math to find the answer to Exercise 4.

Independent Practice

Leveled Practice In **9** through **18**, use mental math to complete the calculation.

9. 400 − 227

400

227	3	70	100

10. 500 − 89

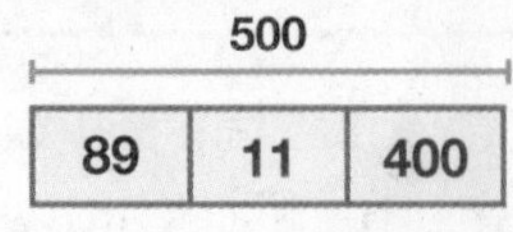

11. 906 − 289

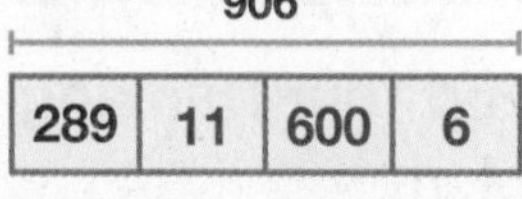

12. 7,000 + 2,130

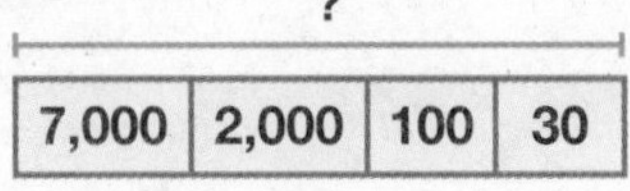

13. 583 + 317

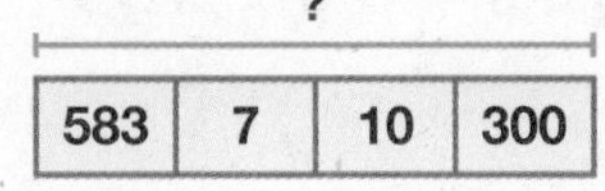

14. 125 + 28

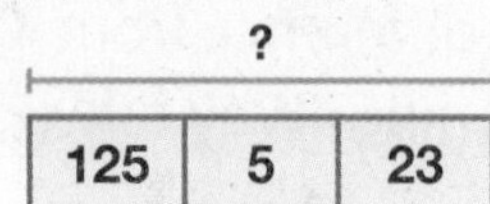

15. 1,700 − 315 **16.** 2,000 + 4,996 **17.** 438 − 129 **18.** 0 + 284

*For another example, see Set A on page 151.

Problem Solving

19. Which state has the greatest land area in square miles? Write its area in word form.

20. Round the land area of the smallest state listed in the chart to the nearest ten thousand.

DATA

State	Total Square Miles
Alaska	571,951
California	155,959
Montana	145,552
New Mexico	121,356
Texas	261,797

21. Ms. Gomez's class collected pencils for the community school supplies drive. Ethan's group brought in 143 pencils and Marcelina's group collected 78 pencils. How many pencils did these two groups contribute?

A 65 pencils
B 204 pencils
C 221 pencils
D 245 pencils

22. An adult human body has a total of 206 bones. There are 300 bones in a child's body because some of the bones fuse together as a child grows. How many more bones are in a child's body than in an adult's body?

300	
206	?

23. **Reason** Is 881 − 262 greater than or less than 500? Explain how you can tell using mental math.

24. **Explain** How can you use mental math to subtract 158 − 29?

25. **Extend Your Thinking** Garry needs to solve the following problem: 422 − 145 − 45. First he uses the Associative Property to group 145 and 45 together. Then he subtracts their difference from 422. Do you agree with Garry's reasoning? Why or why not?

Garry's Work

422 − 145 − 45
422 − (145 − 45)
422 − 100
322

Name ______________________

Homework 2-1
Using Mental Math to Add and Subtract

Another Look!

There are different strategies for adding and subtracting with mental math.

Addition Strategies

Using breaking apart to find 235 + 158:

235 + 158	Break apart 158. 158 = 5 + 153
235 + 5 = 240	Add one part to make a ten.
240 + 153 = 393	Add the other part.

Using compensation to find 235 + 158:

235 + 160	Add 2 to make 160. 158 + 2 = 160
235 + 160 = 395	
395 − 2 = 393	Subtract 2 from the answer because 2 was added earlier.

Subtraction Strategies

Using compensation to find 162 − 48:

162 − 50	Add 2 to make 50. 48 + 2 = 50
162 − 50 = 112	
112 + 2 = 114	Since you subtracted 2 too many, add 2 to the answer.

Using counting on to find 400 − 185:

400 − 185	Add 5 to make 190.
185 + 5 = 190	
190 + 10 = 200	Make the next 100.
200 + 200 = 400	Add 200 to make 400.
5 + 10 + 200 = 215	Find the total that you added on.

In **1** through **8**, add or subtract. Use mental math.

You can choose the mental math strategy you think will work best.

1. 67 + 31 = ______

2. 86 − 14 = ______

3. 29 + 43 = ______

4. 206 − 78 = ______

5. 89 + 46 = ______

6. 101 − 49 = ______

7. 722 + 158 = ______

8. 120 − 33 = ______

9. Reason How can you write 52 + (8 + 25) to make it easier to add?

10. How many more red and green marbles are in the collection than blue and yellow marbles?

11. How many more red and yellow marbles are in the collection than green and blue marbles?

Marble Collection	
red	425
blue	375
green	129
yellow	99

12. Connect Selena's family went on a trip. The total hotel bill was $359. The cost of the airfare was $633. Use mental math to find the total cost for the hotel and the airfare.

13. One year, 76 people helped at the town cleanup. The next year, 302 people helped. How many more people helped in the second year? Use mental math to find the answer.

14. Stanley wants to collect 900 sports cards. So far, he has collected 428 baseball cards and 217 football cards. How many more cards does Stanley need to complete his collection?

A 255

B 472

C 645

D 683

15. Explain Explain how you could add 678 + 303 using mental math.

16. Justify Use a mental math strategy to find 290 + 602. Explain how to check your answer using a different strategy.

17. Extend Your Thinking Janella bought 345 orange beads, then 130 yellow beads. Find the total number of beads she has. Explain what properties you used to find your answer.

Name ______________________

Solve & Share

Vera went on a 3-day trip in which she traveled 336 miles the first day, 423 miles the second day, and 357 miles the third day. About how many miles did she travel on her trip? ***Solve this problem any way you choose.***

Lesson 2-2

Estimating Sums and Differences of Whole Numbers

TEKS 4.4G Round to the nearest 10, 100, or 1,000 or use compatible numbers to estimate solutions involving whole numbers.
Mathematical Process Standards 4.1B, 4.1C, 4.1F, 4.1G

Digital Resources at SavvasTexas.com

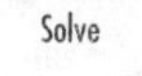

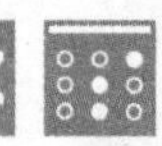

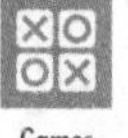

You can **estimate.** You do not need an exact answer to this problem. ***Show your work in the space below!***

Look Back!

Mental Math About how many more miles did Vera travel the second day than the first day?

How Can You Estimate Sums and Differences of Whole Numbers?

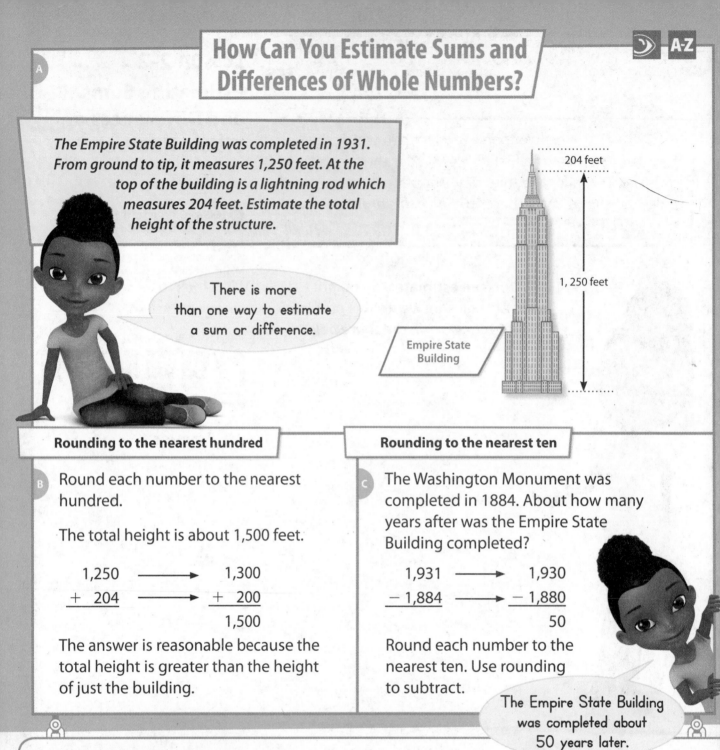

A

The Empire State Building was completed in 1931. From ground to tip, it measures 1,250 feet. At the top of the building is a lightning rod which measures 204 feet. Estimate the total height of the structure.

There is more than one way to estimate a sum or difference.

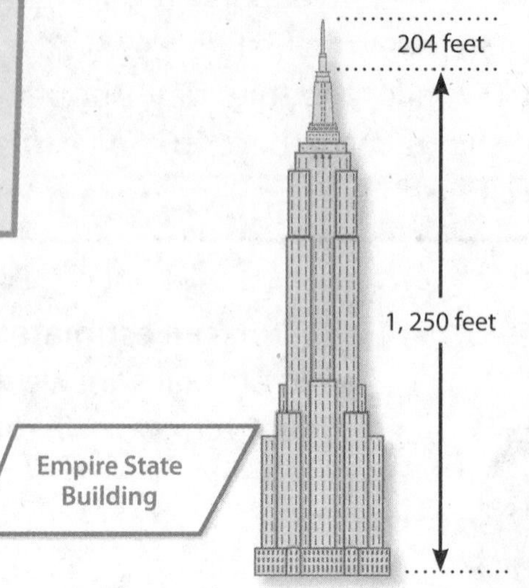

Rounding to the nearest hundred

B Round each number to the nearest hundred.

The total height is about 1,500 feet.

1,250	→	1,300
+ 204	→	+ 200
		1,500

The answer is reasonable because the total height is greater than the height of just the building.

Rounding to the nearest ten

C The Washington Monument was completed in 1884. About how many years after was the Empire State Building completed?

1,931	→	1,930
− 1,884	→	− 1,880
		50

Round each number to the nearest ten. Use rounding to subtract.

The Empire State Building was completed about 50 years later.

Do You Understand?

Convince Me! In the example above for 1,250 + 204, can you estimate by rounding each number to the nearest 1,000? Explain.

Name ___________________________

Homework 2-2
Estimating Sums and Differences of Whole Numbers

Another Look!

Rounding can be used to estimate sums and differences.

To estimate 1,436 + 422:	To estimate 3,635 − 1,598:
Rounding to the nearest hundred.	**Rounding to the nearest thousand.**
1,436 rounds to 1,400	3,635 rounds to 4,000
422 rounds to 400	1,598 rounds to 2,000
1,400 + 400 = 1,800	4,000 − 2,000 = 2,000

In **1** through **11**, estimate each sum or difference.

1. 382 → ☐☐0
− 34 → ☐0

2. 693 → ☐00
+ 117 → ☐00

3. 7,792 → ☐,000
− 3,847 → ☐,000

4. 2,189
+ 388

5. 1,329
+ 45

6. 877
− 475

7. 9,245
− 4,033

8. 788 + 212 = ________

9. 9,769 − 4,879 = ________

10. 65,328 − 14,231 = ________

11. 32,910 + 4,085 = ________

Your estimate may be different from someone else's estimate. That's okay if both estimates are reasonable.

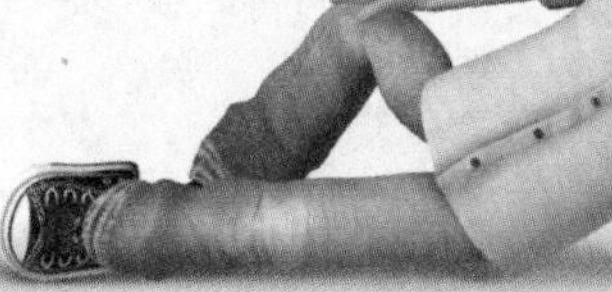

12. About how much greater area does the largest ocean have than the smallest ocean has?

DATA

Ocean Area	
Ocean	**Area (thousand sq km)**
Arctic Ocean	14,090
Atlantic Ocean	82,400
Indian Ocean	65,527
Pacific Ocean	165,760

13. **Connect** Natasha earns $4.30 walking a dog on Friday night. How does $4.30 relate to the decimal number 4.3?

14. **Number Sense** Is 976 − 522 more or less than 400? Explain how you can tell without finding the exact difference.

15. Mallory is a pilot. Last week she flew the following round trips in miles: 2,020; 1,358; 952; 2,258; and 1,888. Which of the following is a good estimate of the miles Mallory flew last week?

A 6,000 mi
B 6,800 mi
C 7,000 mi
D 8,000 mi

16. **Explain** Explain how you would estimate to subtract 189 from 643.

17. **Extend Your Thinking** The fourth graders are helping raise money for the local animal shelter. They hoped to raise $1,000. So far they have made $465 in bake sales and $710 in T-shirt sales. Have they earned more or less than their goal? About how much more or less have they raised?

Name ______________________

Solve & Share

Erica brought 219 bottles to the recycling center. Ana brought 142 bottles. Leon brought 436 bottles. How many bottles did they bring in all? ***Solve this problem any way you choose.***

Lesson 2-3
Adding Whole Numbers

TEKS 4.4A Add and subtract whole numbers and decimals to the hundredths place using the standard algorithm. Also, 4.4G.
Mathematical Process Standards 4.1A, 4.1B, 4.1C, 4.1D, 4.1G

Digital Resources at SavvasTexas.com

Solve

Learn
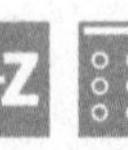
Glossary

Check

Tools
Games

You can **formulate a plan.** What operation can you use to solve this problem? ***Show your work in the space below!***

Look Back!

Check for Reasonableness How can you use estimation to check that your answer is reasonable?

How Do You Add Whole Numbers?

A

A sports stadium with 24,595 seats is increasing in size by 19,255 seats. How many seats will there be in all?

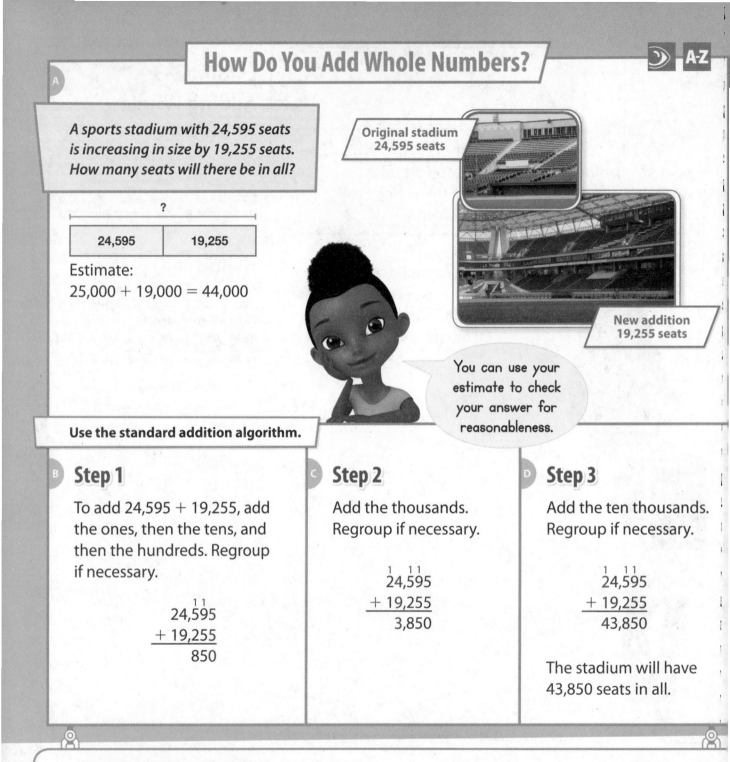

?

24,595	19,255

Estimate:
25,000 + 19,000 = 44,000

You can use your estimate to check your answer for reasonableness.

Use the standard addition algorithm.

B

Step 1

To add 24,595 + 19,255, add the ones, then the tens, and then the hundreds. Regroup if necessary.

$$\begin{array}{r} \scriptstyle 1\,1\;\; \\ 24{,}595 \\ +\ 19{,}255 \\ \hline 850 \end{array}$$

C

Step 2

Add the thousands. Regroup if necessary.

$$\begin{array}{r} \scriptstyle 1\;\;1\,1\;\; \\ 24{,}595 \\ +\ 19{,}255 \\ \hline 3{,}850 \end{array}$$

D

Step 3

Add the ten thousands. Regroup if necessary.

$$\begin{array}{r} \scriptstyle 1\;\;1\,1\;\; \\ 24{,}595 \\ +\ 19{,}255 \\ \hline 43{,}850 \end{array}$$

The stadium will have 43,850 seats in all.

Do You Understand?

Convince Me! If all seats at the basketball arenas below are filled, what is the total number of people in these three arenas?

Basketball Arena	Number of Seats
Memorial Dome	16,285
Park Center	18,187
Central Arena	20,557

Name

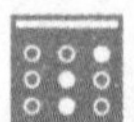

Another Example

Find the sum. 30,283 + 63,423 + 6,538

Estimate:
30,000 + 63,000 + 7,000 = 100,000

```
  11 11
  30,283
  63,423
+  6,538
 100,244
```

The sum is reasonable because it is close to the estimate of 100,000.

Guided Practice*

In **1** through **4**, find each sum.

1. 3,258 + 1,761

2. 16,018 + 135

3. 821 + 4,543

4. 14,926 + 3,832

5. Construct Arguments When adding 36,424 and 24,842, why is there no regrouping in the final step?

6. Volunteer teams identified 73 species of fish, 30 species of coral, and 71 other invertebrate species on a reef. How many species were found in all?

Use estimation to check your answers for reasonableness.

Independent Practice

Leveled Practice In **7** through **14**, find each sum.

7. 78 + 421

8. 617 + 14,312

9. 873 + 4,893

10. 38,911 + 45,681

11. 327 + 886

12. 9,634 + 2,958

13. 4,673 + 262

14. 7,845 + 509 + 3,746

*For another example, see Set C on page 151.

Problem Solving

15. Communicate Explain the mistake made when finding the sum. What is the correct sum?

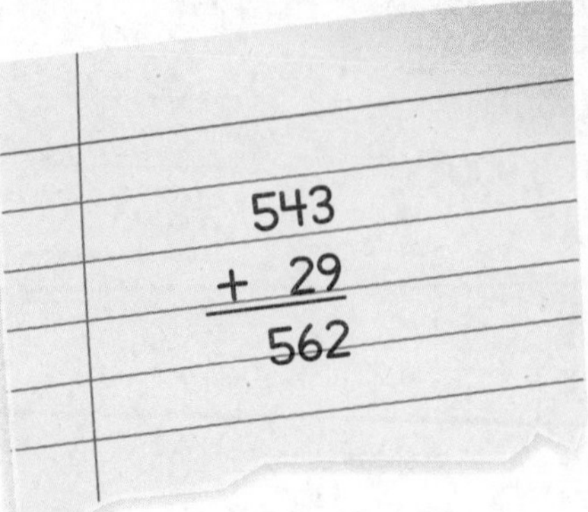

543
+ 29
562

A good math explanation should be clear, correct, and easy to understand.

16. Reason The sum of 86, 68, and 38 is 192. What do you also know about the sum of 68, 38, and 86? Explain.

17. Estimation Maria added 45,273 and 35,687. Will her answer be greater or less than 80,000?

18. A mailman delivers 12,578 pieces of mail on Monday. He delivers 26,229 pieces of mail on Tuesday. How many pieces of mail does he deliver on both days?

A 15,129 pieces of mail
B 26,229 pieces of mail
C 36,239 pieces of mail
D 38,807 pieces of mail

19. Check for Reasonableness Look at the problem and the answer. Using estimation, determine if the given answer is reasonable. Explain.

$$\begin{array}{r} 224 \\ 303 \\ +\ 125 \\ \hline 652 \end{array}$$

20. Extend Your Thinking There were 10,453 items checked out of the public library one week. The next week, 12,975 items were checked out. A week later, 9,634 items were checked out. How many items were checked out during the busiest two weeks?

21. Extend Your Thinking Abby read 235 pages of a book. Joey read 123 more pages than Abby. How many pages did Abby and Joey read in all?

Name ______________________

Homework 2-3
Adding Whole Numbers

Another Look!

You can add two or more numbers when you line up the numbers by place value. Add one place at a time.

Add 3,456 + 139 + 5,547.

Estimate:
3,000 + 100 + 6,000 = 9,100

Step 1	Step 2	Step 3
Line up numbers by place value. Add the ones. Regroup if needed. $\begin{array}{r} \scriptsize{2} \\ 3,456 \\ 139 \\ +\,5,547 \\ \hline 2 \end{array}$ 22 becomes 2 tens and 2 ones.	Add the tens. Regroup if needed. $\begin{array}{r} \scriptsize{1\;2} \\ 3,456 \\ 139 \\ +\,5,547 \\ \hline 42 \end{array}$ Keep digits in neat columns as you add.	Add the hundreds, then the thousands. Continue to regroup. $\begin{array}{r} \scriptsize{1\;\;1\;2} \\ 3,456 \\ 139 \\ +\,5,547 \\ \hline 9,142 \end{array}$ 9,142 is close to the estimate of 9,100.

In **1** through **6**, add.

Use estimation to check your answers for reasonableness.

1. $\begin{array}{r} 945 \\ +\,343 \\ \hline \end{array}$

2. $\begin{array}{r} 2,588 \\ +\;\;866 \\ \hline \end{array}$

3. $\begin{array}{r} 12,566 \\ +\;5,532 \\ \hline \end{array}$

4. $\begin{array}{r} 2,955 \\ 9,017 \\ +\;\;248 \\ \hline \end{array}$

5. $\begin{array}{r} 16,699 \\ 3,311 \\ +\,32,484 \\ \hline \end{array}$

6. $\begin{array}{r} 3,881 \\ 1,735 \\ +\;\;364 \\ \hline \end{array}$

7. What is the combined length of the three longest glaciers shown in the table?

DATA

World's Longest Glaciers

Glacier	Length (miles)
Lambert-Fisher Ice Passage	320
Novaya Zemlya	260
Arctic Institute Ice Passage	225
Nimrod-Lennox-King	180

8. **Connect** A shipping company delivered 4,288 letters and 6,508 packages. How many items did the company deliver?

9. **Analyze Information** Harry has a chest of gold and silver coins. Inside, there are 2,387 gold coins. There are 22 more silver coins than gold coins. How many coins does Harry have in the chest?

A 2,409 coins
B 2,431 coins
C 4,609 coins
D 4,796 coins

10. **Check for Reasonableness** Jill added 450 + 790 + 123 and got 1,163. Is this sum reasonable? Explain.

11. **Number Sense** Leona added 6,641 + 1,482 + 9,879. Should her answer be more than or less than 15,000?

12. A museum has 5,416 items in display cases and 6,986 items in storage. What is the total number of items the museum has?

13. **Extend Your Thinking** Darren jogs 425 meters and runs 650 meters in one workout. He performs this workout three times. What is the total distance covered in the three workouts?

Name

Lesson 2-4

Subtracting Whole Numbers

Solve & Share

During a gardening project, Ruben planted 168 seeds. Jana planted 191 seeds. How many more seeds did Jana plant than Ruben? ***Solve this problem any way you choose.***

You can **formulate a plan.** What operation can you use to solve this problem? ***Show your work in the space below!***

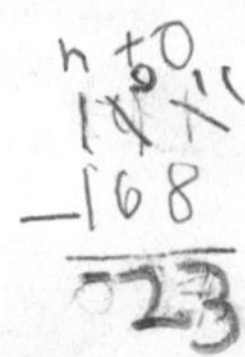

TEKS 4.4A Add and subtract whole numbers and decimals to the hundredths place using the standard algorithm. Also, 4.4G.
Mathematical Process Standards 4.1B, 4.1C, 4.1D, 4.1G

Digital Resources at SavvasTexas.com

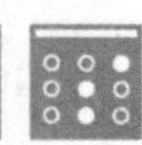

Solve Learn Glossary Check Tools Games

Look Back!

Justify How could you use addition to check your answer?

How Do You Subtract Whole Numbers?

A

Brenda has a total of 221 songs on a computer. Her sister, Susan, has a total of 186 songs on that computer.

How many more songs does Brenda have on the computer than Susan?

This diagram shows the problem.

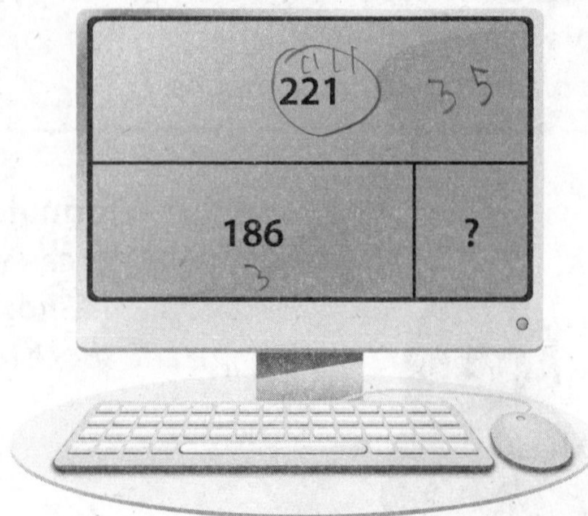

The standard algorithm breaks the calculation into simpler parts.

Use the standard subtraction algorithm.

B

Step 1

Find 221 − 186.

Estimate: 220 − 190 = 30

Subtract the ones.
Regroup if necessary.

$$\begin{array}{r} {\scriptstyle 1\,11} \\ 2\not{2}\not{1} \\ -\;186 \\ \hline 5 \end{array}$$

C

Step 2

Subtract the tens.
Regroup if necessary.

Subtract the hundreds.
Regroup if necessary.

$$\begin{array}{r} {\scriptstyle 1\,11\,11} \\ \not{2}\not{2}\not{1} \\ -\;186 \\ \hline 35 \end{array}$$

D

Step 3

Operations that undo each other are inverse operations. Addition and subtraction have an inverse relationship. Add to check your answer.

$$\begin{array}{r} {\scriptstyle 1\,1\;} \\ 186 \\ +\;\;35 \\ \hline 221 \end{array}$$

Do You Understand?

Convince Me! The work below is NOT correct. What error was made? What is the correct answer?

$$\begin{array}{r} 4{,}248 \\ -\;2{,}764 \\ \hline 1{,}584 \end{array}$$

Name ______________________

Homework 2-4
Subtracting Whole Numbers

Another Look!

Follow these steps to subtract whole numbers.

Find 7,445 − 1,368.

Estimate: 7,000 − 1,000 = 6,000

Step 1	Step 2	Step 3	Step 4
7,445 − 1,368 = 7 (regrouped: 3 tens, 15 ones)	7,445 − 1,368 = 77 (regrouped: 3 hundreds, 13 tens, 15 ones)	7,445 − 1,368 = 077	7,445 − 1,368 = 6,077
You cannot subtract 8 ones from 5 ones. You must regroup. Regroup 4 tens as 3 tens and 10 ones. Subtract 8 ones from 15 ones.	You cannot subtract 6 tens from 3 tens. You must regroup. Regroup 4 hundreds as 3 hundreds and 10 tens. Subtract 6 tens from 13 tens.	Subtract 3 hundreds from 3 hundreds.	Subtract 1 thousand from 7 thousands. You can check your answer using addition. 6,077 + 1,368 = 7,445

In **1** through **8**, find the difference.

1. 624 − 379

2. 759 − 211

3. 814 − 662

4. 391 − 208

5. 4,772 − 1,671

6. 8,335 − 4,188

7. 4,219 − 1,379

8. 5,216 − 2,158

9. Explain The Environmental Club's goal is to collect 1,525 cans by the end of four weeks. The number of cans they collected each week is shown in the table at right. How can you find the number of cans they need to collect in week 4 to meet their goal? How many more cans do they need?

DATA

Week Number	Number of cans collected
1	378
2	521
3	339

10. Estimation Carlos has 2,175 marbles in his collection. Emily has 1,833 marbles in her collection. Carlos says that he has about 1,000 more marbles than Emily. Is Carlos correct?

11. Which of the following best describes the answer to the subtraction problem below?

3,775 − 1,831

A The answer is less than 1,000.
B The answer is about 1,000.
C The answer is greater than 1,000.
D You cannot tell from the information given.

12. A paint company mixed a total of 2,132 gallons of green and blue paint. If they mixed 1,780 gallons of green paint, how many gallons of blue paint did they mix?

13. In a recent election, 547,034 people voted for one of two candidates. There were 338,931 votes cast for the winner. How many votes were cast for the other candidate?

14. Analyze Information Look at the subtraction below. What mistake was made? What is the correct answer?

$$\begin{array}{r} 7{,}392 \\ -\ 4{,}597 \\ \hline 2{,}895 \end{array}$$

15. Extend Your Thinking A restaurant has 2,006 forks, 1,745 knives, and 1,898 spoons. The owner wants to have the same number of each utensil. She can buy more utensils, and donate extra utensils. What should she do?

Name ______________________________

Solve & Share

The Empire State Building is 1,250 feet tall. The Citigroup Center is also in New York and is 915 feet tall. How much taller is the Empire State Building than the Citigroup Center? ***Solve this problem any way you choose.***

Lesson 2-5
Subtracting Across Zeros

TEKS 4.4A Add and subtract whole numbers and decimals to the hundredths place using the standard algorithm. **Mathematical Process Standards** 4.1B, 4.1C, 4.1D, 4.1F, 4.1G

Digital Resources at SavvasTexas.com

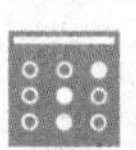

Solve Learn Glossary Check Tools Games

You can **use number sense.** A zero place value can be treated the same way you treat other place values in a subtraction problem. ***Show your work in the space below!***

Look Back!

Check for Reasonableness How can you use estimation to check that your answer is reasonable?

How Do You Subtract Across Zeros?

A-Z

A

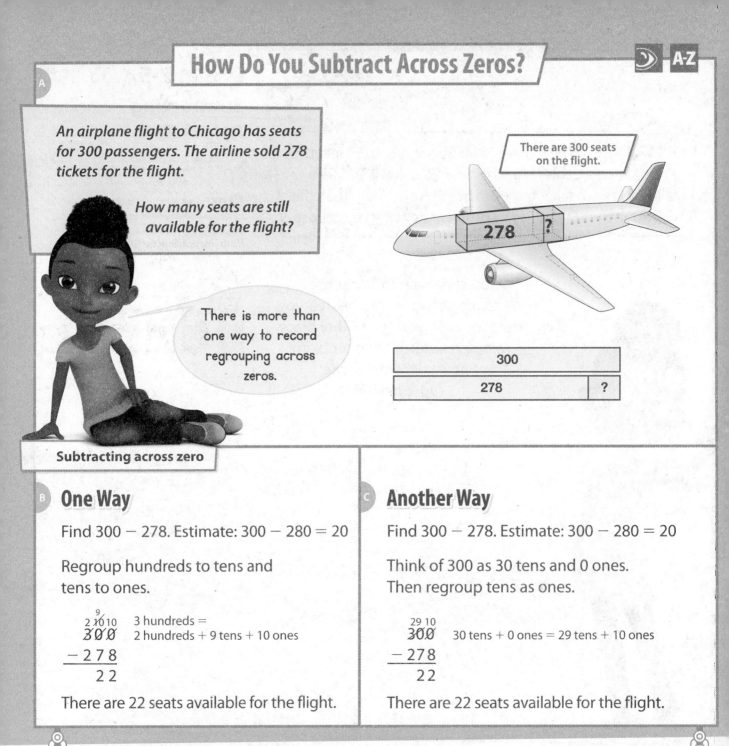

An airplane flight to Chicago has seats for 300 passengers. The airline sold 278 tickets for the flight.

How many seats are still available for the flight?

There is more than one way to record regrouping across zeros.

There are 300 seats on the flight.
278
?

300	
278	?

Subtracting across zero

B

One Way

Find 300 − 278. Estimate: 300 − 280 = 20

Regroup hundreds to tens and tens to ones.

$$\begin{array}{r} \overset{2}{\cancel{3}}\overset{\overset{9}{\cancel{10}}}{\cancel{0}}\overset{10}{\cancel{0}} \\ -\ 2\,7\,8 \\ \hline 2\,2 \end{array}$$

3 hundreds = 2 hundreds + 9 tens + 10 ones

There are 22 seats available for the flight.

C

Another Way

Find 300 − 278. Estimate: 300 − 280 = 20

Think of 300 as 30 tens and 0 ones. Then regroup tens as ones.

$$\begin{array}{r} \overset{29}{\cancel{30}}\overset{10}{\cancel{0}} \\ -\ 2\,7\,8 \\ \hline 2\,2 \end{array}$$

30 tens + 0 ones = 29 tens + 10 ones

There are 22 seats available for the flight.

Do You Understand?

Convince Me! Use both of the ways shown above to find 3,004 − 1,257. Is one way easier for you than the other? Explain.

Name

Guided Practice*

In **1** through **6**, subtract.

1. 600 − 177

2. 1,086 − 728

3. 810 − 638

4. 3,304 − 1,137

5. 1,001 − 868

6. 4,000 − 1,698

7. Connect How would you check if the answer in the example on the previous page is correct?

8. One passenger flew from New York to Phoenix. The flight was 2,145 miles. Another passenger flew from Boston to Los Angeles. The flight was 2,606 miles. How many more miles was the flight to Los Angeles?

Independent Practice

Estimate to check your answers for reasonableness.

Leveled Practice In **9** through **28**, subtract.

9. 902 − 883

10. 502 − 380

11. 3,000 − 673

12. 5,604 − 1,717

13. 1,830 − 722

14. 7,006 − 3,529

15. 1,902 − 903

16. 6,008 − 4,879

17. 450 − 313

18. 5,025 − 178

19. 406 − 381

20. 1,001 − 35

21. 6,090 − 5,130

22. 2,700 − 1,699

23. 10,807 − 4,373

24. 504 − 319

25. 3,000 − 1,047

26. 5,001 − 368

27. 700 − 520

28. 900 − 406

*For another example, see Set E on page 152.

Problem Solving

29. Extend Your Thinking Use the chart on the right. Music City sells CDs. How many more total hip-hop and Latin CDs were sold than total rock and country CDs?

DATA

Music City Sales

Music style	CDs sold
Rock	4,007
Hip-hop	7,097
Country	5,063
Latin	6,203

30. Explain Will the difference between 4,041 and 3,876 be greater or less than 1,000? Explain your answer.

31. Reason In a dart game, Casey scored 42 points, and Maggie scored 28 points. Jesse scored fewer points than Casey but more points than Maggie. Which is a possible score for Jesse?

A 50 points
B 46 points
C 34 points
D 26 points

32. Shawn scored 10,830 points playing a video game. Miguel scored 9,645 points. How many more points did Shawn score than Miguel?

33. Estimation 9,070 cars drove on a highway during rush hour. 4,675 cars drove on the same highway later that night. Estimate the difference by rounding to the nearest thousand.

34. Justify Petulia needed to subtract 375 from 700. Is her answer correct? If not, explain why and write the correct answer.

$$\begin{array}{r} 700 \\ -\,375 \\ \hline 425 \end{array}$$

35. On Thursday, 10,296 people attended a college basketball home game. The following week, 12,000 people attended an away game. How many more people attended the away game than the home game?

Name ______________________

Homework 2-5
Subtracting Across Zeros

Another Look!

You can use these steps to subtract across zeros.

Find 606 − 377.

Estimate: 600 − 400 = 200

Step 1	Step 2	Step 3	Step 4
606 − 377	5 10 ~~6~~~~0~~6 − 377	9 5 ~~10~~ 16 ~~6~~~~0~~~~6~~ − 377	9 5 ~~10~~ 16 ~~6~~~~0~~~~6~~ − 377 229
You cannot subtract 7 ones from 6 ones, so you must regroup.	Since there is a zero in the tens place, you must regroup using the hundreds. Regroup 6 hundreds as 5 hundreds and 10 tens.	Regroup 10 tens and 6 ones as 9 tens and 16 ones.	Subtract. You can check your answer by using addition. 1 1 229 + 377 606 ✓

In **1** through **8**, subtract.

1. 707 − 58

2. 950 − 47

3. 800 − 638

4. 3,506 − 866

5. 4,507 − 3,569

6. 3,076 − 1,466

7. 8,106 − 2,999

8. 6,083 − 1,492

9. **Number Sense** Lexi subtracts 9,405 from 11,038. Should her answer be greater than or less than 2,000? Explain.

Remember to treat zero like you treat any other digit when you subtract.

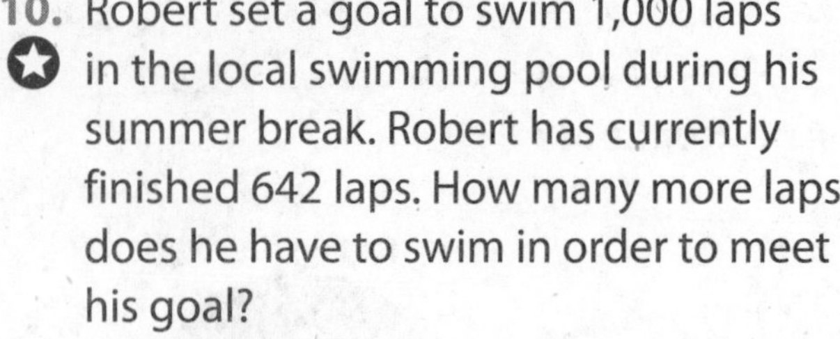

10. Robert set a goal to swim 1,000 laps in the local swimming pool during his summer break. Robert has currently finished 642 laps. How many more laps does he have to swim in order to meet his goal?

A 332 laps
B 358 laps
C 468 laps
D 472 laps

11. **Explain** Fill in the missing numbers:

$694 - 72 =$ ______, and

$622 +$ ______ $= 694$.

Why can you use addition to check subtraction?

12. **Extend Your Thinking** To estimate the difference below, would you round the numbers to the nearest ten, nearest hundred, or nearest thousand? Explain.

$$\begin{array}{r} 8{,}904 \\ -\ 3{,}796 \\ \hline \end{array}$$

13. **Justify** Cory needed to subtract 139 from 800. Is his answer correct? If not, explain why and write the correct answer.

$$\begin{array}{r} 800 \\ -\ 139 \\ \hline 671 \end{array}$$

14. The Mississippi River is 2,530 miles long. The Rio Grande is 1,885 miles long. How much longer is the Mississippi River than the Rio Grande?

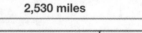

2,530 miles

1,885 miles	?

Name ______________________

Solve & Share

Gloria rode her bicycle 0.75 mile in the morning and 1.10 miles in the afternoon. Make a model to show how many miles Gloria rode in all. ***Solve this problem any way you choose.***

You can **select and use tools.** Use the place-value blocks or other objects to model this problem. ***Show your work in the space below!***

Lesson 2-6
Modeling Addition and Subtraction of Decimals

TEKS 4.4 Develop and use strategies and methods for whole number computations and decimal sums and differences in order to solve problems with efficiency and accuracy.
Mathematical Process Standards 4.1A, 4.1C, 4.1D, 4.1F, 4.1G

Digital Resources at SavvasTexas.com

Solve  Learn  Glossary 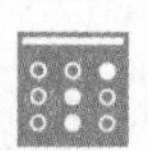 Check  Tools 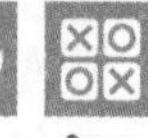 Games

Look Back!

Connect When do you use exact sums and differences of decimals?

How Do You Model Adding Decimals?

A

Use the table to find the total monthly cost of using the dishwasher and the DVD player.

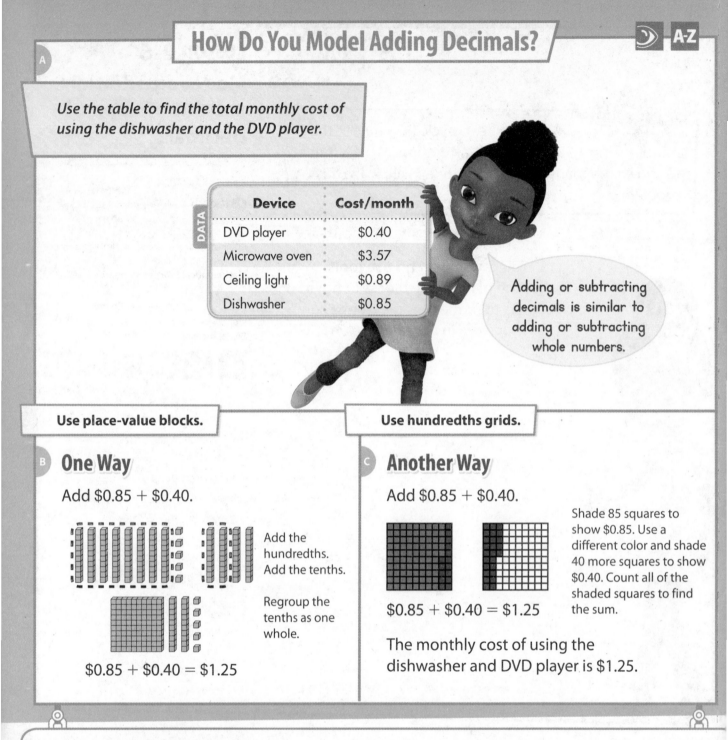

DATA

Device	Cost/month
DVD player	$0.40
Microwave oven	$3.57
Ceiling light	$0.89
Dishwasher	$0.85

Adding or subtracting decimals is similar to adding or subtracting whole numbers.

Use place-value blocks.

B

One Way

Add \$0.85 + \$0.40.

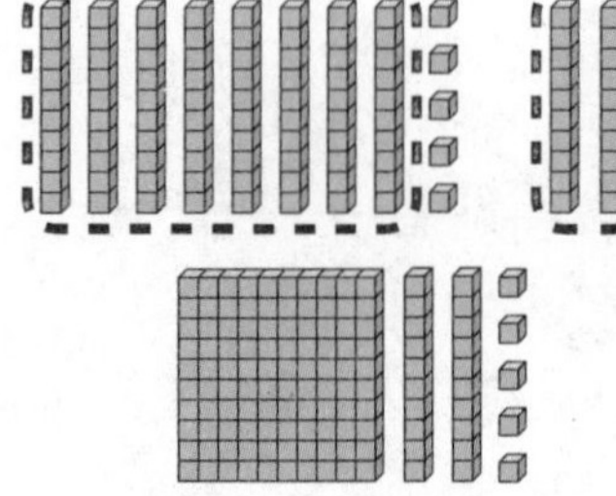

Add the hundredths. Add the tenths.

Regroup the tenths as one whole.

\$0.85 + \$0.40 = \$1.25

Use hundredths grids.

C

Another Way

Add \$0.85 + \$0.40.

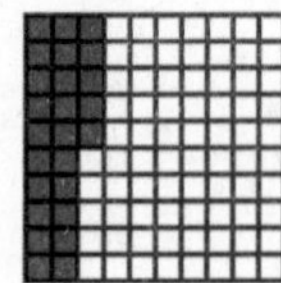

Shade 85 squares to show \$0.85. Use a different color and shade 40 more squares to show \$0.40. Count all of the shaded squares to find the sum.

\$0.85 + \$0.40 = \$1.25

The monthly cost of using the dishwasher and DVD player is \$1.25.

Do You Understand?

Convince Me! Shade the hundredths grids to find 1.25 + 0.54.

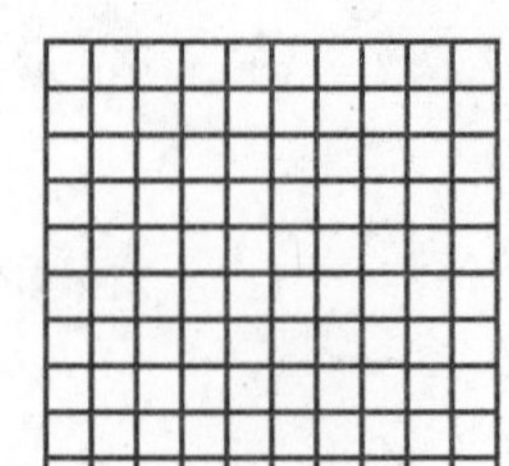

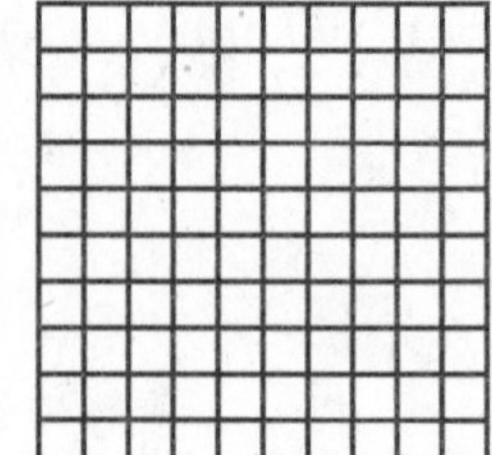

Name ______________________

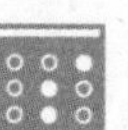

Another Example

Model $3.57 – $0.85.

Using Place-Value Blocks

Subtract 5 hundredths. Regroup one whole as 10 tenths. Subtract 8 tenths.

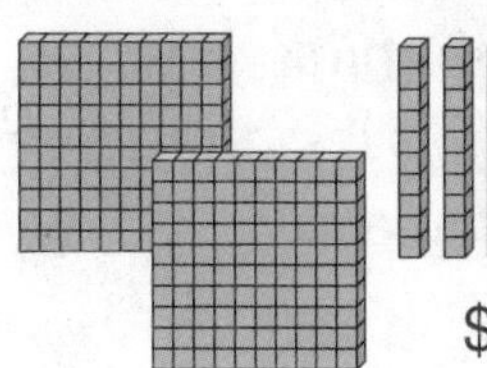
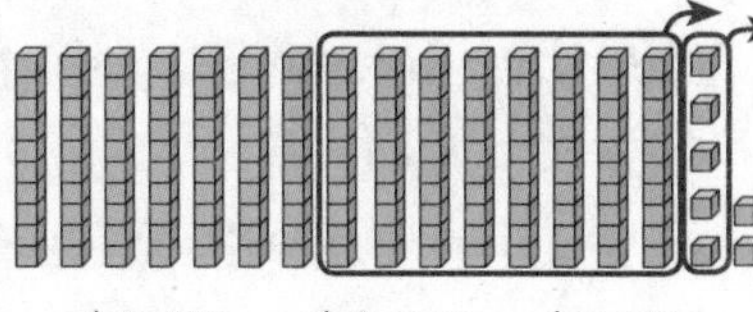

$3.57 – $0.85 = $2.72

Using Hundredths Grids

Shade grids to show 3.57. Then cross out 85 small squares to subtract 0.85.

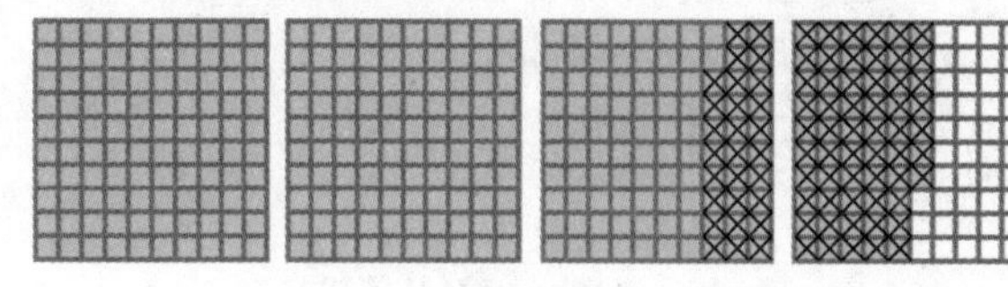

$3.57 – $0.85 = $2.72

Guided Practice*

In **1** through **6**, use place-value blocks or hundredths grids to add or subtract.

1. 1.22 + 0.34 **2.** 0.63 + 0.41

3. 2.73 – 0.94 **4.** 1.38 – 0.73

5. 0.47 – 0.21 **6.** 2.02 + 0.8

7. In the example on the facing page, if you were to shade 40 squares first, and then shade 85 more, would the answer be the same as shading 85 squares and then 40 more? Explain.

Independent Practice

Leveled Practice In **8** through **13**, add or subtract. Use place-value blocks or hundredths grids to help.

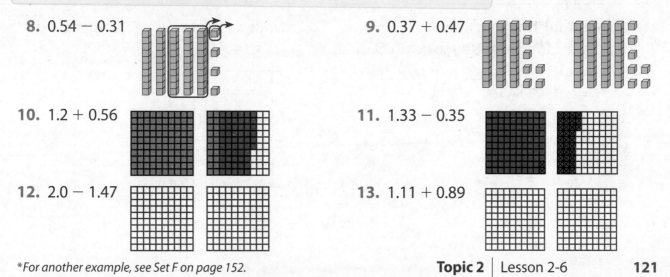

8. 0.54 – 0.31

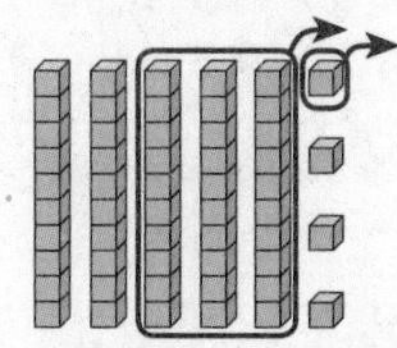

9. 0.37 + 0.47

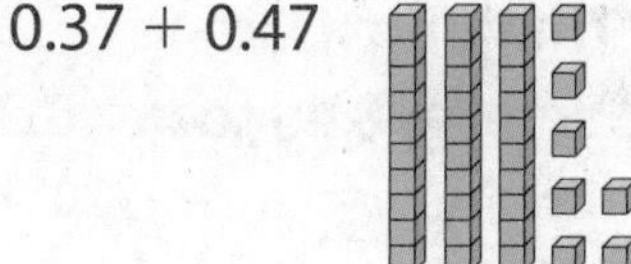

10. 1.2 + 0.56

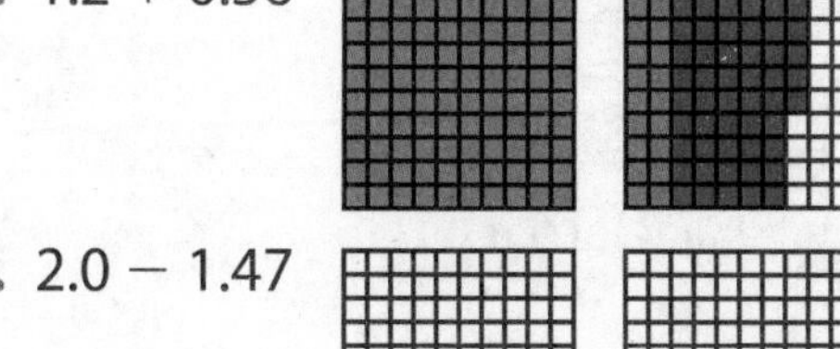

11. 1.33 – 0.35

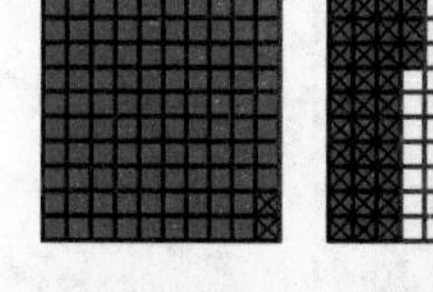

12. 2.0 – 1.47

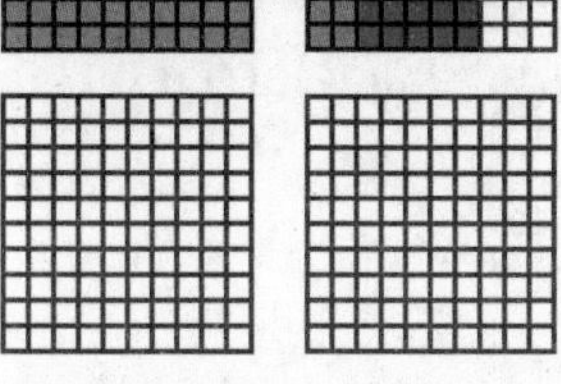

13. 1.11 + 0.89

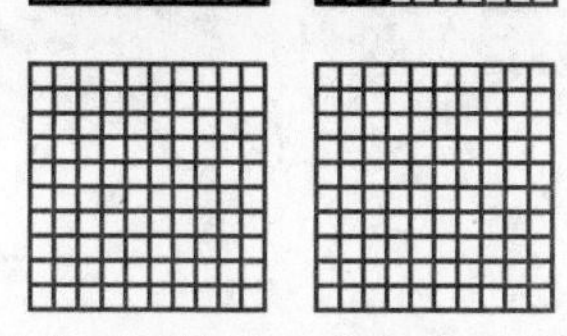

*For another example, see Set F on page 152.

Problem Solving

14. Connect Write the number sentence that is shown by the hundredths grids to the right.

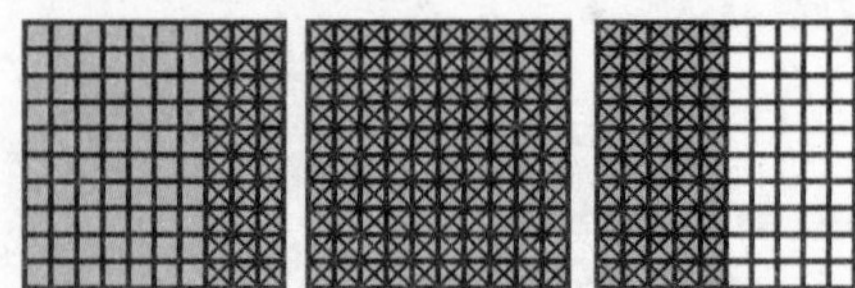

15. Explain How is adding 4.56 + 2.31 similar to adding \$2.31 + \$4.56?

16. Number Sense Do you think the difference of 1.4 − 0.95 is less than one or greater than one? Explain.

17. Number Sense Is the sum of 0.46 + 0.25 less than or greater than one? Explain.

18. Estimation Estimate to decide if the sum of 314 + 175 is more or less than 600.

19. Which choice represents the problem below?

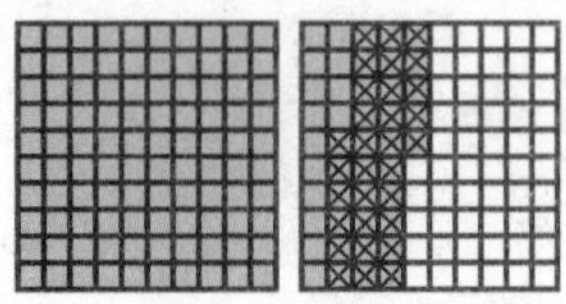

A 2.00 + 0.31
B 1.76 − 0.31
C 1.76 − 1.45
D 1.45 − 0.31

20. Connect Marisa mixed 0.17 gram of salt into a pot of soup. Before she served the soup, Marisa added 0.36 gram of salt. How much salt did Marisa put in the soup in all?

21. Extend Your Thinking Damon subtracted 0.17 from 0.45 to get 0.23. Is his model and answer correct? If not, explain what mistake he made.

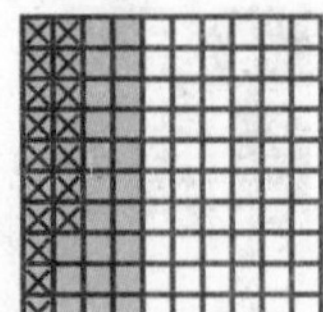

22. Draw a Picture Use a hundredths grid to represent 0.12 + 0.35 + 0.42.

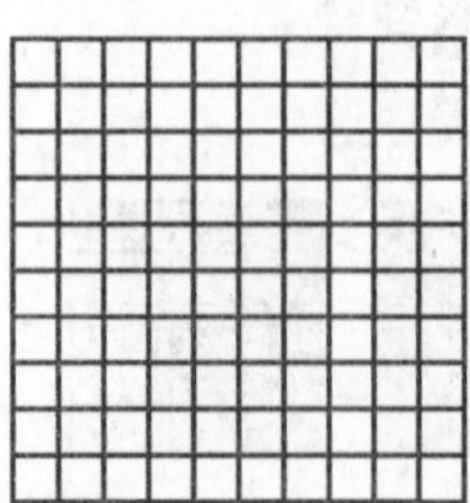

Name ______________________

Homework 2-6
Modeling Addition and Subtraction of Decimals

Another Look!

You can use hundredths grids to help you add or subtract decimals to the hundredths.

Adding decimals using a hundredths grid:	Subtracting decimals using a hundredths grid:
Add 0.32 + 0.17.	Subtract 0.61 − 0.42.
	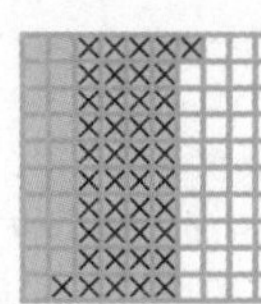
Step 1: Shade 32 squares to show 0.32.	**Step 1:** Shade 61 squares to show 0.61.
Step 2: Use a different color. Shade 17 squares to show 0.17.	**Step 2:** Cross out 42 squares to show 0.42.
Step 3: Count all the squares that are shaded. How many hundredths are shaded in all? Write the decimal for the total shaded squares: 0.49.	**Step 3:** Count the squares that are shaded but not crossed out. Write the decimal: 0.19.
So, 0.32 + 0.17 = 0.49.	So, 0.61 − 0.42 = 0.19.

In **1** through **3**, use the grids to help you add or subtract.

1. 0.22 + 0.35 = ______

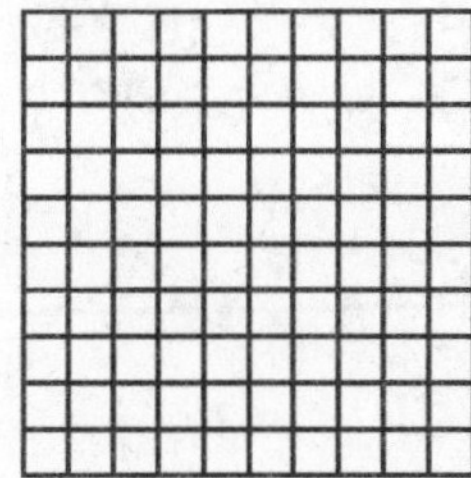

2. 0.52 − 0.41 = ______

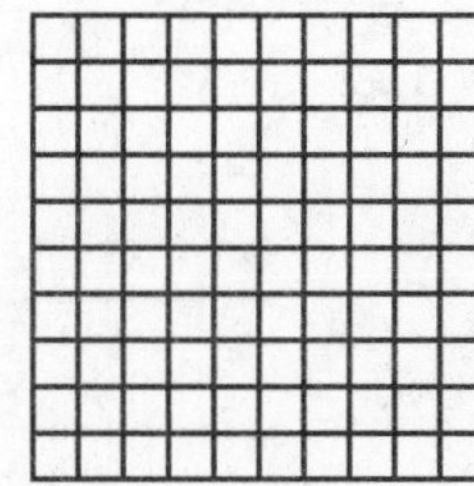

3. 0.85 − 0.1 = ______

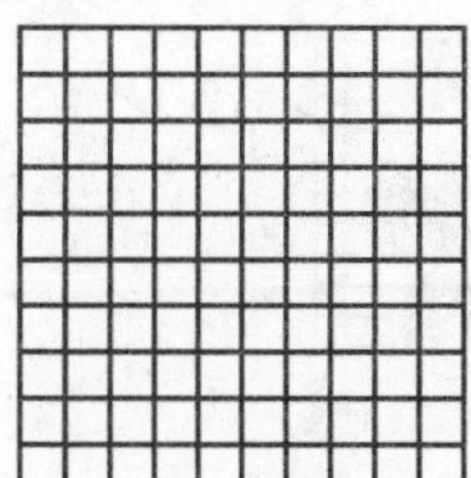

4. **Number Sense** Is the difference of 1.45 − 0.12 less than or greater than 1?

5. A bottle of nail polish holds 0.8 oz. A bottle of perfume holds 0.45 oz. How many more ounces does a bottle of nail polish hold?

6. **Connect** Tim bought 2.7 pounds of potatoes and 1.9 pounds of carrots. How many pounds of vegetables did he buy in all?

7. Jocelyn and Maggie made videos for their Social Studies project. Jocelyn's video was 1.18 minutes long, and Maggie's video was 1.86 minutes long. How long are the videos combined?

A 2.04 minutes
B 2.94 minutes
C 3.04 minutes
D 3.14 minutes

8. **Explain** Explain how you can use a grid to subtract 1.65 − 0.98.

9. **Explain** Each shaded area in the grids below represents a decimal. What is the sum of the decimals? Explain how you found your answer.

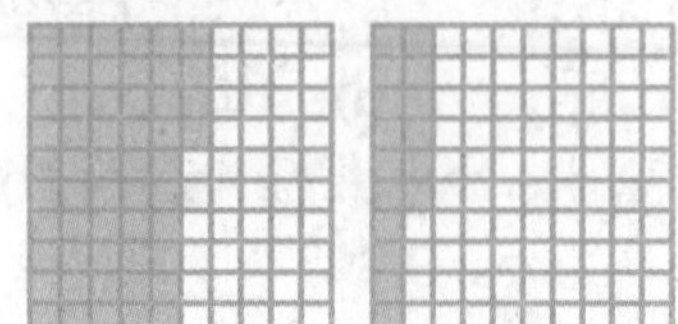

10. **Justify** Jin subtracted 0.57 from 0.7 to get 0.13. Is his model and answer correct? Explain your answer.

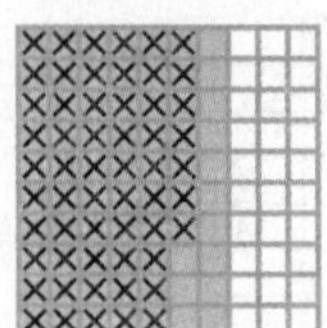

11. **Extend Your Thinking** How could you use what you know about adding whole numbers to add 0.23 + 0.54 + 0.13?

Name ____________________

Lesson 2-7
Adding Decimals

Solve & Share The route Aaliyah walks to work is 1.2 miles long. Walking home, she uses a different route, which is 1.5 miles long. What is the total distance Aaliyah walks to and from work? ***Solve this problem any way you choose.***

TEKS 4.4A Add and subtract whole numbers and decimals to the hundredths place using the standard algorithm. **Mathematical Process Standards** 4.1A, 4.1B, 4.1C, 4.1D, 4.1G

You can **formulate a plan** to decide which operation you should use to solve this problem. ***Show your work in the space below!***

Look Back!

Connect Given the two paths Aaliyah can take to and from work, what is the shortest distance she can walk in a day?

How Can You Add Decimals?

A

The Patel family walked 14.35 kilometers from their cabin to Crystal River. Later, they walked 12.4 kilometers from Crystal River to Lake Dorrance. How far did they walk in all?

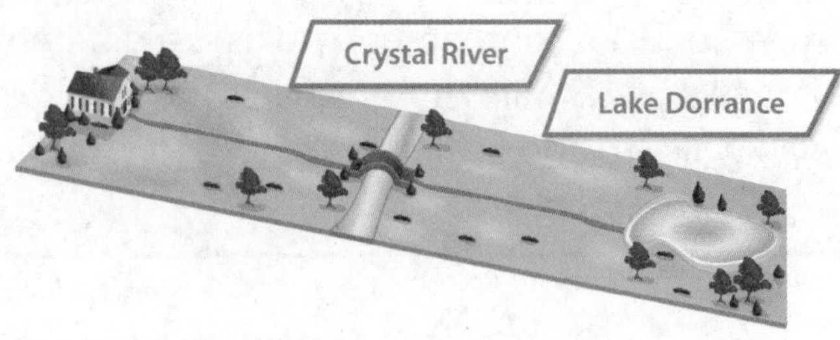

? km

14.35	12.4

You can extend the algorithm you use to add whole numbers.

Add decimals.

B

Step 1

Line up the decimal points. Write zeros as place holders, if necessary.

$$\begin{array}{r} 14.35 \\ +\ 12.40 \\ \hline \end{array}$$

Step 2

Add the hundredths. Regroup if necessary.

$$\begin{array}{r} 14.35 \\ +\ 12.40 \\ \hline 5 \end{array}$$

Step 3

Add the tenths. Regroup if necessary.

$$\begin{array}{r} 14.35 \\ +\ 12.40 \\ \hline 75 \end{array}$$

Step 4

Add the ones, then the tens. Place the decimal point.

$$\begin{array}{r} 14.35 \\ +\ 12.40 \\ \hline 26.75 \end{array}$$

The Patel family walked 26.75 kilometers in all.

Do You Understand?

Convince Me! Without finding the exact answer, is the sum for 23.65 + 20.18 greater than 44? Tell how you know.

Name

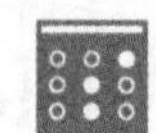 

Guided Practice*

In **1** through **6**, add.

1. $8.24 + 19.16$

2. $5.93 + 87.82$

3. $1.73 + 0.44$

4. $12.55 + 53.59$

5. 7.7 + 0.85

6. 9.12 + 82

7. Explain Sally found a sum of 17.30 for Exercise 1. Explain what mistake(s) she made.

8. Explain Trevor found a sum of 9.94 for Exercise 6. Explain what mistake(s) he made.

Independent Practice

Estimate to check your answers for reasonableness.

Leveled Practice In **9** through **24**, add.

9. $6.8 + 2.4$

10. $35.78 + 70.71$

11. $5.48 + 3.91$

12. $59.32 + 4.31$

13. $17.3 + 98.51$

14. $20.26 + 77.29$

15. $3.7 + 4.67$

16. $0.74 + 6.82$

17. 55.7 + 0.52

18. 9.12 + 82.4

19. 69.63 + 0.99

20. 75.5 + 4.4

21. 93.2 + 38.5

22. 0.98 + 3.1

23. 6.78 + 6.9

24. 2.1 + 2.55

*For another example, see Set G on page 153.

Problem Solving

25. On Oak Street, 66.32 kilograms of trash was collected, and 31.21 kilograms of recyclables were collected in one week. How many kilograms were collected in all?

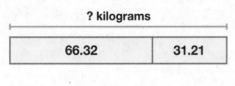

? kilograms	
66.32	31.21

26. Sara found the sum of 35.6 and 42.8 shown below. Is her answer correct? If not, explain her mistake and write the correct answer.

$$\begin{array}{r} 35.6 \\ +\ 42.8 \\ \hline 77.4 \end{array}$$

27. **Reason** Write a number that has a 7 in the tens place and a 9 in the hundredths place.

28. **Extend Your Thinking** Carla used mental math to add 4.7 and 2.3 by adding 0.7 and 0.3 to get 1, then adding $4 + 2 + 1$ to get 7. Use mental math to find the sum of 2.8 and 3.2. Describe your process.

29. **Draw a Picture** Use hundredths grids to show that the sum of 2.4 and 1.2 is 3.6.

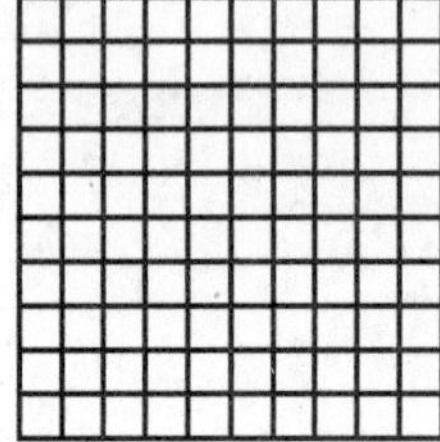
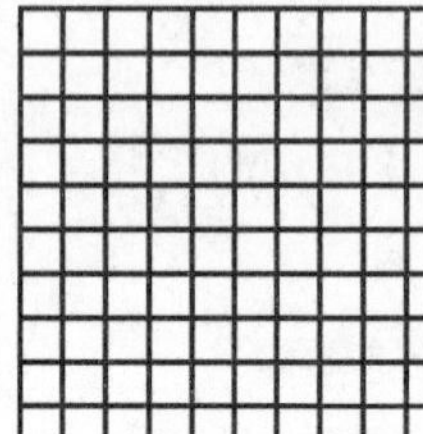
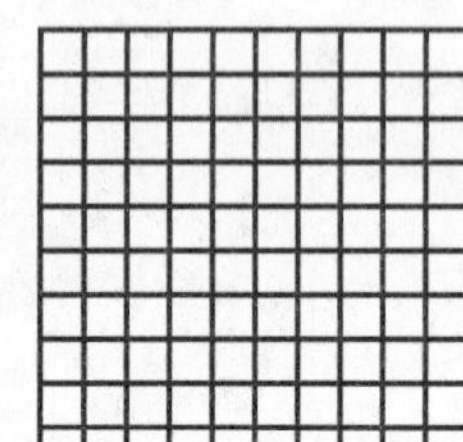
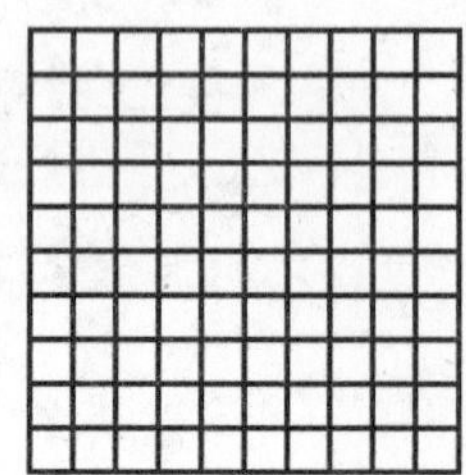

30. **Check for Reasonableness** Abby said that the sum of 323 and 504 is 827. Use estimation to determine if this answer is reasonable. Explain your process.

31. **Connect** A construction company bought 1.15 tons of gravel, 1.3 tons of stones, and 0.47 ton of sand. How many tons of gravel, stones, and sand did the company buy?

A 2.82 tons
B 2.92 tons
C 29.2 tons
D 292 tons

Name ______________________

Homework 2-7
Adding Decimals

Another Look!

Use the steps below to find the sum of 1.35 and 2.4.

Remember to write the decimal point in each sum.

Step 1	Step 2	Step 3	Step 4
Line up the decimal points. Write zeros as placeholders.	Add hundredths. Regroup if necessary.	Add tenths. Regroup if necessary.	Add ones. Place the decimal point.
1.35 + 2.40 ← Remember: 2.4 = 2.40	1.35 + 2.40 5	1.35 + 2.40 75	1.35 + 2.40 3.75

In **1** through **12**, find the sum.

1. $\begin{array}{r} \square \\ 0.3 \\ +\ 2.8 \\ \hline \square.\square \end{array}$

2. $\begin{array}{r} \square\ \ \ \\ 5.6\square \\ +\ 0.56 \\ \hline \square.\square\square \end{array}$

3. $\begin{array}{r} 2.67 \\ +\ 0.45 \\ \hline \end{array}$

4. $\begin{array}{r} 56.3 \\ +\ 26.55 \\ \hline \end{array}$

5. $\begin{array}{r} 73.27 \\ +\ 1.06 \\ \hline \end{array}$

6. $\begin{array}{r} 22.69 \\ +\ 22.72 \\ \hline \end{array}$

7. $\begin{array}{r} 6.33 \\ +\ 0.23 \\ \hline \end{array}$

8. $\begin{array}{r} 15.19 \\ +\ 60.91 \\ \hline \end{array}$

9. $\begin{array}{r} 5.7 \\ +\ 4.38 \\ \hline \end{array}$

10. 32.8 + 0.46

11. 44.37 + 0.99

12. 8.27 + 7.84

13. Explain Explain how you can tell without adding that 4.2 + 0.2 is more than 4.2 + 0.12.

14. Check for Reasonableness Jasmyn said that the difference of 646 and 118 is 438. Use estimation to determine if this answer is reasonable. Explain your process.

15. Maria found the sum of 0.78 and 1.2. Is her answer correct? If not, explain her mistake and write the correct answer.

$$\begin{array}{r} 0.78 \\ +\ 1.2 \\ \hline 0.90 \end{array}$$

16. Draw a Picture Use a hundredths grid to find the sum of 0.56 and 0.12.

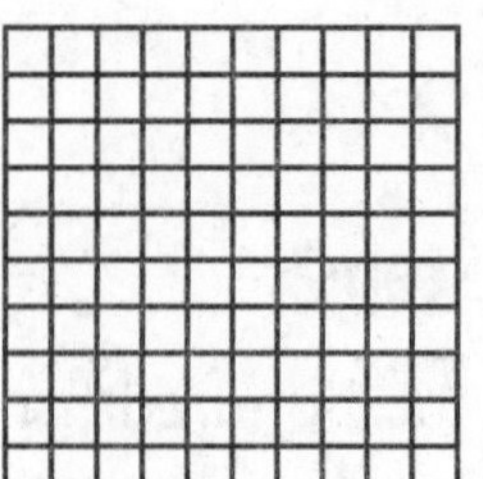

17. Connect On Monday, Benjamin ran 4.2 kilometers. On Tuesday, he ran 5.25 kilometers. On Wednesday, he ran 3.1 kilometers. How many kilometers did Benjamin run in all?

A 12.55 kilometers
B 10.23 kilometers
C 9.25 kilometers
D 5.98 kilometers

18. Estimation Brittany said that the sum of 7.9 and 9.6 is about 18. Do you agree? Explain.

19. Extend Your Thinking Jessica is painting a picture. She has white, red, blue, and yellow paint. Jessica makes three new paints from the paints she already has. She mixes 1.2 mL of white and 1.3 mL of red to make pink. She mixes 1.5 mL of red and 1.1 mL of blue to make purple. She mixes 2.1 mL of yellow and 2.3 mL of blue to make green. How much pink paint does Jessica have? How much purple paint? How much green paint?

Name ______________________________

Solve & Share

A normal body temperature for humans is 98.6°F. If Kali has a fever of 101.3°F, how much above normal is her temperature? ***Solve this problem any way you choose.***

Lesson 2-8
Subtracting Decimals

TEKS 4.4A Add and subtract whole numbers and decimals to the hundredths place using the standard algorithm. **Mathematical Process Standards** 4.1B, 4.1C, 4.1D, 4.1G

Digital Resources at SavvasTexas.com

Solve

Learn

Glossary

Check

Tools

Games

You can **use reasoning** by choosing which operation to use to solve this problem. ***Show your work in the space above!***

Look Back!

Justify How can you check that your answer is correct?

How Can You Subtract Decimals?

A

Roger and Phillip are going on a backpacking trip. How much more mass will Roger be carrying in his backpack than Phillip will be carrying?

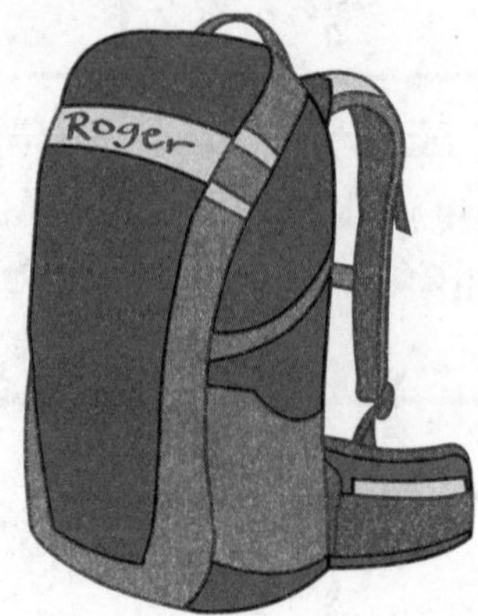

23.23 kilograms

11.6 kilograms

23.23	
11.6	?

You can extend the algorithm you use to subtract whole numbers to subtract decimals.

Subtract decimals.

B

Step 1

Line up the decimal points. Write zeros as placeholders, if necessary.

$$\begin{array}{r} 23.23 \\ -\ 11.60 \\ \hline \end{array}$$

Step 2

Regroup, if necessary. Subtract hundredths.

$$\begin{array}{r} 23.23 \\ -\ 11.60 \\ \hline 3 \end{array}$$

Step 3

Regroup, if necessary. Subtract tenths.

$$\begin{array}{r} 2\ \ 12\ \ \\ 2\not{3}.\not{2}3 \\ -\ 11.60 \\ \hline 63 \end{array}$$

Step 4

Subtract ones and tens, regrouping as necessary. Place the decimal point.

$$\begin{array}{r} 2\ \ 12\ \ \\ 2\not{3}.\not{2}3 \\ -\ 11.60 \\ \hline 11.63 \end{array}$$

Roger's backpack has a mass of 11.63 kilograms more than Phillip's.

Do You Understand?

Convince Me! Find the difference of 43.5 − 26.82. Did you write a zero for a placeholder? Explain.

Name ___

Guided Practice*

In **1** through **6**, subtract.

1. 37.6 − 14.5

2. 62.53 − 43.75

3. 46.81 − 12.43

4. 17.15 − 2.38

5. 0.6 − 0.42

6. 70.1 − 65.81

7. Explain Juan got the answer 19.88 for Exercise 2. Explain what mistakes he made.

8. Draw a Picture Use a hundredths grid to check your answer for Exercise 5.

Independent Practice

Leveled Practice In **9** through **24**, subtract.

Estimate to check your answers for reasonableness.

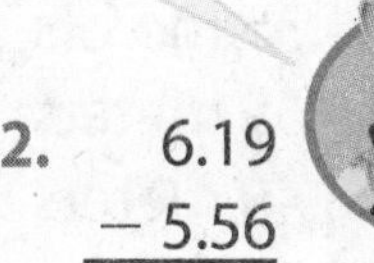

9. 4.8 − 0.5

10. 88.65 − 7.52

11. 9.2 − 2.4

12. 6.19 − 5.56

13. 89.2 − 65.33

14. 44 − 14.4

15. 0.88 − 0.79

16. 62.8 − 9.17

17. 89.82 − 46.3

18. 92.78 − 37.97

19. 39.65 − 17.69

20. 91.5 − 66.13

21. 9.41 − 1.72

22. 37.9 − 3.8

23. 34.8 − 7.46

24. 5 − 2.33

*For another example, see Set H on page 153.

Problem Solving

25. Number Sense Is 8.7 − 0.26 greater or less than 8? Explain.

26. Use a Strip Diagram When Matt left his home in Red Grove, his odometer read 47,283.5 kilometers. By the time he had arrived in Grand City, his odometer read 48,163.7 kilometers. How many kilometers did Matt travel?

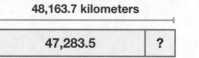

48,163.7 kilometers

47,283.5	?

27. One of the largest dinosaurs ever found, the *Puertasaurus*, measured 39.92 meters long. One of the smallest dinosaurs, the *Compsognathus*, measured 1.43 meters long. What was the difference in length of these dinosaurs?

A 41.35 meters
B 38.59 meters
C 38.49 meters
D 29.49 meters

28. Extend Your Thinking In one week, Jessica spent 2.35 hours walking from her house to work. Together, Jessica and her friend, Constance, will spend 4.21 hours of their week walking from their homes to work. How many hours does Constance spend each week walking from home to work?

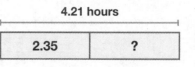

4.21 hours

2.35	?

29. Mental Math How could you use compensation to find 225 + 47?

30. Estimation Estimate the difference of 34.79 − 12.23 by rounding to the nearest whole number. Explain your process.

31. Jackie found the difference of 40.5 and 5.51. Is her answer correct? If not, explain her mistake and write the correct answer.

$$\begin{array}{r} 40.5 \\ -\ 5.51 \\ \hline 2.54 \end{array}$$

32. Draw a Picture Use hundredths grids to find the difference of 1.2 − 0.87.

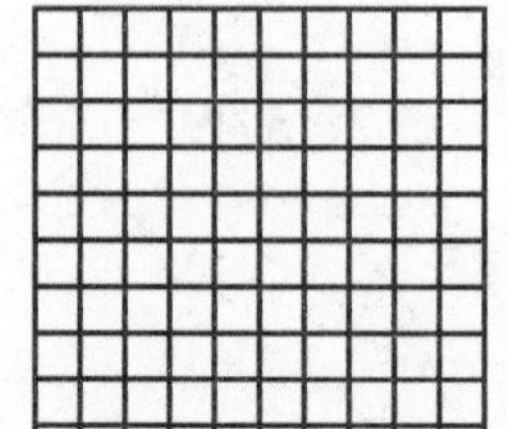

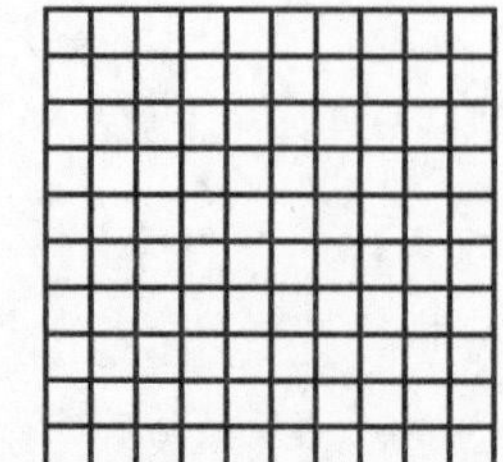

Name ________________

Homework 2-8
Subtracting Decimals

Another Look!

Use the steps below to find the difference of 6 and 1.75.

Step 1	Step 2	Step 3	Step 4
Line up the decimal points.	Write zeros as place holders.	Subtract hundredths. Regroup if necessary.	Subtract tenths and ones. Place the decimal point.
6 − 1.75	6.00 − 1.75	5 9̸ 10 10 6̸.0̸0̸ − 1.75 5	5 9̸ 10 10 6̸.0̸0̸ − 1.75 4.25

1. 3.4 − 2.6 = ☐.☐

2. 4.7☐ − 0.57 = ☐.☐☐

3. 6.9 − 3.25

4. 36.35 − 24.7

5. 32 − 17.43

6. 62.22 − 29.35

7. 37.41 − 16.43

8. 66.34 − 17.55

9. 68.33 − 7.52

10. 54.08 − 45.81

11. 54.28 − 17.7

12. 14.19 − 12.14

13. Number Sense In 1957, rainfall in El Camino was 0.34 inch in the spring and 4.74 inches in the summer. How much more rain fell in the summer than in the spring?

14. Christina walked 44.2 meters. She then walked 19.82 meters more. How many meters did she walk in all?

15. Nelson has $8.82 in his pocket. He spends $4.33 for lunch. Later, he loans $1 to a friend. How much money does Nelson have left?

A $6.49
B $5.49
C $4.49
D $3.49

16. Mario found the difference of 45.3 and 28.6. Is his answer correct? If not, explain his mistake and write the correct answer.

$$\begin{array}{r} 45.3 \\ -\ 28.6 \\ \hline 17.7 \end{array}$$

17. Estimation Braydon said that the difference of 45.03 and 10.12 is about 35. Do you agree? Explain.

How can rounding help you estimate?

18. Use a Strip Diagram A train has completed 52.4 miles of its 135 mile route. How many more miles will the train travel to complete the route?

135 miles	
52.4 miles	?

19. Check for Reasonableness Eliza said that the difference of 845 and 259 is 586. Use estimation to determine if this answer is reasonable. Explain your process.

20. Extend Your Thinking Caterina bought 9.96 ounces of Swiss cheese and 6.06 ounces of Colby cheese. She uses 8.1 ounces of the cheese to make dinner. How many ounces of cheese does Caterina have left?

Name ______________________________

Solve & Share

Reyna had $15.50 on her gift card. She bought one senior ticket and one child ticket. How much was left on Reyna's gift card? Tell how you solve.

Lesson 2-9
Adding and Subtracting Money

TEKS 4.4A Add and subtract whole numbers and decimals to the hundredths place using the standard algorithm. Also, 4.8C.
Mathematical Process Standards 4.1A, 4.1B, 4.1C, 4.1D, 4.1F

Digital Resources at SavvasTexas.com

Solve
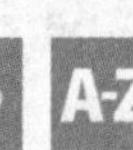
Learn

Glossary

Check Tools

Games

You can **connect ideas.** You know how to add and subtract decimals that aren't money.

Museum Ticket Prices
(including tax)

Seniors	$5.75
Adults	$9.29
Children under 12	$7.49

Look Back!

Estimation How could you tell without finding the exact answer that the total cost of one senior ticket and one child ticket is greater than $12?

How Do You Add and Subtract Money?

A

Kevin has $7.50 on his gift card. He buys a phone case and a screen protector. How much money does he have left on his gift card?

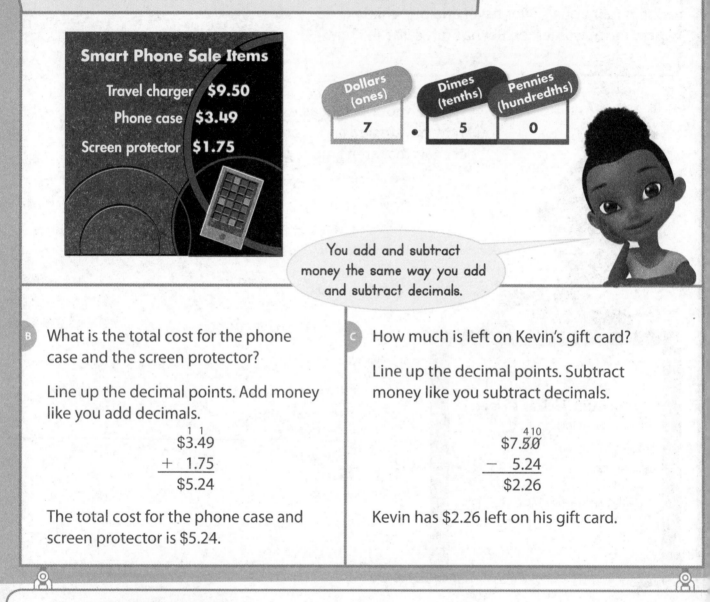

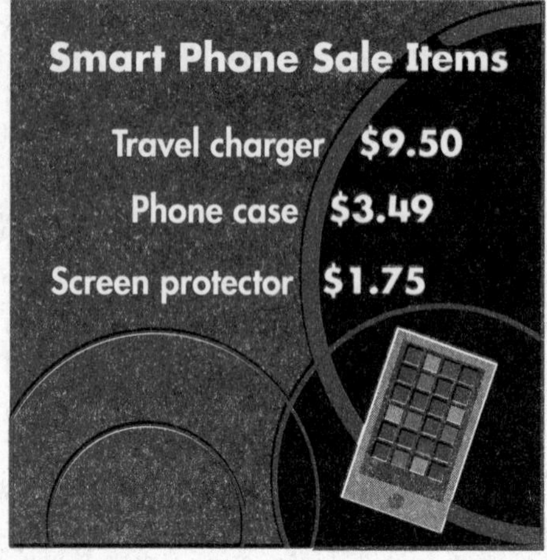

You add and subtract money the same way you add and subtract decimals.

B What is the total cost for the phone case and the screen protector?

Line up the decimal points. Add money like you add decimals.

$$\begin{array}{r} \overset{1\,1}{\$3.49} \\ +\ \ 1.75 \\ \hline \$5.24 \end{array}$$

The total cost for the phone case and screen protector is $5.24.

C How much is left on Kevin's gift card?

Line up the decimal points. Subtract money like you subtract decimals.

$$\begin{array}{r} \$7.\overset{4}{\not{5}}\overset{10}{\not{0}} \\ -\ \ 5.24 \\ \hline \$2.26 \end{array}$$

Kevin has $2.26 left on his gift card.

Do You Understand?

Convince Me! Find the sum of the decimals and then the sum of the money amounts shown at the right. What is the difference between adding decimals and adding money written in this form?

Decimals	Money
24.57	$24.57
+ 18.46	+ 18.46

Name ____

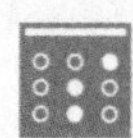 

Guided Practice*

In **1** through **6**, add or subtract.

1. $7.75 + 1.24

2. $8.11 + 7.89

3. $2.32 − 1.45

4. $22.51 − 14.89

5. $5.00 − $1.19

6. $31.45 + $19.76

7. Estimation Round each addend in Exercise 6 to the nearest dollar to estimate the sum. Is your actual sum reasonable? Explain.

8. Brian has $15.00. He wants to buy a book for $7.99 and a set of markers for $5.99. Does Brian have enough money? Show your work.

Independent Practice

Leveled Practice In **9** through **22**, add or subtract.

9. $2.64 + 1.14

10. $4.64 − 1.87

11. $10.48 + 4.55

12. $12.36 − 8.59

13. $12.86 − 8.59

14. $4.23 + 5.67

15. $8.12 − 2.75

16. $9.60 − 2.23

17. $7.81 + $2.62

18. $5.49 − $1.48

19. $7.26 − $4.33

20. $9.09 + $2.78

21. $6.29 − $3.66

22. $6.60 − $4.85

*For another example, see Set I on page 153.

Problem Solving

23. **Connect** How much more is the cost for two adult 5-day tickets than two adult 2-day tickets?

DATA

Theme Park Tickets		
Customer	**5-Day Ticket**	**2-Day Ticket**
Adults	$80.67	$53.60
Children	$75.33	$50.00

24. **Extend Your Thinking** Kyle's father has $25 for movie tickets and popcorn. He plans to take Kyle and Kyle's sister, each under 12, to a movie. Does he have enough money to buy a large box of popcorn for each person? Explain.

DATA

Movie Ticket Prices	
Adults	$7.50
Children Under 12	$4.75

DATA

Drinks and Popcorn Prices			
Item	**Small**	**Medium**	**Large**
Drinks	$1.25	$1.75	$2.10
Popcorn	$0.75	$1.35	$2.25

25. **Mental Math** Use mental math to find the sum of 43 and 57. Explain your thinking.

26. Peter had $20. He bought lunch for $6.39 and a notebook for $4.37. How much money does Peter have left?

A $9.24
B $9.76
C $10.76
D $11.24

27. **Estimation** Estimate the difference of 454 and 125 by rounding to the nearest ten.

28. **Formulate a Plan** Jamie earns $30 babysitting. She spends $12.95 on a new poster. Later, she earns $15 for mowing the lawn. Write a number sentence that shows how to find the money Jamie has left.

29. Norma has $26.20. She buys two packs of pencils for $4.78 each and a notebook for $2.19. How much money does Norma have left?

30. **Personal Financial Literacy** Anne has $435.39 in her savings account. She deposits $25.75 and withdraws $40. How much money is left in her savings account?

Name ______________________

Homework 2-9
Adding and Subtracting Money

Another Look!

You add and subtract money using the same steps you use to add and subtract decimals.

Patrick has $234.57 in his bank account. He deposits $66.87 and then withdraws $80. How much is left in Patrick's bank account?

Step 1	Step 2
Line up the decimal points. Add. $234.57 + 66.87 $301.44	Line up the decimal points. Subtract. $301.44 − 80.00 $221.44

In **1** through **11**, add or subtract.

1. $5.22 + 3.53

2. $7.66 − 1.45

3. $5.45 + 8.07

4. $8.87 − 5.55

5. $8.21 − 6.73

6. $8.20 + 5.43

7. $7.18 − 4.82

8. $7.51 − 6.17

9. $4.33 + $2.61

10. $8.48 − $6.85

11. $8.25 − $7.61

12. Analyze Information Alyssa has $12. She wants to buy a sandwich and a drink for herself and her sister. Does she have enough money? Explain.

DATA

Lunch Menu	
Item	**Price**
Soup	$2.75
Sandwich	$2.95
Chips	$0.99
Fruit Cup	$1.69
Drink	$1.39

13. Extend Your Thinking A "balance" is how much money is in a bank account. Deposits add money, and withdrawals subtract money. The table to the right shows three transactions in a bank account. What is the final balance?

DATA

Bank Account	
Transaction	**Amount**
Starting Balance	$323.78
Deposit	$76.62
Deposit	$34.24
Withdrawal	$100.00

14. Use a Strip Diagram Keith has $35.91. He buys one T-shirt for $15.78 and a cap for $12.19. How much money does Keith have left?

$35.91

$15.78	$12.19	?

15. Mental Math Use mental math to find the sum of 25 and 85. Explain your thinking.

16. Connect The cost for a 5-hour canoe rental is $45.73. The cost for an all-day canoe rental is $60.35. How much more is the cost of the all-day rental than the cost of the 5-hour rental?

17. Sophia bought pens that cost $3.19 and a folder on sale for $0.19. She paid with a $5-bill. How much change did she get back?

A $4.81
B $1.81
C $1.62
D $0.81

Name ______________________________

Solve & Share

Marta's dog weighs 60 pounds. Suso's dog weighs 43 pounds. How much more does Marta's dog weigh than Suso's dog? Draw a picture and write an equation to represent this problem. ***Solve this problem any way you choose.***

Problem Solving

Lesson 2-10

Draw a Strip Diagram and Write an Equation

TEKS 4.1D Communicate mathematical ideas, reasoning, and their implications using multiple representations, including symbols, diagrams, graphs, and language as appropriate. Also, 4.4, 4.5.
Mathematical Process Standards
4.1B, 4.1C

Digital Resources at SavvasTexas.com

Solve

Learn
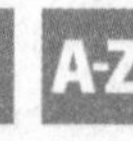

Glossary
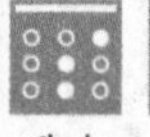
Check
Tools

Games

You can **use a strip diagram** to represent the problem visually. ***Show your work in the space above!***

Look Back!

Formulate a Plan Given the equation you wrote, rewrite this equation into an addition problem.

How Can Diagrams and Equations Help Solve a Problem?

A Analyze

The mass of a human brain is how much greater than the mass of a chimpanzee brain?

The human brain has a mass of 1,350 grams.

Ask yourself, "What do I know?" and "What am I asked to find?"

DATA

Average Masses of Brains	
House cat	30 grams
Chimpanzee	420 grams
Human	1,350 grams
Dolphin	1,500 grams

Draw a strip diagram.

Write an equation.

B Plan

You can use a symbol or letter, called a variable, to represent a number. The human brain has a mass of 1,350 grams. A chimpanzee brain has a mass of 420 grams. Let the variable, x, represent the unknown greater amount of mass of a human brain.

1,350 grams

420 grams	x

C Solve

Use subtraction to find the difference in the sizes of the brains.

$$1{,}350 - 420 = x$$
$$930 = x$$

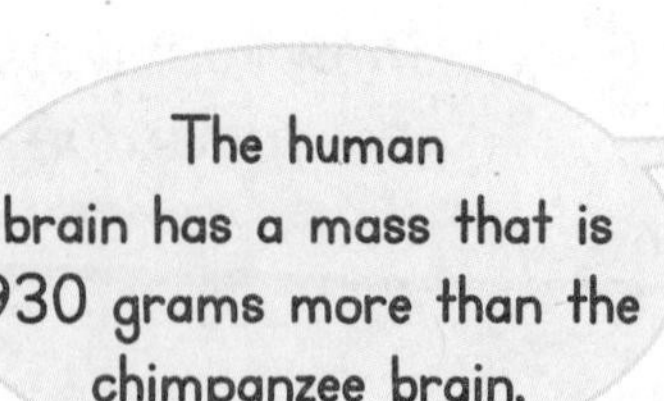

The human brain has a mass that is 930 grams more than the chimpanzee brain.

Do You Understand?

Convince Me! Write a story problem that can be solved using the strip diagram or equation shown below.

2,550

x	875

$$2{,}550 - 875 = x$$

Name ____________________

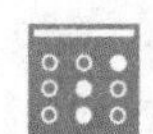

Guided Practice*

1. Sandy earned $36 from babysitting and $15 for doing her chores. Write an equation and find the total amount, *t*, that Sandy earned.

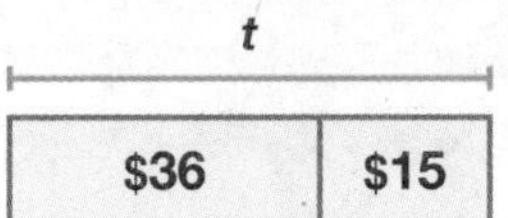

2. A cell phone company has a total of 3,959 customers around the world. If 2,314 of its customers live in the United States, how many of its customers live in other countries? If *x* equals the number of customers in other countries, draw a strip diagram and write an equation to solve.

Independent Practice

In **3** through **5**, use a variable, draw a strip diagram, and write an equation to solve.

3. A monument is made up of 8,361 bricks and 7,990 stones. How many bricks and stones make up the monument?

4. Maddie had $364 in her savings account. She withdrew $75 to buy a new game. How much money, *s*, does Maddie have in her savings account now?

5. A group of students is collecting toys for children. Last week, they collected a total of 3,288 toys. This week, 1,022 toys have been collected. How many toys, *t*, were collected in all?

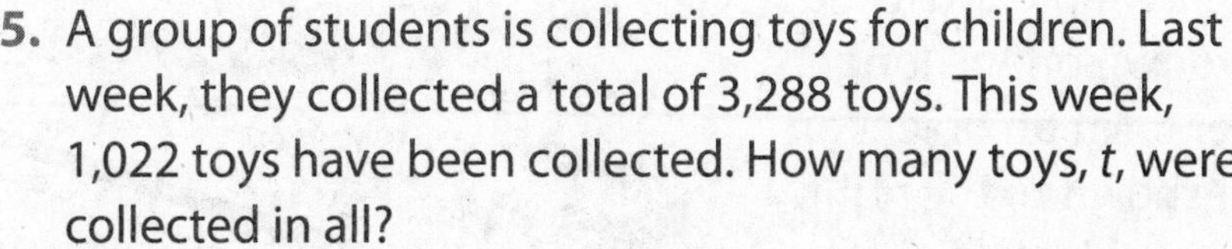

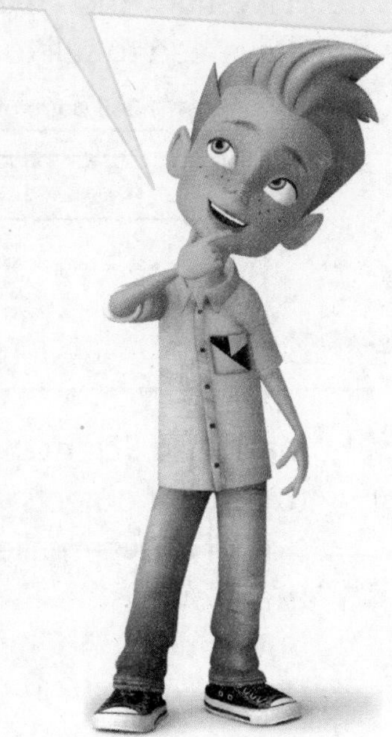

Use a variable, such as x, to equal the total number of bricks and stones.

*For another example, see Set J on page 154.

Problem Solving

6. **Estimation** Estimate the total cost of a shirt, a pair of shorts, and a hat.

Cost of Gym Clothes	
Shirt	\$12
Shorts	\$19
Socks	\$2
Hat	\$15

7. The American Kennel Club recognizes 17 breeds of herding dogs and 26 breeds of terriers. Which equation can be used to find the total number of herding dogs and terriers, *d*?

   A $17 + d = 26$
   B $26 - 17 = d$
   C $26 + d = 17$
   D $17 + 26 = d$

8. **Extend Your Thinking** A parking lot had a total of 243 cars in one day. By 6:00 A.M., there were 67 cars in the lot. In the next hour, 13 more cars joined these. How many more cars, *c*, would come to the lot by the end of the day?

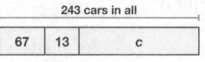

243 cars in all

67	13	*c*

9. **Tools** A shoe store sold 162 pairs of shoes. The goal was to sell 345 pairs. How many more pairs of shoes, *p*, did they need to sell to make their goal?

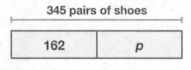

345 pairs of shoes

162	*p*

10. Byron spent \$7.75 on popcorn and a drink at the movie theater. The popcorn was \$4.25. How much was the cost of the drink, *d*?

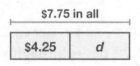

\$7.75 in all

\$4.25	*d*

11. **Math and Science** A lever is a simple tool used to help lift objects. Pushing down on the longer side of a lever makes it easier to lift an object on the shorter side. In the lever shown to the right, how much longer is the longer side than the shorter side?

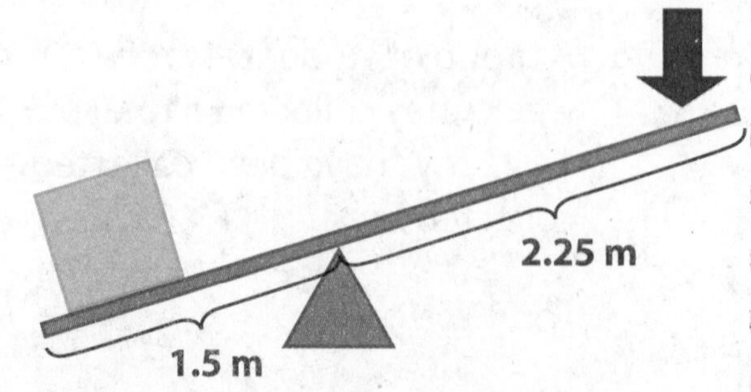

Name

Homework 2-10

Draw a Strip Diagram and Write an Equation

Another Look!

Read the question and follow the steps to develop a problem-solving strategy.

In the morning, a grocery store had 28 apples on display. By the end of the day, 11 apples had been purchased. How many apples were left?

Read/Understand Analyze	Plan	Solve
You know there were 28 apples on display and 11 were purchased. You need to find how many apples were left. You can use a variable, *a*, to represent the number of apples left.	Draw a strip diagram that helps you visualize the problem. 28 in all | 11 | *a* |	Write an equation. $28 - 11 = a$ Solve the equation to answer the problem. $a = 17$ 17 apples were left.

In **1** and **2**, use a variable, draw a strip diagram, and write an equation to solve.

You can use the variable given in each problem.

1. Use a Strip Diagram On Monday, Erika put 12 flakes of fish food in her fish tank before school, and 13 more when she got home. How many flakes, *f*, did she put in the tank that day?

2. Roy is reading a book that is 68 pages. He has read 24 pages so far. How many more pages, *p*, does he have to read to finish the book?

3. **Use a Strip Diagram** There are 29 students in the school band. During practice, 6 new students join the band. How many students, *s*, are in the band now?

s	
29	6

4. **Number Sense** There are 577,850 blue pens and 725,370 red pens in the supply warehouse. Are there greater than a million pens in all? Explain.

You can use mental math.

5. Danny has 45 minutes to take a math test. If Danny finishes half the test in 19 minutes, how many minutes, *m*, does he have left to finish the other half?

45	
19	*m*

6. While shopping, Janet bought a shirt for $8, a pair of jeans for $22, mittens for $5, and a hat for $10. How much money did Janet spend?

A $45
B $32
C $30
D $15

7. **Extend Your Thinking** When Ian's family moved, they packed 108 boxes. They loaded 66 boxes into the moving truck and 20 boxes on a trailer. How many boxes were still left to move?

8. Harold counted 75 different species of fish at the local zoo. He also counted 18 different species of spiders at the zoo. How many more species of fish than species of spiders did he count?

9. Mr. Lee had 62 pencils at the beginning of the school year. At the end of the school year, he had 8 pencils left. How many pencils, *g*, were given out during the year?

62 pencils in all	
8	*g*

Name ______________________________

TOPIC 2 Mixed Problem Solving

Find how many $\frac{1}{6}$s are equal to $\frac{2}{3}$.

You can **select tools** like real objects, manipulatives, technology, and paper and pencil to solve problems.

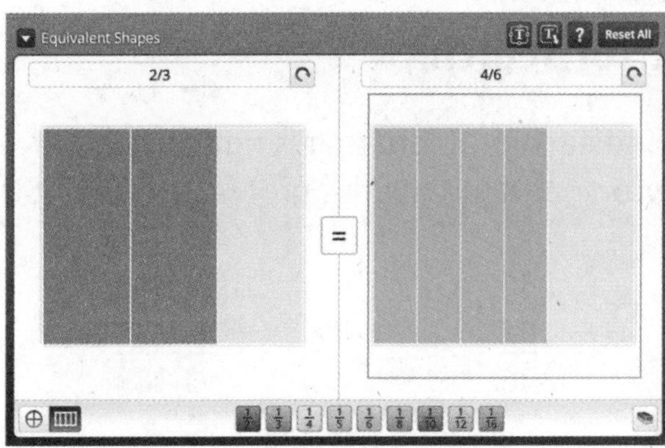

I chose a digital Math Tool for equivalent fractions to find how many $\frac{1}{6}$s are in $\frac{2}{3}$. The tool made it easy to rename the fraction with a different denominator. I could also use objects or manipulatives like fraction strips to compare $\frac{2}{3}$ and $\frac{4}{6}$.

1			
$\frac{1}{3}$		$\frac{1}{3}$	
$\frac{1}{6}$	$\frac{1}{6}$	$\frac{1}{6}$	$\frac{1}{6}$

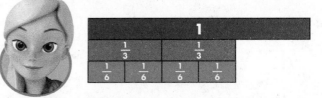

Tell whether you would select real objects, manipulatives, technology, or paper and pencil to solve each problem.

1. How many $\frac{1}{4}$s are equal to $\frac{6}{8}$?

2. **Connect** Morgan found the sum of $22 + 37 + 13 + 18$ by first adding 37 and 13 to get 50, then adding 22 and 18 to get 40, and finally adding 50 and 40 to get 90. Which number properties did Morgan use?

3. **Represent** Eva bought 6 packs of pencils. Each pack contains 4 pencils. How many pencils did Eva buy?

What objects can you use to help?

4. **Personal Financial Literacy** The Higgs family is keeping track of their unplanned spending. What is their total unplanned spending so far?

DATA

Unplanned Spending	
Car repair	$105.90
New water heater	$1,499

Number Sense

Error Search

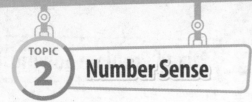

Find each problem that is not correct. Circle what is wrong and rewrite the problem so that it is correct.

1. $\begin{array}{r} 239 \\ +\ 107 \\ \hline 336 \end{array}$

2. $\begin{array}{r} 945 \\ +\ 238 \\ \hline 1{,}183 \end{array}$

3. $\begin{array}{r} 412 \\ +\ 132 \\ \hline 544 \end{array}$

4. $\begin{array}{r} 945 \\ +\ 682 \\ \hline 1{,}527 \end{array}$

Over or Under?

Estimation Circle the better estimate.

5. 716 + 174

over 900

under 900

6. 108 + 308

over 400

under 400

7. 941 + 216

over 1,000

under 1,000

8. 493 − 241

over 300

under 300

9. 869 − 91

over 700

under 700

10. 881 − 86

over 800

under 800

11. 6.55 + 3.48

over 10

under 10

12. 8.22 + 8.17

over 16

under 16

13. 6.83 + 3.35

over 10

under 10

14. 4.59 − 1.85

over 3

under 3

15. 3.5 − 2.13

over 1

under 1

16. 5.8 − 3.16

over 3

under 3

Name ____________________

TOPIC 2

Set A pages 89–94

Add 155 + 38. Use mental math.

Use the breaking apart method. Adding 5 to 155 is easy.

Break apart 38 into 5 and 33.

155 + 5 = 160

160 + 33 = 193

So, 155 + 38 = 193.

Remember to adjust the sum or difference when you use the compensation method.

1. 53 + 88

2. 372 + 226

3. 5,342 + 1,999

4. 283 − 169

5. 676 − 521

6. 1,089 − 961

Set B pages 95–100

Estimate.

$$\begin{array}{r} 1{,}579 \\ +\ 1{,}248 \\ \hline \end{array}$$

Round each number to the nearest hundred.

1,579 rounds to 1,600.

1,248 rounds to 1,200.

Add

$$\begin{array}{r} 1{,}600 \\ +\ 1{,}200 \\ \hline 2{,}800 \end{array}$$

Remember that you can round numbers to the nearest hundred or thousand when estimating sums and differences.

Estimate each sum or difference.

1. 473 + 465

2. 8,352 − 3,421

3. 586 − 483

4. 4,094 + 246

5. 1,440 − 933

6. 748 − 392

7. 981 + 193

8. 725 + 635

Set C pages 101–106

Add 359 + 723.

Estimate: 400 + 700 = 1,100

Add the ones. Regroup if necessary.	Add the tens. Regroup if necessary.	Add the hundreds.
$\begin{array}{r} ^{1} \\ 359 \\ +\ 723 \\ \hline 2 \end{array}$	$\begin{array}{r} ^{1} \\ 359 \\ +\ 723 \\ \hline 82 \end{array}$	$\begin{array}{r} ^{1} \\ 359 \\ +\ 723 \\ \hline 1{,}082 \end{array}$

The answer is reasonable.

Remember to regroup if necessary when adding whole numbers.

1. $\begin{array}{r} 32{,}834 \\ +\ 17{,}384 \\ \hline \end{array}$

2. $\begin{array}{r} 14{,}382 \\ +\ \ 9{,}243 \\ \hline \end{array}$

3. 215 + 8,823

4. 14,296 + 444

5. 2,417 + 3,573

6. 572 + 941

Set D pages 107–112

Find 831 − 796.

Estimate: 830 − 800 = 30

Subtract the ones. Regroup if necessary.	Subtract the tens. Subtract the hundreds.	Add to check your answer.
2 11 8 3̸ 1̸ − 7 9 6 5	7 12 11 8̸ 3̸ 1̸ − 7 9 6 3 5	1 1 7 9 6 + 3 5 8 3 1

The answer is reasonable.

Remember that you may need to regroup to be able to subtract.

1. 651 − 482
2. 18,465 − 6,291
3. 415 − 323
4. 4,978 − 2,766
5. 735 − 255
6. 4,558 − 2,613

Set E pages 113–118

Find 609 − 547.

Estimate: 600 − 500 = 100

Subtract the ones. Regroup if necessary.	Subtract the tens. Subtract the hundreds.	Add to check your answer.
6 0 9 − 5 4 7 2	5 10 6̸ 0̸ 9 − 5 4 7 6 2	1 5 4 7 + 6 2 6 0 9

The answer is reasonable.

Remember that you can think of 100 as 10 tens or as 9 tens + 10 ones.

1. 407 − 239
2. 20,305 − 5,213
3. 400 − 256
4. 5,060 − 3,125
5. 805 − 125
6. 2,008 − 1,605

Set F pages 119–124

Use place-value blocks to find 0.49 − 0.27.

Show 0.49 using blocks.

Subtract 7 hundredths and 2 tenths.

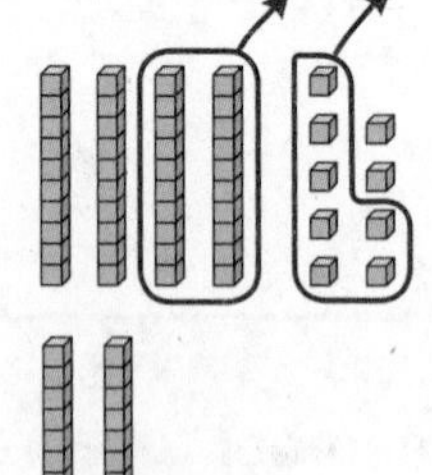

Count the remaining blocks. 0.49 − 0.27 = 0.22

Use place-value blocks to find 0.12 + 0.24.

Show 0.12 using blocks. Add 4 hundredths and 2 tenths.

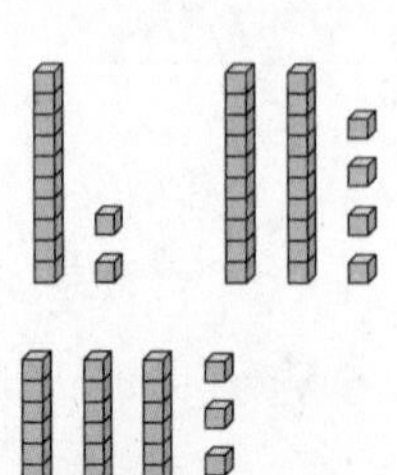

Count the total.

0.12 + 0.24 = 0.36

Remember that adding and subtracting decimals is similar to adding and subtracting whole numbers.

Use place-value blocks or hundredths grids to find each sum or difference.

1. 0.2 + 0.89
2. 0.67 − 0.31
3. 0.28 + 0.64
4. 0.7 − 0.52
5. 0.16 − 0.08
6. 0.28 − 0.25
7. 0.35 + 0.72
8. 0.95 + 0.83

Name ____________________

TOPIC 2

Set G pages 125–130

Add 15.85 + 23.3.

Line up the decimal points. Write zeros as place holders, if necessary.

Add the hundredths.

```
  15.85
+ 23.30
      5
```

Add the tenths.

```
  1
  15.85
+ 23.30
     15
```

Add the ones and tens. Place the decimal point in the answer.

```
  1
  15.85
+ 23.30
  39.15
```

Remember to place the decimal point in the answer.

1. 6.32 + 15.12

2. 43.42 + 15.28

3. 8.34 + 97.25

4. 71.35 + 67.82

5. 5.2 + 0.74

6. 0.8 + 0.56

Set H pages 131–136

Subtract 23.64 − 7.36.

Line up the decimal points.

Subtract the hundredths.

```
     5 14
  23.6̸4̸
−  7.36
      8
```

Subtract the tenths.

```
     5 14
  23.6̸4̸
−  7.36
     28
```

Subtract the ones. Place the decimal point in the answer.

```
  1 13 5 14
  2̸3̸.6̸4̸
−  7.36
  16.28
```

Remember to align the decimal points and write zeros as place holders, if necessary.

1. 19.35 − 8.74

2. 12.3 − 9.7

3. 14.04 − 9.33

4. 7.5 − 3.92

Set I pages 137–142

Sally has $6.95. Jordyn has $8.89. How much more money does Jordyn have than Sally?

You are comparing amounts, so subtract.

```
   7 18
  $8̸.8̸9
− $6.95
  $1.94
```

Jordyn has $1.94 more than Sally.

Remember to read the question carefully to determine which operation to use.

1. Irene had $20. She gave $7.50 to Tom. How much did Irene have left?

2. Kate babysat 3 times last month. She earned $9.50, $16.75, and $12. How much did she earn in all?

Set J pages 143–148

Cathy spent \$8.85 on lunch. She bought a sandwich, a fruit cup, and a milk at the snack bar. She spent a total of \$6.90 on the sandwich and milk. How much did the fruit cup cost?

What do I know?	Cathy had \$8.85. Cathy bought a sandwich, a milk, and a fruit cup. Cathy spent \$6.90 on the sandwich and the milk.
What am I being asked to find?	The amount of money Cathy spent on the fruit cup

You can use a symbol or letter, called a variable, to represent a number.

Let the variable *m* represent the amount of money Cathy spent on the fruit cup. Draw a strip diagram to represent the problem.

\$8.85

\$6.90	*m*

Write an equation.

$m = \$8.85 - \$6.90$
$m = \$1.95$

Cathy spent \$1.95 on the fruit cup.

Remember that you can draw a strip diagram and use it to write an equation to help you solve a problem.

Draw a strip diagram and write an equation to solve.

1. Doug saw 5 agile wallabies and 9 rock wallabies at the zoo. How many wallabies did Doug see?

2. Luz collected 393 tokens from the games at Funland. She needs 500 tokens to win a large stuffed animal. How many more tokens does Luz need to win the large stuffed animal?

3. The clothing Myrna bought totaled \$38.82. How much change did she get if she gave the clerk \$40?

Name ____

1. Joe got 34,867 points playing a video game, and Carlos got 29,978 points. How many more points did Joe get than Carlos?

   A 14,889 points

   B 4,999 points

   C 4,989 points

   D 4,889 points

2. The table shows the number of tickets sold for the school play.

   DATA

Tickets Sold	
Thursday	320
Friday	282
Saturday	375

   Which is the best estimate of the total tickets sold?

   A 1,100 tickets

   B 1,000 tickets

   C 900 tickets

   D 800 tickets

3. David went to a sporting goods store with $4.00 and bought a fishing lure for $2.39, including the tax. How much money did David have left after his purchase?

   A $1.60

   B $1.61

   C $2.60

   D $2.61

4. Luis used compensation to find 572 − 239. First he subtracted 200, and then he subtracted 40. Which should he do next?

   A Add 1.

   B Subtract 1.

   C Add 10.

   D Subtract 10.

5. Manuel has 60 minutes to get to karate class. He takes 27 minutes to get to class and 10 minutes to change into his uniform. How much time does he have before he must leave his house?

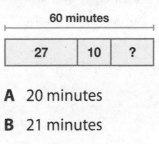

   60 minutes

27	10	?

   A 20 minutes

   B 21 minutes

   C 23 minutes

   D 97 minutes

6. To advertise for the school fun fair, 325 flyers were printed on Wednesday, 468 flyers were printed on Thursday, and 815 flyers were printed on Friday. How many flyers were printed in all?

   A 1,620 flyers

   B 1,608 flyers

   C 1,508 flyers

   D 1,600 flyers

7. Larry spent $1.89 on a bottle of paint and $0.45 on a sponge brush. What was the total amount he spent?

A $2.34

B $1.34

C $1.32

D $1.24

8. Garrett drove 239 miles on Saturday and 149 miles on Sunday. To find 239 + 149, Garrett made a multiple of ten, as shown below. What is the missing number?

239 + 149 = 240 + ☐ = 388

A 129

B 130

C 147

D 148

9. A musical group made 8,000 copies of a CD. So far, they have sold 6,280 copies. How many copies are left?

10. In April, 5,326 books were checked out of the library. In May, 3,294 books were checked out. How many books were checked out in all?

A 8,510 books

B 8,590 books

C 8,610 books

D 8,620 books

11. What number makes the number sentence true?

28 + 79 = ☐ + 28

A 107

B 79

C 51

D 28

12. Betty had 719 pennies in her piggy bank. If she gave her sister 239 pennies, how many pennies did Betty have left?

Name ______________________________

TOPIC 2

13. A penny has a mass of 2.5 grams. A quarter has a mass of 5.67 grams. What is the difference in their masses?

A 2.17 grams

B 3.17 grams

C 5.42 grams

D 8.17 grams

14. The last total solar eclipse seen in Dallas, Texas was in 1623. The next one will not be seen until 2024. Which equation should Tony **NOT** use to find the number of years, *y*, between the eclipses?

A $2024 - 1623 = y$

B $2024 + 1623 = y$

C $y + 1623 = 2024$

D $1623 = 2024 - y$

15. Daria's book has 323 pages. She has read 141 pages. Use the diagram below to find the number of pages, *p*, she has left to read.

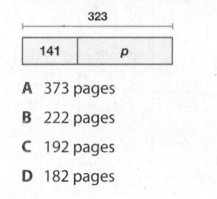

323	
141	*p*

A 373 pages

B 222 pages

C 192 pages

D 182 pages

16. Mr. Miller's class set a goal to read 5,000 pages. So far, they have read 2,898 pages. How many more pages must they read to reach their goal?

A 2,012 pages

B 2,102 pages

C 3,012 pages

D 3,898 pages

17. Mr. Treveses bought 2.72 kilograms of hamburger meat and 1.48 kilograms of turkey meat. How many kilograms of meat did he buy?

A 1.24 kilograms

B 3.10 kilograms

C 4.10 kilograms

D 4.20 kilograms

18. Joe and Sara recorded the number of birds they saw in the park over the summer. How many more birds did they see in 2012 than 2013?

DATA

Birds	
Summer 2012	458
Summer 2013	397

A 47

B 53

C 58

D Not here

19. In 2010, an animal shelter found adoption homes for 1,645 cats and dogs. If 1,218 of the adopted pets were dogs, how many cats, *c*, were adopted in 2010?

1,645 cats and dogs	
1,218	c

A 559 cats

B 532 cats

C 427 cats

D 413 cats

20. Samantha rode her bicycle 6.79 miles on Saturday and 8.21 miles on Sunday. How many miles did Samantha ride during the weekend?

21. Martina has read 89 pages of a book. She has 142 more pages to read to finish the book. How many pages are in the book?

			.		
0	0	0		0	0
1	1	1		1	1
2	2	2		2	2
3	3	3		3	3
4	4	4		4	4
5	5	5		5	5
6	6	6		6	6
7	7	7		7	7
8	8	8		8	8
9	9	9		9	9

22. The average home attendance at a team's baseball games was 17,435. In a larger city, the average number was 46,491. Round to the nearest ten thousand. About how many more people attended games in the larger city?

A About 30,000

B About 40,000

C About 50,000

D About 60,000

23. Compare the expressions. Use $<$, $>$, or $=$.

$12.63 - 5.94 \bigcirc 3.8 + 2.88$

24. For a food drive, Toby collected 38 cans and Quinn collected 44. How many cans did Toby and Quinn collect in all?

			.		
0	0	0		0	0
1	1	1		1	1
2	2	2		2	2
3	3	3		3	3
4	4	4		4	4
5	5	5		5	5
6	6	6		6	6
7	7	7		7	7
8	8	8		8	8
9	9	9		9	9

Number Sense: Multiplying by 1-Digit Numbers

Essential Questions:
How can some products be found mentally?
How can products be estimated?

Penguins use their wings for swimming...

and their legs for walking!

Some penguins walk as far as 50 miles. Here's a project on observing, analyzing, and multiplication.

Math and Science Project: Analyzing the Animal Kingdom

Do Research All birds have two legs. Use the Internet or other sources to research five animals that have more than two legs.

Journal: Write a Report Include what you found. Also in your report:

- Make a chart that includes the type, number of legs, and one interesting fact for each animal.
- Order the animals from least to greatest number of legs.
- For each type of animal, determine the number of legs in a group of 10 and in a group of 100.

Name ______________________________

Review What You Know

Vocabulary

Choose the best term from the box. Write it on the blank.

- repeated addition
- product
- factors
- breaking apart

1. When you write 5×3 as $3 + 3 + 3 + 3 + 3$, you represent multiplication as ______________.

2. When you multiply numbers, you find the ______________.

3. In the number sentence $9 \times 2 = 18$, the numbers 9 and 2 are called ______________.

Multiplication Facts

Find each product.

4. 3×4
5. 7×3
6. 6×5
7. 2×8
8. 4×6
9. 9×5
10. 7×7
11. 8×9

Rounding

Round each number to the nearest ten.

12. 16
13. 82
14. 35
15. 53
16. 24
17. 49
18. 78
19. 97

Round each number to the nearest hundred.

20. 868
21. 499
22. 625
23. 167
24. 341
25. 772
26. 919
27. 552

Subtraction

28. **Check for Reasonableness** Explain the error Tyler made in the problem below. Then show the correct solution.

$$\begin{array}{r} \overset{10}{4,\not{0}58} \\ -\ \ \ 324 \\ \hline 4,734 \end{array}$$

My Word Cards

Use the examples for each word on the front of the card to help complete the definitions on the back.

A-Z

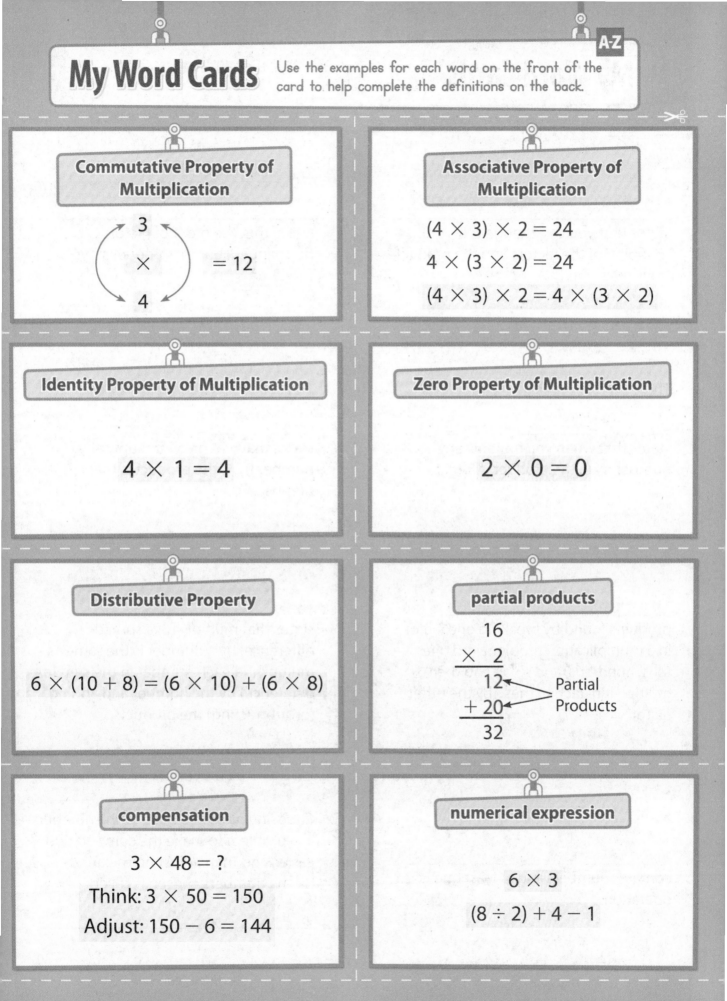

Commutative Property of Multiplication

$3 \times 4 = 12$

Associative Property of Multiplication

$(4 \times 3) \times 2 = 24$

$4 \times (3 \times 2) = 24$

$(4 \times 3) \times 2 = 4 \times (3 \times 2)$

Identity Property of Multiplication

$4 \times 1 = 4$

Zero Property of Multiplication

$2 \times 0 = 0$

Distributive Property

$6 \times (10 + 8) = (6 \times 10) + (6 \times 8)$

partial products

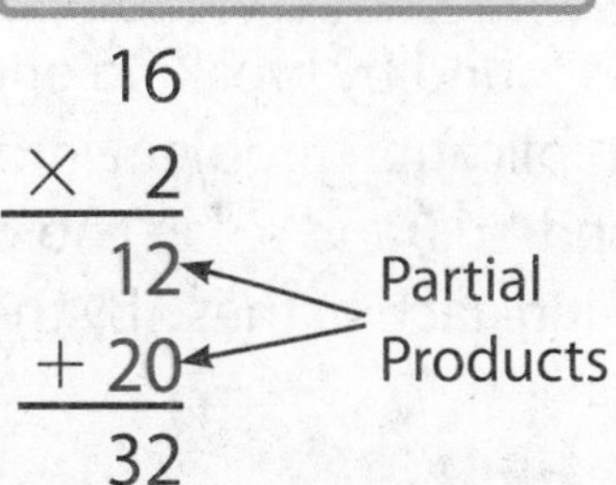

compensation

$3 \times 48 = ?$

Think: $3 \times 50 = 150$

Adjust: $150 - 6 = 144$

numerical expression

6×3

$(8 \div 2) + 4 - 1$

My Word Cards

Complete each definition. Extend learning by writing your own definitions.

The ______________________________

____
states that you can change the grouping of the factors and the product stays the same.

The ______________________________

____
states that the order of factors can be changed, but the product stays the same.

The ______________________________

____
states that when you multiply any number by 0, the product is 0.

The ______________________________

____
states that when you multiply any number by 1, the product is that number.

______________________________ are products found by breaking one factor in a multiplication problem into ones, tens, hundreds, and so on and then multiplying each of these by the other factor.

The ______________________________
states that multiplying a sum (or difference) by a number is the same as multiplying each number in the sum (or difference) by the number and adding (or subtracting) the products.

A ______________________________

____
contains numbers and at least one operation.

Choosing numbers close to the numbers in a problem to make the computation easier, and then adjusting the answer for the numbers chosen is called

______________________________.

Name ____

Guided Practice*

In **1** through **5**, write the multiplication property used in each equation.

1. $100 \times 1 = 100$
2. $45 \times 6 = 6 \times 45$
3. $33 \times 0 = 0$
4. $10 \times 9 = 9 \times 10$
5. $(6 \times 20) \times 5 = 6 \times (20 \times 5)$

6. Using equations, give examples for two properties of multiplication.

7. In the following equations, what number is missing? Which property of multiplication is used?

   a. $40 \times 8 = \_\_\_\_ \times 40$

   b. $1{,}037 \times \_\_\_\_ = 1{,}037$

Independent Practice

In **8** through **13**, write the multiplication property used in each equation.

8. $537 \times 1 = 537$
9. $100 \times 32 = 32 \times 100$
10. $400 \times 0 = 0$
11. $73 \times 14 = 14 \times 73$
12. $5 \times (40 \times 9) = (5 \times 40) \times 9$
13. $1 \times 111 = 111$

In **14** through **19**, determine the number that is missing.

14. $1{,}037 \times \_\_\_\_ = 1{,}037$
15. $5 \times (20 \times 9) = (5 \times 20) \times \_\_\_\_$
16. $(635 \times 47) \times \_\_\_\_ = 0$
17. $8 \times (\_\_\_\_ \times 4) = (8 \times 5) \times 4$
18. $75 \times \_\_\_\_ = 42 \times 75$
19. $(9 \times 6) \times 4 = 9 \times (\_\_\_\_ \times 4)$

*For another example, see Set A on page 213.

Problem Solving

20. Communicate Haley says that she will always know her 0 and 1 multiplication facts. Explain why Haley would say this.

21. Explain How can multiplication properties help you multiply $8 \times 3 \times 1$?

22. Which multiplication property tells you that the following is true?

$7 \times (2 \times 10) = (7 \times 2) \times 10$

A Zero Property
B Identity Property
C Associative Property
D Commutative Property

23. Which multiplication property can you use to multiply $8 \times 7 \times 0$?

24. Represent Naomi orders 2 bottles of water and 1 sandwich. Which expression would you use to find how much Naomi will pay?

A $(2 \times \$1) \times \$3$
B $2 \times (1 \times \$3)$
C $(2 - \$1) + \$2$
D $(2 \times \$1) + (1 \times \$3)$

$1.00
WATE
$3.00

25. Compare. Write >, <, or = for each ◯.

a. 34,304 ◯ 43,403

b. 5.70 ◯ 5.7

c. 21,978 ◯ 21,789

26. Three hundred fifty 10-year-olds registered for a city-wide bowling tournament. If 205 participants are boys, how many are girls?

27. Extend Your Thinking 4 adults and 6 children purchase movie tickets. Does the total cost of their adult tickets equal the total cost of their children tickets? Explain. What multiplication properties did you use?

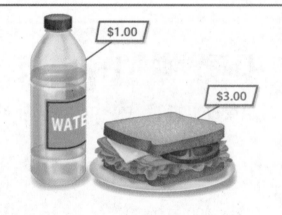

Name ______________________

Homework 3-1
Multiplication Properties

Another Look!

You can use multiplication properties to help you multiply more easily.

Associative Property of Multiplication

You can change the grouping of the factors. The product stays the same.

$(5 \times 2) \times 4 = 10 \times 4 = 40$ $\quad$ $5 \times (2 \times 4) = 5 \times 8 = 40$

Commutative Property of Multiplication

You can change the order of the factors. The product stays the same.

$7 \times 4 = 28$ $\quad$ $4 \times 7 = 28$

Zero Property of Multiplication

When one of the factors is 0, the product is always 0.

$8 \times 0 = 0$ $\quad$ $0 \times 4 = 0$

Identity Property of Multiplication

When one of the factors is 1, the product is always the other factor.

$6 \times 1 = 6$ $\quad$ $1 \times 9 = 9$

In **1** through **4**, identify the multiplication property used in each equation.

1. $18 \times 0 = 0$

2. $6 \times (4 \times 3) = (6 \times 4) \times 3$

3. $9 \times 25 = 25 \times 9$

4. $370 \times 1 = 370$

In **5** through **10**, use the multiplication properties to determine what number is missing.

5. ____ $\times 1 = 37$

6. $9 \times$ ____ $= 7 \times 9$

7. $(100 \times 4) \times$ ____ $= 0$

8. $5 \times (3 \times$ ____$) = (5 \times 3) \times 12$

9. $(23 \times 16) = ($____ $\times 23)$

10. $(57 \times 6) \times 1 = ($____ $\times 57)$

11. The table shows the 2010 population of various states. Which state has the least population? Write the number in expanded form.

DATA

State	2010 Population
Arkansas	2,915,918
Colorado	5,029,196
Louisiana	4,533,372
New Mexico	2,059,179
Oklahoma	3,751,351

12. Explain Darren multiplied $0 \times 1 \times 1 = 1$. Is his answer correct? Explain.

13. If $5 \times 3 \times 8 = 3 \times 8 \times p$, what is the value of p?

A 4
B 5
C 6
D 12

14. Formulate a Plan How can knowing the multiplication properties help you multiply $5 \times (2 \times 6)$?

15. Reason If you multiply any number by 1, can the product ever be greater than that number? Explain.

Use a property in your explanation.

16. Extend Your Thinking Write a definition of the Associative Property of Multiplication in your own words. Explain how you could use this property to compute $2 \times 8 \times 2$ mentally.

Name ______________________________

Lesson 3-2
Multiplying by 10 and 100

Solve & Share

One section in a tennis stadium contains 100 seats. There are 6 sections like this in the stadium. How many seats are there in all? Make a model to explain your answer. ***Solve this problem any way you choose.***

TEKS 4.4B Determine products of a number and 10 or 100 using properties of operations and place value understandings. **Mathematical Process Standards** 4.1B, 4.1C, 4.1D, 4.1E, 4.1G

Digital Resources at SavvasTexas.com

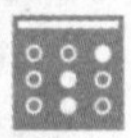

Solve Learn Glossary Check Tools Games

You can **create and use representations.** How can you represent these groups visually? ***Show your work in the space below!***

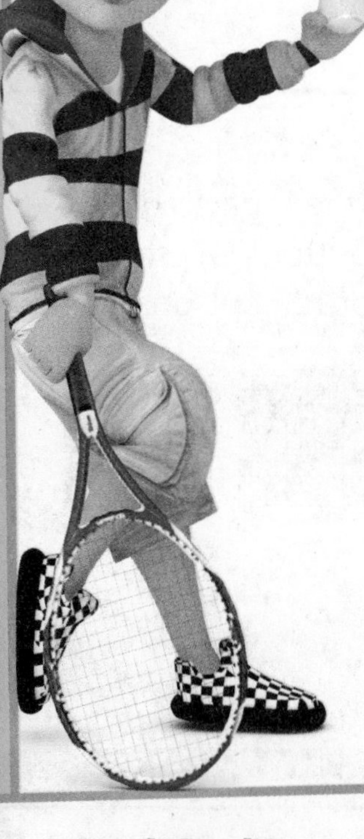

Look Back!

Number Sense How are multiplication and addition related?

How Can You Multiply by 10 and 100?

A

A-Z

Addition and multiplication are related. 4×5 can be written as $5 + 5 + 5 + 5$. Use this idea to multiply by 10 and 100.

How many photo buttons can Dara make if she buys 4 packs of 10 buttons?

Making arrays with place-value blocks helps you visualize the products.

Use place-value understandings.

B Find 4×10.

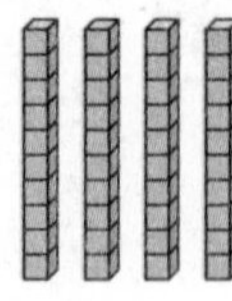

$4 \times 10 = 10 + 10 + 10 + 10$

$= 40$

$4 \times 10 = 40$

Dara can make 40 photo buttons.

C Dara found a website that sells packs of 100 buttons. How many buttons will she have if she buys 2 packs of 100 buttons?

Find 2×100.

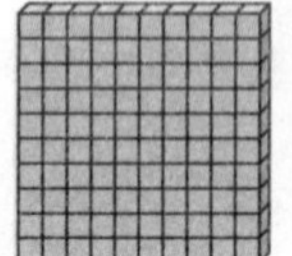
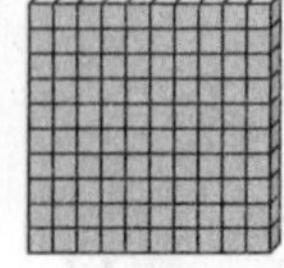

$2 \times 100 = 100 + 100$

$= 200$

$2 \times 100 = 200$

Dara will have 200 buttons.

Do You Understand?

Convince Me! Look for patterns in the multiplication sentences below.

$5 \times 10 = 50$ $5 \times 100 = 500$

$6 \times 10 = 60$ $6 \times 100 = 600$

$7 \times 10 = 70$ $7 \times 100 = 700$

Write a number in each of the blanks below.

The product for 8×10 is an 8 with _____ zero(s) behind it.

The product for 8×100 is an 8 with _____ zero(s) behind it.

Name

Guided Practice*

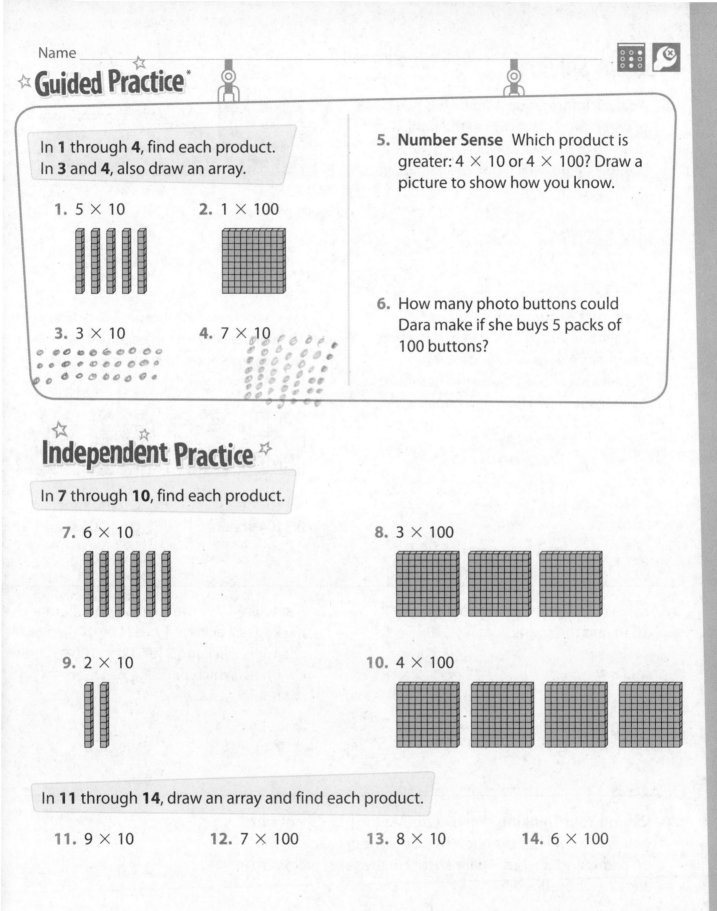

In **1** through **4**, find each product. In **3** and **4**, also draw an array.

1. 5 × 10

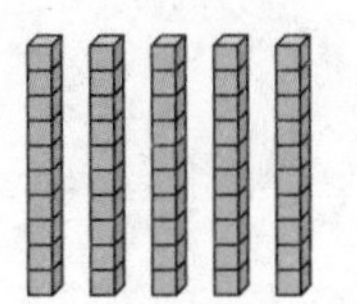

2. 1 × 100

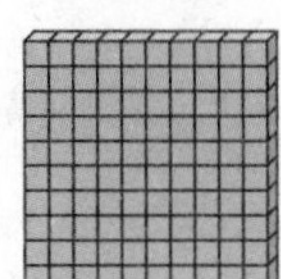

3. 3 × 10

4. 7 × 10

5. **Number Sense** Which product is greater: 4 × 10 or 4 × 100? Draw a picture to show how you know.

6. How many photo buttons could Dara make if she buys 5 packs of 100 buttons?

Independent Practice

In **7** through **10**, find each product.

7. 6 × 10

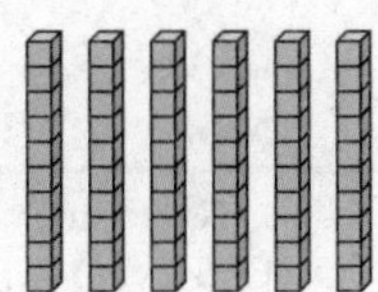

8. 3 × 100

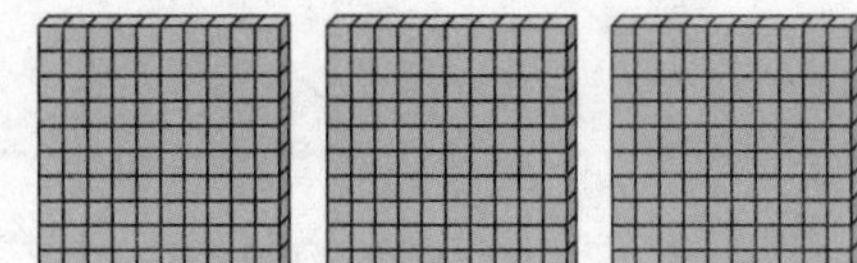

9. 2 × 10

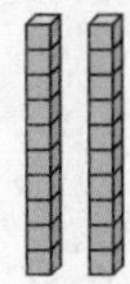

10. 4 × 100

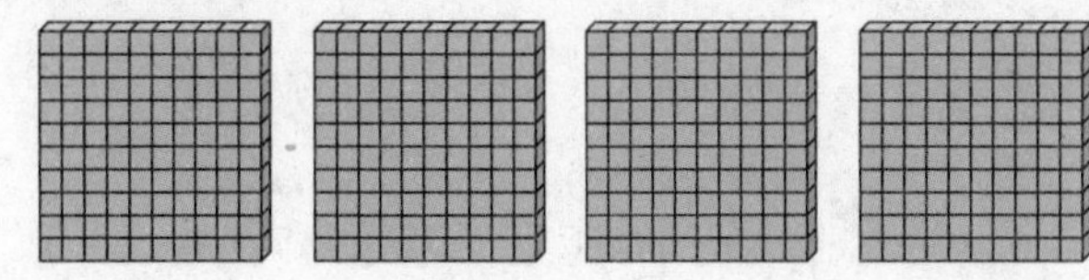

In **11** through **14**, draw an array and find each product.

11. 9 × 10

12. 7 × 100

13. 8 × 10

14. 6 × 100

*For another example, see Set B on page 213.

Problem Solving

15. Analyze Information Wendy has two boxes of party favors, as shown at the right. If she gives 18 of the party favors from the red box to a friend, which box will contain more party favors?

16. Construct Arguments Miki has 6 bags of balloons with 8 balloons in each bag. Karen has 4 bags of balloons with 10 balloons in each bag. Who has more balloons? Explain how you know.

17. Luis has 4 new notebooks. There are 100 sheets of paper in each notebook. How many sheets of paper does Luis have?

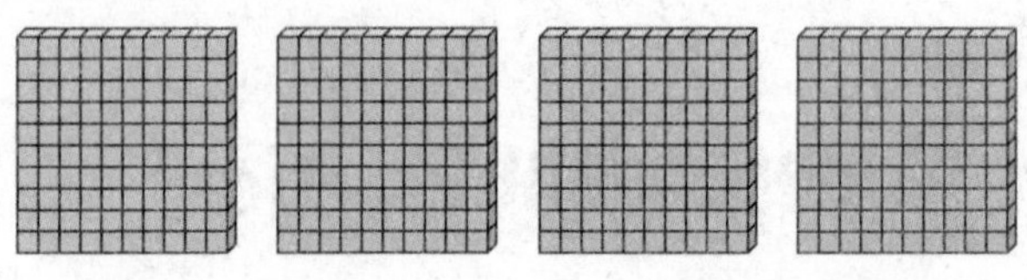

A 40 sheets
B 104 sheets
C 400 sheets
D 4,000 sheets

18. Explain how you can use counting by 10 to find the solution of 7×10.

19. A satellite TV carrier offers two different packages. Package 1 has $(4 \times 100) + 65$ channels. Package 2 has $(2 \times 100) + 198$ channels. Which package has more channels?

20. Extend Your Thinking Jim is counting the number of sabal palms in his neighborhood. His six neighbors each have 10 palms and Jim has 7 palms. How many sabal palms are in Jim's neighborhood?

Name ______________________

Homework 3-2
Multiplying by 10 and 100

Another Look!

You can use addition to help you multiply.

Find 4 × 10.

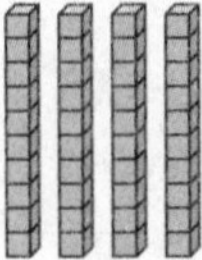

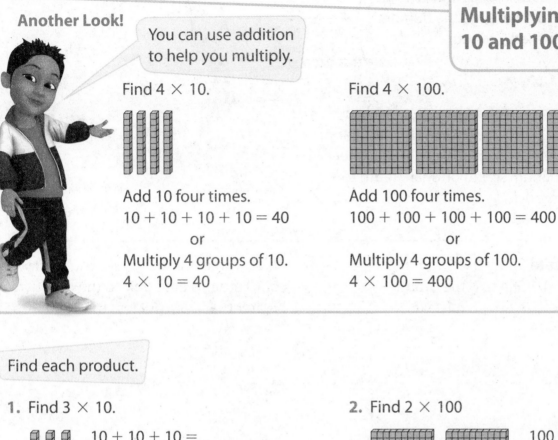

Add 10 four times.
10 + 10 + 10 + 10 = 40
or
Multiply 4 groups of 10.
4 × 10 = 40

Find 4 × 100.

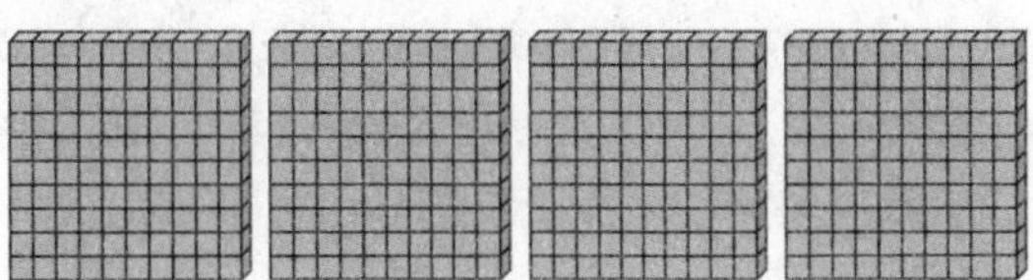

Add 100 four times.
100 + 100 + 100 + 100 = 400
or
Multiply 4 groups of 100.
4 × 100 = 400

Find each product.

1. Find 3 × 10.

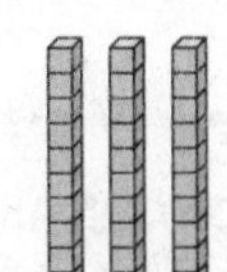

10 + 10 + 10 = ____

3 × 10 = ____

2. Find 2 × 100

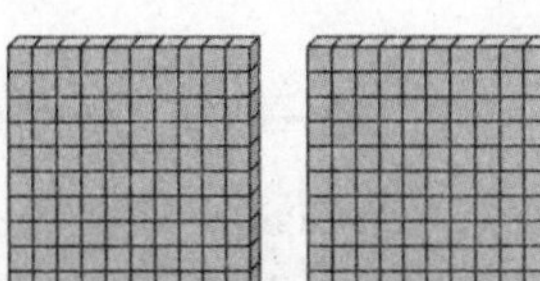

100 + 100 = ____

2 × 100 = ____

3. 5 × 10 = ____

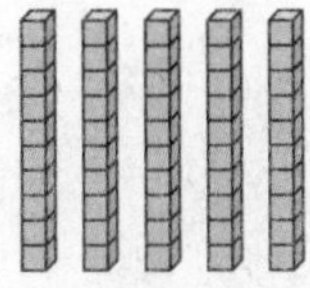

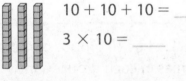

4. 3 × 100 = ____

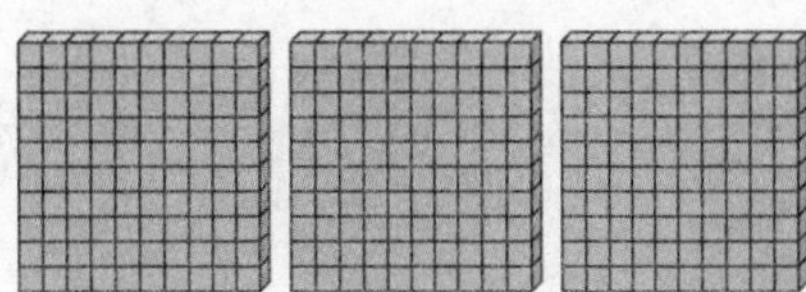

5. 7 × 10 = ____

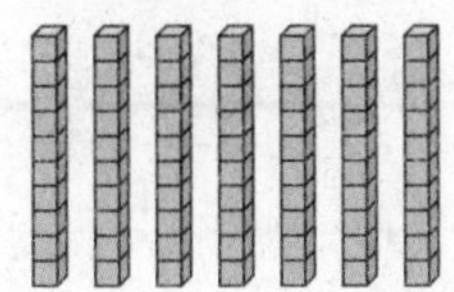

6. 6 × 10 = ____

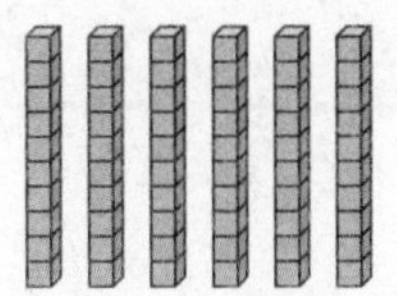

7. 2 × 10 = ____

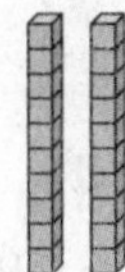

In **8** through **10**, find each product. You may draw an array to help.

8. 9 × 10

9. 6 × 100

10. 5 × 100

11. Represent Use the variable *t* for the number of teeth in one row. Write an expression to determine the number of teeth in a shark's mouth.

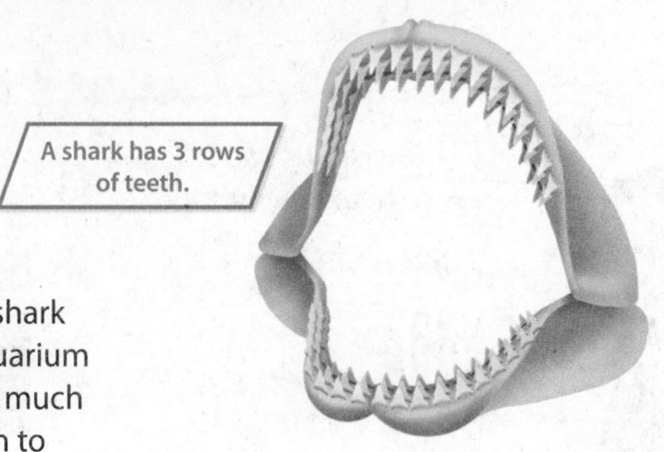
A shark has 3 rows of teeth.

12. An aquarium is creating a display of a shark that has 100 teeth in each row. The aquarium can buy shark teeth for $10 each. How much will the aquarium spend on shark teeth to create the model?

13. Communicate Abby used addition to find 6×10. She said the product was 600. Explain Abby's mistake.

14. What whole number could you use to complete this equation so the product is greater than 700, but less than 900?

$\square \times 100 = \square 00$

15. The distance from Mr. Cavel's home to his work is 5 miles. If he only drives to work and back home each day, how many miles does he drive in 4 days?

A 20 miles
B 30 miles
C 40 miles
D 400 miles

16. Explain Jackie has 10 groups of pennies with 5 pennies in each group. Carlos has 3 groups of pennies with 100 pennies in each group. Who has more pennies? Explain how you know.

17. Extend Your Thinking Look at the products at the right. What patterns do you see?

$1 \times 10 = 10$	$1 \times 100 = 100$
$2 \times 10 = 20$	$2 \times 100 = 200$
$3 \times 10 = 30$	$3 \times 100 = 300$
$4 \times 10 = 40$	$4 \times 100 = 400$

Name ______________________________

Lesson 3-3
Multiplying by Multiples of 10 and 100

TEKS 4.4D Use strategies and algorithms, including the standard algorithm, to multiply up to a four-digit number by a one-digit number.... Also 4.4B. **Mathematical Process Standards** 4.1A, 4.1B, 4.1C, 4.1D, 4.1E, 4.1F, 4.1G

Digital Resources at SavvasTexas.com

Solve

Learn

Glossary

Check

Tools

Games

Find these products.

$3 \times 4 =$ ______

$3 \times 40 =$ ______

$3 \times 400 =$ ______

Solve this problem any way you choose.

You can **analyze relationships.** How can solving the first problem help you to solve the following two problems? ***Show your work in the space below!***

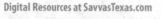

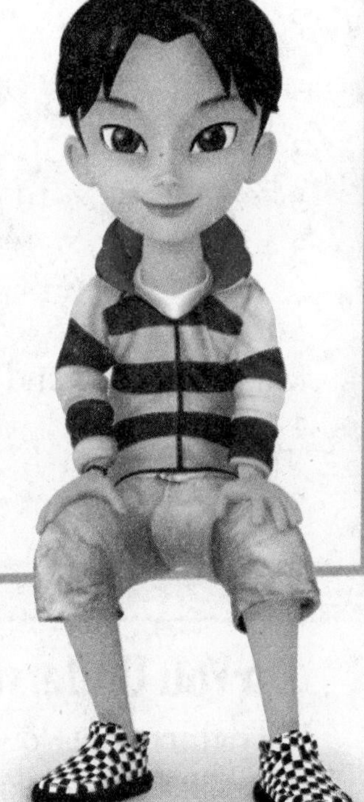

Look Back!

Connect Ideas What pattern do you notice in the three answers?

How Can You Multiply by Multiples of 10 and 100?

A

Find 3 × 50 and 3 × 500 using basic multiplication facts, multiplication properties, and place-value patterns.

Then apply the place-value pattern to find 6 × 50 and 6 × 500.

Understanding why rules work helps you make sense of mathematics.

?

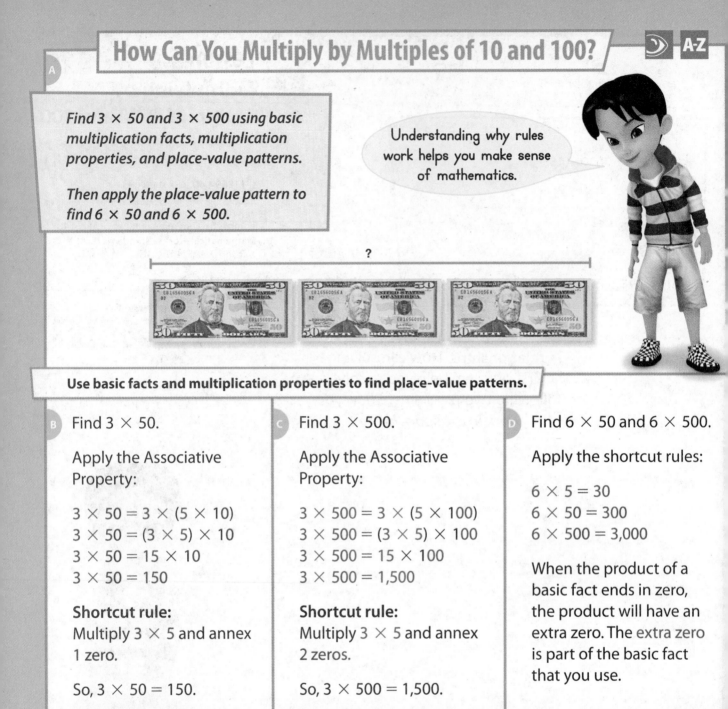

Use basic facts and multiplication properties to find place-value patterns.

B Find 3 × 50.

Apply the Associative Property:

$3 \times 50 = 3 \times (5 \times 10)$
$3 \times 50 = (3 \times 5) \times 10$
$3 \times 50 = 15 \times 10$
$3 \times 50 = 150$

Shortcut rule:
Multiply 3 × 5 and annex 1 zero.

So, 3 × 50 = 150.

C Find 3 × 500.

Apply the Associative Property:

$3 \times 500 = 3 \times (5 \times 100)$
$3 \times 500 = (3 \times 5) \times 100$
$3 \times 500 = 15 \times 100$
$3 \times 500 = 1{,}500$

Shortcut rule:
Multiply 3 × 5 and annex 2 zeros.

So, 3 × 500 = 1,500.

D Find 6 × 50 and 6 × 500.

Apply the shortcut rules:

$6 \times 5 = 30$
$6 \times 50 = 300$
$6 \times 500 = 3{,}000$

When the product of a basic fact ends in zero, the product will have an extra zero. The extra zero is part of the basic fact that you use.

Do You Understand?

Convince Me! How many zeros will be in the product of 5 × 200? Explain how you know.

Name ____________________

Guided Practice*

In **1** through **8**, use basic facts to help you multiply.

1. 8 × 5 = ____
8 × 50 = ____
8 × 500 = ____

2. 4 × 3 = ____
4 × 30 = ____
4 × 300 = ____

3. 7 × 70

4. 2 × 700

5. 3 × 20

6. 9 × 800

7. 7 × 50

8. 8 × 500

9. Explain Show how you can use the basic multiplication fact 5 × 8 = 40 to find the product of 5 × 800.

10. Peter said 4 × 500 = 2,000. Bob said 4 × 500 = 200. Explain who is correct.

11. Use a basic multiplication fact to write a multiplication problem with a product of 7,200.

Independent Practice

Look for patterns.

Leveled Practice In **12** through **27**, find each product.

12. 3 × 7 = ____
3 × 70 = ____
3 × 700 = ____

13. 6 × 4 = ____
6 × 40 = ____
6 × 400 = ____

14. 8 × 5 = ____
8 × 50 = ____
8 × 500 = ____

15. 2 × 8 = ____
2 × 80 = ____
2 × 800 = ____

16. 4 × 20

17. 7 × 40

18. 70 × 2

19. 8 × 60

20. 5 × 500

21. 3 × 600

22. 9 × 700

23. 600 × 6

24. 5 × 40

25. 200 × 6

26. 9 × 50

27. 900 × 4

*For another example, see Set C on page 214.

Problem Solving

In **28** and **29**, use the table to the right.

28. Tina visited Funland with her mom and a friend. They chose Plan C. How much did they save on the two children's tickets by buying combined tickets instead of buying separate tickets?

Funland Ticket Prices

Plans	Adult	Child
Plan A Waterpark	$30	$20
Plan B Amusement Park	$40	$30
Plan C Combined A + B	$60	$40

29. Aimee's scout troop has 8 girls and 4 adults. How much did the troop pay for tickets to the amusement park?

30. **Math and Science** Although "centi" means 100, a centipede does not have 100 legs. In fact, a centipede usually has an odd number of pairs of legs. If a centipede has 17 pairs of legs, how many legs does it have?

31. **Extend Your Thinking** Without calculating the answer, tell which has the greater product, 4×80 or 8×400. Explain how you know.

32. Last year, the fourth graders at Summit School collected 500 cans of food for the food drive. This year's fourth graders want to collect two times as many cans. How many cans do this year's fourth graders hope to collect?

A 250 cans
B 500 cans
C 1,000 cans
D 10,000 cans

33. **Use a Strip Diagram** Ted, Jason, and Angelina are trying to raise $200 for a local shelter. Ted raised $30. Jason raised $90. How much money does Angelina need to raise in order to reach their goal?

$200

$30	$90	?

Name ______________________

Homework 3-3
Multiplying by Multiples of 10 and 100

Another Look!

Patterns can help you multiply by numbers that are multiples of 10 or 100.

$3 \times 7 = 21$	$8 \times 3 = 24$	$9 \times 5 = 45$
$3 \times 70 = 210$	$8 \times 30 = 240$	$9 \times 50 = 450$
$3 \times 700 = 2{,}100$	$8 \times 300 = 2{,}400$	$9 \times 500 = 4{,}500$

When one factor of a multiplication problem is a multiple of 10, first complete the basic multiplication fact. Then write the same number of zeros in the factor that is a multiple of 10. For example:

$4 \times 5 = 20$ $\quad$ $4 \times 50 = 200$ $\quad$ $4 \times 500 = 2{,}000$

Find each product.

Remember, if the product of the basic fact ends in a zero, the answer will have an extra zero.

1. $8 \times 2 =$ ______
   $8 \times 20 =$ ______
   $8 \times 200 =$ ______
2. $9 \times 4 =$ ______
   $9 \times 40 =$ ______
   $9 \times 400 =$ ______
3. $3 \times 9 =$ ______
   $3 \times 90 =$ ______
   $3 \times 900 =$ ______
4. $7 \times 6 =$ ______
   $7 \times 60 =$ ______
   $7 \times 600 =$ ______
5. $5 \times 7 =$ ______
   $5 \times 70 =$ ______
   $5 \times 700 =$ ______
6. $6 \times 5 =$ ______
   $6 \times 50 =$ ______
   $6 \times 500 =$ ______
7. 3×40
8. 300×9
9. 80×3
10. 800×5
11. 8×70
12. 2×90
13. 300×4
14. 7×600
15. 7×800

Complete the sentence.

16. To find 6×800, multiply 6×8, then write ______ zero(s) to form the product ______.

17. Connect Adele has 6 sheets of stickers. Bea has 9 sheets of stickers. How many stickers does Adele have? How many does Bea have?

18. The number of students who attended the basketball game is 4 times the number of students in fourth grade. How many students attended the basketball game?

DATA

School Population	
Grade	**Number of Students**
Fourth Grade	50
Fifth Grade	54
Sixth Grade	60

A 20 students
B 200 students
C 216 students
D 240 students

19. Mr. Young has 30 times as many pencils as Jack. The whole school has 200 times as many pencils as Jack. If Jack has 2 pencils, how many pencils does Mr. Young have? How many pencils does the whole school have?

Mr. Young has ________ pencils.

The whole school has ________ pencils.

20. Number Sense How many zeros will the product of 7 × 50 have? Explain how you know.

21. Analyze Information Jenna has saved $100. She wants to buy 6 games that each cost $20. Does she have enough money? Explain.

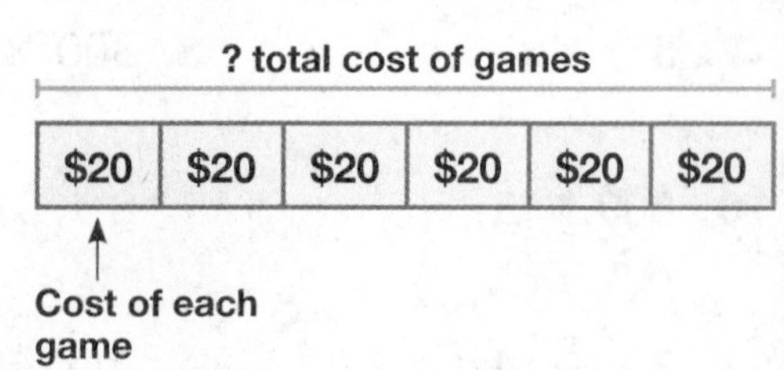

22. Extend Your Thinking Laura says the product of 8 × 50 has one zero. Is she correct? Explain.

Name ______________________________

Lesson 3-4
Distributive Property

Solve & Share Use only the numbers shown on the rectangle and operations symbols (+, −, ×, ÷) to find the area of the unshaded rectangle below. ***Solve this problem any way you choose.***

TEKS 4.4D Use strategies and algorithms, including the standard algorithm, to multiply up to a four-digit number by a one-digit number.... Also, 4.4. **Mathematical Process Standards** 4.1A, 4.1B, 4.1D, 4.1E, 4.1F, 4.1G

Digital Resources at SavvasTexas.com

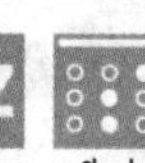

Solve Learn Glossary Check Tools Games

You can **connect ideas.** Remember what you know about finding area to solve this problem. ***Show your work in the space below!***

10

8

4

Look Back!

Justify Are these two problems equal? Explain.

12 × (4 + 2)

(12 × 4) + (12 × 2)

How Can You Use the Distributive Property?

A

A numerical expression contains numbers and at least one operation. What numerical expressions can you write to represent the number of square units inside the rectangle?

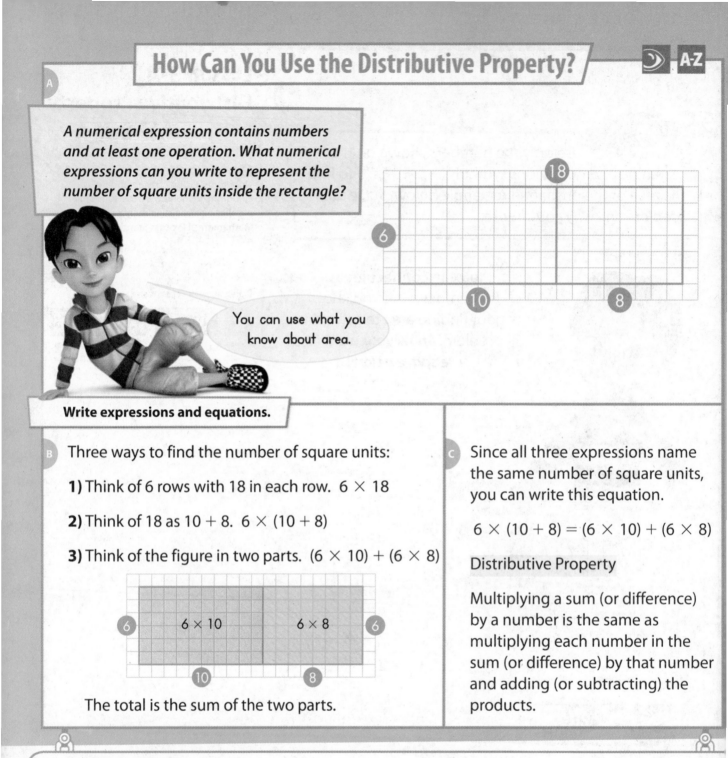

You can use what you know about area.

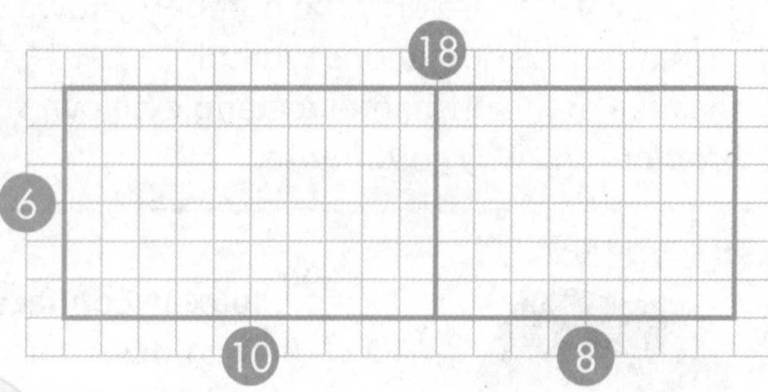

Write expressions and equations.

B

Three ways to find the number of square units:

1) Think of 6 rows with 18 in each row. 6×18

2) Think of 18 as 10 + 8. $6 \times (10 + 8)$

3) Think of the figure in two parts. $(6 \times 10) + (6 \times 8)$

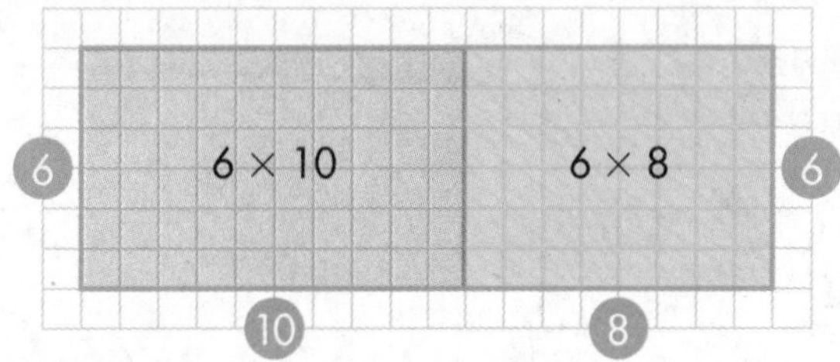

The total is the sum of the two parts.

C

Since all three expressions name the same number of square units, you can write this equation.

$6 \times (10 + 8) = (6 \times 10) + (6 \times 8)$

Distributive Property

Multiplying a sum (or difference) by a number is the same as multiplying each number in the sum (or difference) by that number and adding (or subtracting) the products.

Do You Understand?

Convince Me! Is $12 - (4 \times 2) = (12 - 4) \times (12 - 2)$? Explain your answer.

Name ____________________

Guided Practice*

1. Use the Distributive Property to complete the equation.

   $2 \times 308 = 2 \times (\_\_\_\_ + 8)$

   $= (2 \times \_\_\_\_) + (\_\_\_\_ \times 8)$

   $= \_\_\_\_ + \_\_\_\_$

   $= \_\_\_\_$

2. Show how you can use the Distributive Property to find the product of 4×15.

3. Do these expressions name the same number of square units in the shaded area?

   $4 \times (13 - 5)$ and $(4 \times 13) - (4 \times 5)$

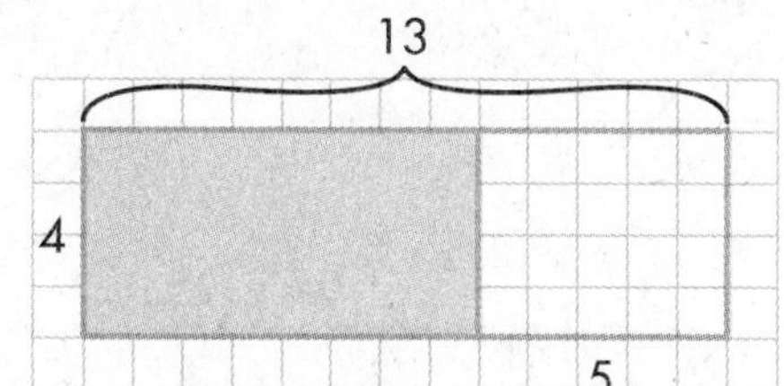

4. **Formulate a Plan** Write another expression for 3×298 to show how multiplication distributes over subtraction. Use $298 = 300 - 2$ and the Distributive Property.

Independent Practice

Leveled Practice Use the Distributive Property to find each product.

5. $509 \times 7 = (500 + 9) \times 7$

   $= (500 \times \_\_\_\_) + (9 \times \_\_\_\_)$

   $= \_\_\_\_ + 63$

   $= \_\_\_\_$

6. $2 \times 47 = 2 \times (50 - \_\_\_\_)$

   $= (2 \times \_\_\_\_) - (2 \times 3)$

   $= 100 - \_\_\_\_$

   $= \_\_\_\_$

7. 7×86

8. 5×420

9. 220×8

10. 4×52

*For another example, see Set D on page 214.

Problem Solving

11. **Represent** Write an expression using the Distributive Property to show how to find the product of 7×382.

12. **Reason** Wyatt said that he used the Distributive Property to write $4 + (8 + 3) = (4 + 8) + (4 + 3)$. Explain Wyatt's error and use math to justify your explanation.

13. **Construct Arguments** Jane and Bob used the Distributive Property to write 8×490 in two different ways. Who is correct? Explain.

Bob's Work

$$8 \times 490 = 8 \times (400 + 90) = (8 \times 400) + (8 \times 90)$$

Jane's Work

$$8 \times 490 = 8 \times (500 - 10) = (8 \times 500) - (8 \times 10)$$

14. **Connect** The total length of a football field, from end post to end post, is 120 yards. What is the total length of a football field in feet?

Remember that there are 3 feet in 1 yard.

15. Todd Mountain is a mountain peak near Tyler, Texas. A ranger hiked 607 ft to and from the peak, each way. The ranger hiked 3 times in the past four weeks. How far did the ranger hike on Todd Mountain the past four weeks?

A 613 ft
B 1,242 ft
C 3,558 ft
D 3,642 ft

16. **Extend Your Thinking** Wendy plans to bring lemonade and iced tea for a school picnic. She will bring 5 gallons of iced tea. Also, for every 10 people, she will bring 2 gallons of lemonade. How many total gallons of lemonade and iced tea does Wendy need for 10 people? Complete the table to find how much she would need for 40 people.

Number of People	Gallons of Lemonade	Total Gallons
10	2	
20		
30		
40		

Name ______________________

Homework 3-4
Distributive Property

Another Look!

Hector's rock collection is in 7 cases. Each case holds 28 rocks. How many rocks are in Hector's collection?

You can use the Distributive Property to find the product of 7×28.

Split 28 into $20 + 8$.
$7 \times 28 = 7 \times (20 + 8)$

OR Split 28 into $30 - 2$.
$7 \times 28 = 7 \times (30 - 2)$

Multiply 7 times each part of the sum.
$(7 \times 20) + (7 \times 8)$
$140 + 56$

OR Multiply 7 times each part of the difference.
$(7 \times 30) - (7 \times 2)$
$210 - 14$

Step 3

Use addition to find the sum.
$140 + 56 = 196$

OR Use subtraction to find the difference.
$210 - 14 = 196$

So, $7 \times 28 = 196$. Hector has 196 rocks in his collection.

Rewrite using the Distributive Property. Then find the product.

1. 8×46
$= 8 \times (40 +$ ______ $)$
$= (8 \times 40) + ($ ______ $\times$ ______ $)$
$=$ ______ $+$ ______ $=$ ______

2. 39×5
$= 5 \times ($ ______ $- 1)$
$= (5 \times$ ______ $) - (5 \times$ ______ $)$
$=$ ______ $-$ ______ $=$ ______

3. 6×310
$= 6 \times (300 +$ ______ $)$
$= (6 \times$ ______ $) + ($ ______ $\times 10)$
$=$ ______ $+$ ______ $=$ ______

4. 9×803
$= 9 \times ($ ______ $+$ ______ $)$
$= (9 \times$ ______ $) + ($ ______ $\times$ ______ $)$
$=$ ______ $+$ ______ $=$ ______

5. 5×108

6. 2×62

7. 4×54

8. 7×508

In **9** and **10**, use the table at the right.

9. **Analyze Information** A party is planned using round dining tables. Six chairs fit around each round table. How many chairs are used for the round tables?

10. **Extend Your Thinking** Eight chairs fit around long dining tables and 4 chairs fit around square dining tables. Which of the three table types allows for the greatest number of people in the banquet room?

DATA

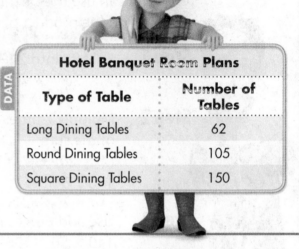

Hotel Banquet Room Plans

Type of Table	Number of Tables
Long Dining Tables	62
Round Dining Tables	105
Square Dining Tables	150

11. **Connect** Lauren read 36 books during the year. If she reads the same number of books for 6 years in a row, how many total books will she read?

12. A parking garage has 8 levels. Each level has parking space for 78 cars. How many cars can park in the garage at one time?

13. The farmer keeps his chickens in 5 coops. Each coop is home to 34 chickens. How many chickens does the farmer have in all?

    A 170 chickens
    B 130 chickens
    C 74 chickens
    D 39 chickens

14. **Connect** A lodge at a state park has 39 rooms. Up to five people may stay in each room. What is the maximum number of people who can stay at the lodge at one time?

15. Joey's class has a goal to collect 250 cans of food for the school canned food drive. There are 26 students in Joey's class. If each student brings in 9 cans of food, will the class reach the goal? Explain.

16. What is the value of the digit 8 in the number 875,421,003?

Name ______________________________

Solve & Share

A parking lot has 4 rows with 23 spaces in each row. How many parking spaces are in the lot? Make a model to help you solve this problem.

Lesson 3-5
Breaking Apart to Multiply

TEKS 4.4D Use strategies and algorithms, including the standard algorithm, to multiply up to a four-digit number by a one-digit number.... **Mathematical Process Standards** 4.1A, 4.1B, 4.1C, 4.1D, 4.1E, 4.1F, 4.1G

Digital Resources at SavvasTexas.com

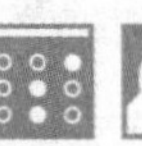

Solve Learn Glossary Check Tools Games

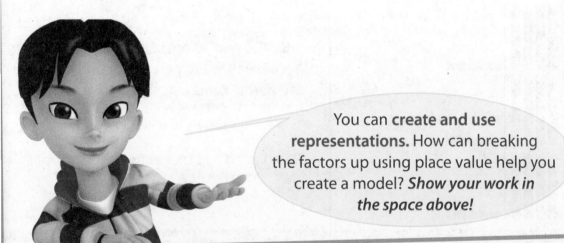

You can **create and use representations.** How can breaking the factors up using place value help you create a model? ***Show your work in the space above!***

Look Back!

Construct Arguments Why might you want to break apart a greater number before you multiply?

How Can You Use Breaking Apart to Multiply?

A

David built 3 toy robots. All of the robots are made of the same number of pieces shown at the right. How many pieces did David use to build the robots?

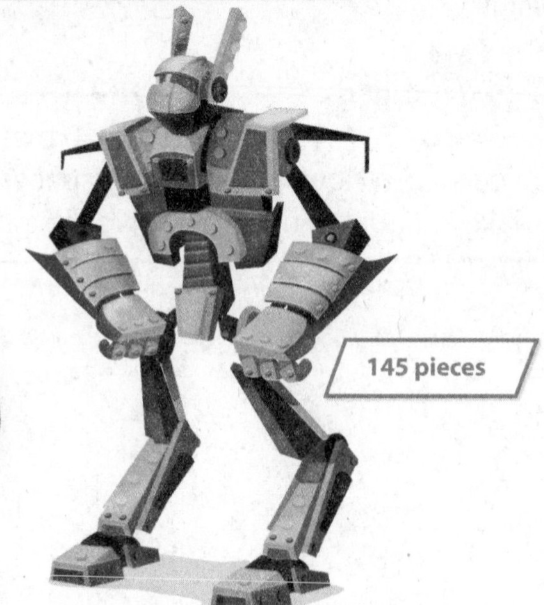

Breaking apart a number makes multiplying simpler.

Use place-value understandings.

B

Find 3 × 145. Break apart 145 into 100, 40, and 5. Then multiply each part by 3.

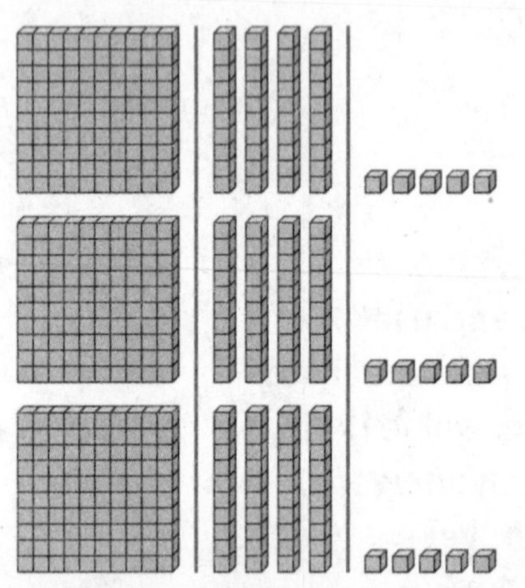

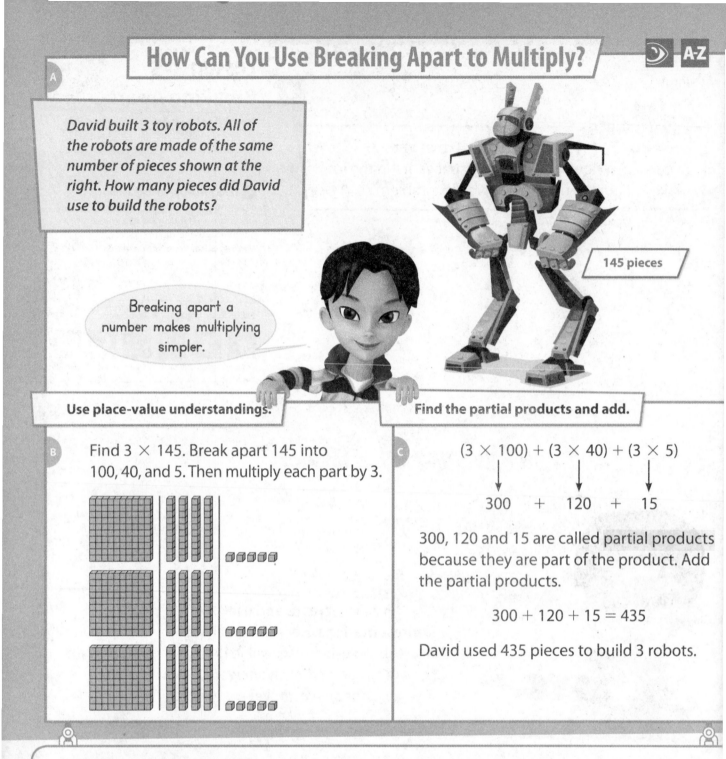

Find the partial products and add.

C

$(3 \times 100) + (3 \times 40) + (3 \times 5)$

$300 + 120 + 15$

300, 120 and 15 are called partial products because they are part of the product. Add the partial products.

$300 + 120 + 15 = 435$

David used 435 pieces to build 3 robots.

Do You Understand?

Convince Me! In the robot example above, what three parts is the array for 3 × 145 broken into? What are the simple calculations used to find the product for each part?

Name ______________________

Guided Practice*

In **1** and **2**, fill in the blanks. You may use place-value blocks or drawings to help.

1. 4 × 365

(4 × 300) = ______

(4 × 60) = ______

(4 × 5) = ______

______ + ______ + ______ = ______

2. 3 × 219

= 3 × (200 + ______ + 9)

= (3 × ______) + (3 × 10) + (3 × ______)

= 600 + ______ + 27 = ______

3. Connect Suri downloads 8 songs onto her MP3 player. Each song uses about 3,584 kilobytes of storage space. Write an expression that you could use to find 8 × 3,584.

4. Explain Why can you break apart numbers to multiply without changing the product?

Independent Practice

Leveled Practice In **5** through **10**, find each product.

5. 8 × 473

= 8 × (400 + 70 + ______)

= (8 × ______) + (______ × ______) + (______ × ______)

= ______ + ______ + ______

= ______

6. 4 × 1,417

= 4 × (______ + 400 + 10 + ______)

= (4 × ______) + (4 × ______) + (4 × 10) + (4 × ______)

= 4,000 + ______ + 40 + ______

= ______

7. 7 × 369

8. 9 × 628

9. 4 × 1,817

10. 3 × 703

*For another example, see Set E on page 215.

Problem Solving

11. **Explain** Use the model to find the product of 3 × 118. Explain how you found the product.

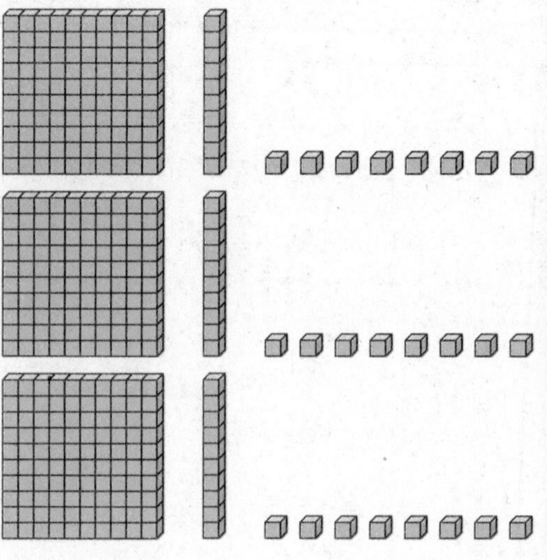

12. **Reason** Which of the following expressions is equal to 5 × 250?

    A (5 × 50) + (2 × 5)
    B 5 × 200
    C (5 × 200) + (5 × 10)
    D (5 × 200) + (5 × 50)

13. **Extend Your Thinking** Find 5 × 1,025. Then find 4 × 1,280. Then name three numbers between these two products.

14. **Check for Reasonableness** A salesman flies from Houston to Junin, Peru, three times each month. The round-trip flight is 6,330 miles. If these are his only trips, how many miles does he fly in 2 months? Use estimation to check whether your answer is reasonable.

15. **Reason** Walt wants to buy shelves that cost $168 each. If he has $500, can he buy three shelves? Explain.

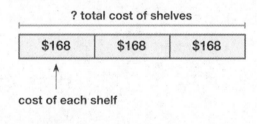

? total cost of shelves

$168	$168	$168

cost of each shelf

16. **Analyze Information** What is the weight of the white rhinoceros in pounds?

There are 2,000 pounds in 1 ton!

A white rhinoceros weighs about 2 tons.

Name ______________________________

Homework 3-5
Breaking Apart to Multiply

Another Look!

Find $2 \times 1{,}234$.

Break apart 1,234 into 1,000, 200, 30, and 4.

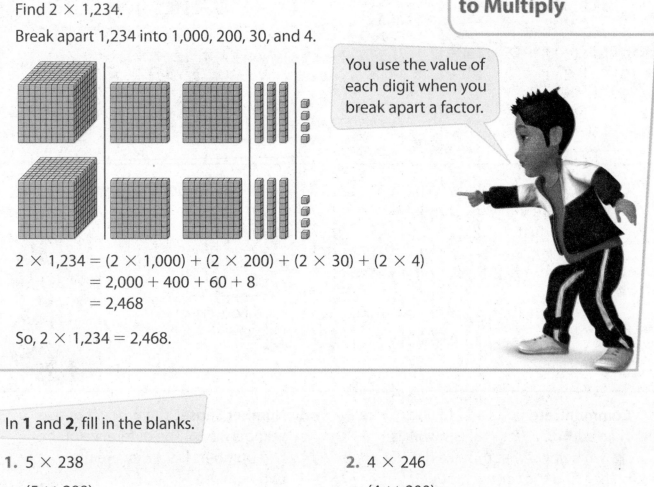

You use the value of each digit when you break apart a factor.

$$2 \times 1{,}234 = (2 \times 1{,}000) + (2 \times 200) + (2 \times 30) + (2 \times 4)$$
$$= 2{,}000 + 400 + 60 + 8$$
$$= 2{,}468$$

So, $2 \times 1{,}234 = 2{,}468$.

In **1** and **2**, fill in the blanks.

1. 5×238

$(5 \times 200) =$ _____

$(5 \times 30) =$ _____

$(5 \times 8) =$ _____

_____ + _____ + _____ = _____

2. 4×246

$(4 \times 200) =$ _____

$(4 \times 40) =$ _____

$(4 \times 6) =$ _____

_____ + _____ + _____ = _____

3. 3×116

4. $6 \times 2{,}140$

5. 3×352

6. $4 \times 1{,}420$

7. $4 \times 7{,}201$

8. 9×276

9. **Reason** The model represents the product of a multiplication problem. Which of the following expressions represents the multiplication problem?

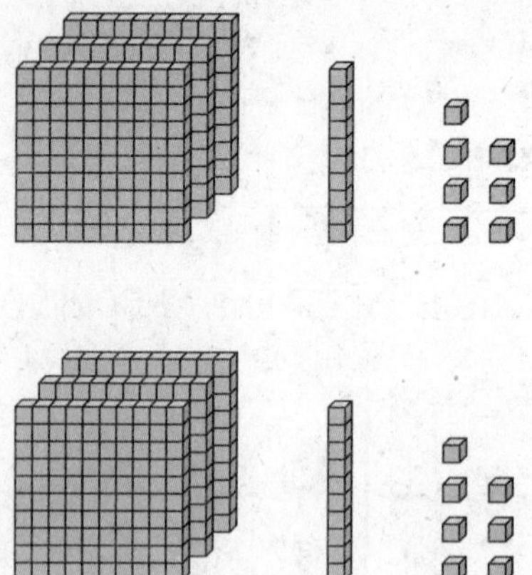

A $3 \times 2 \times 7$
B $300 \times 10 \times 14$
C $(2 \times 300) + (2 \times 10) + (2 \times 7)$
D $(3 \times 300) + (2 \times 20) + (2 \times 14)$

10. Describe how you would find partial products to multiply $6 \times 2{,}194$. Then find the product.

11. The highest point in Colorado is Mount Elbert, at about 3 miles. About how many feet is that?

A mile is equal to 5,280 feet.

12. **Communicate** Joe said, "To find 6×333, I can add $18 + 18 + 18$." His work is shown below. What mistake did Joe make? Find the correct product.

Joe's Work

$$6 \times 333 = (6 \times 3) + (6 \times 3) + (6 \times 3)$$
$$= 18 + 18 + 18$$

13. **Number Sense** The product of two numbers is 36. The difference of the two numbers is 9. What are the two numbers?

14. **Reason** You write the number 3.04. Your friend says he can write a number less than this number using the same digits. Is your friend correct?

15. **Extend Your Thinking** Without multiplying, is the product of 4×999 more than or less than 4,000? Explain how you know. Then check your answer.

Name ______________________

Solve & Share

Suppose Siera has a long commute to work and spends $97 each week on gas. What multiplication sentence can you write to represent the amount of money she spends in 4 weeks? How can you multiply mentally to find the product?

Lesson 3-6
Using Mental Math to Multiply

TEKS 4.4D Use strategies and algorithms, including the standard algorithm, to multiply up to a four-digit number by a one-digit number.... **Mathematical Process Standards** 4.1A, 4.1B, 4.1C, 4.1D, 4.1E, 4.1G

Digital Resources at SavvasTexas.com

Solve

Learn

Glossary
Check

Tools

Games

You can **use mental math.** How can you use an easier number to multiply mentally to solve this problem?

Look Back!

Connect What are some examples of when you might want to multiply mentally?

What Are Some Ways to Multiply Mentally?

A

Anna rode her bicycle 405 miles each month for 3 months. How many miles did she ride in all?

405 miles each month

B

Anna's friend Pam rode her bicycle 298 miles each month for 3 months. How many miles did she ride in all?

298 miles each month

These problems are similar but require different kinds of adjustments.

Substitute a number that is easy to multiply.

C

With compensation you choose numbers close to the numbers in the problem to make the computation easier and then adjust the answer for the numbers chosen.

D

Use compensation to find 3×405.

Substitute 400 for 405 because 400 is easy to multiply.

$3 \times 400 = 1{,}200$

Now adjust.

$400 = 405 - 5$

Add 3 groups of 5, or 15.

$1{,}200 + 15 = 1{,}215$

Anna rode her bicycle 1,215 miles in all.

E

Use compensation to find 3×298.

Substitute 300 for 298 because 300 is easy to multiply.

$3 \times 300 = 900$

Now adjust.

$300 = 298 + 2$

Subtract 3 groups of 2, or 6.

$900 - 6 = 894$

Pam rode her bicycle 894 miles in all.

Do You Understand?

Convince Me! Complete the following.

198×4 is 198 groups of 4.

I know 200 groups of 4 is 800.

198 groups of 4 is ______ less than 800.

$800 - 8 =$ ______

So, $198 \times 4 =$ ______.

Name ______________________

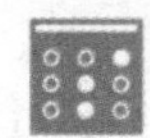

Guided Practice*

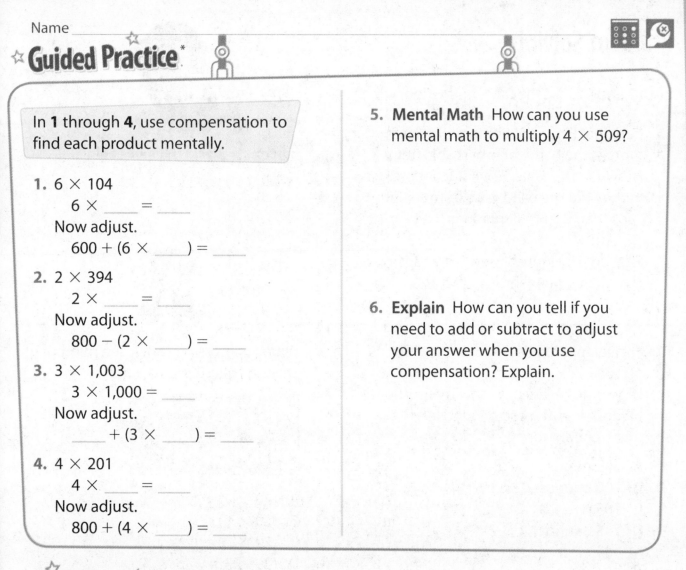

In **1** through **4**, use compensation to find each product mentally.

1. 6 × 104
6 × ____ = ____
Now adjust.
600 + (6 × ____) = ____

2. 2 × 394
2 × ____ = ____
Now adjust.
800 − (2 × ____) = ____

3. 3 × 1,003
3 × 1,000 = ____
Now adjust.
____ + (3 × ____) = ____

4. 4 × 201
4 × ____ = ____
Now adjust.
800 + (4 × ____) = ____

5. Mental Math How can you use mental math to multiply 4 × 509?

6. Explain How can you tell if you need to add or subtract to adjust your answer when you use compensation? Explain.

Independent Practice

Leveled Practice In **7** through **14**, use compensation to find each product.

7. 5 × 102
Substitute:
5 × ____ = 500
Adjust:
5 × ____ = 10
500 + ____ = 510
5 × 102 = ____

8. 2 × 1,998
Substitute:
2 × ____ = 4,000
Adjust:
2 × ____ = 4
4,000 − ____ = ____
2 × 1,998 = ____

You can count backward to subtract.

9. 5 × 109

10. 2 × 599

11. 5 × 1,006

12. 3 × 1,995

13. 6 × 895

14. 4 × 3,002

*For another example, see Set F on page 215.

Problem Solving

In **15** and **16**, use the table at the right.

15. Personal Financial Literacy To raise money, the band members sold items shown in the table. How much more money did the band raise from selling caps than from selling mugs?

DATA

Item	Cost	Number Sold
Caps	$9	36
Mugs	$7	44
Pennants	$8	52

16. Reason How much more do 9 caps cost than 9 pennants?

17. Each elephant at a zoo eats 100 pounds of hay and 5 pounds of fruits and vegetables every day. How many pounds of food does the zoo need to feed one elephant for one week?

A 35 pounds
B 700 pounds
C 705 pounds
D 735 pounds

18. Which expression shows the number of shaded squares?

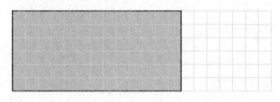

A $(20 \times 7) - (20 \times 6)$
B $(20 \times 6) - (7 \times 6)$
C $(20 \times 6) + (7 \times 6)$
D $(20 \times 13) + (6 \times 7)$

19. Use a Strip Diagram Ashley and 3 friends are planning a trip. The cost of the trip is $599 per person. How much will the trip cost Ashley and her friends? Explain how you found the answer.

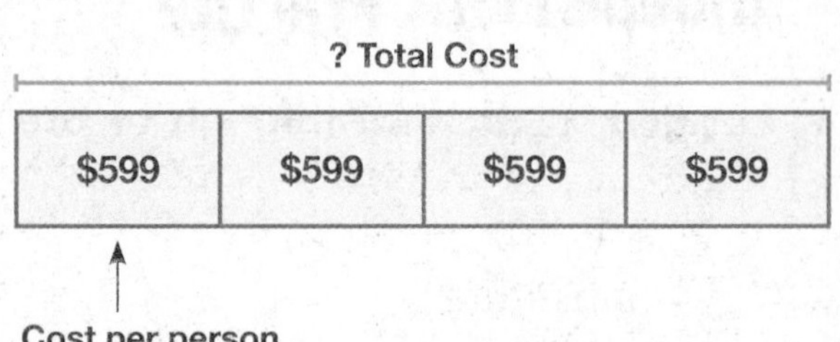

20. Extend Your Thinking A store clerk is stacking soup cans on shelves. He puts 100 cans on each shelf. If he can stack 50 cans in 5 minutes, how long will it take him to stack cans on 4 shelves?

21. Check for Reasonableness Sara says that 6×510 is 2,940. Is her answer reasonable? Explain how you know.

Name ____________________

Homework 3-6
Using Mental Math to Multiply

Another Look!

You can multiply mentally by using compensation. Don't forget to adjust to find the final product.

Use compensation to find 6 × 205.

Substitute a number for 205 that is easy to multiply.
6 × 200 = 1,200

Now adjust. Add 6 groups of 5, or 30.
1,200 + 30 = 1,230

Use compensation to find 4 × 398.

Substitute a number for 398 that is easy to multiply.
4 × 400 = 1,600

Now adjust. Subtract 4 groups of 2, or 8.
1,600 − 8 = 1,592

Leveled Practice In **1** through **12**, use compensation to find each product.

1. 2 × 3,009
   Substitute:
   2 × 3,000 = ____
   Adjust:
   6,000 + ____ = ____

2. 5 × 395
   Substitute:
   5 × ____ = ____
   Adjust:
   2,000 − ____ = ____

3. 4 × 198
   Substitute:
   4 × ____ = ____
   Adjust:
   800 − ____ = ____

4. 2 × 603
   Substitute:
   ____ × ____ = ____
   Adjust:
   ____ + ____ = ____

5. 3 × 598
   Substitute:
   ____ × ____ = ____
   Adjust:
   ____ − ____ = ____

6. 4 × 1,402
   Substitute:
   ____ × ____ = ____
   Adjust:
   ____ + ____ = ____

7. 4 × 1,995

8. 8 × 991

9. 3,004 × 6

10. 404 × 6

11. 5 × 109

12. 5 × 999

13. The longest blue whale on record was about 18 scuba divers in length. Use breaking apart to estimate the length of the blue whale.

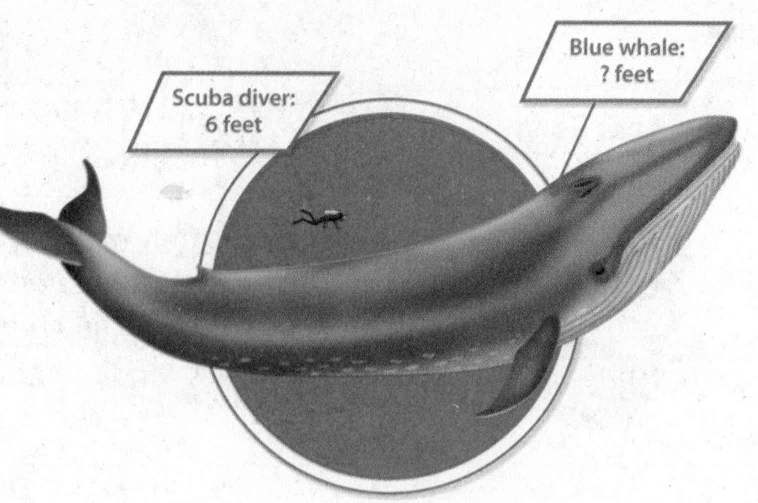

14. Explain how to estimate the length of the whale using compensation.

---

15. **Explain** Find the product of 6×503. Explain how you used mental math to find the product.

16. **Extend Your Thinking** Quinn used compensation to find the product of 4×307. First, she found $4 \times 300 = 1{,}200$. Then she adjusted the product by subtracting 4 groups of 7 to get her final answer of 1,172. Explain her mistake and find the correct answer.

---

17. Davidson's Bakery bakes 108 cookies and 96 muffins every hour. How many baked goods are baked in 4 hours?

A 204 baked goods
B 432 baked goods
C 816 baked goods
D 1,020 baked goods

18. **Number Sense** Alisa's hair is longer than 6.2 inches. Write the shortest length that Alisa's hair could be, using 2 decimal places.

---

19. **Represent** In an election, 589,067 people voted. Write 589,067 in expanded form.

20. **Extend Your Thinking** Do you think it would be better to use breaking apart or compensation to find the product 5×328? Explain why and show how to find the product.

Name ________________________________

Lesson 3-7
Using Rounding to Estimate

Solve & Share

Sarah earns $48 a week babysitting. She has saved all of her money for the past 6 weeks. Estimate to find out about how much money she has saved. ***Solve this problem any way you choose!***

TEKS 4.4G Round to the nearest 10, 100, or 1,000 or use compatible numbers to estimate solutions involving whole numbers.
Mathematical Process Standards 4.1B, 4.1C, 4.1G

Digital Resources at SavvasTexas.com

Solve Learn Glossary Check Tools Games

You can **use estimation.** What mental math technique can you use to find a good estimate?

Look Back!

Construct Arguments Is your estimate more or less than Sarah actually earned? How do you know?

How Can You Estimate When You Multiply?

A

Hoover School is holding a walk-a-thon. Any class that raises more than $500 earns a prize. Mr. Hector and Mrs. Alan both want to know if their class will earn a prize.

Class	Blocks Walked	Pledges per Block
Mr. Hector's	193	$4
Mrs. Alan's	115	$3

Rounding is one way to estimate products.

Use place-value understandings.

B

Mr. Hector's Class

Estimate 4×193 using rounding.

4×193 — Round 193 to 200.

$4 \times 200 = 800$

Mr. Hector's class raised more than 500 dollars.

His class has earned a prize.

C

Mrs. Alan's Class

Estimate 3×115 using rounding.

3×115 — Round 115 to 100.

$3 \times 100 = 300$

Mrs. Alan's class has raised about 300 dollars.

This is not enough to earn a prize.

Do You Understand?

Convince Me! Is the estimate for Mr. Hector's class greater than or less than the exact answer? Explain how you know.

Name ______________________________

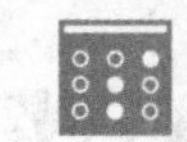

Guided Practice*

In **1** through **8**, estimate each product.

1. 6 × 125
2. 4 × 261
3. 538 × 3
4. 7 × 314
5. 8 × 53
6. 9 × 24
7. 2 × 585
8. 4 × 18

9. Mrs. Alan's class walked 70 more blocks. Estimate to see if her class will now get a prize.

10. **Number Sense** To which place should you round to estimate the product 4 × 1,890? Estimate the product.

Independent Practice

Leveled Practice In **11** through **29**, estimate each product.

11. 3 × 287
    Round 287 to ______.
    3 × ______ = ______

12. 6 × 131
    Round 131 to ______.
    6 × ______ = ______

13. 602 × 9
    Round 602 to ______.
    9 × ______ = ______

14. 486 × 7
    ______ × ______
    = ______

15. 719 × 5
    ______ × ______
    = ______

16. 1,240 × 5
    ______ × ______
    = ______

17. 8 × 3,015
    ______ × ______
    = ______

18. 3,780 × 2
19. 4,365 × 4
20. 8 × 72
21. 5 × 1,108
22. 345 × 2
23. 1,089 × 6
24. 237 × 9
25. 8 × 6,742
26. 8 × 932
27. 65 × 5
28. 4 × 2,907
29. 638 × 7

*For another example, see Set G on page 216.

Problem Solving

30. **Analyze Information** The students at Spring Elementary voted on a school mascot. Which mascot has about 4 times as many votes as the unicorn?

A Lion
B Owl
C Dragon
D Bear

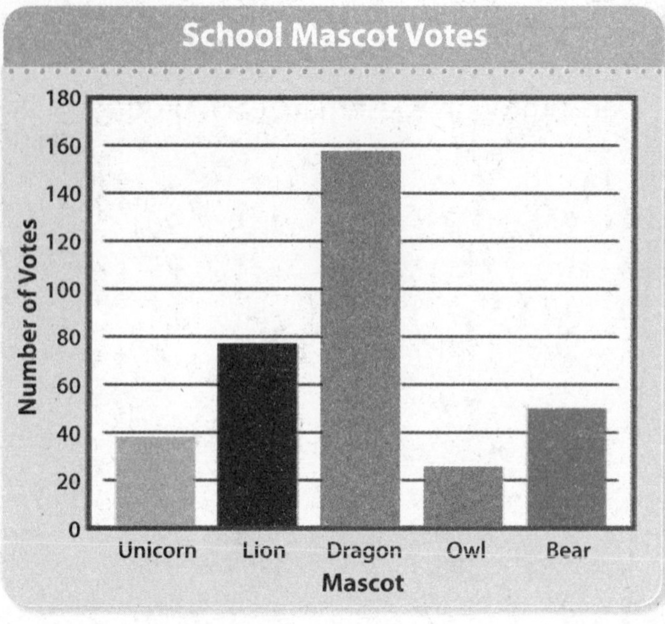

31. **Estimation** Explain how you could estimate the number of students who voted on a school mascot. Then give your estimate.

32. **Estimation** Sam and his two brothers want to fly to Boston. About how much will Sam and his brothers save by buying the less expensive fare?

DATA

Airfare for Round Trip to Boston	
Skies the Limit Airline	$319
In the Clouds Airline	$405

33. **Check for Reasonableness** Ellie estimates that the product of 211 and 6 is 1,800. Is this estimate reasonable? Explain.

34. Estimate the cost of tuition and books for 4 years of college.

DATA

College Costs	
Tuition	$7,200
Room and Board	$5,400
Books	$750

A $28,000
B $32,000
C $36,000
D $48,000

35. **Extend Your Thinking** An adult sleeps about 480 minutes per day. An infant sleeps about 820 minutes per day. About how many more minutes does an infant sleep than an adult in one week? Solve the problem in two different ways. Show your work.

Name ________________

Homework 3-7
Use Rounding to Estimate

Another Look!

Round 3-digit numbers to the nearest hundred and round 4-digit numbers to the nearest thousand to estimate.

Use rounding to estimate 7×215.	Use rounding to estimate $2,885 \times 4$.
First, round 215 to the nearest hundred. 215 rounds to 200. Then, multiply. $7 \times 200 = 1,400$ So, 7×215 is about 1,400.	First round 2,885 to the nearest thousand. 2,885 rounds to 3,000. Then, multiply. $3,000 \times 4 = 12,000$. So, $2,885 \times 4$ is about 12,000.

Leveled Practice In **1** through **15**, estimate each product.

1. 279×4

279 rounds to ______.

______ $\times 4 =$ ______

2. 9×472

472 rounds to ______.

$9 \times$ ______ $=$ ______

3. 8×892

______ rounds to 900.

______ $\times$ ______ $=$ ______

4. 578×8

______ rounds to ______.

______ $\times$ ______ $=$ ______

5. 823×3

______ rounds to ______.

______ $\times$ ______ $=$ ______

6. 7×289

______ rounds to ______.

______ $\times$ ______ $=$ ______

7. 183×4

8. $3 \times 1,675$

9. $8,210 \times 2$

10. $6,392 \times 4$

11. $5 \times 4,688$

12. $7,201 \times 8$

13. 6×674

14. 365×3

15. $2 \times 9,241$

16. Number Sense Estimate to determine whether 5 × 68 is greater than or less than 350. Tell how you decided.

17. The distance between Bill's house and his aunt's house is 485 miles. About how many miles would he drive if he made 4 round trips from his house to his aunt's house and back?

A 5,000 mi
B 4,000 mi
C 3,200 mi
D 2,000 mi

18. Analyze Information Estimate how many of Part B would be made in 3 months.

19. Estimation It costs the factory $4 to make each Part A. About how much does it cost to make Part A each month?

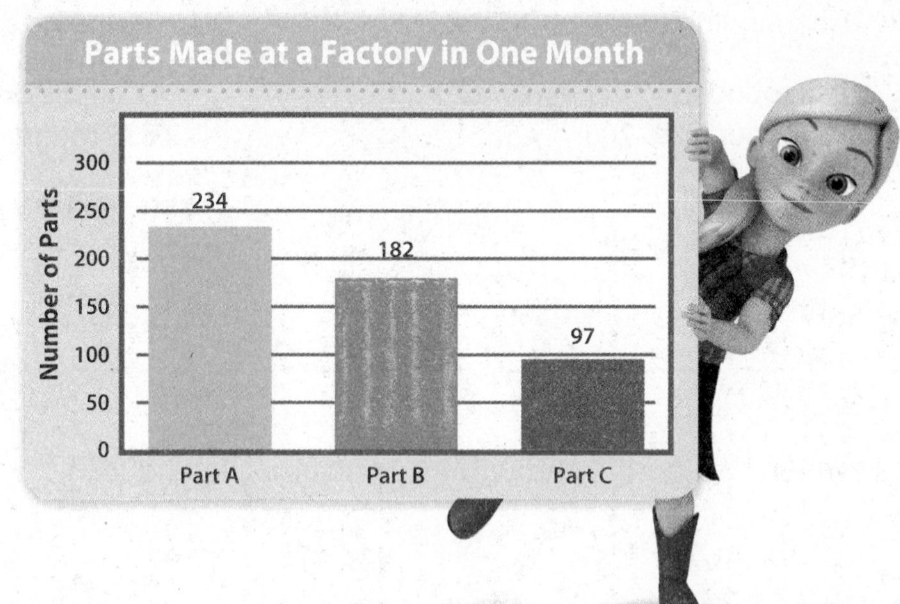

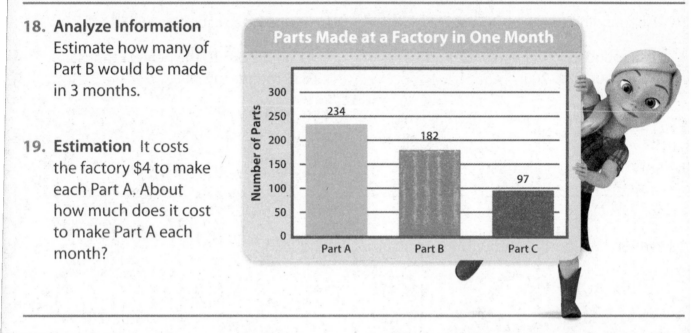

20. Fourth graders chose a read-a-thon as the class fundraiser. Each of the four fourth-grade classes read 408 pages. About how many pages did the fourth graders read?

21. Math and Science Lizards are 4-legged reptiles. Snakes are also reptiles, but snakes do not have legs. Which property of multiplication could you use to calculate how many legs 347 snakes have?

22. Extend Your Thinking A package of all of the individual pictures listed in the chart costs $50. Estimate about how much money is saved by buying a package instead of buying the same number of individual pictures. Show your work.

DATA

Individual Picture Prices	
8 × 10	$18
5 × 7	$14
4 × 6	$10
8 wallets	$18

Name ______________________________

Solve & Share

Susan has $45. She spends $15 on a book for her father, $20 on candles for her mother, and $6 on a board game for her brother. Does Susan have enough money left to buy a box of markers for $5? ***Solve this problem any way you choose.***

You can **formulate a plan.** What operation(s) can you use to solve this problem? ***Show your work in the space below!***

Problem Solving

Lesson 3-8
Multi-Step Problems

TEKS 4.1A Apply mathematics to problems arising in everyday life, society, and the workplace. Also, 4.8C. **Mathematical Process Standards** 4.1B, 4.1C, 4.1D, 4.1G

Digital Resources at SavvasTexas.com

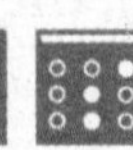

Solve Learn Glossary Check Tools Games

Look Back!

Check for Reasonableness How could you check that your answer is correct?

How Can You Solve Multi-Step Problems?

A-Z

A Analyze

Justine and her father are going on a fishing trip. The prices for supplies, including tax, are shown in the table. Justine and her father have $25. They bought 2 box lunches, 2 bottles of water, 1 pack of hooks, and 1 pack of sinkers. How many pounds of bait can they buy?

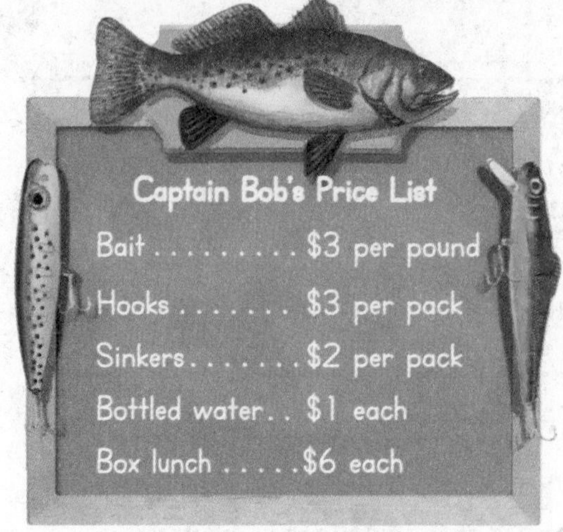

Captain Bob's Price List
Bait . . . . $3 per pound
Hooks . . . . $3 per pack
Sinkers. . . . . . . $2 per pack
Bottled water. . $1 each
Box lunch . . . . .$6 each

Some problems are made up of parts that need to be solved first to be able to answer the question asked.

B Analyze

What do I know?

They bought:

2 lunches for $6 each
2 bottles of water for $1 each
1 pack of hooks for $3 each
1 pack of sinkers for $2 each

What am I asked to find?

The number of pounds of bait they can buy with the money they have left

C Plan and Solve

Find the hidden question. How much money do Justine and her father have left?

The cost of lunches is	$2 \times \$6 = \$12$
The cost of water is	$2 \times \$1 = \$2$
The cost of hooks is	$1 \times \$3 = \$3$
The cost of sinkers is	$1 \times \$2 = \$2$
	The total is $19

$\$25 - \$19 = \$6$ They have $6 left.

Divide to find how many pounds of bait.

$6 \div 3 = 2$ They can buy 2 pounds of bait.

Do You Understand?

Convince Me! What does it mean to "find a hidden question"?

Name ___

Guided Practice*

1. **Connect** Elsa babysits for the Smyth family. She earns $10 per hour on weekdays. She earns $15 per hour on the weekend. Last week, she worked 3 hours during the week and 4 hours on the weekend. How much did Elsa earn last week?

2. **Mental Math** A bus has 12 rows with 1 seat in each row on one side and 12 rows with 2 seats in each row on the other side. How many seats does the bus have?

3. **Analyze Information** What is the hidden question or questions in Exercise 1?

4. **Analyze Information** What is the hidden question or questions in Exercise 2?

Independent Practice

In **5** through **7**, solve each problem.

Look for the hidden questions to answer first.

5. **Formulate a Plan** Gabriella buys 2 sandwiches and 2 drinks. Each sandwich costs $4. Each drink costs $1.50. How much does Gabriella spend?

6. **Analyze Information** Jamie buys 5 packages of red bowls, 3 packages of orange bowls, 4 packages of green bowls, and 7 packages of white bowls. Each package contains 8 bowls. How many bowls does she buy in all?

7. **Number Sense** Carrie says she is thinking of a number between 1 and 10. When she adds 4 to her number and multiplies the sum by 5, the resulting number is 45. What is Carrie's number?

*For another example, see Set H on page 216.

Problem Solving

8. **Analyze Information** Mario and his family went to the county fair. They bought 2 adult passes and 3 children's passes. What was the total cost for the family?

DATA

County Fair Admission	
Adults	$5
Students	$3
Children	$2

9. **Explain** Ashlyn and Brooke went to the arcade with $18. They bought 4 bottles of water, which cost $2 each. They each bought sticker books for $3 each. Ashlyn put $1 in a fundraiser jar. A game of pool cost $3 per game. Did they have enough money left to play a game of pool? Explain how you know.

10. Pedro collects baseball cards. He had 192. His friend Kevin gave him 267 more. His friend Shannon gave him 212 more. How many baseball cards does Pedro have now?

A 771 cards
B 679 cards
C 671 cards
D 579 cards

11. Jorge wants to buy carpet for his living room and bedroom. His living room is 30 square yards and his bedroom is 21 square yards. Carpet costs $9 a square yard. How much will it cost to carpet these rooms?

A $459
B $450
C $359
D $81

12. **Reason** Cyndi and Jewel went shopping for school supplies. They had $14 to spend. They spent $4 on pencils, $3 on pens, and $6 on notebook paper. Cyndi thought she had enough money left over to buy a $2 pencil sharpener. Was she correct?

13. **Extend Your Thinking** Sheila bought four bags of apples and three bags of pears. She paid with a $20 bill. How much change did she receive?

$2 $3

Use picture clues.

14. **Draw a Picture** A grocery store display has 2 boxes of cereal on the top row, 3 boxes in the next row, 4 boxes in the next row, and so on. How many rows are there in the display if there are 44 boxes in all?

Name ______________________

Homework 3-8
Multi-Step Problems

Another Look!

Look for hidden questions that must be solved first.

Analyze

Maggie has $31 to shop for art supplies. She buys 4 paintbrushes, 1 pack of drawing paper, 1 box of crayons, and 3 cans of paint. How many colored pencils can Maggie buy?

DATA

Price List	
Paint	$2 per can
Paintbrush	$3 each
Crayons	$4 per box
Colored Pencils	$2 each
Drawing Paper	$5 per pack

Plan and Solve

How much has Maggie spent so far?

4 paintbrushes for $3 each = $12

1 pack of drawing paper = $5

1 box of crayons = $4

3 cans of paint for $2 each = $6

$12 + $5 + $4 + $6 = $27

Plan and Solve

How much does Maggie have left?

$31 − $27 = $4

How many colored pencils can Maggie buy for $2 each?

$4 ÷ $2 = 2 colored pencils

Maggie can buy 2 colored pencils.

In **1** and **2**, identify the hidden question(s) and solve the problem.

1. Kelly used 6 cups of apples, 4 cups of oranges, and 2 cups of grapes to make a fruit salad. She put an equal amount in each of 6 bowls. How many cups of fruit salad were in each bowl?

2. Muriel started with the same recipe as Kelly used to make her fruit salad. Then Muriel added 1 cup of cherries and 1 cup of bananas. She put 2 cups of fruit salad into each bowl. How many bowls of fruit salad did Muriel make?

In **3** and **4**, use the data at the right.

Just Jerseys	
Number of T-shirts	**Price**
8	$80
24	$240
48	$480

3. Extend Your Thinking Look for a pattern. How much does one T-shirt cost? Explain.

4. Personal Financial Literacy A football team purchases 40 T-shirts. Including sales tax, the bill is $440.50. How much sales tax did the team pay?

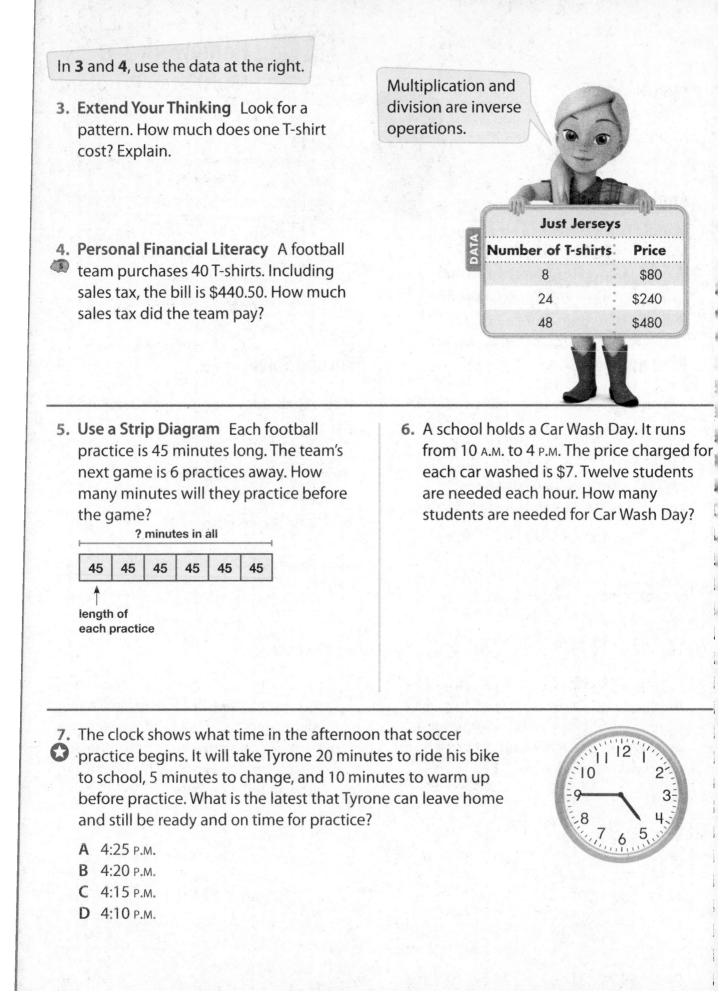

5. Use a Strip Diagram Each football practice is 45 minutes long. The team's next game is 6 practices away. How many minutes will they practice before the game?

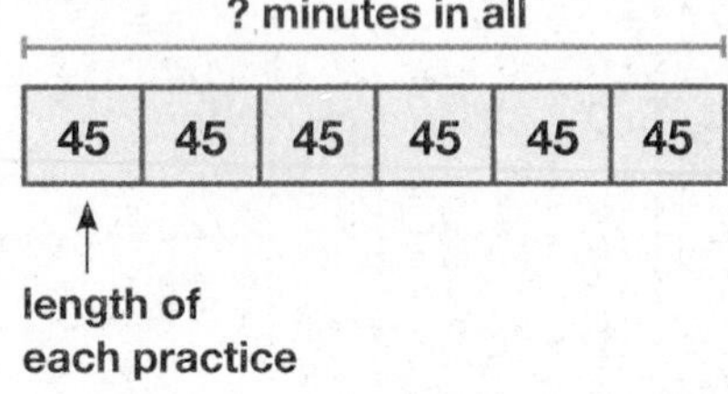

6. A school holds a Car Wash Day. It runs from 10 A.M. to 4 P.M. The price charged for each car washed is $7. Twelve students are needed each hour. How many students are needed for Car Wash Day?

7. The clock shows what time in the afternoon that soccer practice begins. It will take Tyrone 20 minutes to ride his bike to school, 5 minutes to change, and 10 minutes to warm up before practice. What is the latest that Tyrone can leave home and still be ready and on time for practice?

A 4:25 P.M.
B 4:20 P.M.
C 4:15 P.M.
D 4:10 P.M.

Name

Applying Math Processes

- How does this problem connect to previous ones?
- What is my plan?
- How can I use tools?
- How can I use number sense?
- How can I communicate and represent my thinking?
- How can I organize and record information?
- How can I explain my work?
- How can I justify my answer?

1. **Personal Financial Literacy** A hoodie costs \$19. How much do 3 hoodies cost? Tell how to use mental math to solve.

2. **Justify** Use the Distributive Property to show how to solve 6×395.

3. **Extend Your Thinking** Store A has 27 boxes with 8 candles in each. Store B has 31 boxes with 11 candles in each. Sarah estimates that each store has about 300 candles. How can you decide which store's actual number of candles is closer to the estimate?

4. **Represent** Use >, <, or = to make the expression true. Show how you know.

0.9 ◯ 0.90

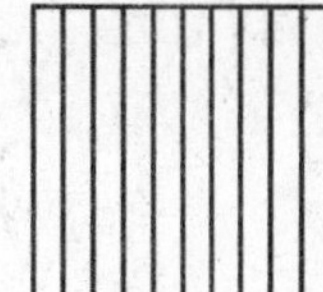
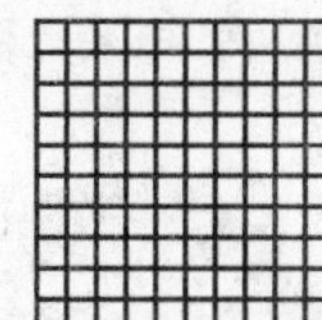

5. **Number Sense** Draw a number line. Place and label points on the number line to show the decimals in order from least to greatest.

W 0.57 *X* 0.53 *Y* 0.55 *Z* 0.59

6. **Connect** When using the Distributive Property to find $9 \times 6{,}031$, which other two properties of multiplication will you use?

Error Search

Find each problem that is not correct. Circle what is wrong and rewrite the problem so it is correct.

1. $5 \times 3{,}070 =$

   $(5 \times 30) + (5 \times 70) = 5{,}000$

2. $2 \times 7{,}088 =$

   $(2 \times 7{,}000) + (2 \times 80) + (2 \times 8) = 14{,}176$

3. $8 \times 492 =$

   $(8 \times 4) + (8 \times 9) + (8 \times 2) = 3{,}936$

4. $6 \times 937 =$

   $(6 + 900) \times (6 + 30) \times (6 + 7) = 124{,}008$

Target Number

Mental Math Using any numbers from the box as addends, list as many sums less than the target number as you can. Numbers in the box may NOT be used more than once in any one sum.

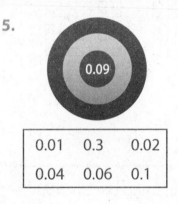

5.

0.01	0.3	0.02
0.04	0.06	0.1

6.

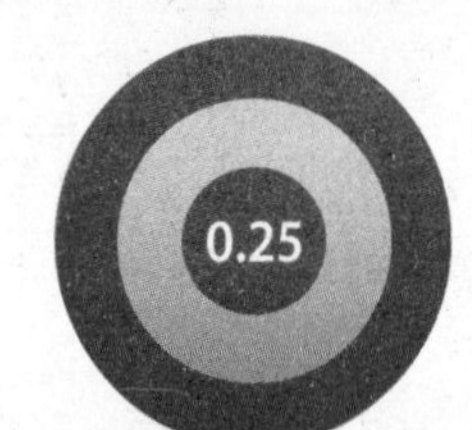

0.06	0.2	0.11
0.09	0.1	0.17

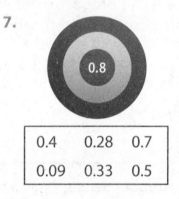

7.

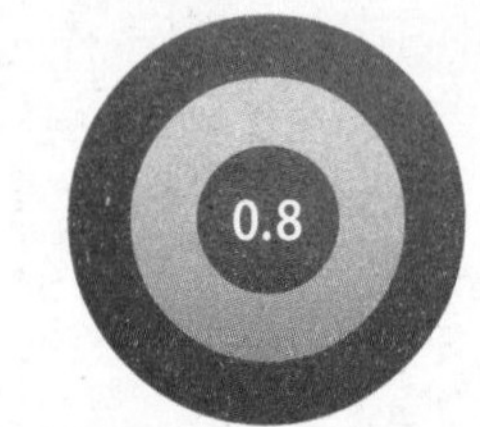

0.4	0.28	0.7
0.09	0.33	0.5

Name ______________________________

TOPIC 3

Set A pages 163–168

DATA

Property of Multiplication	Example
Commutative	$4 \times 8 = 8 \times 4$ $32 = 32$
Associative	$(4 \times 5) \times 6 = 4 \times (5 \times 6)$ $120 = 120$
Zero	$12 \times 0 = 0$
Identity	$9 \times 1 = 9$

Remember to use the multiplication properties to determine what number is missing.

1. $256 \times$ ____ $= 256$

2. $157{,}678 \times 0 =$ ____

3. $7{,}000 \times$ ____ $= 20 \times 7{,}000$

4. $(12 \times 3) \times 4 = 12 \times ($____ $\times 4)$

5. ____ $\times 1 = 799$

6. $(25 \times 7) \times 8 =$ ____ $\times (25 \times 7)$

Set B pages 169–174

Use arrays to multiply by 10 and 100.

Find 3×10.

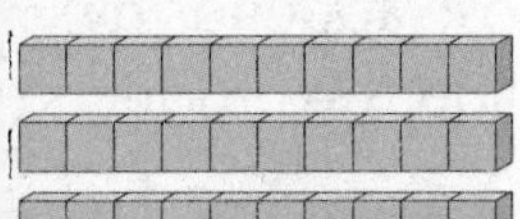

$3 \times 10 = 10 + 10 + 10$
$3 \times 10 = 30$

Find 3×100.

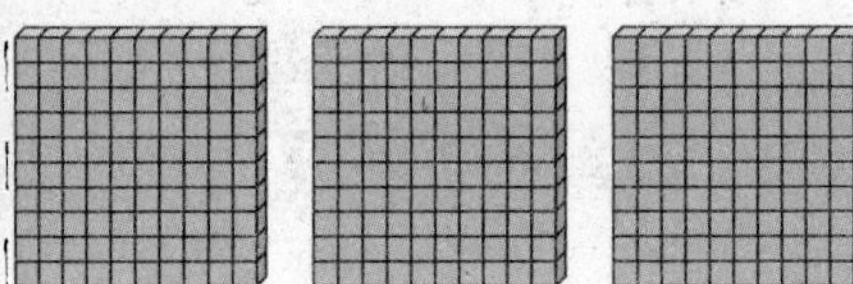

$3 \times 100 = 100 + 100 + 100$
$3 \times 100 = 300$

Remember you can think of multiplication as repeated addition.

In **1** through **4**, write each multiplication as repeated addition to find the product.

1. 5×10

2. 2×100

3. 6×100

4. 4×10

In **5** through **8**, find the product.

5. 7×10 **6.** 8×100

7. 9×100 **8.** 8×10

Set C pages 175–180

Use basic facts and multiplication properties to multiply by multiples of 10 and 100.

Find 4×60.

$4 \times 60 = 4 \times (6 \times 10)$
$4 \times 60 = (4 \times 6) \times 10$
$4 \times 60 = 24 \times 10$
$4 \times 60 = 240$

Shortcut: Multiply 4×6 and annex 1 zero.

Find 4×600.

$4 \times 600 = 4 \times (6 \times 100)$
$4 \times 600 = (4 \times 6) \times 100$
$4 \times 600 = 24 \times 100$
$4 \times 600 = 2{,}400$

Shortcut: Multiply 4×6 and annex 2 zeros.

Remember when the product of a basic fact ends in zero, the answer will have an extra zero.

Find each product.

1. 8×60 **2.** 3×10

3. 6×50 **4.** 5×300

5. 700×4 **6.** 2×900

7. 80×8 **8.** 400×5

9. 30×9 **10.** 5×80

11. 700×8 **12.** 900×6

13. 7×900 **14.** 5×100

Set D pages 181–186

The Distributive Property states that multiplying a sum by a number is the same as multiplying each addend in the sum by the number, and then adding the products.

Use the Distributive Property to find 5×23.

Think of 23 as $20 + 3$.

$5 \times 23 = 5 \times (20 + 3)$
$= (5 \times 20) + (5 \times 3)$
$= 100 + 15 = 115$
$= 115$

So, $5 \times 23 = 115$.

Remember that you write one of the numbers as a sum, multiply each of those addends by the other number, and then add the products.

Use the Distributive Property to find each product.

1. 7×45

2. 29×9

3. 72×6

4. 3×46

5. 37×8

6. 5×95

7. 88×3

Name ______________________________

TOPIC 3

Set E pages 187–192

Use breaking apart to find 4 × 123.

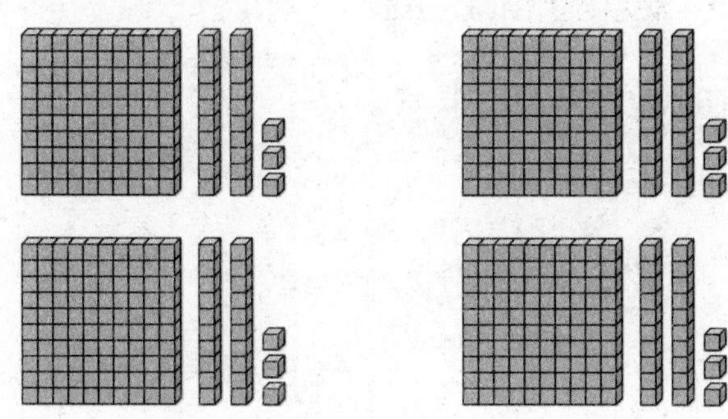

Think of 123 as 100 + 20 + 3.

4 × 123 = (4 × 100) + (4 × 20) + (4 × 3)
= 400 + 80 + 12
= 492

So, 4 × 123 = 492.

Remember you can use place-value blocks or drawings to help you multiply.

Find the product.

1. 4 × 1,173
2. 2 × 1,259
3. 6 × 135
4. 3 × 281
5. 7 × 1,725
6. 5 × 146
7. 8 × 4,204
8. 5 × 354

Set F pages 193–198

Use compensation to find 2 × 297.

First, think of 297 as 300 − 3. Substitute 300 for 297 and find 2 × 300 = 600.

Then adjust by subtracting 2 groups of 3.

600 − 6 = 594

So, 2 × 297 = 594.

Remember to check your answers for reasonableness.

Find the product.

1. 6 × 1,030
2. 3 × 2,004
3. 5 × 397
4. 6 × 3,005
5. 6 × 203
6. 4 × 499

Set G pages 199–204

Use rounding to estimate 9×193.

Round 193 to 200.

9×193
↓
$9 \times 200 = 1{,}800$

So, 9×193 is about 1,800.

Remember to round a three-digit number to the nearest hundred and a four-digit number to the nearest thousand.

Estimate each product.

1. $8 \times 7{,}632$
2. 493×3
3. $9{,}379 \times 5$
4. 678×6
5. 707×4
6. $5{,}703 \times 3$
7. 483×6
8. $6 \times 8{,}166$

Set H pages 205–210

Ann waited 45 minutes in line to ride her favorite roller coaster. While she waited, she listened to music for 5 minutes, played a video game for 12 minutes, and talked to her friend for the remainder of the time. How long did Ann talk to her friend while she waited?

First, add to find how much time Ann listened to music and played a video game.

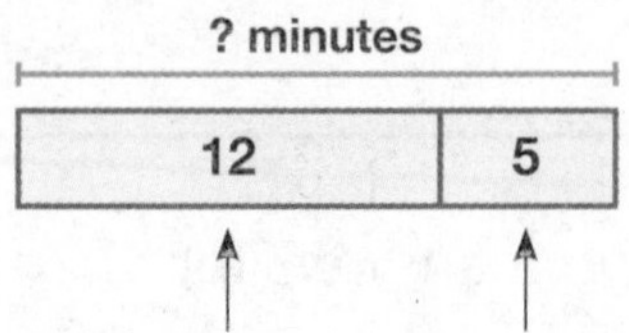

$12 + 5 = 17$ minutes

You know that Ann talked to her friend the rest of the time she waited to ride the roller coaster. She waited 45 minutes total. So subtract 17 minutes from 45 minutes.

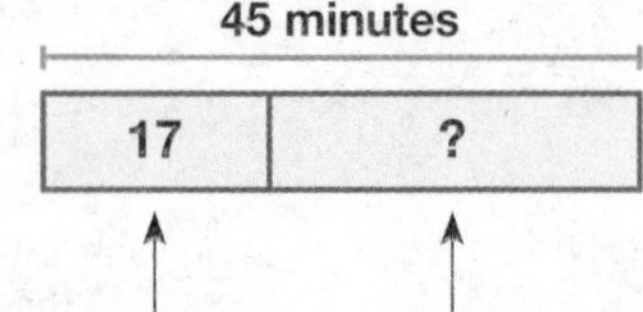

$45 - 17 = 28$ minutes

Ann talked to her for 28 minutes while she waited to ride the roller coaster.

Remember Make sure that you answer the question that the problem is asking. It may require multiple steps to get to the answer. Use strip diagrams to help.

Solve.

1. Isaac has 3 bags of apples. Each bag has 10 apples. He gives an apple to each of his 5 teachers and 1 apple to his sister. After basketball practice, Isaac gives 2 apples to each of his 12 teammates. How many apples does Isaac have left?

2. Elizabeth has 2 dogs. She has 10 times as many fish as she has dogs. She has half the number of cats as she has dogs. How many dogs, cats, and fish does Elizabeth have all together?

3. Tony had \$16 left over after buying 2 notebooks for \$4 each and a calculator for \$25. How much money did Tony start with?

Name ______________________________

1. Mrs. Ortiz can make 50 tortillas using one batch of dough. If she makes 4 batches of dough, how many tortillas can she make?

   A 8 tortillas

   B 20 tortillas

   C 200 tortillas

   D 2,000 tortillas

2. There are usually 365 days in one year. If Jean turned 9 years old today, which is the best estimate of the number of days Jean has been alive?

   A About 2,700 days

   B About 2,800 days

   C About 3,000 days

   D About 3,600 days

3. Alex found 7×132 using breaking apart. Which expression could show his work?

   A $(7 \times 100) + (7 \times 30) + (7 \times 2)$

   B $(7 \times 100) + (7 \times 10) + (7 \times 2)$

   C $(1 \times 100) + (3 \times 10) + (2 \times 1)$

   D 7×100

4. A factory produces 295 cars in one week. How many cars does the factory produce in 4 weeks?

   A 885 cars

   B 1,180 cars

   C 1,200 cars

   D 1,220 cars

5. Sam writes $10 + 10 + 10$ to represent the place-value blocks. Which numerical expression is another way to represent the blocks?

   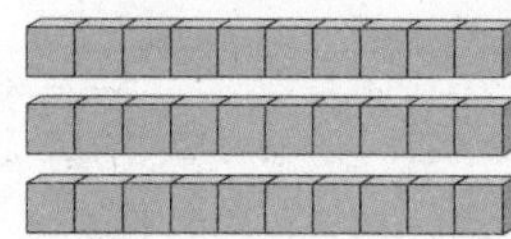

   A $10 \times 10 \times 10$

   B 3×100

   C 3×10

   D 3×1

6. Ed rode the train 198 miles round trip 4 times last month. He used compensation to find the total distance he traveled last month. First, he multiplied $200 \times 4 = 800$. Which number sentence correctly completes the calculation?

   A $800 + 4 = 804$

   B $800 - 4 = 796$

   C $800 + 8 = 808$

   D $800 - 8 = 792$

7. Susanna's school received 5 boxes of books with 108 books in each box. Which is a reasonable estimate of the total number of books?

A 400, because 5×108 is about $5 \times 80 = 400$

B 500, because 5×108 is about $5 \times 100 = 500$

C 800, because 5×108 is about $5 \times 200 = 800$

D 1,000, because 5×108 is about $10 \times 100 = 1{,}000$

8. Ivan earns $240 a month for working at the grocery store. Which is **NOT** a reasonable estimate of the amount of money Ivan would have if he saves all the money he earns for 6 months?

A $1,800

B $1,500

C $1,200

D $500

9. Use the Distributive Property to find 4×293. Show your work.

10. Which numerical expression shows another way to find $100 + 100 + 100 + 100$?

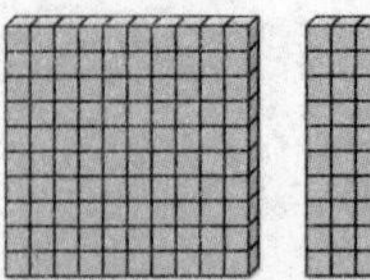
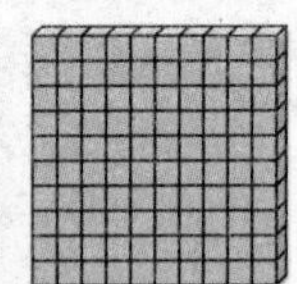
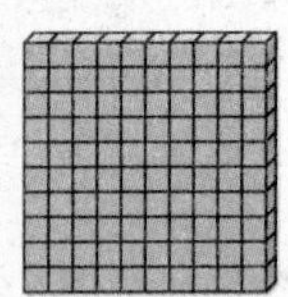
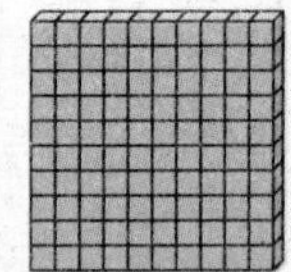

A $4 \times 1{,}000$

B 4×100

C 4×10

D 4×1

11. Mrs. Henderson bought 4 boxes of facial tissues. Each box has 174 tissues. Which number sentence gives the best estimate of the total number of tissues?

A $4 \times 200 = 800$

B $4 \times 100 = 400$

C $200 \div 4 = 50$

D $160 \div 4 = 40$

12. Estimate the product 6×332 by rounding to the nearest hundred.

Name ______________________________

13. Which expression shows how Mia could use breaking apart to find 6 × 135?

A (6 × 100) + (6 × 30) + (6 × 5)

B (6 × 100) + (6 × 3) + (6 × 5)

C (6 × 10) + (6 × 30) + (6 × 50)

D (6 × 1) + (6 × 3) + (6 × 5)

14. A gallon of paint can cover about 400 square feet of wall space. About how many square feet of wall space will 3 gallons cover?

A 120 square feet

B 1,200 square feet

C 12,000 square feet

D 120,000 square feet

15. Cora had $45. She bought a book for $25 and a calculator for $18. How much money does Cora have left?

16. Raul is buying 3 airplane tickets for $185 each. About how much will the 3 tickets cost in all?

A About $300

B About $450

C About $600

D About $650

17. Ricky saves $7 each week. There are 52 weeks in 1 year. Use rounding to estimate the amount he will have saved after one year.

A About $300

B About $350

C About $400

D About $450

18. Use multiplication properties to find 5 × (2 × 8). Show your work.

19. Which expression shows how Tina could use breaking apart to find 5×617?

A $(5 \times 6) + (5 \times 1) + (5 \times 7)$

B $(5 \times 60) + (5 \times 10) + (5 \times 70)$

C $(5 \times 600) + (5 \times 1) + (5 \times 7)$

D $(5 \times 600) + (5 \times 10) + (5 \times 7)$

20. Judy has 5 rolls of stamps. There are 100 stamps in each roll. How many stamps does Judy have?

A 5,000 stamps

B 500 stamps

C 105 stamps

D 50 stamps

21. Ali ran for 19 minutes each day for 7 days. How many minutes did Ali run?

			.		
0	0	0		0	0
1	1	1		1	1
2	2	2		2	2
3	3	3		3	3
4	4	4		4	4
5	5	5		5	5
6	6	6		6	6
7	7	7		7	7
8	8	8		8	8
9	9	9		9	9

22. Nia has 5 piles of paper clips. There are 79 paper clips in each pile. How many paper clips does she have in all?

A 3,995 paper clips

B 3,955 paper clips

C 400 paper clips

D 395 paper clips

23. An auditorium has 136 seats in each row. There are 5 rows in the auditorium. How many seats are in there in all?

A 680 seats

B 700 seats

C 750 seats

D Not here

24. Missy read 10 pages each day for a week. How many pages did she read in all?

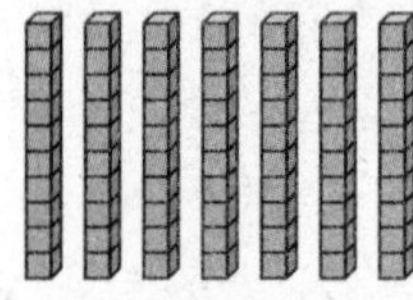

			.		
0	0	0		0	0
1	1	1		1	1
2	2	2		2	2
3	3	3		3	3
4	4	4		4	4
5	5	5		5	5
6	6	6		6	6
7	7	7		7	7
8	8	8		8	8
9	9	9		9	9

Developing Proficiency: Multiplying by 1-Digit Numbers

Essential Questions:
How can arrays be used to find products?
What is a standard procedure for multiplying multi-digit numbers?

When a geyser erupts, steam and water droplets rise hundreds of feet into the air.

There are approximately 700 geysers in the world. Four hundred of those are in Yellowstone National Park.

I'll get my umbrella! Here's a project on matter and multiplication.

Math and Science Project: States of Matter

Do Research Use the Internet or other sources to find information about the different states of matter.

Look around your classroom for examples of the three states of matter: solids, liquids, and gases.

Journal: Write a Report Include what you found. Also in your report:

- Describe water in each of its three states of matter.
- The most famous geyser is Old Faithful. During one of its long eruptions, it shoots out about 8,400 gallons of water. Find $8,400 \times 6$ to calculate about how many gallons of water shoot out during six long eruptions.

Name

Review What You Know

Vocabulary

Choose the best term from the box. Write it on the blank.

- product
- array
- variable
- factors

1. You multiply numbers to find a(n) ________.
2. A(n) ________ shows the number of objects in rows and columns.
3. Two numbers that are being multiplied together are called ________.

Multiplication Facts

Find each product.

4. 4×8
5. 2×9
6. 9×5
7. 6×8
8. 6×4
9. 6×6
10. 8×5
11. 9×9

Rounding

Round each number to the nearest hundred.

12. 164
13. 8,263
14. 351
15. 527
16. 2,498
17. 9,634
18. 7,892
19. 472

Round each number to the nearest thousand.

20. 8,685
21. 4,991
22. 62,549
23. 167,241
24. 77,268
25. 34,162
26. 1,372
27. 9,009

28. **Explain** Explain how to round 608,149 to the thousands place.

You can review rounding in Topic 1, Lesson 4.

Name ____________________

Solve & Share

A museum exhibit has 4 display cases. There are 118 coins in each case. How many coins are there in all 4 cases? ***Solve this problem any way you choose.***

Lesson 4-1
Arrays and Using an Expanded Algorithm

TEKS 4.4D Use strategies and algorithms... to multiply.... Strategies may include mental math, partial products, and the commutative, associative, and distributive properties.
Mathematical Process Standards 4.1C, 4.1D, 4.1G

Digital Resources at SavvasTexas.com

Solve

Learn
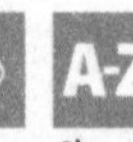
Glossary
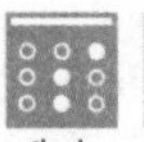
Check

Tools

Games

You can **use tools.** Place-value blocks can help you visualize the problem. ***Show your work in the space above!***

Look Back!

Justify How many partial products did you find? Why did you find that many partial products?

How Can You Record Multiplication?

A-Z

A

A pet store bought 3 large fish tanks to display different types of fish. Each tank is the size shown below. How much water will it take to fill all 3 tanks?

245 gallons

Use partial products.

B

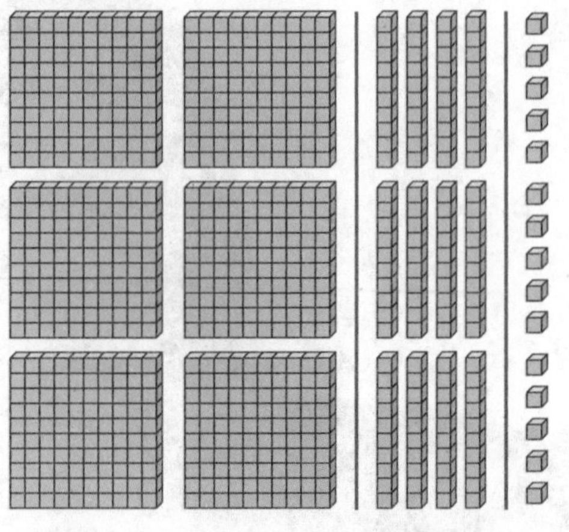

What You Show

6 hundreds   12 tens   15 ones

What You Write

$$
\begin{array}{r}
245 \\
\times \quad 3 \\
\hline
15 \\
120 \\
+\ 600 \\
\hline
735
\end{array}
$$

Partial Products

Those are big fish tanks! It will take 735 gallons of water to fill all three.

Do You Understand?

Convince Me! The array above for 3×245 was broken into three "simpler calculations."

What are these calculations? Why are they "simpler"?

Name

Guided Practice*

In **1** and **2**, use place-value blocks or draw pictures to build an array for each. Complete the calculation.

1. 2 × 124

$$\begin{array}{r} 124 \\ \times \quad 2 \\ \hline \end{array}$$

2. 3 × 218

$$\begin{array}{r} 218 \\ \times \quad 3 \\ \hline \end{array}$$

In **3**, use the array and the calculation.

3. Justify What calculations were used to find the partial products 12, 30, and 300?

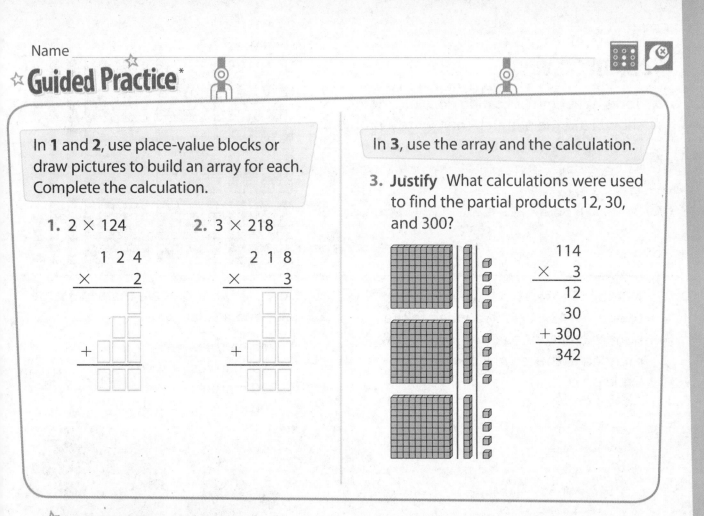

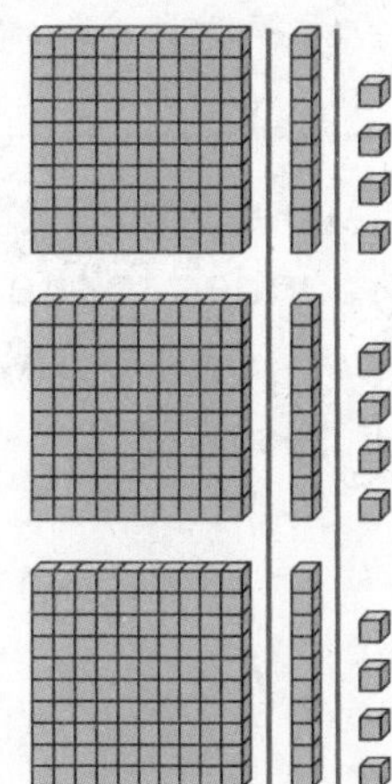

$$\begin{array}{r} 114 \\ \times \quad 3 \\ \hline 12 \\ 30 \\ +\ 300 \\ \hline 342 \end{array}$$

Independent Practice

In **4** and **5**, complete the calculation.

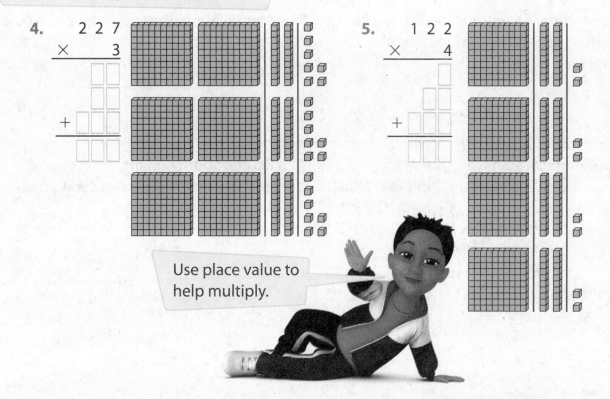

4.

$$\begin{array}{r} 227 \\ \times \quad 3 \\ \hline \end{array}$$

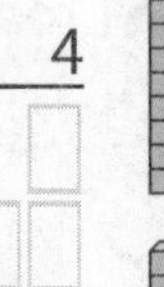

5.

$$\begin{array}{r} 122 \\ \times \quad 4 \\ \hline \end{array}$$

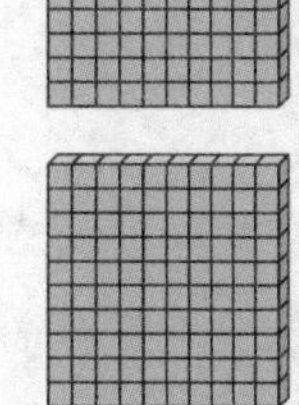

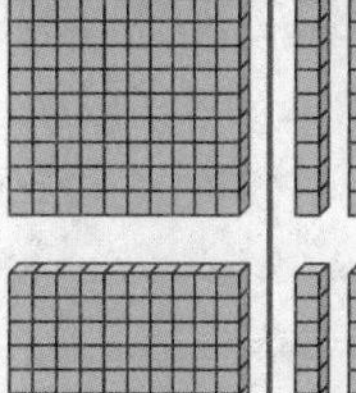

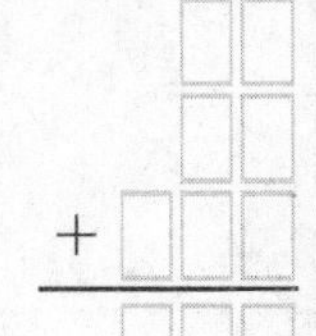

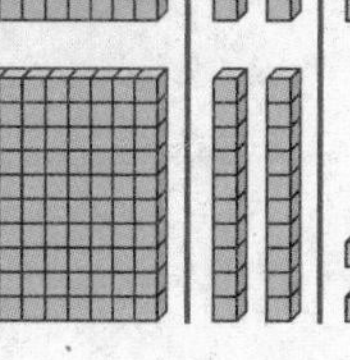

Use place value to help multiply.

*For another example, see Set A on page 267.

Problem Solving

6. **Tools** What multiplication does the model show? Find the product. Then write a problem that could be solved using this model.

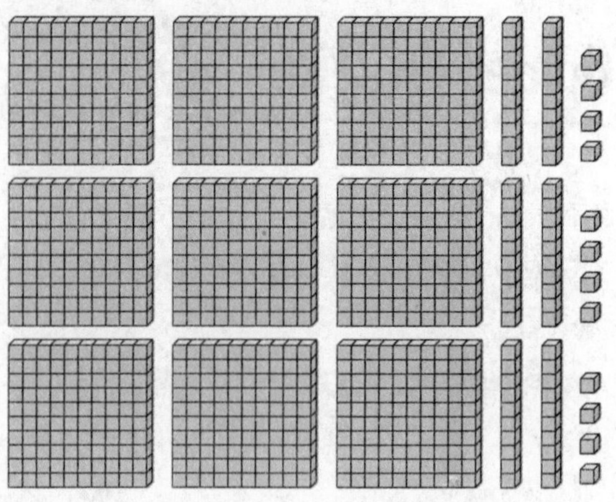

7. **Number Sense** Which would be greater—143,649,525 rounded to the hundred millions place or 105,417,932 rounded to the ten millions place? Explain.

8. How many marbles are there in 3 large bags and 4 small bags?

A 365 marbles
B 345 marbles
C 320 marbles
D 300 marbles

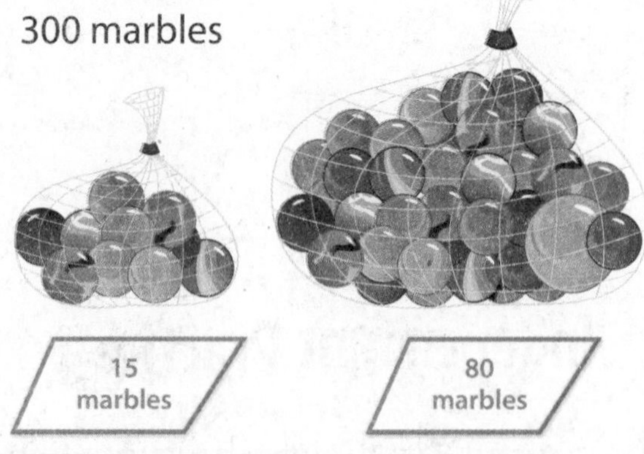

9. **Estimation** Carlos multiplied 3×108 to get 354. Is his answer reasonable? Explain.

10. **Mental Math** Describe how you would multiply 4×300 using mental math.

11. **Communicate** Sonya says that to multiply 824×3, you multiply 800×3, 20×3, and 4×3, and then add the products. Do you agree? Explain.

12. **Extend Your Thinking** How can the Distributive Property be used to find 4×875?

Name ______________________

Homework 4-1
Arrays and Using an Expanded Algorithm

Another Look!

You can use arrays of place-value blocks to multiply.

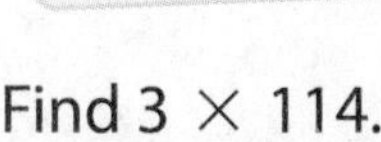

Find 3 × 114.

What You Show

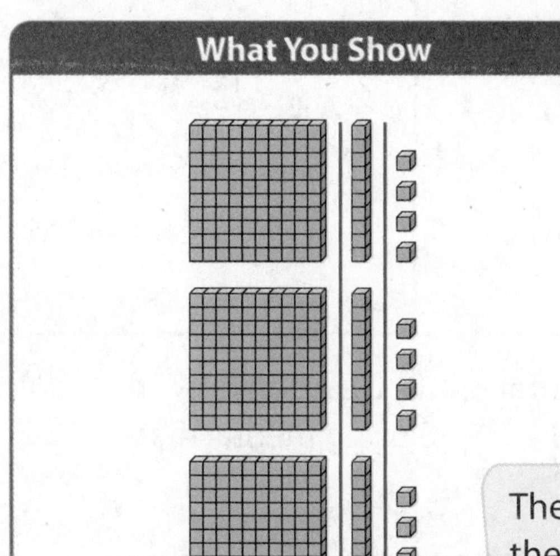

What You Write

$$
\begin{array}{rl}
114 & \\
\times\ \ 3 & \\
\hline
12 & 3 \times 4 \text{ ones} \\
30 & 3 \times 1 \text{ ten} \\
+\ 300 & 3 \times 1 \text{ hundred} \\
\hline
342 &
\end{array}
$$

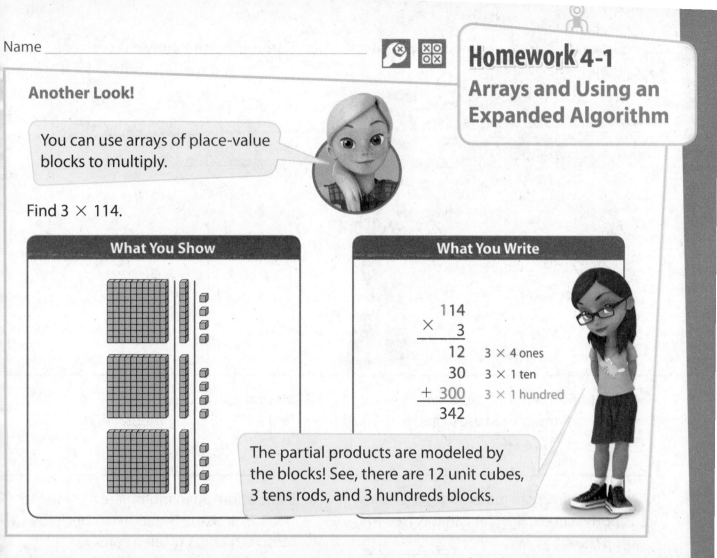

The partial products are modeled by the blocks! See, there are 12 unit cubes, 3 tens rods, and 3 hundreds blocks.

Leveled Practice In **1** through **4**, use place-value blocks or draw an array to help you complete each calculation.

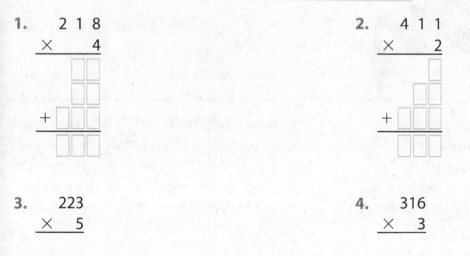

1.
$$
\begin{array}{r}
218 \\
\times\ \ \ 4 \\
\hline
\square\square \\
\square\square \\
+\ \square\square\square \\
\hline
\square\square\square
\end{array}
$$

2.
$$
\begin{array}{r}
411 \\
\times\ \ \ 2 \\
\hline
\square \\
\square\square \\
+\ \square\square\square \\
\hline
\square\square\square
\end{array}
$$

3.
$$
\begin{array}{r}
223 \\
\times\ \ \ 5 \\
\hline
\end{array}
$$

4.
$$
\begin{array}{r}
316 \\
\times\ \ \ 3 \\
\hline
\end{array}
$$

5. Which partial products and final product complete the calculation?

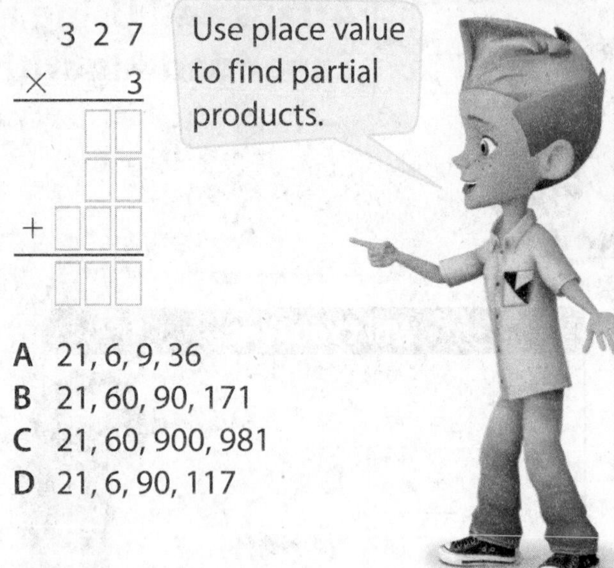

327
× 3
+
Use place value to find partial products.

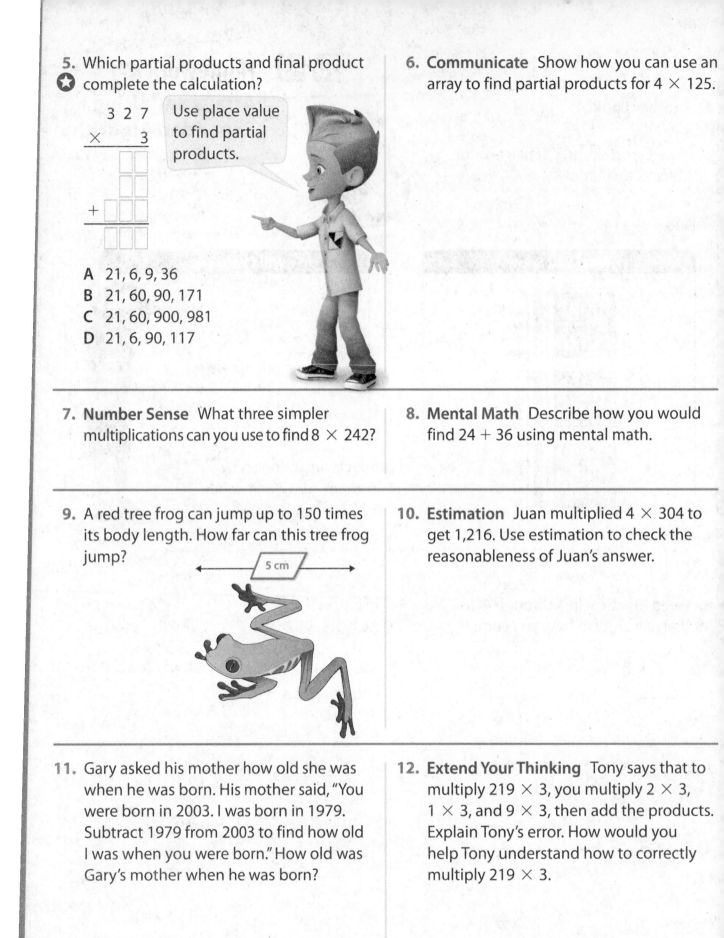

A 21, 6, 9, 36
B 21, 60, 90, 171
C 21, 60, 900, 981
D 21, 6, 90, 117

6. **Communicate** Show how you can use an array to find partial products for 4×125.

7. **Number Sense** What three simpler multiplications can you use to find 8×242?

8. **Mental Math** Describe how you would find $24 + 36$ using mental math.

9. A red tree frog can jump up to 150 times its body length. How far can this tree frog jump?

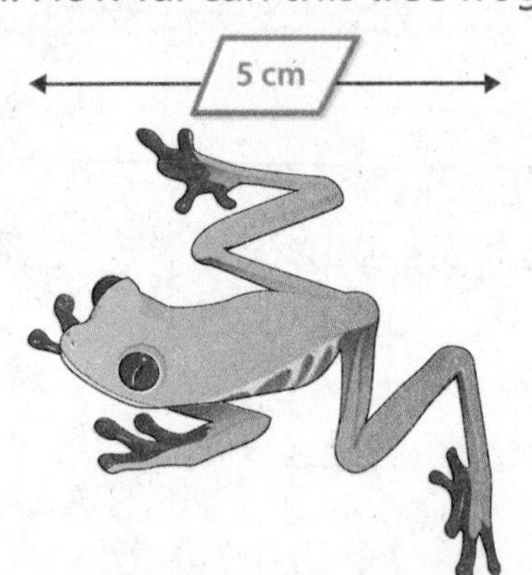

10. **Estimation** Juan multiplied 4×304 to get 1,216. Use estimation to check the reasonableness of Juan's answer.

11. Gary asked his mother how old she was when he was born. His mother said, "You were born in 2003. I was born in 1979. Subtract 1979 from 2003 to find how old I was when you were born." How old was Gary's mother when he was born?

12. **Extend Your Thinking** Tony says that to multiply 219×3, you multiply 2×3, 1×3, and 9×3, then add the products. Explain Tony's error. How would you help Tony understand how to correctly multiply 219×3.

Name

Solve & Share

There are 6 elementary schools in a school district. Each school has 412 students. How many students in all are in the district? ***Solve this problem any way you choose.***

Lesson 4-2
Connecting the Expanded and Standard Algorithms

TEKS 4.4D Use strategies and algorithms … to multiply.… Strategies may include mental math, partial products, and the commutative, associative, and distributive properties.
Mathematical Process Standards 4.1A, 4.1C, 4.1D, 4.1F, 4.1G

Digital Resources at SavvasTexas.com

Solve

Learn

Glossary

Check

Tools
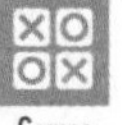
Games

You can **use tools.** How can you use paper and pencil to solve this problem? ***Show your work in the space above!***

Look Back!

Connect Which basic facts helped you solve this problem?

What Are Ways to Record Multiplication?

A

Professional baseballs are hand-sewn and have the number of double stitches shown below. How many double stitches are used to sew 6 baseballs?

Expanded algorithm

B Find 108 × 6. Multiply each place value to find the partial products. Then add the partial products.

```
   108
×    6
    48  ← Partial
     0  ← Products
+  600  ←
   648
```

Standard algorithm

C Find 108 × 6. Multiply each place value, beginning with the ones. Regroup if needed. Add any regrouped values to each place-value multiplication.

Multiply the ones.

```
   4
  108   48 ones
×   6   or 4 tens
    8   and 8 ones
```

Multiply the tens.

```
   4
  108   4 regrouped
×   6   tens added
   48   to 6 × 0 tens
```

Multiply the hundreds.

```
   4
  108
×   6
  648
```

648 double stitches are used to sew 6 baseballs.

Do You Understand?

Convince Me! Mara used the expanded algorithm shown at the right. Is she correct? Explain.

```
   124
×    4
   400
    80
+   16
   496
```

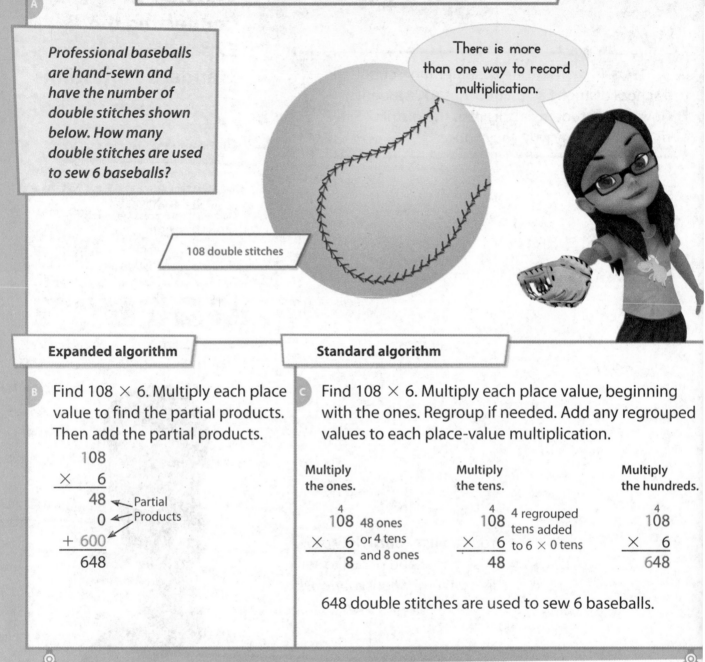

Name ____________________

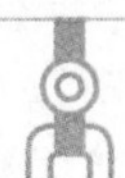

Guided Practice*

In **1** and **2**, find each product using the expanded algorithm. In **3** and **4**, use the standard algorithm.

1. 5 × 117

2. 3 × 243

3. $\begin{array}{r} 129 \\ \times \quad 3 \\ \hline \end{array}$

4. $\begin{array}{r} 288 \\ \times \quad 2 \\ \hline \end{array}$

5. Reason Sara used the standard algorithm to find the product of 374 and 3. Is she correct? Explain.

$\begin{array}{r} 374 \\ \times \quad 3 \\ \hline 1{,}112 \end{array}$

6. A box holds 215 cards. How many cards will 4 boxes hold?

Independent Practice

In **7** through **14**, find each product. Use either method.

7. $\begin{array}{r} 223 \\ \times \quad 5 \\ \hline \end{array}$

8. $\begin{array}{r} 418 \\ \times \quad 8 \\ \hline \end{array}$

9. $\begin{array}{r} 153 \\ \times \quad 3 \\ \hline \end{array}$

10. $\begin{array}{r} 237 \\ \times \quad 7 \\ \hline \end{array}$

11. 6 × 138

12. 7 × 226

13. 8 × 242

14. 5 × 164

For another example, see Set B on page 267.

Problem Solving

15. **Connect** A cat breeder has 6 Sphynx kittens and 7 Persian kittens for sale. If all 13 kittens sell, how much money will the breeder earn?

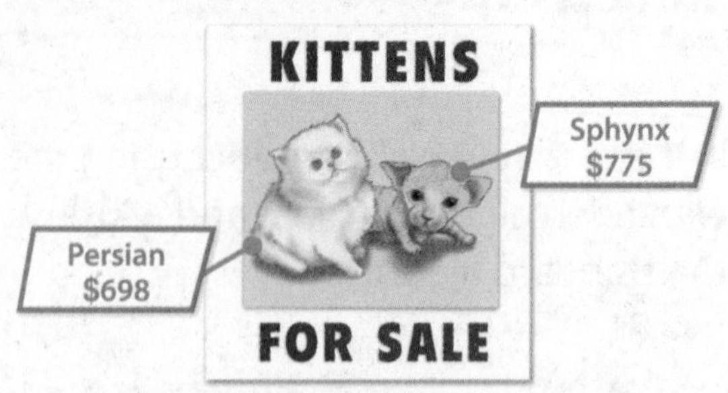

16. **Use a Strip Diagram** The strip diagram shows 4 groups of 225. Find 4 × 225.

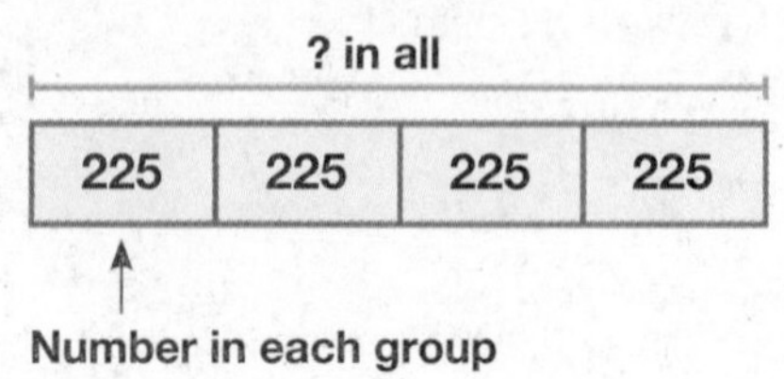

17. **Estimation** Estimate the sum of 382 + 295 + 301 by rounding each number to the nearest hundred.

18. There are usually 365 days in each year. Every fourth year is called a leap year and has one extra day in February. How many days are there in 8 years if two of the years are leap years?

A 2,482 days
B 2,842 days
C 2,920 days
D 2,922 days

19. A charter boat holds 60 adults and 50 children. How many people can go on 4 charter boat rides?

Remember, some problems have multiple steps to solve to answer the question asked.

20. **Extend Your Thinking** Patricia creates a design using 163 tiles. Then she doubles the number of tiles to make a second design. Her third design uses 3 times more tiles than the second design. How many tiles does she use in her third design? Explain how you found the answer.

Name ____________________

Homework 4-2
Connecting the Expanded and Standard Algorithms

Another Look!

There are different ways to find the product for 3 × 145.

Expanded Algorithm

Find the partial products.

$$\begin{array}{r} 145 \\ \times \quad 3 \\ \hline 15 \\ 120 \\ +\ 300 \\ \hline 435 \end{array}$$

Standard Algorithm

$$\begin{array}{r} \scriptstyle{1\,1} \\ 145 \\ \times \quad 3 \\ \hline 435 \end{array}$$

Multiply the ones. Regroup if needed. 15 ones = 1 ten 5 ones

Multiply the tens and hundreds. Regroup and add any extras if needed.

Leveled Practice In **1** and **2**, use the expanded algorithm to multiply.

1.

$$\begin{array}{r} 1\ 8\ 3 \\ \times \quad 4 \\ \hline \end{array}$$

☐☐ partial product
☐☐☐ partial product
+ ☐☐☐ partial product
☐☐☐ product

2.

$$\begin{array}{r} 2\ 5\ 7 \\ \times \quad 8 \\ \hline \end{array}$$

☐☐ partial product
☐☐☐ partial product
+ ☐,☐☐☐ partial product
☐,☐☐☐ product

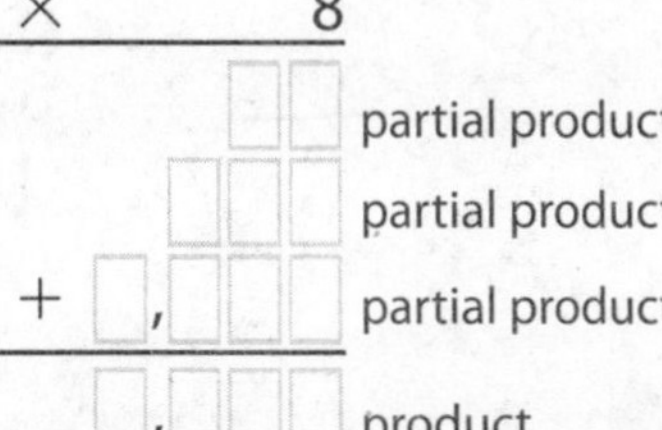

In **3** through **10**, use the standard algorithm to multiply.

3. $\begin{array}{r} 275 \\ \times \quad 6 \\ \hline \end{array}$

4. $\begin{array}{r} 164 \\ \times \quad 5 \\ \hline \end{array}$

5. $\begin{array}{r} 317 \\ \times \quad 9 \\ \hline \end{array}$

6. $\begin{array}{r} 393 \\ \times \quad 4 \\ \hline \end{array}$

7. 7 × 64

8. 96 × 3

9. 531 × 8

10. 5 × 211

11. **Draw a Picture** Complete the model showing how to use the Distributive Property to find the product of 7 and 16. Then write an expression showing how to find the product by using the Distributive Property.

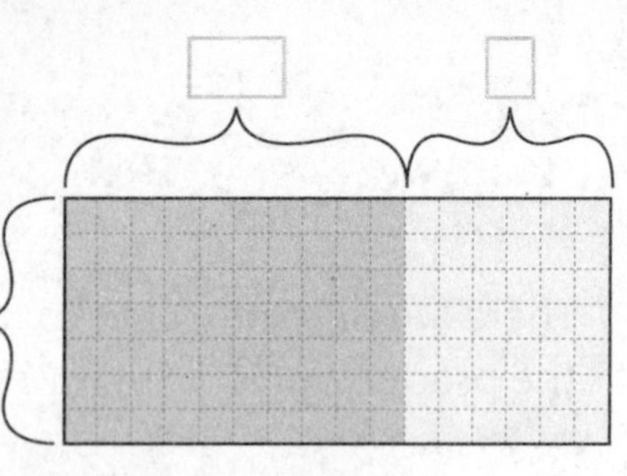

12. **Connect** Find 4 × 135 using the expanded algorithm and then the standard algorithm.

13. At his job, Mr. Martin works 160 hours each month. How many hours does he work in 3 months?

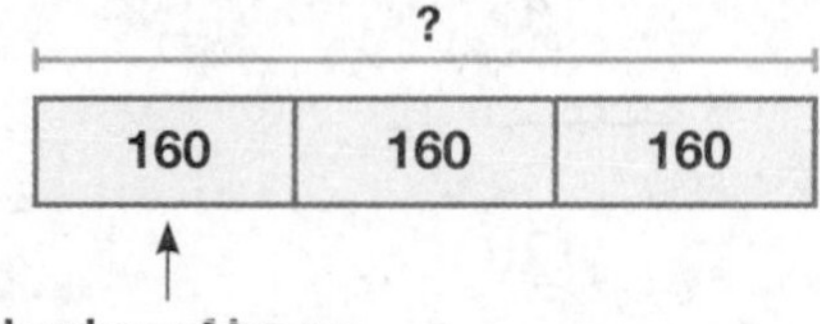

14. **Explain** Josh used the expanded algorithm to find the product for 9 × 239. His work is shown below. Is he correct? Explain.

$$\begin{array}{r} 239 \\ \times \quad 9 \\ \hline 1{,}800 \\ 270 \\ + \quad 81 \\ \hline 2{,}151 \end{array}$$

15. Deshawn multiplies 236 by 9. Which are the three partial products he could add to find the final product?

A 54, 270, and 1,800
B 54, 27, and 1,800
C 54, 270, and 180
D 54, 27, and 18

16. **Estimation** Dalton added 3,402 + 4,950 to get 8,352. Estimate the sum by rounding the addends to the nearest hundred. Is Dalton's sum reasonable? Explain.

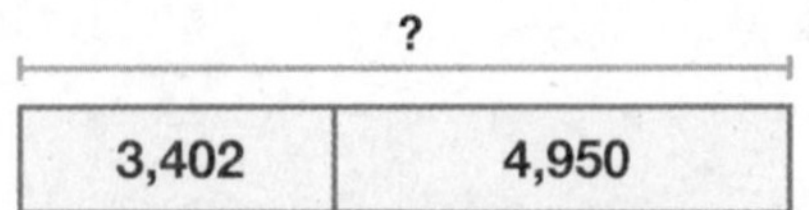

17. **Extend Your Thinking** Suppose you had to teach a friend how to use an algorithm to multiply. Which algorithm would you use, the expanded algorithm or the standard algorithm? Explain why.

Name ____________________

Lesson 4-3
Multiplying 2-Digit by 1-Digit Numbers

Solve & Share

Suppose a school ordered 7 boxes of books. There are 25 books in each box. How can you use paper and pencil to find how many books there are in all? How can you check that your answer is reasonable? ***Solve this problem any way you choose.***

TEKS 4.4D Use strategies and algorithms … to multiply…. Strategies may include mental math, partial products, and the commutative, associative, and distributive properties.
Mathematical Process Standards 4.1A, 4.1B, 4.1C, 4.1D, 4.1G

Digital Resources at SavvasTexas.com

Solve Learn Glossary Check Tools Games

You can **formulate a plan.** How do you use the standard algorithm? ***Show your work in the space below!***

Look Back!

Check for Reasonableness Why are you sure that your answer is reasonable?

What Is a Common Way to Record Multiplication?

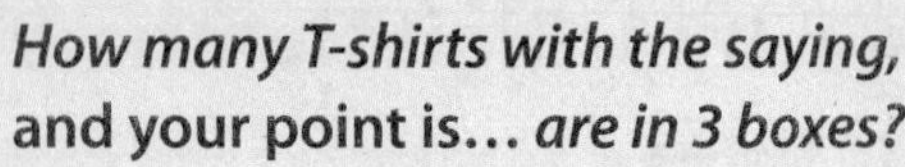

How many T-shirts with the saying, and your point is... are in 3 boxes?

Saying on T-shirt	Number of T-shirts per Box
Trust Me	30 T-shirts
and your point is...	26 T-shirts
I'm the princess that's why	24 T-shirts
Because I said so	12 T-shirts

Choose an operation. Multiply to join equal groups.

Use the standard algorithm.

Step 1

Multiply the ones. Regroup if needed.

$$\begin{array}{r} \scriptstyle 1 \\ 26 \\ \times\ \ 3 \\ \hline 8 \end{array}$$

Step 2

Multiply the tens. Add any extra tens.

$$\begin{array}{r} \scriptstyle 1 \\ 26 \\ \times\ \ 3 \\ \hline 78 \end{array}$$

There are 78 T-shirts in 3 boxes.

Step 3

Estimate to check reasonableness.

3×26 is about
$3 \times 25 = 75$

The answer is reasonable because 78 is close to 75.

Do You Understand?

Convince Me! A student did the calculation for 3 boxes of the T-shirts shown above and got the incorrect answer shown at the right.

What did this student do wrong? What is the correct answer?

Incorrect Answer

$$\begin{array}{r} \scriptstyle 1 \\ 26 \\ \times\ \ 3 \\ \hline 98 \end{array}$$

Name ____________________

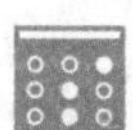

Another Example

Mrs. Stockton ordered 8 boxes of T-shirts with the saying, *I'm the princess that's why.* How many of the T-shirts did she order?

Step 1

$$\begin{array}{r} \overset{3}{2}4 \\ \times\ 8 \\ \hline 2 \end{array}$$

8 × 4 = 32 ones
Regroup 32 ones as 3 tens 2 ones.

Step 2

$$\begin{array}{r} \overset{3}{2}4 \\ \times\ 8 \\ \hline 192 \end{array}$$

8 × 2 tens = 16 tens
16 tens + 3 tens = 19 tens or 1 hundred 9 tens

Mrs. Stockton ordered 192 T-shirts.

The standard algorithm is very useful once you understand why it works.

Guided Practice*

In **1** through **4**, find each product. Estimate to check reasonableness.

1. $\begin{array}{r} 15 \\ \times\ 5 \\ \hline \end{array}$

2. $\begin{array}{r} 34 \\ \times\ 7 \\ \hline \end{array}$

3. 5 × 70

4. 5 × 78

5. Estimation Explain how you would estimate the answer in Exercise 2.

6. Reason Explain how the answer to Exercise 3 can be used to find the answer to Exercise 4.

Independent Practice

In **7** through **14**, find each product. Estimate to check reasonableness.

7. $\begin{array}{r} 12 \\ \times\ 6 \\ \hline \end{array}$

8. $\begin{array}{r} 18 \\ \times\ 7 \\ \hline \end{array}$

9. $\begin{array}{r} 28 \\ \times\ 3 \\ \hline \end{array}$

10. $\begin{array}{r} 43 \\ \times\ 4 \\ \hline \end{array}$

11. 72 × 5

12. 49 × 8

13. 3 × 24

14. 3 × 79

*For another example, see Set C on page 267.

Problem Solving

15. Use the diagram to the right. The Purple Tower Hotel has five times as many floors as the Green Tree Hotel. How many floors does the Purple Tower Hotel have?

    A 60 floors
    B 70 floors
    C 105 floors
    D 1,010 floors

16. **Draw a Picture** Last year, Anthony's grandmother gave him 49 old coins to start a coin collection. Now Anthony has six times as many coins in his collection. How many coins does Anthony have? Complete the strip diagram to show your work.

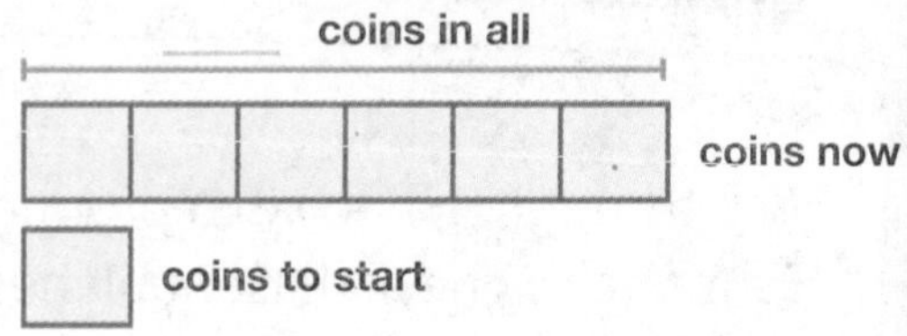

17. Katie made 24 rag dolls. She gave away 8 of them as gifts. Which expression shows the number of rag dolls Katie had left?

    A $24 + 8$
    B 24×8
    C $24 - 8$
    D $24 \div 8$

18. **Personal Financial Literacy** Reese and Wendy need to save \$500 for vacation. They started their savings with \$57. Now they have 7 times that much. How much more money do they need?

19. **Justify** Nan has 15 photos. She says her album will hold 9 times as many photos as she has. She takes 90 photos at her cousin's wedding. Explain whether those photos fit in her album.

20. **Extend Your Thinking** A motor scooter's gas tank holds 3 gallons of gas and gets 87 miles per gallon. A car's gas tank holds 9 gallons of gas and gets 42 miles per gallon. Which vehicle will travel farther on a full tank of gas? How much farther?

Name ________________________________

Homework 4-3
Multiplying 2-Digit by 1-Digit Numbers

Another Look!

Here is how to multiply a 2-digit number by a 1-digit number using paper and pencil.

Find 3 × 24.	**What You Think**	**What You Write**
Step 1 Multiply the ones. Regroup if necessary.	3 × 4 = 12 ones Regroup as 1 ten 2 ones.	$\begin{array}{r} {}^{1}\\ 24 \\ \times\ 3 \\ \hline 2 \end{array}$
Step 2 Multiply the tens. Add any extra tens.	3 × 2 tens = 6 tens 6 tens + 1 ten = 7 tens	$\begin{array}{r} {}^{1}\\ 24 \\ \times\ 3 \\ \hline 72 \end{array}$

Leveled Practice In **1** through **12**, find each product. Estimate to check reasonableness.

1. $\begin{array}{r} 13 \\ \times\ 3 \\ \hline \end{array}$

2. $\begin{array}{r} 17 \\ \times\ 7 \\ \hline \end{array}$

3. $\begin{array}{r} 24 \\ \times\ 5 \\ \hline \end{array}$

4. $\begin{array}{r} 48 \\ \times\ 8 \\ \hline \end{array}$

5. $\begin{array}{r} 62 \\ \times\ 6 \\ \hline \end{array}$

6. $\begin{array}{r} 36 \\ \times\ 5 \\ \hline \end{array}$

7. $\begin{array}{r} 88 \\ \times\ 5 \\ \hline \end{array}$

8. $\begin{array}{r} 52 \\ \times\ 8 \\ \hline \end{array}$

9. 8 × 92

10. 5 × 64

11. 19 × 8

12. 78 × 2

In **13** and **14**, use the table to the right.

13. What is the average length fingernails will grow in 12 months?

A 60 mm
B 50 mm
C 40 mm
D 5 mm

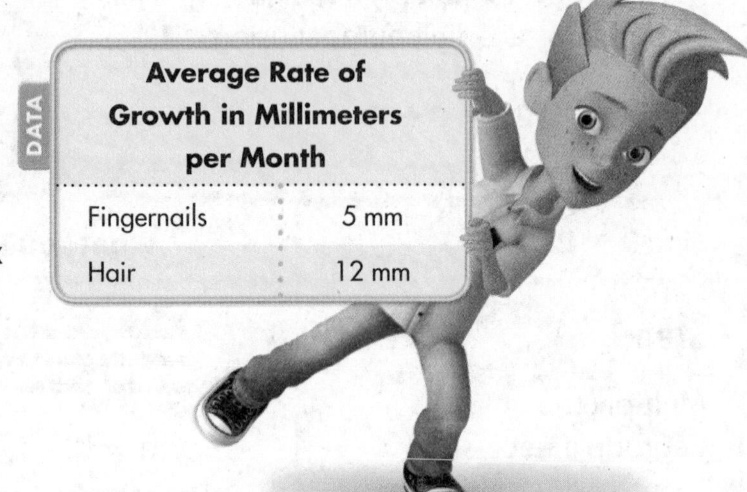

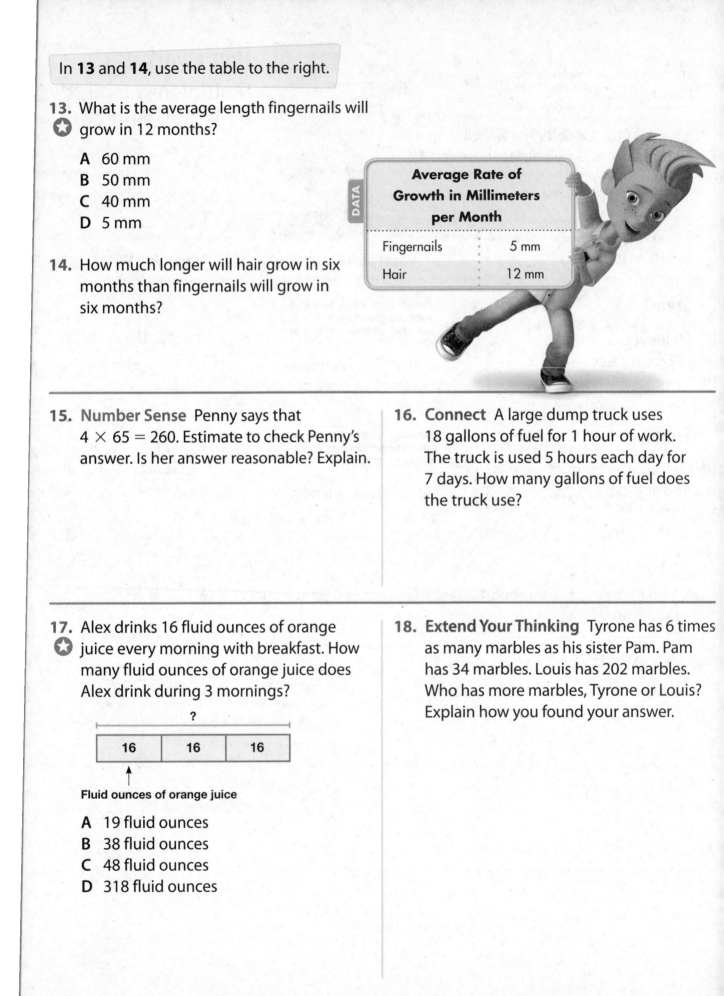

Average Rate of Growth in Millimeters per Month	
Fingernails	5 mm
Hair	12 mm

14. How much longer will hair grow in six months than fingernails will grow in six months?

15. **Number Sense** Penny says that $4 \times 65 = 260$. Estimate to check Penny's answer. Is her answer reasonable? Explain.

16. **Connect** A large dump truck uses 18 gallons of fuel for 1 hour of work. The truck is used 5 hours each day for 7 days. How many gallons of fuel does the truck use?

17. Alex drinks 16 fluid ounces of orange juice every morning with breakfast. How many fluid ounces of orange juice does Alex drink during 3 mornings?

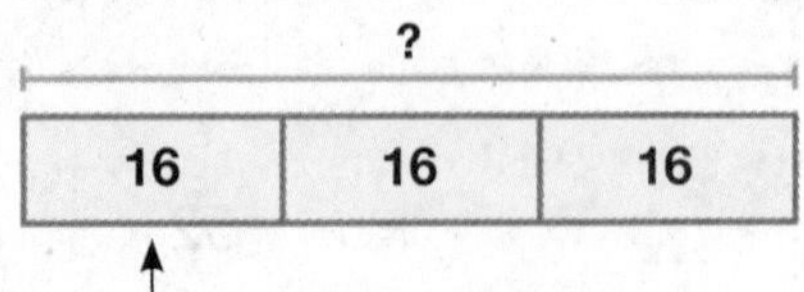

A 19 fluid ounces
B 38 fluid ounces
C 48 fluid ounces
D 318 fluid ounces

18. **Extend Your Thinking** Tyrone has 6 times as many marbles as his sister Pam. Pam has 34 marbles. Louis has 202 marbles. Who has more marbles, Tyrone or Louis? Explain how you found your answer.

Name ______________________________

Bonnie has 4 jars that she wants to fill with pennies. If she puts 231 pennies in each jar, how many pennies does she have all together? ***Solve this problem any way you choose.***

Lesson 4-4

Multiplying 3-Digit by 1-Digit Numbers

TEKS 4.4D Use strategies and algorithms … to multiply…. Strategies may include mental math, partial products, and the commutative, associative, and distributive properties. **Mathematical Process Standards** 4.1B, 4.1C, 4.1D, 4.1F, 4.1G

Digital Resources at SavvasTexas.com

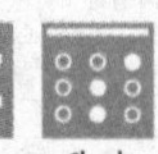

Solve Learn Glossary Check Tools Games

You can **connect ideas** by thinking about the methods you have used to multiply 2-digit numbers. ***Show your work in the space below!***

Look Back!

Number Sense When did you need to regroup?

How Can You Multiply 3-Digit Numbers by 1-Digit Numbers?

A-Z

A

Juan guessed that the larger bottle had 3 times as many pennies as the smaller bottle. What was Juan's guess?

Choose an operation. Multiply to find "3 times as many."

You can use the standard algorithm to multiply hundreds the same way you use it to multiply tens.

Use the standard algorithm.

B

Step 1

Multiply the ones.
Regroup if needed.

$$\begin{array}{r} {}^{1} \\ 264 \\ \times 3 \\ \hline 2 \end{array}$$

3×4 ones $= 12$ ones or
1 ten 2 ones

C

Step 2

Multiply the tens.
Add any extra tens.
Regroup if needed.

$$\begin{array}{r} {}^{1\,1} \\ 264 \\ \times 3 \\ \hline 92 \end{array}$$

$(3 \times 6$ tens$) + 1$ ten $= 19$ tens or
1 hundred 9 tens

D

Step 3

Multiply the hundreds.
Add any extra hundreds.

$$\begin{array}{r} {}^{1\,1} \\ 264 \\ \times 3 \\ \hline 792 \end{array}$$

$(3 \times 2$ hundreds$) + 1$ hundred
$= 7$ hundreds

Juan's guess was 792 pennies.

Do You Understand?

Convince Me! Calle said, "Here's another way to show the problem above."

Is she correct? Explain what she did.

Calle's Way

$$\begin{array}{rrr} 100 & 10 & \\ 200 & 60 & 4 \\ \times & & 3 \\ \hline 700 & 90 & 2 \\ & 792 & \end{array}$$

Name ______________________________________

Guided Practice*

In **1** through **4**, find each product. Estimate to check for reasonableness.

1. 519 × 4

2. 378 × 2

3. 138 × 5

4. 746 × 3

5. Reason In Exercise 2, 2 × 7 tens is 14 tens. Why is a 5 recorded in the tens place of the product?

6. A band performed 4 sold-out shows. All 730 seats were filled for each show. How many people saw the 4 shows?

Independent Practice

In **7** through **15**, find each product.

7. 423 × 2

8. 942 × 4

9. 271 × 3

10. 159 × 5

11. 125 × 2

12. 196 × 3

13. 265 × 4

14. 129 × 5

15. 784 × 9

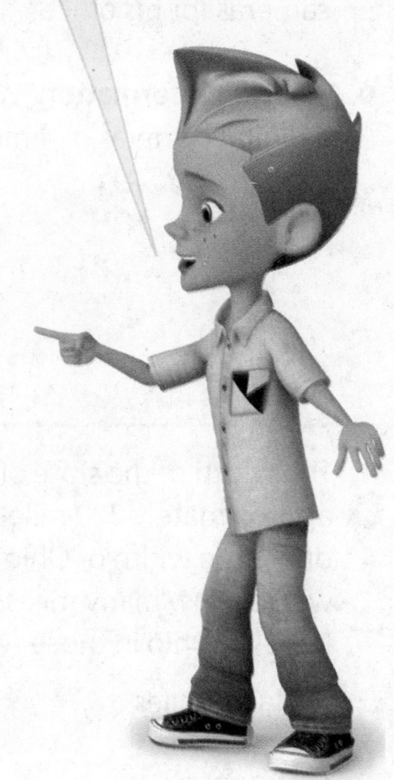
Estimate to check your answers for reasonableness.

*For another example, see Set D on page 268.

Problem Solving

In **16** through **18**, use the information in the pictures below to find the weight of each animal.

16. Horse **17.** Rhino **18.** Elephant

Elephant:
Weighs 9 times as much as the bear

19. Estimation About how much did Dr. Sims spend if he bought 3 digital cameras for his office?

20. Analyze Information Which costs more, 2 digital cameras or 4 mobile phones? Explain.

DATA

Electronics Sale	
Mobile Phone	$135
Digital Camera	$295
Laptop Computer	$1,075
Flat-Screen TV	$1,650

21. The width of the state of Ohio is approximately 220 miles. A truck driver drove the width of Ohio 5 times in two weeks. How many miles did the driver travel in Ohio in those two weeks?

A 1,000 miles
B 1,100 miles
C 1,200 miles
D 1,300 miles

22. Extend Your Thinking Do you think you could use the standard algorithm for multiplication to multiply a 4-digit number by a 1-digit number? Explain.

Name ______________________

Homework 4-4
Multiplying 3-Digit by 1-Digit Numbers

Another Look!

The steps below show how to multiply 3-digit numbers by 1-digit numbers.

Step 1	Step 2	Step 3
Multiply the ones. Regroup if necessary.	Multiply the tens. Add any extra tens. Regroup if necessary.	Multiply the hundreds. Add any extra hundreds.
$\begin{array}{r} {}^{1} \\ 154 \\ \times\ 4 \\ \hline 6 \end{array}$	$\begin{array}{r} {}^{2\,1} \\ 154 \\ \times\ 4 \\ \hline 16 \end{array}$	$\begin{array}{r} {}^{2\,1} \\ 154 \\ \times\ 4 \\ \hline 616 \end{array}$

In **1** through **12**, find the product.

Remember to regroup if necessary.

1. $\begin{array}{r} 185 \\ \times\ 4 \\ \hline \end{array}$ **2.** $\begin{array}{r} 517 \\ \times\ 4 \\ \hline \end{array}$ **3.** $\begin{array}{r} 741 \\ \times\ 3 \\ \hline \end{array}$

4. $\begin{array}{r} 413 \\ \times\ 6 \\ \hline \end{array}$ **5.** $\begin{array}{r} 625 \\ \times\ 6 \\ \hline \end{array}$ **6.** $\begin{array}{r} 812 \\ \times\ 5 \\ \hline \end{array}$

7. $\begin{array}{r} 711 \\ \times\ 8 \\ \hline \end{array}$ **8.** $\begin{array}{r} 381 \\ \times\ 5 \\ \hline \end{array}$ **9.** $\begin{array}{r} 352 \\ \times\ 3 \\ \hline \end{array}$

10. $\begin{array}{r} 482 \\ \times\ 8 \\ \hline \end{array}$ **11.** $\begin{array}{r} 385 \\ \times\ 4 \\ \hline \end{array}$ **12.** $\begin{array}{r} 632 \\ \times\ 5 \\ \hline \end{array}$

13. Extend Your Thinking Suppose Player A scores the same number of runs for 8 seasons, Player B scores the same number of runs for 9 seasons, and Player C scores the same number of runs for 7 seasons. Which player scores the most runs?

DATA

2013 Baseball Statistics

Player	Runs Scored
A	128
B	113
C	142

---

14. If Chuck's Sports sells 124 fishing poles each month, how many fishing poles will be sold in four months?

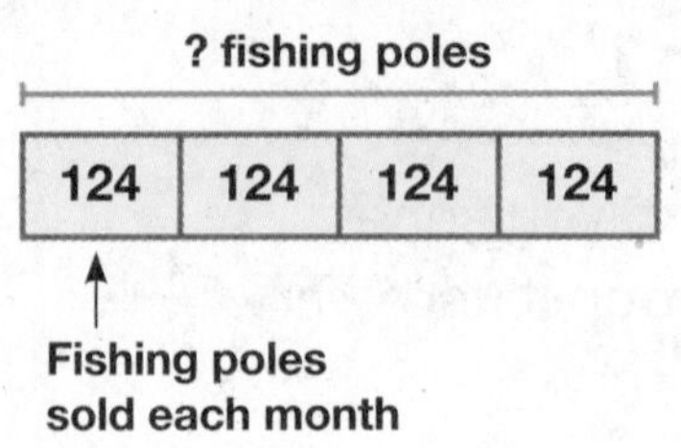

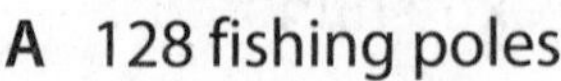

A 128 fishing poles
B 372 fishing poles
C 486 fishing poles
D 496 fishing poles

---

15. A pet store has 9 large fish tanks. In each fish tank, there are 423 fish. How many fish are in all the fish tanks?

A 3,600 fish
B 3,687 fish
C 3,807 fish
D 3,825 fish

16. Math and Science Old Faithful may be the most famous geyser in Yellowstone National Park. A 2-minute eruption is typically followed by an inactive interval of about 50 minutes. How many minutes would it take this eruption pattern to occur 7 times?

---

17. Explain Martin multiplied 423 by 7 and says that the product is 2,841. Is Martin correct? If not, explain what mistake he may have made and give the correct answer.

18. Mental Math How can you use the Distributive Property and mental math to find 8×320?

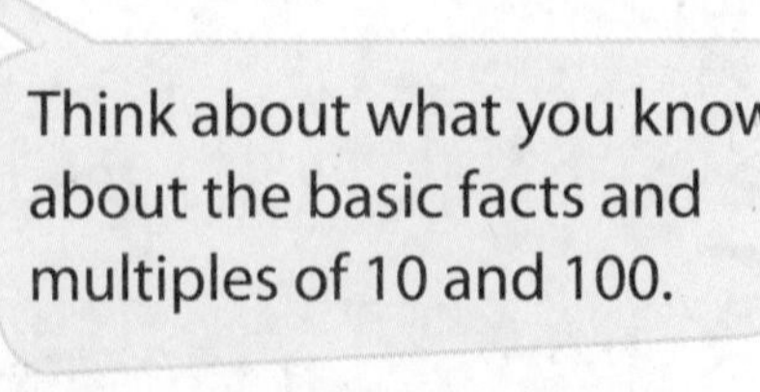

Think about what you know about the basic facts and multiples of 10 and 100.

Name

Solve & Share

A floor pattern contains 5,835 tiles. The same pattern is used 7 times. How many tiles are used all together? ***Solve this problem any way you choose.***

You can **reason.** How are 3-digit numbers like 4-digit numbers? How are they different? ***Show your work in the space below!***

Lesson 4-5
Multiplying 4-Digit by 1-Digit Numbers

TEKS 4.4D Use strategies and algorithms ... to multiply.... Strategies may include mental math, partial products, and the commutative, associative, and distributive properties.
Mathematical Process Standards 4.1A, 4.1B, 4.1C, 4.1D, 4.1G

Digital Resources at SavvasTexas.com

Solve

Learn

Glossary
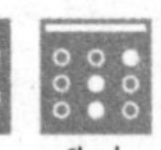
Check

Tools
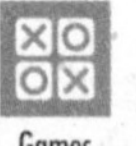
Games

Look Back!

Number Sense How many times did you regroup?

How Can You Multiply 4-Digit Numbers by 1-Digit Numbers?

A wildlife center budgets the amount shown below for food and veterinary expenses each month. What is the budget for food and veterinary expenses for a 3-month period?

You can use the standard algorithm to multiply thousands the same way you use it to multiply hundreds or tens.

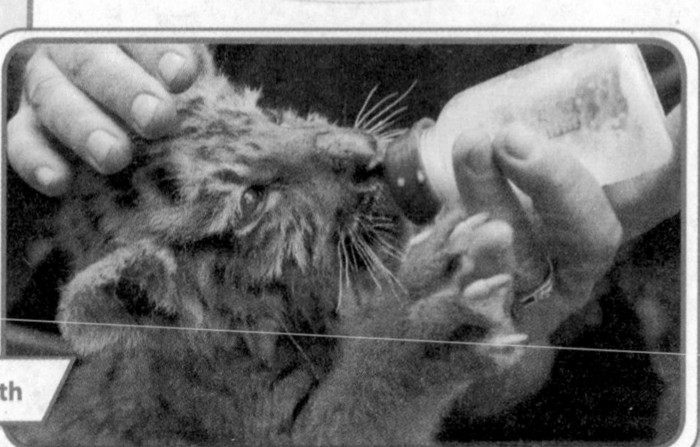

$2,746 each month

Use the standard algorithm.

Find 3 × 2,746.

Step 1

Multiply the ones.
Regroup if necessary.

$$\begin{array}{r} {\scriptstyle 1} \\ 2{,}746 \\ \times \quad 3 \\ \hline 8 \end{array}$$

Step 2

Multiply the tens.
Add any extra tens.
Regroup if necessary.

$$\begin{array}{r} {\scriptstyle 1\,1} \\ 2{,}746 \\ \times \quad 3 \\ \hline 38 \end{array}$$

Step 3

Multiply the hundreds.
Add any extra hundreds.
Regroup if necessary.

$$\begin{array}{r} {\scriptstyle 2\,1\,1} \\ 2{,}746 \\ \times \quad 3 \\ \hline 238 \end{array}$$

Step 4

Multiply the thousands.
Add any extra thousands.
Regroup if necessary.

$$\begin{array}{r} {\scriptstyle 2\,1\,1} \\ 2{,}746 \\ \times \quad 3 \\ \hline 8{,}238 \end{array}$$

The budget for food and veterinary expenses for 3 months is $8,238.

Do You Understand?

Convince Me! For the problem above, how can you use estimation to decide if the product is reasonable?

Guided Practice*

In **1** through **4**, use the standard algorithm to find the products.

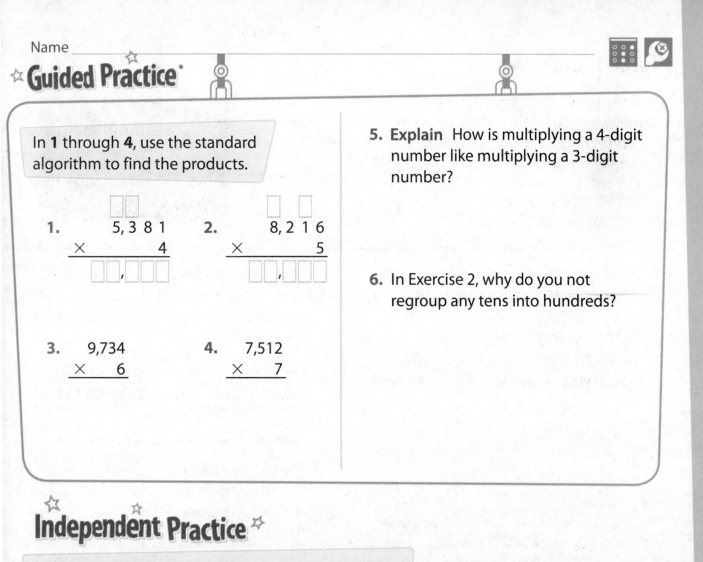

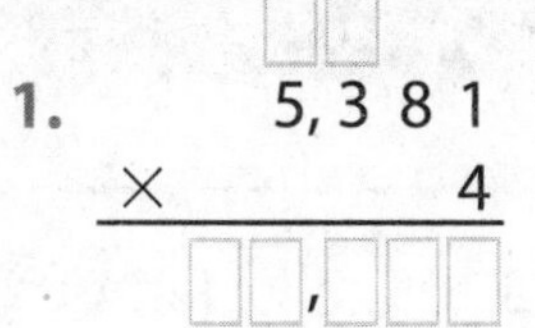

1. 5,381 × 4 = ☐☐,☐☐☐

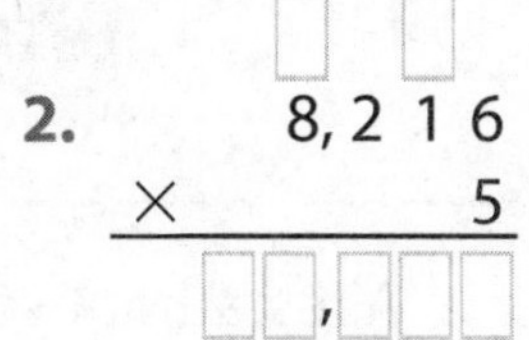

2. 8,216 × 5 = ☐☐,☐☐☐

3. 9,734 × 6

4. 7,512 × 7

5. Explain How is multiplying a 4-digit number like multiplying a 3-digit number?

6. In Exercise 2, why do you not regroup any tens into hundreds?

Independent Practice

Leveled Practice In **7** through **18**, find each product.

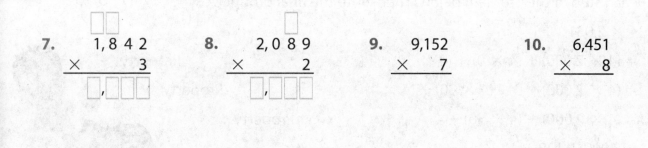

7. 1,842 × 3 = ☐,☐☐☐

8. 2,089 × 2 = ☐,☐☐☐

9. 9,152 × 7

10. 6,451 × 8

11. 3,287 × 1

12. 8,721 × 6

13. 1,428 × 3

14. 3,756 × 9

15. 6,912 × 4

16. 7,856 × 8

17. 4,005 × 5

18. 1,624 × 2

*For another example, see Set E on page 268.

Problem Solving

19. **Connect** There are 5,280 feet in 1 mile. How many feet farther is it to Pickens Corner than Hobbs Landing? Explain how you found your answer.

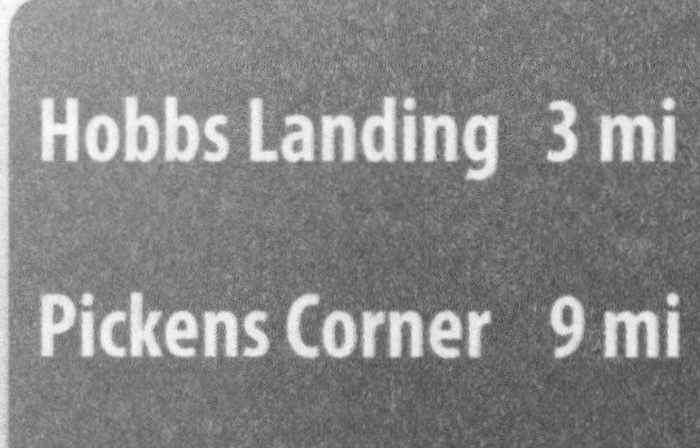

20. **Justify** A semi-truck trailer has a load capacity of 25,900 pounds. A trucker is asked to haul 5 crates on the trailer. Each crate weighs 4,450 pounds. Can the trucker haul all 5 crates in one load? Explain your answer and show your work.

21. A restaurant sells 3,125 of its famous veggie burgers each month. At this rate, how many veggie burgers will be sold in 6 months?

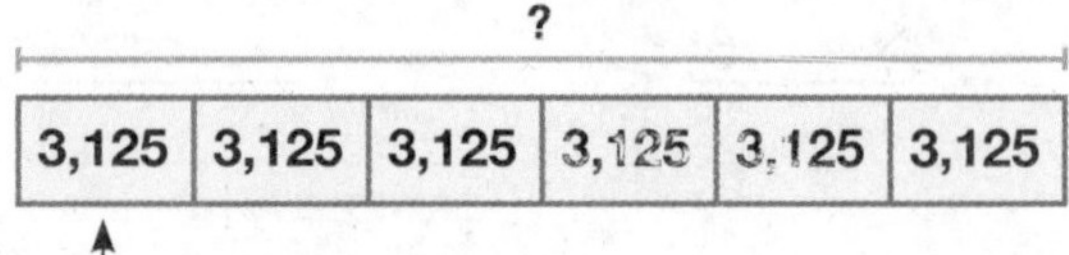

A 18,750 burgers
B 18,620 burgers
C 18,525 burgers
D 18,125 burgers

22. **Communicate** Name the property of multiplication used in each step of the problem below. Then write the final product.

Look at what math has been done to decide which property is used.

$4 \times 2{,}031$

$= (4 \times 2{,}000) + (4 \times 0) + (4 \times 30) + (4 \times 1)$ ______________ Property

$= (4 \times 2{,}000) + 0 + (4 \times 30) + (4 \times 1)$ ______________ Property

$= (4 \times 2{,}000) + (4 \times 30) + 4$ ______________ Property

$= 8{,}000 + 120 + 4 =$ ______________

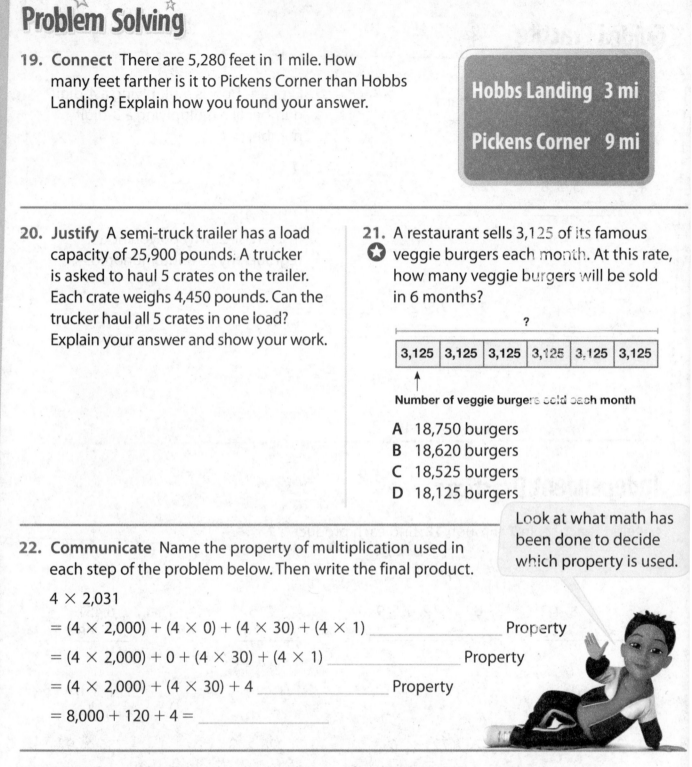

23. **Extend Your Thinking** The driving distance from Boston, MA, to Colorado Springs, CO, and back again is 4,084 miles. A salesperson has already made the trip back and forth twice. A salesperson may drive up to 12,500 miles each month. Can she make the trip again and remain below the monthly miles allowed? If so, how many miles will she have left for the month?

Name ____________________

Homework 4-5
Multiplying 4-Digit by 1-Digit Numbers

Another Look!

The steps below show how to multiply greater numbers.

Keep your regrouped place values neatly in place.

		Example
Step 1	Multiply the ones. Regroup if necessary.	$\begin{array}{r} {}^{2} \\ 1{,}214 \\ \times \quad 7 \\ \hline 8 \end{array}$
Step 2	Multiply the tens. Add any extra tens. Regroup if necessary.	$\begin{array}{r} {}^{2} \\ 1{,}214 \\ \times \quad 7 \\ \hline 98 \end{array}$
Step 3	Multiply the hundreds. Add any extra hundreds. Regroup if necessary.	$\begin{array}{r} {}^{1\ \ 2} \\ 1{,}214 \\ \times \quad 7 \\ \hline 498 \end{array}$
Step 4	Multiply the thousands. Add any extra thousands.	$\begin{array}{r} {}^{1\ \ 2} \\ 1{,}214 \\ \times \quad 7 \\ \hline 8{,}498 \end{array}$

In **1** through **8**, find the product.

1. $\begin{array}{r} 1{,}324 \\ \times \quad 2 \\ \hline \end{array}$

2. $\begin{array}{r} 5{,}618 \\ \times \quad 7 \\ \hline \end{array}$

3. $\begin{array}{r} 4{,}810 \\ \times \quad 3 \\ \hline \end{array}$

4. $\begin{array}{r} 9{,}018 \\ \times \quad 6 \\ \hline \end{array}$

5. $\begin{array}{r} 2{,}721 \\ \times \quad 4 \\ \hline \end{array}$

6. $\begin{array}{r} 7{,}183 \\ \times \quad 2 \\ \hline \end{array}$

7. $\begin{array}{r} 8{,}734 \\ \times \quad 5 \\ \hline \end{array}$

8. $\begin{array}{r} 6{,}451 \\ \times \quad 7 \\ \hline \end{array}$

9. Bailey rode Coaster B four times. How many feet did she ride?

10. **Analyze Information** Janna rode each of the four roller coasters listed in the table twice. How many feet of roller coaster did she ride?

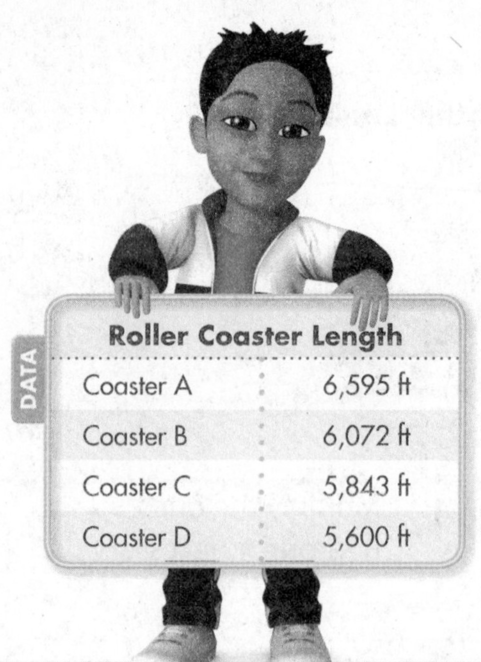

Roller Coaster Length	
Coaster A	6,595 ft
Coaster B	6,072 ft
Coaster C	5,843 ft
Coaster D	5,600 ft

11. The Appalachian Trail is 2,174 miles long. If a group of 7 people hike the entire trail, how many combined miles do they hike?

A 14,851 miles
B 14,868 miles
C 15,198 miles
D 15,218 miles

12. **Estimation** Use the information in Exercise 10. About how long would a trail be if it were 3 times the length of the Appalachian Trail?

?

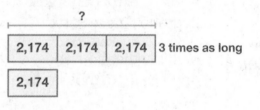

2,174	2,174	2,174	3 times as long

2,174

13. **Extend Your Thinking** Describe two different ways to solve the problem below.

Each wheel on a roller coaster turns around 3,999 times during the ride. Each ride lasts 4 minutes. How many times will each wheel turn around during 2 rides?

14. **Communicate** Explain the mistakes in the solution below. Show the correct solution.

$$\begin{array}{r} 1{,}892 \\ \times \quad 4 \\ \hline 8 \\ 36 \\ 320 \\ +\,4{,}000 \\ \hline 4{,}364 \end{array}$$

Name

Solve & Share A cineplex contains 4 movie theaters. Each theater can seat 312 people. How many people can the cineplex seat in all? ***Solve this problem any way you choose.***

Lesson 4-6
More Multiplying by 1-Digit Numbers

TEKS 4.4D Use strategies and algorithms ... to multiply.... Strategies may include mental math, partial products, and the commutative, associative, and distributive properties. Also, 4.4H, 4.8C. **Mathematical Process Standards** 4.1A, 4.1B, 4.1C, 4.1G

Digital Resources at SavvasTexas.com

Solve

Learn

Glossary

Check

Tools
Games

You can **check for reasonableness.** Is your estimate close to the answer you found? ***Show your work in the space above!***

Look Back!

Number Sense If the cineplex had 8 movie theaters with 312 seats each, how many seats would the cineplex have?

What Are the Steps to Record Multiplication?

A

Paying for pothole damage to cars can be costly. The table shows some of the repair costs.

Use the table to answer each question.

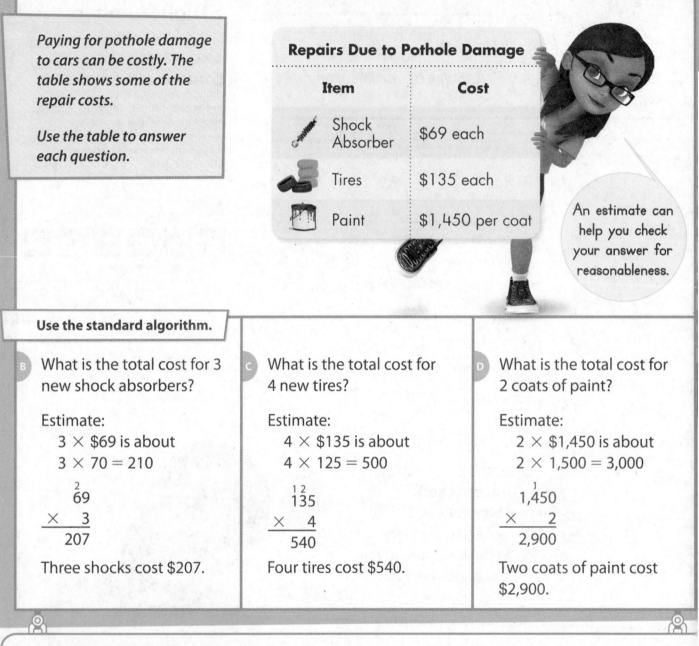

Repairs Due to Pothole Damage

Item	Cost
 Shock Absorber	\$69 each
 Tires	\$135 each
Paint	\$1,450 per coat

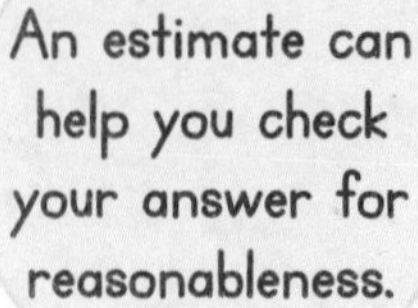

An estimate can help you check your answer for reasonableness.

Use the standard algorithm.

B What is the total cost for 3 new shock absorbers?

Estimate:
3 × \$69 is about
3 × 70 = 210

$$\begin{array}{r} \scriptstyle 2 \\ 69 \\ \times \quad 3 \\ \hline 207 \end{array}$$

Three shocks cost \$207.

C What is the total cost for 4 new tires?

Estimate:
4 × \$135 is about
4 × 125 = 500

$$\begin{array}{r} \scriptstyle 1\,2 \\ 135 \\ \times \quad 4 \\ \hline 540 \end{array}$$

Four tires cost \$540.

D What is the total cost for 2 coats of paint?

Estimate:
2 × \$1,450 is about
2 × 1,500 = 3,000

$$\begin{array}{r} \scriptstyle 1 \\ 1{,}450 \\ \times \quad 2 \\ \hline 2{,}900 \end{array}$$

Two coats of paint cost \$2,900.

Do You Understand?

Convince Me! Find each product at the right. Does the multiplication process change as the value of one factor increases?

$$\begin{array}{r} 21 \\ \times \; 4 \\ \hline \end{array} \qquad \begin{array}{r} 321 \\ \times \; 4 \\ \hline \end{array} \qquad \begin{array}{r} \scriptstyle 1 \\ 4{,}321 \\ \times \quad 4 \\ \hline \end{array}$$

Name

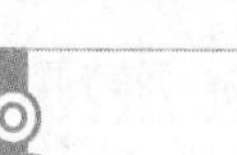

Guided Practice*

In **1** through **6**, find the product.

1. $\begin{array}{r} 74 \\ \times\ \ 6 \\ \hline \end{array}$

2. $\begin{array}{r} 819 \\ \times\ \ \ 5 \\ \hline \end{array}$

3. 4 × 309

4. 3 × 175

5. 8 × 218

6. 6 × 1,741

7. A road repair crew can usually fix 825 potholes each week. How many potholes can they fix in 6 weeks?

8. Explain A tire shop sells 3 tires at $175 each and includes a fourth tire for free. Is this more or less expensive than buying 4 tires at $135 each?

Independent Practice

In **9** through **20**, find the product. Estimate to check reasonableness.

9. 6 × 77

10. 5 × 83

11. 4 × 62

12. 7 × 89

13. 3 × 245

14. 9 × 318

15. 2 × 736

16. 8 × 314

17. 4 × 4,347

18. 6 × 2,716

19. 7 × 1,287

20. 3 × 1,942

*For another example, see Set E on page 268.

Problem Solving

21. Maura's dance team wants to buy costumes that cost $56 each. They have $523. How much money will they have left in the fund after they buy 9 costumes?

A $69
B $58
C $21
D $19

What is the hidden question you have to answer first?

22. **Connect** Elaine rents a car for 5 days. It costs $44 each day to rent the car and $7 each day for insurance. At the end of the trip she spends $35 to fill the car with gas. How much does it cost Elaine to rent the car in all?

23. At the Math Club awards ceremony, 8 guests sat at each table. All of the 17 tables were filled. If each guest received 2 awards, how many awards were given out at the ceremony?

24. **Math and Science** Water erupting from geysers can reach a temperature of 244°F. The average temperature in Yellowstone National Park is 35°F. Use compensation to find the difference between these two temperatures.

25. **Extend Your Thinking** On Monday, Paolo sold 21 tickets to the dance. On Tuesday, he sold three times as many tickets as he did on Monday. On Wednesday, he sold twice as many tickets as he did on Tuesday. How many total tickets did he sell in the three days?

26. **Personal Financial Literacy** Mr. Tran would like to buy a new sofa that costs $934. He can pay the total all at once, or he can make a $125 payment each month for 8 months. Which plan costs less? Explain.

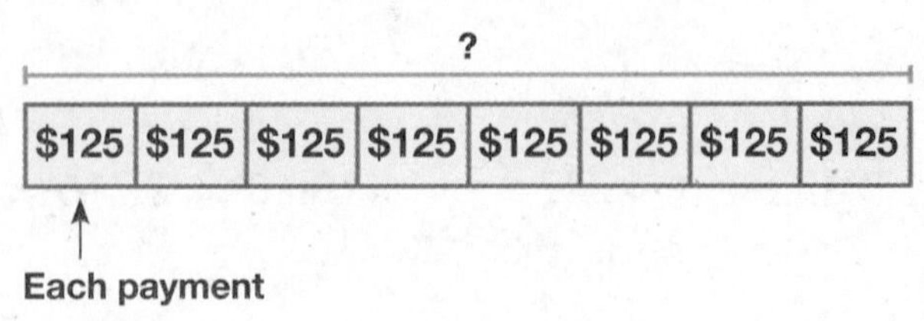

Name ____________________

Homework 4-6
More Multiplying by 1-Digit Numbers

Another Look!

Estimate the products first. Then multiply and check your answer against your estimate.

What is 78 × 4?

Estimate:

78 × 4 is about

80 × 4 = 320

$$\begin{array}{r} \overset{3}{7}8 \\ \times\ \ 4 \\ \hline 312 \end{array}$$

What is 2,802 × 2?

Estimate:

2,802 × 2 is about

2,800 × 2 = 5,600

$$\begin{array}{r} \overset{1}{2},802 \\ \times\quad 2 \\ \hline 5,604 \end{array}$$

In **1** through **12**, find each product.

1. $\begin{array}{r} 538 \\ \times\ \ 4 \\ \hline \end{array}$

2. $\begin{array}{r} 214 \\ \times\ \ 8 \\ \hline \end{array}$

3. $\begin{array}{r} 3,721 \\ \times\quad 7 \\ \hline \end{array}$

Remember to use estimation to check your answers for reasonableness.

4. $\begin{array}{r} 7,956 \\ \times\quad 8 \\ \hline \end{array}$

5. 4 × 92

6. 8 × 37

7. 6 × 505

8. 3 × 589

9. 5 × 6,384

10. 2 × 9,497

11. 7 × 3,218

12. 9 × 1,938

13. Formulate a Plan A grocery store orders 47 bags of onions and 162 bags of potatoes. The onions cost $2 per bag, and the potatoes cost $3 per bag. How much is spent on onions and potatoes?

14. Number Sense The animal shelter charges $119 to adopt a pet. On Saturday, 2 dogs and 7 cats were adopted. How much money did the animal shelter receive on those adoptions?

15. Dave sold 719 tickets. How much money did Dave bring in?

16. Zoe has 1,500 beads. Zoe wants to make 6 friendship bracelets. She needs 215 beads for each bracelet. How many beads will Zoe have left after making all the bracelets?

A 210 beads
B 240 beads
C 360 beads
D 1,290 beads

17. Formulate a Plan Steve packed 350 containers of mealworms for the fishing store. Of those containers, 237 hold 6 mealworms each. The rest of the containers hold 8 mealworms each. How many mealworms did he pack in all?

18. Extend Your Thinking Bo is selling 23 video games at a yard sale. He plans to donate the money to a local charity. What is the least whole dollar amount he should charge for each game in order to reach his goal of donating $200?

In a multi-step problem, look back to be sure that you answer the question asked.

Name ___________________________

Solve & Share Kevin took 248 photos on a field trip. Marco took 2 times as many. How many photos did Marco take? Use your recording sheet. ***Solve this problem any way you choose.***

You can **create and use a representation** such as a strip diagram to help you solve problems like this. ***Show your work!***

Problem Solving

Lesson 4-7
Draw a Strip Diagram and Write an Equation

TEKS 4.1D Communicate mathematical ideas, reasoning, and their implications using multiple representations.… Also, 4.5.
Mathematical Process Standards 4.1A, 4.1B, 4.1C, 4.1E, 4.1F

Digital Resources at SavvasTexas.com

Solve Learn Glossary Check Tools Games

Look Back!

Check for Reasonableness Is the answer you found reasonable? Explain why.

A **Analyze**

What Are Some Strategies You Can Use to Solve a Problem?

A-Z

Each artist at a large art show is assigned to a team of 5 judges. There are 9 teams of judges at the show. If each team reviews the work of 27 artists, how many artists attend the show?

Some problems have extra information.

Draw a strip diagram.

Write an equation.

B **Plan**

There are 9 teams of judges. Each team reviews 27 artists. The total number of artists at the show is unknown.

number of artists

27	27	27	27	27	27	27	27	27

↑ number of artists for each team of judges

C **Solve**

Let a = the number of artists at the show.

$9 \times 27 = a$

$a = 243$

$$\begin{array}{r} \overset{6}{2}7 \\ \times \ 9 \\ \hline 243 \end{array}$$

There are 243 artists at the show.

Do You Understand?

Convince Me! Kathy's grandmother bought a ring for $275 in 1962. A jeweler told her the value of the ring today is 4 times what she paid for it. How much is the ring worth today?

Draw a strip diagram and write an equation to solve the problem.

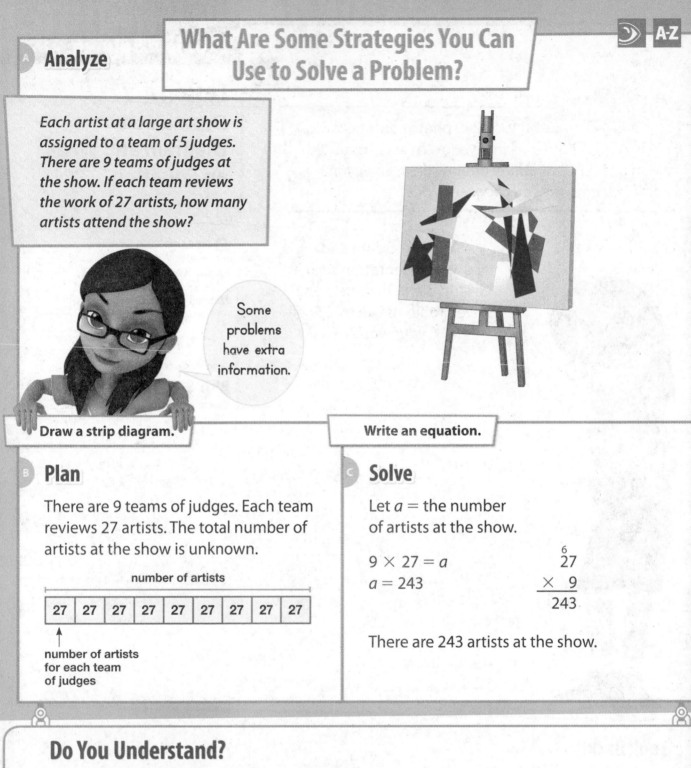

Name ____

Guided Practice*

In **1** and **2**, complete the strip diagram. Then write an equation and solve.

1. Use a Strip Diagram Sharon's Stationery Store has 219 boxes of cards. May's Market has 3 times as many boxes of cards. How many boxes, b, does May's Market have?

b boxes of cards

May's | | | | 3 times as many

Sharon's | |

2. Tools Gamal helped his dad clean the garage and attic over the weekend. They took eight 15-minute breaks. How many minutes, m, did they spend on breaks?

m minutes on break

| | | | | | | | | 8 breaks

↑

____

Independent Practice

In **3** and **4**, draw a diagram and write an equation to help you solve the problem.

3. Use a Strip Diagram A pencil factory ships 4 boxes each containing 144 pencils to an office supply store. How many pencils does the manufacturer ship in all?

Let p equal the number of pencils shipped.

4. Annie has 6 albums of stamps in her stamp collection. Each album contains 440 stamps. How many stamps does Annie have in her collection?

Let s equal the number of stamps in the collection.

*For another example, see Set F on page 268.

Problem Solving

5. **Use a Strip Diagram** The distance between two cities is 280 miles. A trucker drives back and forth between the two cities 8 times while making 4 round trips. What is the total distance driven on these trips?

6. An aquarium has 725 tropical fish and 588 freshwater fish. The total number of animals the aquarium has is 5 times as great as the total number of tropical and freshwater fish. How many animals does the aquarium have in all?

   A 1,318 animals
   B 3,665 animals
   C 4,213 animals
   D 6,565 animals

7. **Personal Financial Literacy** Jordan got $25 from each of two grandparents for her birthday. She spent $39, shared $5, and saved the rest. How much did she save? Tell how you found the answer.

8. **Number Sense** Order the numbers from greatest to least.

   25,439,517
   25,435,917
   25,493,715
   25,439,751

Align the numbers by place value, then compare.

9. Vaughn is trying to estimate the number of paper clips in a jar. If his guess is within 25 of the actual number of paper clips, he will win a prize. He knows that there are about 75 paper clips in one box. He estimates that the jar contains about 9 boxes of paper clips. There are actually 683 paper clips in the jar. Will Vaughn win a prize? Explain.

10. **Extend Your Thinking** A truck can haul 2,700 gallons of gasoline at one time. The storage tank at a gas station holds 9 times that amount. The truck delivers a full load of gasoline to the station 3 times in one week. What is the difference between the amount of gasoline the storage tank can hold and the total amount of gasoline delivered in one week?

Name ______________________________

Homework 4-7

Draw a Strip Diagram and Write an Equation

Another Look!

Analyze

A hardware store ordered 9 packs of screws from a supplier. Each pack contains 150 screws. How many screws did the store order?

What do you know?

The store ordered nine packs of screws.

Each pack contained 150 screws.

What are you trying to find?

The total number of screws ordered.

Plan and Solve

Draw a picture of what you know.

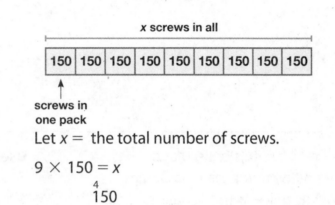

***x* screws in all**

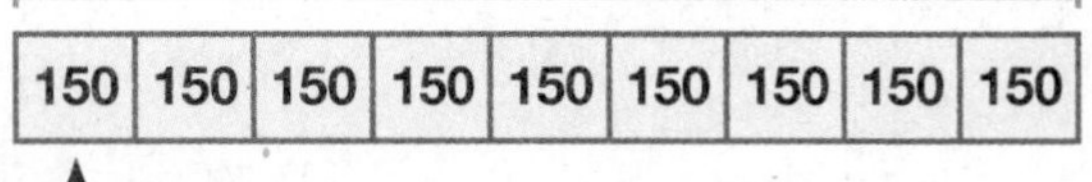

screws in one pack

Write an equation.

Let $x =$ the total number of screws.

$9 \times 150 = x$

Multiply.

$$\begin{array}{r} \overset{4}{1}50 \\ \times \quad 9 \\ \hline 1{,}350 \end{array}$$

The store ordered 1,350 screws.

In **1** and **2**, complete or draw a strip diagram. Then write an equation and solve.

1. **Use a Strip Diagram** When Mary was born, she weighed 8 pounds. When she was 10 years old, she weighed 10 times as much. How much did she weigh when she was 10 years old?

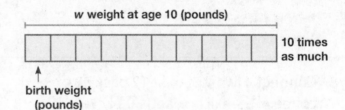

***w* weight at age 10 (pounds)**

10 times as much

birth weight (pounds)

2. **Number Sense** A factory makes 264 parts in one minute. How many parts are made in 3 minutes? In 30 minutes?

3. **Use a Strip Diagram** A state aquarium has display tanks that contain 75 fish each. Three of these tanks are at the entrance. How many fish are on display at the entrance?

4. **Number Sense** Name the rule and find the next two numbers in the pattern.

   10, 70, 490, ________, ________

5. **Connect** Sherry has $28 in her piggy bank. Samantha has saved 6 times as much money. How much money have Sherry and Samantha saved together?

6. Daniel has 12 tennis balls. Manuel has twice as many tennis balls as Daniel. Kendra has twice as many balls as Manuel. How many tennis balls do they have in all?

   A 24 tennis balls
   B 36 tennis balls
   C 84 tennis balls
   D 96 tennis balls

7. **Use a Strip Diagram** Company A ships 749 packages each day. Company B ships 4 times as many packages each day. How many packages does Company B ship each day?

8. **Connect** Hwong can fit 12 packets of coffee in a small box and 50 packets of coffee in a large box. How many packets of coffee can he fit into 5 small boxes and 3 large boxes?

9. **Extend Your Thinking** Ms. Allen bought 15 packs of pens and 18 packs of pencils. If each pack of pens costs $4 and each pack of pencils costs $3, how much did Ms. Allen spend in all?

Name ______________________________

Topic 4 Mixed Problem Solving

Applying Math Processes

- How does this problem connect to previous ones?
- What is my plan?
- How can I use tools?
- How can I use number sense?
- How can I communicate and represent my thinking?
- How can I organize and record information?
- How can I explain my work?
- How can I justify my answer?

1. **Personal Financial Literacy** For a new game system, Debbie must make 9 payments of $39 each. How much does she have to pay in all?

2. **Extend Your Thinking** During a basketball game, the winning team made 8 three-point baskets, 23 two-point baskets, and 21 one-point baskets. How many points did the team score in all?

3. **Number Sense** On Friday, 1,250 people visited the zoo. Four times as many people visited on Saturday as on Friday. How many people visited the zoo on Friday and Saturday?

4. **Formulate a Plan** Janice bought 3 bags of peanuts and 4 bags of pretzels. If each bag of peanuts holds 223 peanuts and each bag of pretzels holds 375 pretzels, how many peanuts and pretzels did Janice buy?

5. **Mental Math** Each roll of stamps has 100 stamps. Jerome bought 4 rolls of stamps and Henry bought 2 rolls of stamps. How many stamps did Jerome and Henry buy?

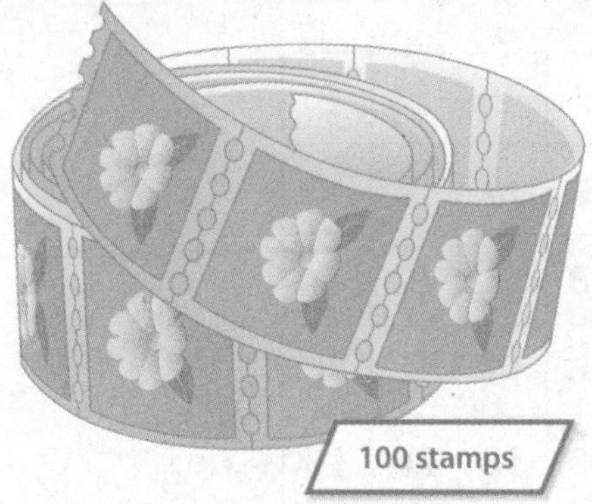

6. The animal park has 12 zebras, 25 monkeys, and some giraffes. If the total number of zebras, monkeys, and giraffes at the park is 50, how many giraffes are there?

   A 10
   B 13
   C 15
   D 23

Error Search

Find each problem that is not correct. Circle what is wrong and rewrite the problem so it is correct.

1.
$$\begin{array}{r} 23 \\ \times\ 4 \\ \hline 12 \\ +\ 80 \\ \hline 92 \end{array}$$

2.
$$\begin{array}{r} 362 \\ \times\ 5 \\ \hline 10 \\ 30 \\ +\ 15 \\ \hline 55 \end{array}$$

3.
$$\begin{array}{r} 273 \\ \times\ 7 \\ \hline 21 \\ 490 \\ +\ 140 \\ \hline 651 \end{array}$$

4.
$$\begin{array}{r} 1{,}328 \\ \times\ 6 \\ \hline 48 \\ 120 \\ 1{,}800 \\ +\ 6{,}000 \\ \hline 7{,}968 \end{array}$$

Compatible Numbers

Mental Math Draw loops around two or more numbers next to each other, across or down, with a sum of 10 or 30. Look for compatible numbers (numbers that are easy to compute mentally).

5. Find sums of 10.

2.3	1.7	6	5.5	4.5
3.7	2.8	2.1	3.9	6.1
4.2	8.2	4.4	5.6	1.6
2.1	1.8	3.5	4.4	4.3
8.9	3.8	5.1	1.1	4.1

6. Find sums of 30.

4	6	4	12	8
8	3	19	15	15
12	13	7	10	8
13	18	17	4	4
5	12	13	26	18

Number Sense: Multiplying by 2-Digit Numbers

Essential Questions:
How can greater products be found mentally?
How can greater products be estimated?

Let's jump right in! Here's a project on animal jumps and multiplication.

Many animals can jump a distance that is a multiple of their size.

Did you know grasshoppers, fleas, frogs, and rats are among the world's greatest jumpers?

Math and Science Project: Animal Facts Mulitplication

Do Research Use the Internet or other sources to find the length of jumping animals such as grasshoppers, tree frogs, kangaroo rats, and South African cockroaches. Then calculate about how many times their own length they can jump.

Journal: Write a Report Include what you found. Also in your report:

- Choose three animals.
- Set up a table that includes each animal's length and jump distance.
- Write and solve multiplication problems based on your data.

Name ______________________________

Review What You Know

Vocabulary

Choose the best term from the box. Write it on the blank.

- equation
- factors
- product
- round

1. A(n) ____________ is another word for a number sentence.

2. One way to estimate a product is to ____________ each number.

3. A(n) ____________ is the answer to a multiplication problem.

4. In the equation $9 \times 5 = 45$, 9 and 5 are both ____________.

Multiplication Facts

Find each product.

5. 3×9
6. 5×6
7. 4×8
8. 6×9
9. 7×4
10. 9×8
11. 8×7
12. 6×3

Rounding

Round each number to the nearest hundred.

13. 864
14. 651
15. 348
16. 985
17. 451
18. 749

Properties of Multiplication

19. Gina wants to multiply $(9 \times 2) \times 5$. What multiplication property can Gina use to regroup the factors to make it easier to multiply? Show how Gina would rewrite the expression.

20. Julio rewrites 7×475 as $(7 \times 400) + (7 \times 70) + (7 \times 5)$. What multiplication property does he use?

21. Henry is thinking of a whole number. He multiplies the number by 5, but the result is less than 5. What number is Henry thinking about? What multiplication property does he use?

A-Z

My Word Cards

Use the example for the word on the front of the card to help complete the definition on the back.

compatible numbers

24 is close to 25
52 is close to 50

My Word Cards

Complete the definition. Extend learning by writing your own definition.

Numbers that are easy to compute mentally are called ______________ ______________.

Name ______________________________

Solve & Share

There are 10 teams in a baseball league. Each team has 25 players on the roster. How many players are there in all in the league? ***Solve this problem any way you choose.***

Lesson 5-1

Arrays and Multiplying 2-Digit Numbers by Multiples of 10

TEKS 4.4C Represent the product of 2 two-digit numbers using arrays, area models, or equations, including perfect squares through 15 by 15.
Mathematical Process Standards 4.1A, 4.1B, 4.1C, 4.1D, 4.1E, 4.1F

Digital Resources at SavvasTexas.com

Solve Learn Glossary Check Tools Games

You can **use tools.** Place-value blocks or grid paper can help you visualize the problem. ***Show your work in the space above!***

Look Back!

Connect Ideas How do the digits in a number being multiplied by 10 compare to the digits in the product?

How Can You Use a Model to Multiply?

A

Max's Moving Company has boxes for packing books. If each box holds 24 books, how many books would fit into 10 boxes?

Choose an operation. Multiply to join equal groups.

Use place-value blocks.

Making an array with place-value blocks provides a way to visualize and find the partial products.

B

Step 1

Use a model to find 10×24.

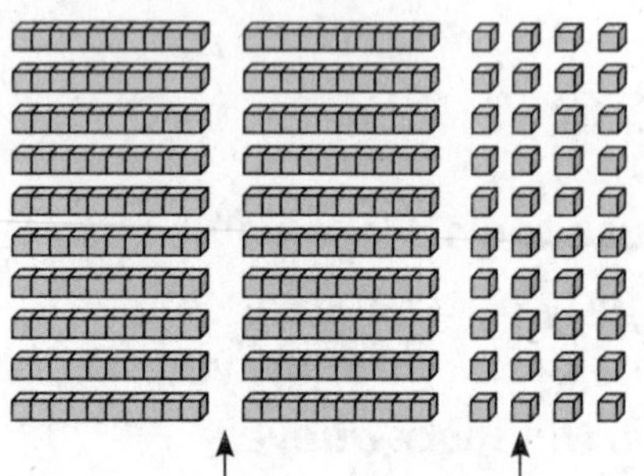

10 groups of 20 = 200 10 groups of 4 = 40

C

Step 2

Add to find the total.

$$\begin{array}{r} 200 \\ +\ 40 \\ \hline 240 \end{array}$$

$10 \times 24 = 240$

240 books will fit into 10 boxes.

Do You Understand?

Convince Me! Use the grid to model 20×25. What is the product?

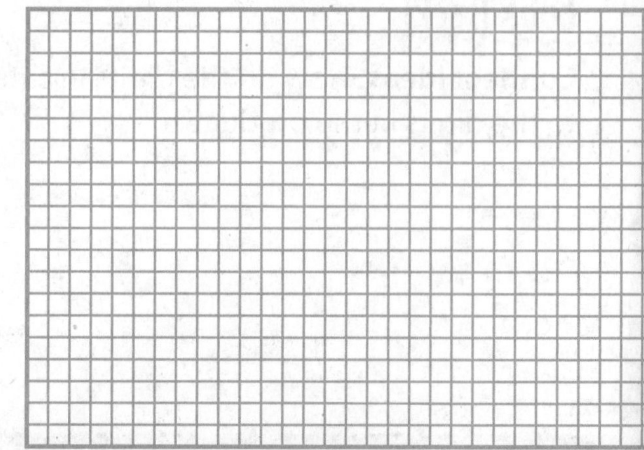

Name

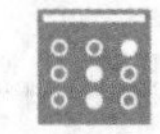

Guided Practice*

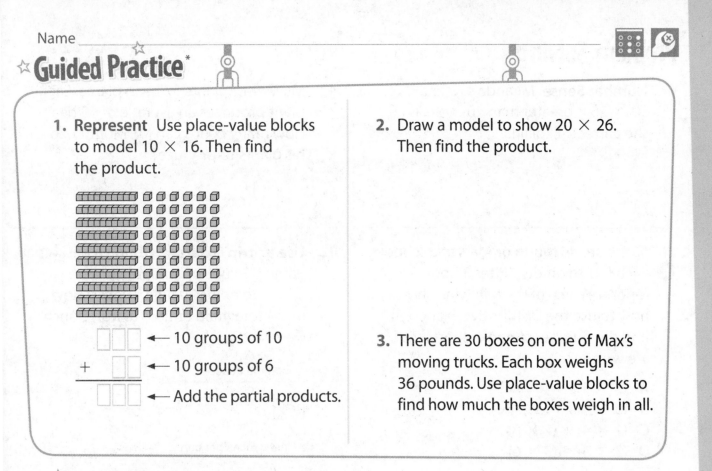

1. **Represent** Use place-value blocks to model 10 × 16. Then find the product.

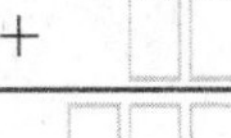

☐☐☐ ← 10 groups of 10
+ ☐☐ ← 10 groups of 6
☐☐☐ ← Add the partial products.

2. Draw a model to show 20 × 26. Then find the product.

3. There are 30 boxes on one of Max's moving trucks. Each box weighs 36 pounds. Use place-value blocks to find how much the boxes weigh in all.

Independent Practice

Leveled Practice In **4** through **9**, use place-value blocks or draw models to find each product.

You can use a sheet of grid paper to draw arrays.

4. 10 × 22

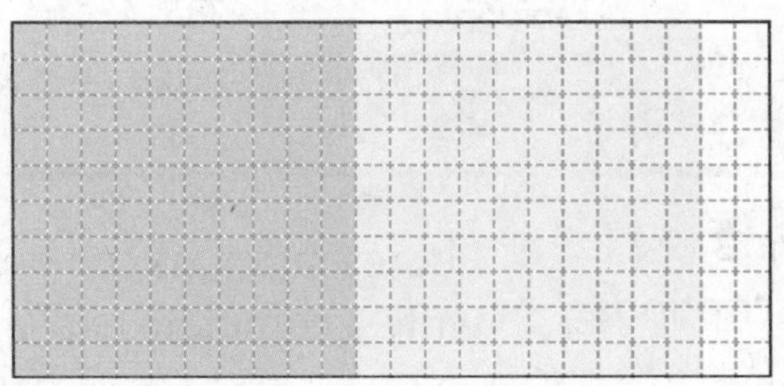

5. 10 × 13

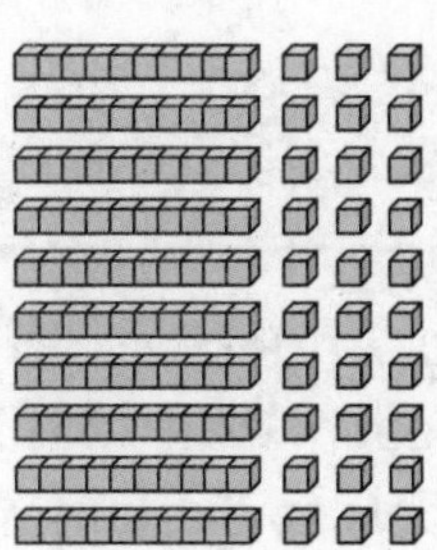

6. 20 × 35

7. 20 × 41

8. 30 × 29

9. 40 × 37

*For another example, see Set A on page 307.

Problem Solving

10. **Number Sense** Miranda says that 30×26 is greater than 20×36. Is she correct? Explain.

11. Mr. Moffitt plants 57 bean plants. Each plant produces an average of 60 beans. How many beans can Mr. Moffitt expect his plants to produce?

12. There are 46 fourth graders at a school. Each fourth grader writes 3 book reports. Which of the following shows how to use the Distributive Property to find the number of book reports that are written?

A $(3 \times 40) + (3 \times 6)$
B $(3 \times 46) + (3 \times 46)$
C $(1 \times 4) + (2 \times 6)$
D $(3 \times 4) + (3 \times 6)$

13. **Use a Strip Diagram** During a basketball game, 75 cups of fruit punch were sold. Each cup holds 20 fluid ounces. How many total fluid ounces of fruit punch were sold?

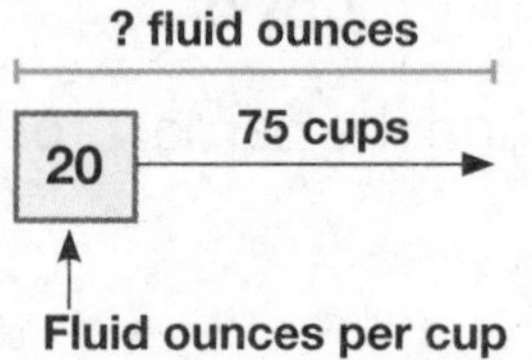

14. **Reason** In the first 3 months of the year, an electronics store sold 1,446 cameras. How many cameras did they sell in March?

DATA

Camera Sales

Month	Number Sold
January	486
February	385

15. **Extend Your Thinking** Angel sold 15 magazine subscriptions for \$30 each. Walt sold 22 subscriptions for \$20 each. Use models to explain who raised more money.

Representations can help you write a complete explanation.

Name ______________________

Homework 5-1
Arrays and Multiplying 2-Digit Numbers by Multiples of 10

Another Look!

Use an array to find the product of 20 × 14.

20 × 14 means 20 groups of 14, or
20 groups of 10 + 20 groups of 4.

Add the partial products from the array.

20 groups of 10 = 200
20 groups of 4 = 80

200 + 80 = 280

So, 20 × 14 = 280.

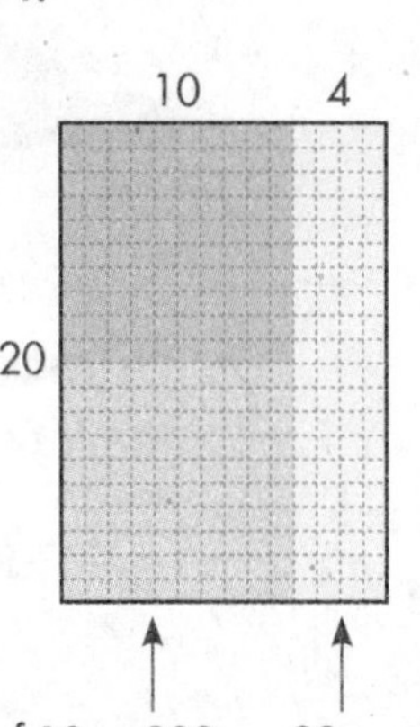

10
4
20

20 groups of 10 = 200   20 groups of 4 = 80

You can break apart numbers to multiply.

In **1** and **2**, use the array to find each product.

1. 10 × 12

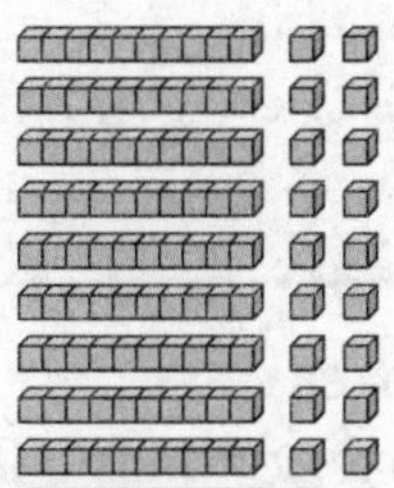

10 groups of 10 = ______

10 groups of 2 = ______

______ + ______ = ______

So, 10 × 12 = ______.

2. 20 × 18

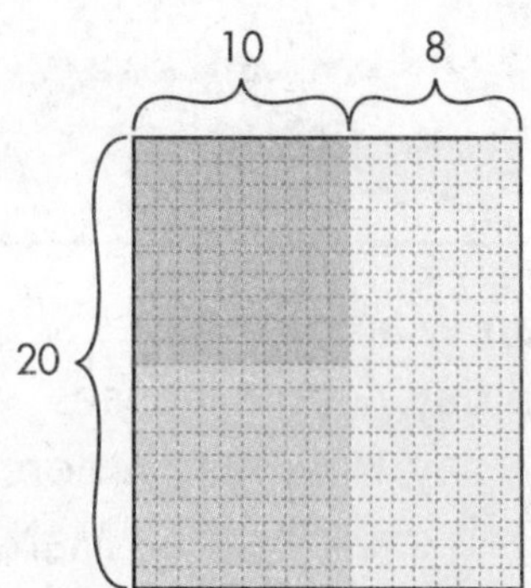

10
8
20

20 groups of 10 = ______

20 groups of 8 = ______

______ + ______ = ______

So, 20 × 18 = ______.

In **3** through **6**, find each product. Draw a model to help.

3. 50 × 15   **4.** 40 × 22   **5.** 30 × 39   **6.** 60 × 21

7. **Connect** The height of each story of an

apartment building is measured from the bottom of one floor to the bottom of the next floor. Each story has a height of 18 feet. How tall is the building?

A 48 feet
B 300 feet
C 480 feet
D 540 feet

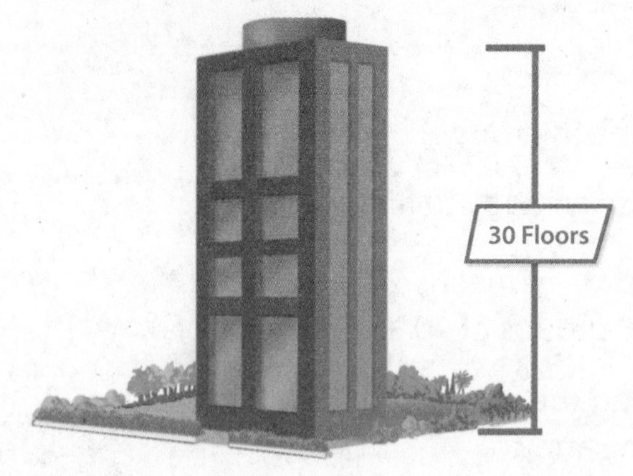

8. The American bison is the heaviest land mammal in North America. Bison live in groups of up to 20. What is the greatest number of bison there could be in 12 groups?

9. **Number Sense** Order the decimals from least to greatest.

0.42, 0.05, 0.41

10. What multiplication sentence is modeled by the array at the right?

11. **Formulate a Plan** Marta exercises 30 minutes each day. Greg exercises 40 minutes each day. How many more minutes does Greg exercise than Marta in a month that has 31 days?

12. The dentist orders 20 boxes of toothbrushes and 15 boxes of floss each month. Toothbrushes are sold 25 to a box and floss is sold 30 to a box. How many items does the dentist order each month?

13. **Extend Your Thinking** Without multiplying, which product is greater: 45 × 10 or 50 × 10? Explain how you know.

14. **Analyze Information** Mrs. Harrigan ordered 30 boxes of glasses for her restaurant. Each box holds 16 glasses. She also ordered 30 boxes of plates. There are 25 plates in each box. How many glasses and plates did she order altogether?

Name ____________________

Solve & Share

The principal of your school needs to order supplies for 20 new classrooms. Each classroom needs the following items: 20 desks, 30 chairs, and 40 pencils. How many of each item does the principal need to order? ***Solve this problem any way you choose.***

You can **formulate a plan.** What basic facts can you use to help solve this problem? ***Show your work in the space below!***

Lesson 5-2

Using Mental Math to Multiply 2-Digit Numbers

TEKS 4.4D Use strategies and algorithms ... to multiply a two-digit number by a two-digit number. Strategies may include mental math, partial products, and the commutative, associative, and distributive properties.
Mathematical Process Standards 4.1A, 4.1B, 4.1C, 4.1D, 4.1F, 4.1G

Digital Resources at SavvasTexas.com

Solve Learn Glossary Check Tools Games

Look Back!

Connect Ideas Look at the factors and products you found. What patterns do you notice?

How Can You Multiply by Multiples of 10?

A

How many adults under 65 visit the Sunny Day Amusement Park in 20 days? How many children visit the park in 30 days? How many adults 65 and over visit the park in 50 days?

Choose an operation. You can use a pattern to multiply by a multiple of 10.

Average number of visitors each day

Use basic facts and place-value patterns.

B **Adults under 65 in 20 days**

To multiply 20×60, use a pattern.

$$2 \times 6 = 12$$
$$20 \times 6 = 120$$
$$20 \times 60 = 1{,}200$$

1,200 adults under 65 visit the park in 20 days.

C **Children in 30 days**

The number of zeros in the product is the total number of zeros in both factors.

$$30 \times 80 = 2{,}400$$

1 zero 1 zero 2 zeros

2,400 children visit the park in 30 days.

D **Adults 65 and over in 50 days**

If the product of a basic fact ends in zero, include that zero in the count.

$$5 \times 4 = 20$$
$$50 \times 40 = 2{,}000$$

2,000 adults 65 and over visit the park in 50 days.

Do You Understand?

Convince Me! Write the missing numbers for each of the following. Tell how you decided.

___ × 7 = 280 ___ × 40 = 1,600 ___ × 50 = 3,000

Name ___

Guided Practice*

In **1** through **6**, use basic facts and patterns to find the products.

1. 30 × 10

2. 50 × 10

3. 20 × 10

4. 60 × 20

5. 40 × 90

6. 80 × 50

7. Reason When you multiply 40 × 50, how many zeros are in the product?

8. In cold weather, fewer people go to Sunny Day Amusement Park. November has 30 days. If the park sells 30 tickets each day in November, how many would they sell for the whole month?

Independent Practice

In **9** through **20**, multiply using mental math.

9. 20 × 70

10. 70 × 90

11. 40 × 20

12. 40 × 30

13. 70 × 40

14. 20 × 30

15. 60 × 40

16. 60 × 90

17. 70 × 80

18. 50 × 50

19. 60 × 60

20. 70 × 30

In **21** through **24**, find the missing factor using mental math.

21. 10 × ___ = 100

22. ___ × 20 = 1,600

23. 20 × ___ = 1,000

24. ___ × 90 = 8,100

For another example, see Set B on page 307.

Problem Solving

25. **Tools** Are the decimals 0.05 and 0.5 equivalent? Use the decimal models to show why.

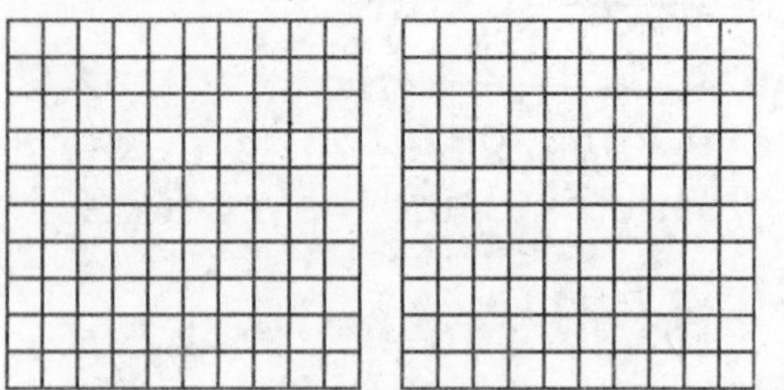

26. **Reason** The product of two factors is 4,200. If one of the factors is 60, what is the other factor? How do you know?

27. **Extend Your Thinking** Explain why the product of 50 and 80 has three zeros when 50 has one zero and 80 has one zero.

28. **Connect** Bob leaves the water running while brushing his teeth. He uses about 2 gallons of water. How many cups of water did Bob use while brushing his teeth?

There are 16 cups in 1 gallon.

29. **Mental Math** James walked 30 minutes each day for 90 days. Show how you can use mental math to find how many minutes James walked in all.

30. **Formulate a Plan** Ms. Kim travels 10 weeks a year for work. She stays in her hometown the other 42 weeks. There are 7 days in 1 week. Which of the following expressions can she use to mentally find the number of days she is home?

A $(7 \times 2) + (4 \times 10)$
B 7×100
C $(7 \times 40) + (7 \times 10)$
D $(7 \times 40) + (7 \times 2)$

Name ______________________________

Homework 5-2
Using Mental Math to Multiply 2-Digit Numbers

Another Look!

A kindergarten teacher wants to buy individual boxes of crayons for her students. Each box contains 50 crayons. How many crayons will she have if she buys 30 boxes of crayons?

Find 50×30.

Use a pattern to find 50×30.

$5 \times 3 = 15$
$50 \times 3 = 150$
$50 \times 30 = 1{,}500$

So, $50 \times 30 = 1{,}500$.

The kindergarten teacher will have 1,500 crayons.

You can multiply with mental math by using basic facts and patterns.

In **1** through **9**, use basic facts and patterns to find the products.

1. $2 \times 2 =$ ______
$20 \times 2 =$ ______
$20 \times 20 =$ ______

2. $6 \times 3 =$ ______
$60 \times 3 =$ ______
$60 \times 30 =$ ______

3. $5 \times 6 =$ ______
$50 \times 6 =$ ______
$50 \times 60 =$ ______

4. 30×80

5. 60×60

6. 50×90

7. 30×70

8. 70×60

9. 40×50

In **10** through **12**, find the missing factor.

Use number sense and mental math when you multiply.

10. $10 \times$ ____ $= 200$

11. $40 \times$ ____ $= 3{,}600$

12. $50 \times$ ____ $= 4{,}000$

13. Ms. Marks records the number of words each student can type in 1 minute. Which student types the fastest? How many words would that student type in 30 minutes?

DATA

Typing Rates in 1 min

Student	Words
Lavon	50
Jerome	40
Charlie	60

14. **Reason** The product of two numbers is 7,200. If one of the numbers is 90, what is the other number?

A 8,000
B 800
C 80
D 8

15. **Explain** There are 30 players on each high school football team. Explain how you can find the total number of players if there are 40 teams.

16. **Use a Strip Diagram** If in one year a city recorded a total of 97 rainy days, how many of the days did it NOT rain? Write and solve an equation.

365 days in one year

97	*d*

17. **Communicate** Amy says, "To find 50×60, I multiply 5 by 6 and then place the total number of zeros in both factors at the end." Do you agree with her? Explain.

18. **Extend Your Thinking** Name two 2-digit factors whose product is greater than 200 but less than 600.

19. **Extend Your Thinking** Of every 30 minutes of television air time, about 8 minutes are commercials. If 90 minutes of television are aired, how many minutes of commercials will be played?

Name

Solve & Share

You need a product that is as close to 1,600 as possible. You can choose two factors from the numbers 18, 42, 56, and 81. Which numbers can you select so that the product is closest to 1,600? ***Solve this problem any way you choose.***

Lesson 5-3
Using Rounding to Estimate

TEKS 4.4G Round to the nearest 10, 100, or 1,000 or use compatible numbers to estimate solutions involving whole numbers.
Mathematical Process Standards 4.1A, 4.1B, 4.1C, 4.1D, 4.1G

Digital Resources at SavvasTexas.com

Solve

Learn

Glossary

Check

Tools

Games

You can **estimate.** How can rounding help you choose two factors? ***Show your work in the space below!***

1,600

Look Back!

Mental Math What do the numbers you multiplied mentally have in common?

How Can You Use Rounding to Estimate?

A

The workers at Mrs. Piper's apple grove picked 87 dozen apples.

There are 12 apples in one dozen.

About how many apples did the workers pick?

1 dozen apples

Some problems don't need an exact answer.

Replace the factors with the closest multiple of 10 or 100.

B Round both numbers in 87×12.

Round 87 to the nearest ten.

$7 > 5$, so round 87 to 90.

Round 12 to the nearest ten.

$2 < 5$, so round 12 to 10.

C Estimate the product.

87×12

$\downarrow \quad \downarrow$

$90 \times 10 = 900$

The workers picked about 900 apples.

Do You Understand?

Convince Me! Sue said that 870 is a reasonable estimate for 87×12, and her teacher agreed. How could Sue get 870 as an estimate?

Think about what numbers are easy to multiply.

Name ____________________

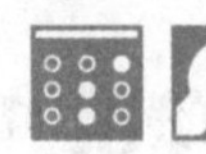

Guided Practice*

In **1** through **4**, estimate each product.

1. 24 × 18 rounds to
   _____ × _____ = _____.

2. 33 × 31 is close to
   _____ × _____ = _____.

3. 38 × 22

4. 45 × 48

5. **Explain** In the example on page 288, how do you know that you only need an estimate of how many apples were picked and not an exact answer?

6. **Communicate** Howie used rounding to estimate the product of 35 × 42 and got 1,200. What did he do wrong?

Independent Practice

Leveled Practice In **7** through **18**, estimate each product.

7. 39 × 19 rounds to
   _____ × _____ = _____.

8. 28 × 27 rounds to
   _____ × _____ = _____.

9. 32 × 42 rounds to
   _____ × _____ = _____.

10. 72 × 48 rounds to
    _____ × _____ = _____.

11. 64 × 13

12. 42 × 17

13. 82 × 36

14. 54 × 18

15. 66 × 41

16. 34 × 52

17. 74 × 34

18. 57 × 49

*For another example, see Set C on page 307.

Problem Solving

In **19** through **21**, use the table.

19. Reason Mr. Gonzalez has the same number of which two types of trees? Explain.

DATA

Mr. Gonzalez's Trees

Type of Orange Tree	Number of Rows	Number of Trees in Each Row
Hamlin	28	38
Temple	38	28
Valencia	31	46

20. Explain About how many more Valencia orange trees than Temple orange trees does Mr. Gonzalez have? Show your work.

21. About how many orange trees does Mr. Gonzalez have in all?

A 1,100 trees
B 1,600 trees
C 3,000 trees
D 3,900 trees

22. Extend Your Thinking Juan wants to buy a pack of cards for $3.58 and a model car for $6.98. He has $15.00. Does Juan have enough money? If so, how much money will he have left? If not, how much more money does Juan need?

$15.00		
$3.58	$6.98	?

23. Check for Reasonableness Lenore rounds each factor to the nearest ten to estimate that the product of 52×38 is 1,500. Is her estimate reasonable? Explain.

24. Connect Other than money, when might rounding factors to estimate a product be useful?

Name ____________________

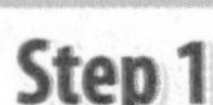

Homework 5-3
Using Rounding to Estimate

Another Look!

Use rounding to estimate 28 × 36. Replace the factors with the closest multiple of 10 or 100.

Not all problems need an exact answer.

Step 1	Step 2
Round both numbers in 28 × 36. Round 28 to the nearest ten. 8 > 5, so round 28 to 30. Round 36 to the nearest ten. 6 > 5, so round 36 to 40.	Estimate the product. 28 × 36 ↓ ↓ 30 × 40 So, the product is about 1,200.

In **1** and **2**, round each factor. Then estimate the product.

1. 31 × 12

31 rounds to ______.

12 rounds to ______.

______ × ______ = ______

2. 28 × 17

28 rounds to ______.

17 rounds to ______.

______ × ______ = ______

In **3** through **11**, use rounding to estimate the product.

3. 54 × 14

4. 44 × 22

5. 45 × 19

6. 34 × 48

7. 39 × 37

8. 25 × 81

9. 64 × 76

10. 15 × 38

11. 88 × 23

12. About how many books in all does Corner Books sell each year?

Corner Books Weekly Sales	
Type of Book	**Number of Books**
Fiction	72
Nonfiction	38
Children's	55

There are 52 weeks in 1 year.

13. Number Sense List the numbers from 50 to 60 that would make this number sentence true.

$85 + 54 > \underline{?} + 85$

14. Estimation A deep-sea fisherman went fishing 14 times last month. He caught 28 fish each time. About how many fish did he catch altogether last month?

15. Math and Science The world's smallest snake, the thread snake, can be 4 inches long. The world's largest snake, the anaconda, can be 60 times as long. How many inches long can an anaconda be?

?

4 — 60 times as long →

16. Explain The art teacher has 30 boxes of crayons with 16 crayons in each box. She gives the students 10 of the boxes to use. Explain how to find how many crayons the teacher has left.

17. Reason A park ranger in Everglades National Park counted the number of alligator eggs in 28 nests. On average, there were 40 eggs in each nest. About how many alligator eggs did he count?

A 80 eggs
B 120 eggs
C 800 eggs
D 1,200 eggs

18. Extend Your Thinking Eric estimated 28×48 by finding 30×50. His estimate was 1,500, but he says the actual product will be greater than that amount. Is he correct? Explain.

Name ______________________________

Solve & Share

You need a product that is as close to 1,600 as possible. You can choose two factors from the numbers 24, 32, 61, and 78. Which numbers can you select so that the product is closest to 1,600? ***Solve this problem any way you choose.***

Lesson 5-4
Using Compatible Numbers to Estimate

TEKS 4.4G Round to the nearest 10, 100, or 1,000 or use compatible numbers to estimate solutions involving whole numbers.
Mathematical Process Standards 4.1B, 4.1C, 4.1D, 4.1E, 4.1G

Digital Resources at SavvasTexas.com

Solve

Learn

Glossary
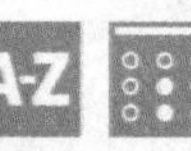
Check

Tools

Games

You can **estimate.** What ways do you know to estimate a product? ***Show your work in the space below!***

Look Back!

Justify Why did you choose the two numbers that you did?

How Can You Use Compatible Numbers to Estimate?

A-Z

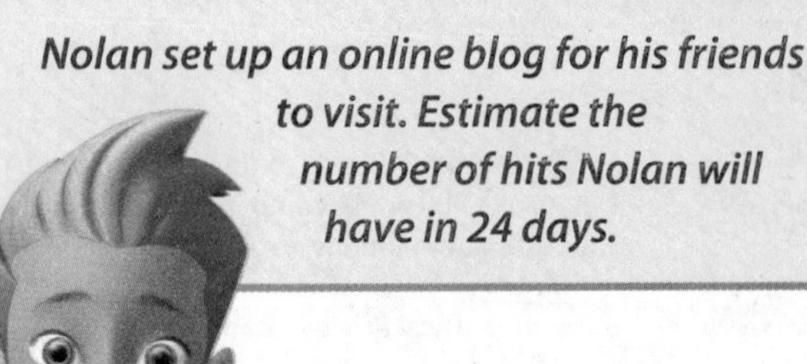

Nolan set up an online blog for his friends to visit. Estimate the number of hits Nolan will have in 24 days.

There is more than one way to estimate.

Replace the factors with numbers that are close and easy to multiply.

Estimate 24 × 41.

Rounding to the nearest ten gives

20 × 40 = 800 as an estimate.

However, you can get a closer estimate by using compatible numbers, which are numbers that are easy to compute mentally.

24 is close to 25 41 is close to 40

It is easy to find 25 × 40, since 25 and 40 are compatible numbers. Remember that:

25 × 4 = 100

So, 25 × 40 = 1,000.

Nolan will have about 1,000 hits in 24 days.

Notice that 24 is closer to 25 than to 20.

So, 25 × 40 gives a better estimate than 20 × 40. However, either method can be used to find an estimate.

Do You Understand?

Convince Me! To estimate 76 × 24, which student's explanation is correct?

Michelle's Answer

I rounded 76 to 80 and 24 to 20. 80 × 20 = 1,600, so 76 × 24 is about 1,600.

Diana's Answer

I used compatible numbers. 76 is close to 80 and 24 is close to 25. 80 × 25 = 2,000, so 76 × 24 is about 2,000.

Name ___

Guided Practice*

In **1** through **3**, estimate each product.

1. 24 × 18
24 is close to 25.
18 is close to ___.
Multiply 25 × ___ = ___

2. 24 × 37

3. 52 × 27

4. In the example on page 294, suppose the average number of hits per day was 61. If you estimate 24 × 61 as 25 × 60, what is the estimate?

5. Reason Rounding would give 20 × 60 as an estimate for 24 × 61. Why does 25 × 60 give a better estimate than 20 × 60?

Independent Practice

In **6** through **20**, estimate each product.

Practice using compatible numbers when you estimate.

6. 26 × 43 **7.** 31 × 46 **8.** 21 × 25

9. 58 × 12 **10.** 22 × 26 **11.** 78 × 21

12. 36 × 49 **13.** 66 × 31 **14.** 64 × 24

15. 21 × 19 **16.** 76 × 39 **17.** 32 × 24

18. 89 × 43 **19.** 79 × 79 **20.** 46 × 18

*For another example, see Set D on page 308.

Problem Solving

21. **Represent** Write an equation for the model using the Distributive Property to find the product of 4 × 16.

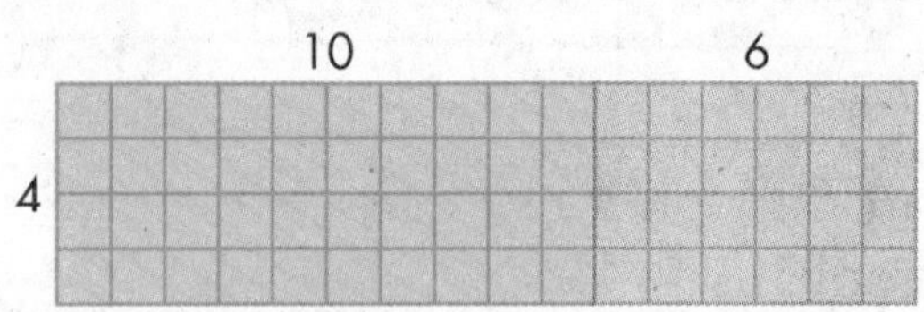

22. **Estimation** An electronics store sells about 45 computers a day, 7 days a week. About how many computers could they sell in 4 weeks?

23. A company ordered 28 cartons of tape. Each carton contained 24 rolls. Which is the best estimate of the total number of rolls of tape ordered?

    A About 280 rolls
    B About 400 rolls
    C About 750 rolls
    D About 900 rolls

24. **Explain** Show how you would use estimation to decide which has the greater product, 39 × 21 or 32 × 32.

25. **Estimation** Mason swims about 55 minutes each day. Estimate the number of minutes he swims in 14 days.

26. **Analyze Information** In 1858, two ships connected a telegraph cable across the Atlantic Ocean for the first time. Using the diagram below, estimate the total distance of cable used.

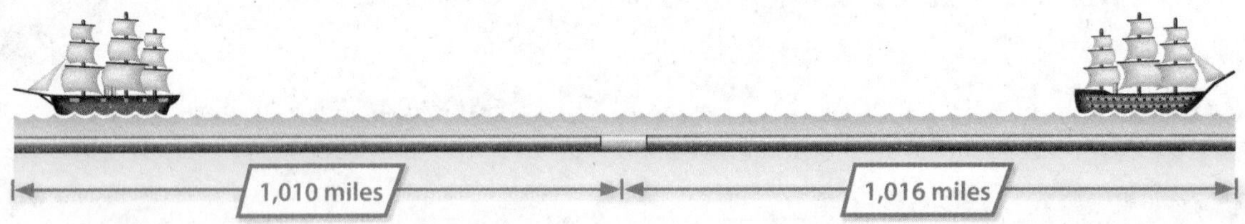

27. During her summer job at the local grocery store, Vivian earned $247 per week. If she worked for 6 weeks, how much money did she earn in all?

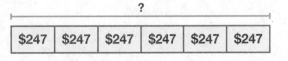

    ?

$247	$247	$247	$247	$247	$247

28. **Extend Your Thinking** How is using compatible numbers to estimate similar to using rounding? How is it different?

Name ______________________

Homework 5-4
Using Compatible Numbers to Estimate

Another Look!

A rollercoaster has 38 seats for passengers. The rollercoaster runs 24 times each hour. About how many passengers can ride the rollercoaster each hour?

Pick numbers close to 38 and 24 that you can multiply mentally.

Step 1	Step 2
Pick compatible numbers. • 24 is close to 25. • 38 is close to 40. 24×38 ↓ ↓ 25×40	Multiply the compatible numbers. $25 \times 40 = 1{,}000$ So, 24×38 is about 1,000. About 1,000 passengers can ride the rollercoaster each hour.

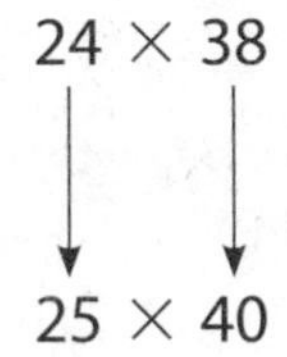

In **1** through **11**, estimate each product.

There can be more than one way of estimating a product. Be sure that the estimate is reasonable.

1. 23×12

23 is close to 25.

12 is close to ______.

$25 \times$ ______ $=$ ______

2. 24×31

24 is close to 25.

31 is close to ______.

______ $\times$ ______ $=$ ______

3. 19×24

4. 51×17

5. 82×78

6. 24×62

7. 48×29

8. 53×39

9. 53×54

10. 68×39

11. 29×43

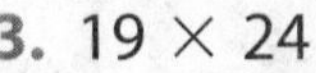

12. There are 16 cups in 1 gallon. About how many cups of water does the bathtub hold?

13. **Personal Financial Literacy** Yoko wants to set aside \$2,000 this year for a vacation. She plans on saving \$48 dollars each week. There are 52 weeks in a year. Explain whether her savings plan is reasonable.

14. **Number Sense** Marc estimates 67×36 by finding 70×40. Will his estimate be greater than or less than the actual product? Explain.

15. **Communicate** Tia and Jamal both estimate 17×32. Tia says $20 \times 30 = 600$, so 17×32 is about 600. Jamal says $15 \times 30 = 450$, so 17×32 is about 450. Can both Tia and Jamal be correct? Explain.

16. A certain tour guide leads groups of 26 people through a museum. She led 42 groups last year. Using compatible numbers, which is the best estimate for the number of people she led last year?

A About 1,000 people
B About 1,092 people
C About 1,200 people
D About 2,500 people

17. **Extend Your Thinking** What might you consider when deciding whether to use rounding or compatible numbers to estimate? Explain.

18. **Analyze Information** A skyscraper has 49 floors. There are 26 offices on each of the bottom 31 floors. The top 18 floors each have 38 offices. About how many offices are there in the skyscraper altogether?

Name ______________________________

Solve & Share

Four friends bought a $36 present for Joan. How much less would each friend pay if 6 friends shared the cost equally rather than 4? ***Solve this problem any way you choose.***

You can **formulate a plan.** What additional information do you first need to find? ***Show your work in the space below!***

Problem Solving

Lesson 5-5
Multi-Step Problems

TEKS 4.1A Apply mathematics to problems arising in everyday life, society, and the workplace.
TEKS 4.5A Represent multi-step problems involving the four operations with whole numbers using strip diagrams and equations with a letter standing for the unknown quantity.
Mathematical Process Standards 4.1B, 4.1C, 4.1D, 4.1F, 4.1G

Digital Resources at SavvasTexas.com

Solve

Learn

Glossary

Check

Tools

Games

Look Back!

Connect Ideas Which operation do you use to find equal shares?

How Can You Solve a Multi-Step Problem?

A-Z

Analyze

Paul and Libby sold some sock monkeys for a total of $72. Libby sold 5 monkeys from her collection. Paul sold 3 monkeys from his collection. If they sold each sock monkey for the same amount, how much did they sell each monkey for?

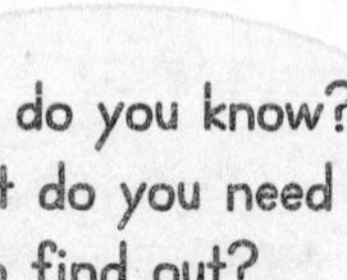

What do you know? What do you need to find out?

Find the hidden question and use the answer to solve the problem.

Step 1

How many sock monkeys did Paul and Libby sell in all?

Let m = monkeys sold in all.

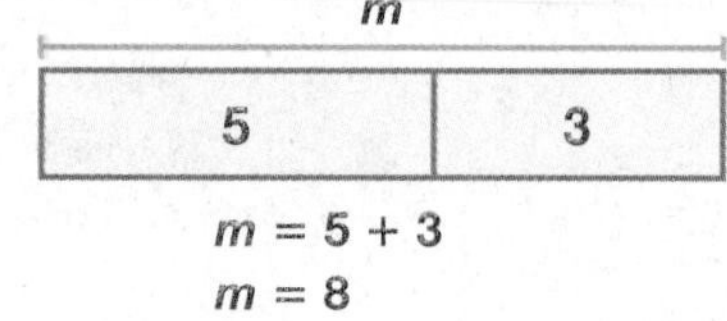

$m = 5 + 3$
$m = 8$

They sold 8 monkeys.

Step 2

They sold each sock monkey for the same amount.

How much did they sell each monkey for?

Let c = cost of 1 monkey.

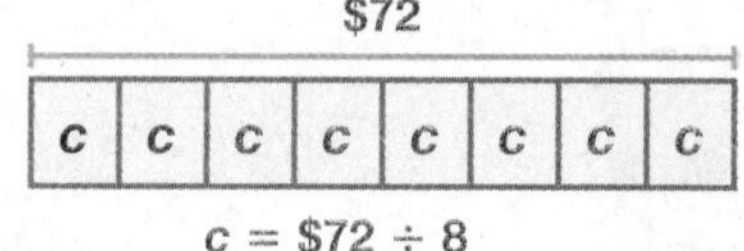

$c = \$72 \div 8$

Paul and Libby sold each monkey for $9.

Do You Understand?

Convince Me! Fana has 48 sock monkeys. She gave 5 to her sister, 2 to her cousin, and 4 to her best friend, Chuck. She sold the rest for $10 each. How much money did Fana receive?

Name

Guided Practice*

1. Adult admission to the museum is $7. Child admission to the museum is $3. How much would it cost 2 adults and 4 children to enter the museum?

2. **Formulate a Plan** A bus has 12 rows with 1 seat in each row on one side and 12 rows with 2 seats in each row on the other side. How many seats does the bus have in all?

3. **Analyze Information** What is the hidden question or questions in Problem 1?

4. **Communicate** Write a problem that contains a hidden question.

Independent Practice

In **5** through **7**, answer the hidden question or questions. Then solve the problem.

5. **Analyze Information** Charlie and Ashley like to walk around the perimeter of their town park. The perimeter is 2 miles long. Last week Charlie walked around the perimeter 4 times and Ashley walked around it 5 times. How many more miles did Ashley walk than Charlie last week?

Writing a good explanation is important with multi-step problems.

6. **Connect** Abby buys 15 sunflower plants and 12 petunia plants to plant in her garden. She plans to plant 3 flowers in each row. How many rows of flowers will Abby plant?

7. **Mental Math** Craig walked 5 dogs on Saturday and 7 dogs on Sunday. He earns $3 for each dog he walks. How much did Craig earn in all for the weekend?

*For another example, see Set E on page 308.

Problem Solving

8. **Analyze Information** Mario and his family go to the county fair. They buy 2 adult passes and 3 child passes. What was the total cost for the family? What are the hidden questions?

County Fair Admission	
Adult	$5
Student	$3
Child	$2

9. **Communicate** Fourteen students in Ms. Engel's class have 2 pets. Three students have 1 pet. There are 3 students that do not have any pets. How many pets does the class have altogether? Write an equation to solve.

10. **Construct Arguments** The gym teacher has 4 yoga DVDs. She has 3 times as many dance DVDs as yoga DVDs. Tyrone says the gym teacher has 12 DVDs in all because $4 \times 3 = 12$. Do you agree? Explain.

11. On one trip, 49 people and 82 cars rode the ferry. About how much money did the ferry service collect for all the tickets?

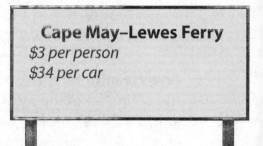

Cape May–Lewes Ferry
$3 per person
$34 per car

12. Aspen is setting up chairs for a concert. One section will have 5 equal rows of 5 chairs each. The other section will have 8 equal rows of 2 chairs each. How many chairs will there be in all?

   A 41 chairs
   B 36 chairs
   C 35 chairs
   D 20 chairs

13. **Extend Your Thinking** Write a problem that has a hidden question using this information.

   A single load of laundry costs $2, and a double load costs $4. The machines only accept quarters.

   Show how you would solve your problem.

Name ______________________________

Homework 5-5
Multi-Step Problems

Another Look!

Chad and Amy cut lawns in their neighborhood to earn money. They charge \$20 per lawn. One weekend, Amy cut 4 lawns, and Chad cut 3 lawns. How much money did they earn altogether?

There is often more than one way to solve a multi-step problem.

Solution One

Hidden Question: How many lawns did they mow altogether?

Chad cut 3 lawns, Amy cut 4 lawns.
$3 + 4 = 7$
They cut 7 lawns.

Question in the Problem: How much money did they earn altogether?

7 lawns × \$20 = \$140

Solution Two

Hidden Question 1: How much money did Chad earn for cutting lawns?

3 × \$20 = \$60

Hidden Question 2: How much money did Amy earn for cutting lawns?

4 × \$20 = \$80

Question in the Problem: How much money did they earn altogether?

\$60 + \$80 = \$140

So, Chad and Amy earned \$140 altogether.

1. **Connect** Keisha sold 8 ribbons and 6 pins at a craft fair. She sold the ribbons for \$3 each and the pins for \$2 each. How much money did Keisha earn?

2. **Analyze Information** Ken uses 6 apples and 2 bananas to make a fruit salad. He puts twice as many oranges as bananas in the salad. How many pieces of fruit will Ken use to make 2 fruit salads?

3. Analyze Information Amber and her family bought 3 chicken sandwiches, 2 salads, and 1 baked potato. They spent $4 on drinks. How much did they spend in all?

DATA

Diner Delight	
Hamburger	$4
Chicken Sandwich	$5
Baked Potato	$2
Salad	$3

4. Check for Reasonableness Estimate sum of 8,237 + 504 + 4,730 + 1,823. Then find the actual sum. Is your estimate reasonable? Explain.

5. Rose has 18 pictures of birds. She has twice as many pictures of birds as pictures of trees. She has 3 times as many pictures of flowers as trees. How many pictures of birds, trees, and flowers does Rose have?

A 9 pictures
B 27 pictures
C 18 pictures
D 54 pictures

6. Analyze Information Terrence and Jennifer went to Al's Discount Music Store. Terrence bought 12 CDs and two 15-packs of blank CDs. Jennifer bought 8 DVDs, 3 CDs, and one 15-pack of blank CDs. Together, how much did they spend?

Al's Discount Music Store	
15-pack blank CDs	$7
DVDs	$5
CDs	$3

7. Communicate Grace ran 8 laps and walked 3 laps around the gym track. Grace ran twice as many laps as Tami ran. Then Tami walked twice as many laps as Grace walked. Who made more laps around the track? How many more? Explain.

8. Extend Your Thinking A tennis pro has 12 cans of tennis balls. There are 3 balls in each can. He gives an equal number of balls to each of 4 players. After the lesson, he realizes that each player lost 3 balls. How many tennis balls are left?

Name ______________________

Applying Math Processes

- How does this problem connect to previous ones?
- What is my plan?
- How can I use tools?
- How can I use number sense?
- How can I communicate and represent my thinking?
- How can I organize and record information?
- How can I explain my work?
- How can I justify my answer?

1. **Use a Strip Diagram** Zebras can run at a speed of 35 miles per hour. At this speed, how far would a zebra run in 5 hours?

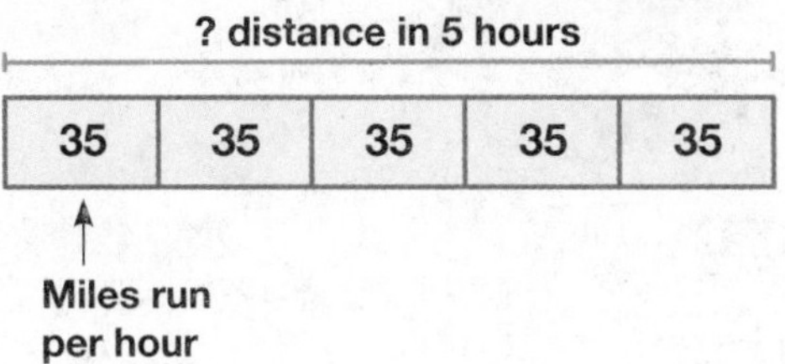

2. **Reason** Write whether Valerie's statement below is true or false. Explain your reasoning.

   The product of 5,892 and 5 is less than 25,000.

3. **Personal Financial Literacy** Teri earns $9 for each piano lesson she gives. She gave 4 lessons this week. She plans to spend $28 on a dress. How much money will she have left? Tell how you found the answer.

4. **Mental Math** Elizabeth bought 10 packs of pencils. There are 20 pencils in each pack. How many pencils did Elizabeth buy?

5. **Analyze Information** A cafeteria has 12 rows of 8 tables and 10 rows of 6 tables. 100 of the tables have been cleaned. How many tables are left to clean?

6. **Estimation** A clothing store has 45 racks for shirts. Each rack can hold 27 shirts. The store manager wants to display 900 shirts on racks. Estimate whether there are enough racks.

Error Search

Find each problem that is not correct. Circle what is wrong and rewrite the problem so it is correct.

1.	2.	3.	4.
$\begin{array}{r} 5{,}432 \\ \times \quad 6 \\ \hline 32{,}592 \end{array}$	$\begin{array}{r} 8{,}316 \\ \times \quad 3 \\ \hline 24{,}938 \end{array}$	$\begin{array}{r} 3{,}792 \\ \times \quad 4 \\ \hline 12{,}168 \end{array}$	$\begin{array}{r} 2{,}894 \\ \times \quad 9 \\ \hline 26{,}046 \end{array}$

Reasoning

Write whether each statement is true or false. If you write false, change the numbers or words so that the statement is true.

5. The number sentence that uses compatible numbers to estimate 38 × 52 is 40 × 50 = 2,000.

6. The best estimate for 52 × 44 is 50 × 40 = 200.

7. The sum of 8,673 and 4 is 34,692.

8. The product of 7,315 × 5 is 10 less than 7,305 × 5.

9. The expression 8 × 1,705 is the same as (8 × 1,000) + (8 × 700) + (8 × 5).

10. In the number 875,458,215, the digit 7 is in the ten millions place.

Name ______________________________

Set A pages 275–280

Use a model to multiply 20 × 14.

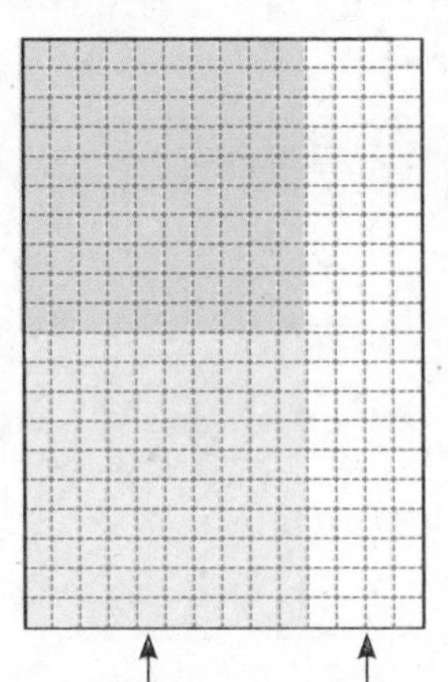

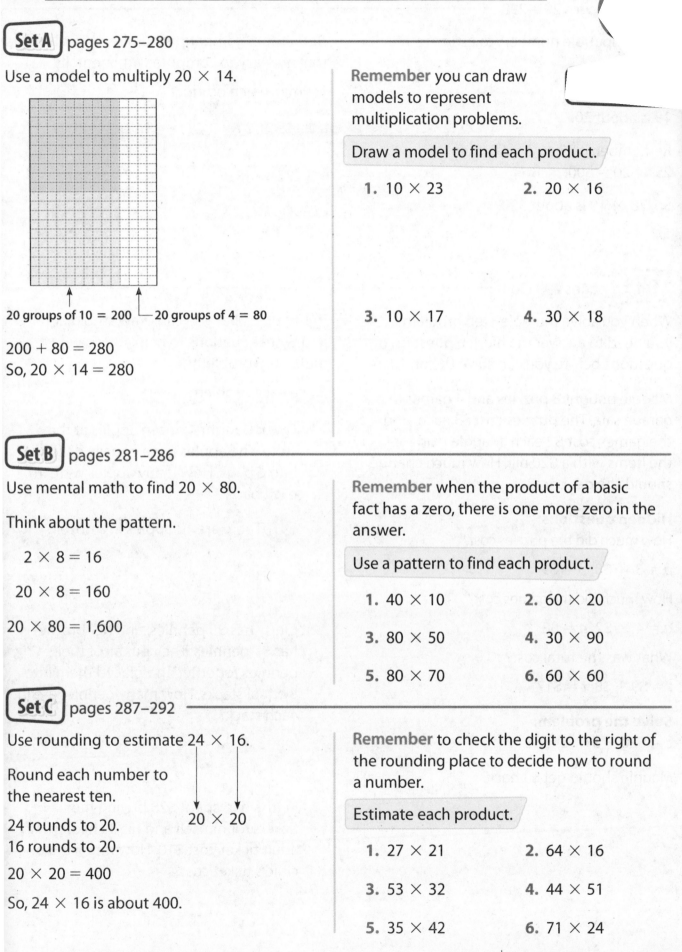

20 groups of 10 = 200 | 20 groups of 4 = 80

200 + 80 = 280
So, 20 × 14 = 280

Remember you can draw models to represent multiplication problems.

Draw a model to find each product.

1. 10 × 23 **2.** 20 × 16

3. 10 × 17 **4.** 30 × 18

Set B pages 281–286

Use mental math to find 20 × 80.

Think about the pattern.

2 × 8 = 16

20 × 8 = 160

20 × 80 = 1,600

Remember when the product of a basic fact has a zero, there is one more zero in the answer.

Use a pattern to find each product.

1. 40 × 10 **2.** 60 × 20

3. 80 × 50 **4.** 30 × 90

5. 80 × 70 **6.** 60 × 60

Set C pages 287–292

Use rounding to estimate 24 × 16.

Round each number to the nearest ten.

20 × 20

24 rounds to 20.
16 rounds to 20.

20 × 20 = 400

So, 24 × 16 is about 400.

Remember to check the digit to the right of the rounding place to decide how to round a number.

Estimate each product.

1. 27 × 21 **2.** 64 × 16

3. 53 × 32 **4.** 44 × 51

5. 35 × 42 **6.** 71 × 24

Set D pages 293–298

Use compatible numbers to estimate 28 × 19.

28 is about 25.
19 is about 20.

Remember, if 25 × 2 = 50, then 25 × 20 = 500.

So, 28 × 19 is about 500.

Remember compatible numbers are numbers that are easy to compute with mentally.

Estimate each product.

1. 29 × 31
2. 42 × 49
3. 73 × 18
4. 24 × 38
5. 19 × 31
6. 63 × 87

Set E pages 299–304

When you solve multiple-step problems, you need to answer the hidden question or questions before you can solve the problem.

Maggie bought 3 puzzles and 4 games at a garage sale. The puzzles cost $3 each, and the games cost $2 each. Maggie paid for the items with a $20 bill. How much change should she get back?

Hidden questions:
How much did the puzzles cost?

p = 3 × $3; *p* = $9

How much did the games cost?

g = 4 × $2; *g* = $8

What was the total cost?

t = $9 + $8; *t* = $17

Solve the problem:
c = $20 − $17; *c* = $3

Maggie should get $3 back.

Remember that you can draw strip diagrams and write equations to help you solve multi-step problems.

Solve each problem.

1. Gwen bought 4 dozen apples at the store. The apples were equally divided into 6 bags. How many apples were in each bag?

   Tip There are 12 apples in a dozen.

2. Cindy has 35 pennies, and her brother has 37 pennies. They put all of their pennies together and placed them into 8 equal stacks. How many pennies are in each stack?

3. Keith's dad spent $28 buying movie tickets for himself and his 3 children. An adult ticket cost $10. How much did one child's ticket cost?

Name ____________________

1. Don works 18 hours a week at the library. Which shows the best way to use rounding to estimate how many hours Don will work in 52 weeks?

   A 10 × 50

   B 10 × 60

   C 20 × 50

   D 18 × 60

2. A Virginia opossum can have up to 21 babies at one time. Suppose 10 Virginia opossums had babies all at the same time. How many baby opossums could there be?

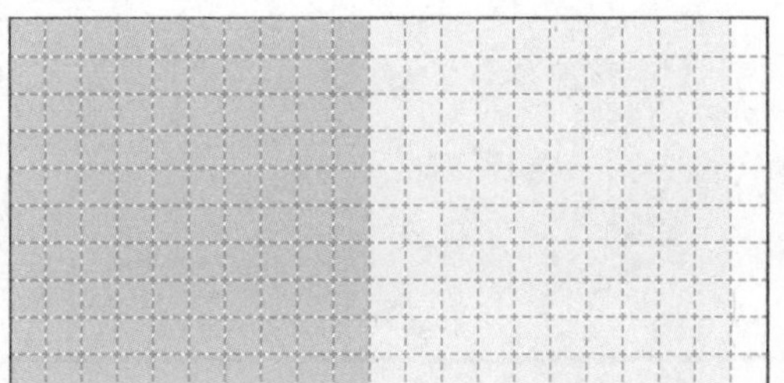

   A 320 opossums **C** 110 opossums

   B 240 opossums **D** Not here

3. There are 21 rows in an auditorium. Each row has 42 seats. Use rounding to estimate the total number of seats.

4. There are 24 schools competing in a cheerleading contest. There are 18 cheerleaders on each team. Which is **NOT** a good way to use compatible numbers to estimate the number of cheerleaders that are competing?

   A 20 × 20 **C** 10 × 10

   B 25 × 20 **D** 30 × 20

5. A movie theater sells 50 tickets for each showing of a movie. They showed the movie 40 times last week. How many tickets did they sell?

   A 20,000 tickets

   B 2,000 tickets

   C 200 tickets

   D 20 tickets

6. Elaine is making 20 pinecone wreaths to sell at a fair. She needs 13 pinecones for each wreath. How many pinecones does she need in all?

7. Mr. Hans bought 40 boxes of tiles for his kitchen floor. Each box of tiles cost $30. How much money did Mr. Hans pay for the tiles?

A $120

B $700

C $1,200

D $7,000

---

8. A florist makes centerpieces for an event. He puts 22 roses in each centerpiece. Which is the best way to use compatible numbers to estimate the number of roses he needs for 26 centerpieces?

A $10 \times 25 = 250$

B $20 \times 25 = 500$

C $25 \times 30 = 750$

D $30 \times 30 = 900$

---

9. Justine's plant stand has 6 shelves. Each shelf holds 4 plants. Justine has already placed 16 plants on her stand. How many more plants can fit on the plant stand?

			.		
⓪	⓪	⓪		⓪	⓪
①	①	①		①	①
②	②	②		②	②
③	③	③		③	③
④	④	④		④	④
⑤	⑤	⑤		⑤	⑤
⑥	⑥	⑥		⑥	⑥
⑦	⑦	⑦		⑦	⑦
⑧	⑧	⑧		⑧	⑧
⑨	⑨	⑨		⑨	⑨

10. A school building is 32 feet tall. There are 12 inches in a foot. About how many inches tall is the building?

A About 94 inches

B About 300 inches

C About 500 inches

D About 700 inches

---

11. Elizabeth is making 20 necklaces. Each necklace has 16 beads. How many beads does she need to make all of the necklaces?

A 320 beads

B 300 beads

C 36 beads

D 32 beads

---

12. Margo hiked 5 miles 3 times last week. She hiked 4 miles 4 times this week. How many miles did she hike in all during the past two weeks?

			.		
⓪	⓪	⓪		⓪	⓪
①	①	①		①	①
②	②	②		②	②
③	③	③		③	③
④	④	④		④	④
⑤	⑤	⑤		⑤	⑤
⑥	⑥	⑥		⑥	⑥
⑦	⑦	⑦		⑦	⑦
⑧	⑧	⑧		⑧	⑧
⑨	⑨	⑨		⑨	⑨

Developing Proficiency: Multiplying by 2-Digit Numbers

Essential Questions: How can arrays be used to find greater products? What is a standard procedure for multiplying multi-digit numbers?

Natural resources like water and coal come from the Earth.

Water is a renewable resource because it can be used over and over again.

I'll get a giant straw! Here's a project on water usage and multiplication.

Math and Science Project: Water Usage

Do Research Use the Internet or other sources to find how much water is used for household activities like taking a shower, taking a bath, using a dishwasher, hand washing dishes, and using a washing machine.

Journal: Write a Report Include what you found. Also in your report:

- Choose 3 of the activities. Estimate how many times each activity is done each week in your household.
- Estimate the weekly water usage for each activity. Organize your results in a table.
- Make up and solve multiplication problems based on your data.

Name ______________________________

Review What You Know

Vocabulary

Choose the best term from the box. Write it on the blank.

- rounding
- Commutative Property of Multiplication
- compatible numbers
- Distributive Property

1. ______________________ are easy to compute mentally.

2. Breaking apart a multiplication problem into the sum or difference of two simpler multiplication problems is an example of using the

   ______________________.

3. You can use __________ when you do not need an exact answer.

Estimating Sums

Estimate each sum.

4. 16 + 13
5. 688 + 95
6. 1,511 + 269
7. 3,246 + 6,243
8. 283 + 178
9. 1,999 + 421

Multiplying by 1-Digit Numbers

Find each product.

10. 53 × 9
11. 127 × 7

12. Norma has 3 photo albums. There are 215 photos in each album. How many photos does Norma have in her albums?

13. The principal bought 5 computers. Each one cost $914. What was the total price?

   A $919 **C** $4,570
   B $4,550 **D** $4,580

Partial Products

14. **Explain** Explain why the array shown below represents 3 × 21.

Writing to Explain

15. **Tools** Each crate of apples weighs 178 pounds. How much does 4 crates of apples weigh? Explain which tool—a digital tool, objects, manipulatives, or paper and pencil—you would select to solve this problem. Then solve.

My Word Cards

Use the example for the word on the front of the card to help complete the definition on the back.

A-Z

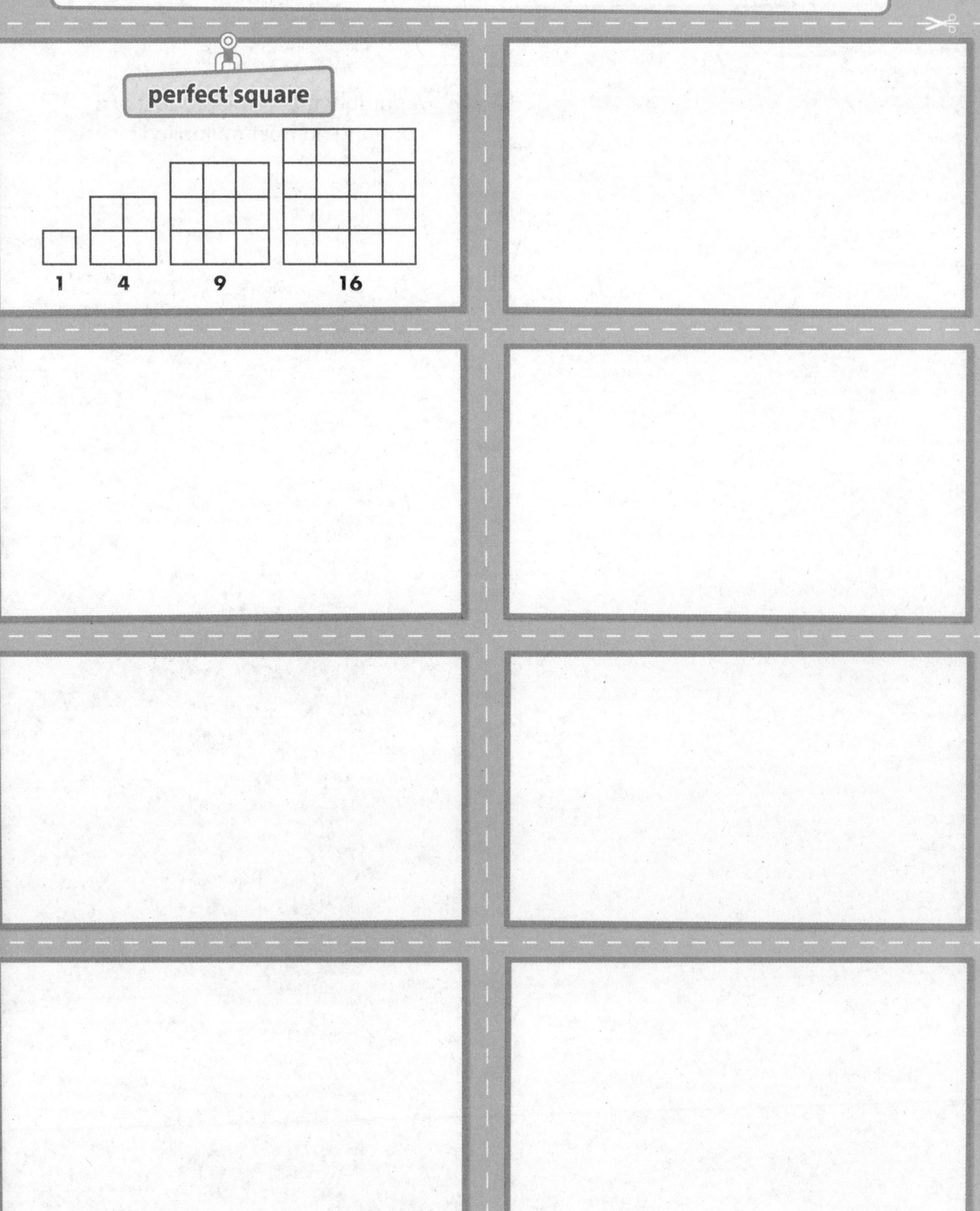

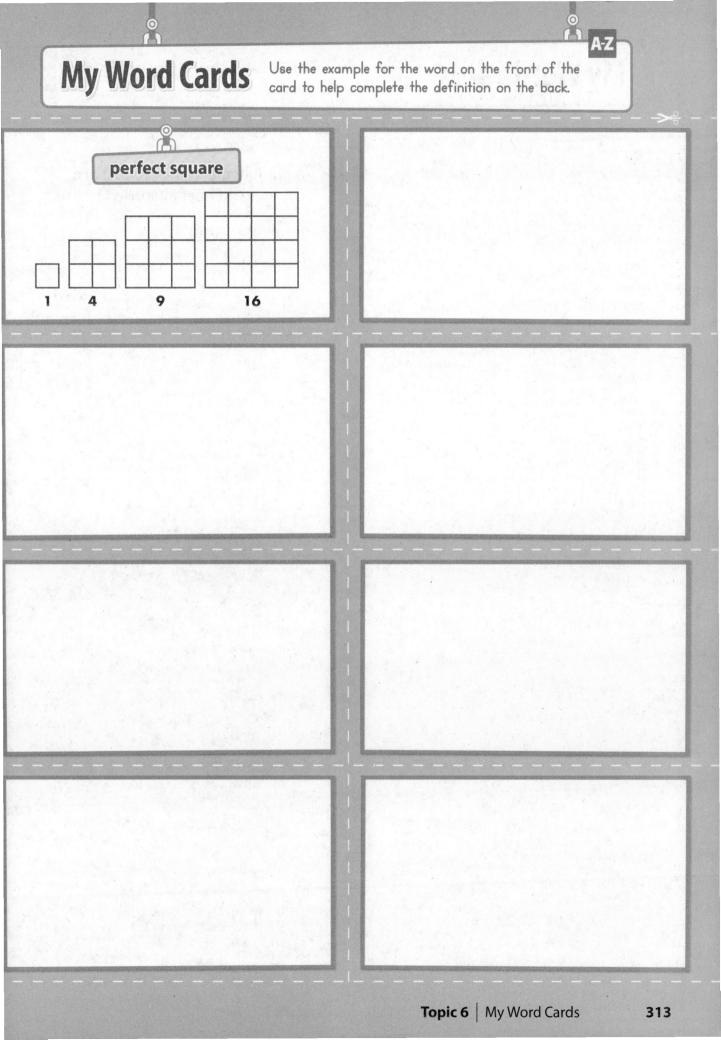

My Word Cards

Complete the definition. Extend learning by writing your own definition.

A number that is the product of a counting number multiplied by itself is called a ______________________.

Name

Lesson 6-1

Arrays and Multiplying 2-Digit Numbers

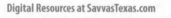

TEKS 4.4C Represent the product of 2 two-digit numbers using arrays, area models, or equations, including perfect squares through 15 by 15. Also, 4.4D. **Mathematical Process Standards** 4.1A, 4.1B, 4.1D, 4.1E, 4.1G

Digital Resources at SavvasTexas.com

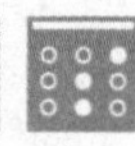

Solve Learn Glossary Check Tools Games

Solve & Share

A theater has 14 rows of seats with 23 seats in each row. How many seats are there in all? ***Solve this problem any way you choose.***

You can **create and use representations.** How can you use grid paper to model the problem?

Look Back!

Connect What kinds of things do you see neatly arranged in rows and columns, or in arrays?

How Can You Multiply Using an Array?

A

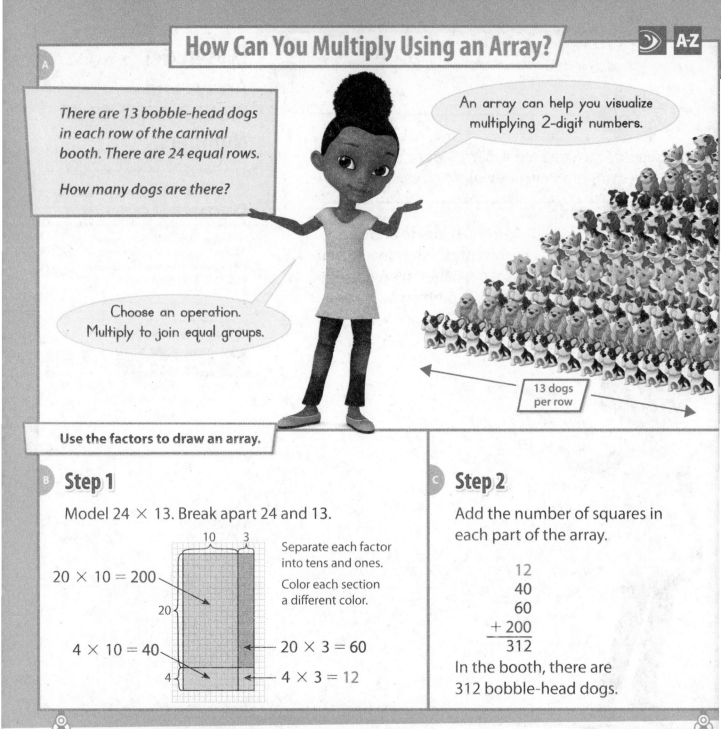

There are 13 bobble-head dogs in each row of the carnival booth. There are 24 equal rows.

How many dogs are there?

An array can help you visualize multiplying 2-digit numbers.

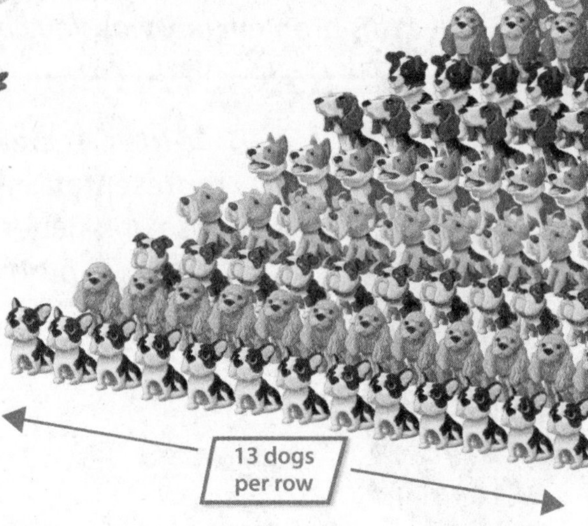

Choose an operation. Multiply to join equal groups.

Use the factors to draw an array.

B

Step 1

Model 24 × 13. Break apart 24 and 13.

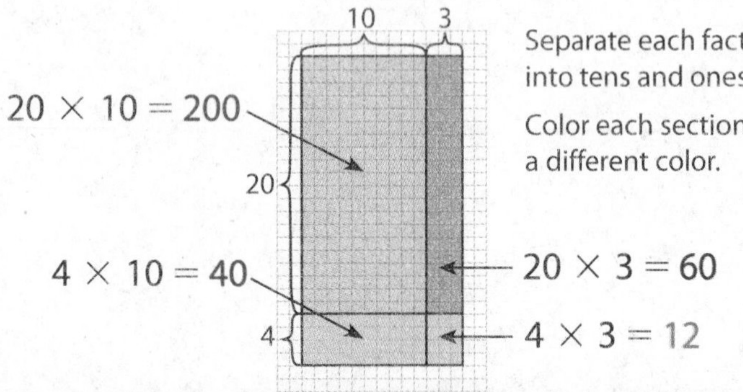

Separate each factor into tens and ones.

Color each section a different color.

C

Step 2

Add the number of squares in each part of the array.

$$\begin{array}{r} 12 \\ 40 \\ 60 \\ +\ 200 \\ \hline 312 \end{array}$$

In the booth, there are 312 bobble-head dogs.

Do You Understand?

Convince Me! What 2-digit by 2-digit multiplication is shown by the model at the right?

What is the product?

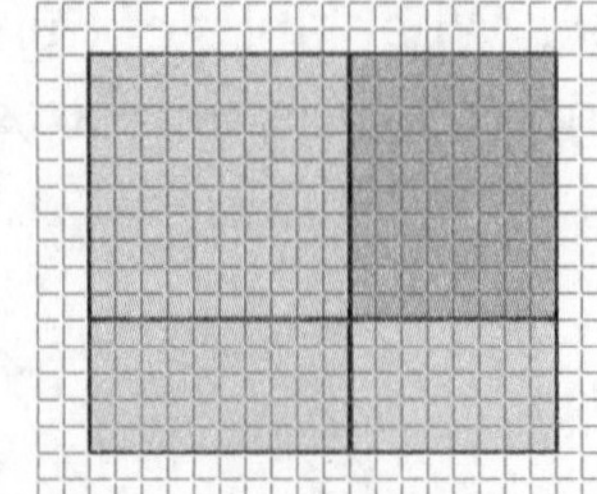

Name ______________________________

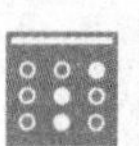

Guided Practice*

In **1** and **2**, use the grid to find the product.

1. 17 × 13

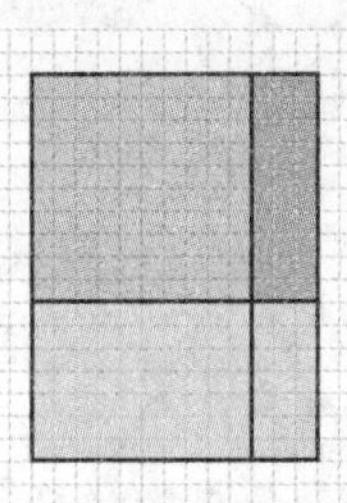

2. 24 × 16

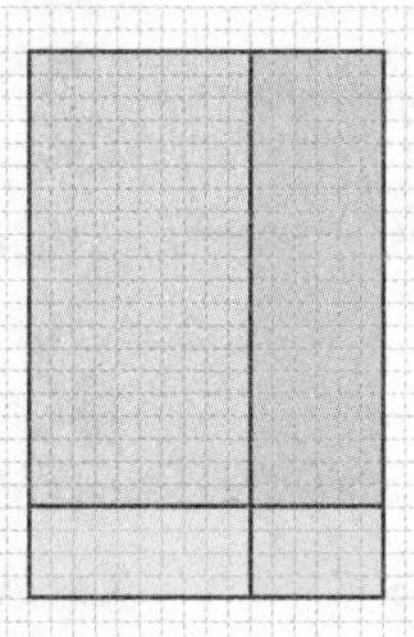

3. In Exercise 1, what four simpler multiplication problems were used to find 17 × 13?

4. Why does it make sense to separate each factor into tens and ones?

Independent Practice

In **5** through **8**, use a grid to find the product.

5. 14 × 21

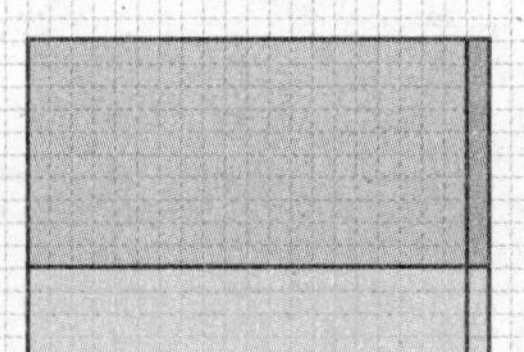

6. 14 × 12

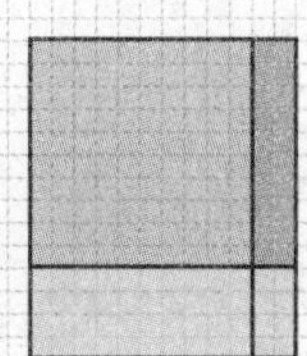

7. 18 × 18

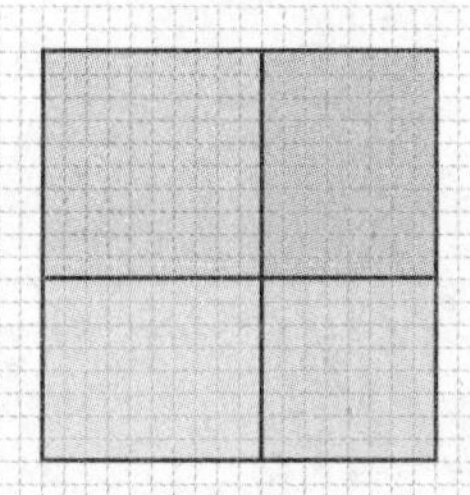

8. 13 × 15

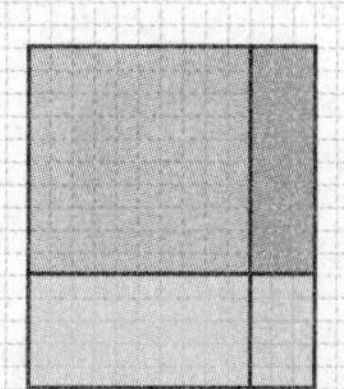

You can solve the simpler problems in any order.

*For another example, see Set A on page 359.

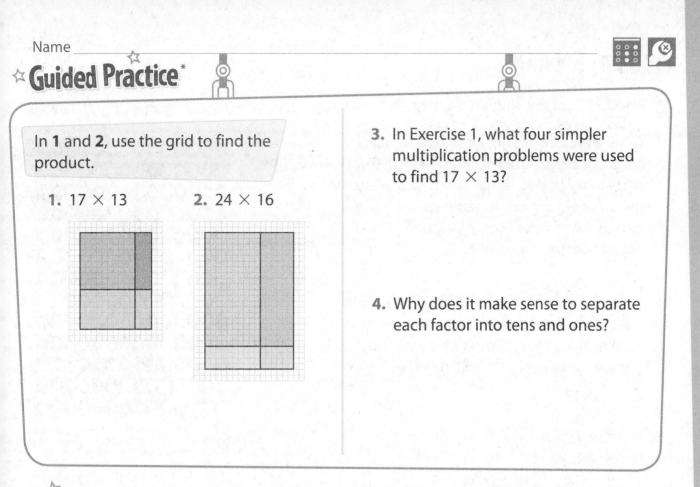

Problem Solving

In **9** and **10**, use the diagram to the right.

9. Draw a Picture Maggie is making a balloon game for the school fair. Students will throw darts to try to pop the balloons. Draw lines on the array of balloons to separate each factor into tens and ones. How many balloons are used to set up the game?

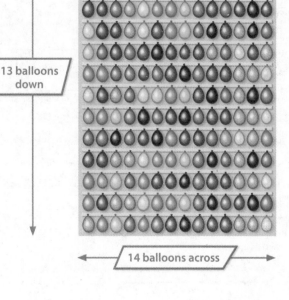

13 balloons down

14 balloons across

10. Maggie knows that she will have to completely refill the balloon board about 15 times in all. Which expression shows how to find the number of balloons she will need?

A 15×13
B 15×14
C $15 \times (13 \times 14)$
D $15 \times (13 + 14)$

11. A theater has 1,918 seats in all. Section A has 7 rows with 14 seats in each row. How many seats are in Section A?

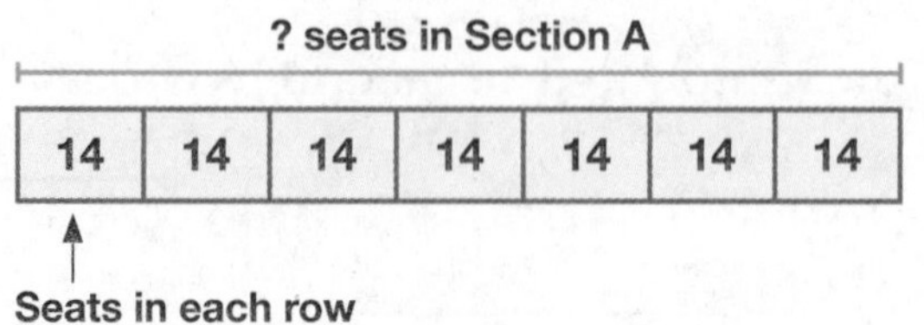

12. Connect The flagpole in front of City Hall in Luis's town is 35 feet tall. How many inches tall is the flagpole?

Remember,
12 inches = 1 foot.

13. Extend Your Thinking Why is the product of 15×32 equal to the sum of 10×32 and 5×32?

Name ________________________________

Homework 6-1
Arrays and Multiplying 2-Digit Numbers

Another Look!

One way to find the product of 12 × 24 is by using an array.

Draw a rectangular model with 12 rows of 24 units.

Divide the model into tens and ones for each factor. Find the number of squares in each smaller rectangle. Then add the number of squares in the four small rectangles.

The array shows the four simpler problems you solve.

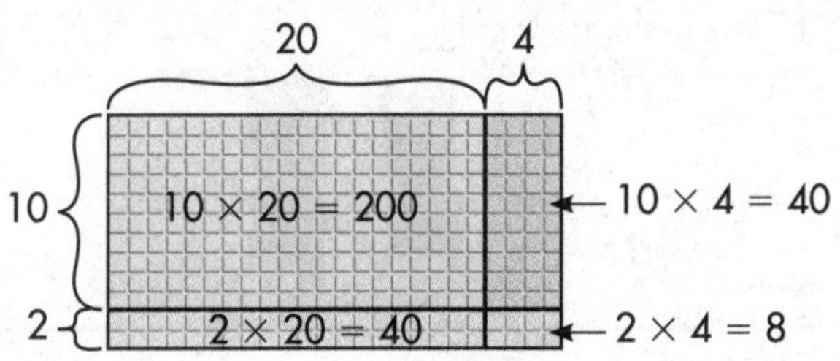

$$\begin{array}{r} 8 \\ 40 \\ 40 \\ +\ 200 \\ \hline 288 \end{array}$$

So, 12 × 24 = 288.

In **1** through **4**, find each product. Use the grids to help.

1. 26 × 18

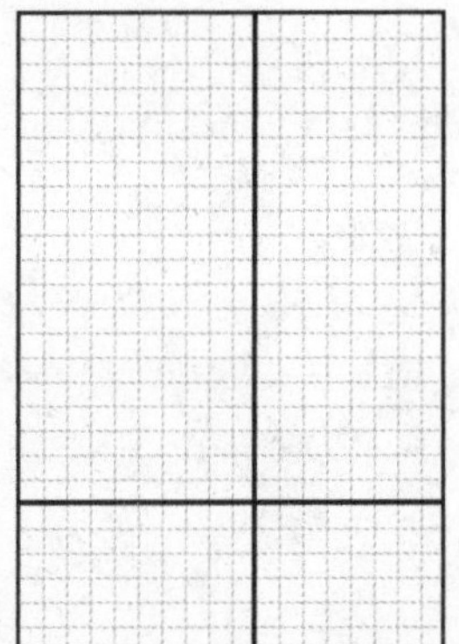

2. 23 × 23

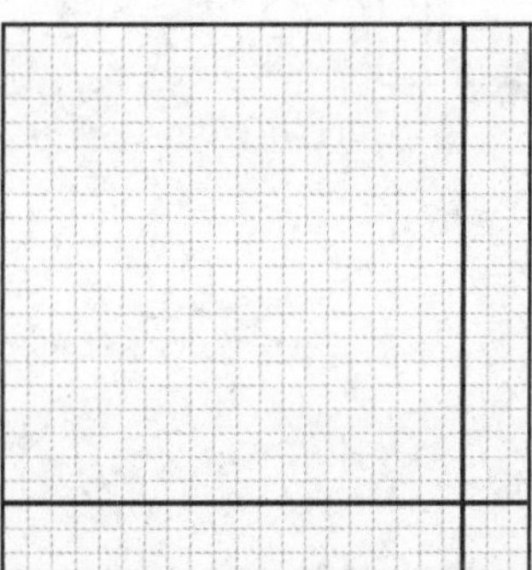

3. 19 × 27

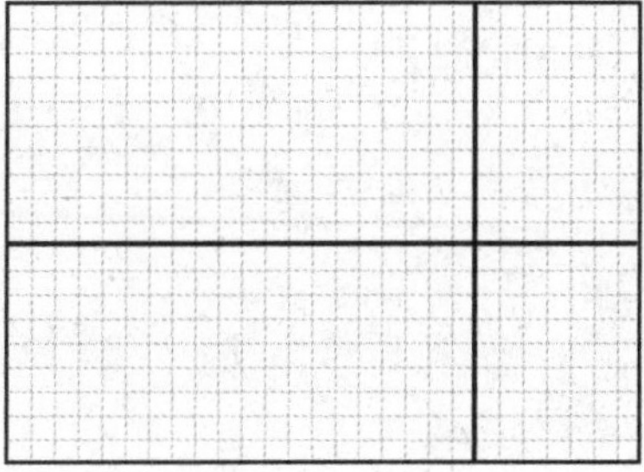

4. 11 × 16

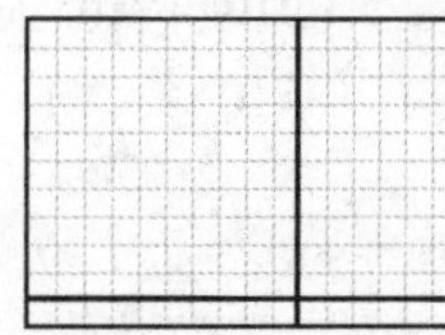

5. **Connect** The prices at Nolan's Novelties store are shown at the right. If 27 boxes of neon keychains and 35 boxes of glow-in-the-dark pens were sold, what was the total sales in dollars?

6. **Justify** Which would cost more, 10 boxes of neon keychains or 15 boxes of glow-in-the-dark pens?

DATA

Item	Price per box
Neon keychains	$15
Glow-in-the-dark pens	$10

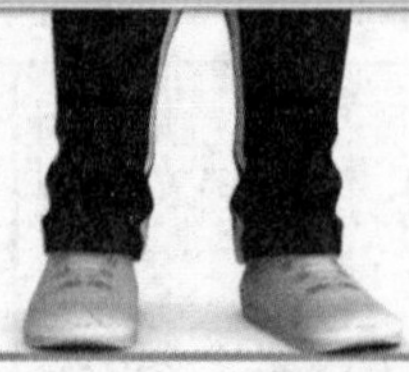

7. Barb exercises for 14 hours each week. How many hours does she exercise in 22 weeks? Use the grid to help.

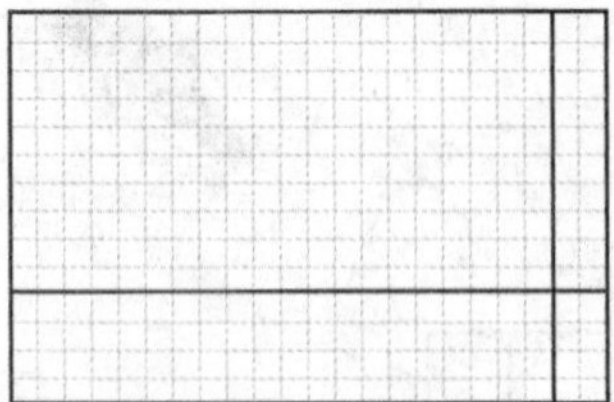

A 296 hours
B 308 hours
C 320 hours
D 424 hours

8. **Check for Reasonableness** Teri used the expanded algorithm to find the product below. Is Teri's answer reasonable? Explain.

$$\begin{array}{r} 4{,}296 \\ \times \quad 7 \\ \hline 42 \\ 630 \\ 1{,}400 \\ 2{,}800 \\ \hline 4{,}872 \end{array}$$

9. **Explain** How can you use a grid to break apart the problem 16 × 34 into four simpler multiplication problems?

10. **Extend Your Thinking** How can you use arrays to show breaking apart to find the product of 18 and 12?

Name ______________________________

Solve & Share There are 11 regular players and 5 substitute players on a professional soccer team. How many players are there in all on 15 soccer teams? ***Solve this problem any way you choose.***

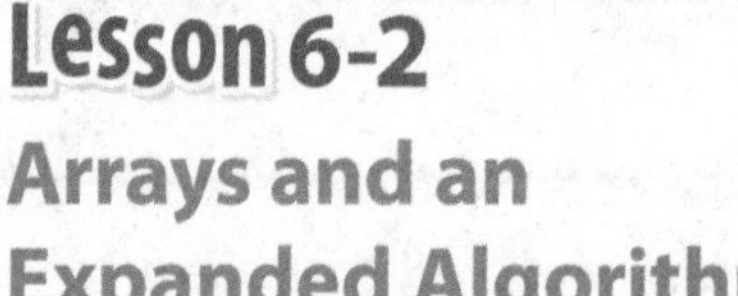

Lesson 6-2

Arrays and an Expanded Algorithm

TEKS 4.4D Use strategies and algorithms, including the standard algorithm, ... to multiply a two-digit number by a two-digit number.... Also 4.4C. **Mathematical Process Standards** 4.1B, 4.1C, 4.1D, 4.1E, 4.1G

Digital Resources at SavvasTexas.com

Solve Learn Glossary Check Tools Games

You can **create a representation.** Grid paper can help you multiply 2-digit numbers. ***Show your work in the space below!***

Look Back!

Estimation How could you have estimated the product for this situation?

How Can You Record Multiplication?

A

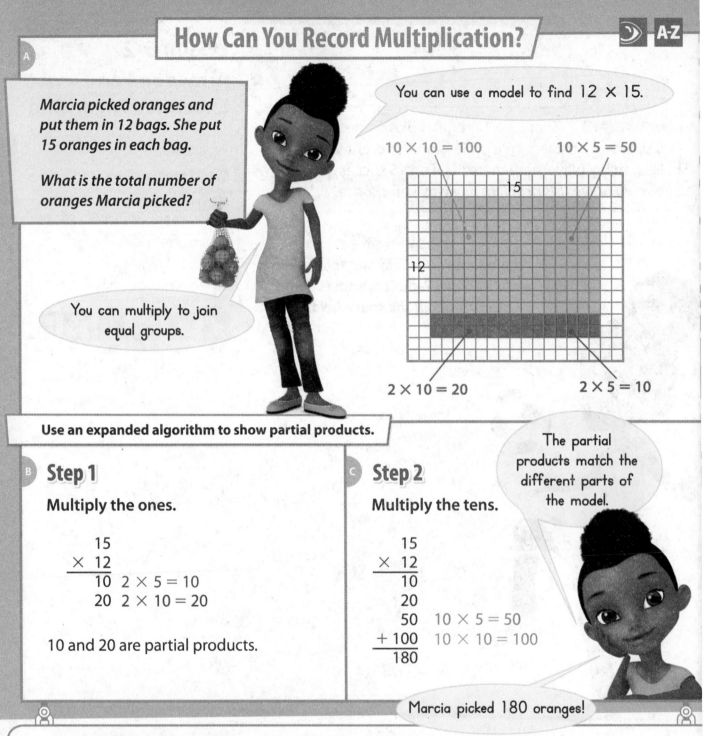

Marcia picked oranges and put them in 12 bags. She put 15 oranges in each bag.

What is the total number of oranges Marcia picked?

You can use a model to find 12 × 15.

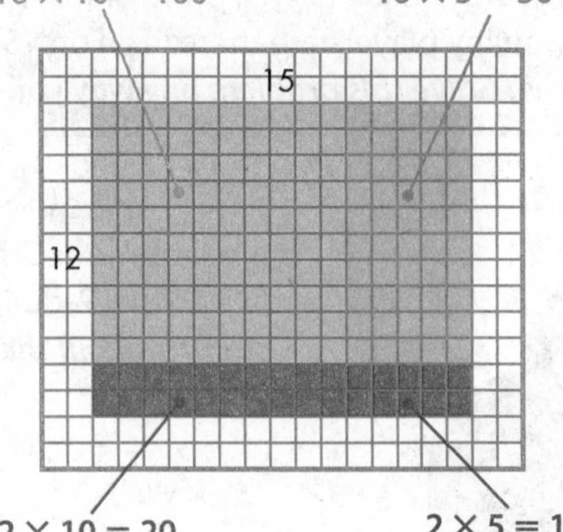

2 × 10 = 20

2 × 5 = 10

You can multiply to join equal groups.

Use an expanded algorithm to show partial products.

B

Step 1

Multiply the ones.

$$\begin{array}{r} 15 \\ \times\ 12 \\ \hline 10 \\ 20 \end{array} \quad \begin{array}{l} \\ \\ 2 \times 5 = 10 \\ 2 \times 10 = 20 \end{array}$$

10 and 20 are partial products.

C

Step 2

Multiply the tens.

$$\begin{array}{r} 15 \\ \times\ 12 \\ \hline 10 \\ 20 \\ 50 \\ +\ 100 \\ \hline 180 \end{array} \quad \begin{array}{l} \\ \\ \\ \\ 10 \times 5 = 50 \\ 10 \times 10 = 100 \\ \\ \end{array}$$

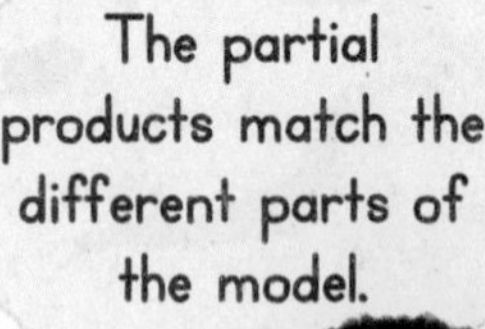

The partial products match the different parts of the model.

Marcia picked 180 oranges!

Do You Understand?

Convince Me! Use the model. Draw lines to show that the partial products are correct. What is the final product?

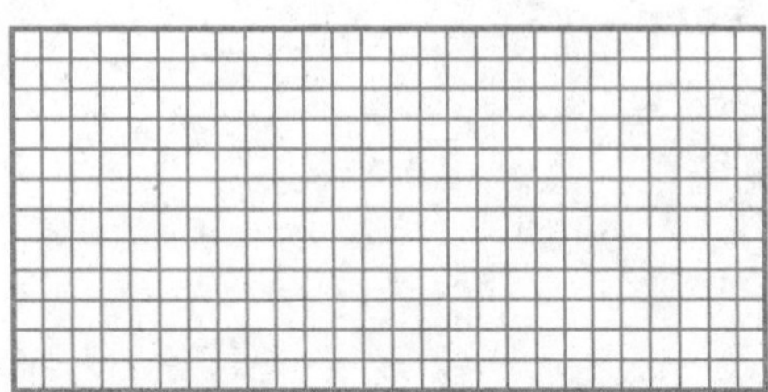

$$\begin{array}{r} 26 \\ \times\ 12 \\ \hline 12 \\ 40 \\ 60 \\ +\ 200 \\ \hline \end{array} \quad \begin{array}{l} \\ \\ \text{2 rows of 6} \\ \text{2 rows of 20} \\ \text{10 rows of 6} \\ \text{10 rows of 20} \\ \textbf{Final product} \end{array}$$

Name

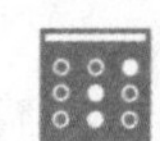

Guided Practice*

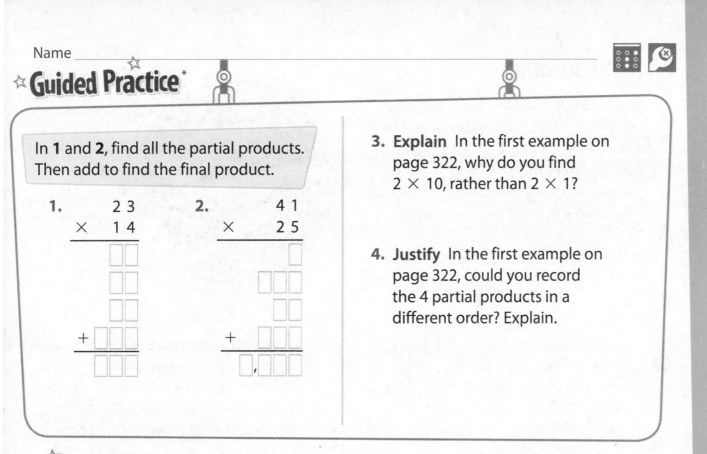

In **1** and **2**, find all the partial products. Then add to find the final product.

1. 23 × 14

2. 41 × 25

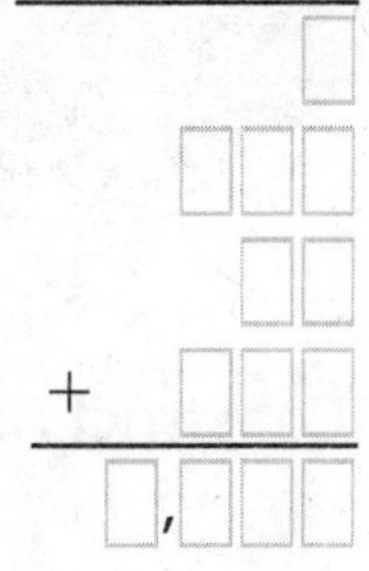

3. Explain In the first example on page 322, why do you find 2 × 10, rather than 2 × 1?

4. Justify In the first example on page 322, could you record the 4 partial products in a different order? Explain.

Independent Practice

Leveled Practice In **5** through **12**, find all the partial products. Then add to find the final product.

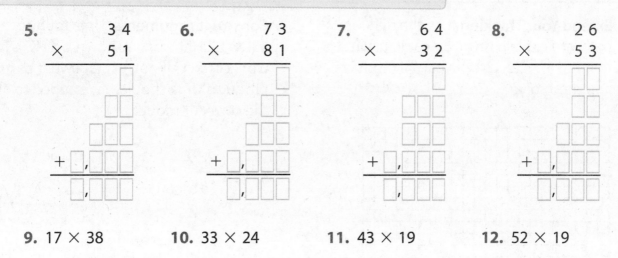

5. 34 × 51

6. 73 × 81

7. 64 × 32

8. 26 × 53

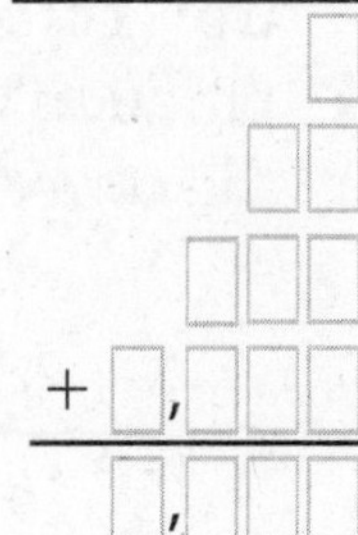

9. 17 × 38 **10.** 33 × 24 **11.** 43 × 19 **12.** 52 × 19

*For another example, see Set B on page 359.

Problem Solving

13. The Castillo de San Marcos is a Spanish fortress that was built between 1672 and 1695.
    a. Rounded to the nearest ten thousand, how many pesos did it cost to build the fortress?
    b. How many years did it take to build the fortress?

It cost 138,375 pesos to build this fortress.

14. A pair of one type of shoes weighs 15 ounces. The shoebox they come in weighs 2 ounces. Which is the total weight of 15 pairs of these shoes, including the boxes?

    A 147 ounces
    B 155 ounces
    C 225 ounces
    D 255 ounces

15. **Construct Arguments** A school has two large patios. One is rectangular and is 24 feet long by 18 feet wide. The other is square and each side is 21 feet long. Which patio has a greater perimeter? Explain.

16. **Extend Your Thinking** Use the diagram below to explain how you could use it to find 14×22. List the partial products and then solve.

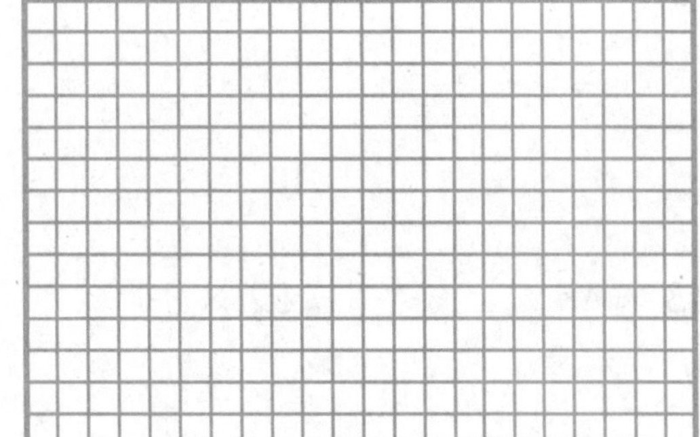

17. **Construct Arguments** Uma found 62×13. Her work is shown below. Is her work correct? If not, explain what partial products Uma should have added to find the correct product.

$$\begin{array}{r} 13 \\ \times\ 62 \\ \hline 6 \\ 2 \\ 180 \\ +\ 60 \\ \hline 248 \end{array}$$

Name ______________________

Homework 6-2
Arrays and an Expanded Algorithm

Another Look!

Golf balls come in boxes of 12 costing $12.95 each. How many golf balls are in 14 boxes?

What You Show

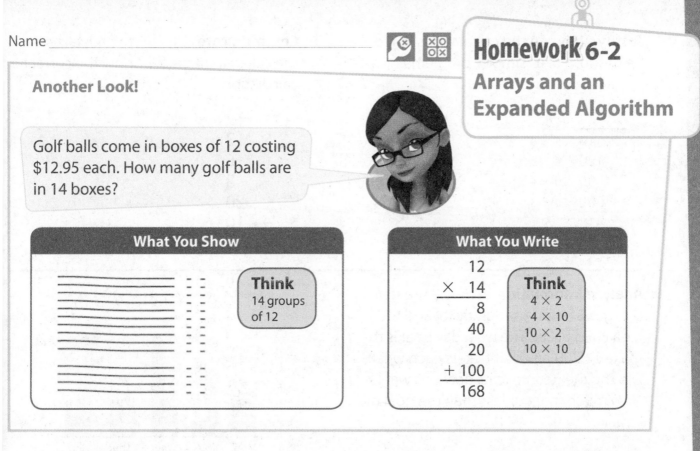

Think
14 groups of 12

What You Write

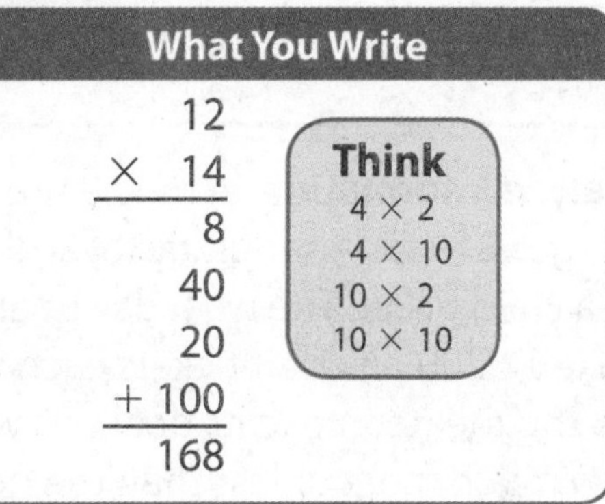

$$\begin{array}{r} 12 \\ \times\ 14 \\ \hline 8 \\ 40 \\ 20 \\ +\ 100 \\ \hline 168 \end{array}$$

Think
4 × 2
4 × 10
10 × 2
10 × 10

1. Draw an array for 15 × 16.
Use the array to complete the calculation.

$$\begin{array}{r} 16 \\ \times\ 15 \\ \hline \square\square \\ \square\square \\ \square\square \\ +\ \square\square\square \\ \hline \square\square\square \end{array}$$

2. $$\begin{array}{r} 16 \\ \times\ 12 \\ \hline \square\square \\ \square\square \\ \square\square \\ +\ \square\square\square \\ \hline \square\square\square \end{array}$$

3. $$\begin{array}{r} 19 \\ \times\ 13 \\ \hline \square\square \\ \square\square \\ \square\square \\ +\ \square\square\square \\ \hline \square\square\square \end{array}$$

4. $$\begin{array}{r} 24 \\ \times\ 12 \\ \hline \square \\ \square\square \\ \square\square \\ +\ \square\square\square \\ \hline \square\square\square \end{array}$$

5. $$\begin{array}{r} 32 \\ \times\ 23 \\ \hline \square \\ \square\square \\ \square\square \\ +\ \square\square\square \\ \hline \square\square\square \end{array}$$

6. Justify Why can the calculations in red be thought of as simpler problems?

$$
\begin{array}{rl}
34 & \\
\times\ 24 & \\
\hline
16 & 4 \times 4 \\
120 & 4 \times 30 \\
80 & 20 \times 4 \\
+\ 600 & 20 \times 30 \\
\hline
816 &
\end{array}
$$

7. Communicate Explain the mistakes in the calculation below. Show the correct calculation.

$$
\begin{array}{r}
12 \\
\times\ 13 \\
\hline
6 \\
3 \\
20 \\
+\ 10 \\
\hline
39
\end{array}
$$

8. Analyze Information A movie theater charges $10 for an adult ticket and $9 for a child ticket. The weekday goal is to make $1,200 on adult tickets each week. Did the theater make its goal this week? How much more or less than the goal did it make?

9. A group of 12 adults and 14 children bought tickets to Play-Land for a day. Which expression can you use to find the total cost of the tickets?

A $(12 \times 18) + (14 \times 15)$
B $(12 \times 15) + (14 \times 12)$
C $(12 + 15) \times (14 + 12)$
D $(12 + 14) \times 10$

Play-Land Fun Park
Adults $18 each
Children $15 each
Seniors $12

10. Extend Your Thinking A golf practice range has only 245 balls. The owner bought a carton of golf balls. How many golf balls did the owner have after buying the carton?

Golf Balls
12 balls to a box
15 boxes to a crate
5 crates to a carton

Name ____________________

Lesson 6-3
Multiplying 2-Digit Numbers by Multiples of 10

Solve & Share In January, Tim's aquarium had 23 guppies. A year later, he has 90 times as many guppies. How many guppies does Tim have now? ***Solve this problem any way you choose.***

TEKS 4.4D Use strategies and algorithms, including the standard algorithm,... to multiply a two-digit number by a two-digit number.... Also, 4.4C. Mathematical Process Standards 4.1B, 4.1C, 4.1D, 4.1F, 4.1G

Digital Resources at SavvasTexas.com

Solve

Learn

Glossary

Check

Tools
Games

You can **use reasoning.** How can breaking up each number using place value help you solve this problem? ***Show your work in the space below!***

Look Back!

Connect Ideas How is multiplying 23 by 90 like multiplying 23 by 9?

How Can You Multiply by Multiples of 10?

Mr. Jeffrey buys 20 rock identification kits for his science classes. If each kit has 28 rocks, how many rocks are there in all?

Choose an operation. Multiply to find the number of rocks.

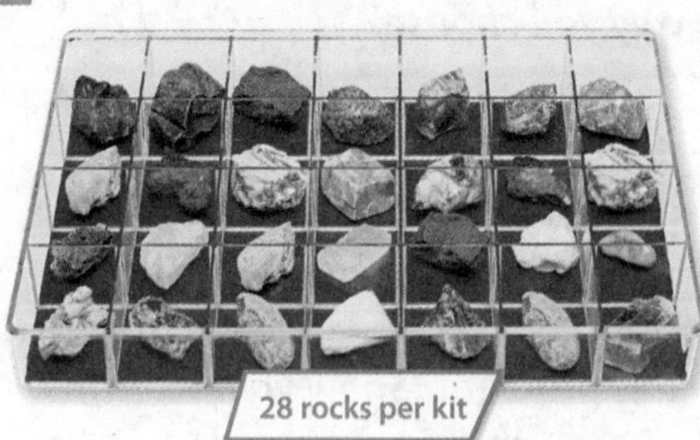

Use a model or use the standard algorithm.

One Way

Find 20 × 28.

Break 28 into tens and ones: **28 = 20 + 8**.

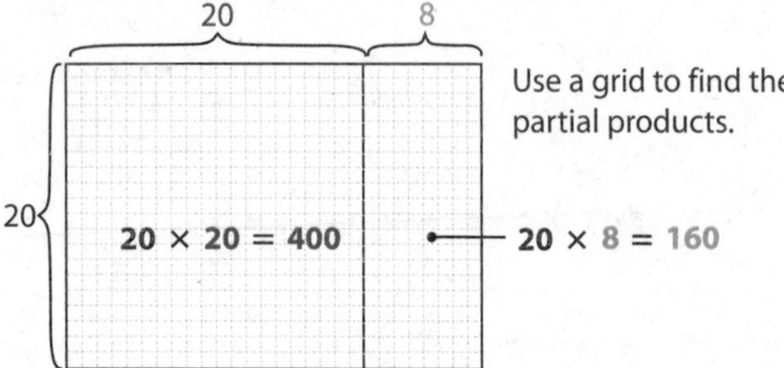

Use a grid to find the partial products.

Add the partial products to find the product.

400 + 160 = 560

Another Way

Find 20 × 28.

Multiply 2 tens × 28.

$$\begin{array}{r} \overset{1}{2}8 \\ \times\ 20 \\ \hline 560 \end{array}$$

Record a 0 in the ones place of the answer. This shows how many tens are in the answer.

There are 560 rocks in all.

Do You Understand?

Convince Me! Amanda said, "To find 68 × 30, I'll just find 68 × 3 and write a 0 at the end."

Is Amanda correct? Explain.

Name ______

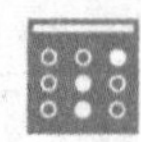

Guided Practice*

In **1** through **6**, multiply to find each product.

1. $\begin{array}{r} 12 \\ \times\ 20 \\ \hline \square\square 0 \end{array}$

2. $\begin{array}{r} 21 \\ \times\ 30 \\ \hline \square\square 0 \end{array}$

3. 35 × 20

4. 63 × 20

5. 27 × 60

6. 66 × 40

7. Explain When you multiply by 20, why is there a zero in the ones place of the product?

8. Number Sense What simpler multiplication problem can help you find 38 × 70?

9. Extend Your Thinking Each year, Mr. Jeffrey's school orders 100 rock kits. Each kit contains 28 rocks. How many rocks are there in all of the kits?

Independent Practice

Leveled Practice In **10** through **22**, multiply to find each product.

10. $\begin{array}{r} 12 \\ \times\ 30 \\ \hline \square\square 0 \end{array}$

11. $\begin{array}{r} 24 \\ \times\ 50 \\ \hline \square,\square\square 0 \end{array}$

12. $\begin{array}{r} 33 \\ \times\ 20 \\ \hline \square\square 0 \end{array}$

13. $\begin{array}{r} 71 \\ \times\ 30 \\ \hline \square,\square\square 0 \end{array}$

14. $\begin{array}{r} 63 \\ \times\ 40 \\ \hline \square,\square\square 0 \end{array}$

15. 18 × 30

16. 20 × 51

17. 32 × 30

18. 40 × 22

19. 24 × 40

20. 34 × 50

21. 40 × 73

22. 88 × 30

*For another example, see Set C on page 359.

Problem Solving

23. A roller coaster ran 50 times one afternoon and reached speeds of 70 miles per hour. If all of the rides were full, how many people rode the roller coaster that afternoon?

A 160 people
B 1,500 people
C 1,600 people
D 2,240 people

8 rows of
4 people

24. It took Davina 45 minutes to clean her room. How many seconds did it take her?

There are 60 seconds in one minute.

25. Reason Rex's class raised frogs from tadpoles. The class has 21 students, and each student raised 6 tadpoles. All but 6 of the tadpoles grew to be frogs. Write a number sentence to show how many frogs the class raised.

26. Construct Arguments Keri simplified the expression below. Is her answer correct? How could she have simplified the expression to multiply by a multiple of 10?

$$57 \times (37 - 7) =$$
$$(57 \times 37) - (57 \times 7) =$$
$$2{,}109 - 399 = 1{,}710$$

27. Extend Your Thinking Jared says it is easier to place a number with 0 ones as the second factor rather than the first. Jasmine says it does not matter which order the factors are placed. Who do you agree with? Explain.

Name ____________________

Homework 6-3
Multiplying 2-Digit Numbers by Multiples of 10

Another Look!

Find 30 × 26.

One way to find 30 × 26 is to use a grid. Show 30 rows with 26 squares in each row.

Break apart 26 into tens and ones: 26 = 20 + 6.

Multiply to find the partial products:
30 × 20 = 600 and 30 × 6 = 180.

Add the partial products:
600 + 180 = 780. So, 30 × 26 = 780.

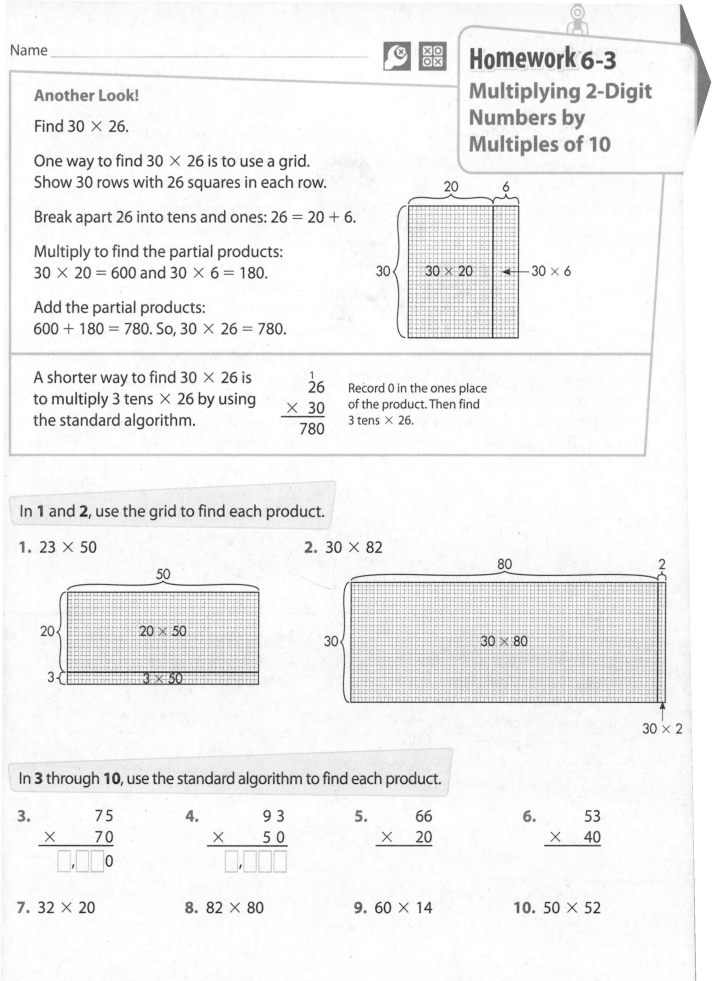

20 | 6
30 | 30 × 20 | 30 × 6

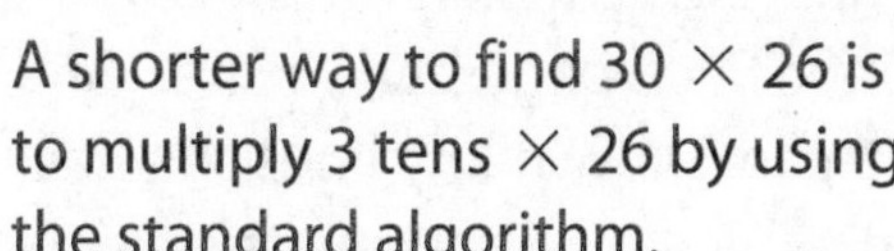

A shorter way to find 30 × 26 is to multiply 3 tens × 26 by using the standard algorithm.

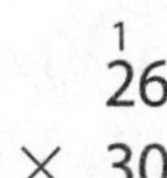

$$\begin{array}{r} \overset{1}{2}6 \\ \times\ 30 \\ \hline 780 \end{array}$$

Record 0 in the ones place of the product. Then find 3 tens × 26.

In 1 and 2, use the grid to find each product.

1. 23 × 50

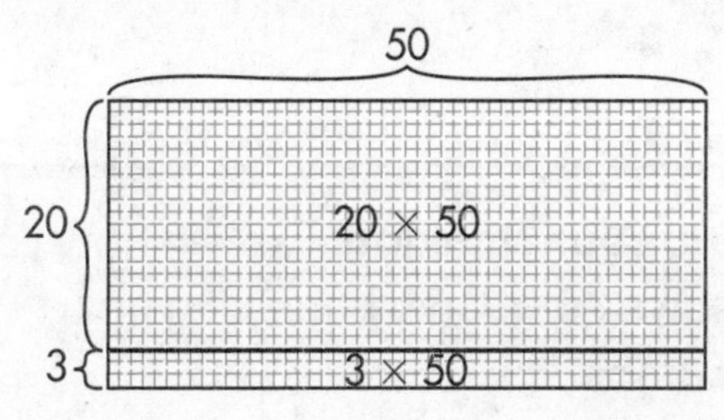

2. 30 × 82

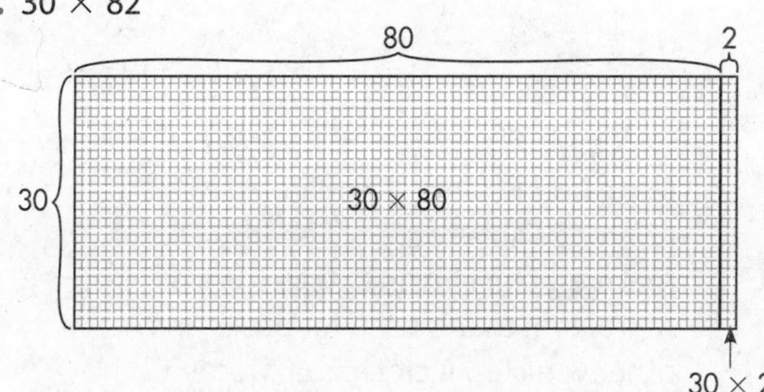

In 3 through 10, use the standard algorithm to find each product.

3. $\begin{array}{r} 75 \\ \times\ 70 \\ \hline \square,\square\square 0 \end{array}$

4. $\begin{array}{r} 93 \\ \times\ 50 \\ \hline \square,\square\square\square \end{array}$

5. $\begin{array}{r} 66 \\ \times\ 20 \\ \hline \end{array}$

6. $\begin{array}{r} 53 \\ \times\ 40 \\ \hline \end{array}$

7. 32 × 20

8. 82 × 80

9. 60 × 14

10. 50 × 52

11. **Number Sense** How many fossil kits with 10 samples each have the same number of fossils as 30 fossil kits with 8 samples each?

A 20 fossil kits
B 24 fossil kits
C 200 fossil kits
D 240 fossil kits

12. **Use a Strip Diagram** Colleen made 73 bracelets on Friday, Saturday, and Sunday. If she made 29 bracelets on Friday and 34 bracelets on Saturday, how many bracelets did Colleen make on Sunday?

73

29	34	?

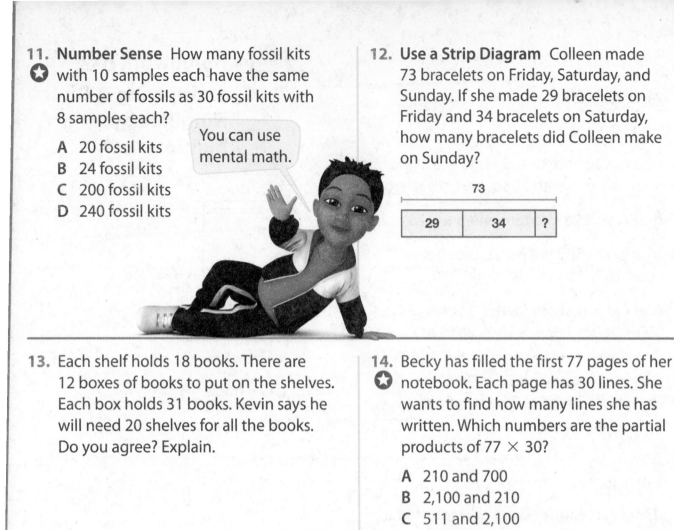

13. Each shelf holds 18 books. There are 12 boxes of books to put on the shelves. Each box holds 31 books. Kevin says he will need 20 shelves for all the books. Do you agree? Explain.

14. Becky has filled the first 77 pages of her notebook. Each page has 30 lines. She wants to find how many lines she has written. Which numbers are the partial products of 77×30?

A 210 and 700
B 2,100 and 210
C 511 and 2,100
D 4,900 and 210

15. **Math and Science** Petroleum is a nonrenewable source of energy. Diesel fuel is an efficient and clean form of petroleum that is used for buses and other vehicles. A city has 60 buses. Each bus can carry 34 passengers. If all of the buses are running, how many passengers can ride the buses at one time?

16. **Extend Your Thinking** Explain how you can solve 40×16 by breaking apart the numbers.

Name

Solve & Share

Ms. Silva has 12 weeks to train for a race. Over the course of one week, she plans to run 15 miles. If she continues this training, how many miles will Ms. Silva run before the race? ***Solve this problem any way you choose.***

Lesson 6-4

Multiplying 2-Digit by 2-Digit Numbers

TEKS 4.4D Use strategies and algorithms, including the standard algorithm,... to multiply a two-digit number by a two-digit number.... **Mathematical Process Standards** 4.1A, 4.1B, 4.1C, 4.1D, 4.1F

Digital Resources at SavvasTexas.com

Solve

Learn
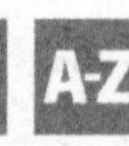
Glossary
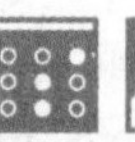
Check

Tools

Games

You can **formulate a plan.** How can you use partial products to solve this problem? ***Show your work in the space above!***

Look Back!

Check for Reasonableness Suppose someone estimated 60 miles as an answer to the above problem. Is this estimate reasonable? If not, what mistake do you think was made?

What Is a Common Way to Record Multiplication?

A

A ferry carried an average of 37 cars per trip on Saturday. If the ferry made 24 one-way trips, how many cars did it carry?

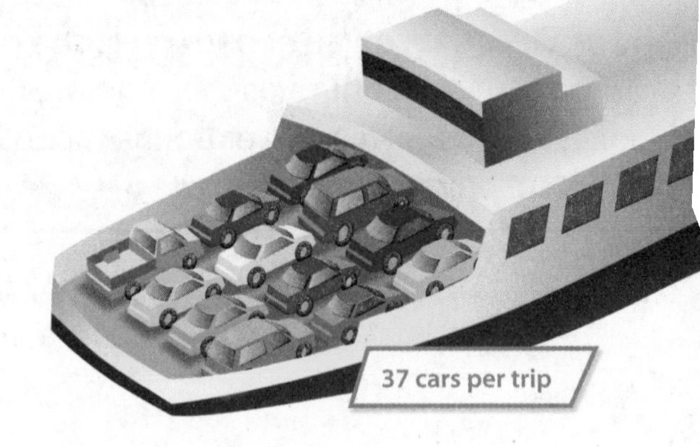

Choose an operation. Multiply to join equal groups.

The standard algorithm is a shortcut for the expanded algorithm.

Use the standard algorithm.

B

Step 1

Find 24×37.

Estimate: $20 \times 40 = 800$

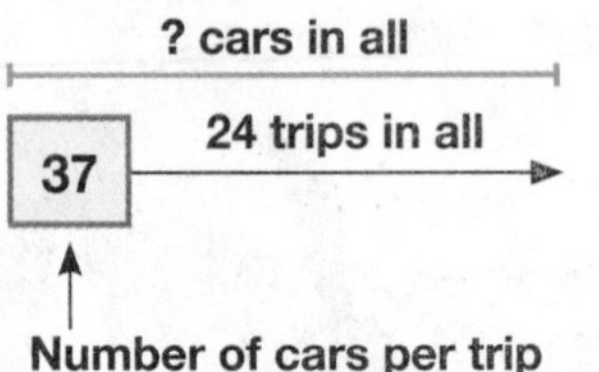

C

Step 2

Multiply by the 4 ones. Regroup if necessary.

$$\begin{array}{r} \scriptstyle 2 \\ 37 \\ \times\ 24 \\ \hline 148 \end{array}$$

D

Step 3

Multiply by the 2 tens. Regroup if necessary.

$$\begin{array}{r} \scriptstyle 1 \\ \scriptstyle 2 \\ 37 \\ \times\ 24 \\ \hline 148 \\ +\ 740 \\ \hline 888 \end{array}$$

Add the partial products.

The ferry carried 888 cars on Saturday.

Do You Understand?

Convince Me! Nannette said, "The example above broke 24×37 into two simpler problems like this."

$$\begin{array}{r} 37 \\ \times\ 20 \\ \hline \end{array} \qquad \begin{array}{r} 37 \\ \times\ 4 \\ \hline \end{array}$$

Is Nannette correct? What are the products for the simpler problems? What is the product for 24×37?

Name ____________________

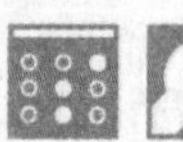 

Guided Practice*

In **1** and **2**, find the product. Estimate to check for reasonableness.

1.
```
     4 1
  ×  2 3
  ------
    1 2 □
  + □ 2 0
  ------
    9 □ □
```

2.
```
      6 3
  ×   3 1
  -------
      □ 3
  + 1,8 □ □
  -------
    1,9 5 □
```

3. The ferry made 36 one-way trips on Sunday and carried an average of 21 cars on each trip. How many cars were ferried on Sunday? Use estimation to check your answer for reasonableness.

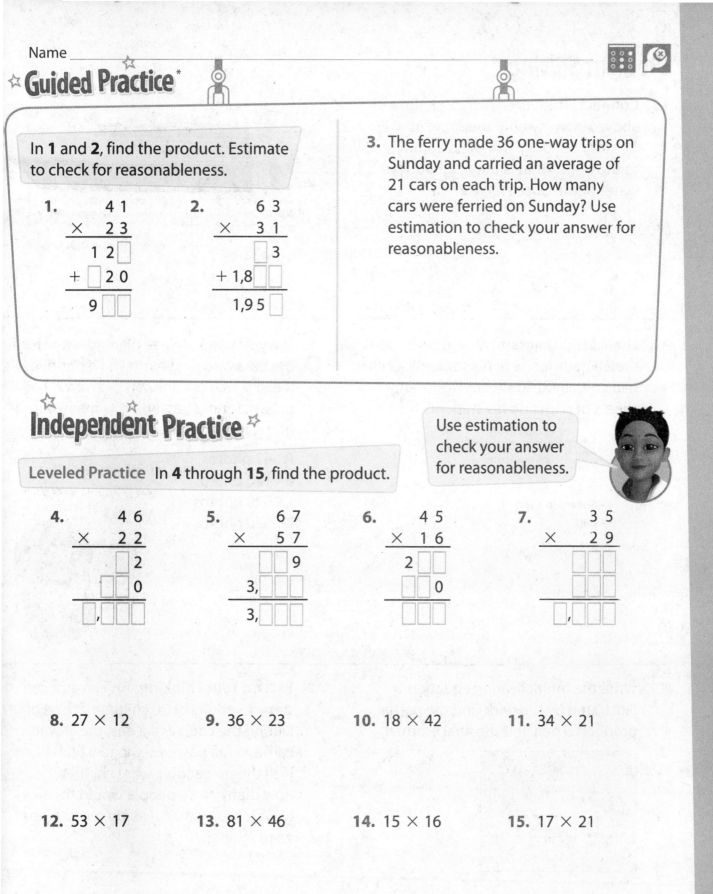

Independent Practice

Use estimation to check your answer for reasonableness.

Leveled Practice In **4** through **15**, find the product.

4.
```
      4 6
  ×   2 2
  -------
      □ 2
    □ □ 0
  -------
  □,□ □ □
```

5.
```
       6 7
  ×    5 7
  --------
     □ □ 9
  3,□ □ □
  --------
  3,□ □ □
```

6.
```
     4 5
  ×  1 6
  ------
   2 □ □
   □ □ 0
  ------
   □ □ □
```

7.
```
      3 5
  ×   2 9
  -------
    □ □ □
    □ □ □
  -------
  □,□ □ □
```

8. 27 × 12 **9.** 36 × 23 **10.** 18 × 42 **11.** 34 × 21

12. 53 × 17 **13.** 81 × 46 **14.** 15 × 16 **15.** 17 × 21

For another example, see Set D on page 360.

Problem Solving

16. **Connect** The *Queen Mary 2*'s height above water is about the same as a 14-story building. Use the diagram to the right. What is the height above water of the *Queen Mary 2*?

17. **Use a Strip Diagram** Mr. Morris bought sketch pads for 24 of his students. Each pad contained 50 sheets. How many sheets of paper do his students have?

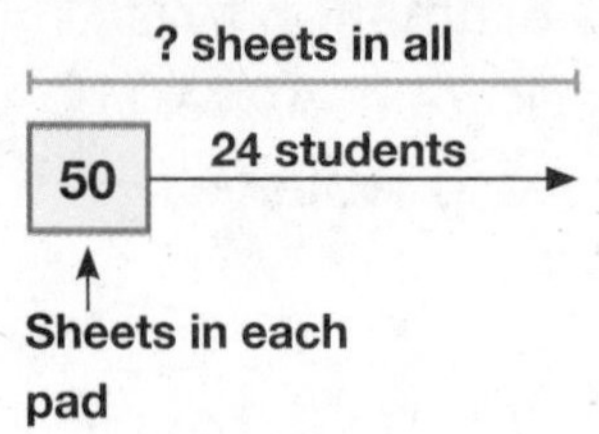

18. Ten years ago Melissa planted a tree in her backyard. She has taken a photo of it every week so she can see how it has grown as time passed. How many photos of the tree does Melissa now have?

A 62 photos
B 120 photos
C 520 photos
D 620 photos

There are about 52 weeks in one year.

19. Write the multiplication equation illustrated by the grid. Find the partial products. Then find the final product.

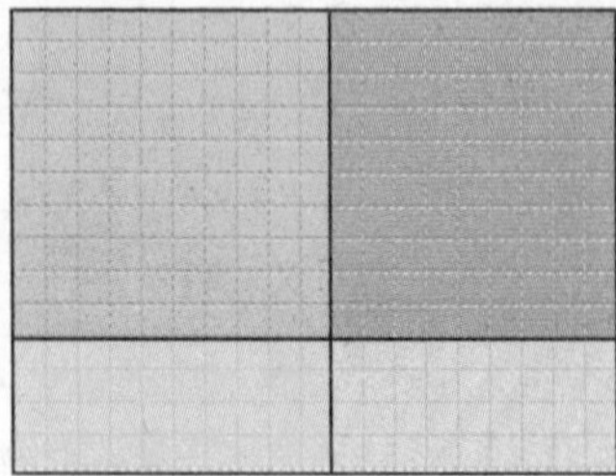

20. **Extend Your Thinking** An elevator can carry 15 adults or 20 children at one time. During the course of a day, the elevator carries a full passenger load 52 times. If all the passengers were children, how many more people would the elevator carry than if all the passengers were adults?

Name ____________________

Homework 6-4
Multiplying 2-Digit by 2-Digit Numbers

Another Look!

There are 24 cars in a race. Each car has 13 workers in the pit area. How many pit-area workers are at the race in all?

Step 1	Step 2	Step 3
Multiply by the ones. Regroup if necessary.	Multiply by the tens. Regroup if necessary.	Add the partial products.
$\begin{array}{r} 24 \\ \times\ 13 \\ \hline 72 \end{array}$ ← 3×24	$\begin{array}{r} 24 \\ \times\ 13 \\ \hline 72 \\ 240 \end{array}$ ← 10×24	$\begin{array}{r} 24 \\ \times\ 13 \\ \hline 72 \\ +\ 240 \\ \hline 312 \end{array}$ $24 \times 13 = 312$, so there are 312 pit-area workers at the race.

In **1** through **9**, find the product.

Estimation is one way to check your answer for reasonableness.

1. $\begin{array}{r} 38 \\ \times\ 26 \\ \hline \square\square\square \\ +\ \square\square 0 \\ \hline \square\square\square \end{array}$

2. $\begin{array}{r} 67 \\ \times\ 27 \\ \hline \square\square\square \\ +\ \square,\square\square\square \\ \hline \square,\square\square\square \end{array}$

3. $\begin{array}{r} 47 \\ \times\ 85 \\ \hline \square\square\square \\ +\ \square,\square\square\square \\ \hline \square,\square\square\square \end{array}$

4. $\begin{array}{r} 88 \\ \times\ 32 \\ \hline \end{array}$

5. $\begin{array}{r} 53 \\ \times\ 48 \\ \hline \end{array}$

6. $\begin{array}{r} 18 \\ \times\ 77 \\ \hline \end{array}$

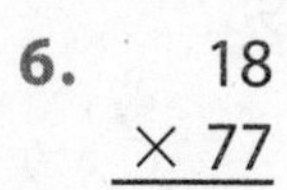

7. $\begin{array}{r} 67 \\ \times\ 34 \\ \hline \end{array}$

8. $\begin{array}{r} 91 \\ \times\ 46 \\ \hline \end{array}$

9. $\begin{array}{r} 56 \\ \times\ 31 \\ \hline \end{array}$

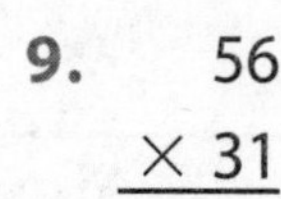

10. Connect An ultralight airplane tracked monarch butterflies migrating to Mexico. The month of September has 30 days. How many miles did the butterflies travel in September?

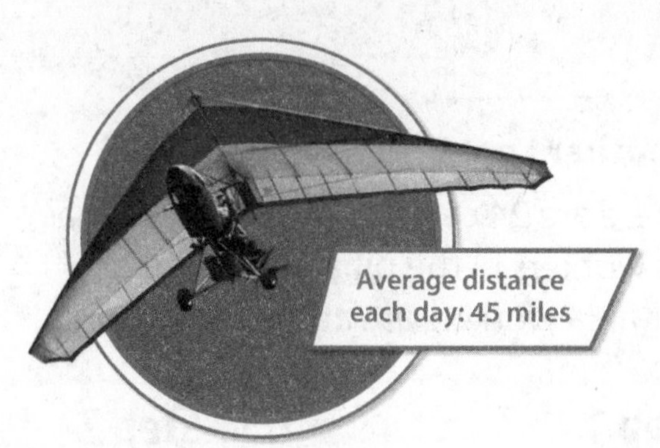

11. Connect The airplane continued to track the monarch butterflies in October. The month of October has 31 days. How many miles did the butterflies travel in October? Explain.

---

12. Analyze Information How much do 21 bushels of sweet corn weigh?

13. Analyze Information How much do 18 bushels of asparagus weigh?

DATA

Vegetable	Weight of 1 Bushel
Asparagus	24 pounds
Beets	52 pounds
Carrots	50 pounds
Sweet corn	35 pounds

14. Mental Math How much do 7 bushels of carrots weigh?

---

15. Which of the following is a reasonable answer for 92 × 98?

A 1,816
B 9,016
C 18,016
D 90,016

16. Extend Your Thinking Corina multiplied 62 × 22 and found a product of 1,042. Is Corina's answer reasonable? Explain.

Name

Solve & Share

The sports club at Carmel School bought 24 grandstand tickets. The sports club at Valley School bought 34 infield tickets. Which group paid more? How much more? ***Solve this problem any way you choose.***

You can **formulate a plan.** Choose the operations you need to solve the problem.

Lesson 6-5

More Multiplying by 2-Digit Numbers

TEKS 4.4C Represent the product of 2 two-digit numbers using arrays, area models, or equations, including perfect squares through 15 by 15. Also, 4.4D, 4.4H. **Mathematical Process Standards** 4.1B, 4.1C, 4.1D, 4.1G

Digital Resources at SavvasTexas.com

Solve

Learn

Glossary
Check

Tools

Games

DATA

Baseball Ticket Prices

Seat	Price
Outfield	$12
Infield	$18
Grandstand	$24
Home plate	$45

Look Back!

Estimation How could you estimate the products for this problem?

How Can You Use Multiplication To Solve Problems?

A-Z

A large garden has a park with a walkway around it. What is the area of the walkway?

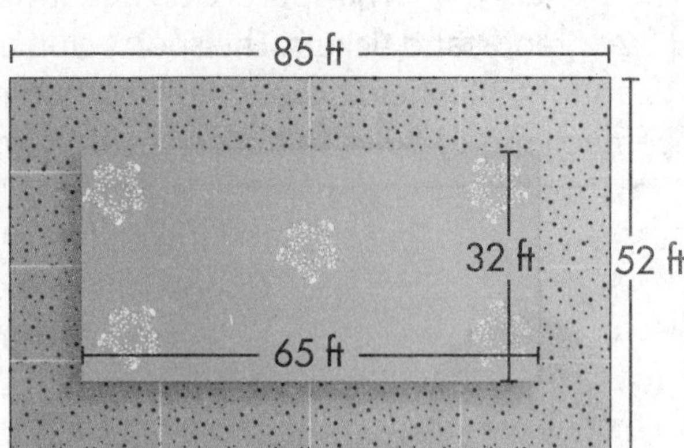

You can multiply the length times the width to find the area of each rectangle.

Step 1

Find the area of the whole park.

$85 \times 52 = ?$

$$\begin{array}{r} \overset{2}{\overset{1}{}}85 \\ \times \quad 52 \\ \hline 170 \\ +\ 4{,}250 \\ \hline 4{,}420 \end{array}$$

The area of the park is 4,420 square feet.

Step 2

Find the area of the part that is not the walkway.

$65 \times 32 = ?$

$$\begin{array}{r} \overset{1}{\overset{1}{}}65 \\ \times \quad 32 \\ \hline 130 \\ +\ 1{,}950 \\ \hline 2{,}080 \end{array}$$

The area that is not the walkway is 2,080 square feet.

Step 3

Find the area of the walkway.

Subtract: 4,420 − 2,080

$$\begin{array}{r} \overset{3\,12}{4{,}\not{4}\not{2}0} \\ -\ 2{,}080 \\ \hline 2{,}340 \end{array}$$

The area of the walkway is 2,340 square feet.

Do You Understand?

Convince Me! Sally's work is shown below. How is her work different than the work above? Is Sally's work correct? Explain.

$$\begin{array}{r} \overset{2}{\overset{1}{}}85 \\ \times \quad 52 \\ \hline 170 \\ +\ 4{,}25 \\ \hline 4{,}420 \end{array}$$

Name

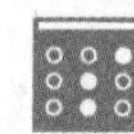 

Guided Practice*

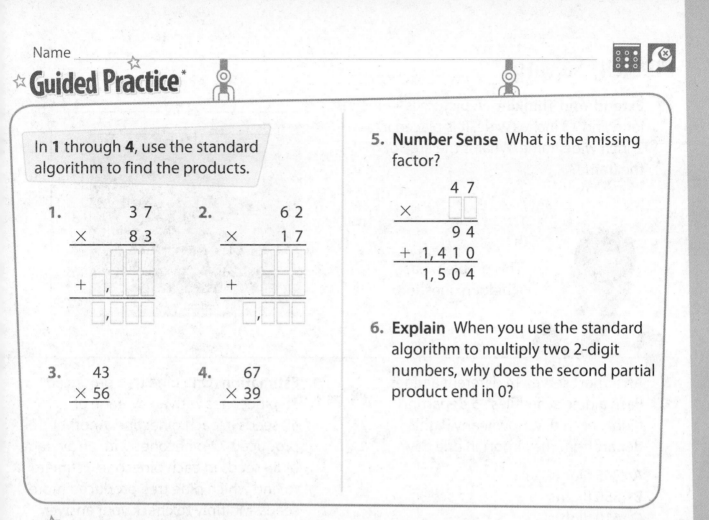

In **1** through **4**, use the standard algorithm to find the products.

1. 37 × 83

2. 62 × 17

3. 43 × 56

4. 67 × 39

5. Number Sense What is the missing factor?

$$\begin{array}{r} 47 \\ \times \square\square \\ \hline 94 \\ +\ 1{,}410 \\ \hline 1{,}504 \end{array}$$

6. Explain When you use the standard algorithm to multiply two 2-digit numbers, why does the second partial product end in 0?

Independent Practice

In **7** through **18**, find each product.

7. 36 × 29 **8.** 84 × 37 **9.** 47 × 46 **10.** 71 × 63 **11.** 89 × 52

12. 25 × 64 **13.** 77 × 33 **14.** 92 × 19 **15.** 54 × 64 **16.** 75 × 35

17. 18 × 21 **18.** 72 × 55

*For another example, see Set D on page 360.

Problem Solving

19. Extend Your Thinking A picture is 17 inches long and 13 inches wide. It is placed in a 2-inch wide frame. What is the area of the frame?

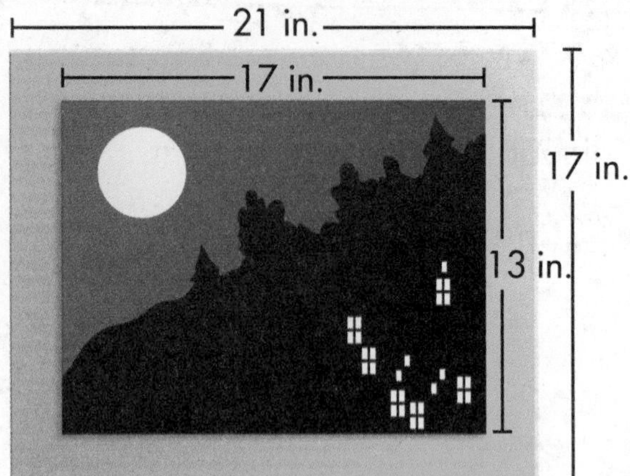

This problem has a hidden question.

20. An airport serves 14 different airlines. Each airline schedules 45 departing flights each day. How many flights depart from the airport in one day?

A 205 flights
B 550 flights
C 610 flights
D 630 flights

21. Estimation One pine tree produced 78 pinecones with an average of 42 seeds in each pinecone. Another tree produced 72 pinecones with an average of 53 seeds in each pinecone. Estimate to find which pine tree produced more seeds. Multiply to check your answer.

22. Fill in the missing digits to complete the calculation.

$$\begin{array}{r} 3\,7 \\ \times \;\square\,6 \\ \hline 2\,\square\,\square \\ +\;7\,4\,0 \\ \hline 9\,\square\,2 \end{array}$$

Which digit must go in the ones place of the first partial product?

23. There are 13 bike racks at the park. Each bike rack holds 18 bicycles. There are 93 bikes in the racks already. How many more bikes can the bike racks hold?

Name ______________________________

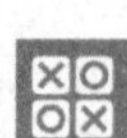

Homework 6-5
More Multiplying by 2-Digit Numbers

Another Look!

An office building is 27 stories tall, and each story has 42 windows that need washing. How many windows need washing?

$27 \times 42 = ?$

Multiply to join equal groups.

$$\begin{array}{r} \overset{1}{4}2 \\ \times\ 27 \\ \hline 294 \\ +\ 840 \\ \hline 1{,}134 \end{array}$$

294 ← Multiply by 7 ones
+ 840 ← Multiply by 2 tens
1,134 ← Add the partial products

1,134 windows need washing.

The standard algorithm for multiplying by 2-digit numbers is an extension of the algorithm for multiplying by 1-digit numbers.

Remember to write a zero in the ones place when multiplying by tens.

In **1** through **15**, find the product.

Use estimation to check your answers for reasonableness.

1. $\begin{array}{r} 70 \\ \times\ 39 \\ \hline \end{array}$ **2.** $\begin{array}{r} 58 \\ \times\ 90 \\ \hline \end{array}$ **3.** $\begin{array}{r} 97 \\ \times\ 42 \\ \hline \end{array}$ **4.** $\begin{array}{r} 64 \\ \times\ 88 \\ \hline \end{array}$

5. $\begin{array}{r} 51 \\ \times\ 47 \\ \hline \end{array}$ **6.** $\begin{array}{r} 62 \\ \times\ 69 \\ \hline \end{array}$ **7.** $\begin{array}{r} 34 \\ \times\ 82 \\ \hline \end{array}$ **8.** $\begin{array}{r} 98 \\ \times\ 23 \\ \hline \end{array}$

9. $\begin{array}{r} 59 \\ \times\ 44 \\ \hline \end{array}$ **10.** $\begin{array}{r} 13 \\ \times\ 31 \\ \hline \end{array}$ **11.** $\begin{array}{r} 85 \\ \times\ 18 \\ \hline \end{array}$ **12.** $\begin{array}{r} 36 \\ \times\ 29 \\ \hline \end{array}$

13. 24×31 **14.** 62×48 **15.** 36×93

16. Explain Courtney said she can see 48 and 240 in the model. Explain what Courtney means.

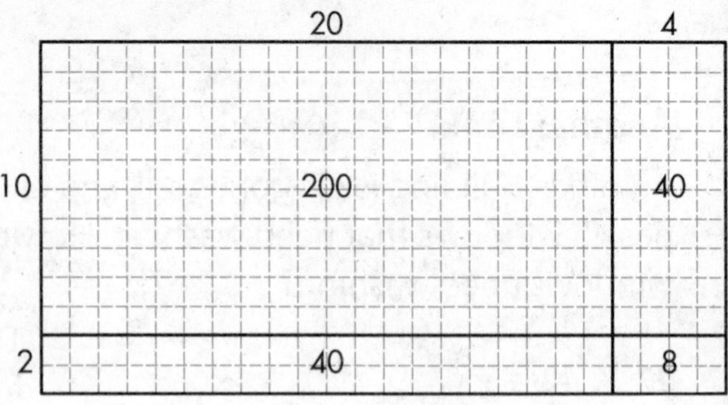

17. Admission to a science museum is \$22 for adults. The cost for children is \$5 less than the cost for adults. What would be the total cost of admission for 12 adults and 15 children?

18. Estimation Bags of potatoes weigh 35 pounds each. Boxes of books weigh 19 pounds each. Estimate which would weigh more: 23 bags of potatoes or 32 boxes of books.

19. Use a Strip Diagram An average person in the U.S. eats about 17 gallons of popcorn each year. How many gallons of popcorn does the average person eat in 12 years? Complete the strip diagram at the right.

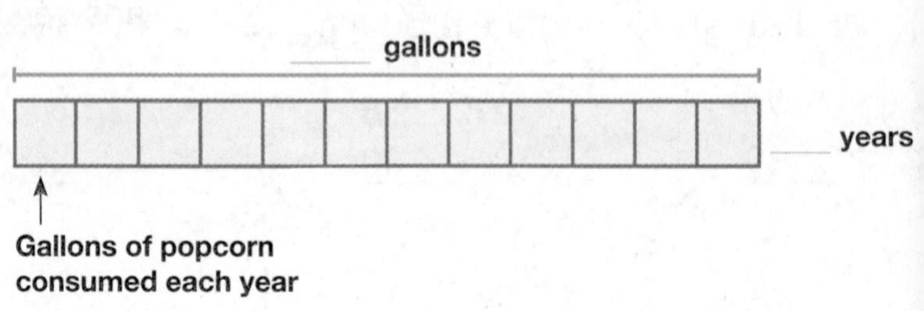

20. A train is pulling 59 cars. Each car has 32 large boxes of freight. Which is the best estimate for the number of boxes on the train?

A 3,600 boxes
B 2,000 boxes
C 1,800 boxes
D 1,500 boxes

21. Extend Your Thinking How is using partial products to find the product of two 2-digit factors similar to how you have used partial products in the past? How is it different?

Name ____________________

Lesson 6-6
Perfect Squares

TEKS 4.4C Represent the product of 2 two-digit numbers using arrays, area models, or equations, including perfect squares through 15 by 15. **Mathematical Process Standards** 4.1A, 4.1C, 4.1D, 4.1E, 4.1G

Digital Resources at SavvasTexas.com

Solve Learn Glossary Check Tools Games

Solve & Share

Each of the larger squares can be filled exactly with small squares. How many small squares are needed to fill each larger square? ***Solve this problem any way you choose.***

1 square ____ squares ____ squares ____ squares

You can **select and use tools.** You may want to use centimeter tiles or draw a picture.

Look Back!

Justify If you extend the sequence of squares above, how many small squares would be in each of the next two squares? Tell how you decided.

What Is a Perfect Square Number?

A

The product of a whole number and itself is called a perfect square.

Is 30 a perfect square?

When the lengths of the sides of a square are whole numbers, the area of the square is a perfect square.

Here are some examples of perfect squares.

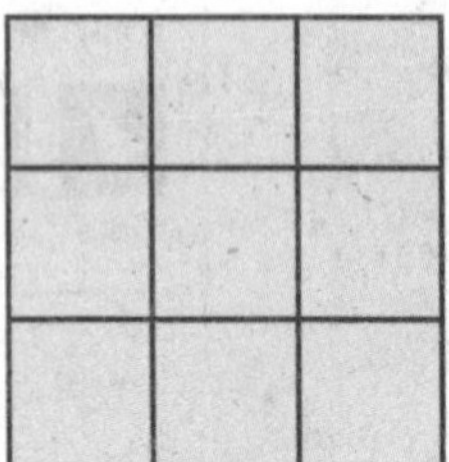

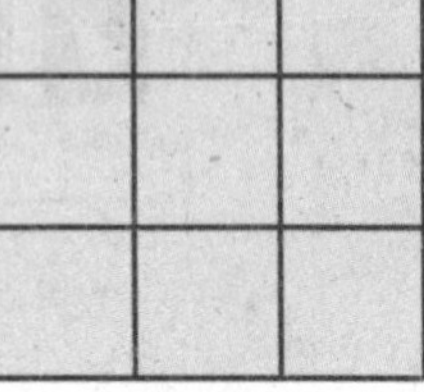

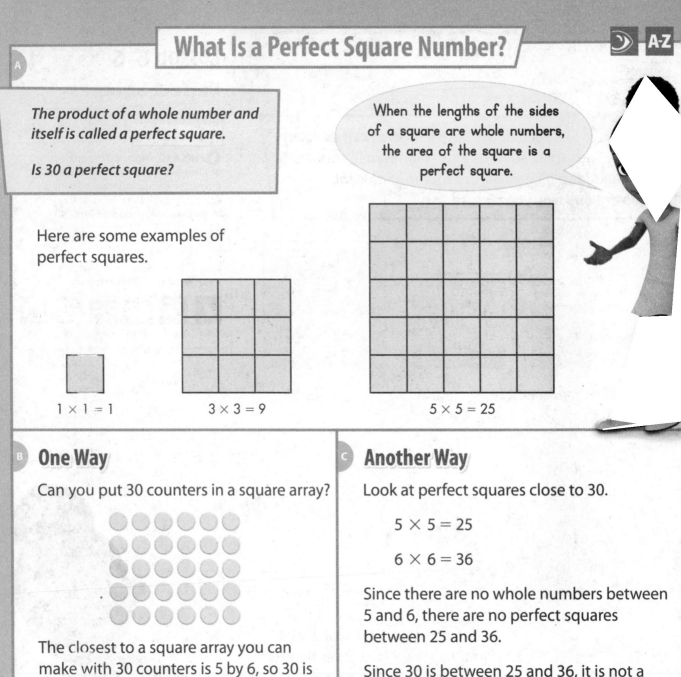

$1 \times 1 = 1$ $\quad$ $3 \times 3 = 9$ $\quad$ $5 \times 5 = 25$

B

One Way

Can you put 30 counters in a square array?

The closest to a square array you can make with 30 counters is 5 by 6, so 30 is not a perfect square.

C

Another Way

Look at perfect squares close to 30.

$5 \times 5 = 25$

$6 \times 6 = 36$

Since there are no whole numbers between 5 and 6, there are no perfect squares between 25 and 36.

Since 30 is between 25 and 36, it is not a perfect square.

Do You Understand?

The area of a square is the product of the length of one side and itself. What are the lengths of the sides of a square with an area of 225 square meters? Explain your thinking.

____ × ____ = 225 square meters

Area = 225 square meters

Name ______________________________

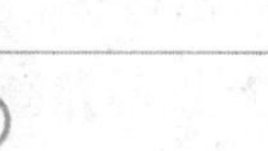

Guided Practice*

In **1** through **3**, write *yes* if the number is a perfect square. Write *no* if it is not a perfect square.

1. 81 **2.** 144 **3.** 50

4. Use the grid to draw an area model of a perfect square greater than 100. Then write an equation for that number.

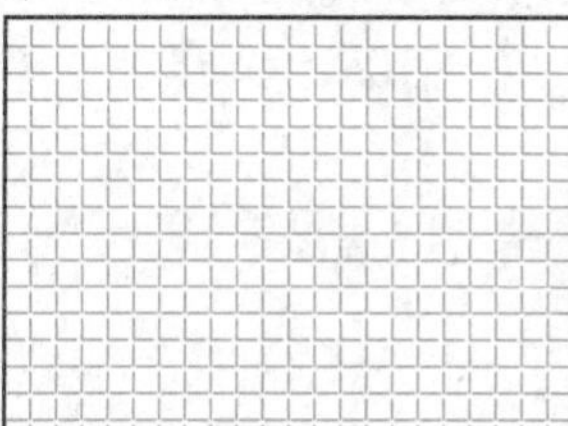

5. Justify Were any of the numbers in Exercises 1 through 3 not a perfect square? If so, justify your reasoning.

6. Reason Sahil wrote that 7 is a factor of a perfect square. What is the other factor? What is the perfect square?

Independent Practice

In **7** through **9**, write the perfect square number for each array.

7. 10 × ____ = ____

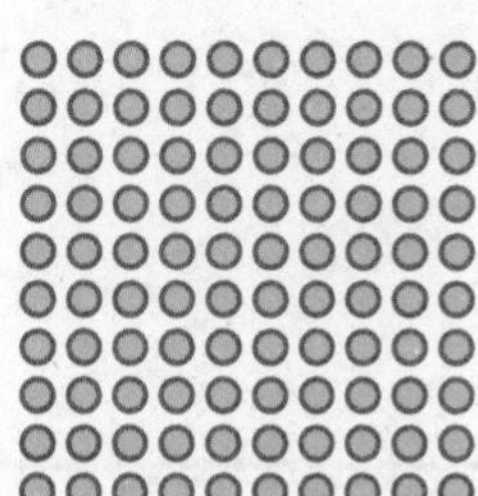

8. ____ × ____ = ____

9. ____ × ____ = ____

In **10** through **12**, write the square number shown by each grid.

10.

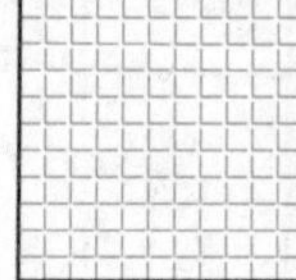

____

11.

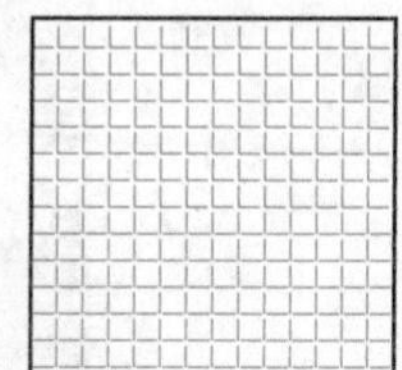

____

12.

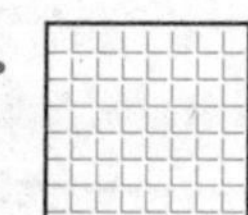

____

*For another example, see Set E on page 360.

Problem Solving

13. Represent Fill each of the larger triangles completely with the smallest triangle. How many smaller triangles are needed to fill each triangle? What pattern do you notice?

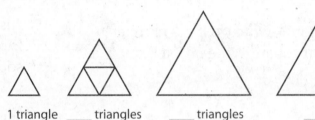

1 triangle

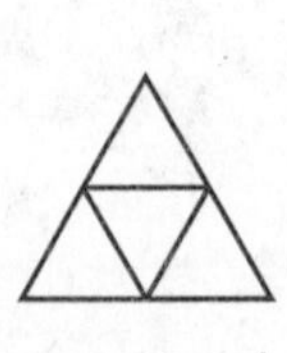

____ triangles

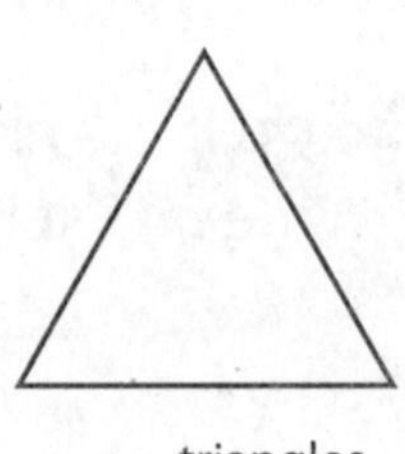

____ triangles

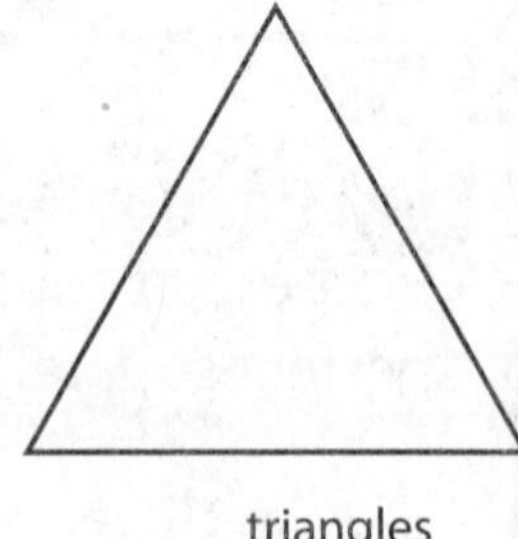

____ triangles

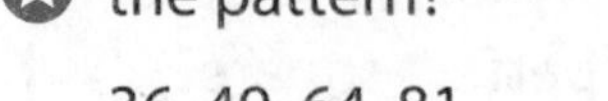

14. Which would be the next number in the pattern?

36, 49, 64, 81, ____

A 98
B 100
C 121
D 145

15. Explain A house covers 196 square meters of land. Could the shape of the house be a square? How do you know?

16. On average, fourth-grade students have 28 teeth. There are 25 students in a fourth-grade class and they all have the average number of teeth. How many teeth in all do the students of that class have?

17. Extend Your Thinking A square number is between 160 and 170. What is the number?

18. Communicate How does the figure show the first 4 perfect squares?

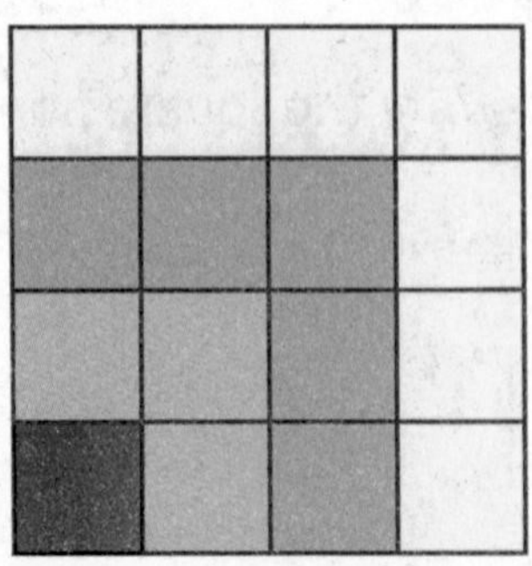

Name ______________________________

Homework 6-6
Perfect Squares

Another Look!

Is 74 a perfect square?

A perfect square is the product of a number and itself.

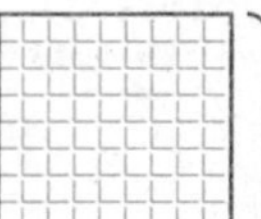

Think: Can you make a square array using 74 counters? Is there a number that can be multiplied by itself and get a product of 74?

8 $8 \times 8 = 64$ 9 $9 \times 9 = 81$

There is no square array with 74 square units and there is no whole number between 8 and 9 that can be multiplied by itself to get a product of 74. So, 74 is not a perfect square.

In **1** through **4**, write *yes* if the number is a perfect square. Write *no* if it is not a perfect square.

1. 90 **2.** 225 **3.** 49 **4.** 130

In **5** through **7**, write the area of a square with the given side length.

5. 9 yards

_____ square yards

6. 10 meters

_____ square meters

7. 3 feet

_____ square feet

In **8** through **10**, complete an equation for each square number shown.

8.

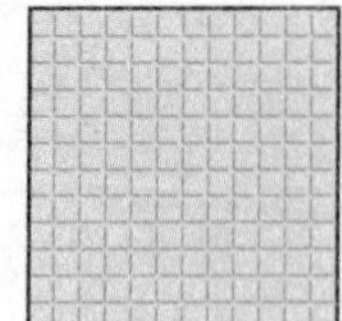

$12 \times$ ____ = ____

9.

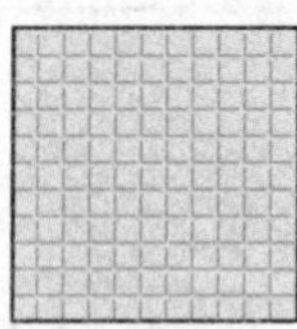

____ $\times$ ____ = ____

10.

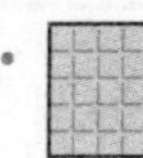

____ $\times$ ____ = ____

11. **Connect** A landscaper built a square patio using 2 feet by 2 feet paver bricks. What is the area of the patio?

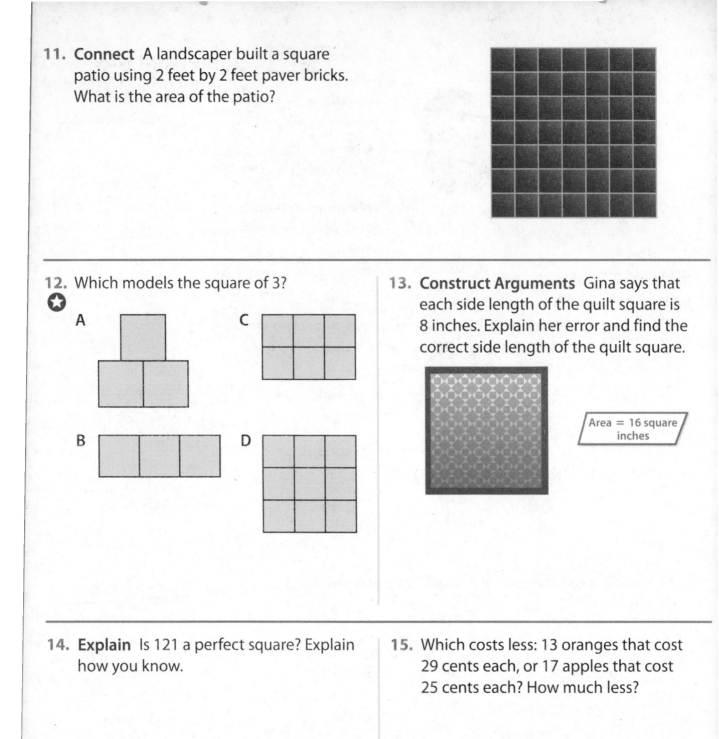

12. Which models the square of 3?

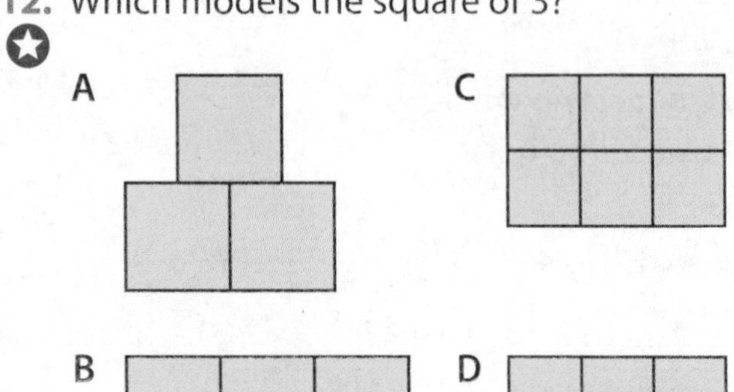

13. **Construct Arguments** Gina says that each side length of the quilt square is 8 inches. Explain her error and find the correct side length of the quilt square.

Area = 16 square inches

14. **Explain** Is 121 a perfect square? Explain how you know.

15. Which costs less: 13 oranges that cost 29 cents each, or 17 apples that cost 25 cents each? How much less?

16. **Extend Your Thinking** Look at the figure at the right. Find the number pattern. Complete the bottom row. Describe the number pattern.

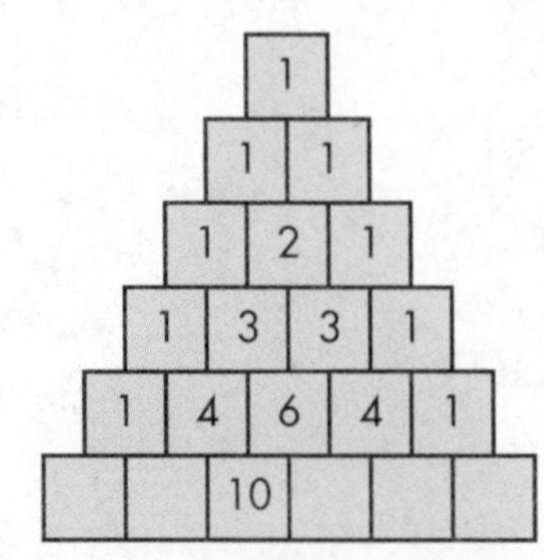

Name

Solve & Share

Susan walked 3 miles and Maxine walked 2 miles to raise funds for a charity. A sponsor donated $50 for each mile they walked. How much did the sponsor donate? ***Solve this problem any way you choose.***

You can **formulate a plan.** Think about the question you are answering and what your first step should be to solve this problem. ***Show your work in the space below!***

Problem Solving

Lesson 6-7

Multi-Step Problems

TEKS 4.1A Apply mathematics to problems arising in everyday life, society, and the workplace.
TEKS 4.5A Represent multi-step problems involving the four operations with whole numbers using strip diagrams and equations with a letter standing for the unknown quantity.
Mathematical Process Standards 4.1B, 4.1D, 4.1E, 4.1G

Digital Resources at SavvasTexas.com

Check

Look Back!

Connect When have you had to answer one question before you could answer another question?

How Can You Solve a Multi-Step Problem?

A-Z

A Analyze

Maya and José are preparing for a bike race. On Wednesday, they rode their bicycles 32 miles in the morning and 22 miles in the afternoon. Maya and José bicycled the same number of miles on Thursday, Friday, and Saturday as they had on Wednesday.

How far did they ride during the 4 days?

Sometimes you have to answer one problem to solve another problem.

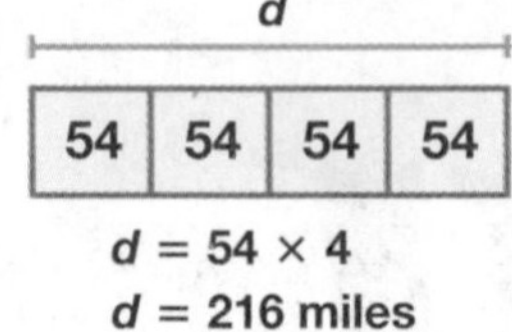

Rode the same distance 4 days in a row

B Plan and Solve

First, find how many miles Maya and José rode on Wednesday.

Let m = miles rode on Wednesday.

m	
32	22

$m = 32 + 22$
$m = 54$ miles

You can use addition to join unequal parts or groups.

C Plan and Solve

Use the answer in the first step to find how far they rode in 4 days. Let d = distance rode in 4 days.

d			
54	54	54	54

$d = 54 \times 4$
$d = 216$ miles

And you can use multiplication to join equal groups. Maya and José rode 216 miles in 4 days.

Do You Understand?

Convince Me! For one tournament, fifteen tennis balls were used out of a carton. How many tennis balls are left in the carton? How do you know?

Tennis Ball Packaging
3 tennis balls in a can
12 cans in a box
18 boxes in a carton

Name ______________________________

Guided Practice*

1. Formulate a Plan Julia used 3 memory cards to take pictures on her vacation. Each memory card holds 28 pictures. She printed 2 copies of each picture.

a. What steps do you need to take to find how many pictures Julia printed?

b. How many pictures did Julia print?

2. Analyze Information Each student purchased a box of 24 crayons and 18 colored pencils. There are 20 students in the class.

a. Explain what operations you would use to find the total number of crayons and colored pencils the class purchased.

b. How many crayons and colored pencils did the class purchase?

Independent Practice

In **3** and **4**, complete the strip diagrams to help you solve.

3. For lunch, Martin buys a sandwich for $4, an apple for $1, and a drink for $2. How much change will Martin receive if he pays with a $20 bill?

t = total cost

sandwich | apple | drink

$20

total cost | ?

change

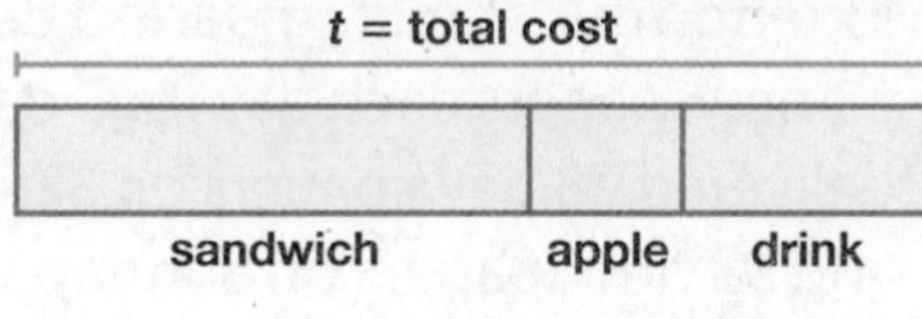

Each step has a different strip diagram.

4. Sally and Byron mow lawns in the summer. Sally mows 5 lawns each week. Byron mows three times as many lawns each week as Sally. Byron gets paid $20 for each lawn he mows. How much money does Byron get paid each week?

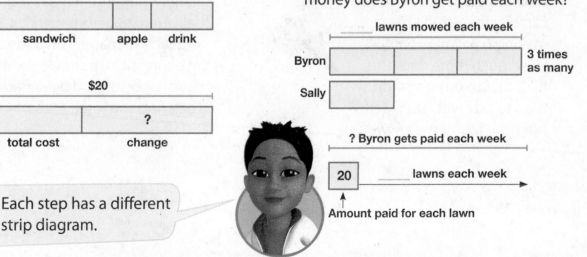

____ lawns mowed each week

Byron | 3 times as many

Sally

? Byron gets paid each week

20 ____ lawns each week

Amount paid for each lawn

*For another example, see Set F on page 360.

Problem Solving

5. **Analyze Information** June's mom brought 3 bags of plain popcorn and 2 bags of caramel popcorn to the park. Each bag contained 16 servings. Did June's mom bring more than or less than 95 servings of popcorn to the park? How do you know?

6. **Connect** Dave tiled his porch floor. He bought 25 black tiles and 23 white tiles. Each tile costs $2. How much money did Dave spend to tile his porch floor?

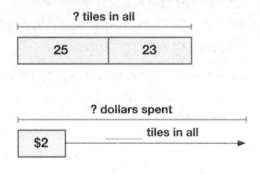

? tiles in all

25	23

? dollars spent

$2 ____ tiles in all

7. The Florida panther is known to sleep about 18 hours a day. About how many hours would a Florida panther sleep in 3 weeks?

   A 478 hours
   B 378 hours
   C 252 hours
   D 54 hours

   Remember that there are 7 days in 1 week.

8. **Math and Science** Wind is a renewable source of energy. Wind farms use large wind turbines that produce electricity. Suppose 25 new wind farms are built, and each wind farm has 18 wind turbines. How many wind turbines are built?

9. **Personal Financial Literacy** A bike costs $126. Mehmet can buy it on credit by making 6 payments of $23. How much more does the bike cost to buy on credit than to buy with cash? Tell how you found the answer.

10. **Extend Your Thinking** Jarrod delivered 63 newspapers each day for 5 days. He delivered 78 newspapers on Saturday and 93 newspapers on Sunday. Write an expression to show how many newspapers Jarrod delivered that week. Then find the total.

Name ______________________________

Mixed Problem Solving

1. Estimation Sara estimated 23 × 43 by using 20 × 40. Sam estimated 23 × 43 by using 25 × 40. Whose method will give an estimate closer to the exact answer? Tell how you decided.

2. Explain Marla wants to buy a new tablet that costs $565, including tax. She saved $15 per week for 25 weeks. Does Marla have enough money saved to buy the tablet? Explain.

Applying Math Processes

- How does this problem connect to previous ones?
- What is my plan?
- How can I use tools?
- How can I use number sense?
- How can I communicate and represent my thinking?
- How can I organize and record information?
- How can I explain my work?
- How can I justify my answer?

3. Analyze Information

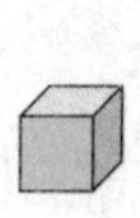
1st

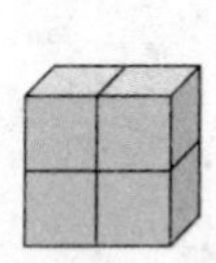
2nd

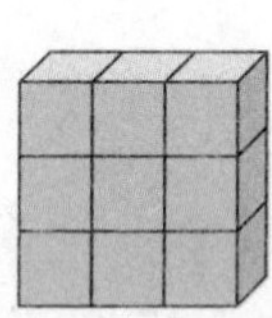
3rd

How many small cubes will the 5th tower have? Explain.

4. Personal Financial Literacy Quincy earns $9 an hour mowing grass and $7 an hour doing laundry. He has 4 hours to work. How much more could he earn mowing grass than doing laundry? Tell how you found the answer.

5. Represent Use the grid below to find 14 × 22. List the partial products and then solve.

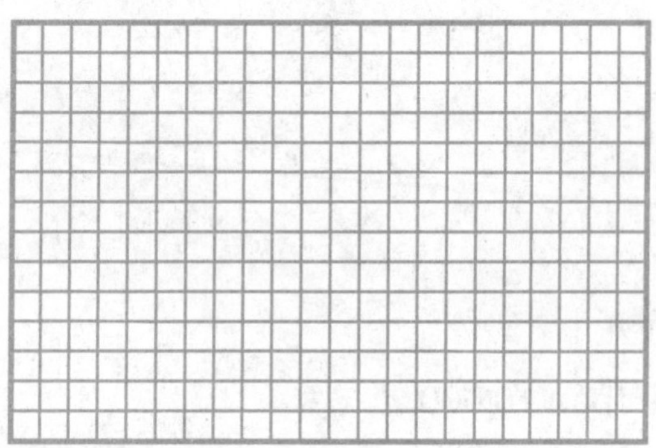

6. Extend Your Thinking Mr. Buckham is teaching vocabulary to a class of 27 fourth graders. There are 63 new words. Each student will write each word on an index card. Mr. Buckham has 1,500 index cards. Find out how many extra or how many more index cards he needs.

Error Search

Find each problem that is not correct. Circle what is wrong and rewrite the problem so it is correct.

1.
$$\begin{array}{r} 543 \\ +\ 29 \\ \hline 562 \end{array}$$

2.
$$\begin{array}{r} 6{,}043 \\ +\ 972 \\ \hline 7{,}025 \end{array}$$

3.
$$\begin{array}{r} 76{,}248 \\ +\ 19{,}046 \\ \hline 95{,}294 \end{array}$$

4.
$$\begin{array}{r} 956 \\ +\ 834 \\ \hline 122 \end{array}$$

Reasoning

Write whether each statement is true or false. If you write false, change the numbers or words so that the statement is true.

5. The number 213,753 is ten thousand more than 223,753.

6. The sum of 6,823 and 1,339 is greater than 7,000 but less than 9,000.

7. The sum of 42,239 and 11,013 is less than 50,000.

8. The difference of 7,748 − 989 is greater than 7,000.

9. The sum of 596 + 325 is 4 less than 925.

10. The difference of 11,968 and 2,856 is closer to 9,000 than 10,000.

Name ______________________________

Set A pages 315–320

Find 14 × 12. Draw a 14 × 12 array.

Separate each factor into tens and ones. Color each section a different color. Add each part to find the product.

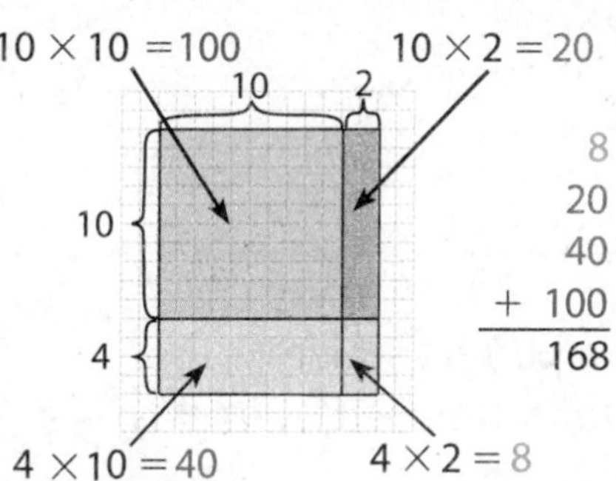

$$\begin{array}{r} 8 \\ 20 \\ 40 \\ +\ 100 \\ \hline 168 \end{array}$$

Remember you can solve the simpler problems in any order and the answer will remain the same.

Find each product. Use grid paper to help.

1. 14 × 32
2. 64 × 12
3. 56 × 17
4. 72 × 15
5. 26 × 63
6. 47 × 27

Set B pages 321–326

Find 16 × 35. List the partial products.

Multiply the ones:

$$\begin{array}{r} 16 \\ \times\ 35 \\ \hline 30 \\ 50 \end{array}$$

30 ← 5 × 6
50 ← 5 × 10

Multiply the tens:

$$\begin{array}{r} 16 \\ \times\ 35 \\ \hline 30 \\ 50 \\ 180 \\ +\ 300 \\ \hline \end{array}$$

180 ← 30 × 6
300 ← 30 × 10

Add: 30 + 50 + 180 + 300 = 560

Remember that to multiply two 2-digit factors, you can find four partial products.

Find each product.

1. 18 × 34
2. 51 × 15
3. 53 × 17
4. 26 × 28
5. 22 × 66
6. 41 × 54
7. 64 × 86
8. 32 × 71
9. 93 × 44
10. 57 × 91

Set C pages 327–332

Find 16 × 30.
Multiply 16 × 3 tens.

$$\begin{array}{r} \overset{1}{1}6 \\ \times\ 30 \\ \hline 480 \end{array}$$

The 0 in the ones place shows that the product is a multiple of 10.

Remember to check that your answer has a 0 in the ones place.

1. 39 × 10
2. 56 × 30
3. 41 × 20
4. 60 × 30

Set D pages 333–344

Use the standard algorithm to find 14 × 19.

Multiply the ones. Regroup if necessary.

$$\begin{array}{r} \overset{3}{1}9 \\ \times\ 14 \\ \hline 76 \end{array}$$

Multiply the tens. Regroup if necessary.

$$\begin{array}{r} 19 \\ \times\ 14 \\ \hline 76 \\ +\ 190 \\ \hline 266 \end{array}$$

Add the partial products.

Remember to regroup if necessary.

Find each product. Estimate to check for reasonableness.

1. $\begin{array}{r} 53 \\ \times\ 36 \\ \hline \end{array}$

2. $\begin{array}{r} 23 \\ \times\ 18 \\ \hline \end{array}$

3. $\begin{array}{r} 73 \\ \times\ 33 \\ \hline \end{array}$

Set E pages 345–350

Is 64 a perfect square? Explain how you know.

Yes, you can make an 8 × 8 square array with 64 counters.

Remember that a perfect square is the product of a factor multiplied by itself.

1. Is 84 a perfect square? Explain how you know.

2. What are the lengths of a square with an area of 144 square feet?

3. What square number has 13 as a factor?

Set F pages 351–356

When you solve multi-step problems, solve one part first. Then you can use that answer to help you solve the problem.

It costs \$3 for a ticket to the pool and \$7 for a ticket to the water park. How much more does it cost 4 people to go to the water park than to the pool?

Cost of 4 pool tickets:

4 × \$3 = \$12

Cost of 4 water park tickets:

4 × \$7 = \$28

\$28 − \$12 = \$16

It costs \$16 more.

Remember to use the information in each step to solve the problem.

1. Rose visited 14 cities on her vacation. She bought 8 souvenirs in each city to send to her friends. Rose paid \$2 in postage for each souvenir she sent. How much did it cost Rose to send all of the souvenirs that she bought on vacation?

2. Mrs. Conrath bought 9 packages of colored pencils for her classroom. Each package has 8 pencils. She saved 25 pencils for the after-school Math Club. How many pencils were used for her classroom?

Name ______________________________

TOPIC 6 Test

1. Tess has 15 pages in her coin collector's album. Each page holds 32 coins. Tess wants to find how many coins will fit in her album. Which partial product is missing from her work?

   300
   20
   10
 + ____

A 15

B 150

C 315

D 480

2. LuAnn is practicing using strategies to prepare for her school's math olympiad. Which shows one way LuAnn can use partial products to find 60×78?

A $(60 \times 70) + (60 \times 8)$

B $(60 \times 70) + (60 \times 78)$

C $(60 \times 70) + (60 \times 80)$

D $(6 \times 70) + (6 \times 8)$

3. Jonah bought 25 postcards that cost 17 cents each. He used partial products to find the total cost in cents. Which is **NOT** one of the partial products Jonah found?

A 35

B 140

C 170

D 200

4. There are 35 trees in each of the 94 rows of an orchard. There are 30 rows of cherry trees. All other rows are apple trees. How many apple trees in all are in the orchard?

A 1,240 trees

B 2,140 trees

C 2,240 trees

D 2,340 trees

5. The librarian ordered 24 sets of bookmarks. Each set contained 20 bookmarks with different designs. How many bookmarks did the librarian order?

6. Loren drew a model to find how much flooring he needs to replace tile in a room that is 15 feet by 29 feet. Which product does the model of 15×29 represent?

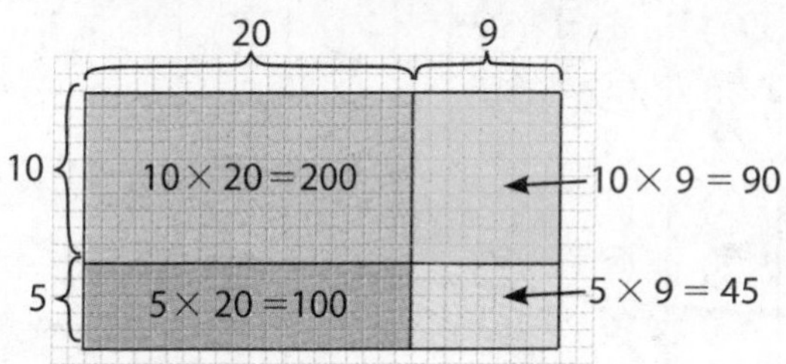

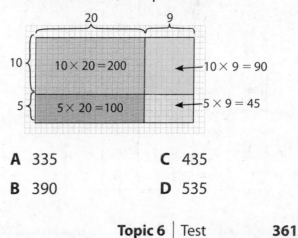

A 335

B 390

C 435

D 535

7. A school has 28 new microscopes for its students to use. The price for each microscope was $87. How much did the microscopes cost in all?

A $1,436

B $1,756

C $2,336

D None of the above

8. Jack's landscape service charges $78 to plant a tree. What is the total cost to plant 18 trees on Tuesday and 23 trees on Wednesday?

9. Tori's goal is to learn 15 new Spanish words each day. If Tori meets her goal, how many new Spanish words will she have learned after 40 days?

			.		
0	0	0		0	0
1	1	1		1	1
2	2	2		2	2
3	3	3		3	3
4	4	4		4	4
5	5	5		5	5
6	6	6		6	6
7	7	7		7	7
8	8	8		8	8
9	9	9		9	9

10. Philip earns $11 an hour. He worked 15 hours last week and 25 hours this week. Which equation shows how to find how much money, *m*, Philip earned in all?

A $m = \$11 + \$15 + \$25$

B $m = 15 \times \$11$

C $m = 25 + \$11$

D $m = 40 \times \$11$

11. Which number is a perfect square?

A 110

B 120

C 121

D 141

12. Large tables in the library have 8 chairs and small tables have 6 chairs. How many students can sit at 5 large tables and 9 small tables if each seat is filled?

			.		
0	0	0		0	0
1	1	1		1	1
2	2	2		2	2
3	3	3		3	3
4	4	4		4	4
5	5	5		5	5
6	6	6		6	6
7	7	7		7	7
8	8	8		8	8
9	9	9		9	9

TOPIC 7

Number Sense: Dividing by 1-Digit Divisors

Essential Questions: How can mental math be used to divide? How can quotients be estimated?

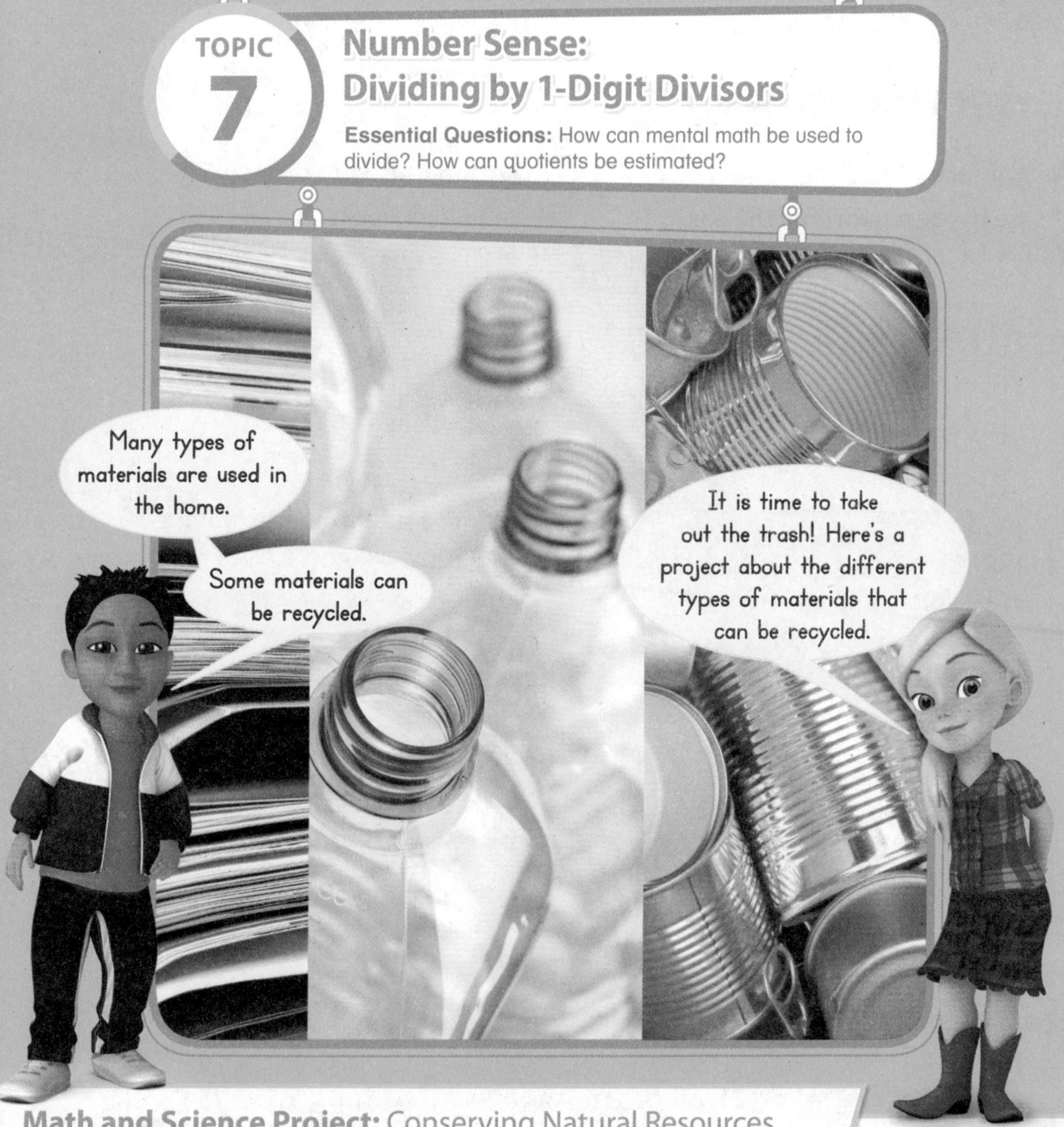

Many types of materials are used in the home.
Some materials can be recycled.
It is time to take out the trash! Here's a project about the different types of materials that can be recycled.

Math and Science Project: Conserving Natural Resources

Do Research Use the Internet or other sources to find out about the different types of materials that can be recycled.

Journal: Write a Report Include what you learned about recycling. Also in your report:

- Include examples of what can be recycled.
- Include examples of what cannot be recycled.
- Set up a recycle bin for your classroom and collect items that can be recycled for 3 days. Estimate the quotient of the total number of items collected divided by 3.

Name ______________________________

Review What You Know

Vocabulary

Choose the best term from the box. Write it on the blank.

- dividend
- divisor
- quotient
- product

1. The ______________ is the answer in a division problem.

2. The number being divided is the ______________.

3. The ______________ is the number that tells into how many groups something is being divided.

Multiplication Facts

Find each product.

4. 8×4

5. 7×6

6. 3×9

7. 5×5

8. 2×6

9. 3×1

10. 8×7

11. 9×4

Addition and Subtraction Facts

Write a subtraction fact for each addition fact.

12. $8 + 8 = 16$

13. $4 + 7 = 11$

14. $6 + 6 = 12$

15. $9 + 5 = 14$

16. Write a subtraction fact for the array below.

17. **Explain** How can you subtract $146 - 18$ using mental math?

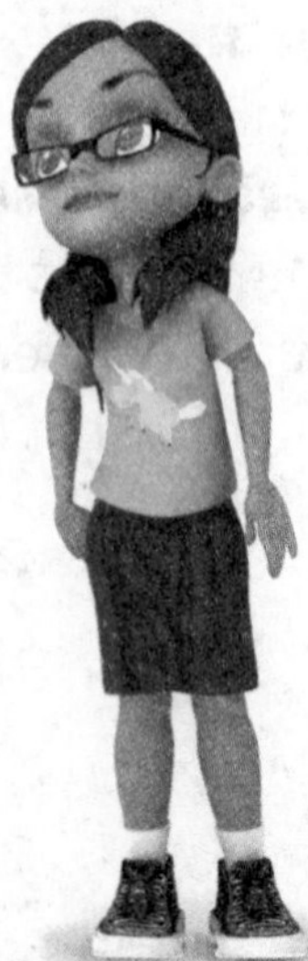

A-Z
ple for the word on the front of the
complete the definition on the back.

My Word Cards

Complete
your own

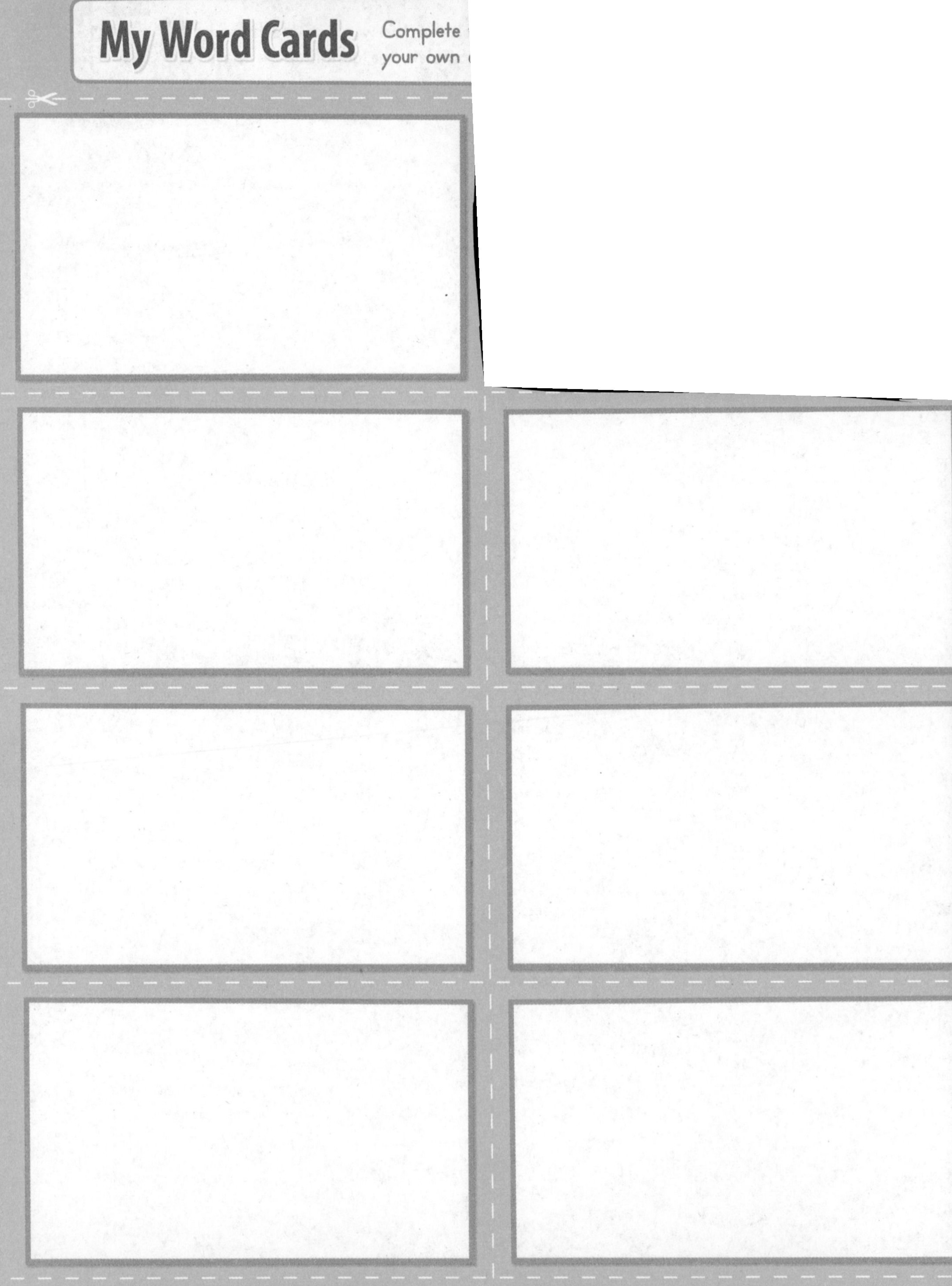

Name ______________________________

Solve & Share

José has 270 hockey cards to arrange in 9 boxes. Each box is to hold the same number of cards. How many cards should he place in each box? ***Solve this problem any way you choose.***

Lesson 7-1
Using Mental Math to Divide

TEKS 4.4F Use strategies and algorithms, including the standard algorithm, to divide up to a four-digit dividend by a one-digit divisor. **Mathematical Process Standards** 4.1A, 4.1B, 4.1C, 4.1D, 4.1E, 4.1F, 4.1G

Digital Resources at SavvasTexas.com

Solve

Learn

Glossary

Check

Tools

Games

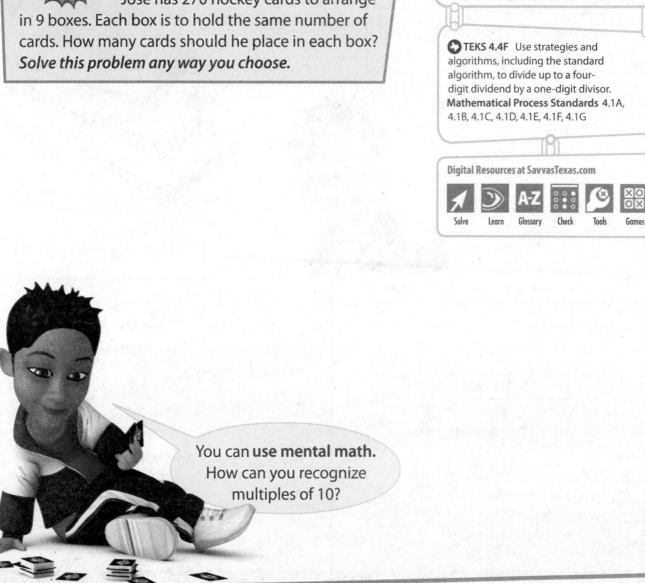

You can use mental math. How can you recognize multiples of 10?

Look Back!

Create and Use Representations What equation could you use to represent this problem?

A

How Can You Divide Mentally?

Mr. Díaz ordered a supply of 320 pastels. He needs to divide them equally among four art classes.

How many pastels does each class get?

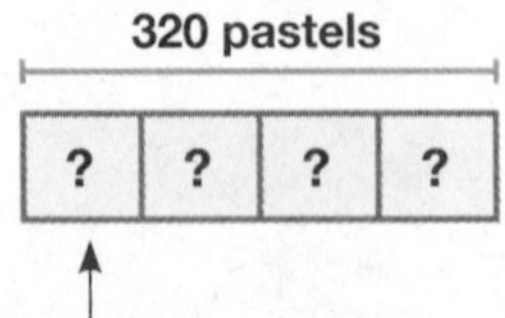

Choose an operation.
Division is used to make
equal groups.

Use basic facts and place-value patterns.

B Find 320 ÷ 4.

320 pastels

?	?	?	?

pastels for each class

The basic fact is 32 ÷ 4 = 8.

32 tens ÷ 4 = 8 tens or 80.
320 ÷ 4 = 80

Each class will get 80 pastels.

C Mr. Díaz wants to divide 400 erasers among 8 classes. How many erasers will each class get?

Find 400 ÷ 8.

The basic fact is 40 ÷ 8.

40 tens ÷ 8 = 5 tens or 50.
400 ÷ 8 = 50

Each class will get 50 erasers.

Do You Understand?

Convince Me! Write the missing numbers for each of the following.

Tell how you decided.

_____ ÷ 7 = 70   _____ ÷ 8 = 50   _____ ÷ 4 = 800

Name ____________________

Guided Practice*

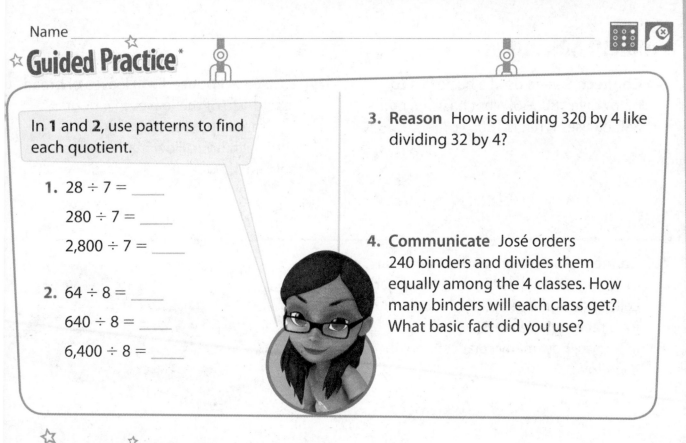

In **1** and **2**, use patterns to find each quotient.

1. 28 ÷ 7 = ____

280 ÷ 7 = ____

2,800 ÷ 7 = ____

2. 64 ÷ 8 = ____

640 ÷ 8 = ____

6,400 ÷ 8 = ____

3. Reason How is dividing 320 by 4 like dividing 32 by 4?

4. Communicate José orders 240 binders and divides them equally among the 4 classes. How many binders will each class get? What basic fact did you use?

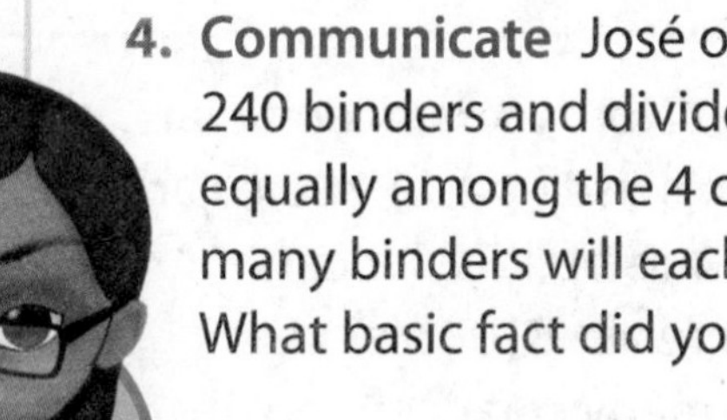

Independent Practice

Leveled Practice In **5** through **8**, use patterns to find each quotient.

5. 36 ÷ 9 = ____	**6.** 10 ÷ 2 = ____	**7.** 45 ÷ 5 = ____	**8.** 24 ÷ 8 = ____
360 ÷ 9 = ____	100 ÷ 2 = ____	450 ÷ 5 = ____	240 ÷ 8 = ____
3,600 ÷ 9 = ____	1,000 ÷ 2 = ____	4,500 ÷ 5 = ____	2,400 ÷ 8 = ____

In **9** through **23**, use mental math to divide.

9. 200 ÷ 5	**10.** 360 ÷ 4	**11.** 540 ÷ 9	**12.** 160 ÷ 4	**13.** 160 ÷ 2
14. 900 ÷ 3	**15.** 320 ÷ 8	**16.** 360 ÷ 6	**17.** 180 ÷ 3	**18.** 210 ÷ 7
19. 720 ÷ 8	**20.** 500 ÷ 5	**21.** 350 ÷ 7	**22.** 6,300 ÷ 9	**23.** 4,800 ÷ 6

*For another example, see Set A on page 399.

Problem Solving

24. **Connect** Selena used a basic fact to help solve 180 ÷ 6. What basic fact did Selena use? What is 180 ÷ 6?

25. A bakery produced 160 loaves of bread. It sold 120 of the loaves in 4 hours. The same number of loaves were sold each hour. How many loaves were sold each hour?

26. **Connect** At the North American Solar Challenge, teams use up to 1,000 solar cells to design and build solar cars for a race. If there are 810 solar cells in 9 rows, how many solar cells are in each row?

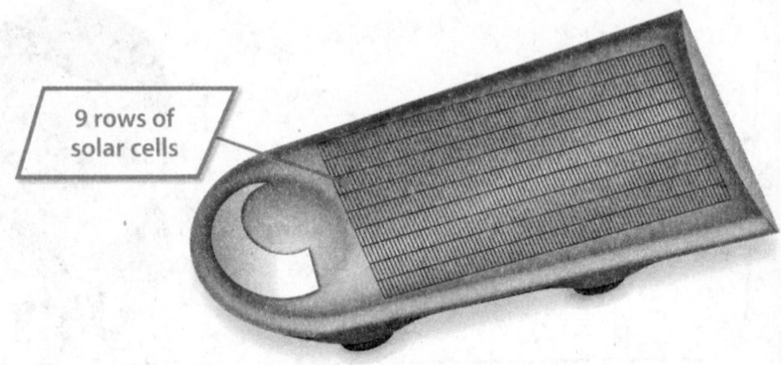

27. **Use a Strip Diagram** On Saturday afternoon, 350 people attended a play. The seating was arranged in 7 equal rows. How many people sat in each row? Explain.

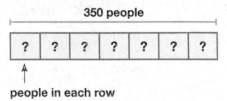

350 people

?	?	?	?	?	?	?

people in each row

28. **Explain** If you know that 20 ÷ 5 = 4, how does that fact help you find 200 ÷ 5?

29. Three dock workers load 240 crates equally onto 8 ships. How many crates are loaded onto each ship?

A 3 crates
B 10 crates
C 30 crates
D 80 crates

30. **Extend Your Thinking** Molly and five friends picked a total of 300 oranges. If each girl picked the same number of oranges, how many did each girl pick? Explain how you found your answer.

Name ______________________________

Homework 7-1
Using Mental Math to Divide

Another Look!

When dividing numbers that end in zero, you can use basic division facts and patterns to help you divide mentally.

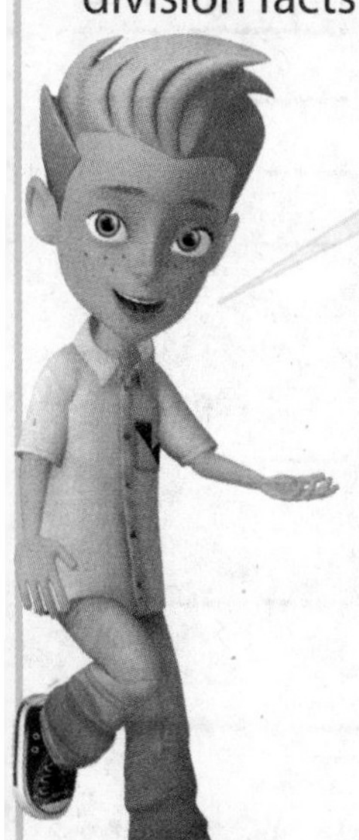

Follow these steps when using mental math to divide.

Find 210 ÷ 7.	Find 4,200 ÷ 6.
Find the basic fact.	Find the basic fact.
Think **21** ÷ **7** = 3, so	Think **42** ÷ **6** = 7, so
21 tens ÷ **7** = 3 tens or 30.	**42** hundreds ÷ **6** = 7 hundreds or 700.
210 ÷ 7 = 30	4,200 ÷ 6 = 700

In **1** through **19**, use patterns to find each quotient.

1. 25 ÷ 5 = ____
250 ÷ 5 = ____
2,500 ÷ 5 = ____

2. 14 ÷ 2 = ____
140 ÷ 2 = ____
1,400 ÷ 2 = ____

3. 30 ÷ 5 = ____
300 ÷ 5 = ____
3,000 ÷ 5 = ____

4. 16 ÷ 4 = ____
160 ÷ 4 = ____
1,600 ÷ 4 = ____

5. 120 ÷ 6

6. 720 ÷ 9

7. 200 ÷ 4

8. 2,800 ÷ 7

9. 810 ÷ 9

10. 5,000 ÷ 5

11. 240 ÷ 8

12. 3,600 ÷ 4

13. 1,600 ÷ 2

14. 270 ÷ 3

15. 4,200 ÷ 7

16. 640 ÷ 8

17. 2,000 ÷ 5

18. 320 ÷ 8

19. 1,200 ÷ 2

In **20** through **22**, use the graph and mental math.

20. Analyze Information Barry charged $4 for each copy of *Return of the Dinosaurs*. How many total copies did Barry sell?

21. Tools Barry charged $9 for each copy of *America's National Parks*. How many total copies did Barry sell?

22. Mental Math Barry charged $7 for each copy of *Musa the Great*. How many total copies did Barry sell?

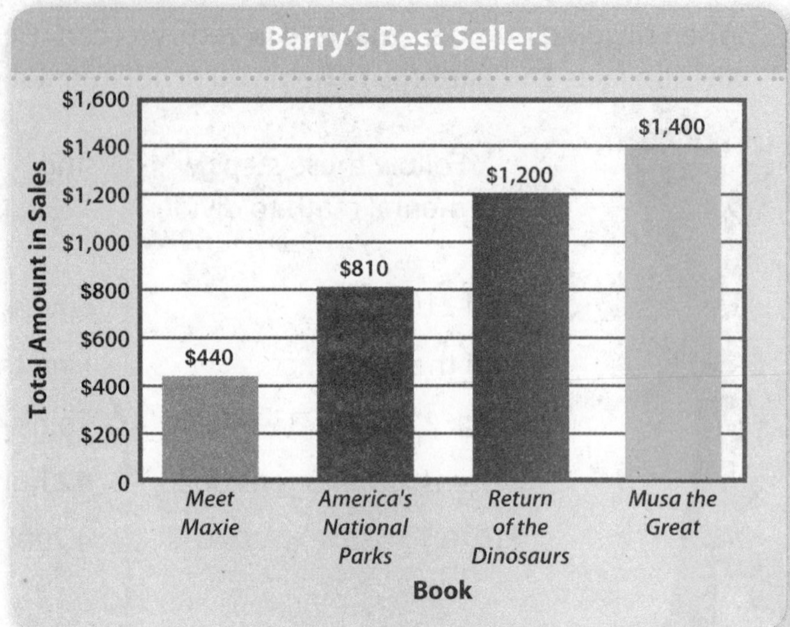

23. Explain Explain why the following answer is incorrect:
1,000 ÷ 5 = 2,000.

24. Reason There are 7 days in 1 week. Some months have 30 days. How many weeks are in 210 days?

25. ✪ Jessica had 120 stamps in a collection. She bought 60 more. Jessica wants to place the stamps equally on six pages of a book. How many stamps will be on each page?

A 20 stamps
B 25 stamps
C 30 stamps
D 40 stamps

26. Extend Your Thinking The band boosters collected $2,400 from the sales of hamburgers and hot dogs. The amounts earned from hamburgers and hot dogs were equal. Hamburgers sold for $3 each, and hot dogs were $2 each. How many of each were sold?

Name

Solve & Share

Three friends at a video arcade win a total of 248 tickets. They decide to share the tickets equally. About how many tickets will each friend get? ***Solve this problem any way you choose.***

Lesson 7-2
Estimating Quotients

TEKS 4.4G Round to the nearest 10, 100, or 1,000 or use compatible numbers to estimate solutions involving whole numbers.
Mathematical Process Standards 4.1A, 4.1B, 4.1C, 4.1D, 4.1F, 4.1G

Digital Resources at SavvasTexas.com

 Solve  Learn  Glossary 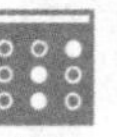 Check Tools  Games

Compatible numbers can help you **estimate** the quotient. ***Show your work in the space below!***

Look Back!

Connect What are some other situations when you might want to estimate the answer of a division problem?

How Can You Estimate Quotients to Solve Problems?

A

Max wants to make 9 rubber band balls. He bought a jar of 700 rubber bands. Estimate to find about how many rubber bands he can use for each ball.

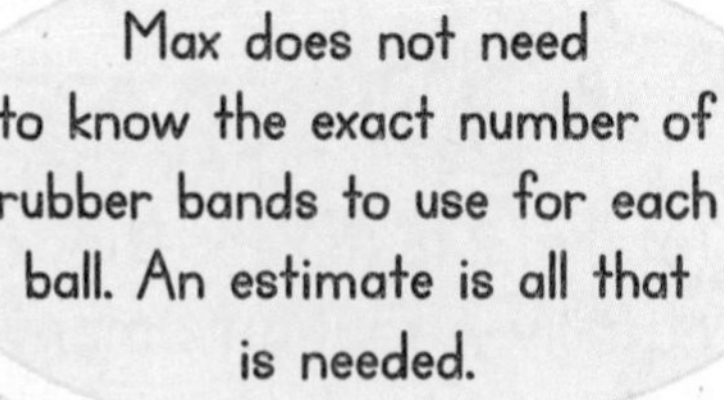

Max does not need to know the exact number of rubber bands to use for each ball. An estimate is all that is needed.

There is more than one way to estimate a quotient.

700 rubber bands

Use compatible numbers or multiplication.

B

One Way

Use compatible numbers.

What number close to 700 is easily divided by 9?

Try multiples of ten near 700.

710 is not easily divided by 9.

720 is 72 tens and can be divided by 9.

$720 \div 9 = 80$

C

Another Way

Use multiplication.

9 times what number is about 700?

$9 \times 8 = 72$,

so $9 \times 80 = 720$.

So $700 \div 9$ is about 80.

A good estimate is about 80 rubber bands for each ball.

Do You Understand?

Convince Me! What compatible numbers can you use to estimate $132 \div 6$? Why is rounding not an effective technique for finding $132 \div 6$?

Name ______________________________

Guided Practice*

In **1** through **8**, estimate each quotient. Use multiplication or compatible numbers. Show your work.

1. 48 ÷ 5 **2.** 235 ÷ 8

3. 547 ÷ 6 **4.** 192 ÷ 5

5. 662 ÷ 8 **6.** 362 ÷ 3

7. 41 ÷ 2 **8.** 211 ÷ 4

9. Explain In the problem on the previous page, will Max be able to make more or fewer balls than he estimated?

Think of basic division facts to help you find compatible numbers.

10. Check for Reasonableness Max decides to use the 700 rubber bands to make 8 balls. Is it reasonable to say that each ball would contain about 90 rubber bands?

Independent Practice

In **11** through **30**, estimate the quotient.

11. 430 ÷ 9 **12.** 620 ÷ 7 **13.** 138 ÷ 5 **14.** 232 ÷ 6

15. 342 ÷ 8 **16.** 652 ÷ 6 **17.** 599 ÷ 9 **18.** 813 ÷ 8

19. 637 ÷ 6 **20.** 481 ÷ 4 **21.** 747 ÷ 8 **22.** 232 ÷ 9

23. 552 ÷ 7 **24.** 527 ÷ 5 **25.** 392 ÷ 2 **26.** 625 ÷ 3

27. 416 ÷ 7 **28.** 347 ÷ 5 **29.** 626 ÷ 9 **30.** 357 ÷ 6

For another example, see Set B on page 399.

Problem Solving

In **31** and **32**, use the chart at the right.

31. Connect Ada sold her mugs in 3 weeks. About how many did she sell each week?

32. Ben sold his mugs in 6 weeks. About how many did he sell each week?

33. Number Sense Complete by writing > or < in the ◯. Without dividing, explain how you know which quotient is greater.

$930 \div 4 \bigcirc 762 \div 4$

34. The International Space Station takes 644 minutes to orbit Earth 7 times. About how long does each orbit take?

A About 80 minutes
B About 90 minutes
C About 95 minutes
D About 100 minutes

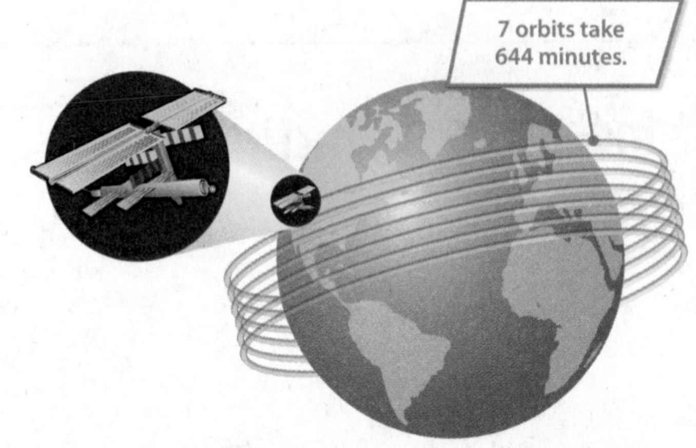

35. Extend Your Thinking Explain how to find a better estimate of $260 \div 5$ than the one shown below.

Round $260 \div 5$ to $300 \div 5$.
$300 \div 5 = 60$, so $260 \div 5$ is about 60.

36. Check for Reasonableness Kaylee wanted to divide 133 pieces of candy into 7 boxes. She decides to put 19 pieces in each box. Use estimation to determine if this answer seems reasonable.

Name ______________________

Homework 7-2
Estimating Quotients

Another Look!

Estimate 460 ÷ 9.

Here are two ways to estimate quotients.

You can use compatible numbers.	You can also estimate by thinking about multiplication.
Ask yourself: What is a number close to 460 that can be easily divided by 9? Try 450.	Ask yourself: Nine times what number is about 460?
$450 \div 9 = 50$	$9 \times 5 = 45$, so $9 \times 50 = 450$.
So, 460 ÷ 9 is about 50.	So, 460 ÷ 9 is about 50.

In **1** through **16**, estimate each quotient. Show your work.

1. 165 ÷ 4 **2.** 35 ÷ 4 **3.** 715 ÷ 9 **4.** 490 ÷ 8

5. 512 ÷ 5 **6.** 652 ÷ 8 **7.** 790 ÷ 9 **8.** 200 ÷ 7

9. 311 ÷ 6 **10.** 162 ÷ 2 **11.** 418 ÷ 6 **12.** 554 ÷ 7

13. 92 ÷ 3 **14.** 351 ÷ 7 **15.** 4,977 ÷ 5 **16.** 61 ÷ 2

Thinking about basic facts and multiples of 10 can help you find compatible numbers to use to estimate quotients.

In **17** through **19**, use Franny's To-Do List.

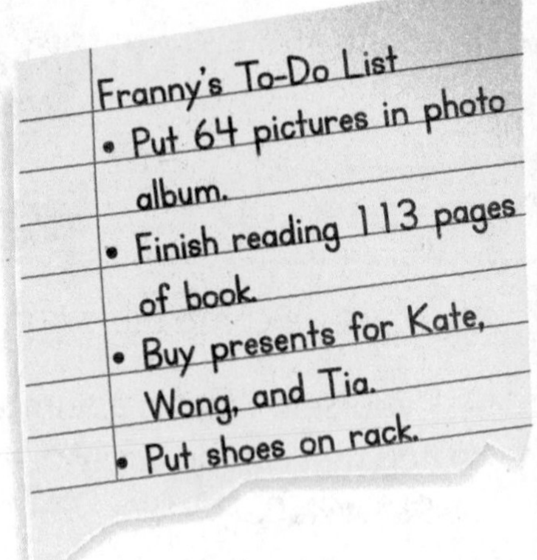

Franny's To-Do List
• Put 64 pictures in photo album.
• Finish reading 113 pages of book.
• Buy presents for Kate, Wong, and Tia.
• Put shoes on rack.

17. Estimation Franny wants to place the pictures in a photo album. She has 5 pages left in the album. About how many pictures can she place on each remaining page?

18. Estimation Franny plans to spend 4 hours reading. About how many pages would she need to read each hour to finish the book?

19. Connect Franny wants to spend an equal amount of money on the presents for her friends. If she has $62, about how much money can she spend on each present?

---

20. Use a Strip Diagram The veterinary clinic has seen 47 dogs, 19 cats, 7 exotic birds, and 3 horses this week. Complete the strip diagram and use it to help find the total number of animals seen by the clinic this week.

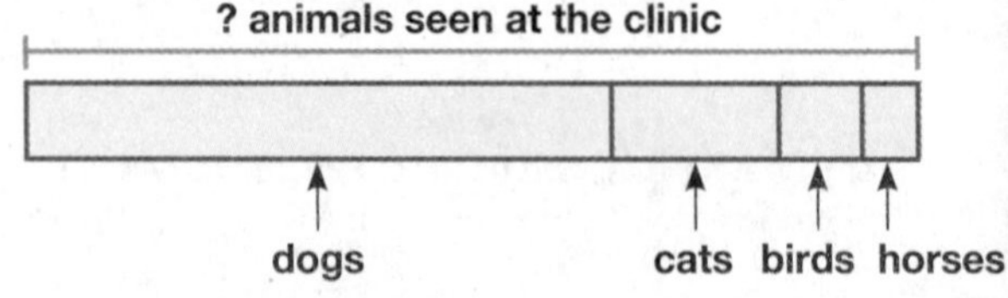

---

21. Personal Financial Literacy Trent earned the following amounts running errands: $4.50, $4.75, and $4.57. Which amount is the greatest?

22. Explain Monika baked 148 cookies. She wants to give them out so that everyone receives the same number. Is an estimated answer good enough? Explain.

---

23. Wayne has 303 marbles. If he gives away 123 of the marbles equally to 3 friends, about how many marbles will he give each friend?

A About 3 marbles
B About 30 marbles
C About 40 marbles
D About 100 marbles

24. Extend Your Thinking Tessa wants to separate 187 ears of corn into bags of six ears each. She has 35 bags. Estimate to find whether Tessa has enough bags. Explain how you found your answer.

Name ________________________________

Solve & Share

Jimi has 3,000 tickets for rides at the school carnival. Jimi needs to pack small plastic bags with 8 tickets in each bag. About how many bags will he need? ***Solve this problem any way you choose.***

Lesson 7-3
Estimating Quotients for Greater Dividends

TEKS 4.4G Round to the nearest 10, 100, or 1,000 or use compatible numbers to estimate solutions involving whole numbers.
Mathematical Process Standards 4.1A, 4.1B, 4.1C, 4.1D, 4.1F, 4.1G

Digital Resources at SavvasTexas.com

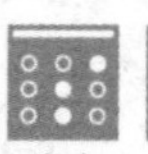
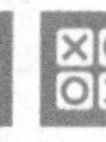

Solve Learn Glossary Check Tools Games

You can **use mental math.** Dividing compatible numbers makes it easier to estimate.

Look Back!

Connect Ideas What basic fact did you use to solve this problem?

A

How Can You Estimate Quotients Using Place Value?

On a "Clean Up Your Town Day," 1,320 people volunteered to clean up the Springville parks. They were divided equally into teams to work in each of the town's parks. About how many people were on each team?

Multiplication and division are related. Mentally multiplying by tens or hundreds can help you estimate the quotient of a multi-digit division problem.

Use multiplication patterns and division facts.

B

One Way

Use multiplication patterns. Ask yourself:

"6 times what number is about 1,320?"

You know $6 \times 2 = 12$, so
$6 \times 20 = 120$ and
$6 \times 200 = 1{,}200$.

1,200 is close enough to 1,320 for this estimate.

C

Another Way

Use division facts and place value patterns to find compatible numbers. Estimate the quotient $1{,}320 \div 6$.

You know $12 \div 6 = 2$, so
$120 \div 6 = 20$ and
$1{,}200 \div 6 = 200$

$1{,}320 \div 6$ is about 200. Each team is made up of about 200 people.

Do You Understand?

Convince Me! Complete the calculations at the right. Explain how you can use the calculations to estimate $1{,}296 \div 4$.

$4 \times 100 =$ ______

$4 \times 200 =$ ______

$4 \times 300 =$ ______

$4 \times 400 =$ ______

Name ______________________________

Another Example

One Way

Rounding the dividend

Estimate: 357 ÷ 8
Round: 400 ÷ 8 = 50

So, 357 ÷ 8 is about 50.

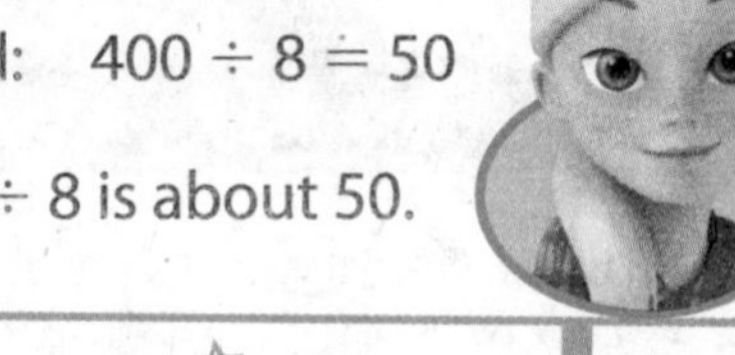

Sometimes you can use rounding to estimate quotients.

Another Way

Rounding the dividend and divisor

Estimate: 5,712 ÷ 9
Round: 6,000 ÷ 10 = 600

So, 5,712 ÷ 9 is about 600.

Guided Practice*

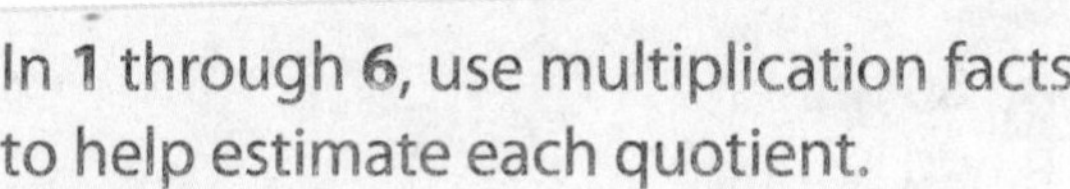

In **1** through **6**, use multiplication facts to help estimate each quotient.

1. 3,340 ÷ 8 **2.** 2,943 ÷ 7

3. 552 ÷ 9 **4.** 776 ÷ 4

5. 2,013 ÷ 5 **6.** 281 ÷ 3

7. Construct Arguments When estimating 1,320 ÷ 6, why is rounding not a good strategy?

8. Reason When dividing a 4-digit number by a 1-digit number, how many digits can the quotient have?

Independent Practice

In **9** through **20**, estimate each quotient.

9. 779 ÷ 7 **10.** 7,779 ÷ 7 **11.** 3,688 ÷ 6

12. 5,684 ÷ 9 **13.** 5,346 ÷ 6 **14.** 508 ÷ 7

15. 647 ÷ 3 **16.** 3,958 ÷ 8 **17.** 224 ÷ 3

18. 497 ÷ 8 **19.** 4,971 ÷ 8 **20.** 2,438 ÷ 5

For another example, see Set B on page 399.

Problem Solving

21. **Connect** Laura's dog eats 1 bag of dog food every 6 days. About how many bags will he eat in 1 year?

There are 365 days in 1 year.

22. In 1999, an 89-year-old woman walked 3,055 miles across the United States. She walked about 9 miles each day. About how many days did it take her to walk across the United States?

23. Ramón's older sister wants to buy a car that costs $7,993. She earns $9 for every hour she works. About how many hours must she work to earn enough money to buy the car?

    A 80 hours
    B 90 hours
    C 700 hours
    D 900 hours

24. **Check for Reasonableness** Eight students can fit at one cafeteria table. About how many tables are needed for 231 students? Does your answer make sense? How do you know?

25. **Extend Your Thinking** At Camp Summer Fun, 4 campers share each tent. The camp is expecting 331 campers. About how many tents will they need? Will the number of tents they actually need be more or less than the estimate? How do you know?

26. **Math and Science** It is estimated that the average American uses about 650 pounds of paper per year. About how many pounds of paper does an average American use each month?

About 650 lb of paper each year

Name ______________________

Homework 7-3
Estimating Quotients for Greater Dividends

Another Look!

Find 294 ÷ 5.

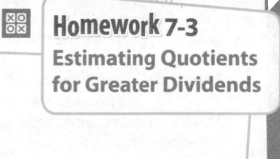

You can also use compatible numbers or rounding to estimate quotients.

Think of multiples of 5: 5, 10, 15, 20, 25, 30

Underline the first two digits of 294.

Find the multiple of 5 that is closest to 29. That multiple is 30.

$6 \times 5 = 30$
$60 \times 5 = 300$

$300 \div 5 = 60$

So, 294 ÷ 5 is about 60.

Here is another way to estimate quotients.

Estimate each quotient.

1. 1,561 ÷ 8

Think of multiples of 8: 8, 16, ________, ________, 40, ________

Underline the first two digits of 1,561.

Which multiple of 8 is closest to 15? ________

What is 200 × 8? ________

What is 1,600 ÷ 8? ________

So, 1,561 ÷ 8 is about ________.

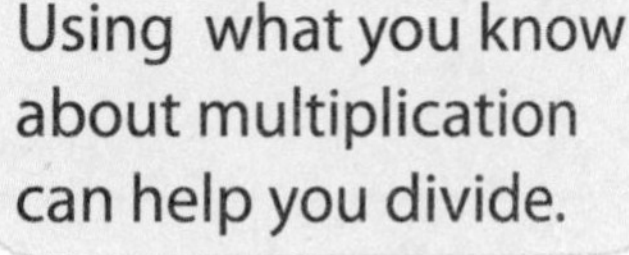

Using what you know about multiplication can help you divide.

2. 461 ÷ 9 **3.** 2,356 ÷ 6 **4.** 5,352 ÷ 9 **5.** 279 ÷ 9

6. 2,449 ÷ 8 **7.** 3,124 ÷ 6 **8.** 4,519 ÷ 5 **9.** 915 ÷ 3

10. 2,120 ÷ 5 **11.** 423 ÷ 4 **12.** 3,305 ÷ 7 **13.** 1,803 ÷ 2

Bob and Kate are making bracelets to sell at a craft fair. Each bracelet uses 6 blue beads, 9 silver beads, 3 rose beads, and 7 white beads.

14. **Estimation** Determine about how many bracelets Bob and Kate can make with each color of bead. Complete the table.

Color	Number of Beads	Beads per Bracelet	Estimated Number of Bracelets
Blue	258	6	
Silver	428	9	
Rose	102	3	
White	258	7	

15. About how many bracelets can they make before they run out of at least one color of bead? Which color of bead will they run out of first?

This table shows how many beads they have of each color. A table helps organize data.

16. Daniel's family grows pecans. They have harvested 1,309 pounds of pecans. If they package the pecans in 3-pound bags, about how many bags will they fill?

A About 40 bags
B About 50 bags
C About 400 bags
D About 500 bags

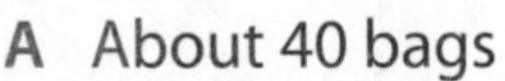

17. **Explain** What is the first step when estimating the answer to a division problem?

18. **Reason** The students who run the school store ordered 1,440 pencils. They are putting them in packages of 6 pencils. About how many packages can they make? Will the exact answer be more or less than the estimate? Explain.

19. **Extend Your Thinking** Find two estimates for 4,396 ÷ 4 by rounding the dividend to the nearest hundred and also to the nearest thousand. Compare the estimates.

Name

Lesson 7-4
Understanding Remainders

Solve & Share

Suppose you are making gift baskets of fruit. You have 14 apples, and you plan to put 4 apples in each basket. How many baskets can you fill? Will there be any apples left over? If so, how many? ***Solve this problem any way you choose.***

TEKS 4.4E Represent the quotient… using arrays, area models, or equations. **TEKS 4.4H** Solve with fluency one- and two-step problems involving…division, including interpreting remainders. **Mathematical Process Standards** 4.1A, 4.1C, 4.1D, 4.1E, 4.1F, 4.1G

You can **create and use representations.** Draw a picture to model the problem. ***Show your work in the space below!***

Digital Resources at SavvasTexas.com

Solve

Learn

Glossary

Check

Tools

Games

Look Back!

Connect Ideas How many apples in all are in the baskets? Write a number sentence to represent these apples.

After Dividing, What Do You Do With the Remainder?

When you divide, any number that remains after the division is complete is called the remainder.

Ned has 27 soccer cards in an album. He can put 6 cards on each page. He knows that 27 ÷ 6 = 4 with 3 left over as the remainder.

Use an R to write a remainder: 27 ÷ 6 = 4 R3

What should Ned do with the remainder?

The remainder must be less than the divisor.

Use the question asked to interpret the remainder.

One Way

27 ÷ 6 = 4 R3

How many pages can Ned fill?

To answer this question, find how many groups of 6 there are. The remainder can be ignored.

Ned can fill 4 pages.

Another Way

27 ÷ 6 = 4 R3

How many pages will Ned work on?

To answer this question, find how many groups are filled or started. Add 1 to the quotient without the remainder.

Ned will work on 5 pages.

Another Way

27 ÷ 6 = 4 R3

How many cards will Ned put on the fifth page?

The answer to this question is the remainder.

Ned will put 3 cards on the fifth page.

Do You Understand?

Convince Me! How can you tell at a glance that the calculation at the right is not correct? What error was made? What is the correct answer?

45 ÷ 6 = 6 R9

Name ______________________________

Another Example

Use counters to find 20 ÷ 3.

Write the quotient including the remainder.

What You Show

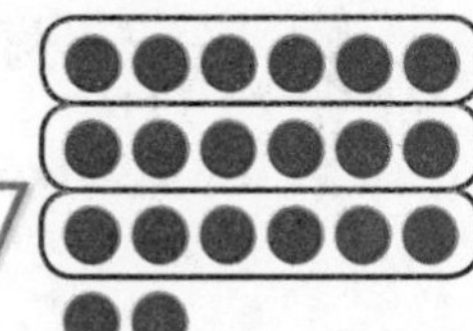

What You Write

6 with 2 left over

20 ÷ 3 = 6 R2

Guided Practice*

In **1** and **2**, use counters or draw a picture to find the number of groups and the number left over.

1. 17 oranges, 3 oranges in each box

17 ÷ 3 = ____ with ____ left over

2. 9 ÷ 2 = ____ with ____ left over

3. Explain Can the remainder be greater than the divisor? Explain.

4. Reason Dave is packing 23 sweaters into boxes. Each box will hold 3 sweaters. How many boxes will he fill? How many boxes will he need in all?

Independent Practice

Leveled Practice In **5** through **10**, find the number of groups and the number left over.

5. 18 jars, 4 jars in each box

18 ÷ 4 = ____ with ____ left over

6. 22 shirts, 6 shirts in each box

22 ÷ 6 = ____ with ____ left over

7. 27 ÷ 7 = ____ with ____ left over

8. 13 ÷ 2 = ____ with ____ left over

9. 31 ÷ 8 = ____ with ____ left over

10. 32 ÷ 9 = ____ with ____ left over

In **11** through **13**, interpret each remainder.

11. 7 football cards, 3 cards on each page
How many pages can Alex complete?

12. 11 baseball cards, 4 cards on each page
How many cards are on the 3rd page?

13. 34 stickers, 5 stickers on each page
How many pages will have some stickers?

For another example, see Set C on page 400.

Problem Solving

In **14** and **15**, use the table on the right.

14. Samuel has 45 prize tickets. How many marbles can he get?

15. Inez got 3 rings and 2 stickers. How many tickets did she use?

DATA

Ticket Exchange

Prize	Number of Tickets
Yo-yo	8
Ring	9
Marble	7
Sticker	4

16. Connect Keiko makes necklaces like the one in the picture on the right. She has 19 blue beads and 13 red beads. How many necklaces can she make? How many of each color of bead will be left over?

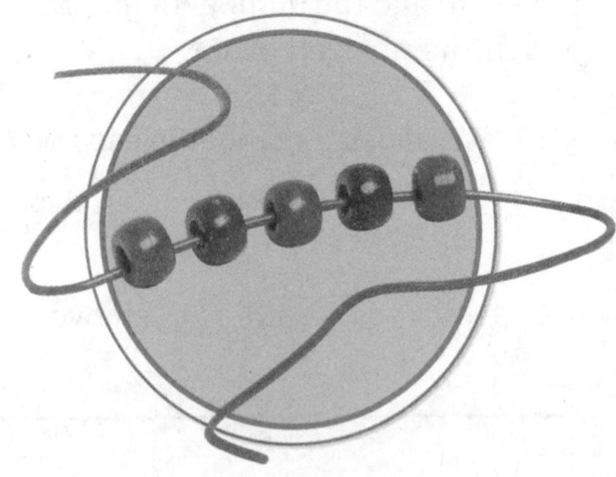

17. Number Sense Amanda found that $34 \div 8 = 3$ R10. Is her answer correct? If not, what is the correct answer? Explain.

18. Jack is making muffins. He plans to use 5 raisins to decorate some of the muffins. If he has 21 raisins, how many muffins can he decorate?

19. Extend Your Thinking Write a problem that requires adding 1 to the quotient when interpreting the remainder.

20. There are 39 children at a park. They want to make teams with 9 children on each team. 2 of the children go home. How many teams can they make?

A 3 teams
B 4 teams
C 30 teams
D 48 teams

Name ______________________________

Homework 7-4
Understanding Remainders

Another Look!

Jamal has 20 marbles that he is putting into bags. He is going to put 6 marbles in each bag. Find 20 ÷ 6.

The remainder is the number left after the division is complete. Remember, the remainder must be less than the divisor.

Jamal can fill 3 bags. There will be 2 marbles left over.

There are 3 ways to interpret a remainder.

The remainder can be ignored.	The remainder can be the answer.	You need to add 1 to the quotient.
How many bags did Jamal fill? 3 bags	*How many marbles are not in bags?* 2 marbles	*How many bags are needed for all the marbles?* 4 bags

In **1** through **3**, find the number of equal groups and the number left over.

1. 16 ÷ 5 = ____ with ____ left over

2. 34 ÷ 6 = ____ with ____ left over

3. 31 ÷ 8 = ____ with ____ left over

In **4** through **6**, divide. Then interpret the remainder.

4. 17 apples
3 apples in each bag
17 ÷ 3 = ____ with ____ left over
How many apples are not in bags?
____

5. 21 cards
5 cards in each box
21 ÷ 5 = ____ with ____ left over
How many boxes are needed for all cards?
____

6. 19 model cars
4 cars on each shelf
19 ÷ 4 = ____ with ____ left over
How many shelves are full?
____

7. **Explain** Why must the remainder be less than the divisor?

8. There are 25 students in Ms. Morris's class. She wants to divide the class into 3, 4, or 5 equal teams. Which number of teams can she have? Explain.

9. How many basketball teams can be made with 18 people if each team must have at least 5 people? Explain.

10. **Number Sense** There are 14 girls trying out for cheerleading. Each team will have 6 cheerleaders. How many full teams will be made? How many girls will not make a team?

11. **Use a Strip Diagram** How many strings are used to make 4 guitars like the ones in the picture? Draw a strip diagram to show how you found your answer.

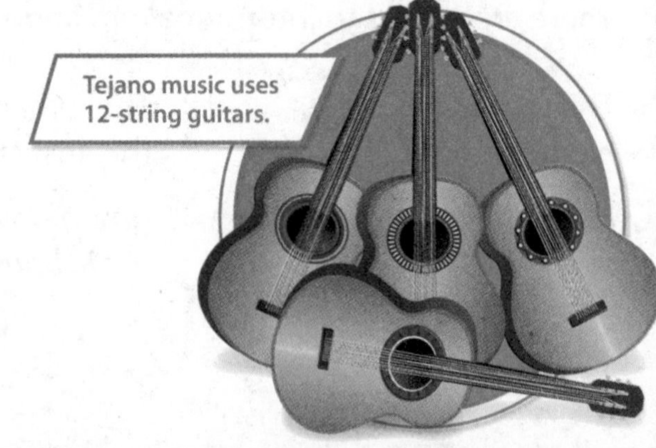
Tejano music uses
12-string guitars.

12. **Extend Your Thinking** Carl puts his coins on pages in a book. He has 22 coins. He can put 4 coins on each page. How many coins will Carl put on the last page? Explain how you found the answer.

13. There are 26 students in Dante's class. One student is out sick today. They want to split into teams of six for a game. How many full teams can they make?

A 2 teams
B 4 teams
C 6 teams
D 20 teams

14. Jada bought a bag of 8 apples. She and her 3 sisters will share the apples equally. How many apples will each person get? Will there be any apples left over? If so, how many?

Connecting the information you are given to what you are asked to find can help you interpret a remainder.

Name ______________________________

Solve & Share

Maggie needs to wrap 30 presents this week. She plans on wrapping 5 presents each day. If instead she wraps 10 presents each day, how much sooner will she finish? ***Solve this problem any way you choose.***

Problem Solving

Lesson 7-5
Draw a Strip Diagram and Write an Equation

TEKS 4.1D Communicate mathematical ideas, reasoning, and their implications using multiple representations, including symbols, diagrams, graphs, and language as appropriate. Also, 4.5.
Mathematical Process Standards 4.1A, 4.1B, 4.1C, 4.1F, 4.1G

Digital Resources at SavvasTexas.com

Solve

Learn

Glossary

Check

Tools

Games

You can **create and use representations.** Draw strip diagrams to help solve this problem. ***Show your work in the space above!***

Look Back!

Reason What equation can you write to help you solve this problem?

A Analyze

What Steps Can You Use To Solve a Problem?

Ruben's scout troop is making 4 milk-jug birdfeeders. Each birdfeeder will use the same number of wooden dowels. If they have 24 dowels in all, how many dowels will be used for each feeder?

How could you use a strip diagram to show the information in this problem?

B Analyze

What do I know? There are 24 dowels. There are 4 birdfeeders. Each birdfeeder has the same number of dowels.

What am I asked to find? The number of dowels used for each birdfeeder.

C Plan and Solve

Draw a picture.

Let $n =$ number of dowels used for each birdfeeder.

24 dowels

n	*n*	*n*	*n*

Write an equation: $n = 24 \div 4$

$n = 6$

There are 6 dowels for each birdfeeder.

D Justify

Check the answer by multiplying.

Each birdfeeder has 6 dowels.
There are 4 birdfeeders.

$4 \times 6 = 24$

The answer checks.

Do You Understand?

Convince Me! Ben has $55 to buy helium balloons for the end-of-summer camp party. The balloons cost $9 per pack.

How many packs of balloons can Ben buy? How much money will Ben have left?

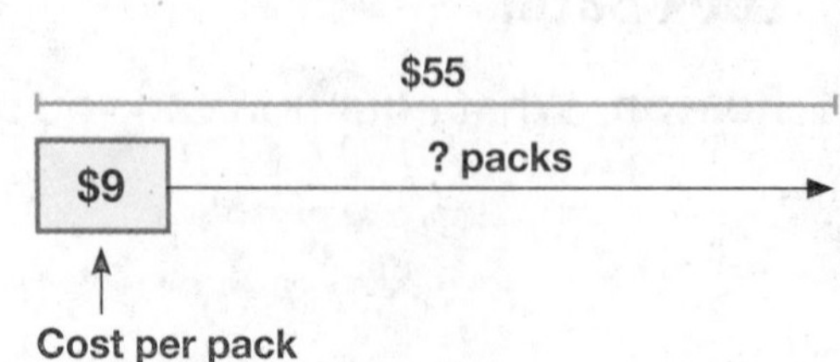

Name ____

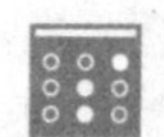

Guided Practice*

1. **Use a Strip Diagram** Tina put 32 flowers into eight bouquets. How many flowers were in each bouquet if each had the same number of flowers?

   Let n = number of flowers in each bouquet.

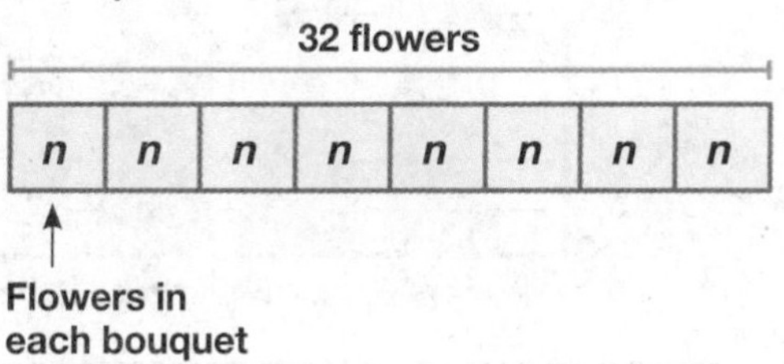

2. **Explain** How did the strip diagram in Problem 1 help you to write an equation?

3. **Communicate** Write a problem about sharing items that you can solve by drawing a picture. Then solve.

Independent Practice*

4. **Use a Strip Diagram** Kylie bought a bag of 30 beads to make bracelets. Each bracelet requires 5 beads. How many bracelets can Kylie make?

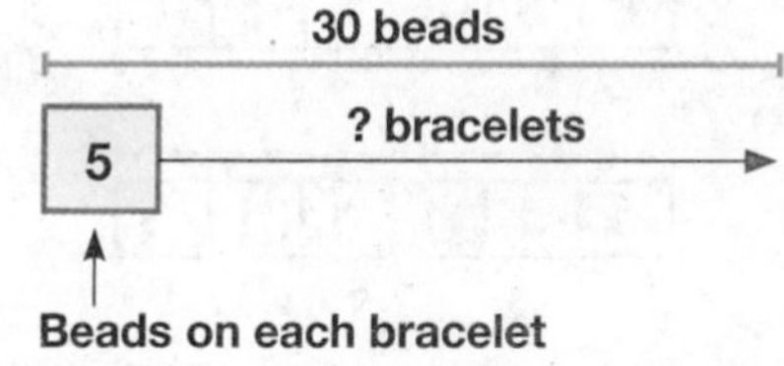

5. **Reason** If Kylie needs 7 beads for each bracelet, how many bracelets can she make? What equation could you write to solve this problem?

6. **Use a Strip Diagram** Jodi is bundling newspapers. She has 54 newspapers and puts 6 newspapers in each bundle. How many bundles does Jodi make?

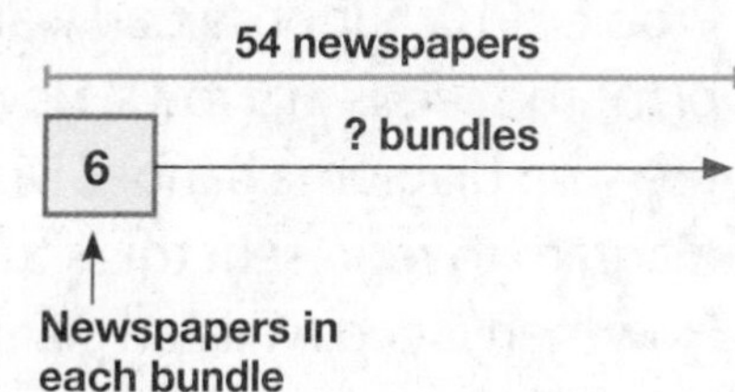

7. **Mental Math** Jenna bought 36 pencils to give to her friends before the first day of school. If each friend received 6 pencils, how many friends did Jenna buy pencils for?

*For another example, see Set D on page 400.

Problem Solving

In **8** and **9**, use the bar graph on the right.

8. Analyze Information How much more money did Katie save in September than in October?

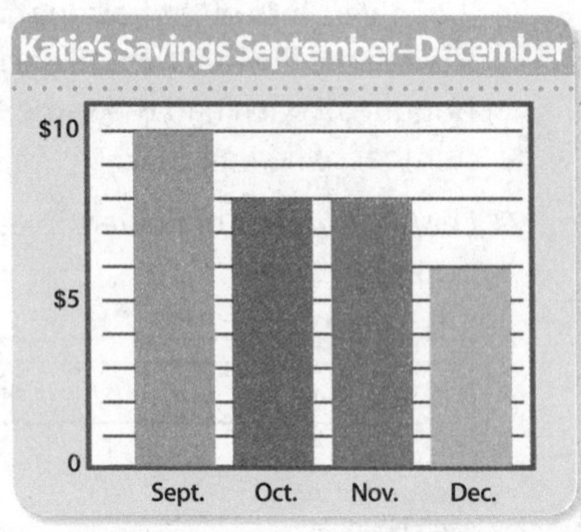

9. Connect Katie used all of the money she saved in November and December to buy two presents. If the presents cost the same amount, how much did each present cost?

---

10. Use a Strip Diagram Carl is planting seeds. He has 36 seeds that he wants to plant in 6 rows. Which shows the number of seeds that will go into each row?

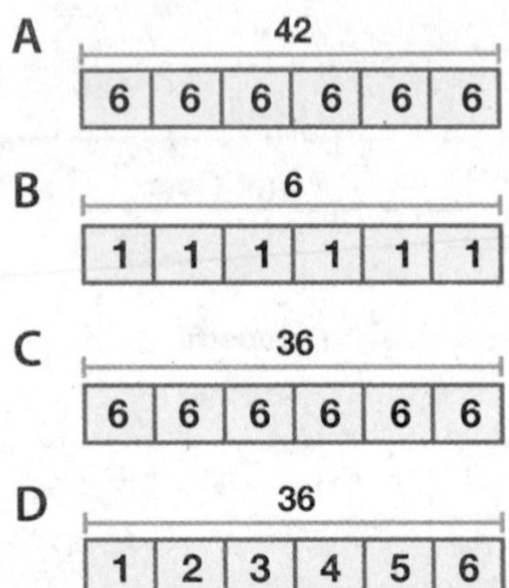

11. Shauna has a collection of 9 paintings. The paintings are worth $81. If each of the paintings is worth the same amount, how much is each painting worth?

A $729
B $90
C $10
D $9

---

12. Extend Your Thinking Look back at Problem 10. Suppose Carl wants to plant the seeds in 9 rows. How would the strip diagram change? Draw a strip diagram to represent this situation. How many seeds will Carl plant in each row?

13. Reason Sheena is packing 18 paperweights in boxes. She packs them in 6 boxes with the same number of paperweights in each box. How many paperweights are in each box?

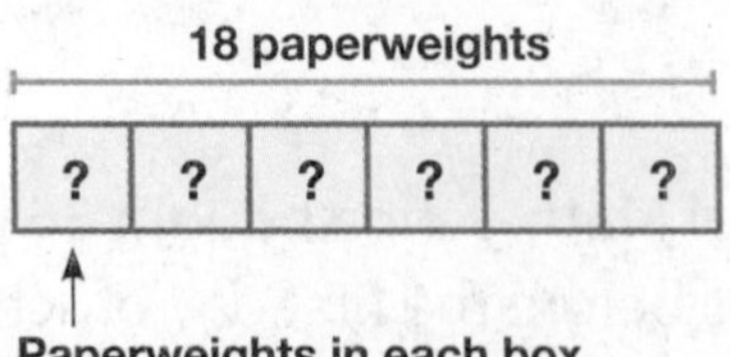

Name ______________________________

Homework 7-5
Draw a Strip Diagram and Write an Equation

Another Look!

Bryan has 24 bottles of water. He and his friends have 8 backpacks. If he puts the same number of bottles into each backpack, how many bottles would each backpack hold?

Follow the steps to solve.

Analyze	Plan and Solve	Justify
• *What information do you know?* There are 24 bottles of water and 8 backpacks. • *What are you asked to find?* The number of bottles in each backpack • *What operation do you use?* Division	• Draw a strip diagram to help you visualize the problem. 24 bottles b | b | b | b | b | b | b | b • Write an equation. $24 \div 8 = b$ • Solve. $b = 3$ bottles	3 bottles in each backpack Check: $3 \times 8 = 24$ The answer checks. I answered the question that was asked.

1. **Formulate a Plan** Joeli has 10 quarters. She wants to buy postcards to mail to her friends. Each postcard costs 2 quarters. How many postcards can she buy?

   a. What information do you know?

   b. What are you asked to find?

   c. Write an equation. Solve and check.

2. **Communicate** Mack has 36 photos. His album can hold 9 photos per page. Write and solve an equation to find how many pages he will need to use. Check your answer.

3. **Communicate** There are 7 vans taking 56 students on a field trip. If each van takes the same number of students, how many students are in each van? Write and solve an equation. Then check your answer.

In **4** through **7**, use the strip diagram to write an equation and solve each problem.

4. Use a Strip Diagram Terrence has 16 trophies and he wants to put an equal number on 4 shelves. How many trophies will he have on each shelf?

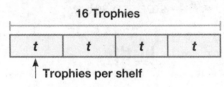

16 Trophies

t	*t*	*t*	*t*

Trophies per shelf

5. Use a Strip Diagram Mrs. Parker has 21 bookmarks that she wants to give to her 7 reading club members. How many bookmarks will each member receive?

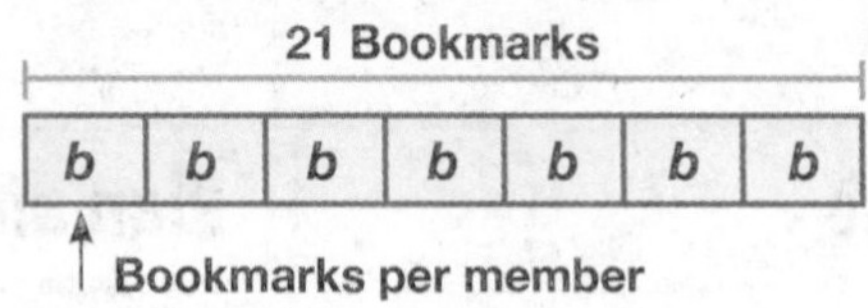

6. Use a Strip Diagram Lisa has 45 megabytes of space left on her flash drive. She has 5 files that are the same size that will fill up the space. How many megabytes is each file?

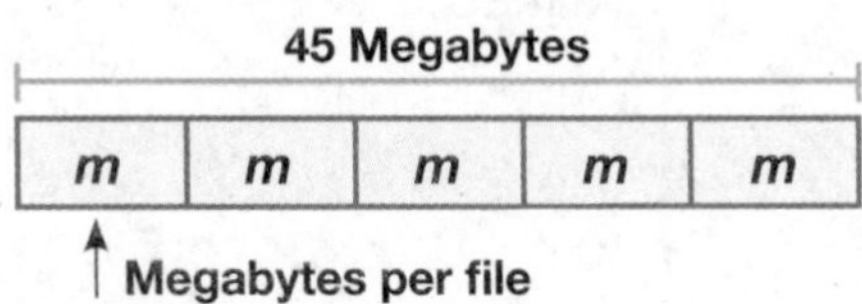

7. Use a Strip Diagram A store is displaying boxes of a new video game in 7 rows. If the store has 49 copies of the game, how many games are in each row?

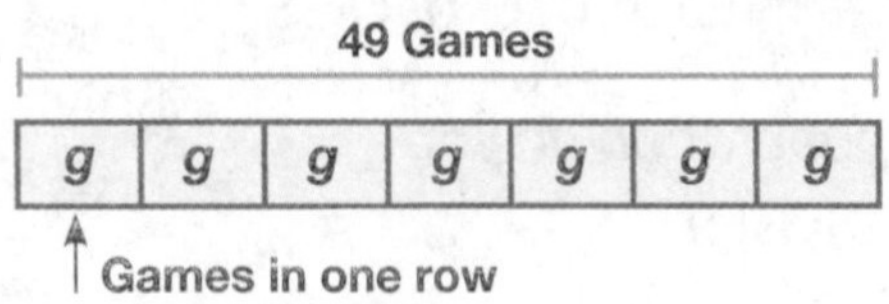

8. Connect Remy is 8 years old. She is twice as old as her younger sister. Which expression below shows how old Remy's sister is?

A 8×2
B $8 \div 2$
C $8 + 2$
D $8 - 2$

9. A food drive collected 140 cans of food. The cans were being distributed equally to four different food banks. How many cans were sent to each food bank?

A 30 cans
B 33 cans
C 35 cans
D 40 cans

10. Extend Your Thinking Jillian wants to organize her shell collection into wooden crates. Each crate holds 8 shells. Jillian has 48 shells. How can she use a picture to find how many crates she needs?

Name

Mixed Problem Solving

1. Number Sense Jonah used a basic fact to find 240 ÷ 8. What basic fact did Jonah use? What is the quotient Jonah found?

2. Use a Strip Diagram A golf course needs to order 300 golf balls. If there are 6 balls in each package, how many packages should the golf course buy?

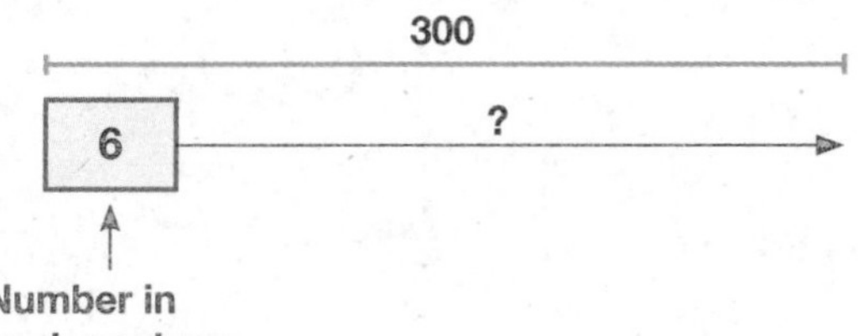

Applying Math Processes

- How does this problem connect to previous ones?
- What is my plan?
- How can I use tools?
- How can I use number sense?
- How can I communicate and represent my thinking?
- How can I organize and record information?
- How can I explain my work?
- How can I justify my answer?

3. There are 720 students in a school. The school has 9 grades, including kindergarten. If each grade has an equal number of students, how many students are in each grade?

A 90 students
B 80 students
C 9 students
D 8 students

4. Personal Financial Literacy Wyatt earns $8 an hour babysitting. He babysat for 3 hours. How much did he earn?

5. Check for Reasonableness Kailen said that the quotient of 1,530 ÷ 5 is 306. Use estimation to check the reasonableness of Kailen's answer. Explain your reasoning.

6. Extend Your Thinking There are 43 students going on a field trip. Each van being used must include one adult chaperone. If each van holds 9 passengers, how many vans will they need? Explain.

A chaperone is also a passenger.

Error Search

Find each problem that is not correct. Circle what is wrong and rewrite the problem so it is correct.

1. $123 \div 4$
   $120 \div 4 = 30$
   $123 \div 4 = \text{about } 30$

2. $81 \div 3$
   $60 \div 3 = 20$
   $81 \div 3 = \text{about } 20$

3. $410 \div 8$
   $560 \div 8 = 70$
   $410 \div 8 = \text{about } 70$

4. $628 \div 7$
   $630 \div 7 = 90$
   $628 \div 7 = \text{about } 90$

Target Number

Mental Math Using any pair of numbers from the box, list as many quotients equivalent to the Target Number as you can. Numbers in the box may be used more than once.

5.

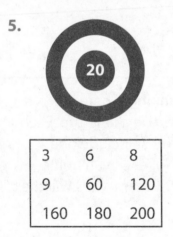

3	6	8
9	60	120
160	180	200

6.

2	4	5	7
60	80	120	210

7.

3	5	7	9
180	240	300	540

Name ______

TOPIC 7

Set A pages 367–372

A class shares 270 pens equally among 3 groups of students.

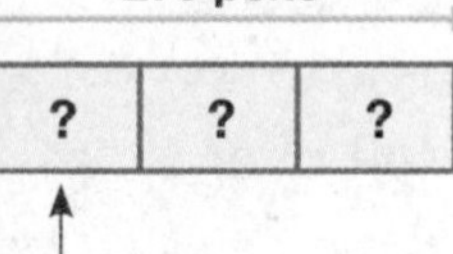

Pens for each group of students

Find $270 \div 3$.

The basic fact is $27 \div 3 = 9$.

27 tens $\div$ 3 = 9 tens or 90

So, $270 \div 3 = 90$ pens.

Remember you can use place-value patterns to divide multiples of 10.

1. $250 \div 5$
2. $810 \div 9$
3. $3{,}200 \div 4$
4. $4{,}200 \div 7$
5. $1{,}000 \div 2$
6. $240 \div 4$
7. $450 \div 5$
8. $720 \div 9$
9. $3{,}600 \div 4$
10. $4{,}900 \div 7$
11. $2{,}000 \div 2$
12. $280 \div 4$
13. $2{,}100 \div 7$
14. $560 \div 8$

Set B pages 373–384

Use estimation to find $420 \div 8$.

8 times what number is about 420?

$8 \times 5 = 40$,
so $8 \times 50 = 400$.

So, $420 \div 8$ is about 50.

Use estimation to find $135 \div 7$.

What number close to 135 is easily divided by 7?

Try multiples of ten near 135:

135 is close to 140.

140 is 14 tens and can be divided by 7.
$140 \div 7 = 20$

So, $135 \div 7$ is about 20.

Remember to try rounding the dividend to a number that is easily divided by the divisor.

Estimate each quotient.

1. $718 \div 8$
2. $156 \div 4$
3. $482 \div 8$
4. $174 \div 3$
5. $843 \div 7$
6. $321 \div 2$
7. $428 \div 6$
8. $811 \div 9$
9. $561 \div 8$
10. $723 \div 8$
11. $632 \div 9$
12. $362 \div 9$
13. $331 \div 4$
14. $1{,}222 \div 6$
15. $2{,}511 \div 5$
16. $362 \div 6$
17. $4{,}940 \div 7$
18. $9{,}312 \div 3$

Set C pages 385–390

Tom is putting 14 apples into bags. Each bag holds 4 apples. How many bags can Tom fill? Will any apples be left over?

Use counters to make an array that models $14 \div 4$.

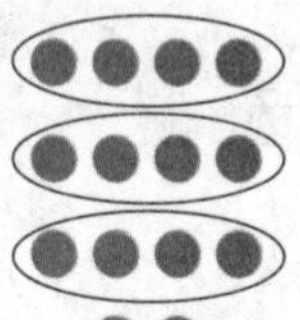

$14 \div 4 = 3$ with 2 left over

Tom can fill 3 bags. There will be 2 apples left over.

Remember to make sure you put the correct number of items in each group.

Make or draw arrays or area models to help.

1. 21 books, 5 books in each box
   $21 \div 5 =$ ____ with ____ left over
2. 40 stickers, 6 stickers on each page
   $40 \div 6 =$ ____ with ____ left over
3. 23 days, 7 days in each week
   $23 \div 7 =$ ____ with ____ left over

Set D pages 391–396

What do I know? Mrs. Collins has 36 pairs of scissors. She puts the same number of scissors in each of 6 drawers. How many pairs of scissors are in each drawer?

What am I being asked to find? The number of scissors in each drawer

Draw a strip diagram.

36 scissors in all

?	?	?	?	?	?

Scissors in each drawer

Write a division equation to find the number of scissors in each drawer.

$36 \div 6 = \square$

$36 \div 6 = 6$

There are 6 pairs of scissors in each drawer.

Remember to draw a strip diagram to help you write an equation.

Draw a strip diagram and write an equation to solve.

1. Winnie buys 20 bookmarks for herself and three of her friends. Each person receives the same number of bookmarks. How many bookmarks does each person receive?

2. Marla has 6 boxes of markers with the same number of markers in each box. If she has 54 markers in all, how many markers are in each box?

Name ________________________________

TOPIC 7

Test

1. A stadium has 3,000 seats and 6 gates. How many seats are served by each gate if each gate serves the same number of seats?

A 5 seats

B 50 seats

C 500 seats

D 5,000 seats

2. Each costume requires 3 yards of material. How many costumes can Beth make out of 26 yards? How much material will she have left?

A 8 costumes; 0 yards left

B 8 costumes; 2 yards left

C 9 costumes; 1 yard left

D 9 costumes; 2 yards left

3. A cyclist rides 2,823 miles in four weeks. He rides an equal distance each week. About how many miles does he ride each week?

A about 1,200 miles

B about 800 miles

C about 700 miles

D about 400 miles

4. A case of plastic spoons has 4,800 spoons. There are 8 boxes of spoons in the case. How many spoons are in each box?

A 400 spoons

B 600 spoons

C 800 spoons

D 4,000 spoons

5. Philip has 52 new stickers. If he puts an equal number of stickers on each of 6 blank pages in his sticker book, how many stickers does he have left over?

A 8 stickers

B 5 stickers

C 4 stickers

D None of the above

6. Robert earned \$184 by mowing 8 lawns. He earned the same amount for each lawn. Which number sentence does **NOT** show a reasonable estimate of the amount he earned for mowing each lawn?

A \$200 ÷ 5 = \$40

B \$160 ÷ 8 = \$20

C \$180 ÷ 9 = \$20

D \$200 ÷ 10 = \$20

7. Olivia has 36 daisies and 6 vases. She puts the same number of daisies in each vase. Which equation shows how to find the number, n, of daisies she can put in each vase?

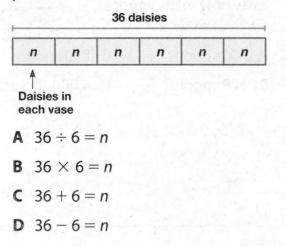

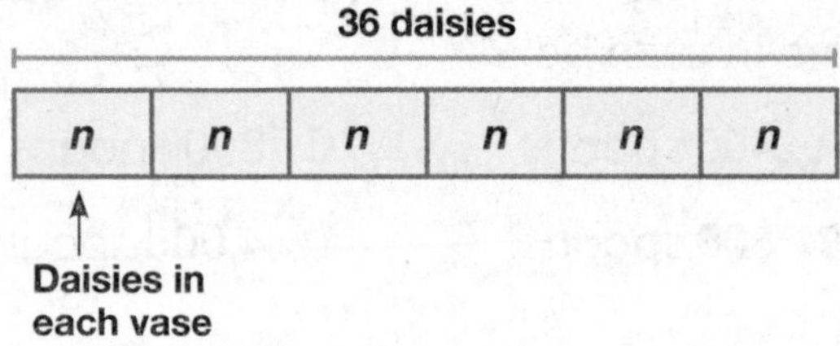

A $36 \div 6 = n$

B $36 \times 6 = n$

C $36 + 6 = n$

D $36 - 6 = n$

8. Holly uses 7 sheets of tissue paper to make one flower. If she bought a package with 500 sheets of tissue paper, about how many tissue flowers will she be able to make? Use compatible numbers to find your answer.

9. The soccer club has one package of 360 paper cups to use in the concession stands. If the cups are split equally among the 4 concession stands, how many cups would each stand have?

			.		
⓪	⓪	⓪		⓪	⓪
①	①	①		①	①
②	②	②		②	②
③	③	③		③	③
④	④	④		④	④
⑤	⑤	⑤		⑤	⑤
⑥	⑥	⑥		⑥	⑥
⑦	⑦	⑦		⑦	⑦
⑧	⑧	⑧		⑧	⑧
⑨	⑨	⑨		⑨	⑨

10. Alex has 27 photos of his friends that he wants to display on 3 pages in his photo album. If he puts an equal number of photos on each page, which equation shows how many photos, n, he can put on each page?

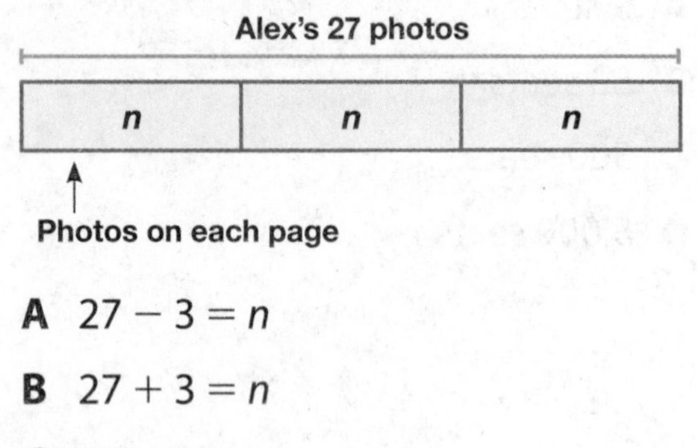

A $27 - 3 = n$

B $27 + 3 = n$

C $27 \div 3 = n$

D $27 \times 3 = n$

11. There are 49 students on a tour. Each guide can take 5 students. How many guides are needed? Explain.

12. Rory's older brother is saving to buy a used motorcycle that costs $2,400. He saves an equal amount of money each month for 6 months. How much does he need to save each month to buy the motorcycle?

			.		
⓪	⓪	⓪		⓪	⓪
①	①	①		①	①
②	②	②		②	②
③	③	③		③	③
④	④	④		④	④
⑤	⑤	⑤		⑤	⑤
⑥	⑥	⑥		⑥	⑥
⑦	⑦	⑦		⑦	⑦
⑧	⑧	⑧		⑧	⑧
⑨	⑨	⑨		⑨	⑨

Developing Proficiency: Dividing by 1-Digit Divisors

Essential Questions: How can the steps in dividing be explained? How can partial quotients be used to divide? What is the standard procedure for dividing multi-digit numbers?

Horsepower was originally used to compare the output of steam engines to the output of horses.
Did you know that horsepower is still used to rate engine performance in cars and other machines?
Hold your horses! Here's a project on horsepower.

Math and Science Project: Work, Power, and Energy

Do Research Use the Internet or other resources to research what horsepower represents. Include in your research which scientist first defined the term *horsepower* and give examples of machines that are rated in horsepower.

Journal: Write a Report Include what you found. Also in your report:

- Choose your favorite kinds of cars or other machines and find how much horsepower they have.
- Give an example of a car or other machine that has a horsepower rating that can be divided equally by 2, 4, and 5.

Name

Review What You Know

Vocabulary

Choose the best term from the box. Write it on the blank.

- array
- compatible numbers
- factors
- partial product

1. An arrangement of objects in rows and columns is called a(n) ______.
2. When multiplying a two-digit number by a two-digit number, a ______ is found by multiplying the first factor by the ones digit of the second factor.
3. Numbers that are easy to compute mentally are called ______.

Division Facts

Divide.

4. $15 \div 3$
5. $64 \div 8$
6. $72 \div 8$
7. $35 \div 7$
8. $12 \div 4$
9. $45 \div 9$

Multiplying by 10 and 100

Find each product.

10. 62×10
11. 24×100
12. 65×100
13. 14×10
14. 35×100
15. 59×10

Arrays

16. Write a multiplication equation for the array at the right.

17. **Explain** Is an array for 4×3 the same as or different from the array shown above? Explain.

No matter which way you model multiplication in an array, the product stays the same. That's the Commutative Property of Multiplication.

My Word Cards

A-Z

Use the example for the word on the front of the card to help complete the definition on the back.

My Word Cards

Complete the definition. Extend learning by writing your own definition.

Name ______________________

Solve & Share

A certain bird feeder holds 6 cups of bird feed. How many times can this feeder be filled using a 72-cup bag of bird feed? ***Solve this problem any way you choose.***

Lesson 8-1
Using Partial Quotients to Divide

TEKS 4.4E Represent the quotient of up to a four-digit whole number divided by a one-digit whole number using arrays, area models, or equations. Also, 4.4F.
Mathematical Process Standards 4.1A, 4.1B, 4.1C, 4.1D, 4.1G

Digital Resources at SavvasTexas.com

Solve

Learn

Glossary

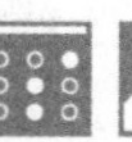
Check

Tools

Games

You can use **number sense.** Think about how many times you can take away groups of six from your original number. ***Show your work in the space below!***

Check for Reasonableness How can you decide if your answer is reasonable?

What Are Some Ways to Record Division?

A

Each row on an airplane can seat 3 people. If there are 63 people waiting in line and each seat will be taken, how many rows of seats are needed?

This strip diagram shows the problem.

63 people

3 | ? rows

people in each row

3 seats per row

Find partial quotients and add.

B

One Way

$3\overline{)63}$	Estimate: How many 3s are in 63? Try 10.
$-\ 30$	Multiply 10×3 and subtract.
33	Estimate: How many 3s are in 33? Use 11.
$-\ 33$	Multiply 11×3 and subtract.
0	

Add the partial quotients. $10 + 11 = 21$, so there are 21 3s in 63.

C

Another Way

$3\overline{)63}$	Estimate: How many 3s are in 63? Try 20.
$-\ 60$	Multiply 20×3 and subtract.
3	Estimate: How many 3s are in 3? Use 1.
$-\ 3$	Multiply 1×3 and subtract.
0	

Add the partial quotients. $20 + 1 = 21$.

21 rows are needed to seat 63 people.

Do You Understand?

Convince Me! A "gross" is twelve dozen or 144. If a gross of apples is placed into bags holding 6 apples each, how many bags are used?

Think: How many 6s are in 144?

Name ______________________________

Another Example

Find 119 ÷ 7.

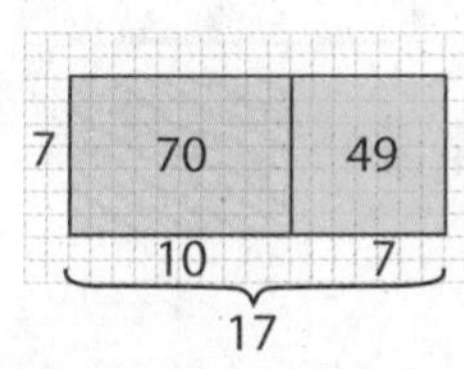


```
7)119
 - 70  | 10
   49  |
 - 49  |  7
    0    17
```

Here is a simple way to record your work.

Guided Practice*

In **1** and **2**, use partial quotients to divide. Show your work.

1. 4)48

2. 9)153

3. Reason Show one way of using partial quotients to solve 69 ÷ 3.

4. Reason Show another way of using partial quotients to solve 69 ÷ 3.

Independent Practice

Leveled Practice In **5** through **10**, use partial quotients to divide. Show your work.

5.
```
 6)78    Try 10.
 - 60    Multiply ___ × 6 and subtract.
   18    Use 3.
 - 18    Multiply ___ × 6 and subtract.
    0
```
Add partial quotients: ___ + ___ = ___

6.
```
 4)84    Try 20.
 - 80    Multiply ___ × ___ and subtract.
    4    Use 1.
  - 4    Multiply ___ × ___ and subtract.
    0
```
Add partial quotients: ___ + ___ = ___

7. 6)90

8. 7)126

9. 5)120

10. 7)84

*For another example, see Set A on page 457.

Problem Solving

11. Use a Strip Diagram A collection of 64 stickers is being placed into 4 equal piles. How many stickers will be placed in each pile?

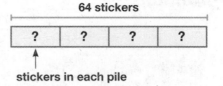

64 stickers			
?	?	?	?

stickers in each pile

12. Connect A car repair shop charges $65 an hour for labor. If a repair requires $120 in parts and 3 hours labor, what is the total cost of the repair?

13. Georgena has 84 pictures she wants to organize in a photo album. How many more pages of the album will be used if Georgena puts 4 pictures on each page than if she puts 6 pictures on each page?

A 7 pages
B 8 pages
C 10 pages
D 14 pages

14. Construct Arguments Amanda thinks that she can stack her books into 4 piles with 6 books each and 6 piles with 3 books each. Is Amanda's reasoning correct? Explain.

15. Mental Math There are 2 dozen eggs in the kitchen. A chef is baking cookies for 3 parties. For each party, the chef uses the same number of eggs. What is the greatest number of eggs the chef can use for each party?

16. Extend Your Thinking How can you use partial quotients to find 366 ÷ 3? Explain.

Name ____________________

Homework 8-1
Use Partial Quotients to Divide

Another Look!

For City Clean-Up Day, 48 people volunteered to clean up the city park. The volunteers worked in groups of 3 people. How many groups of volunteers cleaned up the city park?

Work	Partial quotients	Steps
$3\overline{)48}$		Try 10.
− 30	10	Multiply 10 × 3 and subtract.
18		Use 6.
− 18	6	Multiply 6 × 3 and subtract.
0	16	Add the partial quotients.

There were 16 groups of volunteers.

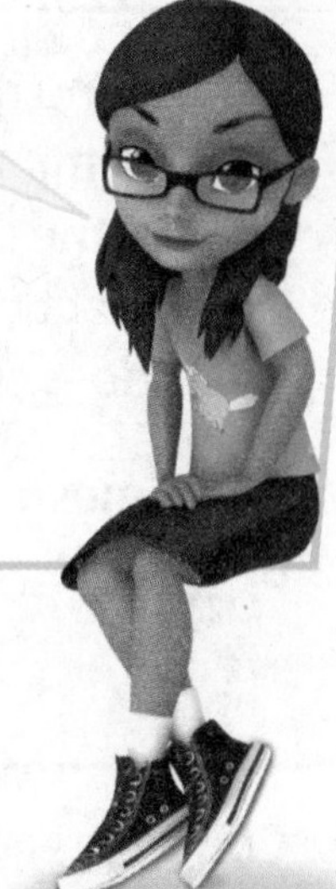

Use partial products to divide. Show your work.

1.

Work	Partial quotients	Steps
$7\overline{)98}$		Try 10.
− ☐☐	___	Multiply 10 × 7 and subtract.
☐☐		Use 4.
− ☐☐	___	Multiply ____ × 7 and subtract.
☐	___	Add the partial quotients.

2. $5\overline{)75}$ 3. $3\overline{)72}$ 4. $6\overline{)96}$ 5. $8\overline{)112}$

6. $4\overline{)92}$ 7. $6\overline{)126}$ 8. $3\overline{)75}$ 9. $2\overline{)36}$

10. $7\overline{)91}$ 11. $4\overline{)124}$ 12. $9\overline{)135}$ 13. $6\overline{)108}$

14. Use a Strip Diagram Jon has 32 trading cards. He puts the cards into piles of 8 cards. How many piles does he make?

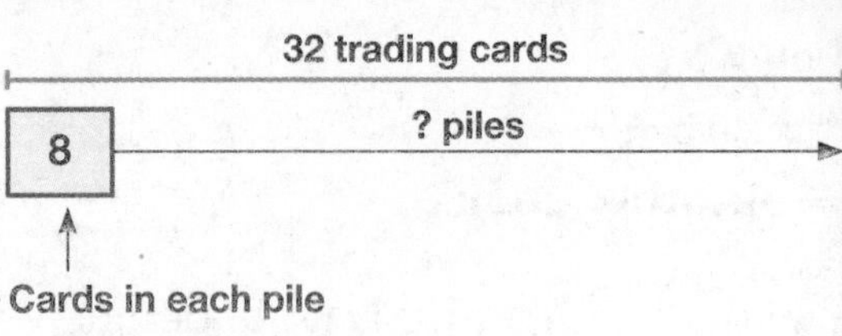

15. For a piano recital, Jessie is playing a song that is 3 minutes long. She practices by playing the song several times in a row. If she practices for 21 minutes, how many times does she play the song?

A 6 times
B 7 times
C 8 times
D 9 times

16. Construct Arguments Ryan has a total of 85 pennies. Will he be able to give away his pennies equally to 4 of his friends? Explain.

17. Connect A teacher forms groups of 4 students to work on a project. There are 13 girls and 11 boys in the class. How many groups are formed?

18. A local baker made 132 bagels one day. The baker sells bagels in packages of 6 bagels. He sold all of the bagels. How many packages of bagels did he sell?

19. Analyze Information Jamal had $25 with him when he went to the fun center. He bought a lunch and one ticket for the batting cages. How much money does Jamal have left?

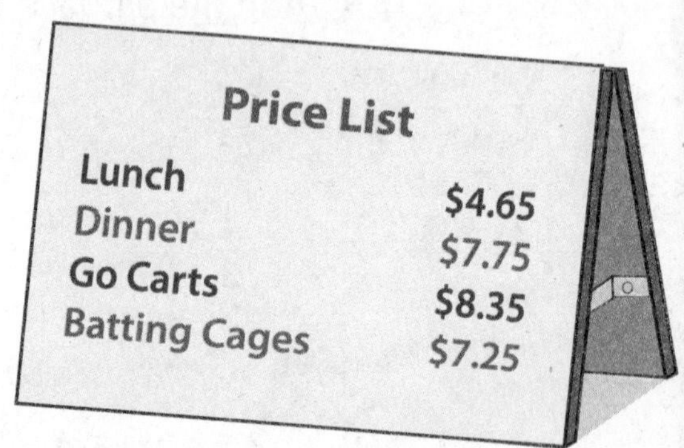

Price List
Lunch $4.65
Dinner $7.75
Go Carts $8.35
Batting Cages $7.25

20. Number Sense Jon, Jenny, and Hoyt are in charge of the party favors for the class party. Jon brings 17 party favors, Jenny brings 25 favors, and Hoyt brings 18. They want to put 6 party favors in each bag. How many bags can they fill?

21. Extend Your Thinking Use partial quotients to find $784 \div 7$. Explain the steps you took.

Name ______________________________

Solve & Share

Paulo has 39 patches from states that he and his relatives have visited. He wants to pin them onto a board and arrange them equally in 3 rows. How many patches will be in each row? ***Solve this problem any way you choose.***

Lesson 8-2
Division as Sharing

TEKS 4.4F Use strategies and algorithms, including the standard algorithm, to divide up to a four-digit dividend by a one-digit divisor. **Mathematical Process Standards** 4.1A, 4.1C, 4.1D, 4.1G

Digital Resources at SavvasTexas.com

Solve

Learn

Glossary

Check

Tools
Games

You can **use reasoning.** Think about using place value to help you divide. ***Show your work in the space above!***

Look Back!

Connect When might you need to divide into equal groups in everyday life?

How Can Place Value Help You Divide?

A

Mrs. Lynch displayed 57 student drawings on 3 walls in her classroom. If she divided the drawings equally, how many drawings are on each wall?

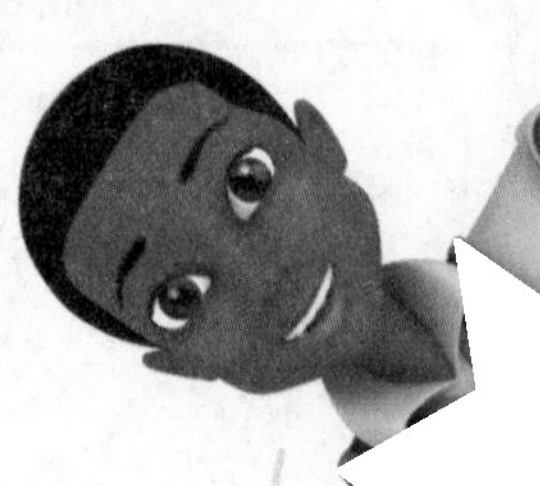

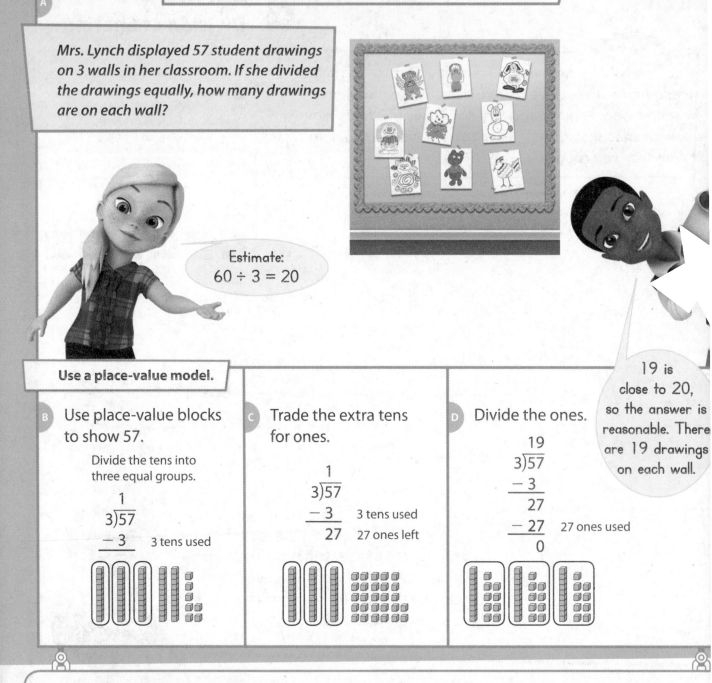

Estimate:
$60 \div 3 = 20$

19 is close to 20, so the answer is reasonable. There are 19 drawings on each wall.

Use a place-value model.

B Use place-value blocks to show 57.

Divide the tens into three equal groups.

$$\begin{array}{r} 1 \\ 3\overline{)57} \\ -3 \\ \hline \end{array}$$

3 tens used

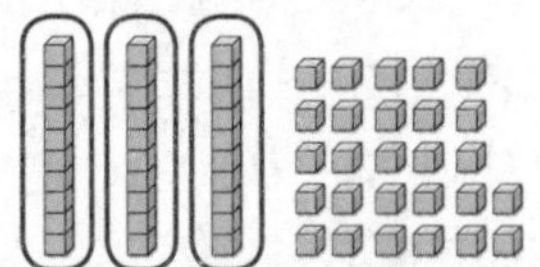

C Trade the extra tens for ones.

$$\begin{array}{r} 1 \\ 3\overline{)57} \\ -3 \\ \hline 27 \end{array}$$

3 tens used
27 ones left

D Divide the ones.

$$\begin{array}{r} 19 \\ 3\overline{)57} \\ -3 \\ \hline 27 \\ -27 \\ \hline 0 \end{array}$$

27 ones used

Do You Understand?

Convince Me! Tell how you would evenly divide the money shown among 4 people only using \$10 bills or \$1 bills.

Name ______________________

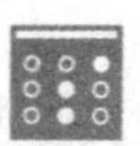

Another Example

Find 55 ÷ 4.

- Divide the tens.
- Regroup 1 ten as 10 ones and then divide the ones.
- There are 3 left over.

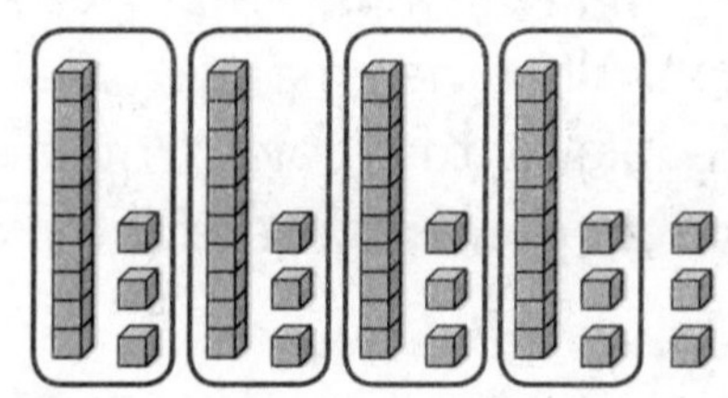

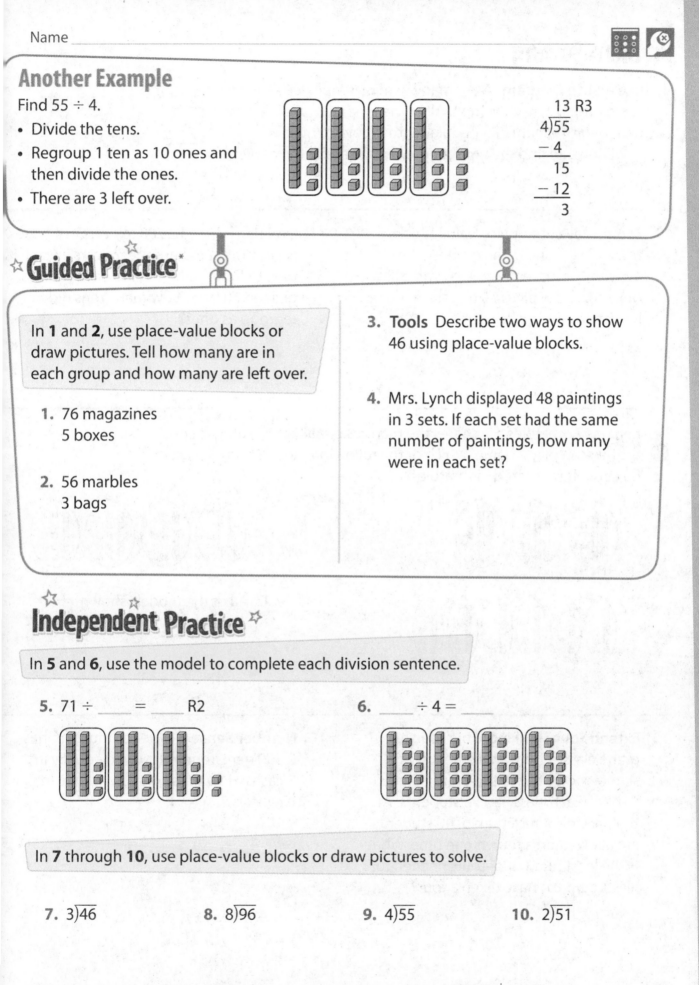

$$\begin{array}{r} 13 \text{ R3} \\ 4\overline{)55} \\ -4 \\ \hline 15 \\ -12 \\ \hline 3 \end{array}$$

Guided Practice*

In **1** and **2**, use place-value blocks or draw pictures. Tell how many are in each group and how many are left over.

1. 76 magazines
   5 boxes

2. 56 marbles
   3 bags

3. **Tools** Describe two ways to show 46 using place-value blocks.

4. Mrs. Lynch displayed 48 paintings in 3 sets. If each set had the same number of paintings, how many were in each set?

Independent Practice

In **5** and **6**, use the model to complete each division sentence.

5. 71 ÷ ____ = ____ R2

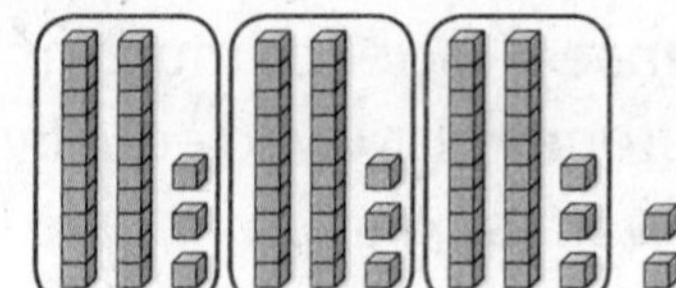

6. ____ ÷ 4 = ____

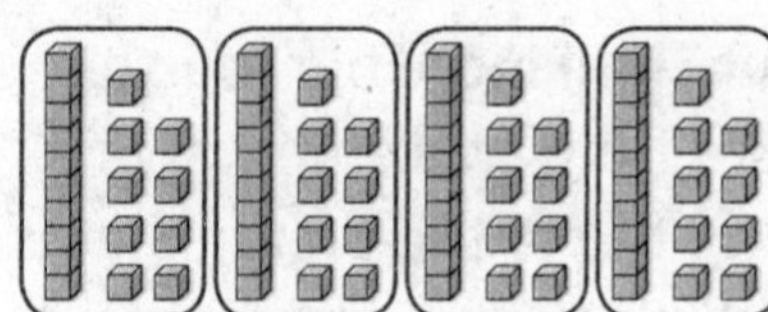

In **7** through **10**, use place-value blocks or draw pictures to solve.

7. $3\overline{)46}$

8. $8\overline{)96}$

9. $4\overline{)55}$

10. $2\overline{)51}$

*For another example, see Set B on page 457.

Problem Solving

11. Use a Strip Diagram A company with 65 employees is moving to a new location. All of the employes are assigned to a team of 5 people for the move. Write an equation and find the number of teams used for the move.

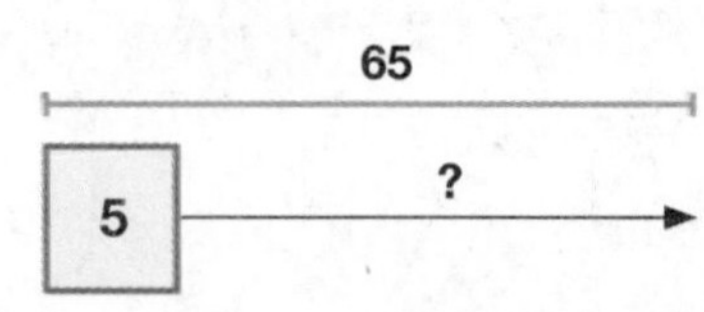

12. Tools Maya used place-value blocks to divide 86. She made groups of 17 with 1 left over. Use place-value blocks or draw pictures to determine how many groups Maya made.

13. Explain Harold has 68 toy cars in 4 boxes. He has the same number of cars in each box. To find the number in each box, he divided 68 by 4. How many tens did he regroup as ones?

14. Ken has 72 marbles. He shares the marbles equally with some friends so they can play a game. Which of the following models shows a way he could have shared his marbles?

A

B

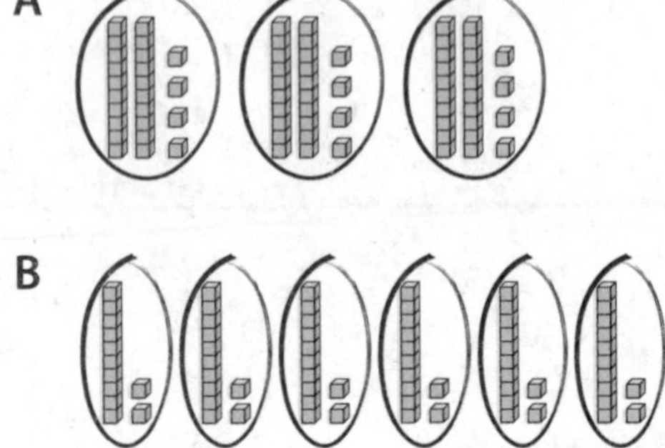

C

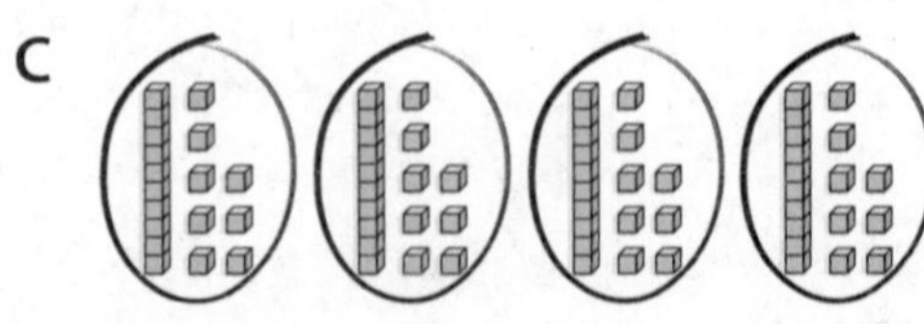

D All of the models shown

15. Extend Your Thinking Four fourth-grade classes from an elementary school took a trip to the United States Capitol. Each class had 25 students. At the Capitol, a maximum of 40 students are allowed on a tour at one time. What is the least number of tours needed for all students to have taken a tour?

16. Number Sense A science museum has 2,400 gemstones displayed equally in 3 cases. How many gemstones are in each case?

Name ______________________

Homework 8-2
Division as Sharing

Another Look!

You can use models to help you solve division problems.
The models below can help you find $78 \div 5$.
Estimate: $80 \div 5 = 16$.

What operations would you use to check your answer?

First, divide the tens.

$$\begin{array}{r} 1 \\ 5\overline{)78} \\ -\;5 \\ \hline \end{array} \quad \text{5 tens}$$

Then, change the tens into the ones.

$$\begin{array}{rl} 1 & \\ 5\overline{)78} & \\ -\;5 & \text{5 tens} \\ \hline 28 & \text{28 ones} \end{array}$$

Lastly, divide the ones.

$$\begin{array}{rl} 15 & \\ 5\overline{)78} & \\ -\;5 & \text{5 tens} \\ \hline 28 & \text{28 ones} \\ -\;25 & \\ \hline 3 & \text{remainder} \end{array}$$

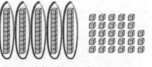

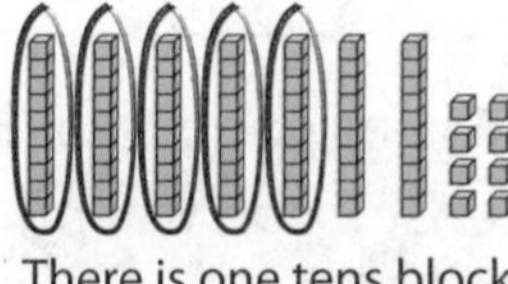
There is one tens block in each of the 5 groups.

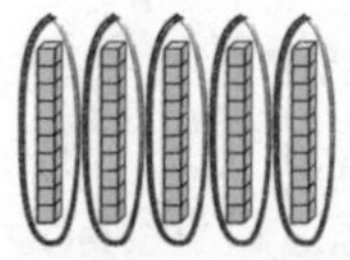
2 tens blocks and 8 ones blocks are equal to 28 ones blocks.

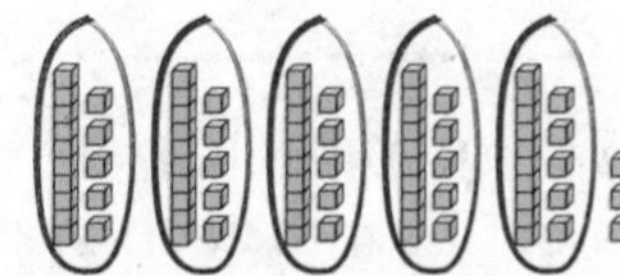
Each of the 5 groups has 1 tens block and 5 ones blocks. There are 3 ones remaining.

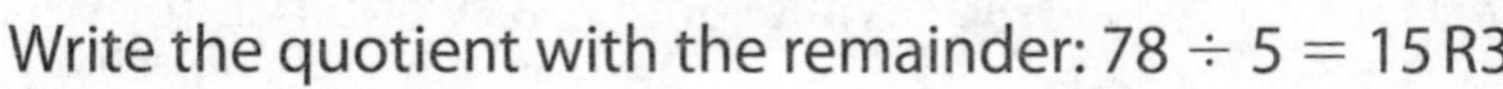
Write the quotient with the remainder: $78 \div 5 = 15\text{R}3$

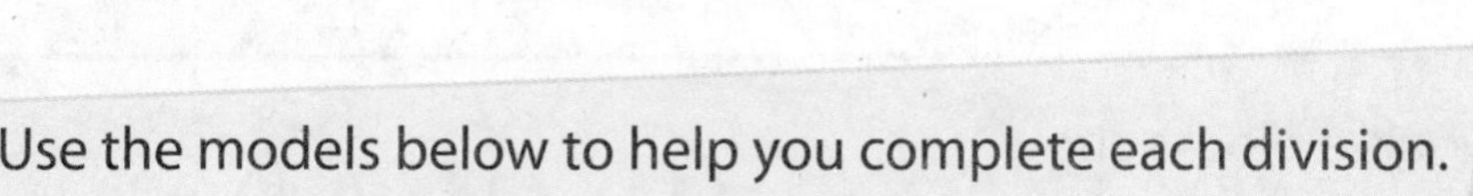
Use the models below to help you complete each division.

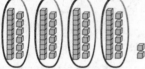

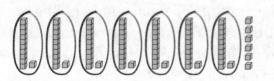

1. $66 \div$ ____ $=$ ____ R2

2. $97 \div 4 =$ ____ R ____

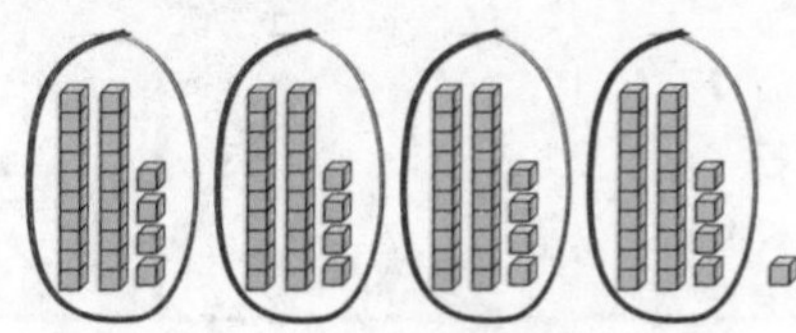

3. ____ $\div 7 =$ ____ R6

4. $76 \div$ ____ $=$ ____ R ____

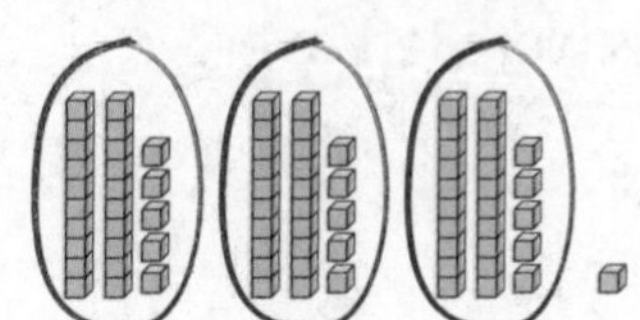

5. **Draw a Picture** Marcos has 78 colored pencils. He arranges the colored pencils into 6 equal groups. How many colored pencils are in each group? Complete the diagram started below to show your work.

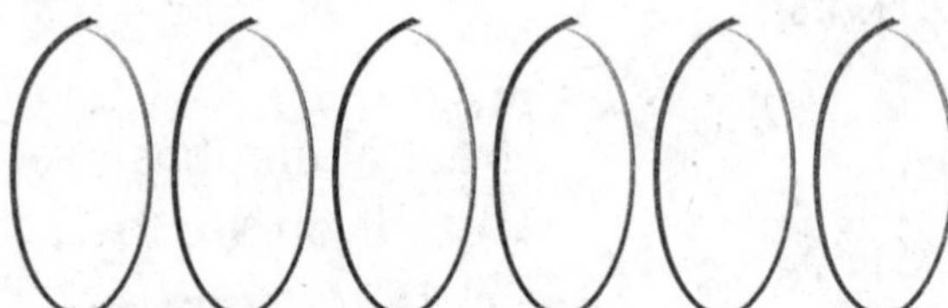

Pictures are tools that can help you solve problems.

6. Anya is putting her 70 baseball cards into piles having 5 cards in each pile. How many piles can Anya make?

   A 5 piles
   B 14 piles
   C 19 piles
   D 21 piles

7. Ben has 62 pictures from vacation. He is putting 6 pictures on each page of an album. How many pages will Ben fill? How many pages will he use?

8. Carlton has 57 CDs. He wants to put an equal number of CDs into each of 8 organizers. How many CDs will be in each organizer? Will there be any CDs left over?

9. **Connect** There are 37 chairs and 9 tables in a classroom. Mrs. Kensington will put an equal number of chairs at each table. How many chairs will she put at each table? Will there be any chairs left over?

10. **Explain** Adrian used the place-value blocks shown to solve a division sentence. What is the division sentence? Explain how you know.

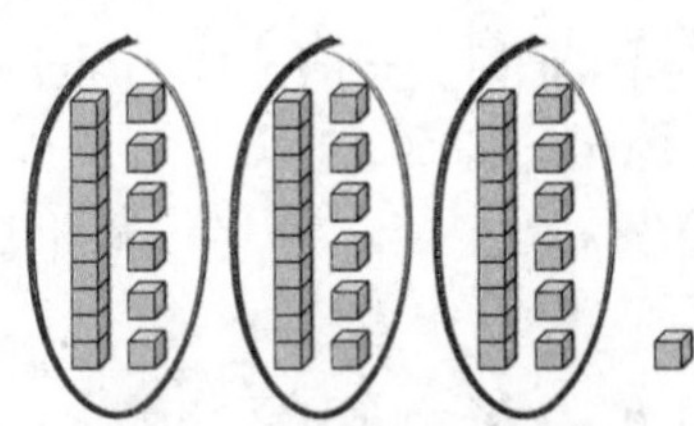

11. **Number Sense** Nancy planted 44 plants in rows. If there are 7 plants in each row, how many plants were left over?

12. **Extend Your Thinking** Mrs. Dryson is dividing her collection of 52 glass bears into groups of equal numbers. She has 1 bear left over. How many groups did Mrs. Dryson make? How many bears are in each group?

Name ______________________________

Solve & Share

Swati is packing T-shirts and shorts into boxes to put away for the winter. There are 42 items to pack. She packs the same number of items into 3 boxes. How many items does Swati pack in each box? ***Solve this problem any way you choose.***

You can **connect ideas.** Recall how your knowledge of place value can help you divide. ***Show your work in the space below!***

Lesson 8-3
Dividing 2-Digit by 1-Digit Numbers

TEKS 4.4F Use strategies and algorithms, including the standard algorithm, to divide up to a four-digit dividend by a one-digit divisor. Also, 4.4E, 4.4H.
Mathematical Process Standards 4.1A, 4.1B, 4.1C, 4.1D, 4.1F, 4.1G

Digital Resources at SavvasTexas.com

Solve

Learn

Glossary

Check

Tools

Games

Construct Arguments Your classmate solved the same problem and said that each box would have 10 items and that there would be 2 items left over. Do you agree or disagree? If you disagree, what did your classmate do wrong?

What Is a Common Way to Record Division?

A

At the school food drive, Al needs to put the same number of soup cans into four boxes.

How many soup cans will go in each box?

The standard division algorithm breaks the calculation into simpler calculations.

Write an equation:
$76 \div 4 = ?$

Use the standard division algorithm.

B

Step 1

Divide the tens.

$$\begin{array}{r} 1 \\ 4\overline{)76} \\ -4 \\ \hline 3 \end{array}$$

There is **1** ten in each group and **3** tens left over.

C

Step 2

Divide the ones.

$$\begin{array}{r} 19 \\ 4\overline{)76} \\ -4 \\ \hline 36 \\ -36 \\ \hline 0 \end{array}$$

Trade the 3 tens for 30 ones. 30 ones and 6 ones make **36** ones.

There will be 19 soup cans in each box.

D

Step 3

Check by multiplying.

$$\begin{array}{r} \overset{3}{1}9 \\ \times\ 4 \\ \hline 76 \end{array}$$

The answer checks.

Do You Understand?

Convince Me! Tell what error was made in the work at the right. Show the correct solution.

$$\begin{array}{r} 27 \text{ R4} \\ 3\overline{)85} \\ -6 \\ \hline 25 \\ -21 \\ \hline 4 \end{array}$$

Name ______________________________ 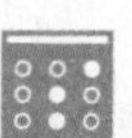 

Another Example

If 58 cans of peas are to be put equally into 4 boxes, how many cans will be put in each box?

- Divide to find equal groups.
- There are 2 left over.

```
   14 R2
 4)58
  - 4
   18
 - 16
    2
```

Remember to interpret the remainder!
14 cans will be put in each box.

Guided Practice*

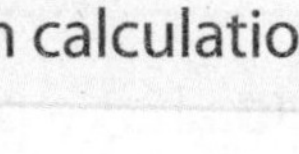

In **1** and **2**, complete each calculation.

```
1.    4 □          2.   □6 R□
   2)9 4             5)8 2
   - □               - 5
     □4                □□
   - 1□              - □□
      0                 □
```

3. **Explain** How would you estimate the answer in Exercise 1?

4. Al has 85 cans of fruit. He puts the same number of fruit cans in 4 boxes. Will he have any cans left over? If so, how many cans?

Independent Practice

Leveled Practice In **5** through **12**, find each quotient.

```
5.   □6        6.   1□ R□      7.   □□        8.   □□ R□
   3)7 8         6)8 0           7)8 4          4)9 3
   - □           - □             - 7            - 8
     □8            □□              □4             □□
   - 1□          - □□            - □□           - 1□
      0              □               0               1
```

9. 3)63

10. 7)88

11. 6)96

12. 4)52

*For another example, see Set C on page 457.

Problem Solving

13. **Reason** Some of the tallest selenite crystals in a cave in Chihuahua, Mexico, are 50 feet tall. Nathan is 4 feet tall. About how many times as tall as Nathan are the tallest crystals?

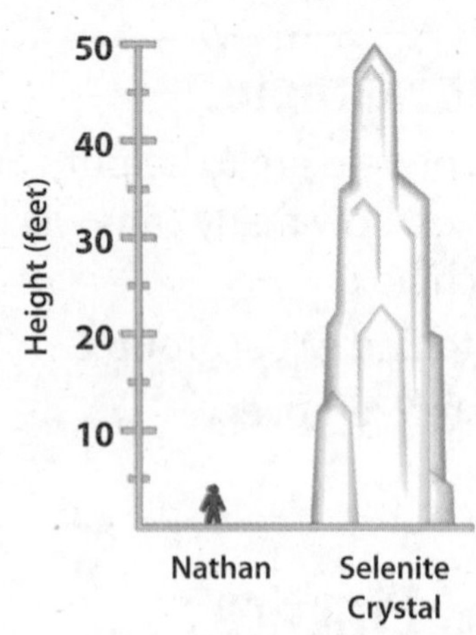

Use an inverse operation to check your answer.

14. **Explain** Why does 51 ÷ 4 have two digits in the quotient, while 51 ÷ 6 has only one digit in the quotient?

15. Zelda has a piece of fabric that is 74 inches long. She wants to divide it into 2 equal pieces. What is the length of each piece?

16. Wendy wants to share 37 pencils equally with 9 people. Explain how to find how many pencils will be left over.

17. **Analyze Information** An art supplies store has received a shipment of paints in 4 boxes. Each box contains 24 packages of paint. Each package contains 5 cans of paint. How many cans of paint did the store receive in all?

18. Every year, the city of San Marcos holds a Cinco de Mayo festival. If 60 students perform in 5 equal groups, how many students are in each group?

A 10 students
B 12 students
C 25 students
D 55 students

19. **Extend Your Thinking** Maggie is making trail mix. She makes 4 batches of the recipe shown. Then she divides it into 3 equal-sized bags. How many ounces are in each bag?

DATA

Tasty Trail Mix	
Granola	8 oz
Nuts	5 oz
Raisins	2 oz
Cranberries	3 oz

Name ______________________________

Homework 8-3
Dividing 2-Digit by 1-Digit Numbers

Another Look!

Find 55 ÷ 3.
Estimate: 60 ÷ 3 = 20.

```
  18 R1
3)55
 - 3
   25
 - 24
    1
```

Check: 18 × 3 = 54.
54 + 1 = 55
The answer checks.

You can divide 2-digit numbers by dividing the tens, and then the ones.

Find each quotient.

1.
```
   2☐
3)8 1
 - ☐
   ☐1
 - ☐☐
    0
```

2.
```
   1☐
4)7 6
 - ☐
   ☐☐
 - ☐☐
    0
```

3.
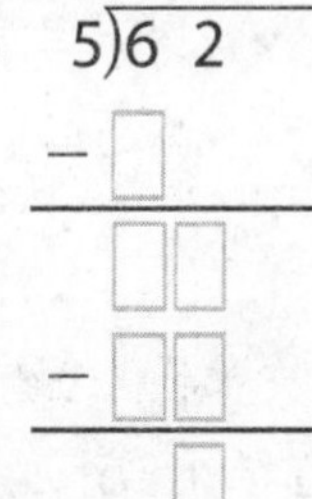
```
  ☐☐ R☐
5)6 2
 - ☐
   ☐☐
 - ☐☐
    ☐
```

4.
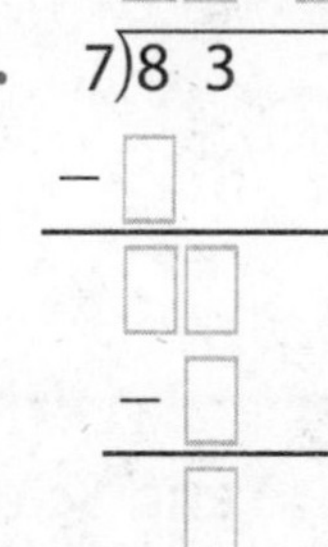
```
  ☐☐ R☐
7)8 3
 - ☐
   ☐☐
 - ☐
    ☐
```

5. 3)91 **6.** 4)86 **7.** 7)94 **8.** 3)39

9. 5)93 **10.** 3)83 **11.** 4)72 **12.** 6)77

13. **Mental Math** Antonio bought 3 soft pretzels and 3 bottles of water. He paid with a twenty-dollar bill. How much change did he receive?

14. Paulo has 78 cattle on his ranch. He wants to divide them equally among 3 pastures. How many cattle will be in each pasture? Will there be any cattle left over?

15. **Connect** There are 84 players at a volleyball camp. Coach Wilson wants to divide the players into teams of 6 players each. How many teams will there be? Will there be any players left over?

16. **Extend Your Thinking** Mrs. Thomas is planning to provide snacks for 96 fourth graders when they go on a field trip to the aquarium. Each student will receive one of each snack. How many more packages of fruit cups does Mrs. Thomas need than packages of applesauce?

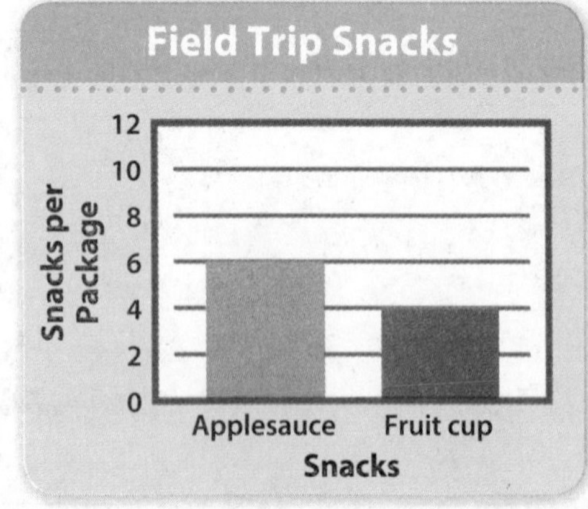

17. **Math and Science** Heat is a form of energy measured in calories. 1 calorie is the amount of energy required to raise the temperature of 1 gram of water by 1 degree Celsius. How many calories are required to raise the temperature of 78 grams of water by 14 degrees Celsius?

18. Celia has 83 beads. She makes bracelets using 6 beads for each bracelet. How many beads does Celia have left over?

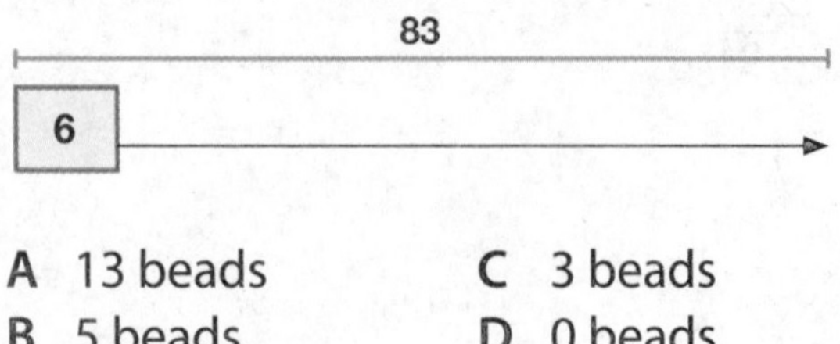

A 13 beads
B 5 beads
C 3 beads
D 0 beads

Name ______________________________

Lesson 8-4
Dividing 3-Digit by 1-Digit Numbers

Solve & Share The local elementary school has 560 students. All 5 grades have the same number of students. How many students are in each grade? ***Solve this problem any way you choose.***

TEKS 4.4F Use strategies and algorithms, including the standard algorithm, to divide up to a four-digit dividend by a one-digit divisor. Also, 4.4E, 4.4H.
Mathematical Process Standards 4.1C, 4.1D, 4.1F, 4.1G

Digital Resources at SavvasTexas.com

 Solve  Learn  Glossary Check  Tools  Games

You can **analyze relationships.** What number sentence could you solve to answer the question? ***Show your work in the space above!***

Look Back!

Communicate How is dividing a 3-digit number by a 1-digit number different from dividing a 2-digit number by a 1-digit number?

How Can You Divide Numbers in the Hundreds?

A factory shipped 378 watches in 3 boxes.

If the watches were equally divided, how many watches were there in each box?

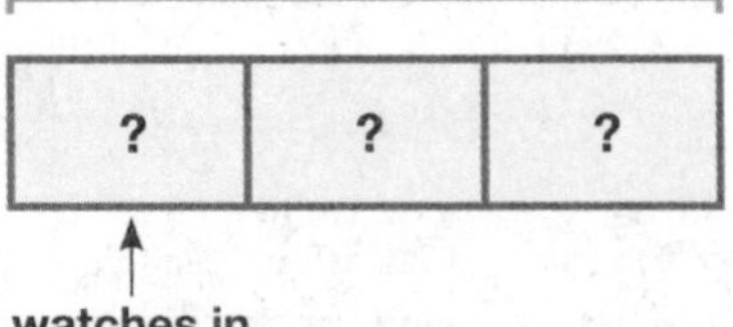

Write an equation:
$378 \div 3 = ?$

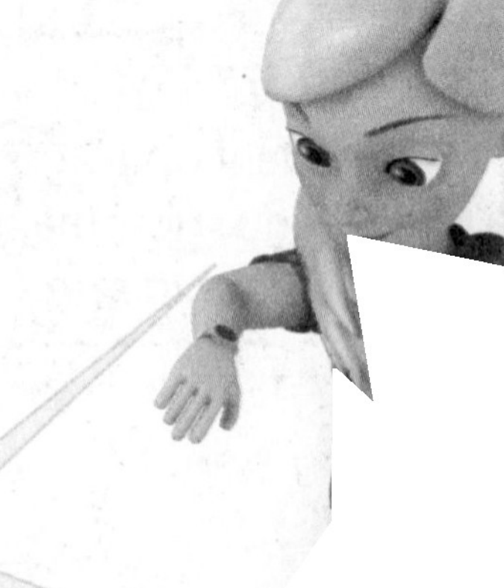

The standard division algorithm works the same way when dividing hundreds.

Use the standard division algorithm.

Step 1

Estimate:

$360 \div 3 = 120$

Divide the hundreds.

```
   1
3)378
 - 3
   7
```

Step 2

Divide the tens.

```
   12
3)378
 - 3
   7
 - 6
   1
```

Step 3

Divide the ones.

```
  126
3)378
 - 3
   7
 - 6
   18
 - 18
    0
```

There are 126 watches in each box.

The answer is reasonable because 126 is close to 120.

Do You Understand?

Convince Me! Carla recorded the problem above this way. Is Carla's work correct? Explain what she did.

```
  126
3)378
- 300
   78
 - 60
   18
 - 18
    0
```

Name

Guided Practice*

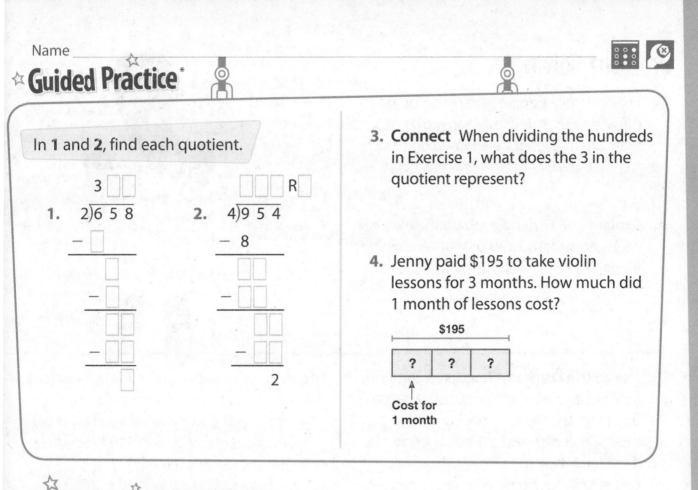

In **1** and **2**, find each quotient.

1. 2)658 — quotient: 3 ☐ ☐

2. 4)954 — quotient: ☐ ☐ ☐ R ☐; first subtraction: − 8; remainder: 2

3. **Connect** When dividing the hundreds in Exercise 1, what does the 3 in the quotient represent?

4. Jenny paid $195 to take violin lessons for 3 months. How much did 1 month of lessons cost?

$195

?	?	?

Cost for 1 month

Independent Practice

Leveled Practice In **5** through **12**, divide.

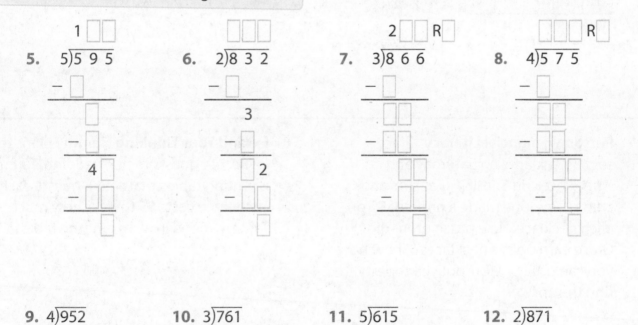

5. 5)595 — quotient: 1 ☐ ☐; partial dividend: 4 ☐

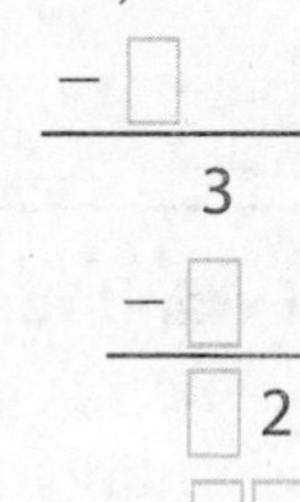

6. 2)832 — quotient: ☐ ☐ ☐; partial dividends: 3, ☐ 2

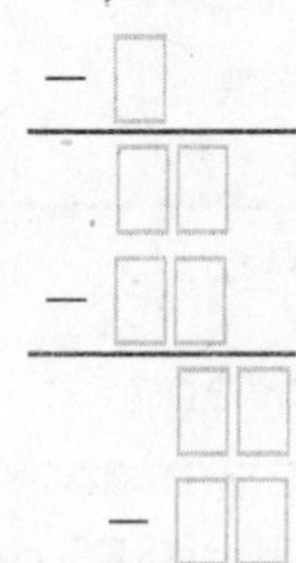

7. 3)866 — quotient: 2 ☐ ☐ R ☐

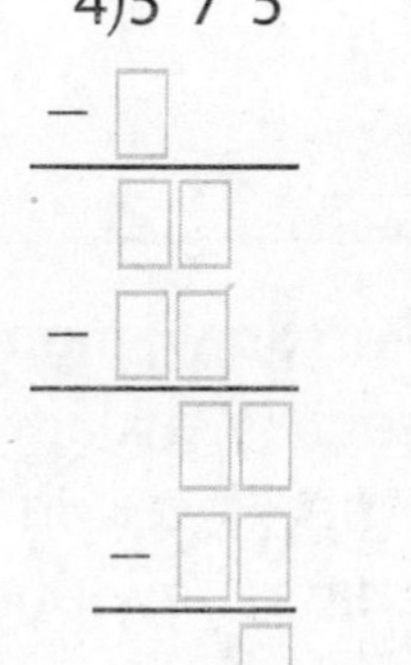

8. 4)575 — quotient: ☐ ☐ ☐ R ☐

9. 4)952

10. 3)761

11. 5)615

12. 2)871

*For another example, see Set C on page 457.

Problem Solving

13. There are 848 people getting on board the *Memphis Belle*. How many rows of seats are needed for every person to sit?

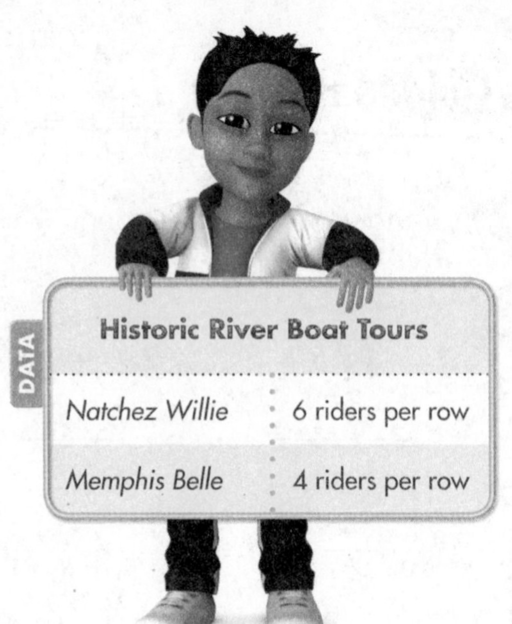

Historic River Boat Tours	
Natchez Willie	6 riders per row
Memphis Belle	4 riders per row

14. **Explain** If 793 people are on the *Natchez Willie*, how many rows of seats are needed for each person to sit? Explain.

15. **Use a Strip Diagram** The Galveston-Port Bolivar Ferry takes cars across Galveston Bay. One day, the ferry transported a total of 685 cars over a 5-hour period. If the ferry took the same number of cars each hour, how many cars did it take each hour?

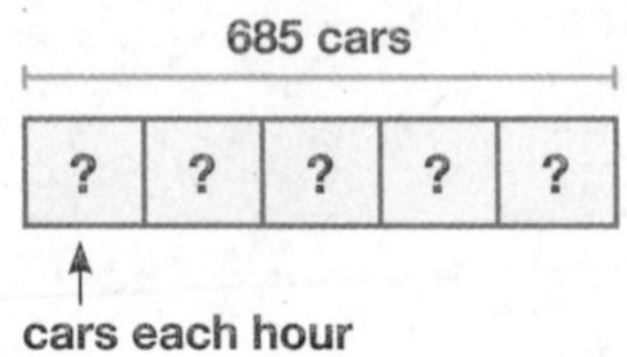

16. In one week, the Green Recycling Center received 784 aluminum cans. They received the same number of cans each day. How many cans did the recycling center receive each day?

A 112 cans
B 114 cans
C 121 cans
D 122 cans

17. **Personal Financial Literacy** Grace sold 8 necklaces on Saturday and 7 necklaces on Sunday at an arts and crafts show. She made a profit of $5 on each necklace. How much profit did Grace earn on the necklaces? Show how you can use the Distributive Property to find the answer.

18. **Extend Your Thinking** Tammy plans to invite 144 guests to her wedding. Tammy is renting tables that seat 8 guests each. If each table costs $5 to rent, how much will Tammy spend in all to rent the tables?

Name ______________________________

Homework 8-4
Dividing 3-Digit by 1-Digit Numbers

Another Look!

You can find 3-digit quotients by breaking apart the problem.

Why is it a good idea to estimate each quotient first?

Find 528 ÷ 4. Estimate 500 ÷ 4 = 125.	Find 575 ÷ 5. Estimate 600 ÷ 5 = 120.	Find 725 ÷ 3. Estimate 750 ÷ 3 = 250.
$\begin{array}{r} 132 \\ 4\overline{)528} \\ -\ 4 \\ \hline 12 \\ -\ 12 \\ \hline 8 \\ -\ 8 \\ \hline 0 \end{array}$	$\begin{array}{r} 115 \\ 5\overline{)575} \\ -\ 5 \\ \hline 7 \\ -\ 5 \\ \hline 25 \\ -\ 25 \\ \hline 0 \end{array}$	$\begin{array}{r} 241 \text{ R2} \\ 3\overline{)725} \\ -\ 6 \\ \hline 12 \\ -\ 12 \\ \hline 5 \\ -\ 3 \\ \hline 2 \end{array}$

In **1** through **8**, divide.

1. $\begin{array}{r} 3\,1\,5 \text{ R}\square \\ 2\overline{)6\,3\,1} \\ -\ \square \\ \hline \square \\ -\ 2 \\ \hline 1\,1 \\ -\ \square 0 \\ \hline \square \end{array}$

2. $\begin{array}{r} \square\square\square \text{ R2} \\ 6\overline{)7\,8\,8} \\ -\ 6 \\ \hline 1\square \\ -\ 1\square \\ \hline \square \\ -\ 6 \\ \hline \square \end{array}$

3. $7\overline{)903}$

4. $4\overline{)890}$

5. $3\overline{)462}$

6. $5\overline{)640}$

7. $8\overline{)889}$

8. $3\overline{)944}$

9. Estimation A toy store receives a shipment of 17 cases of teddy bears. Use compatible numbers to estimate the total number of teddy bears in the shipment.

10. An ant has 6 legs. There are 870 legs in José's ant farm. How many ants are there in his ant farm?

A 14 R5 ants
B 145 ants
C 864 ants
D 5,220 ants

11. Zeeshan has collected 852 autographs. Each autograph is either from a baseball star, a football star, a movie star, or a rock star. He has an equal number of autographs in each group. How many autographs does he have in each group?

12. Harvey has 514 stamps. He places an equal number of stamps in 3 stamp books. How many stamps are in each book? Are there any stamps left over?

13. Explain There are 785 people seated in a large cafeteria. Six people can sit at each table. How many tables are in the cafeteria?

14. Use a Strip Diagram There are 750 eggs in a display at a grocery store. If each carton contains 6 eggs, how many cartons are there in the display?

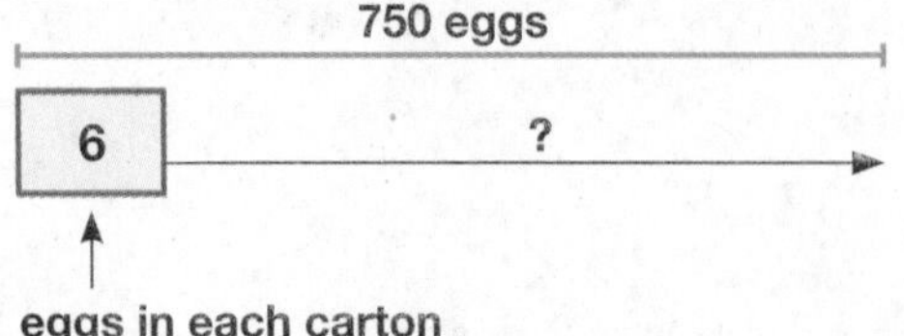

15. Extend Your Thinking You can use the standard division algorithm to divide 2-digit and 3-digit numbers by 1-digit numbers. Explain how you could use the algorithm to divide a 4-digit number by a 1-digit number. What is $4{,}561 \div 3$?

Name ______________________________

Solve & Share

Roberto is using craft sticks to make picture frames. He has 152 craft sticks and he uses 6 sticks for each frame. How many frames can he make? ***Solve this problem any way you choose.***

Lesson 8-5

Deciding Where to Start Dividing

TEKS 4.4F Use strategies and algorithms, including the standard algorithm, to divide up to a four-digit dividend by a one-digit divisor. Also, 4.4H. **Mathematical Process Standards** 4.1A, 4.1D, 4.1F, 4.1G

Digital Resources at SavvasTexas.com

Solve

Learn

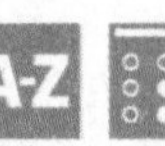
Glossary
Check

Tools

Games

You can **analyze relationships.** What can you do if there are not enough hundreds to divide evenly? ***Show your work in the space below!***

Look Back!

Justify How could you check that your answer is correct?

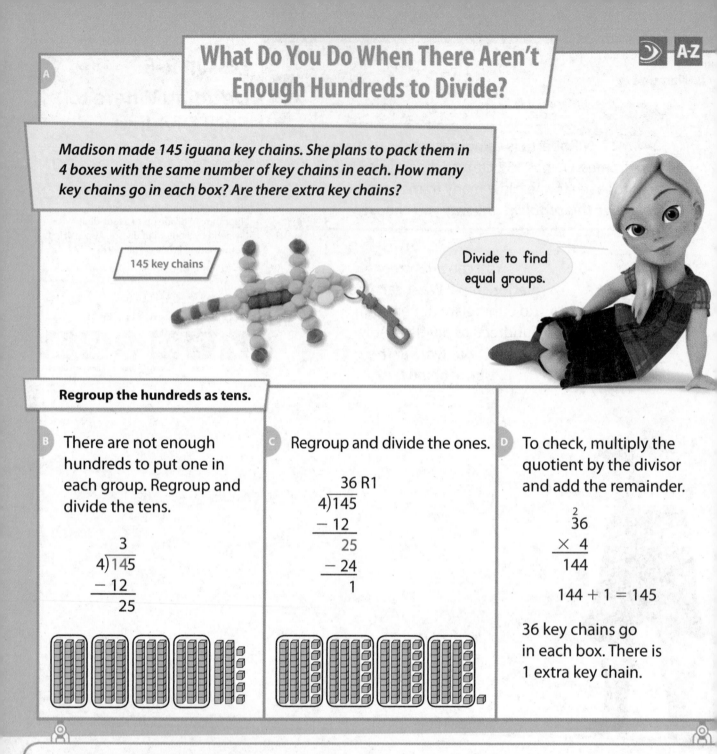

What Do You Do When There Aren't Enough Hundreds to Divide?

A

Madison made 145 iguana key chains. She plans to pack them in 4 boxes with the same number of key chains in each. How many key chains go in each box? Are there extra key chains?

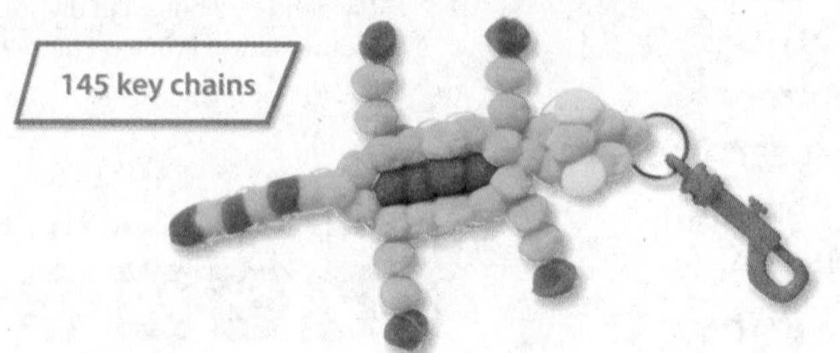
145 key chains

Divide to find equal groups.

Regroup the hundreds as tens.

B There are not enough hundreds to put one in each group. Regroup and divide the tens.

$$\begin{array}{r} 3 \\ 4\overline{)145} \\ -\,12 \\ \hline 25 \end{array}$$

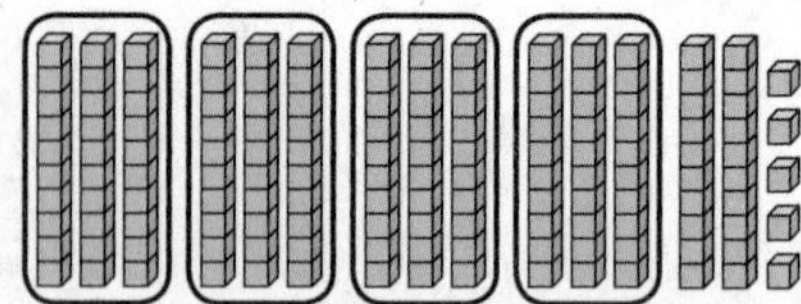

C Regroup and divide the ones.

$$\begin{array}{r} 36 \text{ R}1 \\ 4\overline{)145}\phantom{\text{ R}1} \\ -\,12\phantom{\text{ R}1} \\ \hline 25\phantom{\text{ R}1} \\ -\,24\phantom{\text{ R}1} \\ \hline 1\phantom{\text{ R}1} \end{array}$$

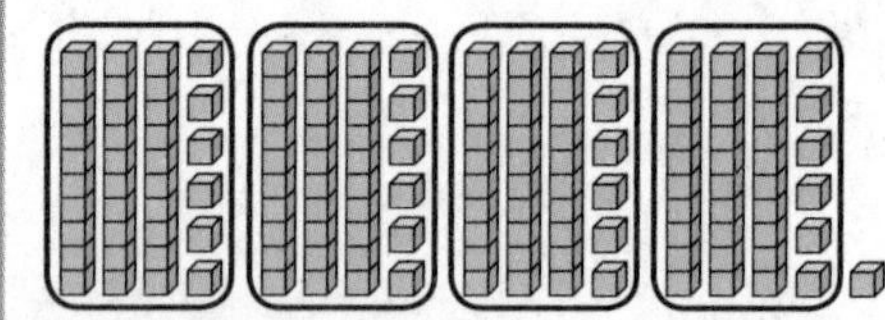

D To check, multiply the quotient by the divisor and add the remainder.

$$\begin{array}{r} \overset{2}{3}6 \\ \times\;\;4 \\ \hline 144 \end{array}$$

$144 + 1 = 145$

36 key chains go in each box. There is 1 extra key chain.

Do You Understand?

Convince Me! Explain how an estimated quotient can help you decide where to start dividing 424 ÷ 6.

$6\overline{)424}$

Name ______________________________

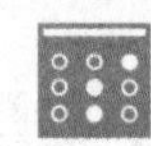

Guided Practice*

In **1** and **2**, complete each calculation.

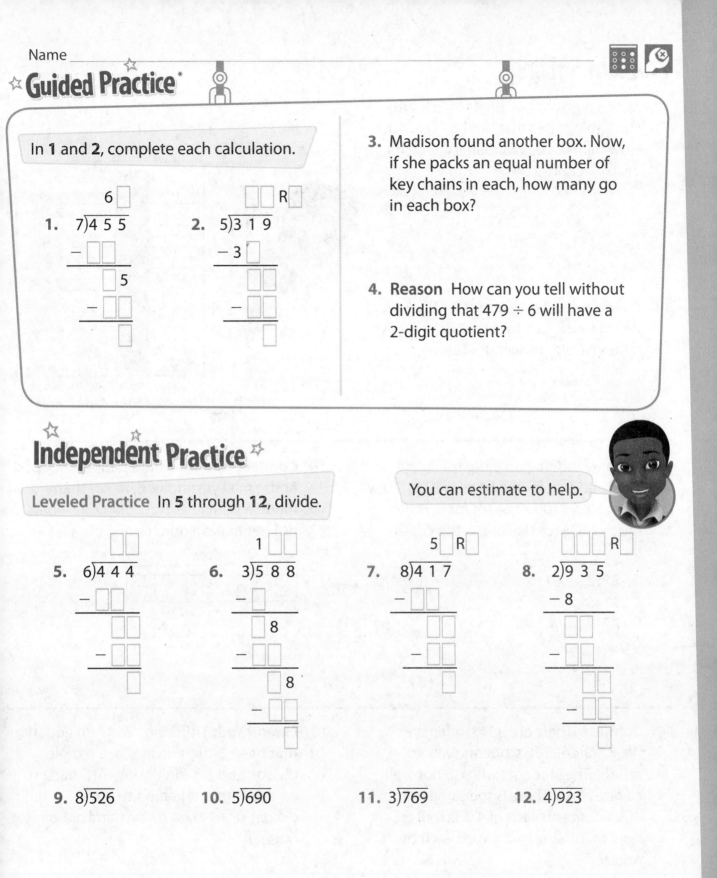

1. 7)455

6☐
−☐☐
☐5
−☐☐
☐

2. 5)319

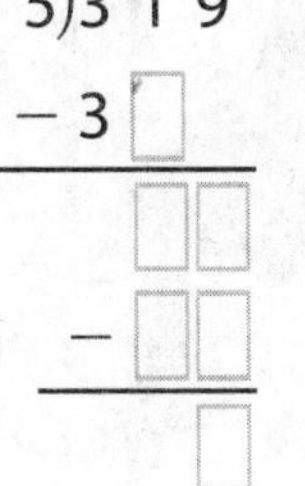

☐☐ R☐
−3☐
☐☐
−☐☐
☐

3. Madison found another box. Now, if she packs an equal number of key chains in each, how many go in each box?

4. Reason How can you tell without dividing that 479 ÷ 6 will have a 2-digit quotient?

Independent Practice

Leveled Practice In **5** through **12**, divide.

You can estimate to help.

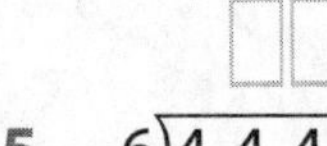

5. 6)444

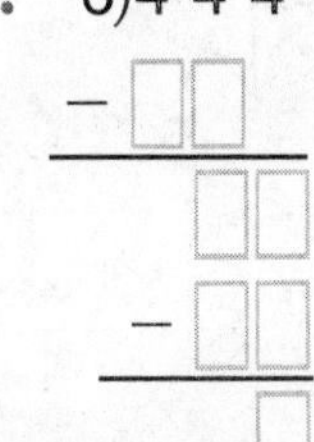

☐☐
−☐☐
☐☐
−☐☐
☐

6. 3)588

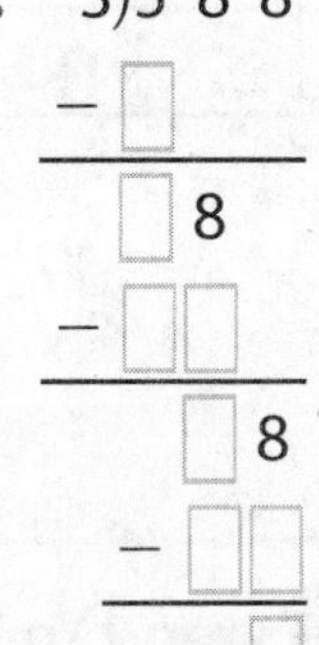

1☐☐
−☐
☐8
−☐☐
☐8
−☐☐
☐

7. 8)417

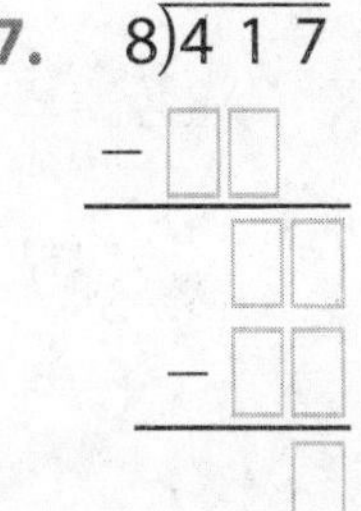

5☐ R☐
−☐☐
☐☐
−☐☐
☐

8. 2)935

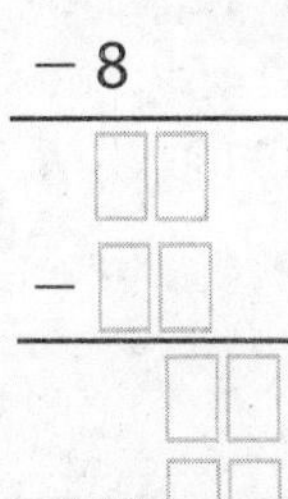

☐☐☐ R☐
−8
☐☐
−☐☐
☐☐
−☐☐
☐

9. 8)526

10. 5)690

11. 3)769

12. 4)923

*For another example, see Set D on page 458.

Problem Solving

13. James plans to put all of his CDs into stackable cubes that hold 8 CDs each. How many cubes will James need for his collection?

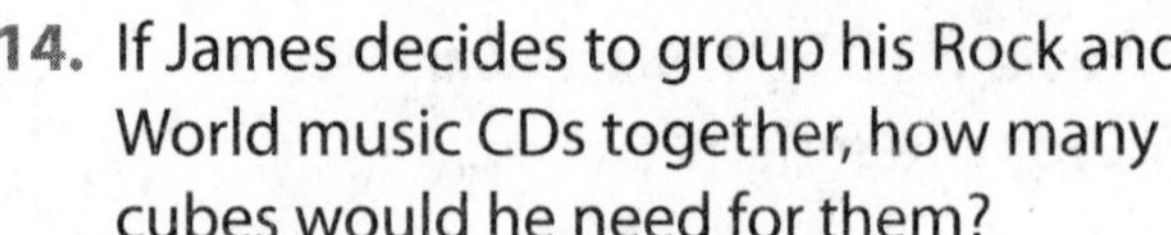

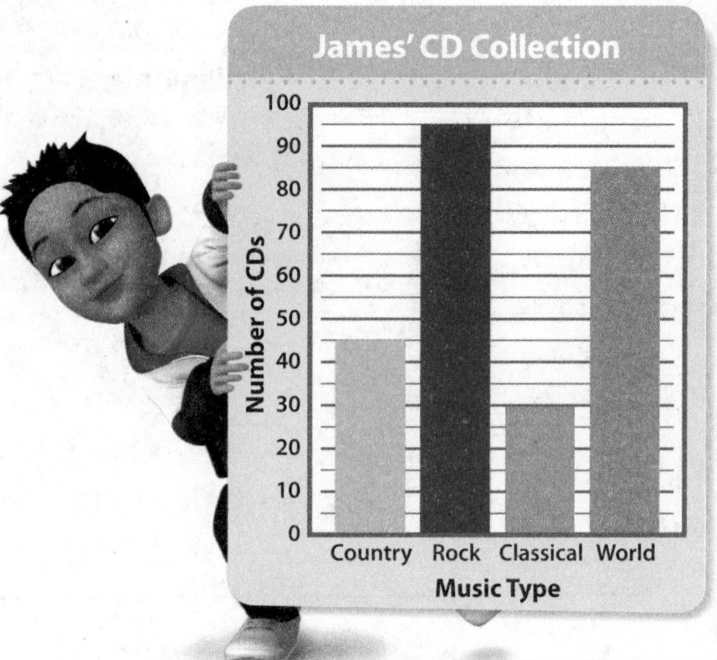

14. If James decides to group his Rock and World music CDs together, how many cubes would he need for them?

15. A family is going on a trip for 3 days. The total cost for the hotel is $336. They budgeted $100 a day for food. How much will each day of the trip cost?

A $33
B $112
C $145
D $212

16. **Connect** Ten thousand people shopped at the mall yesterday. 6,405 of them made a purchase. How many shoppers did not make a purchase?

10,000	
6,405	?

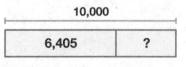

17. **Connect** There are 324 students at West School. 176 students walk to school. The students who do not walk all ride a bus. There is the same number of students on each of 4 bus routes. How many students are on each bus route?

18. **Extend Your Thinking** Write an equation that has a 3-digit dividend, a 1-digit divisor, and a 3-digit quotient. Then, write another equation that has a 3-digit dividend, a 1-digit divisor, and a 2-digit quotient.

Name ____________________

Homework 8-5

Deciding Where to Start Dividing

Another Look!

Find 325 ÷ 5.

There are only 3 hundreds.	Divide the tens.	Now divide the ones.
5)325	6 over 5)325; − 30 (30 tens); 2	65 over 5)325; − 30 (30 tens); 25; − 25 (2 tens and 5 ones, no remainder); 0
	With 32 tens, 6 tens can go into each one of the 5 groups.	Each stack has 65 baseball cards.

If you can't divide the hundreds, regroup them as tens.

Leveled Practice In **1** through **12**, divide.

1. 4)334 = 83 R☐; − ☐☐; ☐☐; − 12; ☐

2. 6)148 = ☐☐ R4; − ☐☐; ☐☐; − ☐4; ☐

3. 7)948 = ☐3☐ R3; − ☐; ☐☐; − ☐☐; ☐☐; − ☐☐; ☐

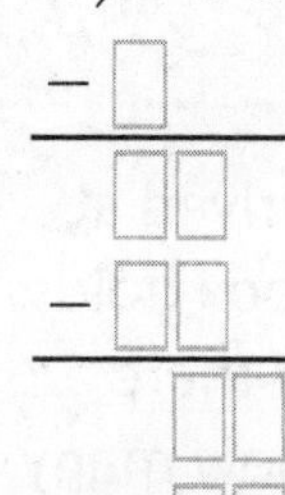

4. 4)179 = 4☐ R3; − ☐☐; ☐☐; − ☐☐; ☐

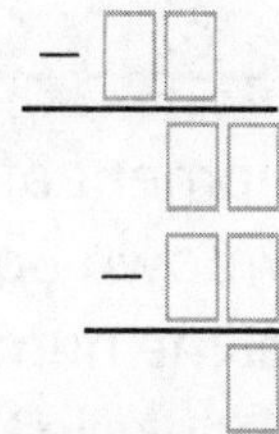

5. 5)125

6. 8)418

7. 2)587

8. 8)747

9. 3)573

10. 6)747

11. 5)750

12. 8)721

13. Communicate Randy performed the division shown at the right. Is Randy correct? What would you tell him?

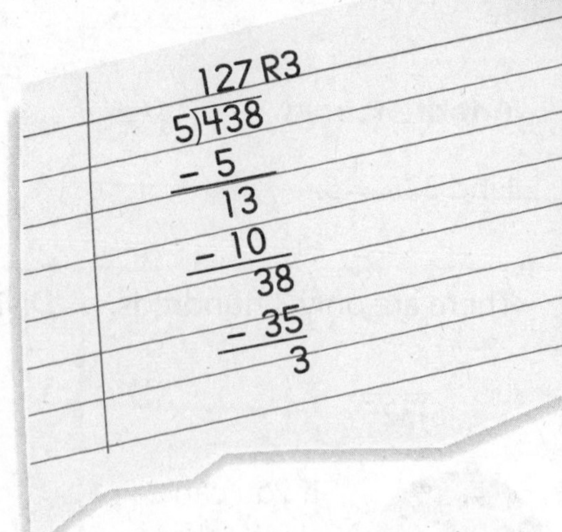

14. Find the correct quotient.

15. Reason Using hundreds, tens, and ones, what are three different ways the number 352 can be modeled other than the way shown below?

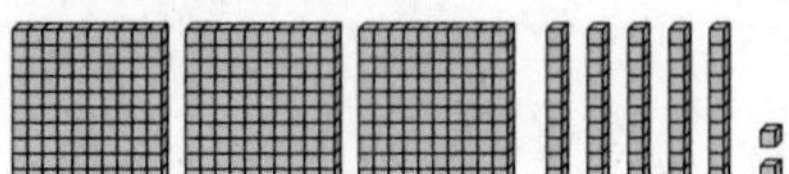

16. There are 144 fourth-graders at Central School. In each of the 6 classes, the number of girls is equal to the number of boys. How many girls are in each class?

A 9 girls
B 11 girls
C 12 girls
D 24 girls

17. A shipment of 8 boxes just arrived at Downtown Bookstore. Each box holds the same number of books. If there are 744 books in the shipment, how many books are in each box?

18. Extend Your Thinking Where would you start dividing to find the quotient of 3,825 ÷ 8? Explain how you know.

19. Construct Arguments Circle the problems that will have 3-digit quotients. Explain how you decided.

a. 2)621 **b.** 3)152 **c.** 4)912 **d.** 5)734 **e.** 6)452

Name ______________________________

Lesson 8-6
Zeros in the Quotient

TEKS 4.4F Use strategies and algorithms, including the standard algorithm, to divide up to a four-digit dividend by a one-digit divisor. Also, 4.4H. **Mathematical Process Standards** 4.1A, 4.1B, 4.1D, 4.1F, 4.1G

Digital Resources at SavvasTexas.com

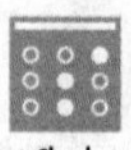

Solve Learn Glossary Check Tools Games

Solve & Share

Carlie has 327 flowers to plant in the park. She wants to plant the same number of flowers in each of 3 flowerbeds. How many flowers should she plant in each bed? ***Solve this problem any way you choose.***

You can **connect ideas.** Think back to regrouping you sometimes do when subtracting numbers. ***Show your work in the space below!***

Look Back!

Communicate When you write a number such as one hundred nine, why do you write a zero in it?

Do Zeros Matter?

A-Z

Liam has 326 nails that he wants to store in 3 containers. He wants to put the same number in each container. How many nails go in each container?

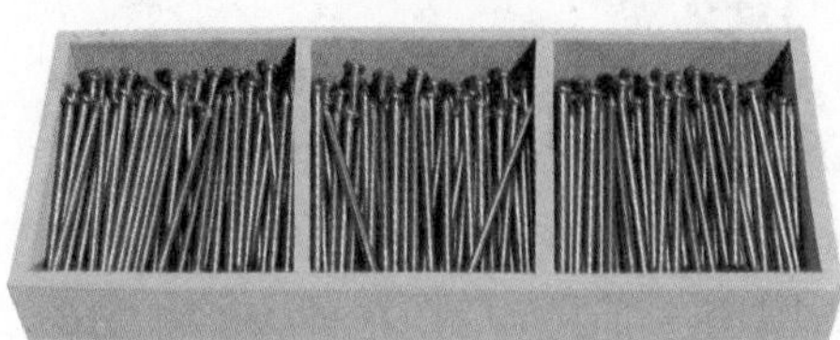

What will you do if there is a remainder?

Record "0" place values the same way you record other place values.

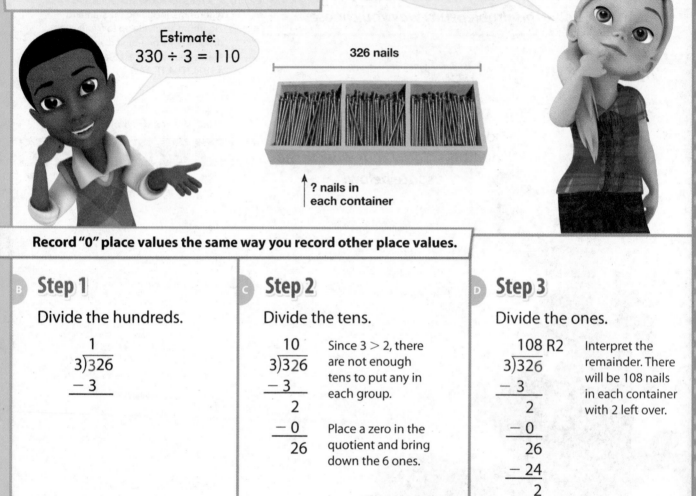

Step 1

Divide the hundreds.

```
   1
3)326
 - 3
```

Step 2

Divide the tens.

```
   10
3)326
 - 3
    2
  - 0
   26
```

Since 3 > 2, there are not enough tens to put any in each group.

Place a zero in the quotient and bring down the 6 ones.

Step 3

Divide the ones.

```
  108 R2
3)326
 - 3
    2
  - 0
   26
 - 24
    2
```

Interpret the remainder. There will be 108 nails in each container with 2 left over.

Do You Understand?

Convince Me! How can you check the answer in the problem above?

Name ______________________________

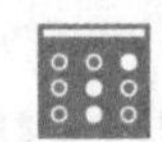

Guided Practice*

In **1** through **4**, divide.

1. $4\overline{)816}$

2. $2\overline{)608}$

3. $2\overline{)213}$

4. $3\overline{)619}$

5. How can you check the answer in Exercise 4?

6. Liam bought some patio bricks at a market and paid $212. If each patio brick cost $2, how many patio bricks did he buy?

Independent Practice

Leveled Practice In **7** through **20**, divide. Then, check your answer.

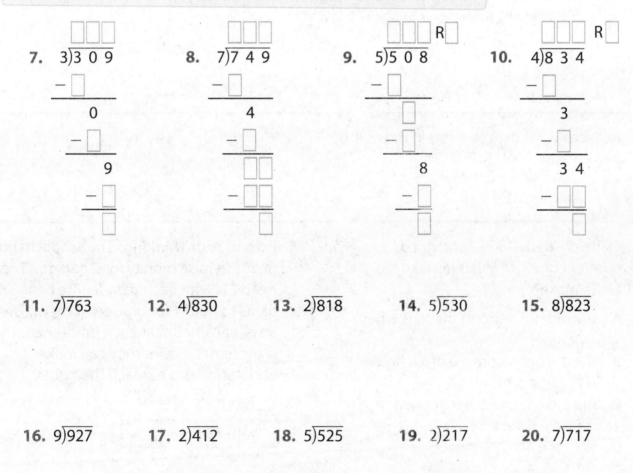

7. $3\overline{)3\ 0\ 9}$

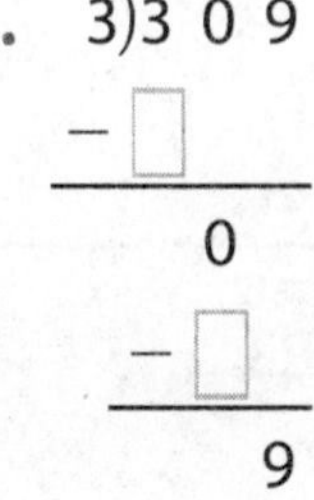

8. $7\overline{)7\ 4\ 9}$

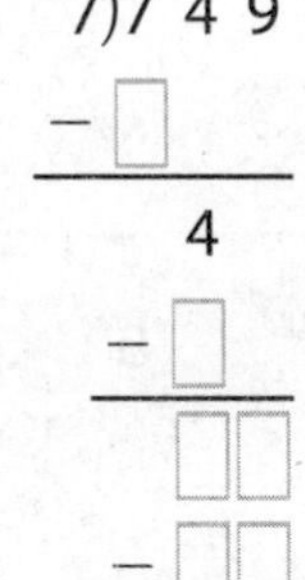

9. $5\overline{)5\ 0\ 8}$

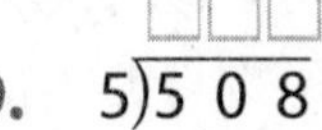

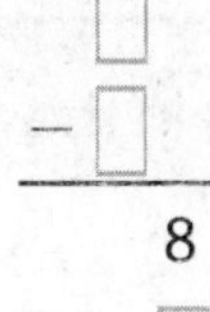

10. $4\overline{)8\ 3\ 4}$

11. $7\overline{)763}$ **12.** $4\overline{)830}$ **13.** $2\overline{)818}$ **14.** $5\overline{)530}$ **15.** $8\overline{)823}$

16. $9\overline{)927}$ **17.** $2\overline{)412}$ **18.** $5\overline{)525}$ **19.** $2\overline{)217}$ **20.** $7\overline{)717}$

*For another example, see Set E on page 458.

Problem Solving

In **21** through **23**, use the information at right.

21. Explain A zookeeper has 540 pounds of hay. Is this enough hay to feed one elephant for 5 days? Explain.

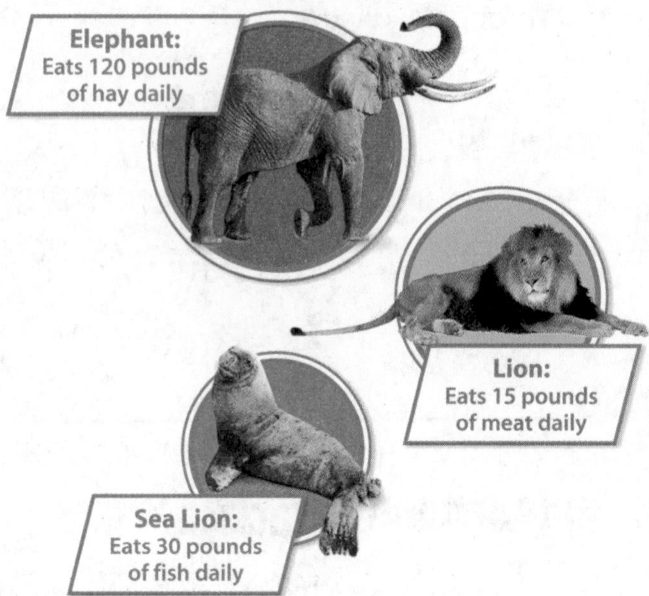
Elephant:
Eats 120 pounds of hay daily
Lion:
Eats 15 pounds of meat daily
Sea Lion:
Eats 30 pounds of fish daily

22. Justify Another zookeeper has 324 pounds of meat. Is this enough to feed 3 lions for a full week? Explain.

23. Communicate Is 654 pounds of fish enough to feed 5 sea lions for 6 days? Explain.

---

24. Reason What digit belongs in the number sentence at the right?

8☐7 ÷ 4 = 206 R3

---

25. Claire divided 415 ÷ 2 and got a quotient of 22 R1. What mistake did Claire make?

- **A** She did not regroup the tens when dividing.
- **B** She did not record a 0 place holder in the quotient.
- **C** She did not check her answer for reasonableness.
- **D** All of the above

26. Extend Your Thinking The school band needs to raise money for 3 parades. They need $276 for each parade. The band plans to hold 4 fundraisers. If they raise an equal amount at each fundraiser, what is the least amount they can make at each fundraiser to reach their goal?

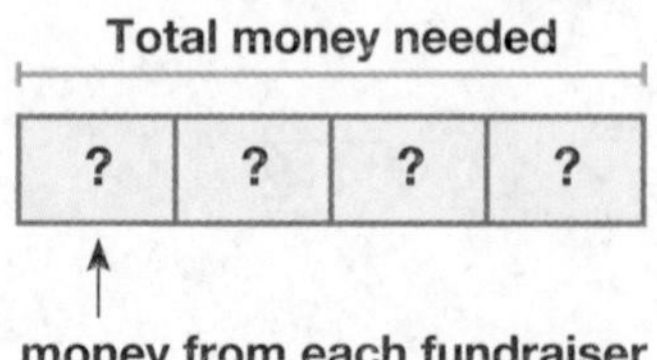
Total money needed
? ? ? ?
money from each fundraiser

Name ______________________________

Homework 8-6
Zeros in the Quotient

Another Look!

A worker at an apple orchard picked 956 apples. He filled 9 bushel baskets with the same number of apples. How many apples were in each bushel basket?

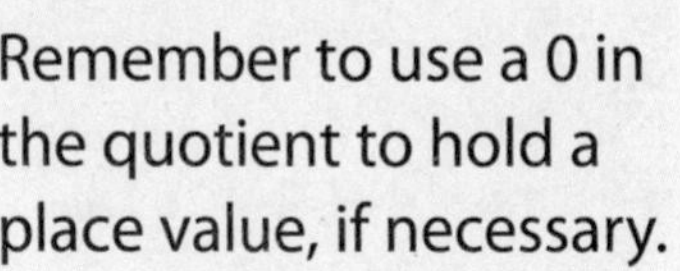

Remember to use a 0 in the quotient to hold a place value, if necessary.

Find 956 ÷ 9.
First estimate: 900 ÷ 9 = 100.

Step 1	Step 2	Step 3	Check
Divide the hundreds.	Bring down the tens. There are not enough tens, so place a zero in the quotient.	Bring down the ones and divide.	Multiply the quotient by the divisor and add the remainder.
$9\overline{)956}$, quotient 1 − 9 Multiply. 0 Compare. 0 < 9	$9\overline{)956}$, quotient 10 − 9 05 Multiply. − 0 Subtract. 5 Compare. 5 < 9	$9\overline{)956}$, quotient 106 R2 − 9 05 − 0 56 Multiply. − 54 Subtract. 2 Compare. 2 < 9	106 × 9 = 954 (regroup 5) 954 + 2 = 956 The answer checks.

In **1** through **8**, divide. Then, check your answer.

1. $7\overline{)742}$ **2.** $5\overline{)520}$ **3.** $2\overline{)813}$ **4.** $4\overline{)121}$

5. $3\overline{)326}$ **6.** $6\overline{)658}$ **7.** $3\overline{)922}$ **8.** $9\overline{)970}$

9. Check for Reasonableness A basketball team scored a total of 600 points in 5 games. The team scored the same number of points in each game. Ned divided to find out how many points the team scored in each game. He did not think his answer was reasonable. What was Ned's error?

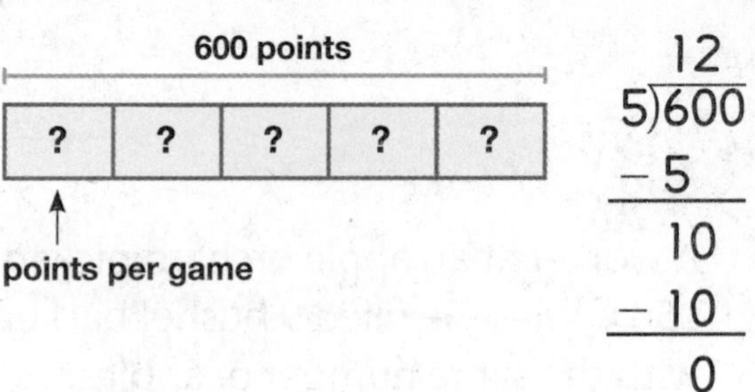

10. Connect How can 102 students best be divided equally into 5 classrooms?

11. The distance from Tom's house to the school is 545 yards. Tom's goal is to walk to school in 5 minutes. How many yards does he need to walk each minute to meet his goal?

12. Owen has had a dog walking business for the last 3 years. He has taken 927 walks during that time. If he took the same number of walks each year, how many walks did Owen take each year?

A 300 walks
B 309 walks
C 330 walks
D 390 walks

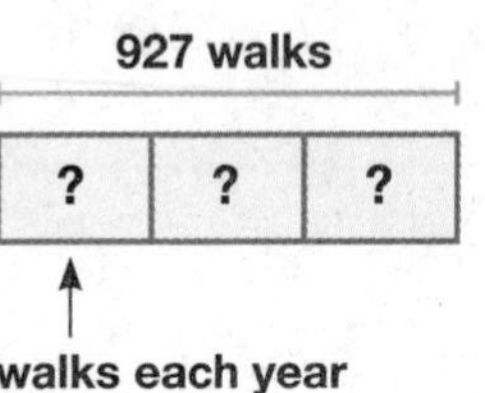

13. Personal Financial Literacy Yani spent $19 on a bike at a yard sale. He also spent $8 on books. Tell how to use mental math to find how much he spent in all.

14. Extend Your Thinking Gabrielle needs $336 to register for a week of summer horse camp. She earns $8 per hour working at the local pool. She has worked 30 hours so far this summer. If she has saved all of her earnings, does she have enough to register for horse camp? If not, how many more hours does Gabrielle need to work?

Have you answered all of the questions asked?

Name ______________________

Solve & Share

A high school football stadium has 6 sections that each seat the same number of people. A total of 1,950 people can be seated in the stadium. About how many people can be seated in each section? Is your estimate greater than or less than the actual answer will be? ***Solve this problem any way you choose.***

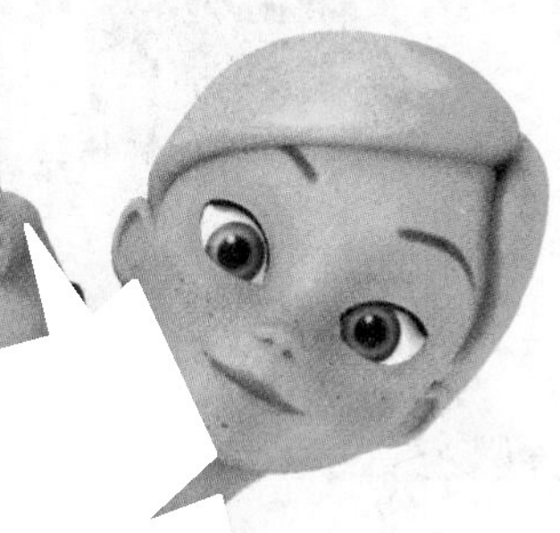

You can use **estimation.** What does the word "about" in the problem tell you? ***Show your work in the space below!***

Lesson 8-7

Dividing 4-Digit by 1-Digit Numbers

TEKS 4.4F Use strategies and algorithms, including the standard algorithm, to divide up to a four-digit dividend by a one-digit divisor. Also, 4.4E, 4.4H.
Mathematical Process Standards 4.1A, 4.1C, 4.1D, 4.1F, 4.1G

Digital Resources at SavvasTexas.com

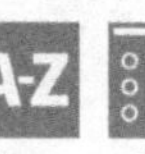
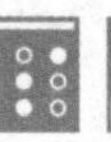

Solve Learn Glossary Check Tools Games

Look Back!

Connect Ideas Using your estimate, in which place will you start dividing to find the actual quotient?

How Can You Find Larger Quotients?

A

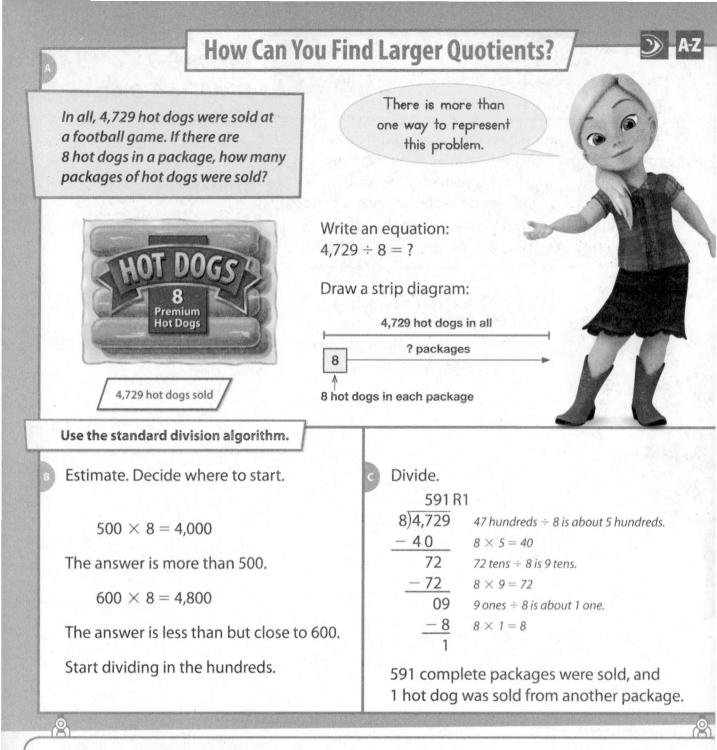

In all, 4,729 hot dogs were sold at a football game. If there are 8 hot dogs in a package, how many packages of hot dogs were sold?

There is more than one way to represent this problem.

4,729 hot dogs sold

Write an equation:
$4{,}729 \div 8 = ?$

Draw a strip diagram:

4,729 hot dogs in all

? packages

8

8 hot dogs in each package

Use the standard division algorithm.

B Estimate. Decide where to start.

$500 \times 8 = 4{,}000$

The answer is more than 500.

$600 \times 8 = 4{,}800$

The answer is less than but close to 600.

Start dividing in the hundreds.

C Divide.

591 R1	
8)4,729	*47 hundreds ÷ 8 is about 5 hundreds.*
− 40	*8 × 5 = 40*
72	*72 tens ÷ 8 is 9 tens.*
− 72	*8 × 9 = 72*
09	*9 ones ÷ 8 is about 1 one.*
− 8	*8 × 1 = 8*
1	

591 complete packages were sold, and 1 hot dog was sold from another package.

Do You Understand?

Convince Me! Use estimation to decide which of the division problems have a quotient between 300 and 400. Tell how you decided.

4)1,174 5)1,988 6)2,146 7)2,887

Name ____________________

Homework 8-7
Dividing 4-Digit by 1-Digit Numbers

Another Look!

Use the same steps for dividing a 4-digit number that you used for dividing 3-digit numbers.

Find 5,490 ÷ 6.

Estimate first. You can use compatible numbers to divide mentally.	Divide to find the actual quotient.	Compare. Is the estimate close to the quotient?
54 is a multiple of 6. 5,400 is close to 5,490, and 5,400 ÷ 6 will be easy to divide. 5,400 ÷ 6 = 900	$\begin{array}{r} 915 \\ 6\overline{)5{,}490} \\ -\,54 \\ \hline 9 \\ -\,6 \\ \hline 30 \\ -\,30 \\ \hline 0 \end{array}$	The estimate of 900 is close to to the actual quotient of 915, so the answer is reasonable. 915 people attended each show.

In **1** through **8**, estimate first. Then find each quotient.

1. Divide 4,318 ÷ 7.

Estimate: ______ ÷ ____ = ______

4,318 ÷ 7 = ______

2. Divide 4,826 ÷ 5.

Estimate: ______ ÷ ____ = ______

4,826 ÷ 5 = ______

3. $8\overline{)4{,}377}$

4. $9\overline{)7{,}192}$

5. $6\overline{)2{,}750}$

6. $4\overline{)6{,}208}$

7. $7\overline{)2025}$

8. $5\overline{)9{,}490}$

9. Estimation Mr. Girard traveled 527 miles from Jacksonville to Miami. He made 6 stops at equal intervals, including his final stop. About how many miles did he travel between stops?

10. Sam's father has an orchard of 3,429 grapefruit trees that are arranged in 9 equal rows. How many grapefruit trees are in each row?

11. Connect At the airport, there are a total of 1,160 seats in the waiting areas. There are 8 separate, same size, waiting areas. How many seats are in each waiting area?

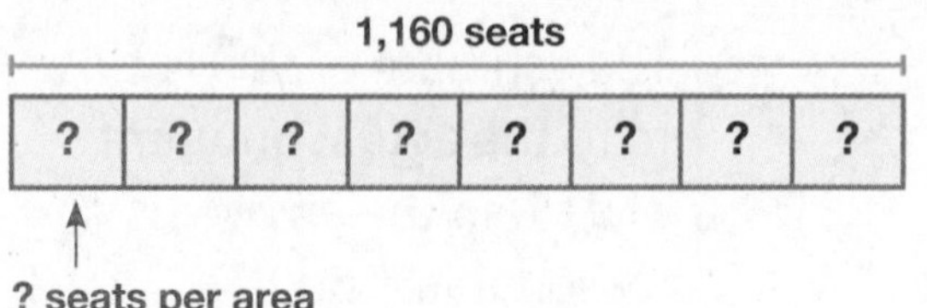

12. A fence around the school football field is 1,666 feet long. Seven teams of students will paint the fence. Each team will paint an equal length of the fence. What length of the fence will each team paint?

A 200 feet
B 228 feet
C 238 feet
D 11,662 feet

13. Math and Science Sound travels in waves, and sound waves are a form of energy. In dry air at 20° Celsius, sound travels about 343 meters in one second. How many meters will sound travel in 7 seconds?

14. Explain Lilly estimated a quotient of 120 and found an actual quotient of 83. What should she do next?

15. Extend Your Thinking Mr. Conners put a fence around the outside of his rectangular yard shown at the right. He put a fence post every 6 feet. How many fence posts did he use?

330 ft

102 ft

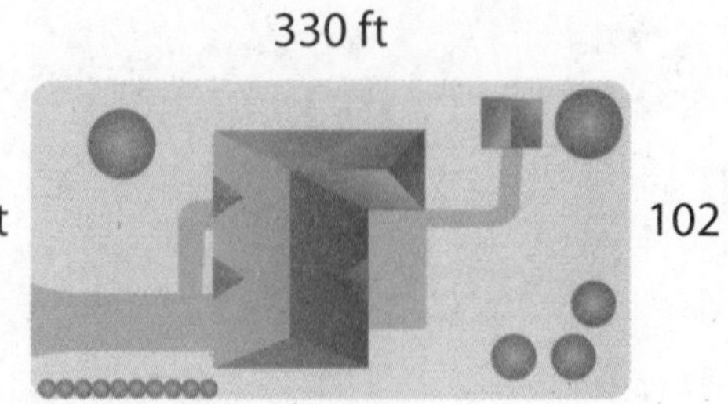

102 ft

330 ft

Name

Solve & Share

Jennifer and Anna are going on a road trip. They have 7,134 miles to drive over 9 days. Jennifer says that they will need to drive about 400 miles each day. Is her answer reasonable? Explain your answer. ***Solve this problem any way you choose.***

Problem Solving

Lesson 8-8

Reasonableness

TEKS 4.1B Use a problem-solving model that incorporates ... evaluating the problem-solving process and the reasonableness of the solution. Also, 4.4G. **Mathematical Process Standards** 4.1C, 4.1D, 4.1G

Digital Resources at SavvasTexas.com

Solve

Learn

Glossary

Check
Tools

Games

You can use estimation to **check for reasonableness.** ***Show your work in the space above!***

Look Back!

Reason If Anna estimates the solution by computing 8,000 ÷ 10, can she determine whether her estimate is greater or less than the actual answer? Explain.

A-Z

Analyze

How Can You Evaluate the Reasonableness of an Answer?

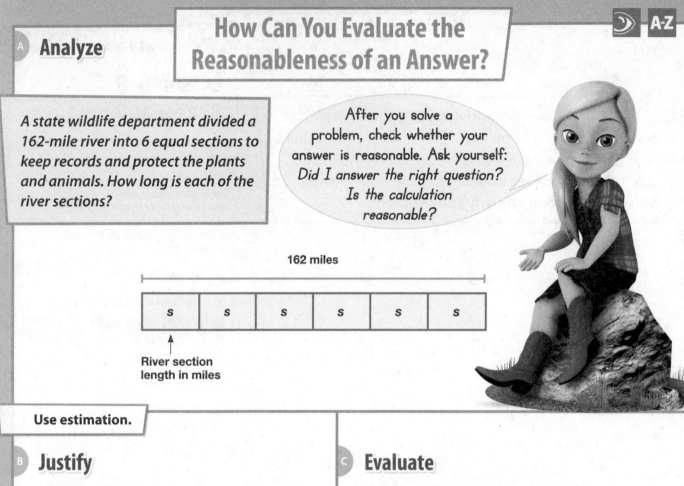

A state wildlife department divided a 162-mile river into 6 equal sections to keep records and protect the plants and animals. How long is each of the river sections?

After you solve a problem, check whether your answer is reasonable. Ask yourself: *Did I answer the right question? Is the calculation reasonable?*

162 miles

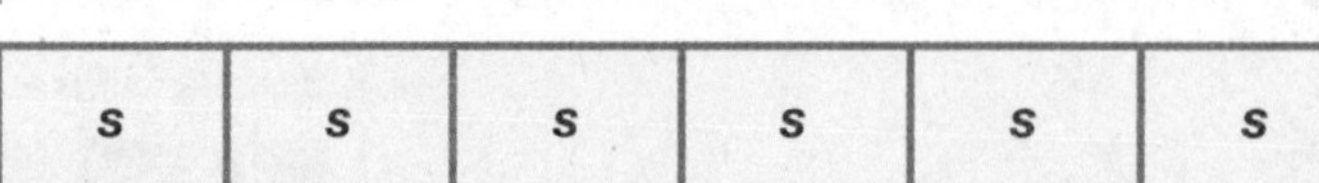

River section length in miles

Use estimation.

Justify

Julie's answer: Each river section is 27 miles long.

Use compatible numbers to estimate $162 \div 6$: $180 \div 6 = 30$

Julie's answer is reasonable because 30 is close to 27. The right question was answered, and the calculation is reasonable.

Evaluate

Maria's answer: Each river section is 17 miles long.

Use compatible numbers to estimate $162 \div 6$: $150 \div 5 = 30$

Maria's answer is not reasonable because 30 is not close to 17. The right question was answered, but the calculation is not reasonable.

Do You Understand?

Convince Me! The table shows the number of people entered in a walkathon. If all of the people entered are divided into 6 equal groups, is the answer below reasonable? Explain.

Answer: Each group will have 57 people.

DATA

Walkathon

People	Number
Children	141
Adults	201

Name ____________________

Guided Practice*

Solve. Then estimate to show that your answer is reasonable.

1. A fish store has 8 empty tanks. After a delivery, 328 fish were divided equally among the tanks. How many fish were put in each tank?

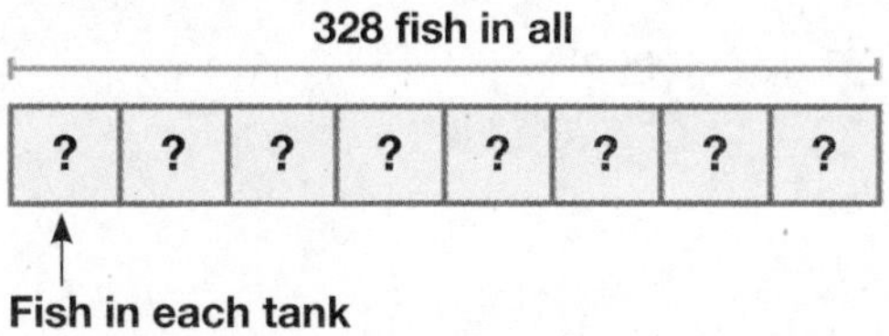

2. **Mental Math** How could you use mental math to divide 328 ÷ 8?

3. A local sports club has 108 fourth graders sign up to play soccer. There are 9 teams, and each team will have the same number of players. How many players will be on each team? Estimate to show that your answer is reasonable.

Independent Practice

In **4** through **6**, use the data table at the right.

4. About how much money does it cost to feed an 11-year old child for 1 week?

5. **Reason** A family spends about $300 to feed their child for 8 weeks. How old is the child likely to be?

6. **Check for Reasonableness** Is your answer for Exercise 5 reasonable? Did you answer the right question? How do you know?

DATA

Age of Child	Average Monthly Cost to Feed a Child
1–2 years	$108
3–5 years	$124
6–8 years	$168
9–11 years	$196

A month is about 4 weeks.

*For another example, see Set F on page 458.

Problem Solving

7. **Justify** Hilary walked 654 feet in 3 minutes. She says that she must have walked about 200 feet per minute. Is Hilary's estimate reasonable? Explain.

8. There were 1,278 people at the last basketball game. The stands were divided into 6 sections. The same number of people sat in each section. How many people sat in each section? Estimate to check whether your answer is reasonable.

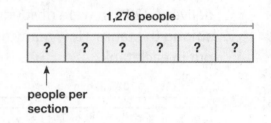

1,278 people

?	?	?	?	?	?

people per section

9. This year, Mary's troop sold 9,462 boxes of greeting cards. Each of the 6 members sold the same number of boxes. This year, each troop member sold 125 more boxes than they sold last year. How many boxes of greeting cards did each troop member sell last year?

   A 750 boxes
   B 1,452 boxes
   C 1,577 boxes
   D 1,702 boxes

10. How many seconds are there in 28 minutes? Show that your answer is reasonable.

There are 60 seconds in 1 minute.

11. **Check for Reasonableness** The student council is planning a dance. They order 284 balloons to make the table decorations shown at the right. How many tables can they decorate? Explain how to check your answer for reasonableness.

12. **Extend Your Thinking** Why is it useful to estimate an answer even if you have already calculated an exact answer?

Name ______________________________  

Homework 8-8
Reasonableness

Another Look!

A bus completed a 432-mile trip in 9 hours. If the bus traveled the same number of miles each hour, how many miles did the bus travel each hour?

After solving, check that you have answered the question. Then, use compatible numbers to be sure your answer is reasonable.

Find 432 ÷ 9.

Step 1	Step 2	Step 3
Divide. $\begin{array}{r} 48 \\ 9\overline{)432} \\ -36 \\ \hline 72 \\ -72 \\ \hline 0 \end{array}$	Answer the question. The bus traveled 48 miles each hour.	Use compatible numbers to be sure the answer is reasonable. 450 ÷ 9 = 50 50 is close to 48. The answer is reasonable.

In **1** through **4**, solve each problem. Then estimate to show that your answer is reasonable.

1. Marcus traveled 126 miles on his bike in 3 days. If he traveled the same number of miles each day, how many miles did he travel each day?

2. There are 327 students at Bob's school. The same number of students eat lunch during the three lunch periods each day. How many students eat lunch during each lunch period?

3. An apple orchard has 8 different varieties of apples. One week, 5,488 apples were picked. If an equal number of each variety was picked, how many apples of each variety were picked that week?

4. A bakery sells packages of 4 pastries. Last weekend, the bakery sold a total of 420 pastries. How many packages were sold?

5. **Analyze Information** The total attendance figures for one day at the Triplex movie theater are shown in the table. A movie is shown on each of the theater's three screens at each show time. If the same number of people saw each movie shown at 1:00, how many people saw each movie at 1:00? Estimate to check that your answer is reasonable.

DATA

Triplex Theater	
Show Time	Number of People
1:00 P.M.	459
3:15 P.M.	347
5:30 P.M.	562

6. **Reason** Could the audiences for the movies at 3:15 have the same number of people in each of them? Could the audiences for the movies at 5:30 have the same number of people in each of them? Explain.

7. **Check for Reasonableness** Sebastian ran around the track 4 times. He ran a total of 1,624 meters. How many meters is one lap around the track? Estimate to show that your answer is reasonable.

8. At the orange grove, the Wilson family picked 258 oranges. They filled 6 boxes and part of a seventh box. If all of the boxes are the same size, which statement is true?

A Each box can hold up to 30 oranges.
B Each box can hold up to 35 oranges.
C Each box can hold up to 40 oranges.
D Each box can hold up to 45 oranges.

9. A company packages every basketball in a cardboard cube. The cardboard cubes are packed equally into 8 large boxes for shipping to different stores. If the company packs 432 basketballs in one day, how many basketballs in cardboard cubes are in each large box?

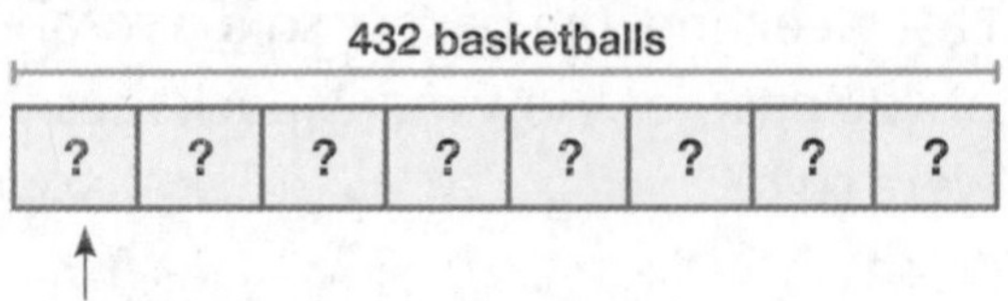

10. **Extend Your Thinking** There were 975 people in the audience at opening night of the school play, 1,263 people on the second night, and 1,035 people on the third night. The next three shows had the same total number of people attend as the first three shows. There were the same number of people in the audience for each of the last three shows. How many people saw the sixth performance? Show that your answer is reasonable.

Name ______________________________

1. Analyze Information For a party, Glenn bought 3 pizzas. Each pizza has 8 slices. There are 8 other people at the party, and everyone ate the same number of slices. What is the greatest number of slices each person ate? How many slices are left over?

Applying Math Processes

- How does this problem connect to previous ones?
- What is my plan?
- How can I use tools?
- How can I use number sense?
- How can I communicate and represent my thinking?
- How can I organize and record information?
- How can I explain my work?
- How can I justify my answer?

2. Formulate a Plan During the California Gold Rush, the demand for cattle was so great that a steer was worth $14 in Texas, but $95 in California. How much more did 5 steers cost in California than in Texas?

3. Use a Strip Diagram 756 people attend a concert on Sunday. On Saturday, four times fewer people attended. How many people went on Saturday?

756

Sunday → | ? | ? | ? | ? |

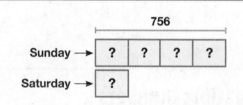

Saturday → | ? |

4. Personal Financial Literacy Asia wants to save $456 in 8 months. How much does she need to save each month?

5. Connect Amelia is canning 104 pears and 126 apples. Each jar holds 8 pears or 6 apples. How many jars does she need?

A 13 jars
B 21 jars
C 29 jars
D 34 jars

6. Extend Your Thinking Trevor has 152 postcards. He shared them all equally among 8 friends. Colton has 133 postcards. He shared them all equally among 7 friends. Jamie received postcards from both Trevor and Colton. Who gave Jamie more postcards?

Error Search

Find each problem that is not correct. Circle what is wrong and rewrite the problem so it is correct.

1.

$$\begin{array}{r} 32 \\ 3\overline{)906} \\ -9 \\ \hline 06 \\ -6 \\ \hline 0 \end{array}$$

2.

$$\begin{array}{r} 300 \\ 7\overline{)210} \\ -21 \\ \hline 0 \end{array}$$

3.

$$\begin{array}{r} 493\text{ R1} \\ 7\overline{)3{,}452} \\ -28 \\ \hline 65 \\ -63 \\ \hline 22 \\ -21 \\ \hline 1 \end{array}$$

4.

$$\begin{array}{r} 4{,}014 \\ 5\overline{)2{,}070} \\ -20 \\ \hline 07 \\ -5 \\ \hline 20 \\ -20 \\ \hline 0 \end{array}$$

Compatible Numbers

Mental Math Draw loops around two or more numbers next to each other, across or down, with a product of 36 or 360. Look for compatible numbers (numbers that are easy to compute with mentally).

5. Find products of 36.

2	9	2	3	2
6	3	12	3	3
3	2	2	4	2
2	18	2	15	3
4	9	9	6	6

6. Find products of 360.

20	3	3	20	2
18	2	60	3	30
90	2	2	120	2
10	9	40	3	2
36	3	6	20	3

Name ______________________________

Set A pages 407–412

Each letter Mary mails needs 2 stamps. If she has a total of 30 stamps, how many letters can Mary send?

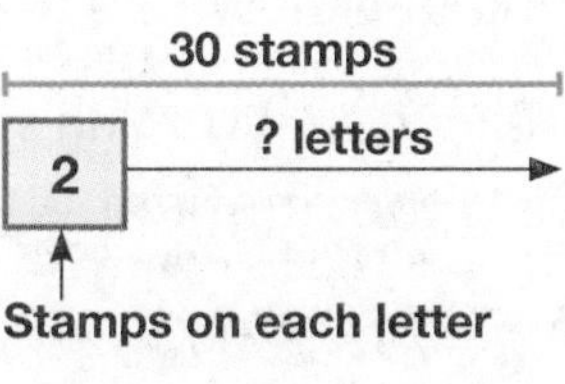

Use partial quotients to find the number of letters.

$$\begin{array}{rl} 2\overline{)30} & \text{Estimate: How many 2s are in 30? Try 10.} \\ -20 & \text{Multiply } 10 \times 2 \text{ and subtract.} \\ \hline 10 & \text{Estimate: How many 2s are in 10? Use 5.} \\ -10 & \text{Multiply } 5 \times 2 \text{ and subtract.} \\ \hline 0 & \end{array}$$

$10 + 5 = 15$ There are 15 2s in 30.

Mary can mail a total of 15 letters.

Remember to add the partial quotients to find the actual quotient.

Use partial quotients to solve.

1. There are 81 chairs in 3 equal groups. How many chairs are in each group?
2. The soccer club has 91 soccer balls for all the teams to share equally. If each team gets 7 soccer balls, how many teams are there?

Set B pages 413–418

Tom divides 54 pennies equally among 4 stacks. How many pennies are in each stack? How many are left over?

Use place-value blocks.

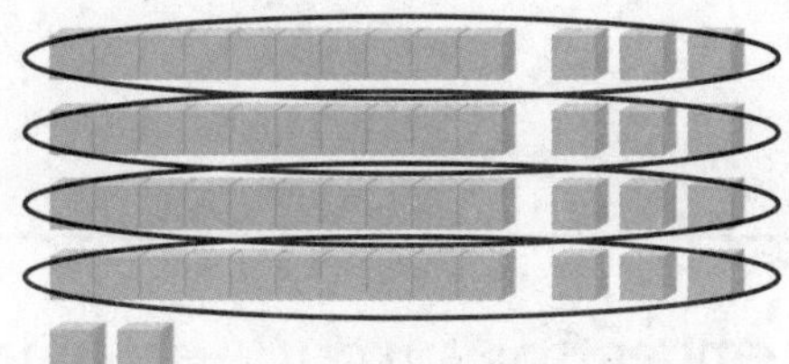

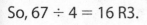

Each stack has 13 pennies.
Two pennies are left over.

Remember to divide the tens and then the ones.

Tell how many are in each group and how many are left over.

1. 38 CDs; 5 stacks
2. 42 nickels; 3 stacks
3. 62 dimes; 4 stacks
4. 77 nickels; 6 stacks

Set C pages 419–430

Find $67 \div 4$.

$$\begin{array}{rl} 16 & \\ 4\overline{)67} & \text{There is 1 ten in each group and} \\ -4 & \text{2 tens left over.} \\ \hline 27 & \text{Trade the 2 tens for 20 ones.} \\ -24 & \text{20 ones and 7 ones make 27 ones.} \\ \hline 3 & \text{There are 6 ones in each group} \\ & \text{and 3 ones left over.} \end{array}$$

So, $67 \div 4 = 16$ R3.

Remember to multiply and add the remainder to check your answer.

Divide. Check your answer.

1. $43 \div 7 = ?$
2. $33 \div 2 = ?$
3. $19 \div 5 = ?$
4. $53 \div 2 = ?$
5. $389 \div 2 = ?$
6. $723 \div 4 = ?$
7. $415 \div 3 = ?$
8. $999 \div 5 = ?$

Set D pages 431–436

Find 566 ÷ 6.

```
   94 R2
 6)566
 − 54
   26
 − 24
    2
```

There are not enough hundreds to divide. Regroup the hundreds as tens and divide.

Regroup the tens as ones and divide.

Remember to estimate the quotient to help you decide where to start dividing.

Tell where you will start dividing. Then find the quotient.

1. 710 ÷ 9 **2.** 601 ÷ 5

3. 398 ÷ 8 **4.** 429 ÷ 2

5. 470 ÷ 6 **6.** 255 ÷ 4

Set E pages 437–448

Find 8,351 ÷ 8.

```
   1,043 R7
 8)8,351
  − 8
    3
   − 0
    35
   − 32
     31
    − 24
      7
```

Divide the thousands.

There are not enough hundreds to divide. Put a 0 in the quotient. Bring down the tens and divide.

Bring down the ones and divide.

Remember to write zeros in the quotient when needed.

1. 4,241 ÷ 4 **2.** 9,143 ÷ 3

3. 8,427 ÷ 6 **4.** 6,381 ÷ 9

5. 4,173 ÷ 2 **6.** 3,812 ÷ 5

Set F pages 449–454

Ty bought 100 roses to place in 6 vases. Ty said that each vase would hold 10 roses. Is this a reasonable number of roses in each vase?

What do I know? Ty has 100 roses and 6 vases.

What am I asked to find? Is it reasonable for Ty to put 10 roses in each vase?

Estimate to determine reasonableness.

6 is close to 5, and 100 and 5 are compatible numbers. 100 ÷ 5 = 20

20 is not close to 10, so the number of roses in each vase is not reasonable.

Remember that you can use compatible numbers or rounding to estimate.

1. Mitch earns $8 an hour for delivering newspapers. Last week, Mitch earned $90. He said that he must have worked about 11 hours. Is the number of hours Mitch worked reasonable? Explain.

2. Joan has $78 to spend on envelopes. Each pack of envelopes costs $4. Joan estimates that at most, she can buy 9 packs of envelopes. Is her decision reasonable? Explain.

Name ______________________________

TOPIC 8

Test

1. For the division problem $689 \div 4$, in what place will you start dividing?

   A Thousands

   B Hundreds

   C Tens

   D Ones

2. Two boxes contain a total of 576 pencils. If each box has the same number of pencils, how many pencils are in each box?

   A 1,152 pencils

   B 328 pencils

   C 288 pencils

   D 238 pencils

3. Susanna's school has 472 students in 6 different grades. Each grade has about the same number of students. Which is **NOT** a reasonable estimate for the number of students in each grade?

   A 50 students, because $472 \div 6$ is about $500 \div 10$

   B 80 students, because $472 \div 6$ is about $480 \div 6$

   C 100 students, because $472 \div 6$ is about $500 \div 5$

   D 150 students, because $472 \div 6$ is about $450 \div 3$

4. Tia has collected 1,005 different types of rocks. She puts the same number of rocks in each of 5 display cases. How many rocks does Tia place in each case?

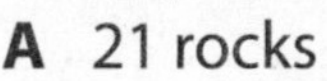

   A 21 rocks

   B 201 rocks

   C 2,001 rocks

   D 2,010 rocks

5. Harold earned $1,468 by mowing lawns for 3 months in the summer. Which number sentence shows the best way to estimate the amount he earned for each month?

   A $\$1{,}500 \div 3 = \$500$

   B $\$1{,}500 \div 5 = \$300$

   C $\$2{,}000 \div 5 = \$400$

   D $3 \times \$1{,}500 = \$4{,}500$

6. Nelly has 40 bricks to outline 3 flower beds. How many bricks will she use for each flower bed if she uses the same number around each?

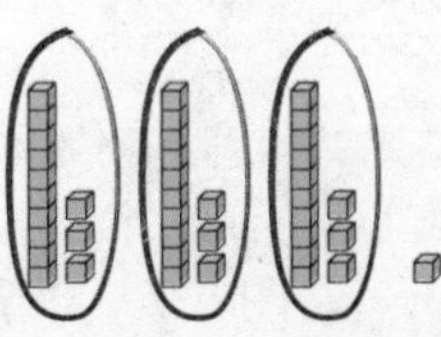

   A Each flower bed will use 11 bricks. There will be 3 left over.

   B Each flower bed will use 12 bricks. There will be 1 left over.

   C Each flower bed will use 13 bricks. There will be 0 left over.

   D None of the above

7. Each costume requires 2 yards of material. How many costumes can Sara make out of 35 yards? How much material will she have left?

A 17 costumes; 1 yard left

B 18 costumes; 1 yard left

C 15 costumes; 5 yards left

D 20 costumes; 5 yards left

8. Ken has 78 pieces of wood for building birdhouses. Each birdhouse needs 6 pieces of wood. How many birdhouses can Ken make?

9. Mason bought a package of 56 wheels. Each model car needs 4 wheels. How many cars can he make?

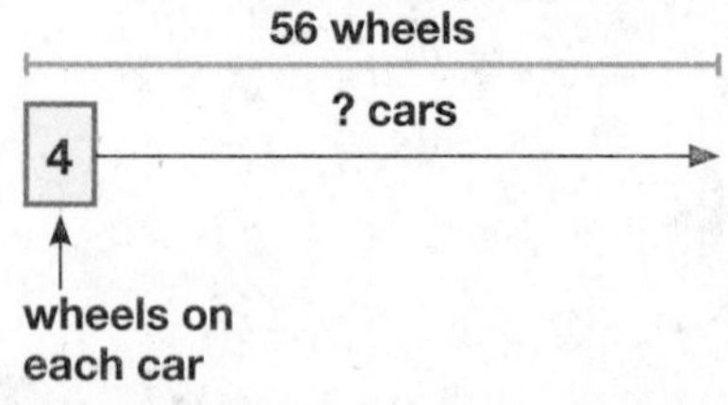

			.		
⓪	⓪	⓪		⓪	⓪
①	①	①		①	①
②	②	②		②	②
③	③	③		③	③
④	④	④		④	④
⑤	⑤	⑤		⑤	⑤
⑥	⑥	⑥		⑥	⑥
⑦	⑦	⑦		⑦	⑦
⑧	⑧	⑧		⑧	⑧
⑨	⑨	⑨		⑨	⑨

10. A baker made 64 rolls. He put an equal number in each of 4 baskets in the bakery. How many rolls did he put in each basket?

A 11 rolls

B 16 rolls

C 36 rolls

D 68 rolls

11. A school has $1,016 for scholarships. The money was awarded equally to 8 students. How much money did each student receive?

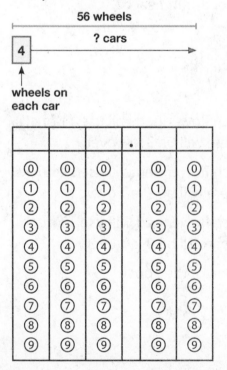

12. Tracey has 453 trading cards. She wants to put an equal number into each of 3 books to display them. How many cards will be in each book?

			.		
⓪	⓪	⓪		⓪	⓪
①	①	①		①	①
②	②	②		②	②
③	③	③		③	③
④	④	④		④	④
⑤	⑤	⑤		⑤	⑤
⑥	⑥	⑥		⑥	⑥
⑦	⑦	⑦		⑦	⑦
⑧	⑧	⑧		⑧	⑧
⑨	⑨	⑨		⑨	⑨

Glossary

acute angle An angle that is less than a right angle.

acute triangle A triangle with three acute angles.

addends The numbers that are added together to find a sum.
Example: $2 + 7 = 9$

Addends

algebraic expression An expression with variables. *Example:* $x - 3$

angle A figure formed by two rays that have the same endpoint.

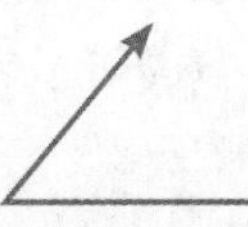

angle measure The number of degrees in an angle.

area The number of square units needed to cover a region.

array A way of displaying objects in rows and columns.

Associative Property of Addition Addends can be regrouped and the sum remains the same.

Associative Property of Multiplication Factors can be regrouped and the product remains the same.

balance The amount of money in a person's bank account.

bar graph A graph using bars to show data.

benchmark fractions Fractions that are commonly used for estimation.
Examples: $\frac{1}{4}$, $\frac{1}{3}$, $\frac{1}{2}$, $\frac{2}{3}$, and $\frac{3}{4}$.

billions A period of three places to the left of the millions period.

breaking apart Mental math method used to rewrite a number as the sum of numbers to form an easier problem.

capacity The amount a container can hold, measured in liquid units.

center A point within a circle that is the same distance from all points on a circle.

centimeter (cm) A metric unit of length. 100 centimeters = 1 meter

century A unit of time equal to 100 years.

circle A closed plane figure in which all the points are the same distance from a point called the center.

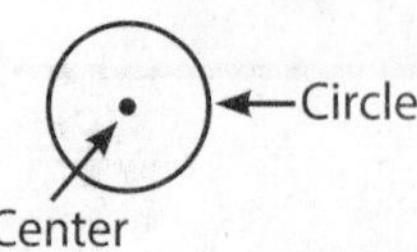

common factor A factor that two or more numbers have in common.

Commutative Property of Addition Numbers can be added in any order and the sum remains the same.

Commutative Property of Multiplication Factors can be multiplied in any order and the product remains the same.

compare Decide if one number is greater than, less than, or equal to another number.

compatible numbers Numbers that are easy to compute mentally.

compensation Choosing numbers close to the numbers in a problem to make the computation easier, and then adjusting the answer for the numbers chosen.

composite number A whole number greater than 1 that has more than two factors.

coordinate grid A grid used to show ordered pairs.

counting on Counting up from the lesser number to find the difference of two numbers.

credit **a.** Money put into a person's account. **b.** Buying something now, but paying for it later.

cup (c) A customary unit of capacity. 1 cup = 8 fluid ounces

customary units of measure Units of measure that are used in the United States.

data Pieces of collected information.

day A unit of time equal to 24 hours.

decade A unit of time equal to 10 years.

decimal A number with one or more places to the right of the decimal point.

decimal point A dot used to separate dollars from cents or ones from tenths in a number.

decimeter (dm) A metric unit of length equal to 10 centimeters.

decomposing To break into parts.

degree (°) A unit of measure for angles. $1° = \frac{1}{360}$ of a circle
Also a unit of measure for temperature.

denominator The number below the fraction bar in a fraction. The total number of equal parts in one whole.

deposit Money put into a person's account.

difference The answer when subtracting two numbers.

digits The symbols used to write a number: 0, 1, 2, 3, 4, 5, 6, 7, 8, and 9.

Distributive Property Multiplying a sum (or difference) by a number is the same as multiplying each number in the sum (or difference) by that number and adding (or subtracting) the products.
Example: $(3 \times 21) = (3 \times 20) + (3 \times 1)$

divide An operation to find the number in each group or the number of equal groups.

dividend The number to be divided.

divisibility rules The rules that state when a number is divisible by another number.

divisible Can be divided by another number without leaving a remainder.
Example: 10 is divisible by 2

divisor The number by which another number is divided.
Example: $32 \div 4 = 8$
↑ Divisor (points to 4)

dot plot A display of responses along a number line with dots used to indicate the number of times a response occurred.

elapsed time The amount of time between the beginning of an event and the end of the event.

equation A number sentence that uses the equal sign (=) to show that two expressions have the same value.
Example: $9 + 3 = 12$

equilateral triangle A triangle in which all sides are the same length.

equivalent Numbers that name the same amount.

equivalent fractions Fractions that name the same region, part of a set, or part of a segment.

estimate To give an approximate value rather than an exact answer.

expanded form A number written as the sum of the values of its digits.
Example: 2,476 = 2,000 + 400 + 70 + 6

expenses The amount of money spent.

fact family A group of related facts using the same set of numbers.

factors The numbers multiplied together to find a product.
Example: $3 \times 6 = 18$
↑ ↑ Factors (point to 3 and 6)

financial institutions Businesses that include banks, savings and loans, and credit unions.

fixed expenses Expenses that occur on a regular basis. Monthly bills are fixed expenses.

fluid ounce (fl oz) A customary unit of capacity.
1 fluid ounce = 2 tablespoons

foot (ft) A customary unit of length.
1 foot = 12 inches

formula An equation that uses symbols to relate two or more quantities.
Example: $A = \ell \times w$

fraction A symbol, such as $\frac{2}{3}$, $\frac{5}{1}$, or $\frac{8}{5}$, used to name a part of a whole, a part of a set, or a location on a number line.

frequency The number of times that a response occurs in a set of data.

frequency table A way to display data that shows how many times a response occurs in a set of data.

G

gallon (gal) A customary unit of capacity. 1 gallon = 4 quarts

gram (g) A metric unit of mass.
1,000 grams = 1 kilogram

greater than symbol (>) A symbol that points away from a greater number or expression.
Example: 450 > 449

H

hexagon A polygon with 6 sides.

hour A unit of time equal to 60 minutes.

hundredth One part of 100 equal parts of a whole.

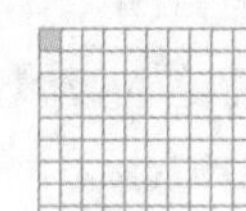

I

Identity Property of Addition The sum of any number and zero is that number.

Identity Property of Multiplication The product of any number and one is that number.

improper fraction A fraction in which the numerator is greater than or equal to the denominator.

inch (in.) A customary unit of length.
12 inches = 1 foot

income Money earned from doing work.

inequality A number sentence that uses the greater than sign (>) or the less than sign (<) to show that two expressions do not have the same value.
Example: 5 > 3

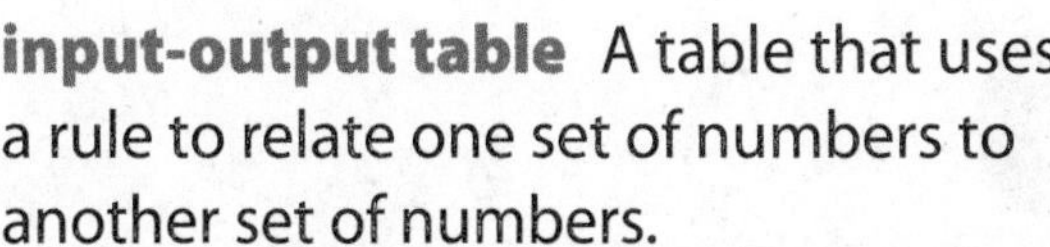

input-output table A table that uses a rule to relate one set of numbers to another set of numbers.

interest Money you pay when you borrow money, or money you receive for having a savings account.

intersecting lines Lines that cross at one point.

interval A number which is the difference between two consecutive numbers on the scale of a graph.

inverse operations Operations that undo each other.
Examples: Adding 6 and subtracting 6; Multiplying by 4 and dividing by 4.

isosceles triangle A triangle that has at least two equal sides.

key Part of a graph that tells what each symbol stands for.

kilogram (kg) A metric unit of mass.
1 kilogram = 1,000 grams

kilometer (km) A metric unit of length.
1 kilometer = 1,000 meters

leaf In a stem-and-leaf plot, a number representing the least place value for the set of data.

leap year A calendar occurrence that happens every four years when an extra day is added to February. Leap years have 366 days.

less than symbol (<) A symbol that points towards a lesser number or expression.
Example: $305 < 320$

line A straight path of points that goes on and on in two directions.

line of symmetry A line on which a figure can be folded so that both halves are the same.

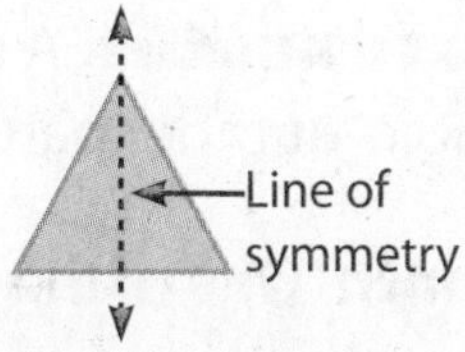

line segment A part of a line that has two endpoints.

liter (L) A metric unit of capacity.
1 liter = 1,000 milliliters

mass The amount of matter that something contains.

meter (m) A metric unit of length.
1 meter = 100 centimeters

metric units of measure Units of measure commonly used by scientists.

mile (mi) A customary unit of length. 1 mile = 5,280 feet

millennium (plural: millennia) A unit for measuring time equal to 1,000 years.

milliliter (mL) A metric unit of capacity. 1,000 milliliters = 1 liter

millimeter (mm) A metric unit of length. 1,000 millimeters = 1 meter

millions In a number, a period of three places to the left of the thousands period.

minute A unit of time equal to 60 seconds.

mixed number A number that has a whole-number part and a fraction part.

month One of the 12 parts into which a year is divided.

multiple The product of a given factor and any whole number.

numerical expression An expression that contains numbers and at least one operation.
Example: 35 + 12

numerator The number above the fraction bar in a fraction.

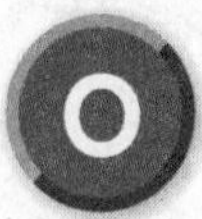

obtuse angle An angle whose measure is between 90° and 180°.

obtuse triangle A triangle in which there is one obtuse angle.

octagon A polygon with 8 sides.

ounce (oz) A customary unit of weight. 16 ounces = 1 pound

outlier A value that is much greater or much less than the other values in a data set.

overestimate An estimate that is greater than the exact answer.

parallel lines In a plane, lines that never intersect.

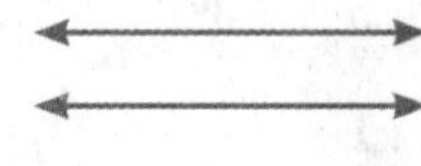

parallelogram A quadrilateral in which opposite sides are parallel.

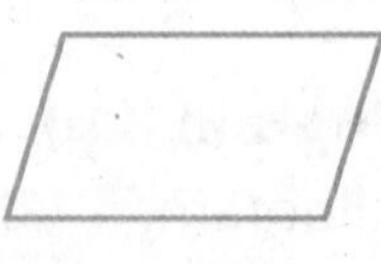

partial products Products found by breaking one factor in a multiplication problem into ones, tens, hundreds, and so on and then multiplying each of these by the other factor.

partial quotients A way to divide that finds quotients in parts until only a remainder, if any, is left.

pentagon A plane figure with 5 sides.

perfect square A number that is the product of a counting number multiplied by itself.

perimeter The distance around a figure.

period In a number, a group of three digits, separated by commas, starting from the right.

perpendicular lines Two intersecting lines that form right angles.

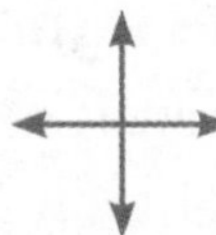

pint (pt) A customary unit of capacity. 1 pint = 2 cups

place value The position of a digit in a number that is used to determine the value of the digit.
Example: In 3,946, the 9 is in the hundreds place. So, the 9 has a value of 900.

plane An endless flat surface.

plane figure A figure that has only two dimensions.

point An exact location in space.

polygon A closed plane figure made up of line segments.

pound (lb) A customary unit of weight. 1 pound = 16 ounces

prime number A whole number greater than 1 that has exactly two factors, 1 and itself.

product The answer to a multiplication problem.

profit The difference between expenses and receipts.

proper fraction A fraction that is less than 1; its numerator is less than its denominator.

protractor A tool used to measure and draw angles.

quadrilateral A polygon with 4 sides.

quart (qt) A customary unit of capacity. 1 quart = 2 pints

quotient The answer to a division problem.

ray A part of a line that has one endpoint and continues endlessly in one direction.

receipts The total money taken in.

rectangle A quadrilateral with 4 right angles.

regroup To name a whole number in a different way.
Example: 32 = 2 tens 12 ones

remainder The amount that is left after dividing a number into equal parts.

repeated addition A way to write a multiplication expression as an addition expression.
Example: $3 \times 5 = 5 + 5 + 5$

rhombus A quadrilateral in which opposite sides are parallel and all sides are the same length.

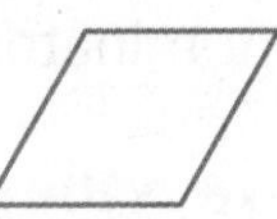

right angle An angle that forms a square corner.

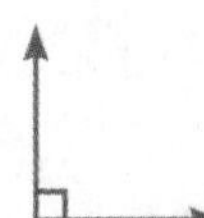

right triangle A triangle in which there is one right angle.

rounding Replacing a number with a number that tells about how many or how much.

rule A mathematical phrase that tells how numbers in a table are related.

saving Putting aside money from current income to buy something in the future.

scale Numbers that show the units used on a graph.

scalene triangle A triangle in which no sides are the same length.

second A unit of time.
60 seconds = 1 minute

sequence A set of numbers that follows a pattern.

sharing Giving money to charity or other people.

side Each of the line segments of a polygon.

simplest form A fraction in which the numerator and denominator have no common factors other than 1.

solid figure A figure with three dimensions that has length, width, and height.

solution The value of the variable that makes an equation true.

solve an equation Find a solution to an equation.

spending Trading money for goods or services.

square A quadrilateral with 4 right angles and all sides the same length.

square unit A square with sides one unit long used to measure area.

standard form A way to write a number showing only its digits. Commas separate groups of three digits starting from the right.
Example: 2,613,095

stem In a stem-and-leaf plot, a number representing the greatest place value for a set of data.

stem-and-leaf plot A display that shows data in order of place value.

straight angle An angle that forms a straight line.

strip diagram A tool used to help understand and solve word problems. It is also known as a bar diagram or a tape diagram.

sum The result of adding numbers together.

survey Collecting information by asking a number of people the same question and recording their answers.

symmetric A figure is symmetric if it can be folded into two halves that fit on top of each other.

tablespoon (tbsp) A customary unit of capacity. 1 tablespoon = 3 teaspoons

teaspoon (tsp) A customary unit of capacity. 3 teaspoons = 1 tablespoon

tenth One of ten equal parts of a whole.

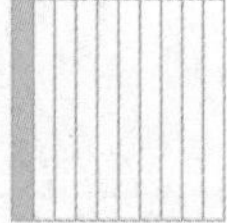

terms Numbers in a sequence or variables, such as x and y, in an algebraic expression.

ton (T) A customary unit of weight. 1 ton = 2,000 pounds

trapezoid A quadrilateral with only one pair of parallel sides.

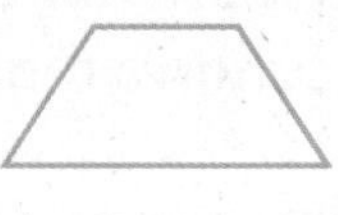

triangle A polygon with 3 sides.

underestimate An estimate that is less than the exact answer.

unknown A symbol or letter, such as x, that represents a number in an expression or equation.

unit angle An angle that cuts off $\frac{1}{360}$ of a circle and measures 1°.

unit fraction A fraction with a numerator of 1.
Example: $\frac{1}{2}$

variable A symbol or letter that stands for a number.

variable expenses Expenses that do not occur on a regular basis.

vertex (plural: vertices) The point where two rays meet to form an angle. Also, the points where the sides of a polygon meet.

volume The number of cubic units needed to fill a solid figure.

week A unit of time equal to 7 days.

weight A measure of how heavy an object is.

whole numbers The numbers 0, 1, 2, 3, 4, and so on.

withdrawal Money taken out of a person's account.

word form A way to write a number in words.
Example: Four thousand, six hundred, thirty-two.

yard (yd) A customary unit of length.
1 yard = 3 feet

year A unit of time equal to 365 days or 52 weeks or 12 months.

Zero Property of Multiplication The product of any number and zero is zero.